THE AUTONOMOUS SELF

The Work of John D. Sutherland

EDITED BY JILL SAVEGE SCHARFF, M.D.

JASON ARONSON INC.
Northvale, New Jersey
London

Production Editor: Judith D. Cohen

This book was set in 10 pt. Baskerville by Lind Graphics of Upper Saddle River, New Jersey, and printed and bound by Haddon Craftsmen of Scranton, Pennsylvania.

10 9 8 7 6 5 4 3 2 1

Library of Congress Cataloging-in-Publication Data

Sutherland, John D. (John Derg)
[Works. 1994]
The autonomous self : the work of John D. Sutherland / edited by Jill Savege Scharff.
p. cm.
Collected works of John D. Sutherland. Includes bibliographical references and index.
ISBN 1-56821-008-6
1. Psychoanalysis. 2. Object relations (Psychoanalysis). 3. Self psychology. 4. Community psychiatry. I. Scharff, Jill Savege. II. Title.
[DNLM: 1. Sutherland, John D. (John Derg) 2. Psychoanalysis—biography. 3. Psychoanalysis—collected works. 4. Object Attachment—collected works. 5. Self Concept—collected works. WZ 100 S96605a 1994]
RC501.2.S88 1994
616.89'17—dc20
DNLM/DLC
for Library of Congress 93-22563

Manufactured in the United States of America. Jason Aronson Inc. offers books and cassettes. For information and catalog write to Jason Aronson Inc., 230 Livingston Street, Northvale, New Jersey 07647.

To

Molly Sutherland

and

The Scottish Institute of Human Relations

THE LIBRARY OF OBJECT RELATIONS

A SERIES OF BOOKS EDITED BY
DAVID E. SCHARFF AND JILL SAVEGE SCHARFF

Object relations theories of human interaction and development provide an expanding, increasingly useful body of theory for the understanding of individual development and pathology, for generating theories of human interaction, and for offering new avenues of treatment. They apply across the realms of human experience from the internal world of the individual to the human community, and from the clinical situation to everyday life. They inform clinical technique in every format from individual psychoanalysis and psychotherapy, through group therapy, to couple and family therapy.

The Library of Object Relations aims to introduce works that approach psychodynamic theory and therapy from an object relations point of view. It includes works from established and new writers who employ diverse aspects of British and American object relations theory in helping individuals, families, couples, and groups. It features books that stress integration of psychoanalytic approaches with marital and family therapy, as well as those centered on individual psychotherapy and psychoanalysis.

Refinding the Object and Reclaiming the Self
David E. Scharff

Scharff Notes: A Primer of Object Relations Therapy
Jill Savege Scharff and David E. Scharff

Object Relations Couple Therapy
David E. Scharff and Jill Savege Scharff

Object Relations Family Therapy
David E. Scharff and Jill Savege Scharff

Projective and Introjective Identification and the Use of the Therapist's Self
Jill Savege Scharff

Foundations of Object Relations Family Therapy
Jill Savege Scharff, Editor

From Inner Sources: New Directions in Object Relations Psychotherapy
N. Gregory Hamilton, Editor

Betwixt and Between: The Understanding and Treatment of the Borderline Marriage
Charles McCormack

Repairing Intimacy: An Object Relations Approach to Couples Therapy
Judith Siegel

Family and Couple Therapy
John Zinner

Close Encounters: A Relational View of the Therapeutic Process
Robert Winer

The Autonomous Self: The Work of John D. Sutherland
Jill Savege Scharff, Editor

Crisis at Adolescence: Object Relations Therapy with the Family
Sally Box, Beta Copley, Jeanne Magagna, and Errica Moustaki Smilansky, Editors

Personal Relations Therapy: The Collected Papers of H. J. S. Guntrip
Jeremy Hazell, Editor

Psychoanalytic Group Therapy
Karl Konig and Wulf-Volker Lindner

Psychoanalytic Therapy
Karl Konig

From Instinct to Self: Selected Papers of W. R. D. Fairbairn
David E. Scharff and Ellinor Fairbairn Birtles, Editors

Treating Developmental Trauma
Jill Savege Scharff and David E. Scharff

Object Relations Individual Therapy
David E. Scharff and Jill Savege Scharff

How to Survive as a Psychotherapist
Nina Coltart

Contents

III COMMUNITY MENTAL HEALTH

IV THE SELF

List of Photographs

Preface and Acknowledgments

My thanks go first and foremost to John D. Sutherland's widow, Molly, who asked David Scharff and me to look through the papers left in her husband's study. We found all his published papers in order, together with some notes extracted from unpublished papers or talks. Molly graciously supplied photographs for a personal touch to the theory of the self, in keeping with Jock's personable teaching style. Molly put us in touch with Sutherland's literary executor, Dr. Alan Harrow, and his literary executive committee at the Scottish Institute of Human Relations, founded by Sutherland in 1970. The committee members were kept busy carrying on the Institute's many projects for training psychotherapists, providing intensive treatment for patients and trainees, building the institution on object relational principles, and integrating the training of their psychotherapy teachers with the standards of the British Psychoanalytic Society. Still mourning the loss of their leader, preoccupied with change, and absorbed by the daily expression of Jock's vision, they were not ready to attend to the task of presenting his work to a wider audience and gladly asked us as series editors of the Object Relations Library if we would be interested in compiling Sutherland's works. I was delighted to be given the honor of being the editor of this collection.

I would like to acknowledge with thanks the cooperation of the following publishers and institutions:

Aberdeen University Department of Mental Health
American Psychiatric Association Library
British Journal of Psychiatry
British Journal of the Philosophy of Science
British Psychoanalytic Institute Bulletin
Bulletin of the Association of Psychoanalytic Medicine
Bulletin of the Menninger Clinic
Contact Journal of the Scottish Pastoral Association
Edinburgh Review
Edinburgh University Department of Psychiatry
Free Association Books

In his study, 1982

Journal of the American Psychoanalytic Association
Macmillan
National Council Social Services
Psychotherapy and Psychosomatics
Routledge Kegan Paul
Royal College of Psychiatrists
Senate House Library, University of London
Tavistock Publications
The American Historical Review
The British Journal of Medical Psychology
The Edinburgh Literary Review
The Hogarth Press
The Institute for Contemporary Psychotherapy, New York
The Institute of Psychiatry, London
The International Journal of Psycho-Analysis
The International Review of Psycho-Analysis
The Journal of Social Issues
The Lauinger Library, Georgetown University
The Menninger Foundation
The National Library of Medicine
The Scottish Institute for Human Relations
The Tavistock Centre Library

The Tavistock Institute of Human Relations
The Washington School of Psychiatry, Washington, D.C.

I am most grateful to J. Alan Harrow, Murray Leishman, Mona Macdonald, and David J. Scott for their support and collaboration. Alan and Murray led the writing effort that resulted in the group's scholarly introduction and they also helped me to mail some requests for permission to reprint from sources at addresses that I could not trace from the United States. It has been a great pleasure to renew old acquaintances and to foster new ties with the Scottish Institute.

I would like to thank Patrick Casement and Terttu Eskelinen de Folch for the use of their clinical material in support of Sutherland's theoretical arguments.

At the publishing house, Jason Aronson was, as usual, unfailingly enthusiastic and yet waited patiently for the published and unpublished papers, transcriptions, and permissions to come together at last. It was a pleasure to work again with Judy Cohen, a delightful, responsive, and well-organized production editor, and with Muriel Jorgensen, the editorial director. Diane Turek handled the book's promotion through the *Psychotherapy Book News* of which she is the managing editor.

Josephine Parker cheerfully managed the office and the correspondence in connection with this book and Rita Leahy enjoyed the demanding job of transcribing the audiotapes from which I created Chapters 24 and 25. Ernest Wallwork helped me to trace some references to works in the field of philosophy and Ruth Selig speedily found me some anthropological references that were evading me. Many librarians responded willingly: Hermi Dauker at the British Psychological Society, Lorraine Fields at the Senate House Library of the University of London, and Margaret Walker at the Tavistock Clinic were particularly helpful. Roger Shapiro enabled me to finish the project on schedule by producing two books that no local library could provide. I am indebted to all of them.

It has meant so much to me to have the opportunity to edit this collection. Trained by Jock as his registrar and senior registrar in community psychiatry in Edinburgh from 1969–1972, taught by him in his seminars on marital and group therapy, and supervised by him on my individual psychotherapy cases, I was imbued with his ideas and felt especially suited to the task of presenting them. What I liked about the training that I got was the breadth and depth made possible by his vision and the extensive explanatory power of object-relations theory. I learned by osmosis and apprenticeship more than by reading theory. Since then I have been interested to read of the ideas and now take great pleasure in sharing them. Section 1 features Sutherland's theoretical contributions to object-relations theory in individual psychoanalysis. In part 1 of section 2 I have put together papers that demonstrate his object-relations approach to groups and institutions, and in part 2 of section 2 those that deal with its application to community mental health. The final section 3 moves toward a theory of the self and represents the thinking that would have been the basis for Sutherland's book on the self, had he lived to bring it to completion.

As an editor himself he headed the *International Journal of Psycho-Analysis* and the *British Journal of Medical Psychology* and as the editor of books of the British Psychoanalytical Society, he shepherded twenty-eight books to publication for his colleagues, but he modestly did not give his own ideas the same prominence. He addresses the reasons for this in Chapter 25, where he reports on the successful self-analysis of an inhibitory condition of his self-functioning. The part of him that identified with his mother's ambition for him produced a tremendous amount of highly regarded work, but another part that identified with his publisher father's pleasure in a relaxed life kept Jock from devoting himself to the writing of an intellectually ambitious book. Fortunately, Jock's self-analysis was successful in time for him to write his biography of Fairbairn at the age of 83. He had other projects in mind—a biography of Guntrip and a book on the self—but I do not think that he appreciated the importance of a collection of his own work. I would like to thank James Grotstein for sharing my appreciation of Sutherland's work and for generously encouraging me to do this project. I am grateful to the literary executive and to David Scharff for giving me the privilege of editing this volume and therefore of doing for Jock what he has done for so many others.

At home with Molly and Jill Savege Scharff

Introduction

J. Alan Harrow, Murray Leishman, M.A.,
Mona Macdonald, M.A., M. Phil., and
David J. Scott, B.A., M. Phil. C. Psychol. A.B.P.S.

Sutherland Literary Executive,
Scottish Institute of Human Relations

Jock Sutherland's ruling passion was the future. He predicted a poor outlook for the world if there were not to be an enlivening and contributive psychoanalysis. The nearer he got to his own death, the more he looked forward to the dynamic impact on society of such a lively psychoanalysis promulgated by the Scottish Institute of Human Relations of which he was the founder and by like-minded Institutes to which he consulted, particularly in the United States. Sutherland was one of the leading object-relations theorists of the British Independent tradition, and, although he was most influenced by Fairbairn's systematic theory building, he was not at all dogmatic. The danger of starting a school, or worse, a cult, was always in mind. "What matters," he said in his opening address at the Fairbairn Centenary Conference in Edinburgh, 1989, "is not the promotion of Fairbairn's views, but the future of psychoanalysis."

The range in this collection of Sutherland's papers reflects the range of his vision, which understood the many currents of the human condition to be an interconnected whole. Just as self, family, group, organization, institution, and community are all inextricably connected so, naturally, they are all here in this collection, which attempts to embody Sutherland's visionary purpose.

In pursuing this integrative vision, Sutherland himself came to exemplify the manifold and evolving self in society that he sought to identify and to explicate throughout the 60 and more years of his career. The psychologist and philosopher turned to medicine, psychiatry, and psychoanalysis; theory evolved alongside practice. In his relationship with Ronald Fairbairn, as his analyst in the 1930s and later as his friend, the personal core of his psychoanalytical self was formed and helped into being. Fairbairn had realized that psychopathology in the individual was the result of lack of a good relationship, that the growth and strength of the self was relational. The baby was born seeking a related person, not an object of gratification, and the mother's recognition of her baby's self enabled and mediated his personal growth. Sutherland extended this insight to social group functioning. His perspective on the growth of the self in society has led to a new psychoanalysis that is a powerful informing force.

In an experimental unit in the British Army, and, later, as Director of the Tavistock Clinic, Sutherland came into contact with men like Bowlby, Bion, and

Trist who were searching for the roots of disorders in the self in the context of their work with groups and social forces. They enjoyed mutual influence and inspiration as they examined and worked with group institutional and cultural forces. As editor of the *International Journal of Psychoanalysis* among others, Sutherland had the opportunity to expand the breadth of psychoanalytical investigation. In his last 25 years this wider orientation took him beyond his consultative involvement with the Menninger Foundation in Topeka, Kansas, to the Washington School of Psychiatry in Washington, D.C., and the Institute of Contemporary Psychoanalysis in New York, where he also influenced and was affected by the growing number of self theorists in the United States. The final expression of his vision of psychoanalysis was his founding of the Scottish Institute of Human Relations.

Sutherland nurtured, recognized, and gave opportunities to those who had led the field in psychoanalysis, group work, and "socio-technical systems." He preferred to "mother" and "father" brilliant prima donna thinkers rather than to promote himself, yet his own questions were more extensive and his perspectives broader. His ability to make the quantum leap into a new paradigm often surpassed that of those he quotes. A considerable portion of his writing promulgated Fairbairn's object-relations theory, culminating in his psychobiography *Fairbairn's Journey into the Interior*, published in 1989. Sutherland's compassion and perspicacity bring out the essence of Fairbairn as man and thinker; his appraisal of Fairbairn's significance—in relation to Freud before him, to the contemporaneous Klein, to Guntrip, Winnicott, and the American self theorists—is throughout judicious and nothing short of brilliant. In the course of setting forth and evaluating these various contributions, Sutherland himself emerges as the thinker who goes further than those whose thinking he elucidates.

The sheer versatility and complexity of the man were too easily obscured in the profusion of all that he said and did in his many roles. When the chairman of a program in which he had presented a paper concluded the session by saying that for years we had listened with pleasure to Sutherland on Fairbairn, but tonight we heard Sutherland, he might have been acknowledging not only the burgeoning autonomy of Sutherland the thinker, but also the burgeoning capacity in his audience to hear and recognize what he had been saying and doing for a long time.

THE SELF IN OBJECT-RELATIONS THEORY

Sutherland was concerned with the concept of the self in object-relations theory and with establishing it at the core of a modern psychoanalysis. Becoming aware that his own life was close to ending, he worked ever more intensively, as though he wished to ensure that the theory of the self would, through being disseminated as widely as possible, have more of an opportunity to take firm root in psychoanalysis as a whole.

Chapter 21, based on a revision of his paper "Hate and the Autonomy of the Self" (1980a), represents his current theoretical position on the self. Here he develops his ideas on the autonomous self using available clinical data, and combines this with a review of the historical development of the concept of the self. However, his unique contribution in this paper is his attempt to construct an overarching metapsychology of the self based on modern biology and open systems theory.

Why did he think it absolutely vital that such a framework be developed? In order to begin to answer this question it is necessary to examine his interest in and understanding of the theory of *open, self-organizing systems*. This relatively new paradigm in science has as its aim the elucidation of the dynamics of interconnectedness at all levels in the natural world (Jantsch 1980). It represents an alternative view of the world to that of the traditional dualistic and reductionist model which has held sway in the scientific community since Descartes.

OPEN SYSTEMS THEORY

Since the '50s, the phenomenon of system—applying in space through structure, in time through process, in every kind of organic life—has increasingly been charted in a multitude of disciplines. This has the force of a new paradigm that is not limited to the scientific.

> The characteristic state of the living organism is that of an open system. A system is closed if no material enters or leaves it; it is open if there is import and export and therefore change of the components. Living systems are open systems maintaining themselves in exchange of materials with environment, and in continuous building up and breaking down of their components. . . . [von Bertalanffy 1950b, p. 23]
>
> Every organic form is the expression of a flux of processes. It persists only in a continuous change of its components. . . . of chemical compounds in the cell, of cells in multicellular organisms, of individuals in super-individual life units. . . . Every organic system is essentially a hierarchical order of processes standing in dynamic equilibrium. [Von Bertalanffy 1950b, p. 27]

Fairbairn's model of endopsychic structure (1944) clearly parallels emerging system thinking very early in the field. Indeed the explosion of his thinking in his four big papers of the early 1940s finds an explanation in terms of systems thinking, when the new paradigm manifests itself suddenly in insight and gestalt awareness.

Miller (1965a,b) developed Von Bertalanffy's (1950a,b) *general systems theory* using unfamiliar concepts from thermodynamics, information theory, cybernetics (the science of communication and control), and system engineering, yet these are quite recognizable when related to concepts of system in philosophical, psychological, and sociological understanding. Moreover each enhances the meaning of the other.

For example, Deutsch (1963) in "A Simple Cybernetic Model" examines system, group, organization, and learning in the light of cybernetics. Deutsch uses the analogy of Aristotelian teleology for any system using *goal-seeking feedback* and Darwinian evolution for the more complex *goal-changing processes*. These are not new; they have belonged to natural systems since time immemorial. The third, more complex, form of feedback is relatively new. It is that of *human consciousness,* namely self-conscious learning inside the system. Mills and Rosenberg (1970) add to this model concepts having to do with the blocking and jamming of circuits by emotional phenomena.

The concept of *feedback* in conscious systems is as the concept of negentropy in general systems theory and natural systems. In the older mechanistic Newtonian paradigm, the belief was that all living organisms were subject to entropy and naturally ran down. This was the second law of thermodynamics. In the new systems thinking the forces of negative entropy, if allowed to influence the system, create the possibility of maintaining the openness of the system, and its growth. Freud in this sense was the biggest exponent of the new paradigm, naturally but not consciously, when he opened the human system to the possibilities of change through the negentropic feedback of unconscious determinants of behavior.

A METAPSYCHOLOGY OF THE SELF IN THE LIGHT OF OPEN SYSTEMS THEORY

Sutherland came to an understanding of open systems theory through the works of Waddington, Prigogine, and Jantsch. The new paradigm focused broadly on the *process* of change and development rather than narrowly and reductively on systems defined by the structural characteristic of "equilibrium perfection, structural unambiguity and permanence, hierarchical control, and predictability of machine-like structures" (Waddington and Jantsch 1976, p. 2). Put simply and briefly, the new paradigm emphasized the process of *order through fluctuation*: random events or developments, if given a critical level of support in the environment, connect and become an integral part of the existing environmental structure and its evolution. This process can be seen to occur in the realm of ideas; for example, traditional Freudian drive theory clearly gained enough critical support for it to become an accepted part of our culture and our language. But did this happen because the theory was true in an absolute sense? To us the answer is clearly no; rather it succeeded because the theory fit clinical observations, which in turn were themselves affected by the prevailing scientific model of man. Drive theory accorded well with the second law of thermodynamics, with its emphasis on equal and opposite forces and on equilibrium.

In keeping with the new paradigm and its emphasis on processes rather than static structures, Sutherland (1980) produced a lengthy and tightly argued case for the sense of self having evolved with the advent of homo sapiens and in response to the survival requirement of social connectedness. The development of a *sense of self* he saw as a quantum leap in human evolution; he thought that man's self was his "essential organising principle" (p. 10) which, in evolutionary terms, fostered "the flexibility, resilience and persistence of human groups by maximising the potential resources within each individual, and did not confine communities to rigid hierarchical organisations" (p. 25).

Sutherland conceptualized the self as an innately patterned process that allowed the baby to seek out personhood. Babies develop their individuality from their interaction with significant others in their environment. The innate psychic tools for this task include the concept of *matching* in which the baby experiences positive affective tone when its needs for recognition as a person are adequately met from the environment. Stern (1985) and Trevarthen (1980), who have observed, developed, and experimentally validated this process, use the term *intersubjectivity*. The gestalt term of *closure* also describes this process well. Matching allows the baby to begin to develop a sense of otherness—a sense of having a *me shape*, which, through time and further cognitive growth, becomes a primary identity. For Sutherland, this originary self process differs from the subsequent development of various identities. We may experience ourselves as having many different identities in our lives—for example, son, daughter, mother, father, doctor, priest—but the sense of a central me-ness, or core self, transcends these. The core self's status as process rather than established content determines its nature as a felt experience rather than a static structure that is objectively knowable in the traditional sense.

The central core self feeling is a gestalt, a whole, whereas identities are components of that whole and develop through interactive experiences with the environment. As the person grows, identities change or are replaced and new ones are generated throughout the life span. The two concepts of self and identity are inextricably linked but the existence of a core self in interaction with an adequate environment remains the necessary and sufficient condition for adaptive identity development for the individual in a social group.

From this evolutionary scientific perspective Sutherland reviewed the growth and development of the self concept in psychoanalytic theory. In Chapter 21, "The Antonomous Self," he outlines the contributions of Hartmann, Fairbairn, Mahler, Erikson, Lichtenstein, Balint, Winnicott, and Kohut, and notes that, without exception, they all emphasized the crucial importance of the self in their writings. He was concerned, however, that many of these theorists, with the exception of Fairbairn and Lichtenstein and later, Greenberg and Mitchell, tended in varying degrees to view the self as a *product* of drive theory, or make no comment at all on the origins of the self. Sutherland realized that psychoanalytic thinking must not be hampered by continuous theoretical cloning that could sap its vitality. The concept of *developmental tilt* (Mitchell 1988) quoted by Ghent (1992) refers to the tampering with theory that occurs when the preoedipal baby, the baby of object relations theory (which contains much of the current theory of the self) is introduced beneath Freud's baby, without altering the centrality of traditional drive theory. "The traditional model is jacked up, and new relational concepts are slid underneath" (Mitchell 1988, p. 137). Mitchell (1988) and Ghent (1992) pointedly note that this maneuver has the advantage of being politically expedient. However, it threatens the future of psychoanalysis. To survive, it must remain an active, evolving theory that challenges current assumptions.

Sutherland saw the issue as vital. He viewed the traditional psychoanalytic theoretical model as taking in new concepts and accommodating them within its own philosophical system, but never facilitating their separate growth and development. Such a system, looked upon in evolutionary terms, risked growing too large, becoming gross, inflexible, and unable to grow or change. Eventually it would either tear itself apart in a forlorn attempt to integrate new concepts (concepts like the self cannot be integrated without losing their central essence) or be left behind by new thinking because of a lack of relevance and an inability to keep up with developments and changes in the wider scientific, cultural, and social fields.

Stated in very broad terms, Sutherland's aim was to ensure that traditional drive theory was placed within a philosophical perspective. He attempted through his theoretical work to establish a biosocial concept of the self and locate it at the center of psychoanalytic theory rather than as a spin-off of the drives. He had no wish to eliminate drive theory since he was very well aware of its importance in the history of psychoanalysis: rather, he attempted to give drive theory a self perspective and argued for its place as the servant rather than the master of the self process.

Quite literally he wished psychoanalysis to make a new "start from the center of the personality" (1985a, p. 1). In Chapter 24, he argues that in order to succeed in this task, psychoanalysis requires (1) a metapsychology of the self and (2) a metapsychology based on an evolutionary scientific paradigm that seeks to study process rather than structure. He attempts to provide psychoanalysis with an evolutionary arm, an evolutionary perspective to lock it into a much wider and developing system of scientific thought, and thus ensure its preservation as a vibrant, evolving system. It is this aspect of Sutherland's work that is revolutionary. If it were to be given a critical level of support, Sutherland's evolutionary perspective on psychoanalysis could provide a closure concept for psychoanalysis as a whole and a new philosophical foundation for the necessary development and change to facilitate theory and practice toward what has been termed a post-Kleinian or third-phase psychoanalysis (Trist 1991).

SELF AND OBJECT IN THE INSTITUTIONAL SYSTEM FOR TRAINING IN THE CARING PROFESSIONS

"What supports the carer is not encouragement in the conventional sense. . . . It is to be part of a learning system greater than himself" (Sutherland 1979, p. 12, and see Chapter 19, p. 277).

Like Sutherland, Fairbairn, in the mid '40s, believed that popularization of psychoanalysis was not desirable in that it could never be more than superficially understood. Fairbairn thought the influence of psychoanalysis would most probably be exerted through its impact on psychiatry and other sciences. During the last 20 years of Sutherland's life, he became less interested in the possible influence on psychiatry and more concerned with its linkage to other sciences. He followed Fairbairn in thinking that psychoanalysis had influenced contemporary thought in wider fields. Popularization had taken place through the medium of general literature and especially through the novels. Sutherland saw novelists and poets as the real allies of modern psychoanalytic thinkers in the use they made of the fairy tales and myths that enshrine the same themes as symptoms and dreams. Fairbairn's theme was that psychoanalysis should be judged by its scientific rather than by its philosophical achievements. Looked upon in this way psychoanalysis ceased to be merely a method of treatment and became a method of scientific investigation profitably employed within the whole group of psychological and sociological sciences.

Practical application of psychoanalysis is most obviously relevant to the treatment of psychopathological states but it is also helpful in understanding normal development and in securing the upbringing and education of children. At the same time, psychoanalysis contributes to the solution of social problems such as international conflict and social unrest: American psychoanalysts such as Volkan (1988) have made significant contributions to conflict resolution in international politics. Sutherland put his belief in the importance of applied psychoanalytic thought into institutional form. He achieved this in the first place as medical director of the Tavistock Clinic, which became internationally recognized during his directorship, and later as founder of the Scottish Institute of Human Relations.

Creating an institution in Scotland (a country in its own right) was a very different undertaking than managing one in London surrounded by other analysts. It involved establishing for the first time a significant psychoanalytic culture, a way of thinking that was well established in London but unfamiliar to the Scots. Sutherland's establishment of an analytic institute in Scotland involved on the one hand a return to his birthplace (and final place of rest), and on the other, the final interpretation of his own self in his personally and professionally mature years. He entered the richest period of creative thought about how a self develops in the human infant and is sustained in society.

Sutherland's developing understanding of the self was based on Fairbairn's view that the human infant is primarily object seeking and that what the infant (or individual) desires and seeks most deeply is emotional contact with important people (mother, in the first instance). This emphasis on emotional contact with significant others in the surrounding environment suffused the model used by Sutherland as institute builder. He realized that the development of an institution had all the inherent difficulties encountered in the infant's relationship with mother, then father, family, and wider social context. He put theory into practice by considering the nature of the environment in which the newborn institution was to thrive and then by systematically enriching that environment. He took the view from the beginning that the aim of the Scottish Institute of Human Relations was not simply to produce psychoanalysts to meet a Scottish society's emotional needs, but to create an establishment whose primary aim was that of spreading psychoanalytic knowledge throughout the helping and caring professions so as to raise the overall quality of personal health services in Scotland.

Sutherland promoted tolerance of complexity with clarity about goals. He used to say, "The first business of any business is to know what business it is in. So what is the business of psychoanalysis?" He saw, shrewdly, that the difficulty in which the psychoanalytic institutions of the world find themselves arises from failing to ask these questions. Institutes assume at their peril that their sole business is to produce psychoanalysts. According to Sutherland, a psychosocial organism with that primary task has no social relevance. The notion of hundreds of analysts going off merely to reproduce themselves, making their hundreds thousands, could not be the future. "We have instead to get psychoanalytic knowledge of the person across to society," he insisted. Freud, he thought, knew that very well and so wrote books for the intelligent public of his day. But even that wasn't enough—for the simple reason that our commodity, namely psychoanalytic knowledge, is itself disturbing. It compels you to consider your own self in new and unaccustomed ways. That raises deep anxieties and in turn requires the help of other people.

The aim of the Scottish Institute of Human Relations from the first was to increase the level of psychoanalytic knowledge among the caring professions in Scotland. Of course the training of candidates in psychoanalytic psychotherapy was to be a crucial and central part of that, but not the overall task. These principles were stated from the outset so that, for example, in the 2-year Human Relations and Counselling Course, senior and experienced professionals did not come for a personal analysis but for study, reading, and reflection on experience, in an endeavor to get something of the psychoanalytic perspective on their own work. As the theory and the music gets across to them, a turbulence develops and needs to be taken up within the course. As a result, at the end of every year some individuals come to the conclusion that they need to look at this disturbance and go on to undertake a personal analysis. Some of them will specialize as analysts.

Sutherland put object-relations theory into practice in the Scottish Institute of Human Relations. The development and maintenance of the self requires a learning system and the Institute is there in response to that belief, as well as in response to the needs of the community. A steady supply of analytic genius from the psychoanalytic training program at the core of the Institute's identity is needed to maintain and develop the skills of members who are variously involved in education, social work, psychiatry, and voluntary agencies. This model offers a feedback system to the Institute and by embodying the theory makes sense of it.

Sutherland's image of man is that of "an open system with a need to be valued and confirmed, striving to integrate the separate subselves as part of his self, and challenged by the need to deal realistically with a changing environment" (Personal Communication to Murray Leishman, 1980). If the search for objects and persons is a more basic force than the gratification of instincts, then the setting in which this is embodied is crucial. People in key positions in education, medicine, and social work who are in tune with the psychodynamic approach in their own field are needed to keep psychoanalysis on course. An instinct theorist on the old classical lines could never have founded an analytic institute on the model of the Scottish Institute of Human Relations, or carried it through.

Sutherland took the view that the future of psychoanalysis depended upon the development of psychoanalytic training combined with human relations activities in a total institution. The specialist training in psychoanalysis would complement and influence a wider program of learning. Because of its prolonged nature the psychoanalytic method can never meet the needs of society. According to Sutherland, its value was to deepen our understanding of the powerful emotions that affect our well being and consequently our everyday lives. He believed that if knowledge gathered by psychoanalytic research were combined with creative resources in the community, we could learn how to use this knowledge in new ways and make a contribution to improving mental health in a given community. This was the philosophy he believed had a future.

The creation of the Scottish Institute of Human Relations, with its ripple effect on Scottish culture, marks the emergence of Sutherland's own autonomous self. This event, together with his book *Fairbairn's Journey to the Interior* (1989), which he completed in his eighties, clearly helped to release the grip of the internal imagos of his own parents in interchange with the authority figures in the outside world. Of course he spoke consistently in positive terms of admiration and respect for Fairbairn, but he left his mentor behind. Sutherland faced Fairbairn's disappointment when he did not join him in starting an analytically orientated institute in Scotland years earlier, but chose instead to take up the appointment as Director of the Tavistock in 1946 after the War. It is perhaps just as well that Sutherland went to London, for there he applied Fairbairn's object-relational perspectives and learned his trade as an institution builder and thinker in the company of such giants as Eric Trist.

Sutherland was the last to boast about it as an achievement or to idealize it, but that an analytic institute happened at all in Scotland is, like Dr. Johnson's dog, remarkable—an Institute consisting of fourteen different learning projects only one of which is the psychoanalytic psychotherapy training but all sharing a psychodynamic theory, in a country whose culture is still dominated by the Protestant ethic of bearing problems without admitting weakness or bothering anyone else. Remarkable, admired, envied, and denigrated, but always a force for change, integration, and growth.

PERSONAL AUTONOMY AND UNDERSTANDING OF THE SELF

For all his community outreach, friendliness, humor, and sociability, Sutherland was a private man who would not have left among his personal papers anything comparable to Fairbairn's rivetingly interesting diaries of self-analysis and dreams. One must therefore invoke a psychobiographical approach to speculate about his self-development, his insatiable curiosity about the self, and his movement toward a new theory of the self. Because social behavior interacts with the individual's inner world, "biography is our proper mode," he would say. He studied John Buchan's somber last novel, *Sick Heart River*, and made a good case of its being essentially a fictionalized autobiography (Chapter 23). But above all, in his own book, *Fairbairn's Journey into the Interior* (1989a), Sutherland documents psychoanalytic ideas arising not simply from clinical work with patients, but from the growing analytic self of the analyst. For instance, he briefly portrays Klein wrestling the events of her life into theory, and shows that her subsequent paper, "A Contribution to the Psychogenesis of Manic-Depressive States," written following the death of her son, had, in turn, a creatively disturbing effect on Fairbairn, which he used to good purpose in his own self-analysis and theory building. In Chapter 25, he describes the parallel growth in his own analytic self while writing his biography of Fairbairn.

Hate and the autonomy of the self was a principal theme in Sutherland's later thinking. His theoretical work provides an invaluable perspective on his life as it reflects his struggle for autonomy, which he achieved after taking in his own hate. He worked toward developing and sharing a mature capacity to handle hatred and envy within the corporate identity of the Scottish Institute. His dislike of establishment thinking and organization sprang from his democratic intellect nurtured in the generalist philosophy of a Scottish University. He prized Freud's legacy not for its power to confer a spurious esoteric status on psychoanalysts but for its power to disturb the sleep of society.

SUTHERLAND'S CONTRIBUTION TO PSYCHOANALYSIS

Toward the end of his life Sutherland called together a small study group to consider once again the required paradigm shift in psychoanalytic theory for expanded understanding of the self. Wallerstein (1988) had made it quite clear that the period of a single theory and unified analytic enterprise was over. At this stage in our analytic history, he said, we are united by a shared focus on the clinical interactions. When we look back to our explanatory structures, within which we conceptualize the process of therapy, self-functioning, and the reversal of psychopathology, we are in a plural situation with a range of metaphoric expressions. Sutherland, like Wallerstein, positively welcomed the advent of a comparative psychoanalysis expounded by Greenberg and Mitchell (1983), that is, one in which we discern kinds of psychoanalysis in the new situation where there is no monolith. Wallerstein (1988) writes, "Drive theory is linked to the positions of Hobbes and Locke, that man is essentially an individual animal and that human satisfactions and goals are fundamentally personal and individual; the role of the state rests on the concept of 'negative liberty,' that the state adds nothing essential to individual satisfaction as such, but just ensures the possibility of personal fulfillment. . . ." (p. 18 fn), i.e., the current philosophy of governments in the west in this epoch.

But he continues, "Relational theory is linked philosophically on the other hand to the positions of Rousseau, Hegel and Marx, that man is an essentially social animal and that human satisfactions and goals are realizable only within a community; the role of the state here rests on the concept of 'positive liberty,' to provide an indispensable 'positive' function by offering its citizens that which they cannot provide for themselves in isolation. Greenberg and Mitchell state in relation to this that 'the drive/structure model and the relational/structure model embody these two major traditions within Western philosophy' " (Wallerstein 1988, p. 18 fn).

At every step Sutherland insisted on bringing to the fore these theoretical matters, always maintaining that drive theory was putting an impossible strain on psychoanalysis and that it was essential to find a relational theory perspective.

Trist (1991) wrote of Sutherland,

> It appears to us that Jock approached the depressive position through the schizoid/paranoid position as Fairbairn did, though it is not clear that Fairbairn had the complete and distinctive understanding of the depressive position as originally put forward by Melanie Klein. Sutherland did. His original ideas which were only incompletely formulated in his last papers, foreshadow a psychoanalysis which is post-Kleinian. Fundamental for him was the idea of the individual as a person, and of the mother/child relationship as interpersonal. "Object relations" was really too abstract a term for him. The interrelations were for him multi-dimensional from the beginning. One sees here the beginning of a new frame of reference which would probably have led to a third generation of psychoanalysis. [p. 1]

In the clinical appraisal of the person and in institute building, we see Sutherland's view of the person as a dynamic organization of purposes and commitments whose behavior is governed by conscious and unconscious motives and whose development and functioning are inseparably linked to his social environment. Jock Sutherland accused himself of not devoting enough attention to his own ideas. This is our loss, but it may well be that his light touch, as Trist (1991) predicted, will increase his long-range influence.

I

OBJECT-RELATIONS THEORY

1. OBJECT-RELATIONS THEORY AND THE CONCEPTUAL MODEL OF PSYCHOANALYSIS

In recent years there have been two prominent areas of development in psychoanalytic theory:

a. The advances in ego psychology, in which Hartmann, Kris, Lowenstein, and Rapaport in the United States and Anna Freud in the United Kingdom have played a leading part.
b. The work on the role of object relations from what has been called loosely the English school. Although deriving in large part from Melanie Klein, these views have had major contributions from British analysts other than Klein's associates, for example, Fairbairn and Winnicott.

To British analysts it is striking how far apart these two areas of work have remained. (For some years it seemed that the work of Klein had been declared an un-American activity!) There are now signs that this situation is changing. I believe this trend is due to a growing realization that some of the apparent differences do not represent incompatible lines of work, but, on the contrary, can be seen in substantial measure as complementary. In what follows I propose to make use of the conceptual models that have been developed as a result of the theoretical work in these two areas to focus attention on where some of the differences lie and so help to promote a fruitful interchange of viewpoints.

In his book, *Energy and Structure in Psychoanalysis*, Colby (1955, p. 79) prefaces his description of his model of the psychic apparatus with some observations on the status and function of models. Models represent one method of describing the parts of a whole and their organization. They are "visual aids, but they picture only imaginative constructions of organization." Further notes of caution are sounded when he points out that, although they do not constitute a theory but merely help to illustrate it, they are often mistaken for the realities of which they are representations.

The complexities of the massive body of observations and constructs that now characterize psychoanalysis make it most unlikely that any one model would

---

Note: The discussant is Otto Kernberg, M.D.

cover other than limited aspects of its theories, and this is probably one of the reasons that have led psychoanalysts to prefer verbal descriptions of their theories. Nevertheless, the *fons et origo* of psychoanalytic theories, the psychoanalytic process, has universally accepted features which readily suggest the use of models. Karl Menninger (1958), in one of the recent books on this theme, *Theory of Psychoanalytic Technique*, finds a working model of the way in which psychoanalytic therapy operates as a helpful device. The position may be put more strongly. Psychoanalysis is a long-term process that is set in motion deliberately by the analyst. He assumes that only through it will the patient get the necessary conditions for achieving certain changes in his personality functioning. Moreover, the analyst expects to control this process in substantial measure by his activities. A statement in the form of a model, or quasimodel, of the concepts used in the theory and practice that underlie his controls is a necessity if assumptions are to be adequately scrutinized and checked, and hence greater power and precision achieved.

The requirements Colby lists for a model of the psychic apparatus can be taken as a starting point. For him a model should:

1. distinguish the variables of primary importance from others that are secondary or derivative;
2. show how internal biological conditions are integrated with the external environment;
3. allow for maturation and experiential development;
4. provide for individual uniqueness and societal variations;
5. indicate how it works.

Of this list, the first one contains the crux of the matter. What are the *variables of primary importance?* I believe it is the failure to get these right rather than the complexity of the data, that has led to the neglect of conceptual models. Most psychoanalysts have found the models put forward so far to have only limited relevance to their practice; and for those with more theoretical interests, the awareness of this gap between theory and practice has confirmed their lack of enthusiasm for them.

In considering the applications of Hartmann's development of psychoanalytic thought, Rapaport (1960) notes that the essential task of studying a relationship between an explanatory theory and the method of observation by which the data are obtained is rarely pursued. We need to know, for instance, "to what extent does psychoanalytic theory reflect human nature, and to what extent does it reflect Freud's methods of studying human nature?" (p. 79). He then goes on to state that the psychoanalytic relationship . . . may well require a distinction to be made between ". . . a *general* psychoanalytic theory which is little dependent on these methods, and a *specific* psychoanalytic theory which is greatly dependent on them" (p. 79).

It is abundantly clear that in Rapaport's writings, as he himself states, he focuses on those aspects of the theory that are not obviously dependent on the clinical method and tries to avoid concepts that obviously are tied to them, like transference, interpretation, and so forth. A noteworthy instance of this divorce from the clinical findings occurs in Rapaport's earlier paper (1951) on, "The Conceptual Model of Psychoanalysis," ". . . for reasons that lie beyond the scope of this paper—I will not deal here with the relevance or irrelevance of this model to phenomena which are variously referred to as those of conscience, ego ideal, superego, etc." (p. 232).

I believe that some of the differences in the two areas of work may be related to this apparent greater distance between clinical data and theory in the ego-psychology group as compared with the British workers. To quote Rapaport again (1960), "When the rules of thumb of clinical psychoanalysis are equated with the theory of psychoanalysis, the observations and concepts which bridge the gap between the basic concepts and the initial observations are inevitably overlooked" (p. 84). What to my mind is the most important part of this observation is the phrase "the rules of thumb" because it indicates that the psychoanalytic method for him is a rather haphazard one from the scientific point of view. Rapaport further notes that: "The psychoanalytic writer and practitioner is inclined to speak of psychoanalytic concepts and theories in terms of 'content.' " He then adds that ". . . Content is an important '*guide*' to the practitioner," but the "majority of contributions to the literature tend to dwell on content to the neglect of other guides. . . . What is lost sight of—and the practitioner need not necessarily keep this in focus or even in sight, but those interested in theory must—is the functional (and thus also conceptual) relationship *to which* the content is a guide. . . . No content yields its full meaning unless its formal characteristics, and those of the time, place and context of its appearance, are taken into consideration, that is to say, abstracted. . . . The stress on content seems to be one of the main causes for overlooking the relationship between concepts and observables" (pp. 84–85).

Much of this stricture is arresting to the psychoanalyst brought up in the tradition of the British School. For him the distinction that is being made between the content and the formal relationships would not exist, because the focus of his attention all the time is the study of the relationships going on between himself and the patient and to these content is only one guide. For him, too, clinical data are the foundations on which psychoanalytic theory rests. He therefore views theories not closely related to these with reserve; and with regard to the method, he would not accept its status as at the "rule of thumb" level.

THE CLASSICAL CONCEPTUAL MODEL OF PSYCHOANALYSIS AND EGO PSYCHOLOGY

The classical model of psychoanalysis appeared many years ago when Freud (1923) formulated his structural concepts. The ego was the part of the personality concerned with organizing the adaptation of the person to the external environment, regulating the means by which he sought satisfaction for his drives (the id) and reconciling these with a more primitive control system (the superego), which operated unconsciously within the ego. These structures were finally shaped by the experience of the Oedipus conflict according to the first formulations. This theory permitted a considerable advance in psychoanalytic understanding and consequently produced a fresh mass of observations from the widened range of conditions it enabled the psychoanalyst to treat more comprehensively. It seemed to give a foundation for so much that had been obscure, especially the unconscious sources of resistance and guilt. It led to an interest in the structural parts of the personality, the ego and the superego, and to an understanding of how the ego was patterned by its defensive needs. The development of the ego in its earliest phases became increasingly important, a trend related to the fact that data from the neuroses gained in width and depth and also to the new findings of child analysis.

Freud's view of the id as a reservoir of unorganized drive energies with the structured ego and superego trying to regulate their discharge was gradually perceived as an oversimplification. Hartmann began to publish his well-known series of papers, many his own and others with associates, on a new concept of early development according to which the ego and the id were differentiated from the first undifferentiated phase. The ego was structured not only by the experiences of the infant and young child in the satisfaction and frustration of its drives, but also by the maturation of autonomous ego capacities, for example, motility, perception, and so forth. As part of these developments Hartmann took psychoanalysis to be no longer a theory restricted to conflict or to unconscious processes but a general psychological theory. His additions, however, to the theory of ego development and the concept of autonomous ego do not alter basically Freud's model. For him, the id still derives from libidinal and aggressive energies.

The value of Freud's model in relation to the clinical phenomena is obvious enough and so it should be since the component parts were postulated to account for clinical phenomena. On the other hand, the ego-psychology group has tended to regard some of the conceptual usages and developments from these theories, for instance, the superego, as anthropomorphic notions. To quote from Rapaport again, "In the clinical parlance (and even in the theoretical writings) of psychoanalysis, the explanatory concepts are anthropomorphized, reified, or at best presented in existential terms, giving the impression that they refer to entities or at least that each of them refers to a specific behaviour. But this is not consistent with the theory. The tendency to anthropomorphize and reify, and the preference for hypothetical constructs, probably derives from clinical practice, where there is a premium on the 'plausibility' and 'uncomplicated everyday application' of concepts." (1960, p. 40)

There has certainly been a massive move here from what Brierley (1951) has described as the personological level of description to the terms of process theory. Guntrip (1961) in his recent book has dealt with some of the implications

Sutherland in Vienna, August 1937

of this move at length and I shall not devote any attention to it other than to summarize by saying that herein lies the critical issue. In Rapaport's model he combines three primary models designed to explain action or conation, ideation, and affect, each of which was formulated early on by Freud. He then has to outline secondary models, which are concerned with the development of derivative drives. "In contrast to the primary models, all the secondary models involve structuralized delay, that is to say, progressive, hierarchically layered structure development. The structures in question are: defence and control structures, structures which segregate affect charges, and the means structures which subserve secondary action—and thought-processes. A parallel development takes place in the hierarchy of motivations; each step in structure development results in a delay imposed on motivations which in turn gives rise to new derivative motivations and affects. The multifaceted hierarchic development is the development of the ego . . . and involves the differentiation of the ego from the id, and the super-ego from the ego. The id-ego-super-ego trichotomy is the broadest structural articulation of the mental organization and, as such, a crucial conception of the clinical theory of psychoanalysis. Since it can be derived from the models discussed, it is not an independent model and we shall not dwell on it here" (1960, p. 33).

The critical issue as Guntrip (1961) brings out in his discussion may be put this way. While it is true that the eventual organizations that are at the top of the hierarchy can be derived from previous processes, in what sense are we to accept the earlier processes as the primary variables that Colby stipulated as the first requirement in a model? Here we are up against a familiar problem in biological thinking, of the extent to which one may lose sight of essential qualitative differences that supervene at the highest levels of organization by relating these complex phenomena to variables appropriate to lower levels. It is not of course that Rapaport is ignoring this problem. For instance, after noting the steps in psychoanalytic theory in a discussion of the structure of the psychic system from the adaptive point of view he goes on to say that

> the fifth conception of reality, foreshadowed by both Freud's third conception and Hartmann's, is the psychosocial one developed by Erikson. . . . Man is potentially pre-adapted, not only to one average expectable environment, but to a whole evolving series of such environments. These environments to which man adapts are not "objective," but rather social environments which meet his maturation and development halfway: social *modalities* (e.g., the socially accepted forms of "getting") foster, select and harness his developing *modes* (e.g., the incorporative oral mode) of behavior (Erikson 1950). This is the genetic counterpart of Hartmann's systematic formulation; it is thus far the only attempt to conceptualize the phases of epigenesis . . . through which pre-adaptedness becomes effective, and in which processes of adaptation inseparably unite behavior epigenesis and environmental conditions. [p. 61]

For Rapaport, however, the inclusion of the psychosocial point of view is "a mark of systematic weakness, since it is merely a specific aspect of the adaptive point of view" (p. 65). He states that "Hartmann's and Erikson's theories are too new, their implications too little understood, and their relationship to each other too little explored . . . to permit a statement disregarding all but systematic considerations" (p. 66).

In short, therefore, the main theoretical trend deriving from the work on ego psychology has thus far led to a concentration on rather limited concepts for the functioning of the personality. Although the relatedness of the ego to the other parts of the personality is constantly acknowledged amongst the ego-psychology group, the failure to do justice to the structuring in the other parts, especially in that area covered by the term *the id*, has led to the development of concepts that perpetuate, or even increase, a divorce between theory and clinical practice that many analysts have recognized in recent years. One of the main features in ego psychology seems to be a need to formulate theories in terms that are thought to be more appropriate to science, or more accurately, to other scientists. For analysts, however, as for others, theories must be closely linked to their practice, and the data of psychoanalysis do not lend themselves to too much depersonalization.

THE OBJECT-RELATIONS MODEL

The most radical statements of object-relations theory in Great Britain, those of Fairbairn, and the detailed expositions of Fairbairn's theories, together with his own contributions, by Guntrip, adopt a completely opposed standpoint in trying to create a model that operates in a way that can be directly related to clinical data and social interaction. This move in the direction of adopting more anthropomorphized structures, that is, structures that do justice to the phenomena of interpersonal relations, would also appear to be a direct development of the last major trend in Freud's work: the structural theories and the introduction of the superego. It is not, as I suggested earlier, a development incompatible with the ego-psychology work, but a development on a more comprehensive front and one into which the ego-psychology work can, I believe, be fitted.

Several developmental trends in Great Britain have contributed to a particular interest in the structuring of the personality from the very start in terms of the relationships between the infant and its environment. Balint (1952), stimulated by Ferenczi, was one of the first psychoanalysts to make a definite pronouncement on the primacy of object relations. Using observational data from the feeding interaction between mothers and young babies, he linked his inferences from these with the findings from child analysis, the study of psychotics, and the greatly enriched data coming from the psychoanalysis of the neuroses following developments in the use of the transference consequent on Freud's structural theory. The work of Susan Isaacs, Middlemore and Winnicott, and others reinforced this trend.

It was Klein's work, however, that eventually impinged more widely, more profoundly, perhaps because she was the first analyst to make full use of the extraordinary richness and complexity of the phantasy lives of young children. Moreover, whatever reactions her theories may have aroused, there was no question of her data being too much the product of her method because children's phantasies can be studied in considerable detail without analytic intervention provided the observer is prepared to spend time with a young child. Such manifestations required the postulation of a relatively high degree of structural development at early stages.

Klein and her co-workers suggested that from the start of extrauterine existence the painful affects of frustration and the intense aggression associated with these feelings led to the creation within the psyche of developing *imagos* of the early objects. At first the breast was predominant, but the internal objects rapidly extended to the whole of the mother's body and her person. These structures evoked within the child the same feelings of persecutory relationships as had the external object. Alongside these persecutory imagos, there are also being laid down imagos of the good breast-mother.

According to Klein, these inner objects are very real and concrete in the experience of the child. The ego grows in active relationship with them and its successful development is governed by the intensity of the affects in these internal relationships. Much controversy has been engendered on the nature of these internal objects and their role. Because of the concrete qualities she attributed to them, many analysts have felt there was a strong anthropomorphic tinge about Klein's theorizing. Nevertheless, it does not seem that there is anything improbable or unpsychological about such internal imagos developing from the earliest stages, or that these imagos should play a dynamic role. As Brierley (1951), one of the most careful and objective writers amongst British psychoanalysts, puts it, there is no real difficulty in conceiving of an embryonic imago of the object from the start because of the different feelings that must be present when the object, in this case the nipple, is actually present (p. 50). What is of fundamental importance is the function of this inner imago or object. As a built-in part of the relationship between the infant and the object, it appears that it can be used as the object itself—Freud's hallucinated object—or as part of an object-seeking system in which it patterns the perceptual organization. This latter role is what Klein describes as the projection-introjection system of object-relations development. That is to say, outer objects tend to be perceived and responded to in terms of inner ones. Normally, however, the outer objects do not behave as badly as the inner ones. When the former are introjected again they are therefore less persecuting; social learning occurs.

When the affect within the relationship system is too disturbing, the inner objects become too frightening to be used in this projection-introjection system. Relations with the outer world can become seriously restricted. Such systems are then split off within the psyche from the central one in which the transactions with the outer world are proceeding apace. The systems which get segregated retain their bad objects and because of the latter being relatively unmodified by the transactions with the real objects, the frightening qualities of these inner objects remain governed by the primitive affects and phantasies. The internal bad objects for Klein are the precursors of the superego and the severity of superego persecution in many patients, adults and children, supports her view that these structures must have been laid down in very early stages.

The range of inner objects created within the psyche means that the child in Klein's view has an inner microcosm in which strong affective relations with inner objects, good or bad, are the fundamental feature. The child's play and most of its developing cognitive and socially adaptive capacities are determined by these inner relations.

The full implications of Klein's observations and formulations for some of the classical theories of psychoanalysis were not followed through by her, and it remained for Fairbairn (1952a) to point these out in a series of papers beginning in 1940. Although expressing his indebtedness to Klein's views on the importance of inner objects, Fairbairn developed his own ideas in complete independence. The starting point of his thinking was the nature of the difficulties presented by schizoid patients. It has long been known that these patients have pronounced difficulties in their social relations, but what had not been recognized, according to Fairbairn, was the extent to which their inability to make satisfying personal relationships appeared to be the root of their troubles. Moreover, he asserted on the basis of his clinical experience that underneath the symptomatic differences between the various psychoneurotic conditions, there was a severe schizoid problem.

To account for the phenomena of the schizoid disorders, Fairbairn was led to the view that it is the relationship with the object and not gratification of impulse that is the ultimate aim of libidinal striving. The *cri de coeur* of all his patients, he concluded, was for a loving mother or father, and not for the quenching of more limited tensions. In keeping with this longing, the main features of the schizoid patient are defences against the painful affects of not being loved by a parent figure with full acceptance. The conflicts within the primary relationship of the infant and its mother lead to a splitting off or segregation within the originally unitary ego of the intolerable aspects of the relationship. Such a split involves a division of the pristine ego into structures each of which contains (a) a part of the ego, (b) the object that characterizes the related relationship, and (c) the affects of the latter. Fairbairn therefore proposed that the libido theory in its classical form and the concept of unorganized id should be replaced by concepts of dynamic structures derived from a psychology of object relations.

Revisionists of Freud's theories have often been castigated for their failure to give systematic form to their views, and to state how their revisions affect psychoanalytic theory as a whole. It is also commonly said of them that they do not grasp psychoanalytic theory fully. A careful appraisal of Fairbairn's writings removes the grounds for any such criticism being applied to him. He writes with admirable lucidity and reveals the close relationship of his own views to those of Freud. Thus, in his paper on "The Repression and the Return of Bad Objects" (1952a, p. 61) he shows in Freud's own writings how the nature of the repressed can be related to objects. Freud had noted that as well as the internalized relations between the superego and the ego (the relationship of the ego to its "good" internalized objects), the superego also represented an energetic reaction formation against the earliest object choices of the id. The significance of this statement, as Fairbairn points out, is surely to imply that the repressed will be concerned with the relationship of the ego to "bad" internalized objects.

Fairbairn has given an outline of the development of object relations from the dependence of infancy to the mature relationships of later stages. The fact that he has not filled in this development in detail is of little consequence, for the conceptual model of adult behavior which he developed readily permits Colby's requirements to be met. Guntrip has described Fairbairn's final model (1961) and here it is only appropriate to note its main features. These are:

1. a central ego in relation to an ideal object directly repressing the following structures:
2. an antilibidinal ego related to the rejecting object (sadistic primitive superego); and
3. a libidinal ego related to the exciting object.

The repression of this latter structure is further reinforced by (2).

These structures are conceived as interrelated dynamic psychological systems, constantly in active relationship with each other and with the outer world. Each structure has a great complexity in depth into which is built its history. The particular experiences of the person will contribute many subsystems that could, for instance, be precipitates of repressed relations at the oral, anal, or phallic phases of classical theory; but there is a tendency for these constituent subsystems to group or to assume a hierarchical order around the image of one person, even if only loosely. The first manifestations of a bad object relationship in the course of analysis may therefore centre around one or other of these subsystems, but as the analysis proceeds all the components come to the surface.

Fairbairn has retained the adjective *libidinal* to describe the object-seeking tendency of the person. I think his libidinal ego might be more accurately described as the repressed or rejected libidinal relationships, for while it is true that the repressed needs are libidinal in character, not all libidinal relationships are "outside" the central ego.

To minimize the intrusion of possibly confusing theoretical stereotypes I propose to put what I take to be the essence of Fairbairn's conceptual model into a series of statements and propositions. Many of these are about behaviour or at a first level of abstraction from the kind of phenomena met with in human relations in general and in psychoanalytic relationships in particular. Where they contain inferences about the nature of underlying processes I believe these inferences can be clearly recognized.

(1) The person is related to his social environment by means of a number of dynamic psychic structures or systems, which vary greatly in the degree to which they are in open transaction with the social environment.

(2) The word *systems* indicates that these structures are organized and seek to effect certain kinds of relationships. By the term *transaction* is meant an ongoing relationship in which there is a *reciprocal interaction*. Each person is involved in such relationships in an active way with his or her needs constantly affecting the behavior of the other and vice versa.

(3) Systems vary in their mode of activity and in their topological position within the personality as a whole. They fall into two important groups:

a. Those that are felt to belong to that part of the self the individual wants to be. These come within a central organizing structure (the ego).
b. Those that are split off or repressed from this self or central system. (The words split, repressed, dissociated, or segregated are used interchangeably in this context.)

The Central System, or Ego

(4) This system has assimilated and organized much of the experience with significant people in the early environment and hence much of the cultural pattern in which the individual is reared. This central organization (the ego) is characterized by its relatively much greater capacity to learn and by its unique feature, namely that its integrative functions appear closely connected with consciousness.

In the healthy adult, the main needs are sufficiently egosyntonic and of such a character that a manifold set of personal relationships is sought and maintained. The relatively free transactions between the need systems themselves (greater communication) in the healthy person also means that he responds more as a whole, is more integrated in assessing inner and outer reality. The central ego in such a person is therefore being enriched throughout life and this *constant enrichment provides a motivational growth and support*.

Typical of the healthy or strong ego are this freedom of communication between different need systems and the consonance of the main needs over time.

The whole question of the scale and the maturational phases of developments in the human personality is something which only Erikson (1956) has attempted to encompass. Although Fairbairn discounts instincts in the sense in which they have been commonly used in psychology and psychoanalysis, the work of the ethologists has shown that a more flexible and illuminating approach to the instinctive roots of behaviour can be made, particularly in regard to social behaviour and object relations. Bowlby has made a major contribution in this direction concerning the nature and development of the attachment of the child to his mother. The tie between the reproductive pair is almost certainly mediated by a number of response and need systems that allow for the rearing of the family over time. It is this kind of approach that could lay a biological foundation more in keeping with the need for sustained object relations than is the primary model of drives and their tensions conceived so often in hydrodynamic terms and requiring so many derivative structures for the social behaviour that is basic to human survival.

The development of the relationship of the person with himself, his identity, as consolidated by Erikson's epigenetic phases, might well be illumined by future studies incorporating an ethological approach, particularly in revealing the factors contributing to the development of the need for whole person relationships from the point of view of rearing the family. The survival unit of the human being is the family. The interplay of the manner in which the dependent status of the child contributes to the building up of the need for whole person relationships and the extent to which these are reinforced by future needs stemming from the reproductive constellation within the family and of the position of the latter within the social group, provides endless scope for further work.

(5) The capacity of the central ego to tolerate conflicting needs and to organize them appears to be largely an acquired property. Certain kinds of early experience make or mar this capacity in a profound way. What starts off the ego as an adequate independent organizer, in other words, what lays the foundations for an organizing ego, independent of the mother who has been the first organizer, is particularly important.

Fairbairn's inferences about what seems to have gone wrong in his schizoid patients is in line with the work of many psychoanalysts. The importance for the future functional power of the central ego of critical phases in the early mother–child relationship is now very familiar in phases that have become bywords in analytic writings—Balint's primary love, Erikson's basic trust, Winnicott's true self, and so forth.

(6) In the relationships fashioned predominantly by the central ego the identity and reality of the other is fully accepted, that is, the overall acceptance of the person raises the threshold of toleration for unfulfilled expectancies so that the relationship is maintained. If the frustrations in the relationship are too great despite mutual adaptation attempts, it can be ended without destructive behaviour. The concern for the other in adult relationships stems from many sources, one being the patterning of the central ego's actions by the tendency, even though this be very much a latent process, to make the real relationships approximate to that of the ideal ego with its ideal object.

Repressed Needs and Primitive Control Systems

(7) These systems comprise:

a. certain need systems, which may be designated *repressed aspects of object relations*, and

b. *primitive control systems* (the superego) derived from early inhibition of certain need systems.

In contrast with those of the central ego, the relationships sought by the repressed need systems are relatively closed, in other words, the objects sought are not individuals with mature independence but are realizations of the inner figures. In extreme cases, it can be clearly perceived that the individual has a relation with an inner object with whom he is virtually completely identified, that is, who is a part of himself. This is particularly striking in the self-gratifying perversions—the transvestist who has the sexually exciting relation with the woman with a penis by finding her in his mirror image when he is dressed up. More, often the inner object acts as a scanning apparatus, which seeks a potential object in the outer world. The subego of this system then coerces these people into the role of the inner object. Such objects are not permitted to have any real independence or individuality; they have to fit the inner imago. Sadomasochistic perversions illustrate this activity, and the ease with which the individual can change roles in these perversions indicates the switch from the identification with one end of the system to the other.

(8) The goals sought by these subsystems represent *aspects of the total relationship* with the significant figures of infancy and childhood and range from relationships characteristic of early infantile dependent states of development (for example, "oral" needs) to genital behaviour.

(9) These subsystems have been split off because their aims were incompatible with the preservation of the egosyntonic relationship with the needed person. The conflict gives rise to "pain" (fear, anxiety, guilt, depression, and so forth) associated with their activity.

(10) They are excluded from the conscious self by forces of varying resistance. Their dissociation from consciousness means that little or no adaptation or learning occurs within them.

(11) The original frustration apparently leads to many of them containing, in addition to the affect associated with their own aims, for example, genital gratification, intense anger, and destructiveness towards the person sought; in other words they are largely sadistic in character.

(12) They are constantly seeking outlet in ordinary relationship and/or in phantasy and thought, that is, they have the compulsion to repeat.

(13) Their activity is particularly evocative of the superego systems, that is, they are accompanied by varying degrees of anxiety and guilt.

(14) The resistance some of them show to being brought back into consciousness becomes increased:

a. By their finding hidden satisfactions within the self (in which case a part of the self is treated as the object to be loved and/or hated in the forbidden way. For Fairbairn, it is the secret tie to the repressed exciting object which is the explanation of much of the resistance to giving it up. Or

b. when their objects are projected into other people—especially in close relationships.

(15) A particularly important feature of these needs is that, though there is a defensive tendency for the person to take them to other people than those he wishes to maintain his close good relationship with, nevertheless, there is an even more powerful trend for them to come back into any close relationship with one person. That is to say, *the repressed not only returns, but it tends to return to the representative of the more comprehensive relationship from which it was originally split off.*

(16) All of the psychic systems are interrelated functionally and their relative strengths and capacities for securing satisfaction must be conceived as stemming from a continuous process of interrelated development. The boundaries between the systems vary greatly in their "permeability."

These statements, based on Fairbairn's model, describe the functioning of the person in his social relationships and they provide at least the outline of a model for human interaction, particularly for conflict in social behaviour. They are intended primarily to meet Colby's first requirement, that variables should be at the right level, and his other requirements can be readily fulfilled also.

The study of the central ego, its functions, and development, provide ample scope for ego psychology. The interrelatedness of ego function and the intrusive effects of unconscious object-relationship needs suggest that a comprehensive statement of object-relations theory will provide a suitable framework for the development of psychoanalytic theory. I am dubious, however, about the extension of psychoanalysis to be a general psychology. Psychology requires many methods of study of which the psychoanalytic method is one. Psychology is hollow without psychoanalysis, but it has to draw on many methods and data other than those of psychoanalysis.

SOME USES OF THE MODEL

The Aims of Psychoanalysis

The *general aims* of psychoanalysis can be stated in terms of an object-relations model as initiating and maintaining a process whereby repressed relationship-systems are brought back within the organizing system of the ego so that they can be subjected to learning and adaptation. The psychoanalyst secures this process by:

1. Providing a specially designed situation in which there can be freer communication between the parts of the self and between the repressed systems and a special external object, himself. He facilitates these changes by interpreting the hidden aims of the dissociated relationships as these emerge in the spontaneous behavioral and verbal expressions of the individual towards him.

2. The personal relationship he offers enables the dissociated systems, eventually trying to use him as their object, to be brought into awareness with sufficient affect as well as to be tested against the continuing reality of his interest. This bringing of the dissociated need systems into the requisite kind of awareness allows "extinction" of some needs and learning of new objects for others to take place again.

A greater degree of integration is sought through a twofold process, namely:

a. Increasing the integrative capacity of the central ego system through the overall relationship with the analyst by establishing a capacity to transact with people more freely.
b. Bringing back the dissociated systems for new solutions.

A certain intensity of treatment and its special setting are required for this process to be adequately maintained and regulated.

I shall not do other here than to refer to the "setting" of the patient's total life situation as creating obstacles to the analytic relationship. Certain alterations of this may be required for the analyst's aims to be possible. For instance, parents may maintain with a child or one marital partner may exert on the other a pressure to keep a subrelationship in being, thereby requiring the relationship to be altered for the analysis to proceed.

Transference and the Psychoanalytic Relationship

Transference phenomena enter into all human relationships so that their existence within the psychoanalytic relationship is in no way characteristic. All kinds of people are made the pegs on which the objects of repressed relationships are hung. What is it that is specific to the transference in the analytic relationship? I believe the answer to this question is that the analytic process permits a unique setting of the reintegration of the split relationships in the self. The affects and aims of repressed relationships tend to be acted out by all human beings in some of their personal relationships without the discharge of these affects having other than a minimal or negligible effect on their compulsion to repeat. But the analyst, starting as a good object, usually an ideal one, creates the essential feature of the analytic process in that the split relationships are reexperienced with this *one person* who does not reject them intolerantly. This is, of course, no new statement. It is universally agreed that it is the transference experiences within the analytic setting that lead to change. Karl Menninger's (1958) model of the analytic contract describes this process. I believe, nevertheless, that its implications for our structural concepts have not been fully realized. Can we account for this *crucial aspect of the transference relationship* unless it is postulated that what is repressed, as Fairbairn has described them, are bad aspects of an original unitary relationship of one ego with another whole person, the mother? In other words, can we explain why the analytic relationship is sought and maintained by the patient unless there is an original supraordinate structure that is trying to reunite within itself parts that originally belonged to it, and whose segregation is sustained only by constant strain within it?

Rapaport asks if the analytic method does justice to the phenomena of human relationships or whether instead it creates artifacts. It would appear that this inner compulsive striving to unite the original splits in the ego and its object within one relationship is not a product of the analytic process but a general tendency of human personality. The literature of the world points to Fairbairn's conception of the splitting within an original unitary structure as a universal truth; in short, it is the human tragedy that "each man kills the thing he loves"—or, at least, tries it the uttermost. But what Wilde did not know, and what object-relation theory emphasizes, is that the killing is not to destroy but is to make an infantile protest from which the good relationship will reemerge magically.

A source of evidence with which I have had a good deal of experience in recent years and which is very telling in this connexion, is that which stems from work with marital conflicts. The commonest presenting pattern of these is as follows. In the early phases there is an idealized relationship, or at least what is felt to be a good relationship. This phase may last over years and often includes sexual relationships that are satisfying to both partners. There then begins an insidious process, frequently starting with more initiative from one partner, but sooner or later colluded in by both, through which the repressed relationships with the original significant parent figures are brought in. The particular pattern follows, of course, the specific content of the individual's history and it is remarkable at times how closely the settings and *patterns of original relationships* are reproduced. With these cases, there are many complications, but the common characteristic keeps reappearing; namely, of the bringing into the good relationship the repressed bad aspects of the relationships with the parents. In marriage, processes of this kind are universal but they are ordinarily contained by the balance in favour of the good relationship and its enrichment. Where the difficulties become of such an intensity that help is sought, then a further feature emerges. Despite the tensions and often fairly prolonged periods of hostility and mutual recrimination, there remains a strong desire to get the relationship right. Often this is reinforced by external considerations, for example, for children, but this need is usually present without these factors. In view of the frustrations and sufferings of so many of these spouses before marriage, it would be expected that desperate measures would be put into action to preserve in the relationship the goodness of the early phases. What then determines the entry into the good relationship of the repressed bad relationships? The most plausible theory to my mind is that the spouses are trying to undo the experiences of an early relationship in which the bad aspects belonged with the good. Unfortunately when, as so frequently happens, both partners collude in a process of this kind the relationship becomes one in which both are living with their bad objects projected into the other and they remain stuck in this position. Psychotherapy directed towards these collusive forces in the relationship often produces good effects in persons who separately would be regarded as much more difficult prospects for individual psychotherapy.

The Psychoanalytic Method

Under the stimulus of the object-relations concepts as these are expressed in the writings of Bion (1961), Rickman (1957), and Fairbairn, Ezriel (1951) put forward a statement of major importance concerning the study of the psychoanalytic method. Ezriel concluded that most doubts about psychoanalytic theories centre on the validity of the psychoanalytic method. Using tripartite object relation structures as described by Fairbairn, he assumed that the psychoanalytic situation would be dominated at any one time by three forces corresponding to the three systems. Thus, the central ego would seek one relationship with the therapist, the repressed needs would drive the individual to express another, and the inhibiting superego would create a feeling of impending threat, disapproval, or catastrophe. He proposed to conduct therapy without making any historical reconstructions and to confine his comments to how he saw these three relationships determining the behaviour of the patient. In other words, the psychoanalytic session could be treated as an experimental situation provided the therapist stuck to the here-and-now forces operating in the setting.

Not only was this a way of investigating the psychoanalytic method, but in Ezriel's view it provided the much needed theoretical framework on which all interpretations should be based. The verbalizations made by most analysts during sessions can be very different in status and complexity, ranging from simple affirmations, requests to give more material, and so on. His thesis, however, was that the interpretation—the crucial aspect of the analyst's verbalizations—must consist of bringing to the patient's notice the three types of relationship in the situation. Fairbairn (1952b) also wrote a short paper subsequent to Ezriel in which he expressed very similar ideas. That is to say, the analyst must account for what the patient is expressing to him by a response in which three components are discernible, namely: (1) When you say (or communicate by behaviour) *x*, you are striving to maintain relationship *a* with me; (2) but *x* also indicates that you want to express another relationship *b* with me, which you must not admit to *because* you fear (3) relationship *c* in which I shall do something disastrous to you (reject, punish, attack, be sexual with, and so on). Thus the unconsciously sought relationship, the defence against it, and the reason for the defence are incorporated in these three parts.

Social Relations and Group Psychotherapy

Freud's original study on group psychology was a remarkable contribution to our understanding of group processes. Here was one of the early examples of theory in object-relations terms because the group members became related through their common introjection of the leader as their ideal object. Kleinian theory with its multiplicity of internal objects suggested that the social relations created by the individual would reflect situations comparable to those between the ego and his inner objects. Bion (1961), Jaques (1955), Menzies (1960) and others developed these ideas. In a number of contributions they showed how illuminating these primitive object relations of the inner world could be both in understanding and handling intragroup tensions and those between groups.

SUMMARY

I have outlined some features of the object-relations theory of the personality that started in the work of Klein and the advantages of which have been formulated so penetratingly by Fairbairn. Its main aim is to formulate a theory closely related to the phenomena of human conflict and of personal relationships. There is a danger to psychoanalytic theory and practice in trying to reduce the phenomena to components that have the appearance of being more scientific because they avoid errors of anthropomorphism. An object-relations model can be flexible and comprehensive with regard to the understanding of behaviour at any one time in terms of the here-and-now manifestations and of how these are the product of historical layerings. It has the added advantage of giving a more rigorous basis for the study of the psychoanalytic method.

Fairbairn's formulations try to do justice to the phenomena of human interaction and I have suggested that the way the personality seeks to undo its splits within one relationship is only explicable by a theory of the kind Fairbairn has stated, namely that these splits occurred within an originally unitary structure that mediated the relationship between the infant and his first object, the mother.

DISCUSSION BY OTTO F. KERNBERG, M.D.

Sutherland has outlined a conceptual model of psychoanalytic theory derived from the English school of psychoanalysis. He has said in comparing that conceptual model with the formulations in psychoanalytic theory derived from developments in ego psychology, that "Some of the apparent differences do not represent incompatible lines of work but, on the contrary, can be seen in substantial measure as complementary." I believe Sutherland's precise synthesis of the object-relations theory of Fairbairn, and his elaboration of Fairbairn's model, are an important step in the direction of clarifying the relationship between ego psychology and the object-relations theory.

Melanie Klein's contributions to a conceptual model of object-relations theory (as contrasted to her contributions to clinical psychoanalysis) have been open to criticism, mainly perhaps, because of her lack of definition of the relationship between the ego as a whole and the inner objects of the ego. For example, it is not clear to what extent in her theory the inner objects of the ego are forerunners of the superego, to what extent object relationships are simultaneously being built up into superego and ego, or what the relationship is between inner objects of the ego and characterological structure. In connection with her clinical work, Melanie Klein's school has also been criticized for what appears to many as a rather arbitrary utilization of concepts related to very early stages of the ego, in interpretations given during the first few sessions to most patients. This practice gives the impression that her group does not take sufficiently into consideration the later defensive processes of the ego, or the more advanced structure of it.

Sutherland's elaboration and reformation of Fairbairn's model overcomes to a great extent this criticism of the object-relations school. He has described the concept of dynamic psychic structures or systems within the ego, which are units differing to the degree they are in open transaction with the social environment, and which contain an *object relationship* (as well as a part of the ego, and the impulse derivative connected with this relationship). He has also introduced an element of historicity, of longitudinal development, which I feel is lacking as far as advanced ego functions are concerned in Klein's theory, and has also provided a link to ego psychology as represented by Erikson's concept of ego identity.

Sutherland states that only Erikson has attempted to encompass the whole question of the maturational basis of development. The work of ethologists, Sutherland believes, might provide a more flexible and illuminating approach to instinctive behaviour particularly in regard to the roots of social behaviour and of object relations than that implied in Fairbairn's subestimation of instincts. I agree with Sutherland. Also, in contrast to Fairbairn's subestimation of instincts, I believe that Melanie Klein's contribution to instinct theory, her impressive analysis of the importance of aggressive and self-aggressive archaic impulses, is a fundamental pillar of the object-relations theory.

I would like to link the observation of Sutherland on Erikson to one area of possible relationship between the object-relations theory and ego psychology, namely, that of the defensive and adaptive mechanisms of the ego connected with the object systems along the developmental path of the ego.

Erikson describes the precipitation of ego identities out of identifications that center around crises of development of the individual. Thus, there are different identities in the ego, on different levels of development, with the possibility of fusion and structuralizations of identities, as well as of conflicts between ego identities of different stages. These identities are built up of identifications which, especially as far as very early identifications are concerned, in turn develop out of introjections. It is my understanding that Erikson sees introjections as representing early adaptive and cognitive mechanisms of the ego as well as defensive operations, of a "diffuse" type as opposed to the more delimited processes involved in identification. Identifications, as contrasted with the perceptually poor and affect-laden introjections, are closely connected with autonomous cognitive processes of the ego on one hand, with social aspects of the parental figure on the other. Identification involves the identification with roles, that is, with habitual social functions accompanying the interpersonal relationship with the object at the time at which those identifications occur. We could say, then, that the growth of the ego is marked by the building of object relationships that finally constitute ego identities that contain adaptive and defensive mechanisms connected with these object relationships. These mechanisms vary along the developmental path, so that very early object relationships introduced into the ego imply primitive mechanisms of adaptation (introjection), and later ones, more advanced mechanisms of adaptation (identification), all of which serve defensive processes.

Melanie Klein and her co-workers have described the importance of primitive defense mechanisms at very regressed levels of ego functioning connected with early object relationships. I refer especially to Rosenfeld's studies of the mechanism of projective identification and Paula Heimann's investigation into defensive mechanisms in paranoid conditions. Projective identification in Rosenfeld's conception implies projection of an impulse, lack of differentiation between the ego and the external object, and the need to control the external object. One might say that this is, for the school of object-relations theory, an essential mechanism "precipitating" into very early object systems of the ego. Of course, when very threatening impulses (especially those of an archaic aggressive nature) are involved, the early object relationship which is to become an inner object or object system of the ego is such that this system is easily rejected by the central ego system and thus, as Sutherland pointed out, kept out of the influence of later integrative ego mechanisms.

In contrast, at a somewhat later stage of development, when autonomous ego functions of a cognitive nature (especially perception) are more developed, projective identification may turn into projection. By now the ego becomes more aware of the limits between itself and the external objects and thus the projected impulse is disconnected from the ego, and the need to control the object diminishes. Also, the development of memory functions may contribute to mitigate the threatening aspect of the object. Different images of that object throughout time can coexist, thus reducing the fantastic nature of the fear of the object, and again the need to control it implied in projective identification. One might formulate this by saying that memory development helps to overcome splitting. What I am trying to say is that while primary autonomous, especially cognitive, functions of the ego develop, defensive mechanisms connected with introjection of object relations change, and therefore, also the nature of the inner objects of the ego. On the other hand, as inner objects of the ego are built up under the influence of less primitive mechanisms, and identification in the sense of which Erikson uses the term are quantitatively replacing introjections (and other related early mechanisms) as the main mechanisms of adaptation and defence, primitive anxieties connected with rejected early object relationships diminish. The ego has now available more freedom for adaptive purposes; this, in turn, reinforces the cognitive aspects of the later identifications and ego identities, which are easily taken over into the central ego. Thus the adaptive (especially cognitive) and defensive mechanisms of the ego might be visualized as a kind of interstitial tissue that structures the more definite ego identity and the advanced preconscious and conscious functions of the ego.

Trying to reformulate the above in a tentative spatial model, inner objects of the ego might be visualized as precipitates of the ego around which cognitive functions and the adaptive aspect of defensive functions construct a secondary, stable interstitial web. This interstitial web gives strength to the whole structure and preserves the delimitation of early object relationships. On a higher level of organization, these interstitial structures actually give the definite form to the ego as an organization, to the extent that even when temporary reactivation of early object relationships occur, for instance, in the countertransference reactions of the analyst, the higher structures do not break down, but keep the form of the central ego and its advanced identity. Thus the refined interaction with reality is maintained, while at the same time the inner experience can be that of the more diffuse nature of an early object relationship.

In conclusion, I do feel that a possible relationship between object-relations theory and ego psychology exists, and that an analysis of the maturational scale of defensive operations, of the characteristics of early precipitates of object relationships as contrasted with those of later precipitates of such relationships, might be constructed. In such a longitudinal model, the characteristics of early defensive operations and early emotional positions connected with primitive object relationships will have an essential place. I believe that Melanie Klein herself moved into this direction when implicitly describing introjection and projection as early mechanisms of development of the ego as well as of defences against archaic anxiety.

A few final remarks on the implication for the theory of the superego and the theory of the id of this tentative, combined model. In Sutherland's formulation, synthesizing and modifying Fairbairn's concept, an advanced form of superego structure corresponds to the central ego, while a more primitive, sadistic superego is structurally involved in the early ego systems. This involves, I feel, a parallel conception of the superego as being also built up of different levels of object relationships. The sadistic primitive superego thus represents a precipitant of very early superego functions connected with early inner object systems. Such a point of view would be compatible also with Paula Heimann's statement that introjections occur simultaneously into the ego and into the superego. Finally, Sutherland's consideration of the question of the relative organization or lack of organization of the id is very important. The point of view that the id is being "structured into" the archaic object relationships which constitute the inner objects of the ego appears to me an interesting and challenging viewpoint. This conception of the id may appear less surprising if one accepted Kubie's critique of the concept of psychic energy, which implies that energy is distributed diffusely through the psychic apparatus; what determines different levels of energy potential are structural elements within that apparatus and not an external source of energy to it.

2. BALINT, WINNICOTT, FAIRBAIRN, GUNTRIP

From the requests to give talks on the work of these analysts, I assume that the growing interest in it is not simply historical. On the contrary, I believe that the issues that they struggled with have become questions of widespread concern today for the advancement of psychoanalytic theory and practice. The reasons for taking this quartet as a group do not stem from any joint work they did. They did not constitute a group in that sense at all. Guntrip's work is closely derived from, and related to, Fairbairn's; but Balint and Winnicott pursued their paths independently of each other and of the others, and both were rather superficial in their comments on Fairbairn's writings, as were most analysts for many years. What gives point to their being bracketed together is the extent to which their contributions eventually embodied a common development. Even in this respect, however, they preserved their individuality, for while Fairbairn stated clearly that his clinical findings required a recasting of some of Freud's central formulations, Balint and Winnicott did not take this step. Indeed, Winnicott (Winnicott and Khan 1953) shared with Masud Khan the view of Fairbairn's book (1954b) that "if one could escape this claim" by Fairbairn that his theory supplants that of Freud, "one could enjoy the writings of an analyst who challenges everything, and who puts clinical evidence before accepted theory" (p. 329). As Guntrip (1961) tersely observes, this is no way to advance any science!

The independence with which their work progressed adds, of course, to the weight of their similar conclusions. It is remarkable, too, that all were contemporaries, born approximately in the last decade of last century and all dying in their early seventies. Personally, they liked and respected each other, though disagreeing about their theories. I should add here that in using the adjective "British," I am not prompted by the Scottish Nationalist spirit that has become prominent in recent years. It is true that Fairbairn carried out all his work in his native Scotland, but I have used the more comprehensive adjective to distinguish this group from what has been referred to as The English School, a term commonly denoting Melanie Klein and her co-workers.

While restricting this group to these four contributors, I do not imply in any way that they were the only ones who have developed object-relations *theories*. Many others have done so. However, I think these four have been more fundamentally concerned with this theme and have written more explicitly on it. The most notable of my exclusions is obviously Melanie Klein. There is no doubt that her work was highly influential on all of our quartet, though perhaps least on Balint. Guntrip, possibly because of his position outside the formal analytic groups and his interest in the historical development of psychodynamic thought, never ceased to emphasize that in his view it was Melanie Klein who made the first major challenge to the foundations on which Freud's metapsychology rests. Her work with the inner worlds of young children established the need to postulate the structuring of object relations from a much earlier stage than had been thought. Although a remarkably gifted and courageously dedicated research worker in this field of the earliest stages of development, Melanie Klein lacked the kind of intellectual rigor that enabled her to follow through the theoretical implications of her work. Her views therefore remained largely as brilliant presentations of some of the phenomena we have to take into account, phenomena which she failed to systematize convincingly largely through her adherence to the theoretical use of the death instinct. In this way she seems to most analysts to minimize the role of the external object almost to that of confirming the fantasies produced from within by the activity of the instincts. She thus appears at times to create a kind of biological solipsism rather than a conceptual framework for the evolution, from the earliest stages, of structures based on experience with objects.

Winnicott (1958b) certainly acknowledges his debt to Melanie Klein at various points, albeit mainly in relation to specific concepts such as the depressive position. With Fairbairn, however, her influence was more fundamental. It was her use of the concept of multiple internal objects along with her object-related views of the paranoid and depressive positions that led him to break away from the classical position, in which the theory of psychic development was based on the unstructured energies of the id, in order to account for his clinical findings with schizoid patients.

The independent way in which our theorists developed their work allows us the more readily to look at the contribution of Balint and Winnicott separately and then to consider Fairbairn and Guntrip as creating successive phases of the same line of thought.

I shall be relatively brief about Balint and Winnicott, whose work has always been better known since both were prominent members of the analytic movement, locally and internationally. By contrast, Fairbairn worked alone from his isolated position in Scotland and so had few opportunities to discuss his work with a wide range of colleagues. Recognition, especially from international sources, came to him relatively late in life. Guntrip was even more isolated from the analytic scene in that he was not a member of the British Psychoanalytic Society. A much more prolific writer than Fairbairn, his books, however, brought him into a wide range of contacts with analysts and analytical psychotherapists.

MICHAEL BALINT

Theoretical preferences and styles are very much influenced by the personalities and backgrounds of the individual. It might therefore be of interest to make a few remarks about each of our subjects. Balint completed his analytic training with Ferenczi in 1926 and along with his first wife, Alice, concentrated entirely on the early development of the ego. Their backgrounds comprised biology, medicine, anthropology, and education, and their work was intensely mutual. Unable to accept the theory of primary narcissism with its implication that the infant only gradually becomes related to objects, they advanced the quite opposite view of the infant's growth as absolutely dependent on an intense relatedness, biologically and libidinally, with its environment. Alice Balint died soon after their emigration to England in 1939, and Michael continued to develop their early theories. From his analytic work with patients who regressed deeply, he was led to describe a condition that he termed *the Basic Fault* (1968). The patients said they felt a "fault" or "something missing" inside themselves, rather than a feeling of something dammed up and needing to be released; and Balint added "basic" because its effects permeated the whole functioning of the person. He assumed that this fault, which in some measure is universal, is caused by a failure of fit between the needs of the child and the response of the mother; but beyond his description of it as a fault or an "area of the mind," he did not really conceptualize it.

It is from this area that the Oedipus complex develops in response to the increasing experience with parents as maturation occurs. Alongside the oedipal phenomena, however, he postulated an "area of creation" in the mind in which the individual creates objects or artistic products in a private internal way to try to make something more satisfying than the real objects. The basic fault is also a precursor to the emergence of two types of object relations: *ocnophilia* in which objects are cathected with great intensity and so clung to for security and *philobatism* in which the inner world is cathected to provide a degree of independence from the precariousness of objects. These object relations are thus for Balint a defense against the effects of the failure of the environment.

In the treatment of individuals who manifest the basic fault regression to a marked degree, Balint concluded that the standard analytic method of giving only verbal interpretations was unable to alter the stalemate produced in the regression. The patient's state was not one that could be analyzed away, so to speak. What the patient needed from the analyst was the opportunity to make good a deficiency. The analyst had therefore to be the kind of object or environment with which the patient could discover his own way in the world of objects. With all basic fault states, the analyst had to convey through his relationship with the patient that he understood his needs and that in doing so he recognized the patient's own inner life and valued his own unique individuality.

What Balint described by way of theory and practice in these regressions is well known, and my purpose in sketching it again is to draw attention to the main position he reached. From his clinical data, Balint suggests that a critical primary developmental phase has to be surmounted for the individual to emerge with a general capacity to relate to objects and to himself in a reasonably effective and satisfying way. Although Balint eschews any attempt at making an adequate theory, it is clear that the individual who escapes major trouble at this basic fault stage must have achieved a very important *structural change*, a fundamental epigenetic development. As Morse (1972) has put it, Balint appears to have refused "to become a psychoanalytic heretic by attempting to formulate the revised structural theory he needs to explain his data" (p. 498), and because he stopped short, he gives us a metaphorical description instead of an explanatory theory. The new structure must function as a very basic organization for all subsequent development if, as Balint (1968) says, its influence extends probably "over the whole psychobiological structure of the individual, involving in varying degrees both his mind and body" (p. 22). It allows us "to understand not only the various neuroses (perhaps also psychoses), character disorders, psychosomatic illnesses etc., as symptoms of the same etiological entity, but also—as the experiences of our research into general medical practice have shown—a great number of ordinary 'clinical' illnesses as well" (p. 22).

Balint accepts that analysts have worked out an adequate theory and practice to encompass the oedipal conflicts, which arise from the parental triangular situation, as opposed to the problems of the basic fault, which occur in the earlier dyadic relationship. Nevertheless, he does not attempt to show in what way, for instance, the earlier developments might correlate with the oedipal phenomena. Again, while the basic fault failure leads to either a clinging to objects, which are then introjected for support, or to creative activities, we are not really taken much beyond that for we are not offered any views about the structural changes that must underlie the development of persistent patterns of behavior such as ocnophilia or philobatism. Also, while hate for Balint is located in the struggle to overcome the oppressive dependence on the primary object and the giving up of primitive omnipotent wishes—and it is this struggle that makes for the intense positive and negative feelings in the "new beginning" phase of the analysis when the basic fault is reached—he makes no reference to related structural concepts, for example, of internal objects.

Benign regression, which leads to a "new beginning," is contrasted with malignant states. Characteristic of the former is the patient's need to feel he is being recognized and responded to as an individual, an outcome that commonly needs some minimal action from the analyst, for instance, touching hands. The patient does not wish for instinctual gratification, and for this reason Balint implies that the need is of a holistic "personal" nature. In contrast to the benign regression, the patient in a malignant condition moves to insatiable demands for orgiastic gratification and so drives the analysis to a "tragic or heroic finale." Balint does not suggest that these different outcomes arise from different structural features. Instead, he thinks that some malignant regressions may be the result of inadequate experience and skill in the analyst with a recreation of the lack of fit between the infant in the patient and the mother in the analyst.

D. W. WINNICOTT

Winnicott's work (1958b, 1965, 1971) is even more familiar than Balint's, so again I shall merely put what would seem to be the essence of his position as he left it. His approach to the earliest stages of development draws on the unusually rich material available to him from the fact that he combined the role of practicing pediatrician with that of psychoanalyst throughout most of his professional life. He was, too, a great individualist who brought a characteristic poetic and imaginative quality to his theoretical and practical work.

His experience with seriously regressed patients and the correlation of his clinical data with his extensive knowledge of mothers and young children led him to the same kind of problems that preoccupied Balint, namely, those around the earliest structuring of the psyche. As did Balint, he concludes that there is a very early split, which has profound significance for future development. Balint's basic fault is paralleled by Winnicott in his concept of a true and false self, a split that originates in a failed relationship between mother and infant in the earliest stages. Winnicott believes that the innate growth potential of the infant expressed itself in various spontaneous manifestations. When the ordinary good mother responds naturally to these—and she is especially equipped to do so by a specific development around the time of the baby's birth, what he termed her "primary maternal preoccupation"—the fit between her response and the baby's experience gives to the latter an "omnipotent" creative quality. Repeated experiences of this kind establish in the infant a sense of wholeness, of conviction about the goodness of reality, and a "belief in" the world as a rewarding place. This core of feeling gives rise to a "true self" because the full maturational potential, as this emerges in its increasing repertoire of activity, can be actualized in joyful relations. The confidence in the mother also permits the gradual giving up of omnipotence, with the disillusionment this involves and its swings between intense love and hate. For Winnicott this true self brings with its growth a feeling that its core has to be intensely private, "incommunicado" (1965, p. 187), as he put it later. There is an obscurity about this notion in that the core feeling of having a self appears to depend on its being given to the infant by the input from the good mothering, and so the separation of an absolutely private part is difficult to understand. It could relate to the essence of the growing sense of the thrust of autonomy, the sensing of an "I" as apart from the objects, an embryonic affect for the later "I am real, I am going to do my own thing and not someone else's," and a fear of this being interfered with, but Winnicott seems to imply some other factors of a more primary nature.

Frustration beyond a certain level cannot be contained within the affective cohesion of the experiences of the true self, especially when the mother is felt as forcing herself on the infant, as impinging on it, with her own responses out of fit with the spontaneous needs of the child. This kind of negative experience gradually becomes organized to form a "false self," that is, one that complies with the mother's attributes; and as the mismatch between the latter and the infant's responses increases, so does the distortion or stunting of development, with the true-self potential receding more and more from its inherent capacity for relatedness.

Like Balint, Winnicott concluded that the experiences structured into the true and false selves are not those of instinctual gratification. Good experiences of the latter reinforce the true self, but its structuring is founded on the quality of the relatedness between the infant and its mother. The relationship between these structures and Freud's tripartite division remains ambiguous. It is again as if Winnicott, like Balint, stopped short of any radical confrontation between the theories he needed and those so well established. Thus although he refers to this early structuring as very close to the id, he continues to emphasize its complete dependence on the quality of the object relations. Guntrip notes his reverting to *ego relatedness* as the critical contributing factor instead of continuing with his almost complete adoption of the term self. Guntrip suggests that Winnicott may have introduced the ego to denote the part of the self involved in relations, but concluded that this idea could not be maintained. It is more likely that it represents a certain inconsistency in Winnicott's theorizing; and in this connection there are various examples of that. Thus Winnicott notes (1963, p. 83) that his account of the growth from dependence to independence makes no reference to the libido theory. He then adds that we can take all that for granted and his scheme for these early structural developments does not in any way invalidate any statement he might have made in terms of erotogenic zones. In all his later papers, however, there can be little doubt that he has moved from the classical frame of reference to an approach of a general systems theory type, for it is the self that operates as the organizing principle for all future differentiation. The critical property of the self is the creativity that takes place within it through play. Winnicott doubts whether we can explain this creative process, although we can study the very important processes through which creative living can be lost and hence lead to the feeling of life as unreal or without meaning. With his descriptions of the functions of play and creativity (1971) he gives more specific suggestions on the development of the self.

The concept of the transitional object was his first stressing of an activity that occurred in this creative "area" between the subjective and the objectively perceived. Later he widened this area as the one in which play, artistic creativity, religion, and culture were developed, as also were the contents of psychopathological conditions. Again, too, it is in this area of playing, as in the formation of the core self, that the process is spoiled by the intrusion of instinctual excitement, for example, masturbation. Playing is a form of doing, but of a special kind in which there is an interplay of personal psychic reality and the experience of control of actual objects. The appropriate responsiveness of the mother allows her to become a subjective object and, with further good interaction, an objectively perceived object; and the self differentiates as a result of the essential role of play. The capacity for play is very much dependent on the mother's love or her object-relating, at first on her active input and later on her reliable availability, as he described in his paper on "The Capacity to be Alone" (1958a). It is, in other words, founded on trust. Playing is thus the universal facilitator for growth and social relationships and, indeed, for Winnicott, mutual playing is the essence of the psychotherapeutic relationship. It is only in playing that the individual—child or adult— uses his whole personality in creative activity, and it is only in being creative that he discovers this self. The way in which the self is sensed, in other words, its security or otherwise, has to be mirrored back by the trusted parent. A conviction of one's creativity as "fun" that can be shared is the essence of the self that can enjoy living. It is here that theory must again take the object relatedness of the child into account because the emergence of play and creativity is dependent upon the environmental provision, the quality of the mother's love, from the start.

A further elaboration of his views of the first stage of development consists in what he terms the phase of *being* as a necessary precursor to a phase of *doing* for healthy development (1971). In the phase of *being,* the first weeks, the infant acquires from its experience of ordinary good mothering what is apparently a positive affective content to its overall self-feeling. The prototype of this good experience is the relationship with the empathic mother and her breast, and, because the infant is in a relatively passive absorptive state most of the time and because only the mother can give this experience, he terms it, for want of a better, the *female element* in the self. This phase moves on to one of *doing,* which he correspondingly calls the *male element* wherein the object relatedness proceeds to the differentiation of the self and object. Although the terms may not be satisfactory, he has clearly separated two phases in the course of development of the self toward its becoming a subject in relationship with objects.

While Winnicott, like Balint, leaves a great deal of theoretical work to be done, they have both reached a closely similar general position.

I have already referred to Morse's critique (1972) of Balint; he is equally critical of Winnicott, considering his scheme too inconsistent and even contradictory. The importance of both, however, seems to lie in the role they accord to certain basic developmental achievements. If successfully attained, then the individual is established with the capacity to relate effectively to others and himself, whereas failure means restricted or distorted development. A fundamental organizer has been fashioned, not from instinctual satisfactions by themselves, but from these along with the experience of a general fit between the infant's overall psychological needs and the mother's spontaneous acceptance of these. The implications of such a structuring as a template for the future development of the person are profound, and since the same questions arise with our other theorists we shall hold off on answering them until later.

W. R. D. FAIRBAIRN

When we turn to Fairbairn and Guntrip we soon sense a different quality as pervading their thinking. Freud's approach was profoundly rooted in the scientific materialism of the nineteenth century, and though his findings drove him persistently toward the recognition of the psychological level of the organism's activity as an irreducible domain, he never reached the point of feeling it had as much reality as the physiological. Balint and Winnicott also tended to retain this influence, though to a lesser degree. While they could both think of love as a human response at a personal level, not reducible to instinctual gratifications, they kept this "area" of their minds largely separated from the area which the classical libido theory had created. Even with Winnicott's increasing preoccupation in his later work with the phenomena for which he used "the self" rather than the less personal terms of Freud's structural theory, he did not pursue the wider theoretical changes his work was inexorably foreshadowing.

The intellectual backgrounds of Fairbairn and Guntrip were very different from the others. Fairbairn's first academic training was in philosophy, from which he went to Hellenic studies and then to theology. He intended to enter the Church until the First World War interrupted this plan, and by the time he finished his 4 years as a combatant soldier he had decided to take a medical training with a view to becoming a psychotherapist. Freud linked his dislike of philosophers to their speculative *Weltanschauungen*. Perhaps there was sufficient change in the teachings of philosophy by the time Fairbairn came to it, for certainly to him, and even more so to Guntrip, the importance of this influence was the discipline it imposed upon the theorist to criticize rigorously his concepts. Thus Fairbairn always viewed the libido theory and the pleasure principle with the uneasiness that the philosophical criticisms of any hedonistic theory engendered. Also, from his role as teacher in the Psychology Department in the University of Edinburgh, he was influenced by the views on *Instinct in Man* which had been published by Drever (1917), the Professor there. Although armchair in origin, these views had quite a dynamic system nature, for example, any structured propensity that instinct was based on engendered a specific emotional coloring according to whether its aim was being achieved or not. Another influence was gestalt psychology, which did a great deal to reinforce the need to think of the unique properties of the relevant wholes in psychological processes in contrast to the atomistic approach to these fostered by scientific materialism. Guntrip was especially influenced by the philosopher John MacMurray (1961) who expounded the need to conceptualize the personal level and who stressed that one of the most pressing problems for philosophy was a satisfactory conceptualization of the self because for him the self was the essential agent in human behavior.

The papers produced by Fairbairn during the first decade of his psychoanalytic work show that he had carefully assimilated Freud's theories. It was from the treatment of a series of markedly schizoid patients after this period that the primary importance of object relationships struck him. Their impact coincided with another powerful influence, namely, Melanie Klein's writings on the inner object relations of children and adults, and especially her 1934 paper, "A Contribution to the Psychogenesis of Manic-Depressive States." Fairbairn's geographical isolation, with its reinforcement of the independence of his thinking, led him to stress, however, the primacy of the phase earlier than Klein's depressive position. Indeed, he came to think that depression had played too great a part in psychoanalytic theory. It was not, after all, a very common clinical condition, and, moreover, much happened in the developmental period that preceded Klein's critical phase.

The clinical manifestations of his schizoid patients convinced Fairbairn that their etiology consisted in the mother's failure to give the infant an adequate experience of "being loved for himself." This condensed phrase is clearly a very complex package, one that essentially connotes the view that the foundation for subsequent healthy development is not laid in the satisfaction of instincts but in the imparting to the infant that he is "a person," valued and enjoyed as such by his mother. When deprived of this experience, the most serious consequences can occur. The individual, despite his innate longing for object relations, becomes too frightened to make them lest his love be rejected, and so he builds up a compensatory inner world of relationships. There thus develops massive structural splitting within the unitary ego, which is present from the start. At the time of writing his new formulations, Fairbairn was clearly reluctant to alienate other analysts by introducing too many new terms and so he retained the word ego for this pristine unity. Just as Winnicott and Guntrip found they had to adopt *the self* as a more appropriate term, so Fairbairn found it best to restrict *ego* to the part of the self that is adapted to outer reality, thus leaving the *self* for the more comprehensive *psyche* or *person*. He also reverted at times to the entitative *the libido* when, as he later pointed out, it would have been more consistent had he said that it is the individual in his libidinal capacity that seeks objects.

Fairbairn's explicit statement that the development of the person from the very start had to be conceived in terms of dynamic structures based on experience with objects instead of these being derived from unstructured energies was a major challenge to the libido theory. It was one of those changes of standpoint that is simple in principle and yet is soon felt by many as extremely disconcerting. The complexities of psychological phenomena are certainly daunting, and it was Freud's incredible achievement to have provided future investigators with an exploratory instrument. The peculiar feature of the analytic method, however, is that the instrument is the personality of the investigator, informed and supported by his experience, the latter being enlarged through training. Psychoanalytic theory and practice are thus uniquely interdependent, and what Freud's theories had given us were our only anchor points in the uncharted seas that every patient presents. As a result, to challenge Freud's theories has usually been responded to with anxiety, as if a sacrilegious outrage were being perpetrated. Of course we do not change theoretical views lightly, especially when they come from someone of Freud's stature. Nevertheless, his theories, as Freud himself remarked, are the upper stories of the edifice and not the foundations; and Fairbairn certainly had a thorough knowledge of the foundations, which were never in question for him.

The reception accorded to his challenge, which was argued in an impressively compact and tightly logical way, was at first somewhat patronizing, and some of this attitude has persisted. Thus Modell (1968), while acknowledging the value of his clinical findings, regrets that "Fairbairn's theory was not intended to supplement Freud's but to *supplant it*" and so has won very few supporters. Again, "men like Fairbairn, when faced with these problems, would wish to rip out the entire fabric of psychoanalytic thinking and start anew. . . . It would take a man of Freud's genius to rival Freud, and the history of science shows that such men do not appear to every generation; they scarcely appear in every century" (pp. 4–5, 6).

When he was writing his papers, Fairbairn in fact would often say that as he kept going back to Freud's writings he was repeatedly astounded to find Freud constantly on the brink of taking a step that would have cast his formulations into the more appropriate one of keeping strictly to psychological structure. Anyone with less sense of rivalry or of "sacrilegious intent" than Fairbairn would be hard to find. He was one of the most conservative of men, a man of great dignity and integrity. He was, moreover, very strongly against people attributing a new school to himself. For him, psychoanalysis and its development were what mattered; but he did not shrink from suggesting a theory that he considered did more justice to the facts, nor did he feel apologetic in doing so. To him it was more of a sin against Freud's legacy to cling to any part that might be improved than to recast it in the light of further knowledge; and intellectually he was well equipped to appraise the status of the concepts needed to fit the data. Within the past decade, Fairbairn has become more widely recognized in the United States, particularly through the writings of Kernberg, who has appreciated the value of his contribution though not agreeing with some of its tenets (1976, 1980).

The essentials of Fairbairn's views on psychopathology are briefly given with slight modifications of his original terms—for instance, he accepted Guntrip's use of the *self* as appropriate for the early ego (Fairbairn, 1963).

1. The human infant is obect-seeking from the start.
2. This activity is mediated by a unitary ego or self, and the reality principle is operative from the beginning. Impulses cannot exist except through activation of the ego or self, and they cannot be viewed as sources of energy existing apart from structures.
3. Pleasure is an accompaniment of relationships with objects, that is, it has a guiding and selective function and is not the primary aim of activity.
4. Aggression is a reaction to frustration and is intense in the earliest experiences.

5. The original anxiety is separation from the mother and can readily be experienced as of terrifying intensity, for example, when a satisfying object is unavailable.
6. To cope with the unsatisfying original object (breast-mother), this object is internalized by a distinct psychological process and established as a structure within the psyche.
7. This unsatisfying object arouses excitement because it is needed, and frustration because it rejects. With the intensification of these experiences, the exciting and rejecting aspects of the object are split off, along with the part of the self related to them, into subselves, each of which contains the object and the part of the self related to it.
8. The main core of the internalized object then becomes an ideal object or ego ideal, and the part of the ego related to it is termed the central ego (self).
9. There are thus three dynamic systems, each of which acts like a partial self: (a) The central self, related to the ego ideal, which represses both (b) the needy libidinal self in relation to the exciting object and (c) the antilibidinal self linked to the rejecting object.

   Because the antilibidinal self is attached to the rejecting object, it attacks the libidinal self and so reinforces the repression of the latter.
10. The superego covers the complex of (a) the ego ideal, (b) the antilibidinal self, and (c) the rejecting or antilibidinal object. These structures are interrelated dynamic psychological systems, subselves within the person, and it was important to Fairbairn that psychoanalytic theories should be couched in purely psychological terms at the level of personal functioning. To introduce etiological factors at lower levels of the organism's functioning was to abandon the data specific to the analytic situation as well as to depart from the proper level.

In place of the classical developmental scheme of object relations related to erotogenic zones, Fairbairn puts this progression into one governed by the quality of dependence. The infantile dependence at the start is characterized by its incorporative attitudes and by primary identification. The gradual separation from the object throughout childhood and adolescence constitutes a transitional period from which the healthy individual emerges with the capacity for mature dependence in which giving is as important as taking and the differentiation of the object as a separate person with an independent identity characterizes the desired object.

The abandonment of the libido theory as a basis for the development of object relations inevitably means a reconsideration of the nuclear position of the

Oedipus complex. For Fairbairn, the origin of psychopathology lies in the extent to which the pristine self is split. By the time oedipal fantasies are being stimulated by psychosexual development, the individual has a divided self, and it is the extent to which these divisions are present, along with the intensity of their activity, that determines the outcome of the oedipal conflicts. The three dynamic structures are each modified by later experiences, and indeed Fairbairn states that the unsatisfying relationships have to continue into the later years of childhood for the separate systems to become established with the kind of rigidity that makes for the serious psychopathological disorders. The existence of the needy libidinal self leads, under the pressure of the oedipal conflicts, to one parent being put into the position of the exciting object with the other parent as the attacking, rejecting one. Normally, the parent of the opposite sex becomes the exciting object, but lack of acceptance by either or both parents in the early stages readily leads to pathogenic patterns in the antilibidinal figure and so to the establishment of the various psychosexual distortions and inhibitions in both the boy and the girl.

Fairbairn's dynamic structures with their internal objects make good a defect of Balint's and Winnicott's theories in that they give a structural basis for the development of the different psychopathological patterns from the earliest phase. As dynamic systems, they are constantly active. A degree of splitting of the kind he describes is universal, though in ordinary healthy development the central self remains dominant as a learning adaptive system, which can integrate in large measure the activity of the other systems into a more or less coherent scheme of motivation for the self. In such development the self is then largely co-terminous with the ego. When the antilibidinal system is overdeveloped, then a wide range of inhibited behavior is the result. Severe splitting initially, with the associated intensely frustrated relationship needs, made aggressive and sadistic by the pressure to satisfy them, give a good explanatory scheme for the schizoid conditions, while the main pathological modes of relating—the hysterical, paranoid, obsessional, and phobic—are also accounted for in terms of the particular pattern of relationship with the internal objects that become dominant at any one time. Not only is each of the main neurotic patterns accounted for, but the scheme also explains the common finding that so many patients can exhibit more than one of the patterns at different times.

The structuring of the relationship systems also makes clear why resistance to therapy can be such a difficult, and even intractable, problem. In his theory of repressed impulses, Freud took resistance to emanate mainly from unconscious guilt, with the lessening of which the impulses could be brought under the influence of the ego and given a different aim or at least made controllable. In Fairbairn's theory, what is repressed is not a forbidden impulse but an attachment of a subself to a forbidden object and of another subself to a rejecting object which can be frighteningly primitive if this system becomes active. This attachment to bad objects seems at first sight puzzling until it is realized that the infant and child has no choice in his attachments. Bowlby,[1] in his use of ethological concepts to give a developmental scheme for relationships, has brought out this feature in the higher mammals as well as in man, that is, clinging to the mother becomes intensified the less secure the relationship is. In other words, a bad object is infinitely better than no object, the latter state being that of disintegrative anxiety.

For Fairbairn, then, the baby begins with a self system that seeks relationships as its primary need. Within this unitary system there differentiate two subselves in coping with the frustrations of the environment. These two subselves are really not independent in origin since they are both the complementary aspects of the frustrating situation. In other words, the creation of a rejecting inhibiting self goes in parallel with the forbidden relationship needs of the libidinal self. The subselves are maintained as a relatively closed system since in this way the individual seeks to have some control over the objects he needs. The more he remains absorbed in these relationships with inner objects, the less is he involved with the outer world in a mature way. Such relations with external objects as he does try to make in these circumstances are predominantly externalizations of his inner world, that is, people are not individuals in their own right and valued as such, but are figures to be coerced into the mold of the inner object.

The overall self system is thus a reactive matrix dominated at different times by one or another of the self divisions. The central self or reality ego ordinarily tries to preserve consistent adaptive relationships with people in the outer world; and when one of the subselves takes over, neurotic patterns appear. The self as a whole thus has what Kohut (1971) has termed *vertical* splits. But it also has horizontal divisions from the fact that experience can be organized in successive layers as well as fused. In this way each of the self systems can expose its structure as it was at earlier stages, though alteration in one cannot occur without all being involved. The tendency is for each system to acquire a characteristic pattern by the time adulthood is reached. Thus the libidinal ego may have created as its exciting object a perversion which remains relatively stable. In treatment, however, it is usually not long before the earlier object needs can be discerned; and, as Fairbairn further suggested, seeking gratification of impulse tension through part objects develops from the failure and deterioration of object relations.

HARRY GUNTRIP

Guntrip was drawn into a close relationship with Fairbairn's work especially after its appeal led him to undergo analysis with him. The stimulus of this experience

[1]Although Bowlby's work makes him a major contributor to object-relations theory in the British scene, his position in relation to the present group will not be definable until the completion of his current task. What he has published so far (1969, 1973) gives considerable support to the general line of the present group, especially to Fairbairn's views.

was to start him on a very careful study (1961) of Fairbairn's theories in relation to the general analytic scene and particularly of their relationship to Freud and Klein. Guntrip, like Fairbairn, had had a philosophical training as part of his preparation to become a clergyman, and his clinical work, too, had focused on notably schizoid individuals. Perhaps from what he had learned from Fairbairn, his therapeutic experience confronted him with serious regression in several patients. As a result, he began to realize that Fairbairn's picture of the endopsychic structuring of the person failed to do justice to the nature of regressed states. These are characterized by a massive withdrawal from relationships and a deadness that can not be accounted for by Fairbairn's subselves. In the libidinal self, there is commonly, in contrast to apathy and withdrawal, an active seeking of libidinal relations typically sadistic and primitive but nevertheless actively sought, while the antilibidinal self is correspondingly activated. In those threatened with the withdrawn states, there is in part a desperate struggle to keep these subself activities going as a countermeasure against the great dread of sinking into a total apathetic futility equated with dying. For these phenomena, Guntrip postulated—and Fairbairn approved—a split in the libidinal self by which one part takes flight from all object relations, which seemed to him to be like an attempt to go back to the safety of the intrauterine condition. Besides the powerful regressive flight with its aim of this ultimate security, these patients also experience in analysis terrifying anxiety at the loss of their self, a terror based on a fear of total isolation, in which state there is nobody to hold the self together. He thus adds force to Fairbairn's view that relations with internal objects constitute a desperately needed world in which these are figures to relate to, even though they are not external ones. Guntrip gives clinical material to support his view that not only the neuroses but manic-depressive states as well have a primarily defensive function against this basic terror—a desperate attempt through compulsively active internal object relations to keep the self in being. Helping the patient to cope with this anxiety becomes for Guntrip the ultimate psychotherapeutic problem; and the intense anxieties and resistances surrounding it explain the extremely difficult task that psychotherapy can encounter.

In consolidating his views on these primal experiences, Guntrip makes increasing use of Winnicott, with whom he had a period of analysis, which he has described (1975). He brings Winnicott's concepts of the origin of the self into a comprehensive outline of the development of the self from its beginnings with being and doing up to maturity. His scheme gave him a strong sense of a comprehensive psychodynamic image of man, one that illumines his anxieties and fears as the origins of his manifold evasions in regard to self-knowledge. This scheme also conveyed to him a confidence about the scientific status of psychodynamic knowledge, and his paper on this subject (1978) is of particular value to the analyst today when there is not only the challenge to this status but the danger of the right to pursue our research tasks being denied.

Fairbairn's, and much more Guntrip's, accounts of development and its pathology have been thought to have dispensed too drastically with instincts. It is rather, however, that they do not see instincts as the basic determinants of structure in the self. Structures derive from the quality of the relationship experience, and instinctual activity is merely one mode of the activity of structures. Given distortion of the structures, then pathological expression of instinctual activity occurs. Their position in this respect is akin to that of roles for those sociologists who stress these as the structural elements in the person. Roles are universally prescribed, but each individual fills them in a manner determined by his self, in other words, by the way that structures created out of very early experience function.

What emerges, then, as common to this group? In the first place, they all derived their theories from long and testing work with very difficult patients—patients of the kind whose analyses so often end in stalemate or worse. In recent years there have been many critiques of theory and many contributions to its advancement. Some of these have been the work of analysts who have devoted a substantial part of their time to academic study. These critiques and contributions are valuable and always needed. Our four theorists, however, all remained deeply rooted in clinical work. What their theories may lack in academic precision has thus to be balanced against the importance of the data they have exposed and the questions these have raised. Their immersion in clinical work helps to explain another aspect of their approach: they all placed the therapeutic task as paramount. They refused to adhere rigidly to the method when they felt that this might lose the patient. Any parameters introduced were not such as would preclude further understanding. To many, their work would be described as analytical psychotherapy rather than analysis—an issue which, as recent discussions have shown (see Wallerstein, 1969, 1975), may well prove to be a relatively unimportant one if our goal is deeper understanding. Analytical psychotherapy does not necessarily mean the unconscious is no longer being explored.

Balint's description of the basic fault highlighted a critical developmental phase. From the way patients related to him while they struggled with this state, he concluded that it reflected a failure in the earliest mothering, one in which there had not been adequate input of what can appropriately be described as love, that is, interest, affection, and enjoyment at the "personal" level. Physical care can be of a high order, instinctual gratification can be experienced, but without this holistic response from the mother the infant does not prosper. Indeed, as the studies of Spitz, Mahler, Bowlby, and many others have demonstrated, without this maternal love, future development is greatly endangered. Balint, however, while giving us clinical data on the existence of the phase and how it manifested itself plus its damaging ramifications, did not take its conceptualization further nor did he suggest how it linked with future conflict.

Fairbairn also concluded that the seeds of all future psychopathology were sown in this early failure in the mother–baby relationship. He then followed up with a theoretical outline of the subsequent differentiation of dynamic structures within the primary self system and so related later psychopathology to the early phase with a unified framework. His multiplicity of subselves has been criticized, yet the criticisms often appear as resistance to their challenge to traditional theory rather than founded on a careful appraisal of their nature and of the phenomena for whose explanation they were evolved. Here it is noteworthy that Kernberg, who has devoted so much study to patients with marked splits in their personalities, found Fairbairn's approach of considerable value in ordering the manifestations of borderline patients. Fairbairn did not have Hartmann's work available when he produced his theories, and it is striking that two such different endeavors were proceeding almost simultaneously with the common feature of dealing with the inadequacy of the concept of the id as Freud left it. Hartmann retained the notion of energies without structure, a quite untenable concept for Fairbairn and, moreover, one which hampered psychoanalytic development. General systems theory, as it later developed in modern biology, was of course unknown to Fairbairn, though he was familiar with some of its precursors, for example, gestalt psychology. Fairbairn's structures as he described them in his theory of the basic endopsychic situation represent end products. Thus, when he relates the different neuroses to the different patterns of relationships with the internal objects, his references to the latter, for example, as the accepted or rejecting objects, imply the form taken by these objects as they occur nearest to the central self or ego. The complex layering and fusion of the different stages of experience that have produced their final form constitute much of the analyst's task. This endopsychic picture of the self as an overall matrix in which there are these internal "dramatis personae" is a conception that is sometimes thought to be anthropomorphic and so to take analytic theory out of the natural sciences. Guntrip has dealt with that issue, and we can note that one gain of abandoning scientific reductionism and placing conflict on the personal level is that the mutual understanding of the writer and psychoanalyst is greatly facilitated. Whereas Winnicott stressed the importance of creativity as bridging the individual to his object relationships, Fairbairn can be said to describe the specific structures this creativity is driven to make according to the particular relationships the individual is situated in.

Taking Winnicott and Fairbairn together, it would appear that the next step they implicitly point to is the study of the self, the conceptualization of its origin and development—a topic that has become central and controversial for psychoanalysis. When Erikson began to discuss the meaning of identity, it was sometimes thought he was leaving the field of psychoanalysis. Why the center of the person should have been so long in becoming the center of our theoretical concern is itself a fascinating question. Lichtenstein (1977), Weisman (1965), and many others have remarked on the barriers that our Cartesian inheritance has created for us, and even today the self is commonly taken to be too vague a concept to be a profitable line of research. A major difficulty in the past was how this subjective matrix could be linked to its brain; and energy ideas, however metaphorical they were claimed to be, have had an insidiously persistent habit of intruding in a reified way into our thinking. Analysts have tended to lag behind in the assimilation of new developments, although Bowlby (1973), Peterfreund (1971), and Rosenblatt and Thickstun (1977) have made efforts to reformulate theory. Insofar as their work has gone, however, we do not yet have the theoretical basis for the integrative organizing center, thus raising the question whether we shall merely get a kind of psychoanalytic behaviorism.

Ernest Jones in his brief foreword to Fairbairn's (1954b) book showed his characteristic percipience into the vital issue by noting that Fairbairn started at the center of the personality and described its strivings and difficulties in its endeavor to reach an object where it may find support—in contrast to Freud who began with the stimulation of the nervous system and proceeded from the erogenous zones and internal tension from genetic activity. As Jones concluded, "This constitutes a fresh approach in psychoanalysis which should lead to much fruitful discussion" (p. v).

The study of biological systems tells us that development occurs by differentiation and every system has to have an organizing principle in order to keep emerging subsystems in the required relation with each other and with the whole. And with biological systems we have to include the environment as integral to the system. As Winnicott remarked many years ago, there is no such thing as a baby—there are only babies with mothers (1960, p. 39n).

Development in an adaptive learning system is inevitably morphogenic, that is, new structures have to embody new adaptive capacities (see Buckley, 1967). Without a structural basis it is difficult to understand how these changes are made. Thus Jacobson (1964), who gives an excellent account of the later development of the self and its object relations, nevertheless explains the earliest developments in terms of energic changes. But statements, for example, about libido or aggression being turned from object to self are meaningless without some notion of what does the turning. Perhaps Jacobson's reluctance to structure experience of object relations from the start is reinforced by her view that threats to identity are not predominant in the neuroses, a view that is not shared by our theorists nor, I believe, would it be by a growing number of analysts. Angyal (1965) was one of the first psychotherapists to give a conception of personal development based on the systematic organization of experience. For him the *autonomy* of the individual, a powerful inherent impetus from the start, relates to this central organizing principle, while the constant necessity for the interaction with the social environment, if the organism is to survive, he termed its *homonomy*. No consideration of the person made sense without these two being taken together; no autonomy is possible without homonomy. It is the organizing principle, however, we want to know more about. We have learned a great deal about the mature organism, and, as Angyal says, we have to know its structure before we can understand the embryo.

Mischel (1977) comments that the task of understanding what it is for a person to be an agent is a conceptual rather than empirical one. I doubt if we can make this separation, though there is clearly a formidable conceptual task. We know the stimulus–response views of the behaviorist cannot do justice to the way the person is activated by his own meanings, purposes, and goals. It is the latter that play the main part in determining what makes a stimulus, and they are developed as the person internalizes a map or model of his environment. What Fairbairn's endopsychic situation tries to do is to represent this environment as it is structured internally by the subject. Psychoanalysis has gathered an enormous amount of knowledge on how this inner world gets built up, but what was missing was a more holistic dimension. Fairbairn suggests how this inner world is created to make good the deficiencies of the outer one, while Guntrip has taken this further in his view of the ultimate analytic problem as the nature of the unbearable threat to his existence when the person cannot achieve enough homonomy, enough psychic metabolism with his social environment. In connection with this theme, Guntrip (1969) makes the intriguing suggestion that mankind has clung to the belief in a frighteningly powerful impersonal nature within us, the death instinct, for example, or at least an aggressive energy, because of the fear of facing up to the feelings of intolerable helplessness and weakness that characterize the infant, especially in an experience of deprivation.

To imagine an organizing principle at work in the self does not necessarily take us into innate forms or Aristotelian entelechies. What our theorists have brought out is that while the future growth of the person, his creativity, his use of particular talents, and so forth, entail unpredictable emergents from the experiences and opportunities he meets, nevertheless, the potential for this growth is not created without a "personalized" input. The infant at the start presumably fashions from the good enough input an affective field that predisposes it to pursue with interest and enthusiasm its exploration of the world. This is what Winnicott (1971) seems to be saying with his concept of the female element. Yet, however ill-defined the content of this central experience is, it seems to have a quality that we can appropriately describe as a beginning toward being personified. One recalls here Sullivan's (1953) personification of the self system, and there are clearly affinities. The full nature of the dynamic properties of the system, however, are missing from Sullivan's account, especially as the development of the self–object awareness proceeds, for it is at this stage that, all our theorists agree, the roots of intensely aggressive and violent feelings are laid down.

It is when the self system becomes patterned by its dominant relationship modes that the term identity comes to the fore. Lichtenstein (1977) suggests that an identity theme gets *imprinted* on the self at this stage, a pattern determined largely by the unconscious wishes the mother has for her infant's future, and that this remains as a virtually unchangeable template, an invariant for future development, though naturally the particular clothing put onto the skeletal pattern will vary with experience. But whether Lichtenstein's view of the virtual irreversibility of this pattern is akin to imprinting is probably an open question. Fairbairn's view, and this would be reinforced by Guntrip's conceptions, would be that a pattern for the self would be carried by the internal object structures and, though the task of change can be formidable, it may not be irreversible as our knowledge is enlarged. As in most fields of knowledge, a certain stage is reached when new concepts are proposed. The problem of the self has become emergent and already many responses have been appearing independently, with Kohut's (1971, 1977) work perhaps best known.

Our four theorists have found, as analysts have done under the stimulus of Freud's work, that developments in our theoretical understanding must inevitably be reflected in technique. For all, the parallel between therapeutic requirements and the needs of the infant in its relationship with its mother was more and more forced upon their attention. The gap between theory and practice may well underlie some of our therapeutic limitations and failures, and especially our diagnostic appraisals.

The position of the self for Hartmann and ego psychology has been rather in the background, with the ego given all the prominence, albeit restricted to an impersonal group of functions. Nevertheless, if we take the important consideration of who or what is the agent in our actions, the self appears as the most likely candidate. Chein (1972) in a careful discussion of this issue considers the claims of Freud's three structural entities along with the self and the body. The essential psychological human quality for him is "the commitment to a developing and continuing set of unending, interacting, interdependent and mutually modifying long-range enterprises" (p. 289). In such a commitment, all the entities constitute one system, "the person," and so he takes the person to be the actor or active agent at the personal level (compare also Schafer, 1968). Although he chooses the person rather than the self, his decision appears to be based upon his difficulty in envisaging a structural basis for the self. In the ordinary way we use the self it would seem to cover just that overall integrated system he takes as the person—and certainly it is this integrate that our object-relations theorists are speaking about and for which they all envisage or imply a dynamic structure. As a supraordinate structure (Saperstein and Gaines, 1973) of great flexibility and perhaps in the nature of a "field force," its primary function is to contain and organize motives from all the subsystems that have differentiated from it. The higher-level organizations we might call the subegos and their related internal objects all fall within its influence.

The ego or central self is that part of the total system that is most related to *realistic* action, that is, to the recognition of others as independent persons with their own characteristics. The course of ordinary development is such that this system has a high overlap with the supraordinate one. The value of the self conceptualized as the overall dynamic structural matrix is that we can give underpinning to the personal level of action as "I" and yet allow for the self to be dominated at different times and in different situations by any of its subsystems, such as the superego.

What all of our theorists have come to is the view that the innate developmental potential has to be activated by an input of loving empathic care from the mother for it to become the proactive matrix with the positive enjoyment that developmental activity requires. To be able to love and enjoy, the baby has to be loved and enjoyed. It is as if a "positive field of force" is patterned as the core of the self system by the effects of the positive self feeling at one pole and the expectation from a supporting figure at the other, at first external, then internalized. The environment continues to add to the structural differentiations, and a degree of correction of early deficiency may be attained. But as Bowlby mentions (1973, p, 336), drawing upon the biologist Waddington who introduced the theory of epigenesis, there is a general organismic tendency for the individual to maintain whatever developmental pathway he is already on, partly because the internal structural features influence the selection of the environment and partly because the environment, especially within the family, also tends to remain unchanged.

SUMMARY

What I believe to be the essential contribution of this group of analysts may be summarized as follows. The role of object relations has always been a prominent theme in analytic thought and has become much more so in recent years. Instead of grafting the implications of relations onto a theory that started from a different standpoint, what the British group has done is to show that the development of the person has to be conceived as the progressive differentiation of a structure from a unitary matrix that itself interacts at a holistic personal level from the start. While Balint noted clinical data that required this step, he did not put forward a theoretical scheme. Winnicott, who suggested more specifically how the infant's relationships at the earliest stages patterned its whole subsequent personal development, also refrained from following through the theoretical logic of his observations. Fairbairn was the first analyst to expose the questionable logic of a developmental scheme based upon the energic concepts that Freud retained as his theoretical base. Fairbairn's scheme, however, did not account adequately for the earliest developmental stages as these were inferred from the study of regressive states. Guntrip, making full use of Winnicott's views, has sought to make good this limitation.

The British group does not presume to have made anything like an adequate conceptual map for the development of the psyche. The theoretical problems are far too complex for that. They have, however, shown a fruitful direction and have influenced many areas of contemporary psychoanalytic thought.

3. WINNICOTT*

The British object relations theorists Balint, Winnicott, Fairbairn, and Guntrip were all concerned with identifying and understanding a primary developmental failure in the central organizing capacity of the person—that is, in the ego. (Winnicott in his early writings used the terms *ego* and *self* interchangeably.) Patients described this developmental failure as something lacking rather than as conflict, and it emerged only after a good deal of ordinary analytic work had been done with oedipal and sadistic themes. Balint adopted the term the *basic fault,* Fairbairn and Guntrip the *schizoid split*, and Winnicott the *true and false self split* for this stage. All concluded that when the nature of the developmental failure had emerged, the important therapeutic work relied far less on interpretation than the creation of a relationship in which the analyst could be sensed as concerned with and responsive to a need that could only be described in holistic terms, such as being recognized as a person, or liberating his true self. This need was not the seeking of instinctual gratification. On the contrary, there was frequently a negative attitude to such thoughts. It was a powerful need to feel at one with an inner person who was not the constricted person they had been.

Winnicott's terms, in contrast to those of the other object-relations theorists, have become a part of our everyday analytic vocabulary—such concepts as the transitional object, and the true and false self. However, it is doubtful that his work has had as much impact on analytic theory and practice. One speculation is that this is partly because his idiosyncratic approach made him something of a psychoanalytic maverick, and his almost playful quality of thought resulted in many inconsistent views being expressed with the fuller implications being passed lightly by.

WINNICOTT'S FRAMEWORK AND SOME OF HIS TERMS

Winnicott believed that the most difficult behavior, and even illness, in the quite young baby was rooted in what was happening in the *mother–infant relationship*.

*Discussant: Eugene Mahon, M.D. Reporter of this talk by Dr. Sutherland: Marvin Wasserman, M.D.

The ongoing mother–infant interaction established a central organization that governed the well-being of the infant's growth in a profound way. When he listened to what was supposed to be going on in the baby, talked about as an entity, he protested on more than one occasion that there is no such thing as a baby—there are only babies with mothers! In this respect he was very much a modern biological systems theorist.

On review, we note there is often confusion in reviewing Winnicott's writings (which were spread out over 40 years) about the various ways he designated his central concern. He variously referred to the development of the ego, the psyche, the psyche-soma, the self, the true self. At times the initial self and true self are synonymous, though in most of his writings the true self is that part of the self that has not become the false self.

Though Winnicott uses the ego and self as interchangeable in his earliest writings, self is preferable since he means the full developmental potential of the infant to become a person. Winnicott (1960a) commented that if he were to relate his concepts to classical theory, he would have to say that the true self was close to the id since it comes from "the aliveness of the body tissues and the working of body functions" and from the infant's "spontaneous gesture" (p. 148). However, since the true self rapidly acquires integration, personalization, and an embryonic reality sense, this would place it more in the ego category; and on this basis Winnicott may be classified an ego psychologist who does not really differentiate ego and id at the start.

Winnicott used the term *integration* to refer to the gradual merging of separate existences into a continuity of being, and to locating the self in the body. Its opposite is not disintegration but *unintegration* which he seems to have adopted from Glover's ego nuclei. *Disintegration* refers to a pathological state arising subsequent to a degree of integrative development.

EGO RELATEDNESS

In pursuing the concept of *ego relatedness*, Winnicott insisted on the need to see the infant-mother as the essential system. He describes the infant's innate potential as including two main divisions—"the instincts" and the rest. The instincts are the appetitive ones, hunger and sex. Apart from these he refers to ego needs, that is, responses that are required from the mother for an adequate development of a joyous sense of being and for security and confidence toward the social and physical environment. He expressly states that basic ego security does not rest upon instinctual satisfaction, but rather upon the integration and growth of the ego to its full potential. This depends on the appropriate responses from the mother to the spontaneous actions of the infant that are in a broad sense "instinctive" (those associated with hunger and love). After six months of such good maternal interaction, the baby becomes "personalized" (a term Winnicott drops in his later writings).

Winnicott believed, as does Bowlby, that the core of the development of the self does not rest on the feeding relationship having a uniquely important role. The instinctual satisfactions have to be experienced within a self that can experience them as part of itself in action, otherwise they can be used for the development of satisfactions split off from the central developing core. The assimilation into the self of experiences of good mothering give a start to a secure kind of independence which Winnicott suggests can be seen in the capacity to be alone. This is not related to the internalization of good figures in later experience.

Winnicott was preoccupied with what the baby's *experiences* were and how they were organized. His speculations were based on the analysis of a number of borderline and seriously disturbed children and adults as well as on his pediatric experience. He observed that psychoanalysis had little to offer for a theory of positive personal health. Winnicott believed that the mother's ordinary spontaneous empathic response to the infant's gestures established a basis for a secure independent personalized individuality. The state of absolute dependence was one of primary identification of mother and infant. The move to independence implied that the earlier state, in which the object is a subjective one, must be replaced by the objective perception of the object as external. Here we are perhaps involved in the most difficult of all our conceptual tasks, but Winnicott was convinced it had to be tackled.

Winnicott began with Freud's concept of the hallucinated breast, the essential event being the meeting of the infant and mother in a shared experience. He assumed that for the infant the experience was a moment of *illusion* which could be either of his hallucination of the breast or of a thing belonging to external reality. Winnicott was fascinated by illusion, and he felt it was at the root of all self development. Good mothering meant the essential opportunity for this experience by which the baby could feel that it had created its own personal environment. Thus the most real contact with reality began on the basis of this illusion. Yet, paradoxically, it was the security engendered in this experience that enabled the child to proceed with disillusionment, as in weaning. What could be described as omnipotent or magical control could be given up by an infant whose confidence in the external world had been maintained so that he could go on discovering its riches without any loss of the sense of self. It was from this experience of illusion that the *transitional object* could be created and later art, religion, and culture.

TRUE AND FALSE SELF

Winnicott worked with the notion of the false self before he turned his attention to the true self. It stemmed from some of his patients' describing a major life-long inner state of always feeling a kind of false existence. The false self originates not as a defense against instinctual impulses, but as a response to the mother not meeting the needs of the innate developmental potential of the self or ego and therefore not allowing them to have their spontaneous omnipotent expression. The true self is the living reality that grows with the mother's success. The inner activity "joins the infant to the object" (1960a, p. 146). With the failure of the mother's adaptation, the disjunction between the inner and the outer shows itself in functional disturbances such as general irritability in the infant. A seduction of the infant then takes place with the development of a compliant false self which accepts the environmental demands. This process can make an impression of "success" in that the child grows up to be good, "just like mother," and so forth. Imitation rather than real growth becomes permanent. The false self acquires one of its main functions—to conceal and protect the true self. Later it becomes enmeshed with defenses against internal objects and many find ways of allowing the true self to find expression in psychopathology.

Winnicott's idea that the false self served a defensive protective function against impingement on the true self led him to the idea that the true self has a powerful need to preserve an inviolacy, to remain perpetually "incommunicado." Since the growth of the true self is founded on the relationship with the mother this would seem to be an inconsistency. Winnicott explains the retreat of the true self into isolation as reactive to intrusive impingement of the mother and reflective of the need to survive. He also emphasizes that though the healthy self seeks and enjoys communicating there is in everyone an intense need to be secretly isolated that is so intense that violation of this core is the ultimate terror. At the same time the universal dilemma is how to preserve this isolation without insulation. He also suggested that there is communication between the true self and subjective objects that is felt as real because it is from the true self. He thus indicated that in healthy development there is a split between the part of the self that does this silent communicating and the part that relates to the objective world.

TRANSITIONAL OBJECT, CREATIVE IMAGINATION, AND OBJECT RELATIONS

The theoretical importance of Winnicott's *transitional object* lies in its representing the *creation* of something from the unique processes underlying the human imagination. It is the prototype of all art and culture. Three lines of thought developed from this concept: (1) the role of creative imagination in the establishment of the self; (2) the way in which mature object relations develop; (3) application of this concept to some of the puzzling phenomena of transference.

Winnicott was interested in understanding more of the process of experiencing through which every individual separates, yet keeps a close relation between inner and outer reality. Omnipotent control over the transitional object is gradually abandoned and the transitional object just fades away. Control through omnipotence is replaced by control through manipulation. Here we have the use of the illusory object being transferred to the objective object. This bridging is only possible through the continuity of maternal care.

Winnicott saw play as a basic source of development. Play within the mother–child relationship leads to the subjective object being repudiated and then being reaccepted and gradually perceived objectively. It is exciting not because the instincts are involved, but because of the precarious interplay between the omnipotent psychic reality and the experience of control of actual objects. If instinctual excitement becomes too great, play can become frightening because it can no longer contain its own experience. For this reason, the presence of adults is necessary when young children are playing.

The natural developmental function of playing also enables us to see how therapeutic work at times can go ahead without any interpretative work. Psychotherapy is indeed for Winnicott two people "playing" together and when this is not possible it is the therapist's task to enable the patient to "play"—to associate freely. Indeed, Winnicott makes a plea for a much greater withholding of interpretations in order to allow the patient to develop his capacity to play—to do creative analytic work.

Winnicott viewed *creativity* as the universal process underlying everyone's approach to external reality as distinguished from the commonly associated idea of producing works of art. However deeply hidden it may be, there cannot be a destruction of anyone's creativity. Here again, he believed that the capacity for creativity and being an individual were both ultimately related to the quality of the mother–child relationship.

MALE AND FEMALE ELEMENTS AND THE USE OF AN OBJECT

Winnicott described a middle-aged man he treated who impressed him as talking like a girl describing penis envy. Winnicott believed that this had nothing to do with homosexuality. Exploration led to the conclusion that as a baby the patient was seen as a girl by his mother. This understanding was followed by the patient developing an infection which Winnicott took to be the "girl's" resistance to releasing the man, that is, the intense defensive protection of the true self. He pointed out that it was this split-off *female element* that established primary unity with him and so gave the patient a new start in living.

Speculating about the *male and female elements* in regard to object relating, he suggested that the female element relates to the subjective object, to the baby becoming the breast—a process he again emphasizes is not determined by instinctual drives. This relating arises entirely from primary identification and is the foundation of the sense of being. The male element, which occurs later, introduces an object relating or doing based on growing feelings of separateness accompanied by id satisfaction and anger from frustration. To summarize

Winnicott's views about object relating and female and male elements, he believed that object relating in its first stages (female element) had nothing to do with instinctual drives. The classical libidinal stages all belong to the later stages of the male element.

From this position Winnicott made his final statement about object relating. He believed that object relating developed from a stage of experiencing the object as a vehicle for the subject's projections to a stage in which the object is "used." In order to be used the object has to belong to a shared reality and be a thing in itself. "Used" is the opposite of exploitation. The capacity to use objects is not inborn but only develops within a facilitating environment. This change whereby the object is placed beyond the subject's omnipotent control implies, according to Winnicott, the destruction of the object followed by its survival and, importantly, survival means not retaliating. It is as if the subject says, with the experience of disappearance and reappearance, "I destroyed you; I love you, and you have value for me because you have survived my destruction of you." This position can only be reached through the repeated experience of the object becoming real through being destroyed. Thus though we have traditionally conceived of the reality principle as involving anger and reactive destruction, for Winnicott it is the destruction that places the object outside the self, that is, makes reality. The subject, in other words, finds externality through the destructive drive.

The therapeutic implication is that changes in this basic attitude to reality in borderline patients arise from the analyst's nonretaliatory survival of attacks, and from the survival of the analytic situation which operates like the mother's primary holding. The analyst is thus experienced as separate and outside the patient's omnipotent control. His survival of this destructive externalization enables the patient to "use" him. In the sequence that Winnicott is describing, there is no anger but rather joy at the survival of the object. The patient's dependence and destructiveness during these phases can be extremely testing for the analyst, and it is of great importance that he should not hand the care of the patient over to others at this stage if it can possibly be avoided. Winnicott here again stresses that the significant mechanisms for object relating are not drive determined.

CONCLUDING SUMMARY

Dr. Sutherland concluded by summarizing Winnicott's contributions as follows:

1. He conceived of the self or ego as a highly dynamic structure with its own needs. It is not an impersonal structure that can be defined as Hartmann suggested by its functions, but is a highly personalized self.

2. The development and personalization of the ego from absolute dependence to a growing independence with a secure capacity to relate to both subjective and objective objects is entirely a product of the shared experience of the mother and infant. Its effective autonomy is greatly reinforced by instinctual satisfaction but does not rest primarily on it.
3. The successful realization of full developmental potential leads to the establishment of a true self.
4. Without this fit between the infant's needs and maternal input a false self develops through which the individual seeks to comply with the needs the mother has imposed on him. Once this split is established, the false self adopts an intensely defensive function against the exposure of the true self, and often much analytic work is required to make therapeutic contact with the true self.
5. Many analyses become interminable because of the failure to get to the primary level of trauma which involves identifying the true and false selves. Winnicott did not advocate new therapeutic techniques, but relied on the analyst being guided by his increased understanding of these early developmental phases.
6. There are close links between his work and that of Balint, Fairbairn, and Guntrip.
7. Winnicott tried to understand the nature and origins of the unique creativity of the human mind. Instead of a reductionist stimulus-response psychology proposed by behaviorists, he put the human problem nearer the real situation, that is, he reversed the behaviorist approach by attempting to understand what responses create our most significant stimuli.

DR. EUGENE MAHON'S DISCUSSION

Dr. Mahon focused on (1) the "early" as opposed to the "deep" in Winnicott's contributions; and (2) the technical modifications in classical psychoanalytic techniques warranted by Winnicott's work.

He cited Winnicott to clarify the distinction between early and deep: Deep implies "unconscious fantasy or psychic reality; the patient's mind and imagination are involved"; "deeper and deeper takes us to the instinctual roots of the individual, but this gives no indication of early dependence and dependence which has left no trace on the individual, although these characterize early life"; a human infant must travel some distance from early in order to have the maturity to be deep; depth implies conflict, structures, telescoping of memory, and so forth, that the concept of early could never contain— for obvious reasons. Winnicott argues that the early etiological trauma of borderline patients "goes back behind the Oedipus complex and involves a distortion at the time of absolute dependence." He emphasizes influences on the ego that are not instinctual, downplaying id instinct theory and emphasizing ego needs in his definition of early.

Winnicott suggests that "the early" is reached in analysis not by lifting repression but by creating a new setting in which the trauma can be experienced as a projection and interpreted. Dr. Mahon expressed the view that alongside this interpretative approach Winnicott seemed also to be advocating a corrective object-relationship approach. To support this view he cited Winnicott's asserting that after years on the run the true self settles on the couch. Its appearance is perhaps manifested by silence or a gesture. To interpret this as resistance of the false self to continuous revelations would be a reenactment of environmental trauma. However, to recognize it as the first stirrings of spontaneity and aliveness of the true self promotes individuation and development. Mahon seems to be saying that Winnicott's advocacy of recognition without interpretation is an example of a corrective object-relationship approach. As an additional support for the view that Winnicott advocated a corrective object-relations approach, he pointed out that Winnicott made abundantly clear that the analyst must fail in his holding capacity, and believed that it was the genuine expression of anger by the patient to these failures that made a fake analysis real.

Dr. Mahon went on to cite other authors, who disagree with Sutherland's and Winnicott's views that no deviation from classical psychoanalytic technique is required in the treatment of borderline patients. He believes that this issue is at the heart of current psychoanalytic controversy. He cited Cooper, who believes that two different theories of psychoanalytic treatment are required to adequately contain all data; Greenacre, who feels that residues of preanxiety remain even after being understood in analysis, though they are tolerated better; Kernberg, who believes that many borderline patients require a modification of technique; and Freud, who in *Analysis Terminable and Interminable* implied that early contributions of constitution, instinct, and trauma are well nigh impossible to correct through analysis though he agreed with Winnicott that of these factors the contribution of trauma to early ego formation had perhaps the best prognosis.

Mahon went on to point out that there is also a great deal of disagreement among psychoanalysts about the related issue of how much of the early can be recaptured in the transference and analyzed. Winnicott can be criticized for overemphasizing the central role of early object relations to the neglect of drive theory. He tempered this criticism by pointing out that Winnicott often asserted that since acceptance of Freudian drive theory is so firmly established in our analytic identities we can therefore purposely omit it in order to focus on a more object-relations way of describing the phenomena of infancy and dependence. Mahon concluded by agreeing with Sutherland that at times a genius may seem to neglect a certain essential proposition in order to better explicate others.

4. FAIRBAIRN'S CONTRIBUTION

THE SIGNIFICANCE OF FAIRBAIRN'S CONTRIBUTION

Fairbairn played such a prominent part in my life that any judgments I may make about the significance of his work for the development of psychoanalysis may be unduly influenced by this personal factor. I should like to emphasize, however, that Fairbairn was not by nature a zealous proselytiser. His appeal to me rested from the start upon his integrity as a good human being who never lost the primacy of his interest in the well-being of people and this concern was never separated from his thinking about the nature and origin of psychological distress and how it might be alleviated. He communicated these interests readily yet his enjoyment in sharing his ideas was always expressed in open dialogue. In his writings he habitually gives his reasons for suggesting amendments to the views of others. Indeed it is this characteristic of respecting the other person that almost certainly played a fundamental part in shaping his thought around the person in contrast with Freud whose preoccupations became dominated by the impersonal forces of nature. Noteworthy in this connection, too, is his choice as the title for his book: *Psychoanalytic Studies of the Personality*. It was this open-minded attitude toward the understanding of the person that also attracted Guntrip who fashioned his own thinking from the stimulus of Fairbairn's views.

Fairbairn's academic training in philosophy naturally added to his ability to examine critically the principles upon which conceptual schemes were based. For him, if these were unsound then the theoretical structures erected upon them not only became progressively divorced from clinical findings, but they inhibited the expansion of the latter by the constraints they imposed upon the analyst. In its early history, challenges to his theoretical principles led Freud to exclude the prominent dissidents from the psychoanalytic movement. These challenges, however, were accompanied by clinical work that abandoned what Freud deemed to be the essential core of psychoanalysis: "Any line of investigation which recognizes these two facts [of transference and resistance] and takes them as the starting-point of its work has a right to call itself psycho-analysis, even though it arrives at results other than my own" (1914, p. 16). Proceeding from his own metapsychological principles, Freud formulated his structural theory of the personality which brought a period of outstandingly productive cohesion. As in all scientific work, developments inevitably exposed limitations, mainly in the understanding of the ego. Anna Freud (1946), then Hartmann (1958) along with his colleagues in a surge of fresh thinking filled out a conspicuous gap in the structural theory with their creation of ego psychology. Preserving much of Freud's metapsychology, this line of thought was widely adopted as part of a mainstream development. A different fate befell the work of Klein despite her repeated emphasis that it too was evolved directly from Freud's theory of the death instinct. Her findings proved so disturbing that there were early reactions to them as not falling within the scope of psychoanalysis. Thus the suspicion arose at times that inclusion within the analytic fold was to be determined by theoretical conformity to Freud rather than by the careful appraisal of new data, even though the method of gaining these was the psychoanalytic one.

The impact of Fairbairn's papers, published during and immediately after the Second World War, was minimal and this disregard has continued increasingly in the United Kingdom, though progressively less so in the United States. It is particularly striking in that it was he who introduced the term *object relations theory* to describe views that challenged Freud's basic principles. Moreover, it was soon afterwards used widely to cover the work of Balint, Winnicott, and Klein since she too stressed her work as coming within this category. Many factors contributed to this neglect which, I hope to show, has been a serious loss in the development of psychoanalysis.

It was on the self and its vicissitudes that Fairbairn built his general theory of the person. His first observation, that the baby has to be loved for itself, implies an innately structured potential which has to be personified by parental figures responding lovingly to the infant as a person. To do this in a way that matches the innate needs, the mother and father have themselves to be good prototypes as persons. Although the breast gives an especially vivid experience, he rejects the atomistic approach of building the whole from parts. Instead, he asserts the baby's innate sense of the wholeness of the mother and her subjective state from the start; and research studies confirm this view. The feeding of itself does not lead to a thriving infant. Thenceforward, the self via its component instincts builds up a multiplicity of substructures all of which are fitted into what strives to be the coherent whole. It would seem that the innate whole exercises its influence through its affective state. When the environment is deficient, then the resultant state evokes responses whose function is to remedy these. When things go well a personalised self is recognisable from a few months old by observers. The inevitable comment from persons with serious personality problems is that "I never felt I was allowed to be myself."

A first point is the commonly raised issue of the separateness of the infant self from the mother. The autonomy of the self has a powerful dynamic from the start. Frustration of the bodily needs produces manifestly aggressive protests. What we have to recognise is that the same response follows deprivation of relationship needs. Lack of responsiveness from the mother, even though she is present, is felt as rejection and so at this stage frustration and deprivation are synonymous. Even in the absence of frustration, the infant is assertively its own self as is familiar in the way the nursing couple adapts mutually. The self's autonomy requires a sense of its own boundaries. The question of differentiation is, I believe, confused with the constant closeness the infant needs. Bowlby's work (1969) has fully established the need for an attachment to the mother to be structured in the baby's self; but attachment is not fusion or merging. It gives the affective security in the self and the close interactions necessary for personalisation. These later needs may or may not be met by the appropriate input from the parents.

The physical dependence of the infant on the mother brings out the great paradox in the development of the self. The autonomy of the adult implies the opposite of separation from persons. Indeed there is no stage when the self does not need to be related to others for its maintenance and effective functioning. The autonomous self develops from what Fairbairn describes as the state of infantile dependence to that of adult dependence. As mentioned, there is perpetual "autonomy within heteronomy." The adult self enjoys the autonomous feeling of being one's own agent with freedom of choice. But freedom is within the organism's limitations mentally as well as physically, and to be isolated from others is not a choice for the normal adult. Freud's conception of the adult's instincts in an adversarial relationship with his society rests on his inadequate view of the instincts. It can happen, of course, that a particular culture conflicts with them but he must be of the same culture. As has been stressed, Fairbairn's more modern outlook deals with this by adopting the concept of the instinctive potential having been evolved to be a genic inheritance that can only be realised in relatedness.

With this conception of the self as a perpetually dynamic autonomous system needing appropriate relationships, then, since deprivation or prolonged frustration is a threat to its autonomy, that is, to being alive, such a threat instinctively arouses aggression to the point of violence, of a ferocity leading to murderous rage. Freud's death instinct thus becomes for Fairbairn the fight of the self to survive. At this point it is significant to recall that in the adult when the attachment to the ideal object has matured to include the ideals of the group, then attacks on these are tantamount to threats of death. It is in this connection that when Freud could not account for the origin of such primitive rage, he ascribed an elementary character to it in the instincts of death.

In Fairbairn's view, deprivation of mother's enjoyable responsiveness, her loving care, or other frustrations, leads to a split in the self at a very early stage. The pristine personality then establishes an imago of this unsatisfying mother, which is split into a desired, or exciting, imago and a rejecting, or "bad", object; but, in varying degrees, both are changed by phantasies. They also form part of a relationship system within the self. They can moreover be identified with the self. Fairbairn takes the first splitting to be that of the object while a second stage splits off the part of the self related to the object. The splitting in both stages is an active process mediated by hostility from the central part of the self. (Splitting and repression are used interchangeably.) The object relationship that the residual or central self must have is with the good or acceptable aspects of the mother made into an ideal object. These developments constitute a *basic endopsychic situation* in which there is a self containing the unmet urges for the satisfying mother, needs that Fairbairn terms libidinal, and attached to an imago that would meet these needs, that is, a libidinal self seeking a desired or exciting object. Correspondingly there is an antilibidinal self linked to the imago of a bad or rejecting mother, and a central self with an ideal object. The two split off subselves have the dynamic properties of the original unified self and so are constantly seeking satisfaction. They retain in large measure intensity of pressure, that is, the more pressing the needs of the libidinal self, the more hostile is the antilibidinal self response. The repressed systems, although barred from consciousness, remain within the dynamic self. Because they are excluded from the transactions occurring in the central self, they do not change in the way that the central self does.

The effects of deprivation of the needs of the whole self are manifested by a progressive withdrawal of investment in external objects and a turning to satisfactions from the inner world, that is, the schizoid personality is created. This does not necessarily interfere with an effective though partial realisation of self potential by building up special interests and competencies. Such success, however, even when rewarded by a great deal of recognition, often does not alter the deeper emptiness arising from the lack of close personal relations and detachment from people. The inability to love because they feel unlovable is at deeper levels a profound conviction causing wide inhibition.

When activities do not meet the self needs sufficiently, then Fairbairn made an important distinction between depression and the feeling of futility engendered. The futility is commonly described as depression but it is important that this affect be distinguished from melancholic depression originating in guilt. Futility is the expression of a loss of trust in others, what in more extreme degrees becomes the despairing cry from the schizoid patient—"What's the point?" The turning to the inner world is also accompanied by an increase of omnipotence, though this may be covered over.

The less prominent, though equally devastating, characteristic of the schizoid personality is the hate engendered by the frustration of the autonomy of the self, of its right to have a reasonable security and self-confidence. Fairbairn was criticised by Klein for not giving due weight to hate although he makes quite clear that he fully recognises its presence in his theory. Klein's view perhaps had some foundation in that he did not bring out adequately in his earlier papers its clinical significance or manifestations. Fairbairn could not accept the death instinct, which Klein took to be an essential postulate. For him, what was encountered clinically was personal aggression and hate in response to frustration or deprivation of the urge in the self to secure autonomy. The situation was not one of abstracted force, but of persons in an internacine war. And with the frustration felt as a threat of destruction of the self, so was the most violent hatred often evoked. Its persistent presence, moreover, did not require the postulation of the impersonal biological death instinct to account for it being manifest widely, for with the rejecting object being built in, the rage was perpetually activated. It was his rejection of the death instinct that seemed to evoke Klein's rejection of Fairbairn's standpoint. Her expressed disagreement, however, was not given with any reasons.

The fundamental role attributed to the depressive position by Klein does not feature in Fairbairn's scheme because he did not meet it often. Klein relates it to the development of the capacity to perceive the mother as a whole, and to create this whole despite the feeling of abandonment at the weaning stage. However, such recognition can only develop in a self that is sufficiently a personalised whole, that is, when the primal splits are not still precluding its establishment. An aggregate of parts cannot perceive the wholeness of anything else for that needs another whole. Only a gestalt can perceive a gestalt, as Pankow, the philosopher-biologist, states. In my own experience, what I have found is that schizoid personalities, as they gain more freedom from the bad mother, do go through a phase in which there are recurrent dreams of a destroyed world out of which they cannot extricate themselves. As the badness of the internal mother recedes, this massive destruction fades out and compassionate reparative feelings emerge to give a good wholeness.

Despite the existence of the split subselves, the self never ceases to have an overall orientation to itself and to the outer world. The holistic functioning of the self is readily studied in projective tests such as the Rorschach. There the ambiguous stimulus is perceived selectively by all the sections of the self, even though their nature and aims may be unconscious. In short, while the outer world is being scanned by the conscious central self, the subselves are simultaneously searching for opportunities to get into action. The central self nevertheless strives to preserve as much integration as possible. And we have always to remember that it is the whole person who shapes his neurosis.

The structure of the self as described by Fairbairn is analogous to Freud's tripartite structure. The principles underlying Fairbairn's conception are, however, radically different. Freud's basis is in part a nonpersonal psychology founded upon the energies of the biological instincts and the erotogenic zones. Fairbairn's rests on dynamic structures evolved from the experience of the innate potential of the self with the persons this potential needs for its realisation. It will be seen that although he does not specify the nature of the holistic innate potential, it embodies a manifold group of structures seeking an object, yet with each component fitting affectively into the whole sense of itself. Lichtenstein (1977) has commented on this potential self in relation to the concept of narcissism. The urges to relate come paradoxically from the narcissistic position of the primal self. He has suggested that the mother imprints, so to speak, upon this primal potential self a shape it is seeking to encounter. In so far as her personality is responsive to the needs of her baby as a person, so does the infant acquire a reasonable cohesion. When she imposes an identity on the baby from her own needs, or denies its spontaneous expressions, the stage is set for the various distortions of the personality. The endowment of the infant we now know to be such that much of its perceptual activity is much more organised and more holistic than was traditionally conceived. Thus the subselves and internal objects all become personalised, at times with different figures to represent them. The self then comes to contain a cast of characters constantly interacting and changing. It is this scene from which dreams are created and the wish fulfillment there seems to be part of the urge to integration. This urge in Fairbairn's view is also what gives rise to the repetition compulsion, namely, to bring the bad objects back to the central self with the hope of lessening their threats to the integration of the self.

With the rising pressure of sexuality and the central self being inhibited from its mature expression in personal relationships, the self falls back on greatly increased activity in the split selves. The frustrated libidinal self now becomes much more sadistic toward its object as also does the attack on it from the rejecting object and its associated self. The total situation between these subselves is increasingly repressed by the central self so that it becomes much more markedly split off. No external personal object can be approached because of the fear of rejection or of attack, with the result that these two subselves can become locked in a sadomasochistic relationship to provide a degree of gratification by the relief of tension. Pleasure is greatly intensified when instinctive tensions are discharged with depersonalised objects especially in autoerotic or perverse sadistic activities. When relations with the outer world are severely compromised then little or no joy is experienced at a personal level in sexual relations thus producing a depleted self feeling. With the satisfaction missing, the urge to repeat depersonalised pleasures can become an addiction within a closed system with highly secret or repressed gratification. The resistance to these processes being brought within the consciousness of the central self verges on the intractable. The absence of deep relationships with good objects entails the self clinging desperately to the bad objects, for having no objects means unbearable emptiness or the loss of the self, that is, disintegration into madness.

The individual who seeks analysis nevertheless wants to be free of the bad internal objects. To succeed, he has to experience the role of all the defensive positions evolved to protect his self against the deep fears of losing his self by giving up all the false self structures he has hidden behind. The various psychoneuroses become for Fairbairn defences against the disintegration of the self. To account for the origin of the different conditions he suggested that different topological distributions of the inner objects could do this, for example, by projecting or retaining the good or bad objects. In the course of development the self makes perpetual use of the processes of projecting parts of the self, either to be free of them or to alter them by taking them back in a more tolerable form following an external object having contained them.

I believe there is a general resistance to the conceptualisation of the self as our central issue. It seems easier to resort to an impersonal nature for the destructiveness and evil within us than to accept its personal origins. For this means that we have to take full responsibility for these frightening and hated aspects of ourselves. And for our analytic work we need enough freedom from these deeply repressed infantile relationships in ourselves before we can empathise with them in others, and to empathise is to sense the experience of the patient as essentially that of a person in a relationship.

I hope I have given Fairbairn orientation through the basic principles he put forward, which gives us a start toward a theory of the self maturing as a person through the realisation of its innate potential in its relationships. The theory of object relations would be termed accurately a theory of the self, the agency that fashions the relations. We encounter here, however, the fact that the acceptance of the deep implications of this theory for practice is to take us into areas in the past unconscious only recognised by the analyst having come to terms with them in himself.

Fairbairn's theory does not stand alone in its explanatory power, but it constitutes the most systematic statement of a psychoanalytic theory of the personality in nonreductionistic terms. He was inspired by Klein's concepts of the structuring of the inner world, yet he believed that her retention of Freud's instinct theories hampered the full development of her seminal contributions. For him, the individual was motivated by the need for relatedness, not for instinctual discharge. Fairbairn's theory is not a handbook for the future. Its value lies in the opening up of directions that would appear to be eminently productive for expanding our understanding and, especially, for resolving some of the blocks that have tended to keep psychoanalysis tied to its past. There is a general acknowledgment, outside the United Kingdom at least, of the value of his views. I believe they thus form an essential basis for the formulation of what could become the unifying perspective for the next phase in the development of analytic knowledge.

Commemorative plaque outside the Fairbairn residence. "W. Ronald D. Fairbairn, Edinburgh, 1926–1940."

5. THE OBJECT-RELATIONS THEORY OF PERSONALITY

The classical model of psychoanalytic theory appeared over seventy years ago when Freud (1923) formulated his structural concepts. The ego was the part of the personality concerned with organizing the adaptation of the person to the external environment, regulating the means by which he sought satisfaction for his drives (the id) and reconciling these with a more primitive control system (the superego), which operated unconsciously within the ego. These structures were finally shaped by the experience of the Oedipus conflict. This theory permitted a considerable advance in psychoanalytic understanding and consequently produced a fresh mass of observations from the widened range of conditions that the psychoanalyst was enabled to treat. It seemed to give a foundation for much that was obscure, especially the unconscious sources of resistance and guilt. It led to an interest in the structural parts of the personality, the ego and the superego, and to an understanding of how the ego was patterned by its defensive needs. The development of the ego in its earliest phases became increasingly important, a trend related to the fact that data from the neuroses gained in width and depth, and also to the new findings of child analysis.

Freud's view of the id as a reservoir of unorganized drive energies with the structured ego and superego trying to regulate their discharge was gradually perceived as an oversimplification. Hartmann (1964) began to publish his well-known series of papers, many his own and others with associates, on a new concept of early development according to which the ego and the id were differentiated from the first undifferentiated phase. The ego was structured not only by the experiences of the infant and young child in the satisfaction and frustration of its drives, but also by the maturation of autonomous ego capacities, motility, perception, and so forth. Hartmann's additions, however, to the theory of ego development and the concept of the autonomous ego do not alter basically Freud's model. For him, the id still derives from libidinal and aggressive energies.

The relatedness of the ego to the other parts of the personality is constantly acknowledged amongst the ego-psychology group. The failure to do justice to the structuring in the other parts, especially in that area covered by the term *id,* has led to the development of concepts that perpetuate, or even increase, a divorce between theory and clinical practice that many analysts have recognized in recent years. One of the main features in ego psychology seems to be a need to formulate theories in terms that are thought to be more appropriate to science, or, more accurately, to other scientists. Nevertheless, for analysts, as for others, theories must be closely linked to their practice, and the data of psychoanalysis do not lend themselves to too much depersonalization.

Object-relations theory, as described by Fairbairn (1952a) and Guntrip (1961, 1969), adopts the standpoint that the psychological difficulties of patients do not arise basically from the frustration of instinctual impulses, but are the by-products of the individual's failure to develop an adequate capacity to make satisfactory relationships. This capacity for good relationships with others is the end-product of successive stages of development from infancy onwards.

During infantile dependence, the infant needs to be loved unconditionally, to be cared for, fed, and responded to as a unique individual by all the loving, encouraging stimulation that good mothering gives. Growth to more independence, with the capacity to tolerate frustration, is accompanied by the consolidation of an imago of the good mother when she is not there. This representation of the good mother forms one pole of a dynamic structure or system gradually established within the matrix of the mind. The inner mother in the system serves to stimulate an effective basis for the development, at the other pole, of the self as an I who can do many things to maintain the good feelings that she provided. This dynamic structure as a whole (*System A*) thus mediates the pleasure and confidence with which the individual expands his rapidly maturing resources, for example, in motor skills and in speech, during the process of becoming an autonomous person. An extension of this system is evolved later from the relationship with the good powerful father who readily becomes another inner supporting figure. This inner father has a special importance in the general drive towards individuation of the self from the original fusion with the mother.

The foundation of good affective experience which is associated with this system enables the growing personality to distribute appropriately its satisfactions between inner fantasy relationships and activities with the outer world. It also creates an effective balance between satisfactions that need to involve people and those that are derived from creative interaction with the physical environment.

In contrast with what happens as the result of good experiences, two other kinds of inner figures or object-relations systems are established within the mind from feelings of rejection and of weakness and inadequacy, or later, when the individual feels his drive to autonomy or his emerging sexual interest are responded to as "bad." These systems are:

System B: The frustrated self, with needs made "exciting" because their satisfaction is forbidden, and with representations of the parents or parts of them (e.g. breast or penis) that could gratify these needs.

System C: Imagos of parents threatening the self by withdrawal of love or punitive retaliations if the needs in System B are expressed. This system, a precursor of the later oedipal superego, operates as a powerful controller and inhibitor, "forbidding" expression of the repressed needs.

Since the affects associated with the frustrated yet exciting needs evoke anxiety from the activity of the controlling system, both of these systems become incompatible with the positive relationships sought by the central self (*System A*), namely, to be accepted and loved as a person. The resultant segregation splits the original unitary matrix of the self into subselves, each of which seeks another person in the role of the object created in the inner world. This early splitting, which appears to occur through the innate properties of the affects, is of a different order from that which takes place in later stages of development, for example, by repression under the influence of more developed relationships with the parents when the oedipal superego is formed. For our purposes, however, we do not need to differentiate these stages and the terms *segregated* or *repressed* systems can be used interchangeably. Also, the term *object* refers to the imagos of persons, or parts of persons, which represent the nonself pole of the inner relationships.

The segregated systems have at one pole the self, or more strictly the self in a certain state, and at the other pole the corresponding object. This bipolar structure introduces into the systems the important property that the relationships they represent are reversible. The self can be the frustrated person seeking to find the object it needs; but because the object is internalized in the mind, the self can also feel identified with, and hence play the part of, the inner object. Thus the individual can be the dependent baby seeking mothering, or he can adopt the role of being the bountiful mother giving devoted care to himself, or to another person with whom his frustrated self is identified. With increasing experience and maturation, and aided by his own body in providing gratification, he can enact these relationships in fantasy and play with growing richness in thought and feeling. Moreover, the frustrated longings are commonly fused with other reactive feelings, for example, anger, hate, triumphing, controlling. Similarly, the disapproving or hostile parental imago comes to have all the intensity of the child's aggressive feelings, thus leading to severe anxiety, guilt, humiliation, depression, and despair. Frequently, the control system fuses with repressed needs so that, for example, sexual gratification is fused with a punitive aggressive relationship leading to sadistic or masochistic behaviour. Thus the characteristics of the inner objects in the segregated systems, while derived from the experiences with the real parents, are selected, compounded, and added to by fantasy, conscious and unconscious, into unique constructions.

What happens in these internal relationships is interrelated in the closest way. From the start, the central ego develops as that part of the central self that seeks to integrate and adapt to reality the various relationships and activities that provide the most satisfying patterns for living in the individual's environment.

With its capacities for learning, the central ego modifies some of the frustrated needs by finding more acceptable satisfactions leading to a diminution of the retaliatory fantasies. A number of the unacceptable needs remain, however, with a constant tendency to seek gratification. To cope with this inner situation, the ego adds to the defensive function of the primitive superego a variety of other controls—the familiar mechanisms of defence. As a result, many of the segregated needs are completely barred from consciousness and others are recognized only in part or only at certain times. When segregated in this way, these needs fall largely outside the learning processes of the central ego, and they seek to enact the inner relationships, not in a realistic way, but by forcing reality to match the inner needed object. They operate as closed systems in contrast to the open adaptive relationships of the central ego.

As adulthood is reached, the personality is thus structured by a range of dynamic systems, each mediating a relationship with an internal object:

System A: The central self which is related to its ideal objects. It attempts to come to terms with systems B and C, which are segregated at varying "distances" from consciousness.

System B: The frustrated need system containing the unsatisfied needs of earlier phases and therefore immature in character. In it the self, or more accurately a part of the self, seeks to realize the inner exciting object relationships.

System C: The primitive controlling system constituted by the threatening parental imagos forbidding the expression of System B needs.

These relationship-systems constitute the dynamic units of personality functioning. Every individual acquires a unique inner world from the varying content and strengths of these systems. His fantasies and feelings, thoughts and interests, are determined by their activity and their interaction. As action systems, they create relations in the outer world which are largely a reflection of those in the inner world.

Individuals of widely different personality patterns can live effectively and with adequate satisfaction. In the functioning of the person, boundaries between the so-called normal and the neurotic are notoriously unclear. In psychotherapy we are concerned with those whose functioning has become inadequate to the point of motivating them to seek help, and for the task of appraising such dysfunction it is convenient to adopt two broad types (leaving aside the psychoses):

1. Normal or mature functioning;
2. Pathological functioning (as in the psychoneuroses and character disorders).

Within the central ego system, inner object-relationships are represented by flexible structures related to ideal objects and ego-ideals which are constructed from those highly valued aspects of parental and other relationships with which the person wishes to identify. Ideals embody an imago for the self to be realized in relationships with these ideal figures. In the mature person, ideal objects are not so much fixed imagos of particular figures as more generalized representations comprising good values attached to earlier figures. These abstracted values can be related to actual others, thus making the value systems or ideals much more realistic, in other words, the standards expected from others and those set for the self are within normal capacities.

In the course of healthy development, much of the intensity of the segregated systems, both of those concerned with control as well as those containing frustrated needs, is diminished by absorption into the central self. The adaptive compromises thus achieved contribute many of the specific attitudes and character features of the individual or the minor eccentricities and irrationalities in his behaviour. For instance, a latent need to be defiantly assertive through being messy may be dealt with by the central ego adopting tidiness as a general character trait while retaining some activities in which untidiness is expressed. Leisure activities also constitute an important adaptive outlet for repressed needs. With this kind of development, the repressed needs cease to be sources of major conflict and are adopted as relatively benign parts of the self.

The functioning of a mature person in terms of the dynamic object-relations systems can be described as follows:

1. A wide range of relationships and activities, involving both the social and physical environments, and appropriate to the phase of the life cycle, is spontaneously sought and maintained. These relationships and activities reflect an investment in living. Most activities and relationships are enjoyed, because satisfying affects are freely experienced in personal relationships.
2. In close relationships, and particularly in those concerned with the reproductive cycle, satisfactions are found in treating the loved objects as whole persons. The identity and reality of the other is fully accepted, raising the threshold of toleration for unfulfilled expectations and thus increasing the capacity to maintain stable relationships with others, especially in marriage and bringing up children. These mature relationships are *transactional*, that is, the individual constantly influences and is influenced by the other in a mutually adaptive way.
3. In general social attitudes and relationships, the individuality of people is accepted and their way of life and their feelings are respected. The normal constraints and demands of the social environment are accepted with understanding. The needs of others, for example, when they express criticism, or when authority or responsibility has to be accepted, are met in a realistic manner.

4. The free activity of good object-relation systems in the personality maximizes the resources of the central ego by facilitating both the gaining of experience and its use. Perception of reality is relatively free from the distortions that powerful repressed needs induce. Energies are readily available and constantly mobilized. The patterns of personality functioning in thought and in action in major life roles are integrated and consistent. This integrated and consistent quality is not rigid, however, and changes are met by a flexible use of resources.
5. There is a need to participate in the shared social tasks that constitute work and to achieve a socially meaningful status through the contribution made. Work is accepted as a positive relationship with the environment, physical and social, and is therefore maintained with interest as a means of self-realization. Career aspirations and performance match resources.
6. Alongside family, work, and recreational needs, is the whole complex of what might be described as "higher or supra-individual values," a tendency to generalize about life and give it meaning. Social improvement, artistic endeavour, religious beliefs, and so forth, could be said to represent the attempt in man to improve the human lot and give meaning to life. This complex probably provides for the individual a trend towards the highest level of integration he can achieve among his needs and experience.
7. Being spontaneously involved in the world, the mature person acquires a background of confident self feeling without excessive self-reference. His activities engage him with satisfying affects so that he ordinarily loses himself in them. When he does appraise himself, his rich and positively felt experience with others permits him to be realistic and accepting of his own assets and liabilities. Where difficulties arise from external sources, affects aroused are those which are appropriate to good solutions, for instance, extra effort, or aggression for mastery. Negative affects such as anxiety, guilt, grief over loss, humiliation, and so on, are not unduly marked or prolonged.

PATHOLOGICAL FUNCTIONING

In the neurotic patient, by contrast, the conflict between the repressed needs and those of the central self stamps his relations with himself and others. While satisfaction of repressed relationships may often be obtained by fantasy activity, they retain their tendencies to act out, to coerce the external person into the role of the inner object in such a way that the other is not permitted to have much independence or individuality. With relationships based on the repressed need systems there is also the powerful tendency to project the self pole of these relationships and to treat the other as this part of the self. For example, the individual may be a sadistic self towards a masochistic object or he may occupy the masochistic position himself, giving a sadistic role to the other.

As with the repressed needs, the control system also operates both in fantasy and by seeking external relationships. The individual may play the role of the harsh or severe controller towards another who is treated as, and often provoked into behaving like, the unacceptable part of himself. Again, he may manoeuvre authority figures into restrictive relationships of power and control over him.

With the pressures to make the object fit the repressed systems along with the tendency to reverse roles, relationships with others tend to be restricted or unstable. Frequently these relationships have inappropriate affects as in excessive hates and loves. Again, the inability to enter into a relation of full mutuality with the other can lead to sexual interest and gratification being more localized in part-objects rather than linked with the total person.

Because frustration has played such a dominant part in development of the neurotic, he tends to feel the demands of reality as unpleasant constraints. For instance, the role of authority figures or the demands of work arouse a preponderance of negative feelings, a defensive indifference or a degree of resentment.

Perception is distorted, either by blind spots when strong repressed needs have to be inhibited, or by erroneous constructions when they dominate ego functioning. When stability is tenuously achieved by extreme restriction of the environment, underlying insecurity is often exposed by an inability to adapt to changes with normal flexibility. Available energies and the sustaining of effort are also erratic.

The most striking effects of dominant repressed systems are usually to be seen in the area of self-feeling. The self is divided with the result that there is little consistency or confidence in self-feeling. Self-appraisal is not in keeping with reality, in other words, the psychoneurotic is often self-depreciating, and at other times self-exalting. The familiar affective consequences of conflict—anxiety, guilt, and inferiority feelings—are prominent.

The distorted character formations evolved by many patients to deal with strong repressed systems may not show interferences so much within the person as between the person and others. In this kind of development, the central self fails to develop an interest in the individuality of others and a capacity for obtaining satisfaction from a free and flexible range of transactions with them. Instead, it becomes subservient to the dominant segregated needs. Perception of, and relations with, the environment involve a distortion similar to that in the neurotic patient, but the central ego functioning is more stable within the restrictions it has to maintain. Self-feeling, too, although distorted, for example, by over-estimation, tends to be consistent, and the negative affects may not be noteworthy. In self-selected environments such people may function well and consistently. Their limitations emerge only when changes are forced on them by conflicts or failures in the outer environment, for example, from the lack of response by others, or from a growing feeling that they are "different" or are "missing something." When environmental "failure" leads to the breakdown of this type of defensive functioning, more devastating affective disorders, for example, depression, can follow.

THE PROCESS OF PSYCHOTHERAPY

Since the functioning of a person is governed by complex interactions of inner object-relations systems, and by their interaction with the external social and physical environment, breakdown can be seen as an outcome of multiple causation. Sometimes a person is able to recover his functioning by temporarily withdrawing from the disturbing activities or circumstances, or he might be able to make use of the ordinary help, sympathy, and support available. For many people, however, the pressure of these systems, which causes maladaptive relations within the self and with others, drives the individual to seek treatment. More specific measures are then required to alter the properties of the segregated systems in relations to the central ego.

From the object-relations viewpoint, the task of psychotherapy is one of enabling the individual to experience the nature of his segregated systems so that they can be brought within, and modified by, the adaptive powers of the central ego. This goal is achieved by the therapist inviting the patient to talk spontaneously about himself. What is then communicated by the total behaviour of the patient reveals progressively the relationships of his inner world. The skill of the therapist lies in gradually exposing the aims of the segregated relationships and the defences adopted to control them. The central ego then reexperiences in the relationship with the therapist the affective patterns of the forbidden longings and the fears that led to their being split off. A new reality is tested in which the longings can be freely felt and expressed without the previously feared consequences being realized. Thus, learning can take place, needs given up or modified, or new solutions found for their regulation.

To pursue this process throughout the layering of the personality is a major endeavour and one that requires the intensity and length of psychoanalysis. In psychotherapy, the aim is less ambitious and restricted to achieving only a moderate modification of the segregated systems so that the person's capacity for good relationships is eased from the conflicting aims that have hitherto interfered with this potential.

When the therapeutic process is under way, the individual is thrown into a much more open state than previously. Repressed needs begin to be released with the affects and relationships within them. In the early stages, positive affects from feelings of increased freedom, especially in sexual relationships, may predominate. Negative self-feelings with anxiety and guilt may follow, however, from the activity of the repressed controlling system. Relationships with others and within the self are more labile and intense during this phase.

After the termination of psychotherapy, a period of consolidation is often required for the individual to achieve a stable position with the new relationships he has been enabled to make.

The overall effect should be a change towards mature patterns of functioning, with more investment in living and more positive affect experienced in general. Better acceptance of the constraints of the social and physical environment also contributes to better self-feeling. Undue dependence on others, or withdrawal from them, should be replaced by mature social relationships and independent activities. The individual who has experienced the process of becoming conscious of much of his unrecognized inner life is, however, different from the ordinary normal person in his greater awareness of, and attention to, the inner world. Although he may achieve a satisfying involvement with the outer world, this increased self-awareness tends to remain.

6. AN OBJECT-RELATIONS APPROACH TO PSYCHODIAGNOSTIC APPRAISAL*

Psychotherapists hitherto have not devoted much attention to the problem of quantitative assessment. It occurred to us that recent developments in ego psychology, the concept of the self and the theory of object relations might enable a fresh approach to be made, and in this paper we describe some exploratory work in the hope that it may stimulate fresh contributions to this important task.

Psychodynamic appraisals are concerned with the needs that the patient seeks to satisfy in his relationships. Normally when a relationship need is being sought and expressed, the *form* of the associated behavior is appropriate—the posture, gestures, choice of words with their feeling tones, and the manner of speech are of a piece. The resources of the ego established through past experience determine a form of behaviour that expresses the dominant feelings or needs in the most appropriate and integrated manner. Conflicting motives or affects, by contrast, are noted when they create various kinds of incongruous or inappropriate features within the behaviour that fits the consciously sought relationship; and although the ego tries to maintain a control whereby motor behaviour is appropriate to the main relationship it seeks, the conflicting needs are seldom completely blocked from some behavioural manifestations. The total behavioural form thus reflects the interplay of the competing relationship needs activated in the person.

Speech, which is one of the more refined forms of behavioural expression, reveals the same close relationship between its formal aspects and the range of dynamic systems actively associated with it. The choice and arrangement of the expressive words match the underlying affects and can be used to detect the harmony, or otherwise, of these feelings. The role of intrusive conflicting relationships is most familiar in slips of the tongue, but there are clearly many ways in which the formal aspects of verbal communication can be influenced by such conflicts, for instance, in blocking, inhibited phrasing, choice of inappropriate words, the free or restricted use of affective words, and so forth. A good example of studies in this area is one by Lorenz and Cobb (1953). When,

---

*This chapter was co-authored by H. S. Gill and H. Phillipson.

therefore, a test situation is used which demands a specified form of verbal response concerning the individual's experience and mode of relating to others, then the way in which the specified form is met will give information about the relevant strengths of the ego and conflicting systems. Analysis of the form of the response can give a more standardized and quantitative assessment of these competing systems in the functioning of the personality. Furthermore, relating the form to the content helps to identify the interfering systems and to appraise the resources of the ego in achieving a synthesis or otherwise.

In such a test, the stimuli to be presented should be those that are particularly evocative of relations existing between parts of the self and between the self and others. Words and pictures have both been profitably used in the past as stimuli. We chose to work first with words because a series of stimulus words could be prepared much more readily than a series of pictures.

Since we assumed that the basic mode of relating to the self, to others, and to the physical environment is reflected in the syntactical unit of everyday speech, namely the sentence, we decided, in contrast with the traditional use of the word-association test, to ask for the spontaneous personal reaction in the form of a sentence. The sentence has a subject interacting (transitive verb) with an object, or else it depicts a state of being or activity by the use of an intransitive verb. The quality of affect in the relationship is often further indicated by the use of qualifying words, adverbs, and adjectives.

AN EXPLORATORY TEST

Choice of Words for the Stimulus Series

The stimulus words were chosen to emphasize the various roles in a range of human relationships and their associated affects. Preference was given to words that could elicit a variety of relationships through different meanings, for example, BEAT, MEAN, PART. Approximately one-third of the words referred primarily to a person (or part of a person) in the role of subject or object in a relationship, for example, MYSELF, PATIENT, FRIENDS, BOSS. Another third of the words referred to the content of the relationship between the main figures (subject and object), for example, NEED, LOSE, and TEAR. The remaining third of the words were concerned primarily with affects, for examples, EMPTY, EXCITED, AFRAID. An attempt was also made (*a*) to cover relationships at the major stages of human development—infancy, early childhood, later childhood, adolescence, adulthood—by such words as DEPENDENT, CAREER, MANAGE; (*b*) to include words relevant to the major areas of living, such as family, work, and social life, for example, HOME, PARTY, BELIEVE; (*c*) to have approximately the same number of words in positive, negative, and neutral affect categories.

In ordering the stimuli the words from the categories mentioned above were spread as evenly as possible throughout the series. An attempt was also made to ensure that the two halves of the 100-word series, when considered separately, were roughly comparable. Each half of the series (1–50 and 51–100) was begun and ended with the less disturbing words, that is, was started with a few such words to "warm up" and a few at the end to affect a feeling of "closure."

(The final list of stimulus words is given in the case study on pages 87–88.)

The Form of Response Required

As stated, personal reactions were required in the form of a sentence because a sentence with its subject, verb, and object reflects the relationship evoked by a stimulus in the test situation. As the smallest unit expressing a relationship, the sentence provides information of a greater range, within better-defined boundaries, than is possible with the traditional associational words or phrases. Compare, for instance, the following four responses to the stimulus word SUBMIT. The first two would be typical of traditional word associations. The last two represent the majority of responses under instructions to respond with a sentence: (1) Failure. (2) Headmaster. (3) I usually do. (4) One must submit to higher authority.

The statement about the self-sufficiency of a unit of analysis is, of course, a relative one. Often a sentence leaves many questions unanswered. But in our view the most useful approach was to obtain a large number of brief responses to a wide range of stimuli and thus make it possible to assess quantitatively the functioning of the ego in a large variety of relationships.

We found it convenient to ask for written responses and to administer the test in a group setting. The words were printed on large cards and exposed one at a time at intervals of 15 seconds. This time proved suitable to get at the first spontaneous reaction of the subjects and to detect defensive recovery after initial interference.

Selection of Subjects

The most important test of the efficacy of an instrument designed to detect changes in personality functioning will come from studies with the same patients at different stages of treatment—before, during, and after. Analytical psychotherapy, whether conducted through group or individual settings, takes usually 3–4 years to produce substantial effects. As an interim measure, however, comparable groups at different stages of treatment could give sufficient evidence to establish the value of the approach. Satisfactory evidence of reasonable diagnostic power would be obtained if the following results were achieved. (*a*) Significant differences should exist between patients and "normals." (*b*) Comparable groups of patients at different stages of treatment should show a progression towards normality.

We therefore studied the responses of four groups matched for age, sex, intelligence, occupation, and verbal competence,[1] the groups representing a series of stages towards "normal" functioning.

Group A: new patients. Twenty patients at the time of their application to an outpatient clinic.

Group B: patients in treatment. Ten patients currently in weekly analytical group psychotherapy for at least 2 years and rated by their therapist as showing some improvement.

Group C: patients after treatment. Ten patients who for at least 3 years were in weekly group psychotherapy before its termination 2 years ago or earlier, and rated by their therapist as improved.

Group D: nonpatients ("normals"). Twenty adults from nonclinical settings, excluding those who scored highly on a neuroticism inventory. These subjects included staff of industrial management, social workers, teachers, and so forth—all actively interested in psychological studies.

Analysis of Responses and Results

In developing a scoring scheme, considerations as described in the early sections suggested a number of variables concerned both with the content and the form of the responses. Some preliminary work on less well-matched samples of patients and nonpatients helped in making our final choice.

Dimension I: Form of Expression

Briefly, this dimension classified each response as *inhibited* (blanks or single words), *phrase, or sentence* (complete or incomplete). The ability to respond freely with a sentence indicated that the subject was responding with the ego as the predominant source of relationships. Conversely, failure of the ego to regulate a repressed need evoked by the stimulus word would be shown in the disturbed form of the required response.

The results (Figs. 1, 2) show that new patients give more inhibited responses and fewer sentences than the "normal," and that the treated groups show a progression in the expected direction. (A table of results along with the statistical significance of differences is given in an Appendix.)

Dimension II: Syntactical Use of the Stimulus Word

The aim of this dimension was to compare those responses in which the stimulus word was used as the *subject* of the sentence, and those in which it was used as the *object* of the sentence. (In this, and subsequent dimensions, responses which did not fit a category were left unclassified.) In making it the subject of the sentence, the individual would show a spontaneous acceptance of, and absorption in, the

[1]On the Mill Hill Vocabulary Scale—definitions.

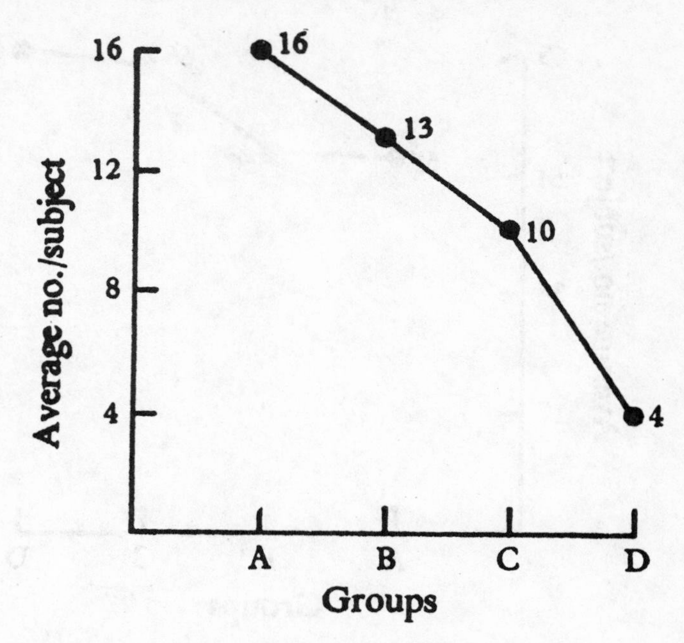

Fig. 1. Inhibited responses

stimulus by placing it in the first part of his response and by making some kind of statement directly about it, for example, WORK—"Work is very enjoyable." In contrast, the stimulus word is placed in a subordinate, more distant position, as the object of the sentence when some other interest intrudes into the responding dynamics and displaces it from its position of primacy within the sentence, for example, WORK—"I can enjoy my work."

In Figs. 3 and 4 it will be seen that new patients use the stimulus word less often as subject and more often as object of the sentence than do the nonpatients. The use of the stimulus word by the treatment groups is similar to that of new patients.

Dimension III: Self and Other References

Responses in this dimension were scored as: (1) those referring to *self*, and (2) those referring to *others only*.

It was expected that nonpatients would be spontaneously more concerned with thinking and feeling about others, and would reveal this interest in others by making more frequent references to them. Conversely, because strong repressed needs create more anxiety about, or preoccupation with, the self, there would be more reference to self in a new patient.

Figs. 5 and 6 show that new patients make more references to themselves and fewer to others compared with nonpatients. Treated patients show a trend

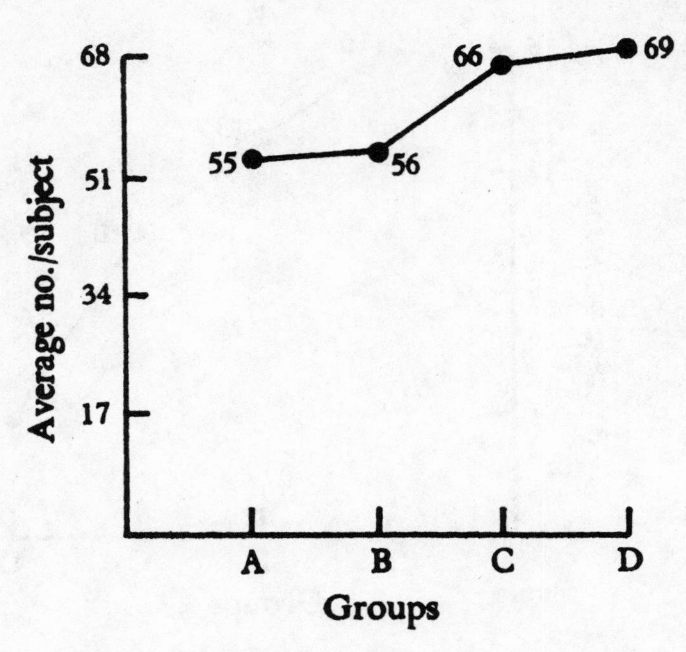

Fig. 2. Sentences

towards more self-reference. Although some such increase was to be expected because of the introspective nature of the therapeutic process, the actual amount of increase is surprisingly large. It would seem that the process of becoming conscious of one's inner life as the result of psychotherapy inevitably leads to greater attention to the self. However, within the self-references, treatment should lead to a decrease in the proportion of negative affects (see dimension V).

Dimension IV: Mode of Communication

The responses were classified as follows:

a. *Generalizations*. Statements in the form of generalizations were put into two categories: (i) those expressing a sound, evaluative judgement—*"adaptive" generalizations*; and (ii) those involving a biased, inaccurate judgement—*"maladaptive" generalizations*.
b. *Personalized statements*. Statements referring to self were classified as: (i) those expressing a positive or constructive attitude—*"adaptive" personal statements*; (ii) those expressing feelings of inadequacy, or antisocial attitudes—*"maladaptive" personal statements*.

In making a generalization the individual is expressing the "learning" from a number of situations in which the self has come to terms with the conflicting feelings present in interpersonal experience. Such a generalization would reflect

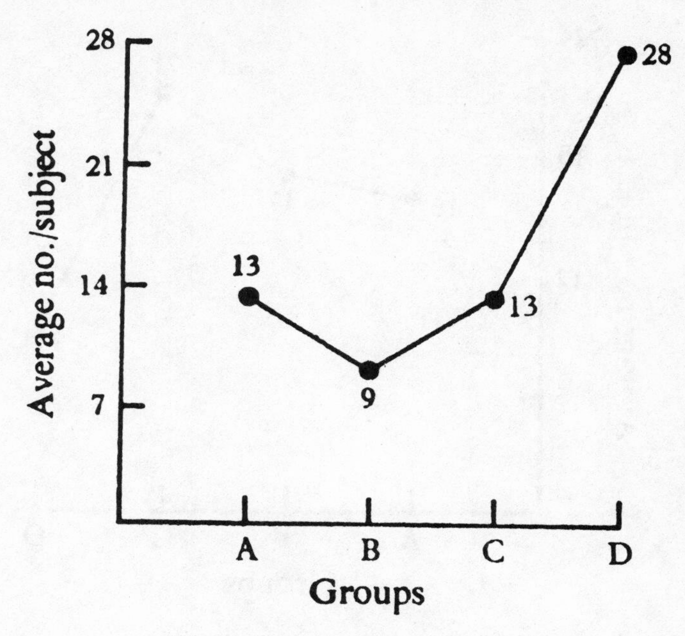

Fig. 3. Stimulus word as subject

shared reality. Thus, painful experience relating to criticism can lead to a reflective generalization indicating that the individual has learned the role of criticism in relating to others, for example:

CRITICISM—"Criticism can be helpful at times."

CRITICISM—"One has to accept criticism in order to improve."

In contrast with an adaptive generalization, a maladaptive one is indicative of a failure to come to terms with major conflicts and associated painful affects involved in living closely with others, for example:

CRITICISM—"Critics should be banned."

BOSS—"Bosses are a real problem."

Figs. 7 and 8 give some of the results. Nonpatients make more generalizations than do the new or the treated patients, and nonpatients also show that a greater percentage of their generalizations are adaptive. The treatment groups do not show a progressive trend towards the normal pattern either in the total number of generalizations or in the percentage of adaptive ones. In contrast, in the percentage of maladaptive personal responses the three patient groups show the expected trend of improvement.

Dimension V: Affective Tone

In this dimension each response was scored, as far as possible, by affect alone, without considering its form or other aspects of content. When an affect was

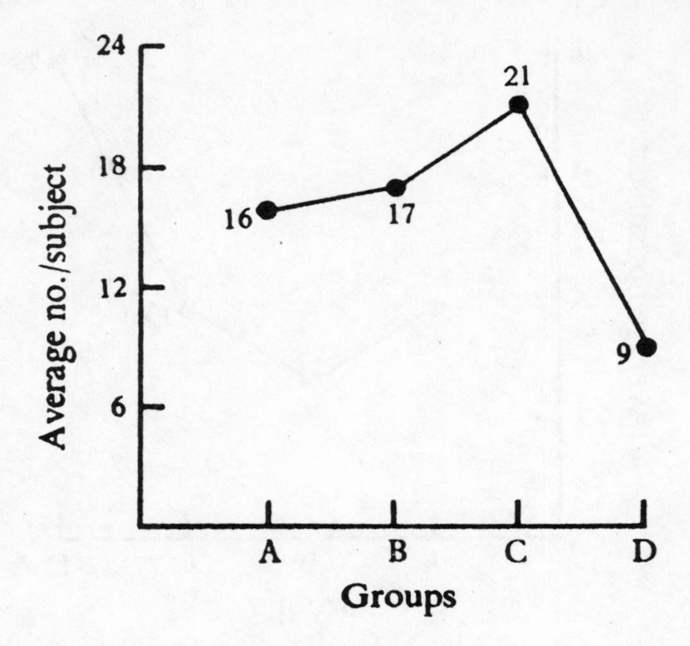

Fig. 4. Stimulus word as object

clearly expressed in a response it was scored as *positive* or *negative*. When the presence of affect was doubtful, or when its positive or negative quality could not be ascertained, the response was left *unclassified*. Affect was scored only on twenty-eight selected words that were particularly evocative of affective expression.

The scores on this dimension are given in Figs. 9 and 10. The balance of positive to negative feeling shows a consistent trend in the expected direction for all the four groups. It would thus appear that psychotherapy is most effective in this area of self-feeling. Presumably the change in self-feeling follows from the diminution in the strengths of the conflicting systems in relation to the central self.

Dimension VI: Specific Affective Reference in Four Key Areas

In this dimension those responses were counted which constituted a simple, direct reference to *dependence, aggression, sex,* or *fear*.

In three areas—dependence, aggression, and sex—the results (Figs. 11–13) are in agreement with our expectation. A new patient experiencing difficulties in these areas is often locked in a conflict about the expression of these feelings. A patient in treatment necessarily goes through a phase where such feelings find more direct expression. With the termination of treatment, and as a stabilized position is reached by the passage of time, the repressed experiences in these

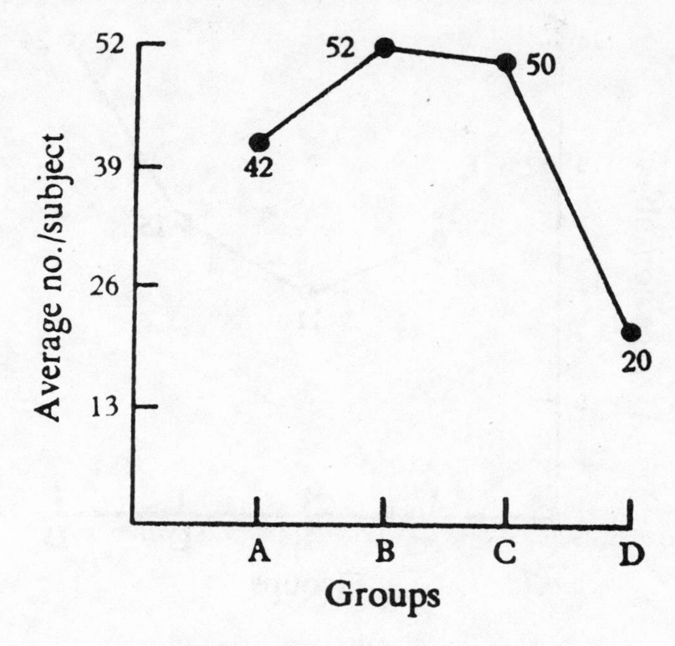

Fig. 5. Reference to self

areas are integrated into the central ego organization and preoccupation with them decreases to the normal level. As Fig. 14 shows, the situation concerning fear is somewhat different. Apparently, the expression of anxious feelings is lessened by the security felt in the relationship with the therapist.

Reliability of Scoring

A set of 100 responses was scored independently by five psychologists. With their more objective system of scoring, dimensions I, II, and III showed a very high level of reliability (over 90 percent in each case). Other dimensions involved a subjective component in judgement and first comparisons led to a relatively low level of agreement. With more practice and sharing of experience in using them, reliability showed considerable improvement and rose to over 80 percent agreement.

Influence of the Clinical Setting

In comparing patients with the nonpatient group the question arises of differing motivations towards the test situation. This question is clearly a complex one and could not be satisfactorily answered within the design of the present study. However, a partial check on the influence of the clinical setting was made as follows. The nonpatient Group D was selected from those subjects who, amongst

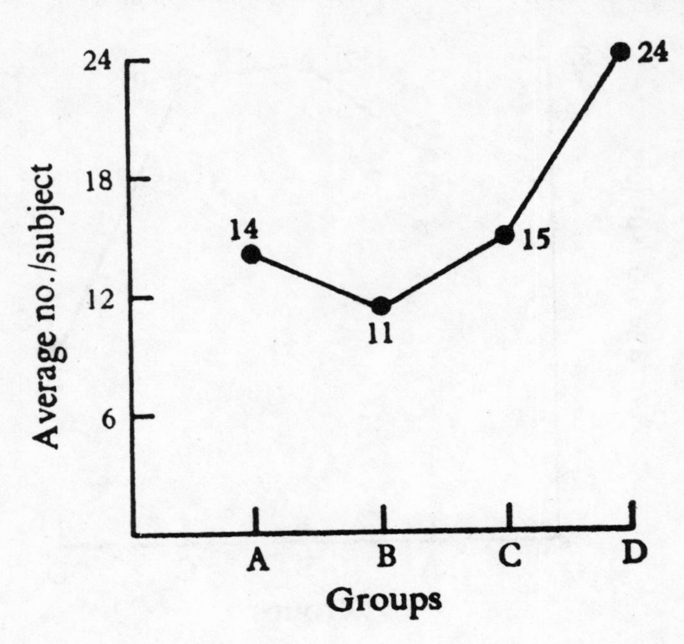

Fig. 6. References to others

a larger number tested, scored within the normal range on a neuroticism inventory (the Eysenck Personality Inventory). From the same pool of nonpatient subjects, we selected another group who had high neuroticism scores, that is, who indicated in their test responses the presence of many neurotic symptoms. The responses of this group to the stimulus words were compared with those of our other groups. In spite of not being in the category of patients, their performance resembled much more that of the new patients than the nonpatient Group D.

CLINICAL USE OF THE TEST: A CASE STUDY[2]

The following case study illustrates the use of the method in formulating the main psychodynamic aspects likely to be involved in treatment.

Mr A. is a married man of 35, separated from his wife. When applying for treatment he supplied in unusual detail a personal history. In it he said: "Basic to my condition is a fundamental negativism, a pessimistic assessment of my capabilities, and an uncertainty about precisely what I want to do. Although the

[2]This is one of the several cases from our sample who went into treatment and whose test findings are being compared with reports from their therapists.

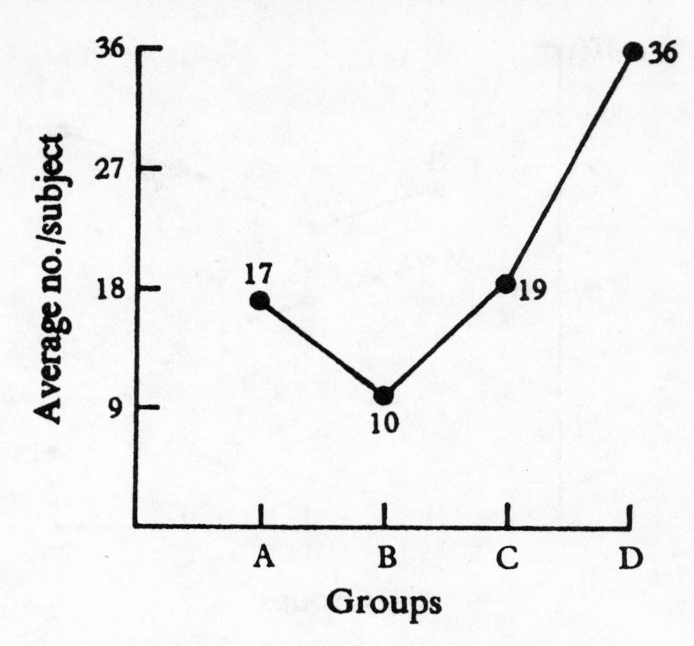

Fig. 7. Total generalizations

drugs help a lot to make life bearable, the underlying groundswell of insecurity remains. The roots of all this in my childhood are not hard to trace. My current difficulties, however, are clearly connected with the recent break-up of my marriage, which, together with the marriage itself, was symptomatic of my condition."

In the initial psychiatric interview he said that his wife was a good mother to his son, though she tended to smother him with kindness. For a large part of the marriage sexual relations were "a flop" because of impotence or premature ejaculation. Later, however, they were "satisfactory." More recently he experienced impotence with a girl, and agreed that he was worried by the competition for this girl and by the feeling that she was testing him out.

Before his operation for undescended testes when 14, a doctor had remarked, in front of students, that he had a very small penis, which had greatly embarrassed him. The psychiatrist discussed his wish for a satisfactory relationship with a woman, his feelings that he was not entitled to such a relationship, and his fears of reprisals from men so that he took a submissive position and avoided competition, though underneath, as in his political life and thinking, he rebelled. It was suggested that in his case an active interest in left-wing politics had enabled him to feel safe, with "comradely" support, in his rebellion against authority. The competitive feelings with his son were seen as a factor in the final break-up of his marriage. The patient readily agreed with these interpretations.

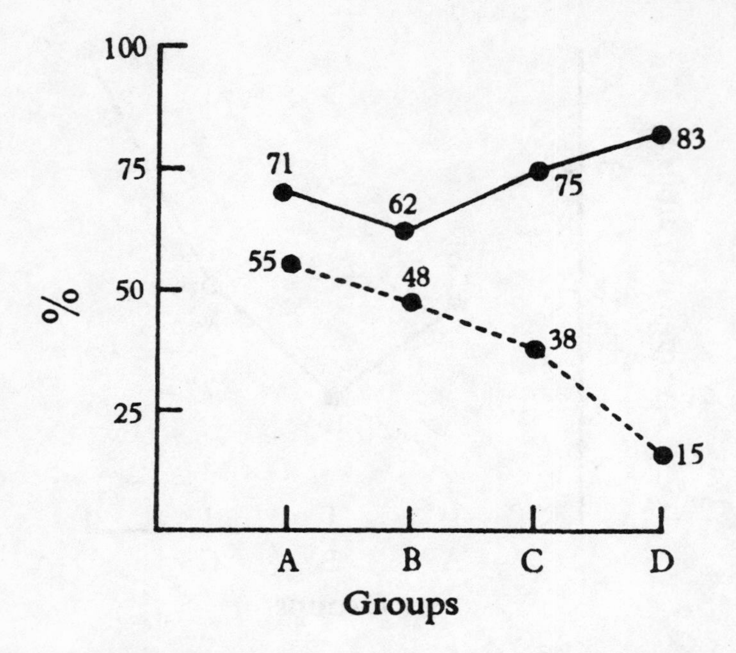

Fig. 8. —, Percentage adaptive generalizations; ---, percentage maladaptive personal statements

Study of Word-association Responses

The patient's responses to the stimulus series are given in Table 1. In studying these, the only information provided for the psychologist was age, sex, and marital status.

Analysis of Scores

Table 2 shows the patient's scores compared with the scores of the average patient and of the average normal.

1. *Form of expression*. He writes ninety-six complete sentences, an unusually high proportion, suggesting verbal fluency and great effort to meet the requirements of the test. The four responses that show marked inhibition in their form must therefore indicate that these stimuli have aroused particularly strong conflicting feelings:

    No. 14. Empty—
    No. 21. Husband—Husbands [can't]
    No. 28. Big—Big people——
    No. 84. Weak—Weakness

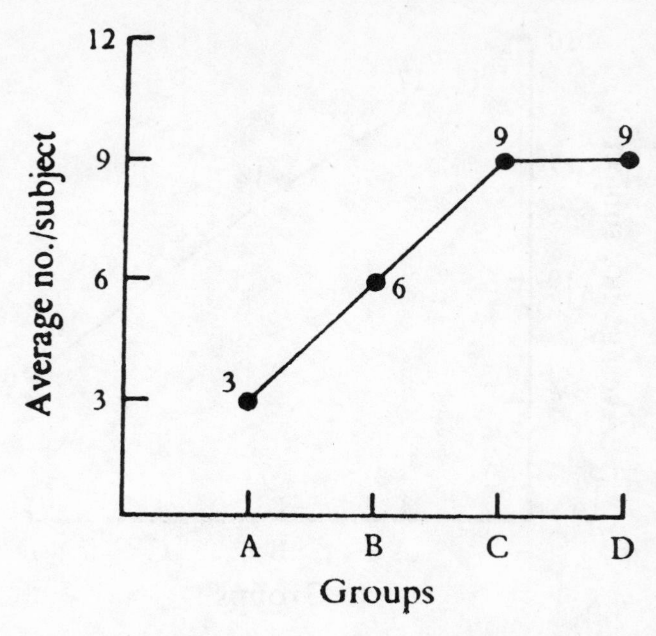

Fig. 9. Positive effect (on twenty-eight selected words)

These responses suggest feelings of inadequacy, in particular masculine inadequacy.

2. *Syntactical use of the stimulus word*. The patient uses the stimulus word as subject twice as often as the average nonpatient. This high score suggests too close an identification and excessive involvement with issues raised by the stimulus word, and may indicate his insecurity in maintaining the boundaries between himself and others.
3. *References to self and others*. The patient's scores in this dimension are between the average of patients and nonpatients for self-reference, and close to the average of nonpatients for reference to others only. He is, therefore, on the surface somewhat less preoccupied with himself than the average patient, and much more able to direct his response to others. His normal amount of reference to others appears to go along with his intellectualizing tendency, as shown in dimension IV. This interest in others may also have common roots with the compulsive involvement mentioned in the previous dimension.
4. *Mode of communication*. The main characteristic of his responses is that in spite of an unusually large proportion of adaptive generalizations, there is a relatively high number of maladaptive personal statements. This contrast suggests that his apparent

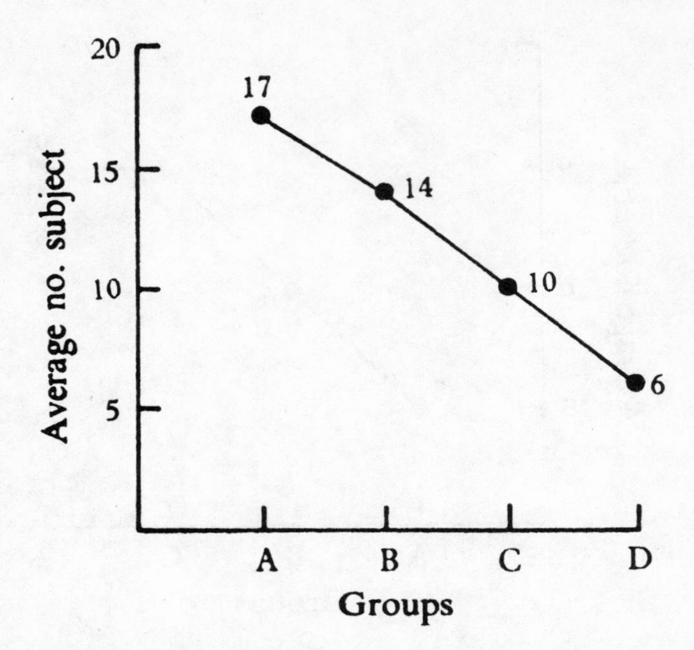

Fig. 10. Negative effect (on twenty-eight selected words)

adaptation may be based on a defensive intellectualizing position, which is his way of avoiding pressing personal difficulties.

5. *Affective Tone*. The balance of positive and negative affect is fairly close to that of the patient sample. The presence of so much negative affect in relation to the adaptive efforts shown in dimension IV further suggests that these efforts are compulsive and defensive in nature.

Personality Functioning from Form and Content of Responses

Dimension IV is the most suitable for examining all the patient's responses in terms of content, yet within formal categories.

1. The fifty-three generalizations may be divided into three groups:
   a. Twenty-eight responses to highly evocative words are in the form of intellectualizations in which the affective values are neutralized in large part, for example, no. 9: COLD—Coldness can be countered by wrapping up; no. 13: TOUCH—Touch is the most important sense (in a way).
   b. Eighteen responses show a need to conform to standards and a tendency to be critical of failure and pretence, for example, no. 7: IDEAL—Ideals[m] are essential; no. 33: FACE—One must face up to things.

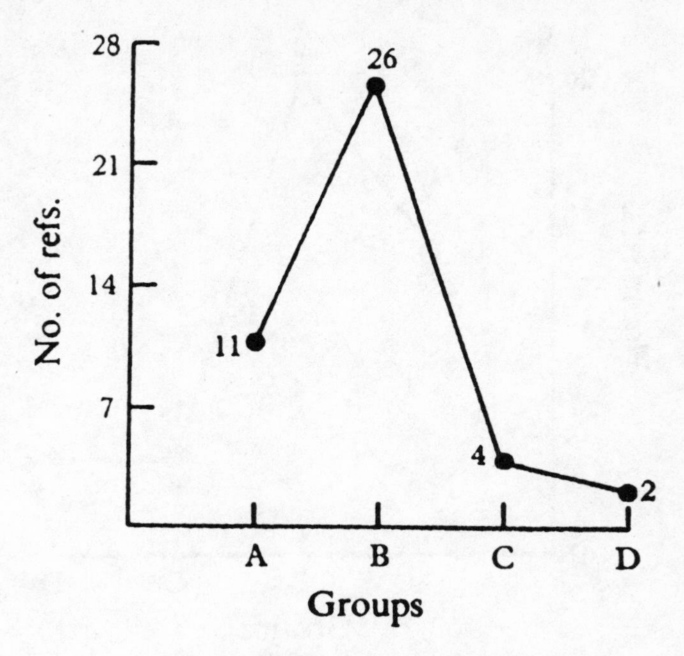

Fig. 11. Reference to dependence

These forty-six responses together show the extent of his intellectualization and strong superego pressure to conform.

c. Seven responses show his sensitivity and insecurity, for example, no. 60: SECRET—Secret thoughts often hurt; no. 80: DEPENDENT—One is dependent on other people's emotions.

2. Of the nine adaptive personal statements, four stress intellectual aspirations, for example, no. 51: MASTER—I should like to master political philosophy. The other five responses show a more interpersonal concern, mainly in a qualified form, for example, no. 2: WORK—I enjoy work on the whole.
3. The nineteen maladaptive personal statements are direct expressions of personal inadequacy and insecurity, for example, no. 46: BOSS—I always fear my boss; no. 54: LONELY—I often feel lonely.
4. The remaining nineteen responses, though made mostly to highly evocative words, show marked avoidance or inhibition of feeling.

The restriction or avoidance of emotional responses by intellectual effort or denial is a dominant characteristic of the record. Intellectual effort is used also to compensate for feelings of inadequacy as a man, and his lonely insecurity. By it he attempts to maintain a self that is effective, conforming to high standards, and to an extent constructive and reparative. On the other hand, he expresses

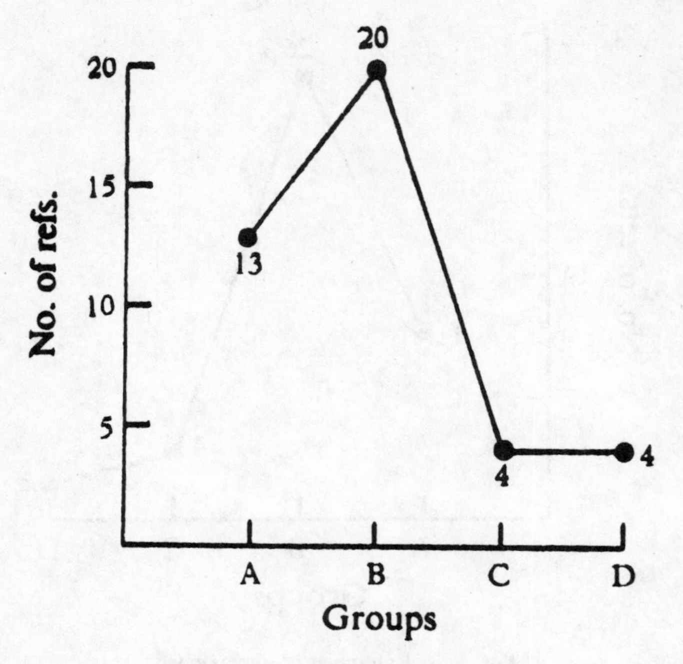

Fig. 12. Reference to aggression

feeling when directly portraying his insecurities and when indirectly angry at pretence in authorities. Expressions of enjoyment and achievement are few and usually accompanied by reservation or qualification.

The contrast between intense needs directly expressed and tight control of feelings suggests the possibility of compulsive acting-out behaviour.

Object Relations in the Content of Responses

The main object relationships can be examined from the content of responses.

Relations with Men

His relationship to men, particularly those in authority, has three main components:

1. On his own, he adopts a position of fear, inadequacy, and submission, for example, no. 46: BOSS—I always fear my boss; no. 65: SUBMIT—I often submit to others. He avoids situations involving physical aggression or hurt, for example, in the following responses "physical" connotations of the stimulus words are denied: no. 10: BEAT—"Beat" people don't wash!; no. 19: WOUND—Wounding people with words is easy.

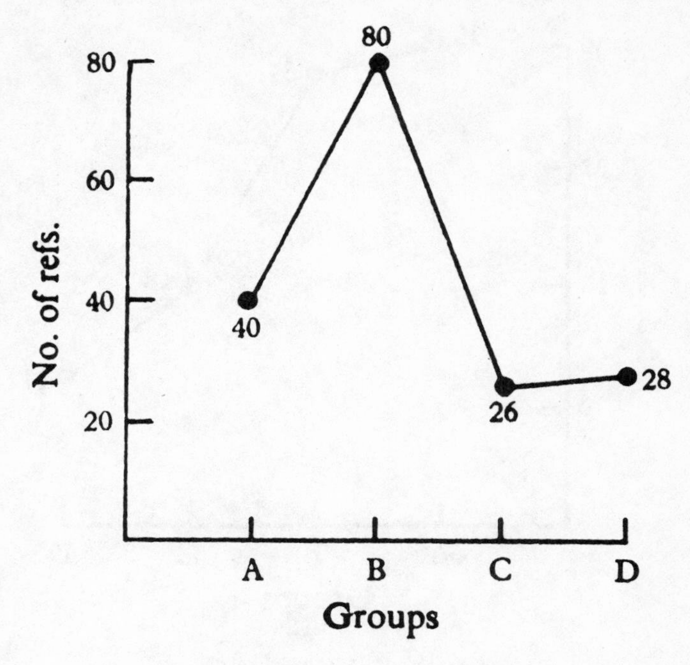

Fig. 13. Reference to sex

2. He can criticize authority, but only is an intellectual form, for example, no. 68: POWER – Power is what most politicians seek; no. 90: UNFAIR – Most societies are "unfair."
3. As part of his conflicting feelings towards authority, there is also a longing for a good relationship with the father figure, for example, no. 31: FATHER – My father was not very close to me; no. 96: DOCTOR – Doctors make fine father-figures.

Relations with Women

4. He has a strong need for a relationship with a woman (mother), but this is expressed in infantile, dependent terms, for example, no. 42: WARM – Warmth is comforting; no. 55: SOFT – Softness is connected with sleep; no. 71: MOTHER – My mother is kind and good. But he is unable to maintain a reciprocal, give-and-take relationship, as is indicated by the following responses where interactional aspects of stimulus words are ignored: no. 5: DEMAND – Demand is the converse of supply (!); no. 12: TRUST – "Trust-busting" *was* an important US occupation.
5. Just as he avoids physical, aggressive connotations of stimulus words (see (1) above), so he avoids also sexual connotations of

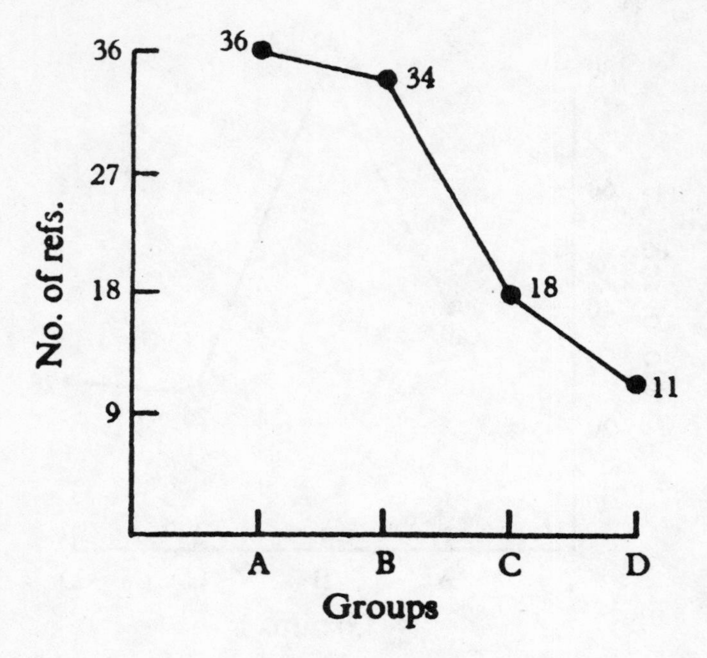

Fig. 14. Reference to fear

most words, for example, no. 48: ORGAN—Bach [on t] played on the organ is superb; no. 63: COUPLE—Couples are natural social units. However, one or two responses contrast sharply with the above by their direct sexual expression: no. 40: BARE—Bareness is socially taboo in the West (!); no. 56: MATE—Mating is very common in animals! This split in his sexual attitudes, his inferiority as a man and his need to test himself would be expected to lead to sexual acting-out.

6. In spite of this conflict, there are indications that he also wants to establish a good relationship with an idealized woman, for example, no. 71: MOTHER—My mother is kind and good; no. 26: DAUGHTER—Daughters are nice to have.

Relations to Self

7. He feels a sense of guilt, but tends to deny shame, for example, no. 34: GUILTY—I often feel guilty; no. 69: ASHAMED—I rarely feel shamed—perhaps I should.
8. There is a need to comply with the demands of his ego ideal, for example, no. 72: STAND—One must make a stand about things in which one believes; no. 82: SERVICE—Service to others is commendable.

Table 1
(The patient's alterations and punctuation are reproduced. Words which were deleted are shown in brackets.)

1. FRIENDS	I haven't many friends. Those I have I like very much.
2. WORK	I enjoy work on the whole.
3. DRINK	I don't drink much these days.
4. LOSE	I tend to lose confidence in certain situations.
5. DEMAND	Demand is the converse of supply (!).
6. ANIMAL	I don't like animals much.
7. IDEAL	Ideals[m] are essential.
8. CLOSE	Some People tend to be very close.
9. COLD	Coldness can be countered by wrapping up.
10. BEAT	"Beat" people don't wash!
11. CLOTHES	Clothes are status symbols
12. TRUST	"Trust-busting" was an important US occupation.
13. TOUCH	Touch is the most important sense (in a way).
14. EMPTY	
15. CARE	One should take care.
16. HEAD	Heads are better than hearts (?).
17. MANAGE	I usually manage to get through the month.
18. LONG	I long for security.
19. WOUND	Wounding people with words is easy.
20. CRITICISM	Criticism takes many forms.
21. HUSBAND	Husbands [can't]
22. SCHOOL	School should be reformed.
23. EXCITED	Excitement is often sought after.
24. DESTROY	The H-Bomb may well destroy us all.
25. MEAN	Meanings can be of several kinds. (etymological, etc.)
26. DAUGHTER	Daughters are nice to have.
27. INTEREST	Interest is a function of saving.
28. BIG	Big people — —
29. AFRAID	I used to be afraid of the dark.
30. PRIVATE	Privacy is [use] essential but probably over rated.
31. FATHER	My father was not very close to me.
32. PLAY	Plays at present aren't up to much (?)
33. FACE	One must face up to things.
34. GUILTY	I often feel guilty
35. STRAIN	Work is sometimes a strain—So are other things.
36. CHILDHOOD	My childhood was on the whole unhappy.
37. ADMIRE	I admire integrated people.
38. NEED	I need stability and affection.
39. DEAD	My father is dead.
40. BARE	Bareness is socially taboo in the West(!)
41. PATIENT	Patience must be cultivated.
42. WARM	Warmth is comforting
43. CHANGE	Changing for dinner is getting old-fashioned
44. SAD	Many things make me feel sad.
45. EXAMINATION	Examinations make me very nervous.
46. BOSS	I always fear my boss
47. SECURE	I wish I felt secure.
48. ORGAN	Bach [on t] played on the organ is superb.
49. HURT	I often feel hurt—without tangible reason

(cont.)

Table 1 (*cont.*)

50. Part	Parting can be hurtful.
51. Master	I should like to master political philosophy
52. Fun	Fun must/can be had spontaneously
53. Pride	Pride is socially bad
54. Lonely	I often feel lonely.
55. Soft	Softness is connected with sleep
56. Mate	Mating is very common in animals!
57. Responsible	Responsibility should be encouraged
58. Favourite	My favourite occupation is reading
59. Greedy	Greedy people eat too much
60. Secret	Secret thoughts often hurt.
61. Home	Home should be happy.
62. Believe	I believe in humanity—I can't say why!
63. Couple	Couples are natural social units.
64. Hate	[The] I don't hate *many* people.
65. Submit	I often submit to others.
66. Son	My son is the only . . . person I really love.
67. Party	Parties are fun. Political parties especially.
68. Power	Power is what most politicians seek.
69. Ashamed	I rarely feel ashamed—perhaps I should.
70. Doubt	Philosophical doubt is important.
71. Mother	My mother is kind & good.
72. Stand	One must make a stand about things in which one believes.
73. Deep	Still waters rarely run deep (in people).
74. Fail	Failure is a constant worry.
75. Burn	Burning is not pleasant.
76. Body	Bodies contain minds.
77. Rich	Richness is a quality.
78. Dream	I don't remember *many* dreams I have.
79. Tear	A tear usually means unhappiness,
80. Dependent	One is dependent on other people's emotions.
81. Myself	I think about myself too much
82. Service	Service to others is commendable.
83. Bed	Bed is great. Sleep is refreshing.
84. Weak	Weakness
85. Trouble	Troubles are often imaginary.
86. Finger	Fingering is important in music.
87. Like	I like to talk & think.
88. Mould	One is moulded by society, largely.
89. Worry	I worry unnecessarily.
90. Unfair	Most societies are "unfair."
91. Wife	My wife & I are separated.
92. Career	I wish I knew for certain about my career.
93. Control	Control over others is finally impossible.
94. Dirt	Dirtiness is deplored.
95. Break	Cups break if dropped (!)
96. Doctor	Doctors are fine father-figures
97. Satisfied	I am rarely satisfied.
98. Key	The key to the Universe will never be found (!!).
99. Dark	Darkness used to frighten me now I rather like it.
100. Habit	Most things are habitual.

Table 2

	Patient's score	Average for patients	Average for normals
(1) Form of expression			
Blanks and single words	2	16	4
Phrases	2	29	27
Sentences	96	55	69
(2) Syntactical use of stimulus word			
As subject	55	13	28
As object	9	16	9
(3) Reverence to self and others			
Self	34	42	20
Others only	23	14	24
(4) Mode of communication			
Generalizations			
Adaptive	46	12	30
Maladaptive	7	5	6
Personal Statements			
Adaptive	9	7	10
Maladaptive	19	23	3
(5) Affective tone			
Positive	27	22	31
Negative	39	45	17

9. Intellectual achievement, particularly in the realm of politics and affairs, tends to be both critical and constructive, and it gives him a sense of power over others, for example, no. 51: MASTER—I should like to master political philosophy; no. 88: MOULD—One is moulded by society, largely.
10. His use of exclamation marks and other unusual punctuation suggest his need to display his intellectual prowess.
11. He experiences, though is little able to express, basic trust in and concern for others, for example, no. 62: BELIEVE—I believe in humanity— I can't say why!

Summary of Findings from the Test Data

The diagnostic picture that has emerged is one of a character disorder in which the predominant problems are oedipal. His duty-driven intellectual effort seeks to dominate, control, and improve others, while avoiding any close emotional ties with them. He thereby attempts to manage his feelings of inadequacy and loneliness. He separates idealized relations with women from his sexual relations in which the woman is treated as faithless and potentially belittling of him. So far his defences have allowed him only vicarious satisfactions in intellectual mastery and in identification with political causes. There are some suggestions in the test that his underlying anger and contempt towards men and women may find more direct but guarded expression in compulsive acting-out behaviour.

Within the tightly woven character structure two kinds of defensive failure can be seen. The first, illustrated in his blank and single-word responses, and later emphasized in the more detailed examination of form and content, is associated with his feelings of impotence and his inability to maintain secure dependent or sexual relations with women. Thus he feels empty, weak, lonely, and depressed, and is driven to seek treatment. The second centres on a compulsive testing out of his potency in self-display, intellectual dominance, and active political interests. With women this testing-out also involves a contempt of them as sexual objects and a denial of any possibility of a close ongoing affectional relation with them. But he gives evidence of a basic trust in others and in his own capacities for good relations with them.

With regard to his ego resources and therapeutic potential, the following points can be noted: (*a*) his strong motivation to get help, as evidenced by his response to the test requirements; (*b*) his readiness to express his difficulties as shown in his maladaptive personal statements; (*c*) his basic trust in good relationships, as seen in the reparative effort implied in many of his generalizations; (*d*) his intellectual aggressiveness, which is largely object oriented, and is not rigid or aloof in a paranoid fashion.

While he will use his intellectual resources widely as agile defences, he has some access to his feelings. This, together with his strong pressure to test himself out with others, should ensure that his problems come into the open in group psychotherapy. Therapeutic work will have to concentrate on: (i) his ambivalence to men in authority and especially his denied belittlement of them; (ii) the split between his dependent and sexual feelings towards women; (iii) his use of intellectual defences to avoid feelings.

Summary of Therapist's Report

The psychiatrist who saw the patient in initial consultation and who subsequently treated him in a therapeutic group was asked to make an independent report after a year.

The patient joined the group a few weeks after it started. At his first attendance he told the group all about himself in a rather exhibitionistic manner, although he was tense and anxious. Later he questioned the other members intimately, often prodding them in a jocular manner. Soon he set himself up as the therapist's assistant and was very submissive towards him, but he attacked authority outside the group. He frequently projected his anger, and after provoking another member into a rage, he would become smug and self-satisfied.

He used his intelligence in an analytical, obsessional manner, but his excessive need to control often interfered with his understanding of other members' problems. He seemed determined to find a solution for his conflicts, and although at times very critical of group therapy he attended regularly and made use of the insights gained. He began to recognize his intolerance and resentment of the relationship between his son and his wife, which he had tried to resolve by leaving them.

He worked hard in the group, progressing in stops and starts and sometimes suddenly bringing out painful material with courage. He described affairs with married women which culminated in their husbands' attacking them and threatening him. He would then abandon the wife, and, though terrified, seek to establish a "friendly" relation with the husband whom he hoodwinked. In these episodes he reported no feelings of anger or violence, though he roundly derided both the husband and wife concerned. He also referred to a longstanding affair with a single woman. When tired of her, he would send her away and then throw himself into work as a way of avoiding his guilty feelings. When this failed he would rationalize his resolutions in regard to her and reembark on a period of uninhibited sexual activity which would again end in rejection of her.

Although ambitious and wanting to write, his achievements were restricted because of oedipal guilt. The exhibitionistic gratification he got from teaching also made him guilty. At times, especially when his obsessional defences failed, he became quite depressed. His motivation to find a solution to his difficulties and to establish better relationships has remained strong and over the year he has changed considerably. In the group he accepts others more seriously, is less of a prima donna and participates more deeply and more sincerely. He has become more assertive, timidly and anxiously at first, but more confidently of late. While previously he would contradict himself and decide the therapist was right in the group, he is now able to disagree with the therapist.

With women he has become more dissatisfied with his sadomasochistic relations and has nearly ended the longstanding, but intermittent, relation referred to earlier. He now expresses the desire for a more settled life with a more suitable woman, in which the quality of the relationship between them would be the important thing, and he is making attempts to establish such a relationship. Whereas he had been deeply depressed over periods for many years, some months ago he stopped taking antidepressant drugs, though occasionally he takes tranquilizers when he cannot sleep. He spends more time with his son and is better able to handle their mutual antagonisms. He has taken practical steps to help his son in various difficulties.

He has completed his first published article for many years and his writing and teaching activities seem to be coming closer together. In the group he has largely stopped pursuing his and other people's problems in a detached intellectual manner and takes much more account of emotional factors as he has grown to understand them.

SUMMARY

An approach to quantitative appraisal of the factors involved in psychotherapy is described. Using the form and content of expressive verbal behaviour in giving a spontaneous personal reaction in the form of a sentence to a series of stimulus words, differences were shown between patients and nonpatients, and to a lesser degree between new patients and patients in, or after, treatment. These initial findings are sufficiently encouraging for further development of this test by including other stimuli such as pictures to increase its discriminative power. With a more comprehensive and sensitive instrument of this type, used before and after analytic treatment, it should be possible to demonstrate objectively the changes resulting from treatment. It should also be possible to compare the effects of different psychotherapeutic approaches and to show the difference between these effects and symptomatic changes produced by other methods or occurring without treatment.

A test approach, such as this one, can also provide objective confirmation of observations based on clinical work. Thus even in the present initial form, and in treatment occurring only once per week, the test confirms the familiar clinical observation that dependent, sexual, and aggressive expressions are heightened during the early phases of treatment. The expression of anxiety, however, does not increase concurrently, presumably because of the support provided by the therapeutic relationship. Again, the psychoanalytic view that difficulties in relating to others play a central part in psychopathology is supported by the fact that the most discriminating words in our stimulus series turned out to be those that made a direct and unavoidable reference to interpersonal demands—CRITICISM, WORK, FRIENDS, NEED, SUBMIT, CONTROL.

With regard to its clinical use, the study of individual cases has shown that test findings closely parallel those that emerge during treatment. Thus, the present test approach seems suitable for delineation of conflict areas, study of the nature and stability of defences, and the assessment of therapeutic potential, an approach that can be of help in the selection of patients for treatment in its different forms. Also, since the patient can see his responses to this test as relevant to his problems it should be easier to make a test of this kind a part of the initial consultation.

APPENDIX

Differences between groups

Dimension and category	A group (N = 20): new patients average/ subject	B group (N = 10): patients in treatment average/ subject	C group (N = 10): patients finished treatment average/ subject	D group (N = 20): non-patients average/ subject
I. Form of expression				
1. Inhibited responses	16	13	10	4
2. Phrases	29	31	24	27
3. Sentences	55	56	66	69

(cont.)

APPENDIX *(cont.)*

Differences between groups

Dimension and category	A group (*N* = 20): new patients average/ subject	B group (*N* = 10): patients in treatment average/ subject	C group (*N* = 10): patients finished treatment average/ subject	D group (*N* = 20): non-patients average/ subject
II. Syntactical use of the stimulus word				
1. Stimulus word as subject	13	9	13	28
2. Stimulus word as object	16	17	21	9
III. Self and other references				
1. Reference to self	42	52	50	20
2. Reference to others only	14	11	15	24
IV. Mode of communication				
1. Generalizations, adaptive	12	6	14	30
2. Generalizations, maladaptive	5	4	5	6
3. Personal statements, adaptive	7	8	11	10
4. Personal statements, maladaptive	23	25	19	3
V. Affective tone (28 words)				
1. Positive affect	3	6	9	9
2. Negative affect	17	14	10	6
	Total no. of references	Total no. of references*	Total no. of references*	Total no. of references
VI. Specific affective reference				
1. Dependence	11	26	4	2
2. Aggression	13	20	4	4
3. Sex	40	80	26	28
4. Fear	36	34	18	11

*In Groups B and C the total numbers are double to make them comparable with Groups A and D.

*Statistically significant differences**

Between groups A and D
Dim. I Cat. 1
Dim. II Cats. 1 and 2
Dim. III Cats. 1 and 2
Dim. IV Cats. 1, 1 + 2, and 4
Dim. V Cats. 1 and 2
Dim. VI Cats. 1, 2 and 4

Between groups B and D
Dim. I Cat. 1
Dim. II Cats. 1 and 2
Dim. III Cats. 1 and 2
Dim. IV Cats. 1, 1 + 2, and 4
Dim. V Cats. 1 and 2
Dim. VI Cats. 1, 2 and 3

Between groups A and C
Dim. V Cats. 1 and 2

Between groups B and C
Dim. IV Cats. 1 and 1 + 2
Dim. V Cats. 1 and 1
Dim. VI Cats. 1 and 2

Between groups C and D
Dim. I Cat 1
Dim. II Cats. 1 and 2
Dim. III Cats. 1 and 2
Dim. IV Cats. 1, 1 + 2, and 4
Dim. V Cat. 2

*Minimum level of significance = 0.05. Mann-Whitney *U* test for Dimensions I to V. Chi-square test for Dimension VI.

7. OBJECT-RELATIONS THEORY AND COGNITIVE PERFORMANCE

THREE CASES OF ANXIETY AND FAILURE IN EXAMINATIONS

Some time ago I was asked to help three male students who had failed repeatedly in examinations although their capacities were sufficient for success and all had devoted adequate time to study. At first none of them mentioned any difficulty other than the failures, yet each was convinced that the trouble was due to a weakness in his personality. Two of them experienced panic feelings during the examinations, and an emotional basis for the failures was suggested by the fact that these two did worse in successive attempts at the same examination despite steady application. Acute symptoms of this kind are of interest to the medical psychologist because they would be expected to provide, on investigation, some insight into the determinants of examination anxiety in general, a strain frequently blamed for the onset of neurotic illness. They are also not without importance to the educational psychologist, since such factors diminish the validity of examinations as measures of knowledge or capacity in these cases. Before making any general observations a brief description of the cases is given below.

> *Case A.* A young man, aged 23, was depressed by having struggled in vain for 4 years to pass the first of his professional examinations. His intelligence as measured was not superior, a fact which he appreciated, but in view of the energy he devoted to his studies he ought to have succeeded in the usual time of 1 year. As a rule he worked with fair progress until an examination approached, whereupon he would become anxious. Inability to recall the essence of what he had read would begin to produce a feeling of panic followed by further agitated attempts to memorize. Finally, during the examination he became so excited and confused that nothing could be reproduced. He blamed his failures on various faculty deficiencies such as a bad memory, poor power of concentration, or a lack of will power. Nevertheless, he realized that his memory for

certain subjects was good, while in reading general literature he concentrated readily, and in the grim determination with which he worked he showed no deficiency of will power. It was clear that the examination was associated with an increasing emotional disturbance that blocked completely a normal flow of thought.

In his first years at school he had a period of difficulty, which was followed by several years of good progress, his class position being always in the upper third. At adolescence his performances deteriorated to such an extent that he was usually near the foot of the class, a humiliation that he lessened by taking an active part in sport and other social activities.

He began his first session by remarking that a friend who was familiar with psychoanalytic treatment had told him about associating and had asked him what the word "murder" suggested. To the patient's amazement he had a vivid picture of a man throttling a woman. Next he spoke of how he had been an only child until he was 10 years old when a brother was born. This brought to mind a series of games he used to play in his early childhood with a girl. In these he played "the doctor," a role which appealed to him because of his strong desire to know about the female body. Even then he felt this interest to be a sexual one.

These first associations as usual referred to his dominant unconscious conflicts. It is interesting to note the association of his brother's birth with the concern about the female body, for Klein (1932) and Schmideberg (1938) have suggested that anxiety over phantasied attacks on the contents of the mother's body may lead to various intellectual inhibitions. Later, A expressed sadistic impulses towards his mother more openly in associations to a dream wherein he felt identified with a man who murdered a woman. Adolescent sexual conflicts alternated with his work failure as the main themes of the early weeks of treatment, with great emphasis on the failure as the cause of his unsatisfactory personality development. He began to masturbate when about 14, and 3 years later was in a state of constant guilt and anxiety over this. He felt that this worry impaired his health and was the cause of a ruptured abscess of the appendix, which almost cost him his life. Subsequent associations suggested that unconsciously this operation was regarded as a punitive castration. For instance, he feared that the surgeon who treated him would think he had a very large penis, doubtless due to his guilty practices; he also thought that circumcision might cure him of the masturbation so he secretly consulted a doctor about this.

While recovering from the operation he developed obsessive fears of contamination by germs and dirt, which have persisted although much diminished. He resolved to expel from his mind all sexual ideas and to work incessantly for the entrance examination to his professional course. It took him 2 years to pass this examination, in other words, four attempts, by the end of which period he had become a very shy inferior person. He was nervous and hesitant in answering anyone and envious of his younger brother's self-confidence which he felt sure made his brother their father's favourite. These personality troubles were attributed entirely by A to his failures, as he thought he had successfully conquered his sexual impulses. Gradually, however, a different picture was revealed. For the past few years he had been disturbed at nights by erections associated with anxiety dreams from which he would awaken with a shout. Each night was dreaded on account of these unpleasant dreams, and his strong guilt over them was seen in his alarm lest anyone should hear what he said. Another besetting dread was that some violent death might overtake him at any moment. When it was suggested that he was still afraid of punishment for his sexual impulses, he suddenly recalled that at the height of his adolescent conflicts he thought he had given himself a venereal disease and planned suicide to escape from the shame. It was with great relief he learned that his fear of such infection was unfounded, but the fright reinforced the intense counteractivities from which he decided never to relax, "for any relaxation was dangerous." Thus work was compulsive activity to keep these sexual thoughts out of his mind.

The patient's reaction to this interpretation of the function of his work brought forth several confirmatory ideas. Despite his repeated failures, he felt he could never give up work because it was "the only thing he had to hold on to," "he must keep up a high standard of work and morals." He had considered at times a career that did not involve study, but this seemed to be far too dangerous. Often he had bemoaned the fact that as long as he was such a failure he could never marry, so he withdraw quickly from any friendships he made with girls. The failures could therefore be regarded as a defensive measure against all sexual behaviour. He *must fail* in examinations because success meant exposure to the dangers of relaxation and possible marriage. The failures also served as a self-punishment for the bad impulses he still possessed. This interpretation led to several references to great disturbances going on during sleep and more dreams were remembered. In the past his unconscious processes had not only given rise to dreams, but also to frequent somnambulistic acts, for example, he would often find that he had locked his bedroom door, or put a light on, or that some piece of furniture had been moved, and such acts now occurred more often. Many dreams contained an evil figure, which represented a force interfering with his work and which was too powerful to fight. Later it became a less disguised symbol of his sexual impulses.

The origin of his intense sexual guilt was now directly related by A to feelings dating from early years. As a child he had always felt that something evil went on between the sexes. Once he found his parents inside their room with the door locked and immediately he became greatly perturbed. On getting into the room he felt in a vague way that his worst fears were confirmed when he rushed to the bed and saw impressions indicating that they had been on it, an experience that produced a strong hatred and envy of them on account of their secret enjoyment.

The revival of these early feelings was followed by several very emotional dreams. In one a scene took place in which A got into a murderous rage with a man who stole his overcoat. This dream brought many associations of aggressive feelings towards various people with whom he connected his father. In his seventeenth session a dream was described in which the patient experienced vividly the conflict he had in examinations. He was required to apply knowledge he had, but which he could not recall, whereupon he became excited. This scene was immediately associated with an actual occasion a few years ago when he had got upset in the same way. His excitement in the examination had grown as he stared at a girl in front of him and had culminated in a seminal emission. The recollection of this incident had passed through his mind in previous sessions but was deemed too unimportant to mention! Later he added that his examination excitement almost always ended in a sexual feeling. The length of time taken to mention this matter indicated the strength of his defences against the significance of his examination difficulties, and with the penetration of these defences a great amount of affect was released. He became embarrassed by the way in which sexual topics displaced his work anxiety. Wildly aggressive phantasies developed accompanied by impulses to tear people in pieces, especially for their sexual misdeeds. As already mentioned, he harboured strong aggressive impulses towards his parents for their sexual relations from which he felt excluded. Thus he dreamt he was made to sit on the bumper of a car while his parents "rode" inside. Later he remembered sleeping at the foot of his parents' bed when about 7 years old and being awakened by the sound of the bed creaking and shaking; he knew they were "up to something wicked." Again, he dreamt of a light at a bedroom window of a nearby house being extinguished. This suggested an elderly couple preparing to go to bed to enjoy sexual relations. When he awoke from this dream he found that he had knocked over his own bedside lamp. From another dream connected with parental intercourse he awoke beating his fists on the bed.

There now began a series of dreams dealing with his father. A felt he could never emulate his father because the latter had "resources" that he could never possess. By this term he thought of intellectual and personal qualities, but the immediate associations of guilt over his large penis showed the unconscious determinants of this inferiority. His attitude to his mother was also brought into his material at this time. Although she always seemed to be emotionally cold to him, he felt identified with her.

A few days before his next attempt at the examination he had a terrifying dream in which he enacted his difficulties. At first he thought he knew how to answer all the questions but then noticed he was short of time and getting unnerved as he hurried from one question to another. Two students near him began to distract his attention by a quarrel. One was a licentious youth with whom he felt identified, while the other was an old school friend who finished his paper in good time and then reproached the rake for his immoral behaviour. A felt the whole scene to be frightfully real, and as he watched this pair he had an emission which he hoped no one would see.

His first associations to this dream produced the usual naîve explanation that he had got excited by the feeling of hurry and it was this that produced the emission. The rake was a fellow-student who was often ragged about having a large penis, a feature which the patient applied to himself. The other represented the ideal person, and A remembered that this youth's father followed the profession that A himself wished to pursue. These two figures had actually been friends until the ideal one turned against the other on account of his sexual behaviour. The dream was interpreted as introducing another motive in the patient's conflict. His ideal self, identified with his father, was opposed to his sexuality. This was gratified, however, in such a manner that not only was A punished by his failure, but he procured a revenge upon his father at the same time. A was reluctant to accept this view of his behaviour until the dreams which followed overcame some of his resistance. In one of these he had to lead his football team after the captain was injured. Then there was a partially repressed scene in which he flirted with a friend of his mother, and from the associations to this dream his Oedipus situation emerged clearly. In another dream the theme of his brother's birth and his mother's body returned. He and his brother climbed through a tiny hole into a cupboard under a staircase where they tried to catch mice. A felt he must not allow any to get out and became anxious at the thought that he might not be able to escape himself. He associated this with the feeling that he had no way out of his work difficulties—his work made him a prisoner. That it dealt with the problem of the arrival of other babies, and in particular of his brother, was made clearer in his next dream. In this he left a house wearing a girl's hat and carrying a dog, which he took without asking the permission of the woman who owned the house. The dog was associated at once with his brother.

When actually on the way to his examination he became obsessed with the thought of sexual intercourse, which made him so anxious that he almost turned back. He noticed he had an erection, and when he saw some girls at the door of the examination room he felt he was about to have an emission. This increased his panic until he suddenly thought of the interpretation of his recent examination dream, whereupon he soon found himself writing the answers without much difficulty. Afterwards he reported his success in a grudging fashion, attributing it to the use of better study methods although these had not been changed.

In his short treatment of about sixty sessions little alteration was made in A's very poor personality development. The deeper trends seen in many of his phantasies, for example, his identification with his mother and passive homosexual attitude to his father, were not interpreted, as he intended to stop treatment after the examination. Sufficient progress was made nevertheless in the interpretation of the motives of his failures in their superficial layers for him to be able to adopt a less compulsive attitude towards his work. Thus he was able for the first time in several years to spend one night a week on some recreation, and though thereby devoting less time to study then previously he succeeded in passing his examination.

Case B. This case presented many of the features of case A. A male student, aged 21, and of average university intelligence, had done progressively worse in three attempts at an examination despite hard work. His personality showed several obsessional trends by which he was able to stifle all emotions because these were sinful to him. At first he discussed his conflicts in a detached manner and only showed strong feeling after a sexual dream occurred. This produced many associations about his painful masturbation guilt, which made him execute various unpleasant tasks and self-denials as an expiation. His failures had often struck him as being like a punishment from God. Another source of conflict was his future, for though he wished to go abroad he felt it his duty to return home after his training was completed in order to support his mother, his father being dead. The prospect of marriage also worried him, as he found it difficult to accept his sexuality. The possible evasion of these problems by his failures was suggested, and he was successful in his next attempt at the examination. As B was seen on twelve occasions only during the three weeks preceding this attempt, it was not possible to gain more knowledge of the deeper motives at work.

Case C. Male, aged 21. A quite different picture was presented by this case. In his first years at the university he had shown outstanding ability, but by the time he reached his final year his performances in class examinations became such that failure in his degree examination was regarded by his teachers as inevitable. There was no lack of energy as an active intellectual and social life was maintained, though any attempt to study for examinations immediately aroused an intellectual "wanderlust." He managed to do a certain amount of preparation, but found that he became flurried when answering the questions. C was distressed by his difficulty and sought help when he found he could not overcome it. Contemptuous of the cultural standards of his fellows, he was also very aggressive towards the Calvinistic values under which he had been reared at home. His mother was a very bigoted person, and his ambivalent feelings towards her gave rise to spells of mild depression. This conflict over her was an old one, and in his associations on this theme he remembered being deeply impressed when she told him some years before that she had never been able to satisfy him as an infant. Throughout childhood he had many nightmares in which villainous witch figures threatened him. His father had died when C was a child, and, as with case B, he was torn between pursuing his own interests and making reparation to his mother on whom he felt very dependent despite their many quarrels. There was no doubt that he had a savage hatred of her which he tried to conceal from himself, and it was likely that his impending failure to get into a position whereby he could help her was an expression of this aggression. When this was interpreted he began to work better and stopped treatment after a few sessions. Probably his deep unconscious aggressive impulses, the intensity of which suggested that he might eventually develop a serious breakdown, were about to prove intolerable.

From the account of these cases there is little doubt that the failures are motivated acts, that is, they serve to gratify various unconscious wishes that are unacceptable to the conscious mind, and thus they are in the nature of neurotic symptoms. Certain motives are apparent in all cases, for example, an unconscious aggressive attitude towards a parent and a self-punishment for this. In the first two cases the failures seem to be designed to prevent the subjects assuming the emotional responsibilities of manhood while at the same time acting as a punishment for bad sexual impulses. Naturally one cannot generalize on the data from so few subjects, but it is interesting to note that in the cases of examination anxiety reported by various psychoanalysts during the past 10 years the same motives of renunciation of manhood, the need for punishment, and revenge upon a parent, occur almost without exception.

The unconscious motives giving rise to such disturbances provide, of course, the answer to the problem of why the examination situation is so commonly an anxiety situation and is so readily exploited by an unconscious conflict. Flugel (1939) has already given an excellent review of the psychoanalytic literature on examination anxiety, and he shows how the history of the examination system confirms Stengel's view that the examination has the unconscious significance of an initiation rite. Their occurrence in our society at the threshold of manhood would give examinations this function and, as mentioned, the conflict over the acceptance of manhood appears to be the important source of anxiety in most of the cases. Some degree of anxiety is to be regarded as usual because of the real importance of the situation; failures are costly in prestige, time, and money. And a little anxiety is not like a little learning. If often acts as a stimulus to adequate preparation and may possibly raise the efficiency of the subject in some cases. The fear of the consequences of failure will obviously provide rationalizations, however, for deeper anxieties of unconscious origin. Frequently the degree of anxiety varies with the form of the examination, for instance, it is usually said to be greater with oral than with written examinations, while oral examinations arouse different amounts of anxiety according to the reputation of the examiner. To some extent these differences have a reality basis; thus the majority of students find it easier to make the most of a limited amount of information in a written examination. The unconscious factors can nevertheless be important in these differences. Stengel (1936) points out the cunning way in which a candidate in an oral examination will expose his weak spots in order to satisfy his need for punishment, especially for forbidden exhibitionistic impulses. Little pieces of information added to an answer to impress the examiner often lead the latter to follow up a topic on which the candidate is poorly informed. This situation involves the unconscious motives of the examiner which will alter the candidate's anxiety according as the examiner derives pleasure from being the loving helpful parent, or from making an aggressive attack upon the unfortunate candidate. (Guilt over unconscious exhibitionistic impulses is probably an important cause of anxiety in interviews and in being examined medically.)

In support of the contention that the examination signifies an initiation rite to the unconscious mind, Flugel quotes many of its irrational features. It implies the testing of a younger by an older person and so provides a situation onto which various conflicts over parents may be projected. Hence, no doubt, the almost universal presence of some amount of irrational anxiety. If the testing of knowledge were its sole function, then on rational grounds the test should be repeated periodically to ensure that the knowledge is being maintained—a point especially applicable to the professional examinations in medicine. Examinations only became systematized with the development of the universities into organized bodies, and it is probable that the degree ceremony grew out of the much more informal initiation among student groups. The ceremony usually involved some bullying of the student, then a welcoming of him as a comrade, and finally a feast must be provided at his expense. Flugel suggests that the first two features contain the castration and guilt motives of all initiation ceremonies and are seen in many of the rituals still preserved in some degree ceremonies. A more readily appreciated irrational feature of all academic degree examinations and initiations which he mentions is the extortion of money, which persists no matter how much the other aspects of the ritual may have become unrecognizable.

The very low incidence of acute examination difficulties does not warrant any recommendations on the desirability of abolishing examinations. The reliability and validity of well-constructed tests are high. It will be noticed, however, that a subject who is always anxious in examinations will not lower the reliability since his performances will be consistently bad; but the validity of the measure in such cases will be low. The unconscious significance of the examination as initiation rite suggests that perhaps many features of the examination system in its present forms are retained to gratify the aggression of the fathers towards the sons rather than to improve its function. In this connexion one thinks of the practice of conducting short oral examinations on knowledge that has already been tested extensively in written papers, a practice to which examiners in the medical curriculum seem to be especially prone. Another feature of this curriculum, which appears to be maintained by the same motivation, is the habit of teaching all clinical work by having one student examine a case while others watch. The time taken in dragging answers from the initiate would certainly be much more efficiently used by the teacher were he to demonstrate the case himself, bring out the main points, and then leave the students to practice the elicitation of these. This unconscious meaning must also be considered as the probable cause of examination worry being blamed for neurotic illnesses, but the cases described, and those of all other writers, show that severe disturbances over examinations are associated with longstanding and usually serious personality disorder. Treatment of these underlying conflicts is naturally a long slow process, yet it was gratifying to find in the cases described that enough insight into the symptom could be gained in a comparatively short time to enable the students to break a very vicious circle.

8. FAIRBAIRN'S CRITICISM OF BASIC PSYCHOANALYTIC CONCEPTS

Freud's metapsychological theories were, as he repeatedly stressed, his speculations on how the phenomena of psychological conflict could be explained keeping in mind not only his clinical findings, but also his knowledge of the central nervous system and of contemporary biological thought. The most striking clinical fact he had to contend with was the intensity of the pressure with which impulses or ideas, discovered to be sexual in nature as a rule, sought discharge against the wishes of the individual. The discharge of these foreign elements characteristically relieved tension, usually accompanied by a feeling of gratification. He therefore thought he had to account for drives or forces of a peculiarly impelling kind in these impulses and for the repression of their origins and nature from consciousness. The final forms his theories took were his concepts of the id, the ego, and the superego. Freud included the instincts in the id, but they were not regarded as giving the id an organization. The id was a chaotic seething cauldron of excitement that acted as a reservoir of energy. Instincts for him did have objects and aims, nevertheless they were so plastic in man that what seemed to matter most for him was the "drive" in them. He therefore retained as the sources of this drive the libido or sexual energy and the destructive energy of the death instinct, both of these psychic energies being derived from transformation of the activities of body cells.

In relating energy to structures in the psychic apparatus in a way that would account for the specific manifestations of psychological conflicts and behaviour, Freud had eventually to create the dynamic structures of the ego and the superego. At birth there was only the id with its plastic instincts determining relatively unstructured behaviour. Within the next few years there developed from it as a result of the experiences of the child the two dynamic structures, the ego and the superego, and the energy for their functions was taken over respectively from "desexualised" libido and the death instinct.

As Fairbairn (1956a) indicates, these concepts present difficulties that can be looked at from two angles, namely, their consistency with the general scientific and biological thought of today and their value in clinical work. These two angles are naturally closely related yet, as in other branches of science, gaps and even inconsistencies between pure and applied theory can exist until certain facts demand changes in one or both. Fairbairn states that changes are now demanded on both grounds.

On the general grounds, it would be widely accepted that the notion of a free energy with an aim is out of step with the views of energy in physical sciences; and from general biological considerations it seems unlikely that the constellation of instinct patterns in man would be so relatively unorganised as is assumed in the id concept and the libido theory. But, as Fairbairn points out, it is the unsatisfactory picture of behaviour given by the libido theory that is more important. It implies that conflicts arise from the need to seek pleasure, an affect which Freud related to the conditions under which id tensions were discharged. There is here, however, a gap between pure metapsychological theory and working clinical hypotheses, and because the level of abstraction of the libido concept is so different from that at which the psychoanalyst works, the difficulty has been largely ignored. At the clinical level, the phenomena of conflict between conscious and unconscious motives are in fact interpreted largely in terms of object relationships. It is incompatibility between the urges to do certain actions with objects, and in particular the conflict between loving and hating relationships, that constitutes the core of analytical work. Thus, most psychoanalysts would accept Fairbairn's view that conflict is essentially related to interpersonal factors. In other words, in accounting for the nature of conflict at the clinical level Freud's divorce between energy and structure hardly enters into consideration. It is, for example, the libidinal or the aggressive impulses *towards the mother or father* that matter rather than the operation of the hypothetical libido or death instinct. Indeed many analysts do not accept the theory of a death instinct. Instead, their instinct theory resembles one that would be more in keeping with instinct theory in animals, that is, it involves impulses to specific actions with objects. At the same time, it would not be true to say that the present instinct theory of the id is not without its influence on clinical work, and here Fairbairn's plea for a more systematic object-relations theory, that is, one in which all drives are conceived as having specific aims with objects, is in my view justified not only in the interest of logical tidiness, but also to alter concepts that may be impeding advances in theory and practice. The fundamental nature of the issues he raises makes it difficult to do justice to his views in a brief statement, and the following points are merely a few of the considerations his views have suggested to me.

1. The large bulk of evidence regarding the nature of neurotic conflict shows increasingly that unconscious motives are unconsciously sought relationships; they represent desired relationships with internal objects, which the individual wishes to achieve in the external world. The work of Klein and her associates, Fairbairn, and others has shown that analysis as an instrument of investigating unconscious activity can be increased greatly in power and scope by the use of a more systematic object-relations theory.

Thus, if we take the phenomena of autoerotism and narcissism, these were formerly, under the influence of the libido theory, regarded as precluding analysis when present in an intense degree because they represented objectless discharge of libido. Klein's work, however, has shown that even severe schizophrenics with markedly narcissistic withdrawal can be kept in an analytic relationship by the constant interpretation of their behaviour in terms of relationships with objects of the most primitive kind. A meaning can be given to the autoerotic and narcissistic behaviour when it is regarded as deriving from the earliest internalised objects, the nipple and breast, and such interpretations permit the subject, at least for a period, to make more externally directed relationships.

2. An object-relations theory is the most useful one in accounting for the most characteristic phenomena of the analytic relationship, namely transference, and for the effects of interpretations. There is a widespread agreement that it is chiefly when the individual experiences towards the analyst the aims of his unconsciously sought relationships that changes in the intensity of these occur and hence fundamental changes in the personality. Yet the full implications of this well-known observation have not been adequately related to the psychoanalytic theory of the personality.
3. A libido type of theory, that is, one in which drive is regarded as divorced from structure in its origins, is still used by some psychiatrists as the basis of their clinical action, but the clinical findings do not confirm the value of the theory. Thus it is on the basis of this type of theory that changing the balance of the sexual hormones, or other biochemical processes, is thought to hold out a means of altering some of the sexual perversions, because through such somatic interference it is hoped to change the libidinal tension. No substantial or consistent changes, however, in the pattern of sexual behaviour have been obtained in this way.
4. The great lack in the theory of personality at present is a framework with which the chief determinants of behaviour can be formulated and assessed. The identification of the main unconsciously sought relations would give a good account of the forms of relationship with people and things that the individual seeks in the external world, and with clearer identification, it should be possible to make even rough quantitative assessments of the strength of these relationships. With such a scheme, better predictions than we are able to make at present could be achieved, especially in regard to the course of events to be expected during analytic treatment where they could be tested. A description of the personality in such terms would also permit of more precise

> meaning being given to such notions as *ego strength*. Hitherto analyses of very disturbed patients have at times had to be given up, or have not been undertaken, on the grounds that the ego was too weak for the unconscious forces the patient had to control. Concepts of ego strength, however, have never been very satisfactory in relation to clinical work and general theory. An object relations theory can make more specific what is missing, usually the structures derived from the normal good experiences of the child. When such relations with good internalized objects are too impoverished, there arises the problem of whether or not the analysis can proceed without some replacement experience. A few analysts—Winnicott and several American analysts—believe that such patients need to be permitted to make a relationship with the analyst in which the latter can be felt more directly as a person, for example, by his being in limited ways more "active." Most analysts at present do not share this view, and only further clinical work with more adequate means of assessing changes in the dynamics of the personality will throw light on this issue.

Fairbairn's case for a psychology of the personality in terms of its object relations is therefore in my view important and timely. His formulations have clearly sharpened his clinical observations and these have been widely regarded by many psychoanalysts as constituting an important contribution. With regard to his particular psychic structures, it is perhaps premature to comment on their value as such views require considerable testing out in practice. It is interesting to note, however, that Winnicott's independent formulations of a *true self*, that is, a self that can give free expression to feeling, and a *false self*, that is, a self that conforms to the inhibiting pressure of the outer environment, closely resemble Fairbairn's structures.

While the libidinal and antilibidinal egos may represent the outcome of the attempt of the personality to reach maximum integration, these structures give the impression of a greater degree of organisation than appears to be the case, at least in some patients. If we take the antilibidinal ego in many severe hysterics, clinical findings would suggest that this has active substructures. Thus, in order to secure libidinal gratification, such persons may identify predominantly with one parent and be persecuted by the attacks of the imago of the other, and then at other times reverse the predominance of the identification. Interestingly enough, too, a common remark of such patients is that they do not really know "who they are," that is, they have no feeling of a stable constellation in either of these larger structures of Fairbairn's.

A last point may be made concerning metapsychology and internal objects. There can be little doubt that it was the inadequate nature of the means at his disposal for relating energy to structure that prevented Freud from solving this problem more to his satisfaction. Had he had available the concepts of modern physics and neurophysiology, he would have been freed from the restricting effects of what Colby (1955) describes as his "hydraulic metaphors." When the cathexis energy of ideas, and so forth, in the psychic apparatus can be related, as Colby has done, to the frequency period, synchrony and dysynchrony of pulsations, then the structural nature of drive can be much more readily illustrated by a model. As a prelude to the description of his model, Colby makes almost the same criticism of the classical id, ego, and superego theory as does Fairbairn. A critical point is that he considers that drive structures must incorporate the notion of purposive aims and the imago of an internal object must be closely related to the aim of a drive schema. The development of Colby's ideas will therefore be of considerable theoretical interest. He is careful to point out that his model merely serves at present as a basis for relating energy and structure, and that there is inevitably a considerable gap between his metapsychological theories and clinical application. Nevertheless, and this is Fairbairn's main thesis, the more the theories at these different levels are in harmony, the better it must be for clinical progress.

II
GROUP RELATIONS

9. SMALL GROUPS, THEIR DISORDERS AND TREATMENT

INTRODUCTION

The rapid spread of interest in recent years in the small group is perhaps due to the development of new methods of studying it rather than to a new awareness of its contribution to the growth and maintenance of the person. Each approach has produced an enormous volume of research, for example, the field theoretical studies of Lewin and his pupils, the large number of researches stimulated by Moreno's sociometric, psychodramatic, and sociodramatic methods, the interaction studies of Bales and his colleagues; and alongside these are the great many descriptive observations from the group therapists.

Faced with this vast volume of research, it seemed to me that the best thing I could do for people like ourselves who have to help individuals in groups was to explore the emergence of unifying concepts—those ideas that make sense of the interrelatedness of the individual being shaped within his family group and then maintaining his growth through his subsequent group memberships. For this purpose I shall consider first the individual in the group, next the group and its task, and then the process of therapy and change in the group.

THE INDIVIDUAL AND THE GROUP

The dynamics of the interaction between the individual and the group present us with the problems for whose solution the lack of an adequate theoretical framework is most apparent. On the one hand we have to account for the fundamental needs of the person for belongingness with others in significant ways. He needs his identity, his achievements, and his value to himself and others to be affirmed by the members of the groups with which he is most related. On the other hand, there are also to be understood the various conflicting attitudes and relationships, at times intensely emotional and irrational, between members, and between members and the group leader or leaders.

Perhaps many of our difficulties in finding a set of concepts we can use to bring order into this complexity stem from the way in which we perseverate in our view of the individual as the unit from which we start, isolating him and building up his future social modes from inferred instinctive endowments and other properties of the organism. If we conceive of the individual as having built into him from the start the properties of the social system in which he is reared, our task of relating him subsequently to the groups in which he functions is greatly simplified.

It is, of course, nothing new to draw attention to the roles of the family in the growth of the person. Nevertheless, the implications of the way in which the family structures the person have not been systematically considered in our theories of the personality, its development, and in its mode of functioning socially. The most helpful concepts are those that are emerging in what is known as the object-relations theory of the person. This theory develops the view of dynamic structures inside the personality built on representations of parental figures on whom the child is dependent. Although the superego, the best known of such internal structures, has proved an indispensable concept in psychoanalytic thinking, it has often been regarded as a theoretical weakness that such an "anthropomorphic" notion has to be imported. The phenomena it relates to, however, are usually admitted to be most aptly described by a highly "personalized" structure of this kind, which operates as an inner parent. For the understanding of the nature of the individual's social interactions I believe, as Fairbairn has suggested, that we must surmount our tendency to cling to speculative neurophysiological notions and postulate more boldly the kinds of dynamic psychic structures our theory needs. Theories of this kind have been developed by several sociologists, notably G.H.Mead (1952), and they have had their most thorough-going and rigorous expression in the recent writings of Parsons and Bales (1955). It is of particular interest that this latter group of some of the most eminent sociologists of to-day, starting from their need to account for the phenomena of family and social interaction, are developing concepts that are of the same kind as those being formulated by some psychoanalysts to give meaning to the phenomena of the individual's relations with himself and with others as these are seen in the consulting room.

Because the most far-reaching object-relations theories of the personality have been developed in Great Britain, especially by Klein and by Fairbairn, I shall draw on their formulations. It is not the work of any particular individual or group I wish to present for your consideration but rather to take from this work what seems to be its common essentials. I propose to outline its form in a way that indicates the comprehensive effects of these in-built relationships in all social behaviour.

The Object-Relations Theory of the Personality

From the time he leaves his mother's body, the emotional experiences of the infant lead to the segregation of their associated imprints in such a way that constellations grow around "good" and "bad" feelings. The earliest good experiences make an idealised good object or imago of the mother who supplies care and satisfaction of needs unconditionally. (The dominance of the infant's experiences with the breast lead in some workers, especially Klein and her school, to the concept of the earliest imagos being more related to part-objects such as the breast, rather than to the mother as a whole.) Correspondingly, painful frustrations and the intensely aggressive feelings associated with the violent attempts to get rid of these pains, begin to build an inner object, which appears to threaten the developing self with devastating disintegration and destruction. Between these two poles of idealised blissful fusion with the good mother and the dread of loss of the self, associated with an attacking mother imago, there grows what can be termed the *central self* in which the more reality-based differentiation between the self and the mother takes place.

Whatever the mechanisms are which contribute to his attachments, the infant by the second half of the first year exhibits a differentiated relationship with his mother. Ethological research may well add new insights here to be considered alongside the inferences the psychoanalyst makes from the study of fantasy and behaviour within the psychoanalytic setting (see Bowlby, 1960). For the present it is sufficient to appreciate this first crucial qualitative change, namely, that an interrelated internal and external social system has been established, and that there is a high degree of interdependence between the relations going on in this inner world and those that are made with the outer world. The infant's resources for tolerating frustration grow because he can now use this inner world in which the inner good mother is part of himself. He can feel that he is playing the part of his own desired mother and so fulfil his longings in fantasy or in play with his own body or with his rudimentary toys. It is the satisfactions from his real mother, of course, that consolidate the inner imago. Should his tensions become painful, he tends to feel he is the object of a fantasy attack, which can be terrifying at times, from the internal persecuting mother. Ordinarily, the experiences with his real mother, especially in times of stress, will keep the effects of the threatening experiences within manageable limits. A preponderance of painful tensions, however, will induce too frequent evocation of this frightening inner figure with desperate attempts to defend himself against what are felt as its attacks. By projecting it outside he can secure a fantasy safety, perhaps reinforced by a clinging to the idealised internal object as well as by the development of the defence of avoiding the objects onto which the frightening figures have been projected. But the price of this phobic defence is that the outer world becomes the place where his dreaded objects are located and so his interaction with it becomes restricted. Again, in managing his interactions, he may tend to assume the role of the attacking imago and turn his anger on himself and his own longings.

An immense range of possibilities exists for variation in the patterns that may get consolidated according to the different properties of the particular infant interacting with his particular mother. It would appear that although relations with his mother may be centred around a variety of activities and bodily contacts, the common pleasurable affective and erotic experiences create the generalised image of her as a whole person. Similarly, the common affective elements in painful experiences seem to fuse these so that what may be termed a generalised "bad" mother imago develops.

With the movement from complete dependence to increasing autonomy, a process in which weaning and the development of locomotor abilities and speech play central parts, the father begins to play a second major role. A similar development takes place leading to the creation in the inner world of structures mediating the relationships with the good powerful father who readily becomes the prototype of independent achievement. And, as before, an idealised father along with a more threatening one are also differentiated in the inner world. The addition of these father imagos permits of a great range of inner relationships and identifications and the appearance of sexual interests and fantasies makes for the most intense use of these systems. Sibling relations and identifications with other figures in later childhood, often from stories as well as from objects in the real world, also add to the population of the inner world.

The Inner World and Social Relationships

The multiplicity of these inner object relations and the variety of needs which go into them do not require elaboration here. Of most importance to us are the ways in which the adult seems to function in his social relations as a result of their creation. The following summary account puts in condensed fashion some of the main concepts.

1. The individual personality is patterned by its growth within the family into a number of dynamic object-relations systems which seek to effect certain kinds of interaction with others (that is, they are personal need-systems). Each of these systems represents a part of the self related to an inner object which defines in varying degrees the "other" in the sought relationship. The presence of the internal object within the system has two consequences. First, it can be taken as an object for part of the self so that the person can in fantasy play the dual roles of self and object thereby dispensing with the uncertainties of the real external object. Second, the internal object can be used as a mould for selecting people who will fit into it, or for coercing others into it by various manipulations. Thus, the husband who unconsciously wants to settle old scores in regard to his sexually rejecting mother will pursue a course of conduct with his wife that will lead her to frustrate him even though she is a tolerant and sympathetic partner, that is, he will fit her into this unconsciously needed role. Again, in the therapeutic group, a number of passive dependent members will often collude actively to get one member to monopolise the

therapist's interest before they make resentful complaints about being put into the rejected position.

2. These systems vary in their mode of activity and in their degree of consciousness according to their position within the hierarchial organisation of the person.
3. Those which are felt to belong to that part of the self the individual wants to be, come within a central organising structure of the self, the part we usually refer to as the ego. This overall system leads to a range of relationships being sought and maintained and it is characteristic of these relationships that they are largely reality based, that is, the different identity and reality of others is accepted and mutual adaptation and learning takes place within these relations. The internal objects of this central system appear to be very plastic in keeping with the acceptance of the differentiated identity of the other person.
4. Two sets of relationships systems are separated from this central part of the self: (a) those containing certain repressed needs and (b) those concerned with primitive control.
5. Repressed relationships contain drives to satisfactions that were sought within the original comprehensive relations with parent figures but which were incompatible with the preservation of these relationships. Because they brought threats of parental loss or retaliation, of varying severity and hence associated with different intensities of anxiety, these relations are segregated by different degrees of "psychic distance" from the central part of the self. They also tend because of the original rejection of their aims to have angry and destructive components. Their separation from consciousness means that little or no learning occurs through their activity. They are, however, constantly ready to go into action. Normally their aims are realised in hidden substitute ways but more direct expression tends to emerge in close ongoing relationships with individuals or in groups.

A particularly important way of realising their aims is by the mechanism of projective identification. That is to say, the others who are in ongoing relationships are used not only as potential objects of repressed needs, but they can also be manipulated to play the part of the self that wants the forbidden relationship. For example, an aggressive individual in a group may be apparently unwittingly provoked and encouraged by the others in order to express their hostility to the leader; or a dependent person may similarly be unconsciously pressed into the role of the "sick one" to give vicarious satisfaction to the dependent needs of members. The boundaries of "the person" at these times have to include "the other."

The personality can therefore be regarded as an overall system that maintains its continuity and consistency, its identity, through social interactions.

(The results of the sensory deprivation experiments show how readily the organisation of the personality can be disturbed and acute anxiety experienced when the normal constellating inputs are removed. Those exceptional individuals who can withstand prolonged isolation appear to do so because they maintain a relation with an inner object, or substitute object such as a social or religious ideal. Even in these cases, there are at least transient periods when the fight to keep sane is nearly lost or abandoned.)

The central ego in the person is normally engaged in a process of unceasing growth. Concepts of homeostasis in regard to the individual are apt to lose sight of the fact that the person embodies the need to progress through a life cycle with changing achievement goals. In other words, the future is a constant reference point affecting behaviour.

The fundamental structures of his being represent needs for attachment and for achievement, and for defining himself in cooperative relations with others. These needs require membership of different groups for their satisfaction and also that the social climate of the groups permit their satisfaction.

The integrity and value systems of the central self for most people are achieved only by some degree of splitting off of the inevitably conflicting aims of repressed needs. The common range of defence mechanisms does not succeed as a rule in extinguishing these needs and there is an unconscious compulsion to re-create social relationships in which they can be satisfied. This leads almost universally to the selection of others in groups for appropriate partial identifications. Each person tends to choose a number of members to whom he is attached in this way and these choices reflect Moreno's concept of the social atom that each individual patterns for himself in his groups.

Repressed relationships are to be seen particularly clearly in therapeutic groups. When a need in several members combines around one individual who is detected as prone to realise it, he is perceived as willing to take the lead in this respect. This member is then cast in the appropriate role, for example, the antileader or "the sick one." If the expression of the need arouses too much guilt or anxiety, then the member being used can be attacked or ejected as a scapegoat.

Whatever the mechanisms involved, group situations appear to release at times less inhibited ways of relating, which can have both positive and negative effects. Most investigators are against postulating any hypothetical "herd instincts" and this parsimony would appear to be justified on the grounds that innate social response mechanisms would have been released and structured within the person during the early stages of his development within the family.

Relations with the Leader

The most striking group relationships are those evoked towards the leader, and many speculations have been made as to why this should be so. Here again the situation in the group seems to tend towards the reactivation of some of the patterns in the family when the immature individual is uncertain of his acceptance and status and of his powers of control. In this connection it is of considerable interest that Bales's work has shown, and sociometric studies tend to confirm, that many groups function best with two leaders, the instrumental leader who maintains the efforts of the group to meet the demands of its task and the emotional-expressive leader who accepts the emotional needs of members while at the same time supporting the instrumental leader.

Bion (1961), whose brilliant descriptions of phenomena observable when the group has no conventional "external" task to perform, postulated certain primitive patterns which he called *basic assumptions*. At first he implied that these ways of responding derived from a specific primitive mental system brought into action in the group situation. Theories which try to relate such phenomena as Bion described by his basic assumptions to innate mental systems or mechanisms would certainly have to consider evidence from group behaviour in cultures widely different from western societies. Later Bion suggested that basic assumption behaviour was related to the earliest object relationships made by the individual, that is, with the prototypes of the leader. The theories used by Foulkes and Ezriel to account for phenomena in therapeutic groups also support the primary role of unconscious object relations with the leader.

These concepts of the intra- and interpersonal dynamics in the group clearly apply only to the small group which is continuing with its structure and culture over time. The small group is usually thought of as comprising approximately five to fifteen members and it may be that the term face-to-face group provides a link with object-relations concepts in regard to these numbers. Below a certain number there may not be enough differences amongst the members to provide for the projective identifications each individual needs. It really does take all kinds to make a world for the individual's needs. Above the limit quoted, the projections may get so diffused that their connections with the self get lost. The term *face-to-face* certainly has an implication of one identity in relation to another, and only when the identity of others can be perceived does it seem that the individual feels his identity affirmed. Some exploratory studies by Rice and Turquet in larger groups (thirty to fifty) suggest that individual behaviour in these groups becomes more disorganised than in the small group, as though individual responses were made anonymously. Apparently to counteract this tendency to loss of identity, the large group tends to break up into small groups of fluctuating boundaries.

THE GROUP AND ITS TASK

The performance of the work group has been the object of an enormous amount of research in which a sociological approach is used, that is, the behavioural manifestations are studied without reference to what is going on inside each member. Various effects on members' behaviour and attitudes through their group attachment and group role have been established, but most writers surveying these contributions have noted that these effects have not been related to the dynamics in the group by any coherent set of concepts.

Much work has centred around the contribution of the leader and the effects of different ways of filling this role. Older approaches in terms of the leader's personality, usually implying an authoritarian relationship between the leader and the group, have tended to be superseded by functional considerations. Thus, although a formal leader may be designated, many studies show that the most effective work is maintained when the leader can allow his function to be shared at times by members so that the latter feel that their needs for status as mature autonomous persons with creative potential are recognised and valued.

A most important line of thought in this area is to be found in the attempts being made by Trist (1963) on the basis of a deeper understanding of the group process to link the structure and organisation of work groups with the member's emotional needs. This development is of particular interest in industry because these studies were initiated to deal with the high incidence of stress manifestations in the groups concerned.

A brief example of this work shows how an organisation based on technological considerations may not match the personal needs of the group members. Traditionally, the task of coal getting had been carried out by a self-selected group which had a high degree of responsible autonomy in carrying out their difficult and often dangerous job. Under the new methods, these groups were divided so that each group had only a limited section of the total task with coordination supplied by an external management. One result was the creation of harmful tensions between and within these groups. After prolonged explorations, a different social organisation was evolved which, while retaining the new technical methods, retrieved some of the "self-regulating" features of the traditional group. That is to say, it permitted the psychological tensions thrown up by the human interactions around the carrying out of this particular job to be handled in an effective way. The members were allowed once more to be responsible people planning their own contribution and relating it to what other groups did. Careful comparisons showed that the new social structure led to a fall in the total absence rates, mainly due to sickness and accidents, from 20 percent to 8.2 percent, and also to a substantial increase in productivity.

The Concept of the Sociotechnical System

To provide a conceptual framework for understanding and handling these situations in which the pattern of group functioning required by the technical procedures for the task must be related to the personal and emotional needs, Trist introduced the term *Sociotechnical System*. Every group organised or existing for a job or task can be regarded as such a system and I think this notion can illumine much of our work with groups other than those we are accustomed to think of as work groups. In particular, I believe it to be a valuable notion in dealing with the tensions raised in the family group, faced with its ever-changing tasks as it proceeds with its developmental schedule over the years.

As an example I should like to refer to a family described by some of my colleagues in one of their recent publications (see Pincus 1960).

> In a middle-aged couple the marital relationship had become the vehicle of primitive projections rather than a collaborative endeavour. This change had become unbearable when the elder child, a daughter, reached adolescence and began to show manifestations of sexual interest. It could be said that this family had "worked" while dealing with young, and in the parents' view sexless, children and failure developed with the appearance of the new task of coping with sexuality in the children. Unable to meet the new task, there was an upsurge of primitive anxieties, which led to mutual projections, especially by the wife, of her intolerable feelings about sexuality. From being a collaborative group concerned with the natural development of the children, the primary task in the family, mainly under the wife's leadership, became the banishment of sexuality. In the few years before they were seen, the wife had increasingly withdrawn from her husband in proportion as she felt he was little more than "dirty sexual needs." In response the husband had reacted by resorting to evenings in the pub with men friends. The daughter in an outburst of resentment with the mother's repressive attitudes over her going out with boys left home.

This kind of situation, of course, can be described in many ways and the value to my mind of putting it into the framework of the sociotechnical system concept is that by so doing we see how similar disturbances can be created by a wide range of new tasks. The family moving to a new environment, should one or more of its members fail to adapt, can begin to show the same kind of change, namely, a stirring up within the family relationships of primitive feelings and anxieties when the previous equilibrium state is upset. Effective help requires the elucidation and linking of the "external" and the "internal" factors before new solutions can be achieved, a process which can be painful and protracted.

THERAPY AND ORGANISATIONAL CHANGE IN GROUPS

The questions all psychotherapists must ask when pondering particular developments in understanding groups will naturally focus on how these help us with our tasks.

Group Therapy

As with the study of small groups in general, the enormous literature on group therapy contains relatively few of what Berne (1963) describes as "creative ideas," the kind of illuminating framework that comes from "creative meditation about nature." Such ideas do exist, though, as he notes, they tend to be ignored by professional researchers because of their "informal character." The significant contributions which he selects, those from Moreno, Burrow, Bion, Foulkes, and Ezriel, reassured me because I found I had made almost identical evaluations. It seems to me that in their formulations of the group process, these writers have in common much of what I have described by the term the object-relations theory of the personality.

The particular value I attach to this view is that it can help us formulate the essential task of psychotherapy whether this is carried out within the *dyadic* relation with the therapist, in the analytic therapeutic *group*, or in a *psychodrama*. The essence of this task consists in the provision of a setting in which the repressed relationship need systems can be brought back within the organising system of the ego where they can then be used for new learning and adaptation. Many analysts have asserted that what is done in therapeutic groups is not to be identified with the therapeutic process in psychoanalysis. I cannot accept this view when we restrict our attention to essentials. Some of our concepts have perhaps contributed to our inability to see the common core of our task, particularly such concepts as "aggressive energy" and transference. Psychotherapists frequently write of transference interpretations when they point out emotions, for example, angry feelings in the patient. Is this, however, enough? Object-relations theory tries to do justice to the crucial aspect of transference phenomena, namely, the need to bring the repressed *relationship* back to the one person relationship from which it was split off. In this way the individual is able to repeat in the here and now of his therapeutic relationship the pattern of the original "there and then" situation and hence he has the possibility of making a new solution. As Ezriel (1950) has put it, object-relations theory requires that interpretations should present to the individual three components in the following form: (1) When you say (or communicate by behaviour) "x", you are striving to maintain relationship "a" with me, (2) but "x" also indicates that you want to express another relationship "b" with me, which you must not admit to *because* you fear (3) relationship "c" in which I shall do something disastrous to you (reject, punish, attack, be sexual with, and so forth). Thus the unconsciously sought relationship, the defence against it, and the reason for the defence are incorporated in these three parts.

In the group situation, the way in which the unconscious relationships are expressed is naturally different. The therapist is, nevertheless, the central figure to whom these unconscious relationships are directed and any therapeutic work that ignores the constant reference of the group towards him is in danger of missing the important dynamics. As a rule, the relationships sought by each member at any one time can be inferred from the common theme occupying the group's interest. The defences adopted by members are different in the group setting, especially through the use of projective identification into other members. The manifold roles, which members fulfil at different times for each other, may make the interpretation work difficult for the therapist, nevertheless, when the therapist is alerted by these considerations his work is facilitated.

The therapy of natural or primary groups such as the marital relationship or the family has become more popular in recent years perhaps as a consequence of our growing appreciation of the embeddedness of the person in his closest social relationships. Here again, various degrees of help can be given by the mere fact of a therapist making a relationship with the family and through which there is some facilitation of communication. More intractable difficulties, however, can often be helped only when the unconscious collusions and projective identifications can be brought into awareness. The aggressive demanding husband in conflict with his dependent passive wife has to be seen in terms of the right unit–the total system constituted by their mutual interaction. The husband and wife may not contain the difficulties within their relationship and then we have to bring in other members of the family.

Organisational Change

Reference to the task of trying to deal with tensions within family relationships brings me to the implications of trying to effect change within the systems established in small groups. If we remind ourselves that the characteristics of each system have been evolved to deal with the threatening tensions within it, then we will be prepared for the consequences of trying to change it. All of us are familiar with the anxieties aroused within the individual when he begins to alter his defence systems and it is inevitable that such alterations within the defensive patterns of a social system will also release anxiety and a degree of acting out. Social systems, like therapeutic groups, can create special difficulties during the change process, but it is also true that they offer considerable positive features in the support that members can give each other. When the group we are trying to help is part of a larger social system, then the effects of the larger organisation on the group have also to be taken into account and vice versa.

New satisfactions have to be experienced and accepted before the old ways can be given up and during this process the role of a therapeutic person or group of persons has a close parallel with the role occupied by the therapist for the individual (See Menzies, 1960, and Sofer, 1961).

THE SMALL GROUP IN MENTAL HEALTH PROGRAMMES

The recognition of the role of group membership as a requirement for personality functioning has stimulated much of our efforts to provide social settings for our patients to which they can either continue to belong or from which they can gain resources to participate in other groups. This topic does not need comment here but in developing more positive mental health programmes two points may be noted.

First, because it has become part of our way of life to live in a rapidly changing environment—and in recent years the psychiatric consequences of dislocation have been a prominent feature in most parts of the world—we may ask if there are ideas which can help to forestall and to equip people to meet these changes. Much useful knowledge has been gained and I merely wish to draw attention here to the role of the family again. Many sociologists have commented on the way in which the family, and especially the marital relationship, are having to bear increasing stresses. The more the family is separated, the more has it to try to resolve by itself the inevitable powerful tensions within its relationships. Appropriate group memberships for the various members at the different stages of their development obviously relieve these stresses and bring increased resources to all. The healthy family itself is probably the best training ground to equip the individual to meet change because it is coping with constant growth and change in the role and status of all its members. We must therefore devote much more attention to the family as our most important unit of study and I have suggested that the object-relations concepts would seem to be most promising.

The second point concerns the role of the work group. Since participation in work groups plays such a large part in our lives, we have to learn much more about making these contribute to the enrichment of the person. The changing nature and role of "work" under the advances of automation will also demand much new thinking. Fortunately, progressive management is moving in the direction which we, as promoters of mental health in the widest sense, want to follow. We as psychotherapists have, however, also a duty to help by elucidating the phenomena of interaction and human needs. I have tried to indicate how the object-relations concepts are illuminating the dynamics of group process in ways that permit social and industrial administration working with the social psychologist to evolve methods of combining our production needs with small group structures that foster the individual's personal growth and well-being.

SUMMARY

Much recent work in psychoanalysis and in sociology points to the value of the object relations theory of the personality for understanding social interaction in the family and in small groups. This theory tries to account for the development of structures within the personality based on the central social relationships that have been experienced. These structures mediate a variety of needed personal relationships, both conscious and unconscious. The theory sheds light on the way in which the individual distributes these needed relationships in the groups to which he belongs and it therefore bridges the gap between personality theory and group process.

10. THE ONE-WAY VISION SCREEN IN ANALYTIC GROUP PSYCHOTHERAPY*

ADVANTAGES AND DISADVANTAGES OF USING THE ONE-WAY VISION SCREEN

The use of the one-way vision screen in analytic group psychotherapy stems from the need to provide students and research workers with a firsthand experience of the phenomena occurring in psychotherapeutic relationships. An alternative practice to the use of the screen is the introduction into the room with the therapist of one or two trainees assuming the roles of (i) a co-therapist, (ii) a participant observer, or (iii) a nonparticipant observer. A co-therapist is involved in the therapy as actively as the group therapist. The division of the patient's feeling between the two therapists, however, proves to be a negative feature in the treatment situation, since the crucial point for psychotherapeutic change seems to be the bringing together of the patient's ambivalent feeling towards the same therapist. The discrepancy in skill, moreover, between a trainee and an experienced therapist introduces further complications. A participant observer in group therapy intervenes only occasionally, remaining silent or taking notes most of the time. A nonparticipant observer takes no part at all in the group's discussions and, unlike the participant observer, sits clearly separated from the group. In comparison with having observers present in the therapy room, observation through a screen has distinct advantages to offer: (i) more trainees can be accommodated, (ii) new observers can easily be introduced during the course of several years' therapy without creating recurrent disturbance in the group, and (iii) it is possible for senior therapists to observe each other's technique in occasional sessions.

A therapist making use of the one-way screen for training purposes is confronted with two kinds of questions: (a) those pertaining to the ethics of the situation, and (b) those concerning the possibly deleterious effects on the treatment. The ethical questions concern the therapist's professional responsibility not to betray the patient's confidence, and have been met in various ways. The patients are given a free choice in the situation: they are told about the

---

*This chapter is co-authored by Harwant S. Gill.

screen and the demands of training; and, in the case of an objection, an alternative group is made available to the patient. The responsibility for proper selection of the observers rests with the therapist; he exercises control over admission to the observation room and only bona fide professional workers are permitted to observe. With these safeguards it is hard to believe that the use of the screen shows less respect for the patient than does the situation in out-patient clinics where an interview may be conducted in front of medical students and allied staff.

While the objections arising from ethical considerations can be met, no easy answers have been possible to questions about the effect of the screen upon therapy or about its dynamic significance for the patients. Prejudgements are common on this matter. The present study was conceived in an attempt to clarify some of the issues involved and to suggest hypotheses based on a careful examination of the tape records available for a therapy group.

Questions concerning the effect of the screen on the therapist, though highly relevant, could not be considered in this study due to insufficient data. The questions that the study hoped to consider were as follows:

General Effects

1. Does the screen exert an overall effect on the group situation?
2. If so, what is the nature of the effect? Thus:
   a. Does the screen act as a general distraction such as a constant unpleasant noise might?
   b. Does it have a general inhibiting effect, for example, by making the members more self-conscious or by inhibiting the expression of more personal and intimate feelings?
   c. Does it become a dynamically significant feature of the situation, the effect of which is more complex than either distraction or social inhibition tend to suggest? For instance, would those disturbed by the screen be using it at least in part as a resistance?
3. Does the screen have a selective psychodynamic effect in evoking certain clusters of phantasies in the group as a particular Rorschach card might, for example, paranoid fears?
4. Are the effects manifested in an obvious form so that concern about the screen is a conscious one, or are they indicated less directly, for example, in dreams?

Differential Effects

5. Does the screen affect only certain patients?
6. If so, how do the effects vary amongst those affected?

a. Do some patients show more intense reaction to the screen than others?

b. Do patients vary in their mode of response, for example, are some affected mainly consciously while others resort to more indirect forms of expression?

7. Are individuals with certain kinds of difficulty or make-up more prone than others to be affected?

Effects of Group Process

8. Do the effects vary at different times?
9. If so, are they associated with any external characteristics of the group situation, for example, times of holiday breaks?
10. Does the prevalence of certain feelings in the group lead more readily to the screen becoming a topic of concern, for example, feelings of dependence or depression?
11. When one member refers to the screen, what purpose does it serve at the time?
12. On each reference, does the screen become a group theme? If sometimes it does and at others it does not, how can these different developments be explained?

It will be clear that many of the above questions are basic to the whole process of group psychotherapy, and answers to them will have an application beyond the screen per se. Such is the case with question 12, for example, which is concerned with differentiating between the times when an issue becomes and when it does not become a group theme. Questions of wider significance for the understanding of group processes have accordingly been given more attention.

While several of the hypotheses suggested might be applicable to group processes in general, some of them might not hold true for all kinds of group structure or where the technique of therapy differed widely from the one used. The present study is exploratory in character and is based on the limited data provided by a single therapeutic group taken by the senior author. The group is described below, along with a brief account of the psychotherapeutic approach commonly used at the Tavistock Clinic.

The Group

The group consisted of four men and four women, ranging in age between 30 and 40, all of superior intelligence and of similar educational background. The difficulties for which they had sought help included the common psychoneurotic symptoms and character problems, for example, inadequacies in social relationships and in work, claustrophobia and exhibitionistic anxiety, obsessional behaviour, and psychosexual difficulties. In all cases, the symptoms were of many years duration; three patients had had in-patient and two of them out-patient psychiatric treatment.

One of the women dropped out of the group after 4 months, so that by the time of the second screen reference in Session 21 there were only four men and three women patients in the group.

The group room was a small one with a screen, 6 feet long by 3 feet high, on one of the longer walls. Two microphones were suspended from the ceiling about 5–6 feet from the floor over the centre of the group circle.

Sessions of 1½ hours were held weekly.

The Therapeutic Method

The therapeutic approach used in this group was the one developed at the Tavistock Clinic and based on the work of Bion (1961) and Ezriel (1956–57). With this approach, the therapist's attention is focused on the transference, that is, the conscious and the unconscious relationships that the patients make with the therapist and with each other in the here and now of the group interaction. The group is allowed to develop spontaneously and the therapist uses the content of the discussion and the behaviour of the group to bring out:

a. The conflicting feelings and motives expressed within a common theme, such as anger with the therapist or longings for a special, intimate relationship with him, along with inhibiting fears such as rejection by the therapist or humiliation before other group members.
b. How each individual tries to deal with the common tensions underlying a topic, that is, the particular defences adopted.

DATA

Typescripts based on tape recordings were available for the 2-year period when the group met behind the screen as well as for ten additional sessions after it had moved from the screen room into the therapist's office where no observers were present. The typed records were read independently by the two investigators, and all instances were noted where either a manifest or a latent reference to the screen was made by any member of the group or by the therapist. There were, in all, thirteen such references, each of which has been summarized below, along with an abridged account of the context in which it occurred. There are also brief notes on the general happenings within the group during the intervening periods. Every summary is followed by brief comments in which are indicated the significant points emerging from each instance.

Sessions 1–5 (October–November)

In the early weeks the group was absorbed in learning how the sessions would be conducted and in getting to know and trust the therapist and each other. A woman member (Miss S) became a preoccupying concern because her compulsive monopolizing of attention and aggressive nagging were difficult to tolerate or alter. Competitive feelings for the therapist's attention with consequent fears of rivalry and of unsympathetic attitudes from other members emerged. At the end of the second meeting Miss C asked for a private session to discuss something which she could not bring out in the group. She was told it would be better to try to bring it up there. During the next few sessions she started a practice of sitting beside the therapist where in addition to being close to him she had her back to the screen.

Reference 1. Therapist's initiative. Session 6. Miss B absent

Towards the end of session 5, the members had discussed whether or not they were a group. Miss C was most expressive of her feelings in saying they were not a group: "Everybody is a separate entity who is only interested really in their own problems. . . . I don't feel part of a group at all." In response to a comment by the therapist about the members' need to be accepted and loved by him, she stated that she was getting into a "state" and that she did want to be loved by him.

At the beginning of Session 6 a member pointed out how Miss C had turned to the exit door instead of towards the therapy room. Miss C remarked it must have been automatic and invited the group to discuss it if they liked. The group, however, ignored her and took up a suggestion that they should use their forenames. This move towards achieving some degree of group cohesion did not last because of Miss S's need to control the proceedings. Later the group became concerned with the way in which strong feelings such as depression and inadequacy tended to overwhelm them and here again Miss S took the lead in exploring these feelings and in questioning others about them.

The therapist commented on how the group members reacted ambivalently to Miss S. On the one hand they resented her need to monopolize, but on the other they colluded to put her into this position. He went on to interpret the role of each member in some detail and in connexion with Miss C referred to her difficulty in feeling a part of the group and her concern over not getting his exclusive attention. Perhaps, too, she felt he was more interested in people behind the screen because she had made a point of sitting close to him with her back to the screen. This reference to the screen was not taken up by any member of the group during the rest of the session.

Comment

In this session the therapist took the initiative in referring to the screen. This arose partly from Miss C having reacted strongly in a preliminary inquiry on possible objections to joining a group that would be observed through the screen. She had then stated that she would be worried about being watched but would accept the situation. In addition, she insisted, rather assertively, on taking the chair next to the therapist, and the one with its back to the screen. She had sought a private interview with the therapist and had declared that she did not feel a part of the group, implying that the other group members (and perhaps also the observers) were in the way of her securing a relationship with the therapist.

The reference to the screen was brought in as a part of a comprehensive comment about the group theme and the role of each member in it. The group members seemed too preoccupied with what was going on inside the group, particularly their feelings about Miss S's domination, for the observers to become a theme of immediate concern.

Sessions 7–20 (November–March)

The hostility to Miss S gradually became more open, as also did the group's collusion in allowing her to continue her domination as the "controlling mother." After she left (Session 15), there was a good deal of guilt worked through over her departure.

Rivalry situations and social difficulties then began to be discussed more directly. Miss C frequently described the triangular situations she got into with other women in her office over their relationships with the boss. The nature of the sexual conflicts in the group became more manifest and fears of uncontrolled sexuality began to be expressed.

Reference 2. Therapist's second reference. Session 21. All members present

In the previous session, the last before a holiday break, Miss O had told the group about a novel she was writing. The story depicted a near-incest situation, in which a man and woman fell in love without knowing that they were a brother and sister who had been separated. Later in the same session dependent feelings of several members, aroused by the break, became prominent. The next day Miss O had such tense feelings that she called the Clinic to ask if the therapist could see her but this was not possible.

In the first session after the break Miss O referred to her disturbed episode and later the group went on to discuss the incest theme in her novel. A few members brought memories of oedipal phantasies from childhood. The therapist pointed to the disturbing thoughts and feelings associated with the incest theme and suggested that the group was perhaps resentful with him for exploring them as well as for heightening such feelings by the break.

Following these comments, there was a short discussion about the significance of the break. Then Miss C mentioned her difficulty in participating in the discussion about incest. She went on to describe her worries about a party where "people will talk about subjects that are beyond me." The therapist pointed out that her difficulties and worries seemed to relate to the incest theme. This was illustrated by the fact that right from the start of the group she had wanted to have a special relationship with him, for example, she came and sat beside him in every session. There she sat with her back to the screen, perhaps to forget the observers and to cover up her guilt.

The therapist's reference to the screen was completely ignored by Miss C and by the group during the remaining 20 minutes of the session, and there was no reference to it in the next session.

Comment

The holiday break had increased the tensions arising from the oedipal phantasies. The resistance to recognizing the sexual longings underlying these phantasies was particularly striking in the case of Miss C, the patient whose acting out of the oedipal situation in the group had begun to irritate the other members. This second reference by the therapist to the observers was intended primarily to breach her massive resistance to recognizing her need to be "the boss's woman."

The group ignored the reference to the observers and remained preoccupied with the impact of the incest theme. To have allowed the screen to assume importance, even had its significance been restricted to Miss C, would presumably have meant admitting embarrassing sexual phantasies about the therapist in the here-and-now situation.

Sessions 22–29 (April–June)

Angry frustrated feelings with the disappointment over magical expectations about treatment became more open. Mr W brought the problem of having become attached to a girl who was homosexual. Oedipal rivalries within the group, in triangular conflicts outside, and with inner parental figures, now featured prominently. In Session 29 Mr W surprised everyone by describing a period of several days in which he had experienced a striking change in himself, namely, affectionate longings for the therapist along with compulsive locking of cupboards, turning off of taps, and so on. The homosexual nature of these feelings and his defences against them were interpreted and discussed.

Reference 3. Miss O's anxiety about observers. Session 30. All present

Discussion developed on the theme of how people draw attention to themselves. Miss O described an amateur dramatic group in which she was passed over when parts were being allocated. Interest continued in the question of how some people grab the parts while others are left out.

The therapist interpreted that they were expressing their own competitive feelings in the group. In the subsequent discussion the rivalry theme was dropped and several members began to talk of their feelings of depression and inadequacy. Miss O said at this point that she knew that some of her colleagues might be coming to the Clinic as part of a social work course. She would hate to have colleagues listening and would be relieved if she were forewarned. In discussing her feelings, some members remarked that it was extremely unlikely that her friends would be there. Miss O stated she really knew this, but she still had a strong feeling of being watched.

The therapist remarked that the concern about the observers stemmed from a fear of humiliation and punishment, which were appropriate to wanting a special relationship with him at the expense of the others. The interpretation was followed by some remarks about how they hated being laughed at, Miss O adding, "especially behind my back." The therapist commented, amongst other remarks, that Miss O seemed to feel that if she brought her longing to him, he would go off with the people behind the screen to laugh at her. Miss O said that she had often wondered whether any observers were actually there, and another woman replied that one night they were heard laughing behind the screen. One of the men (Mr L) added in a casual way that the only thing to do was to develop a sense of humour. A third woman (Miss B) said she did not bother about the screen and asked if this was a peculiarity of hers. Mr T remarked, with obvious tension in comparison with the others, that she was very lucky not to care, and Miss O wondered if she was pretending to herself about this indifference. It was said that if the people behind the screen did laugh at them they would be very unprofessional. Mr T commented that when they felt inadequate, other people might not really be laughing at them at all and added, "Somebody might have fallen off the chair in there" (that is, behind the screen).

Comment

The questions of interest are why one member brought in the observers and why, in contrast to the previous references, they became the object of the group's concern.

Miss O's introduction of the screen presumably represented a displacement of anxiety caused by rivalry with members of the group to external rivals, since to continue the discussion with direct reference to her interest in the therapist would have brought into the open the painful rivalry situation in the group. The group's response to the observers indicated a sharing of Miss O's need to displace anxiety from the group to the feared rivals outside. In the early part of the session, there had been a withdrawal from the longings for the therapist (the sexual aspects of which had been commented on by the therapist at this period), and the group had shared the feelings of inadequacy which the sensing of the inevitable frustration of these sexual longings had brought—"there would be no good parts in the play for them." By using the observers rather than the other group members as the rivals, Miss O provided them with a new opportunity to express their rivalry. For most of the group, however, the thoughts and feelings they described themselves as having in relation to the observers were more influenced by reality than was Miss O's phantasy-determined image of them.

Reference 4. Mr L's Phallic phantasy about the microphones. Session 31. All present

A discussion started about Christianity, morality, and sex, and the questions of freedom and control in sexual matters were then taken up. The therapist commented that the group was anxiously concerned about what would happen if sexual thoughts and feelings were to continue to be freely aired without the group observing the various taboos and prohibitions.

After a brief silence, a group member asked Mr L if he had any views. Mr L said that he was sorry, his mind was distracted, and, pointing to the microphones, he added: "Actually I was wondering what on earth these two balls hanging there are. I am sorry I was not paying attention. Perhaps they are phallic symbols."

The group ignored Mr L's reference to the microphones and went on to discuss further the questions of religion, sex, and morality.

Comment

Although the microphones were obviously there to let the observers listen, Mr L's response to them was, as he himself implied, more to be related to sexual phantasies stirred up by the discussion than to the observers with whom any manifest connexion seemed remote. The directly sexual nature of his reference may also suggest why any latent feelings the group had about the observers had to be suppressed. Sexual feelings could only be brought in as a general topic and, moreover, in the context of how they should be regulated. For the observers to have become an open concern in this context would have meant the expression of sexual thoughts about the therapist and possibly sexual phantasies about him and the observers—themes which were only beginning to emerge and to which there was still strong resistance.

Reference 5. Miss O's implication of continuing tension over the microphones. Session 32. All present

As the group entered, they talked of how they tended to sit in the same places. After they sat down Mr W noted the fact that they had all taken their usual seats and Miss O and Miss B agreed that they had. Miss C, however, asked if Miss O was sitting in her usual place and Miss O answered that she preferred the seat she had, though as a rule she came in too late to get it. Miss B remarked that it was much more comfortable in the waiting room and Miss C added that perhaps the chairs in the waiting room were more comfortable. Miss O pointed to another difference: "No microphones there." After a brief silence one of the women (Miss B) said that the group ought to continue the discussion started in the waiting room.

The therapist commented on how they had preferred the waiting room, including Miss O's observation on its lack of microphones, to the therapy room where he exposed their secret sexual phantasies.

The reference to the observers was not taken any further by the group.

Comment

It was again Miss O who made the second explicit reference to the observers. Strong rivalry feelings had become apparent in the discussion about seats. Miss B wanted to get away from these unpleasant rivalries by her reference to the pleasanter atmosphere of the waiting room. Miss O, also wanting to avoid group rivalries, attempted to displace her resentment onto the observers. For Miss B the observers were too close to the group situation to be allowed into the discussion, so she again brought in external situations.

With regard to why the group did not take up the observers as a common theme on this occasion, it may be noted that there had recently arisen anxious and aggressive feelings resulting from the frustration of repressed sexual wishes towards the therapist, especially amongst the women, and their anger had been displaced to external situations. To have become more openly resentful of the observers and their presumed relationship with the therapist would have entailed too explicit a confrontation of their guilt-laden sexual longings for the therapist, their dangerous hostility to the "rival woman" (the observers) and their humiliated position as rejected "little girls."

Sessions 33–47 (July–November)

More intimate feelings were now pressing for expression with associated anxieties about how these feelings would be received by the group. During this phase dependent longings also became more prominent. The frustration of these longings began to be expressed in lateness, apathy, and despair. Oedipal dreams and some oedipal acting out formed much of the content with the open expression of sexual phantasies.

Reference 6. Miss C's reference to the higher microphones. Session 48. All present

During the first few minutes Miss C was the only woman present with two men. Her opening remark was: "The microphone is higher tonight," but there was no response from the men. After a short pause she continued, "I came in feeling very depressed. I feel a bit more cheerful since I arrived. Must be me." There was again no response to her remarks and she went on to refer to her depressed fits. One of the men rather ostentatiously ignored her by proceeding to discuss with the other man the reasons for the latter being absent for several weeks, and the other members joined in when they arrived. For the rest of the session, the discussion was mainly about the size of the group, a theme stimulated by the fact that in this session all members were present after a few weeks of smaller attendances. Some felt better that everyone was around, others felt that more got done when there were fewer people in the group. The whole group became interested in the issue of crowds, how one avoided them, and how one asserted oneself in them.

Comment

Miss C's early reference to the microphones was, at the manifest level, associated with her depression. The instruments were at most only a few inches higher than usual, yet she appeared to associate this stimulus with a lightening of her depression. With no further elucidation it was not clear what the symbolic connexion with her relief was. Possibly it was a feeling that the "persecuting mother" was further away, a relief that may also have derived from the fact that the other women were absent at the start.

The lack of group response to the microphones in this session seemed predominantly related to the intense triangular situation in the group. One of the men was particularly hostile to Miss C at this period and expressed this feeling by his deliberate ignoring of her. The other man present at the start was also critical of her. The subsequent discussion about the size of the group revealed the continued presence of rivalry feelings in the group.

Sessions 49 and 50
(Second year—November to Christmas break)

There were several references to outbursts of anger with bosses and parents which were associated with the coming Christmas break. Mr W, who had been abroad for some weeks, returned in Session 49. The group members made no comments about his return and later he tended to be contemptuous of the therapist's reference to dependent feelings. He thought he would now give up the group or might well do so after the break. He did not come to the last session before the break and 3 days later he arrived at the Clinic in considerable agitation. As the therapist was unavailable, he was seen by another doctor.

Reference 7. Mr W's disguised reference in a vivid dream.
Session 51. Mr T absent

It was the first group meeting after the break. Miss O talked of her dependence upon her mother and whether or not it would be possible for her to live separately from her. This theme was kept going by others questioning her about steps she might take. The therapist interpreted that the group's interest in her dependence on her mother expressed their own feelings of dependence, as stirred up by the break. This led Mr W to talk at great length about his vacillation between attitudes of independence and dependence. In this context he related a dream that he had had before Christmas, and which he said had greatly disturbed him. In it he was attending a ceremony in the chapel of a university where he was employed. At the end of the commemorative sermon a group of "mass observation observers" turned up to ask the university staff questions about the brands of tea, coffee, wine, and so forth, that they drank. Mr W objected to the introduction of this commercial element into a religious function and refused to answer any questions. The secretary of the university got annoyed and asked him to quit the job. Mr W begged and cried but to no avail, so he decided to kill the secretary by using a long case-opener and then to poison himself before he was caught.

When he finished telling his dream the group members started discussing Mr W's attitudes of independence versus dependence. Miss C soon interrupted to tell the group about a quarrel with her landlady who had let people move into her room to redecorate it without obtaining her permission, or even informing her. She talked of her anger with the landlady about this intrusion, and there was some discussion of how this kind of incident should be handled.

The therapist's interpretations focused on the group's dependent feelings as related to the break; thus, the two women spoke of angry "mothers" intruding on them, while Mr W resented the university secretary bringing him to the chapel and then subjecting him to a mass-observation quiz. Mr W perhaps felt that he was merely another "case" for the therapist to play with in front of the screen.

The group did not take up the interpretation but went on to discuss Miss C's episode with the landlady and a similar humiliation experienced by Miss O at her work. There was no further allusion to the observers.

Comment

Mr W's upset before the break had revealed a large breach in his habitual rigid defences. On his return from his trip abroad he must have felt rejected by the group as well as by the therapist, and at first he tried to deny these feelings by professing independence to the extent of believing he could do without the group. Missing the last session appeared to be a defiance of the therapist, who had been stressing the group's dependent feelings. In keeping with his strongly defensive detachment, the breakthrough of his feelings for the therapist on the night of his defiant absence could appear only in disguise in a dream.

There was no general response on the part of the group to the observers. Instead the discussion switched to external incidents, and the turning away from Mr W's experience was striking. This move away from his experience could be viewed as an attempt to escape from the intolerable dependent feelings for the therapist. To have taken up Mr W's dream and the links with the depriving observers would probably have confronted the other members with conflicting feelings about the therapist that were too painful.

Sessions 52–56
(Second year: January–February)

Delayed resentment about the break and dependent feelings began to be expressed in the form of increasing references to depressed feelings that derived from the release of destructive phantasies towards the frustrating therapist (parent). The strong feelings for the therapist, bosses, and parents required a good deal of working through before these feelings could be accepted. In Sessions 55 and 56 there were several expressions of resentment with members for taking up too much time.

Reference 8: Miss O's anxiety over the unknown observers.
Session 57. Mr L absent

The session started with Miss C coming alone into the room ahead of the others, followed soon by Miss O, who also preferred to walk ahead while the others were waiting downstairs for the elevator. This was in some contrast to the usual practice of the group, which was to come to the room together.

Miss O said that coming to the group made her anxious that evening. She found it hard to talk of a certain problem from her past. If she failed to bring it up in the group she would have to ask for a private session with the therapist. Several group members tried to persuade her to talk of it in the group and she eventually remarked: "I don't mind the lot of you being here but goodness knows who is behind the screen, people I might get involved with in my work." The group then attempted to reassure her about the observers, by such remarks as: "You have talked about so many things with the other people behind there that it should not matter any more." "They can be big hearted enough to realize that all flesh is human." Despite these pressures, Miss O said she did not think she could get it out.

The therapist then pointed to the collusion between Miss O and the rest of the group in developing a situation of coaxing her to speak. They all had feelings that they did not wish to talk about and by fastening on to Miss O they were trying to treat these reluctant bits of themselves.

Following this interpretation Miss O readily described her concern about a homosexual phase in her adolescence and its recurrence in her twenties after a broken engagement. The "analysis" (as she referred to the sessions) had brought this worry about the past back again. The whole group then became absorbed in the theme of homosexuality.

The therapist commented that Miss O was turning to homosexuality as a result of disappointment and frustration with the male therapist. He also pointed out how the group's interest in continuing the discussion on this theme revealed their own concern over similar feelings towards the therapist. He went on to interpret the interest in the people behind the screen as representing their curiosity about "the other parent." The reference in this interpretation to the observers was "ignored" by the group in their subsequent discussion, which concerned Miss C's description of a new feeling she had experienced in the last week or two, namely, an aversion to men.

Comment

Miss O's anxieties about her unconscious drive to get the therapist's exclusive interest had apparently stirred up her dread of the rival "mother" and also her homosexual solution to this situation. The danger of rivals within the group was still too great to bear and led to a displacement to the observers, her phantasy again being that her colleagues would be watching her.

As long as the group felt the observers were being discussed only in relation to Miss O, they gave expression to their feelings about them. When the therapist interpreted later on that the group shared the homosexual phantasies to which Miss O had turned as the result of disappointment with the male therapist, then interest in the observers ceased. To have continued would presumably have meant being confronted with homosexual phantasies in the here and now of the group and they preferred instead the less direct expression of feeling by talking about incidents outside the group.

Sessions 58–62 (March–April)

The freer communication of phantasies about the therapist led to a more active interaction in the group. Guilt and anxiety related to early parental memories appeared.

Reference 9. Mr W's second dream. Session 63. Miss C absent

It was the second last session before the Easter break. At the beginning of the session Mr W brought up a dream in which he was a child taken to a doctor by his mother. "The doctor got out a stethoscope and proceeded to put it against me, but instead of putting the other ends in his ears—the two sort of earpieces—he plugged them into the wall. . . . I said to my mother, 'This man is a phoney. I don't believe he is a doctor at all. . . .' I said, 'Well, I know a doctor who is better than that,' having in mind Dr Sutherland . . . and then, as we were walking along, much to my surprise, I saw you, Dr Sutherland, on the other side of the street. . . . I waved to you several times but you were so busy examining the house numbers that you took no notice of me."

The group went on to discuss various aspects of Mr W's feelings towards his mother, his father, and the therapist. The therapist interpreted that Mr W and the other group members felt the coming break as a rejection. They were all interested in Mr W's dream, which presented two versions of the therapist: "There is one who hides behind all the paraphernalia of medicine, the 'me' that you feel resentful with, because I am inhuman, impersonal. I plug the stethoscope into the wall . . . it sounds like some reference to the observers or to the fact that I am just using you as specimens, that they can watch your feelings, as it were, or listen in to them. . . . The other 'me' that Mr W was trying to get at was also rejecting because I seemed to be so concerned with all the other members and missing him. This feeling too was similar to one Mr W had brought in his dream at the time of the Christmas break."

The interpretation was followed by a long silence. The therapist commented that the thick silence was perhaps due to his having raised the question of dependent feelings and that the group seemed to be making a concerted effort to sulk and to have nothing to do with him.

The group again ignored the therapist's comments and went on to discuss one of the women's (Miss O) feelings of inadequacy and depression when rejected as a child by a school teacher.

There was no mention of observers in the remaining part of this group session nor in the next.

Comment

This session was reminiscent of session 51, when Mr W described his first long dream. Here, too, his feelings about rejection were stirred up by the break, and again they appeared in a vivid dream. On this occasion, however, Mr W's experiences were not ignored. The group explored them in considerable detail, but as though they were something external to themselves. There was no reference to the observers, because it might not only have brought in the humiliated rejected feelings but also anger and resentment over the rejection, feelings which would have created too much anxiety.

Sessions 64–66 (April–May)

Depressed feelings concerned with hostility towards the rival oedipal parent developed and hostility continued to Miss C for her chronic tendency to monopolize the therapist's interest. Mr T, who had said he might not continue, evoked a good deal of pressure from the others to stay.

Reference 10. Mr T's anger. Session 67. Mr L absent

The group members began by inquiring after Mr T's difficulty in bringing up his problems for discussion in the group. The therapist commented that their great enthusiasm to get Mr T to speak was a substitute for speaking about themselves and especially for expressing their resentful feelings to him and to each other. Mr T said that he was angry because he was forced to struggle in order to get to the group on time, because he had to travel a long way, give up an evening, and so on. He needed to come but he resented the position of having to come. He added that he resented most the therapist, because he was the head of the group and, to him, the "instigator."

The group showed surprise at finding in Mr T a strong need to come to the group as it had been their impression that he had no such need. The therapist pointed to the similarity between Mr T's feelings about the group and the feelings of a child towards its parents. One cannot do without parents. One is furiously angry with them at times, yet one is tied to them and continually hoping for something better from them. When Mr T was asked by other members what it might be about the group situation that he resented so much he answered: "Merely that I am forced into this position of having to come here. It seems to me to be humiliating . . . I know Miss O is always worried about her friends being behind the glass and so on, and I sense other people are too."

The group ignored this reference to people behind the screen and continued instead to discuss Mr T's angry feelings towards them as well as towards the therapist.

Comment

Although in the past he had reported that attendance at the group had made him aware of intense pent-up, angry feelings, this was the first occasion on which Mr T brought them directly to the therapist and the group. Just as the fears of what his angry feelings would do had led to his keeping away, so now, when eventually brought to the group, he could only allow them to be directed at first towards the therapist. It seemed that he could not include the group in the angry feelings he revealed towards the therapist, and had to bring in the observers in place of the group members as more remote objects of his hostility. The group, however, inferred from his past aloofness that he also resented them and began to question him about these feelings.

Reference 11. Miss C faces screen. Session 68. Mr L absent

Mr V came in first and took the seat next to the therapist. Miss C, who normally occupied it, took a chair facing the screen, smiled at Mr V and remarked, "A switch around—it feels funny facing the screen—it is the first time I have faced the screen for about a year—I feel self-conscious now."

Miss C next asked Mr V why he had taken her chair. He did not know and inquired whether she felt it was her chair. She answered that she did, and then went on to describe a dream in which she was travelling in an aeroplane with her family and fighting as if for her life with the feeling that the plane was going to crash. The therapist commented on the fight going on in the group itself. He recalled Miss C's concern about being watched from behind the screen and made some further comments about her need to monopolize him. The group ignored the mention of the screen and went on to discuss their interrelationships.

Comment

Here again Miss C seemed to use the observers for the displacement of her hostility from the group. Her resentment was primarily with Mr V for taking her usual chair. The group felt resentment with her and preferred to take up their interrelationships more directly.

Sessions 69–80 (May–October)

Anger and frustration with the therapist over disappointed oedipal longings and oedipal dreams continued to be worked through. The homosexual solution of oedipal rivalries and at times the aggressive manifestations of rivalry in the group became more intense. The summer break on this occasion was 2 weeks longer than usual because the therapist had to be abroad. This fact probably contributed to its provoking stronger feelings than hitherto, with denials at first and then recognition of the role of the dependent longings.

When the reactions to the break had been discussed, the therapist announced that the group would end its period in the screen room and change to his office in 2 weeks' time. There was no response to this announcement until the end of the last session before the change, when on his reminding them of the new room for the next week's session, one of the men (Mr V) asked if that meant the group would no longer be observed.

Reference 12. Change from screen room. Session 81. Miss C and Mr T absent

The members did not arrive together and, unlike the usual pattern, the therapist said good evening to each member individually as they entered his office, and then inquired after the health of one of the men who had been ill. Mr V thought the therapist was "slightly more personal" and that the room had a certain air of domesticity. Miss O reflected: "I am wondering whether the sort of pictures and basins and things are going to be distracting." While the group was engaged in nothing the differences in the therapist's attitude and in the two rooms, Mr V pointed to the additional difference that there were no more people behind the screen.

Miss O said she would have feared being observed by a group of social workers visiting the Clinic that evening (actually a group attending a seminar). Mr V had seen a girl from his office in the Clinic and there was a brief discussion about his concern lest she be admitted as a patient in this group. The therapist commented on the fears about being watched coming, as before, from inside themselves, perhaps increased by the feeling of a closer relationship with him. When they were free from the screen observers, the watchers still came in, colleagues from a course or people with whom they worked.

Miss O said that the new group room was on the same floor as the old one, and that coming here involved the same number of floors on the lift. She went on to say that her claustrophobia was as bad as ever and the group got engaged in discussing her symptoms. The therapist commented that despite the new room the group were finding themselves up against the same old symptoms and difficulties.

Mr V described feeling depressed about his work situation as he had been unable to get away from his malevolent boss to a more satisfying job. Miss B discussed her difficulty in deciding whether or not to take a certain part-time study course. All this time Mr W had been very quiet "because I am sleepy." The therapist pointed out how the various group members, in talking about indecision with regard to taking a study course or changing a job, or in feeling withdrawn from the situation, seemed to express their concern about continuing to attend the group, feeling perhaps that the therapy course was not worth it.

After a long silence one of the men who had been very quiet (Mr L) reinitiated the discussion about the change in the therapist's attitude, namely, the intimate and friendly feeling that had been present at the start. The therapist commented that as he continued to make the usual kind of interpretations, the wishful thinking for a more friendly therapist with the change of room had receded, and that they now wished to recapture this close relationship.

Mr L remarked on how the therapist reminded him of his father. He added: "The more you love them, the more you fear for them that something may happen, that in some way the relationship may be broken." Mr V pointed out that concern about someone's safety often concealed a wish for his death. Next, Mr V described how at the moment he was "very conscious of the outside world in this room, of people creeping about upstairs and laughing and fooling around in the corridors. I seem to be much more conscious of them here than I was in the other room. . . ." The group went on to discuss the differences in quietness and in privacy between the two rooms. Then there was a long silence, which was interrupted by one of the women (Miss B) raising once again the problem of her inability to decide whether or not to join a study course. Mr V commented irritably that he could not focus his mind on the kind of problems that she presented and blamed her for bringing in extraneous issues.

In his next interpretation the therapist pointed out how the group's expectations in the new room of finding in him a more affectionate, a more loving, fatherlike figure were frustrated when he did not conform to this role. The group had felt at the beginning that he was more intimate, more personal, but were later disillusioned when he continued to play the same old role. There was concern about losing him, which Mr V felt might represent an expression of anger and a wish for his death. In his reference to people creeping about outside the room, Mr V was perhaps revealing his fear that some retaliating figures would open the door and interrupt the close relationship they wanted with the therapist.

There was no further mention of the observers in the remaining part of the session.

Comment

On this critical occasion of the group's move from the screen, a striking feature was the transience of "relief" feelings. The new room, with its more personal furnishings and the more friendly greeting of the therapist, reinforced the longings for a more intimate relationship with the therapist. These forbidden longings, however, soon reactivated the inner fear of rivals, with the result that the initial good feeling of closeness to the therapist gave way to increasing tensions about "inner observers." Thus Mr V, who was the first to comment on the newly found intimacy, had to note that the external observers were absent, and soon afterwards he gave more direct expression to his fears about observers by describing his concern about a colleague joining the group. Miss O also showed a similar fear in her comments about her colleagues.

After Mr L had reverted to the earlier theme by declaring his strong feelings for the therapist, it seemed that Mr V's phantasies of the dangerous rivals in the group were intensified but displaced to potential intruders from the corridor outside the room. The limited success of this manoeuvre was seen in the irritability that he expressed towards Miss B for her attempt to divert the discussion to external incidents.

Reference 13. Curiosity about screen room. Session 82. Mr T absent

Miss C, returning to the group after her holiday, started to describe fits of acute depression she had had recently. She then mentioned that she had walked into the old room. Miss O admitted having waited near the observers' room and added that she was "dying to peep and see what was going on." Mr V reported that he too had looked into the observers' room where a film was being shown and so he had quickly withdrawn. Miss O then confessed that she had actually looked into the room and was surprised to see it in darkness.

Miss C reverted to her depressed feelings and described how she had felt isolated from her companions on holiday. The discussion about her feelings continued for some time and Mr V observed that the group had become very depressed—"everyone is looking as if they were going to burst into tears." Shortly afterwards, Mr W noted the apparent contradiction between what had been happening to Miss C on her holiday and the way in which she was monopolizing interest that evening. Several members went on to compare the amount of attention that she was able to command in the group with the little recognition she got from others on her holiday.

In his interpretation, the therapist referred to the group's depression as being intensified by the feeling that the new room had not changed anything. The depression had in turn led to their concern about Miss C, who seemed to represent for them a mother inside the group who had taken possession of the therapist.

There was no further reference to the observers in this or in subsequent sessions.

Comment

Miss C's going to the old therapy room was perhaps due to the fact that the change of room had occurred when she was still on holiday, but the entry of Mr

V and Miss O into the observation room clearly stemmed from their intense curiosity about the observers. The unconscious motivation behind their curiosity could have involved a variety of phantasies that remained unexplored. It was clear, however, that there was an element of latent excitement in their phantasies about what went on behind the screen, as though they felt they would now share the same special relation with the therapist as the observers had done formerly. This excitement died down rapidly with the realization that the possessive mother (Miss C) was back in the group to deprive them of the therapist.

DISCUSSION

General Effects

The first point to emerge from the data is the limited number of references to the screen. The ninety group sessions reviewed, covering a period of more than 2 years, produced no more than thirteen screen references, seven of which were limited to single comments by individuals and evoked little response from the other group members. The group's reaction to the screen remained minimal, in spite of the fact that the therapist was particularly interested to point out any significant impact of the screen on the group, and in fact had taken the initiative in the first two instances to comment about the seat taken by a group member in relation to the observers behind the screen.

It would thus appear that the screen did not constitute to an appreciable extent either a constant source of distraction or a persistent cause of inhibition. What happened instead was that occasionally a group member would complain of distraction (Mr V in Reference 12) or of inhibition (Miss O in Reference 8 and Mr T in Reference 10). All such episodic complaints could be understood in terms of the dynamics of the situation at the time and are best seen as equivalent to other sources of defence or resistance during psychotherapy. Mr V's distraction by "people creeping about . . . in the corridors" represented a resurrection of the observers (when the group had moved out of the screen room into the therapist's office) and conveyed his fear that a retaliating figure would open the door and interrupt his relationship with the therapist. Miss O's stated inability to talk of her problem in the group because of the presence of observers disappeared when the therapist interpreted the nature of her defence; she then proceeded to talk freely about her homosexual difficulties. Mr T's reluctance to speak because of people behind the screen was another instance where the screen was used as a temporary peg on which to hang his resistance, a resistance that was related to his major symptom of exhibitionistic anxiety.

It would therefore seem that when members of the group refer to the screen as either distracting or inhibiting, their references are best understood as a means of resistance and are as amenable to effective interpretation as any other significant feature of a psychotherapeutic situation.

While the screen could conceivably be used as a means of resistance in many ways, it is seen in this study that there are a limited number of typical forms that this resistance tends to assume. A common feeling is that it is difficult or humiliating to talk of personal problems in the presence of people behind the screen who are unknown to the patients, or who might judge them harshly or be unduly critical of their motives and behavior. An allied concern is the fear that the observers might make fun of the patients' problems and difficulties, and that the therapist might join with the observers in laughing at them behind their backs. Another common reaction is to see the observers as stealing the therapist's attention away from the group, so that the patients feel that the therapist's interest in them is subordinate to his primary interest in teaching the observers. Along with such fears and anxieties, the observers are also made the object of interest and curiosity.

It would thus seem that the feelings projected onto the observers are typically those related to phantasies about the role of the other parent. The activation of the internalized conflict with the rival parent can be seen in References 12 and 13 when, in the absence of observers, the group members were unconsciously impelled to re-create the feared observers in a variety of ways.

It is clear from the data given that the group's concern about the screen could be expressed either in a conscious or in an unconscious form. The feelings about the observers in References 7 and 9 were manifested in the first instance through the relating of dreams. Miss C's concern about the intrusion of the observers was also revealed indirectly through her description of a quarrel with her landlady who had let people pry into her room. In addition to these instances of indirect expression, an unconscious component could be seen in the more direct references to the screen also. For example, Miss O's stated inability to talk of her problem because of the people behind the screen in Reference 8 was shown to be unconsciously determined and projective in character by the ease with which she talked freely of her homosexual difficulties immediately following an interpretation.

Differential Effects

The screen had an effect on each group member, though this differed in intensity as well as in mode of response, and was directly related to the particular character structure or symptomatology of each person. The response to the screen of two group members Mr L and Miss B, was minimal. Mr L indicated his concern about the observers only once when, in Reference 3, the group were expressing their fear about being laughed at and he joined in to remark: "The only thing to do is to try to develop a sense of humour." His only other comment, about the microphones, in Reference 4, was ambiguous in meaning, suggestive more of sexual phantasies about the therapist than of any direct reference to the screen. Both of these comments are consistent with his character structure, a prominent feature of which is submission to the sexually potent and powerful father. Miss B never mentioned the screen herself, and when it was brought up she professed to be indifferent to it. In her lack of comment about the screen a process of defensive denial (in keeping with her major character defence of denial) was noticeable on more than one occasion: when the observers were referred to by other group members she manoeuvred towards external topics, which led the discussion away from the observers. At one point, her attempt to deny the effect of the screen was noticed and pointed out by group members themselves (Reference 3).

In direct contrast to the minimal response from Mr L and Miss B, two other group members, Miss O and Mr T, showed intense concern about the screen. Miss O experienced recurrent anxiety about being watched by her colleagues. The reality basis for her fear was that she knew that some members of her profession attended seminars at the Clinic. It was entirely a phantasy on her part, however, that such groups would be behind the screen. Her concern about being watched became acute when her feelings of oedipal rivalry were at their strongest. The oedipal theme was a particularly dominant one for this patient and had appeared in her relationship with her mother over the last few years, following her father's death. It is of particular interest to note that after the group changed from the screen room, and when Miss O was no longer able to use the observers as her feared rivals, she developed an almost unbearable hostility to Miss C. She sought a private interview with the therapist to tell him that she had become friendly with Mr W, but that she could not possibly mention this when Miss C was present. It took many weeks before she was eventually able to discuss this intense rivalry.

Mr T expressed his anxiety about the observers in Reference 3 by his questioning of Miss B's stated indifference to the screen, and in Reference 10 by referring to Miss O's anxiety about being watched from behind the screen. Though less direct in mode of expression, Mr T's anxiety about the observers appeared to be as intense as Miss O's. The responses of both Mr T and Miss O seemed to involve a projection of persecuting inner figures onto the observers, a projection that was in keeping with the fact that both of them suffered from intense phobic anxieties, Miss O experiencing claustrophobic panics, and Mr T having attacks of anxiety in "exhibitionistic" situations (for example, in public speaking). The more intense reaction to the screen of these two members perhaps indicates the existence of a close link between symptoms of phobic anxiety and fear of screen observation.

Unlike Miss O and Mr T, for whom the phantasied observers were frightening, Mr W perceived them to be depriving rather than persecuting, and expressed anger about them rather than anxiety. His mode of response was also radically different, in that both of his references to the screen (7 and 9) appeared in a symbolic form in his dreams. He presented a highly defended intellectualizing front, valued his emotional independence from people, and continually expressed his contempt for the unscientific nature of the therapist's interpretations. However, his repressed longing to be loved by the therapist showed a striking tendency to recur in dreams at the time of breaks. For him the observers represented the other parent responsible for his deprivation. It is interesting to compare his mode of response to the observers with his initial statement in his letter of acceptance when the group was first proposed to him. He wrote: "I would probably be interested in joining the group and I have no *conscious* objection to one-way screen" (our italics).

Mr V's response to the screen was somewhat similar to that of Mr W. Ordinarily, neither would initiate discussion about the observers and when someone else raised the topic, both of them would react to it at the reality level, making rational comments, such as, "It would be extremely unlikely . . ." that Miss O's colleagues would be listening behind the screen (Reference 3); or "I wouldn't let that inhibit you from speaking" (again concerning Miss O's reluctance to speak because of observers in Reference 8). However, under conditions of heightened feeling, both showed intense reaction to the presence of observers. Mr W responded in a symbolic form through his dreams. Mr V experienced anxiety regarding the "people creeping about . . . in the corridors" when he felt he had a more intimate relationship with the therapist and feared that some retaliating figure would come in to interrupt this relationship. His comment about the screen was consistent with his problem of repressed passive homosexual phantasies along with a great fear of the retaliating rival parent.

Finally there was Miss C, the one amongst the group who most strongly demanded a special relationship with the therapist. Right from the beginning she asked for private interviews (which were refused), and sat beside the therapist in a position that also enabled her to keep her back to the observers. When, before the start of the group, she was told about the screen she had shown sharp concern about "being watched and listened to by an unseen audience." In spite of this strong initial reaction, however, her later comments about the screen remained minimal. In the first two references it was the therapist who had referred to her usual sitting position in relation to the screen. In Reference 6 she had simply referred to the microphones being higher that evening. In Reference 11 she had been blocked from sitting beside the therapist and was left facing the screen, which prompted her to speak of her mild discomfort in that position.

Like Miss O, Miss C also had strong oedipal transference feelings to the therapist. Unlike Miss O, however, Miss C engineered in the group (as she also did in external social life and work situations) a self-punishment in which she got isolated and rejected by other group members. It would appear that under the circumstances, Miss C did not "need" to bring in criticism of the observers; for her the observers were much more remote than her rivals within the group itself. The group, in turn, perceived her as striving to possess the therapist and to exclude them. It was perhaps in keeping with the group's perception of her as an immediate rival that on each occasion when she initiated a reference to the observers, the other members were unable to express their feelings about these more distant rivals behind the screen.

Effects on Group Process

The above examination of differential effects concentrated on the role of intrapsychic factors in determining the intensity and the mode of response to the screen and pointed mainly to the differences existing among the diverse screen references. The effects on group process will now be considered in order to elucidate the role of interpersonal and group situational factors, and this will perhaps clarify the common or shared meaning of the group's concern about the screen as seen in the various references.

Among the group situational factors examined were: (1) the size of the group, that is, the number of members present in each session; (2) the duration of time for which the group had been in treatment at the time of each screen reference; and (3) the time around the various holiday breaks. Of these, the size of the group showed no relation to the frequency of the occurrence of references to the screen. The duration of time since the start of the group appeared also to be unrelated to the frequency of references. A priori, it would be expected that most references to the screen would occur when the screen was first introduced, or when another change was made. References 12 and 13 in fact occurred when a change was made and the group was moved away from the screen room. However, reference to the screen did not develop into a group topic until Session 30. That the screen did not become a topic of concern to the group for so long was probably due in part to the following three factors: (i) The process of overcoming initial anxieties about the situation inside the group was relatively slow because most of the members were inhibited in making social relationships. (Of eight people aged 30–40, only two were married.) (ii) The unusual domination by one member (who left after Session 15) made the initial situation a particularly difficult one for this inhibited group to handle. (iii) The screen was present from the start, and by the time mutual knowledge and trust had developed it was part of a familiar setting.

The holiday breaks, on the other hand, were seen to be related to the references to the screen. A reference was judged to occur around a holiday break if it was made after the therapist's announcement of the break, or if made during the group's first meeting at the end of the break. Out of the eleven relevant references (References 12 and 13 being a direct consequence of the group's move from the screen room into a nonscreen room), only four occurred at a time other than just before or just after a holiday break.

The holiday breaks are perhaps significant because of their impact on the group's relationship to the therapist. The separation, or prospect of it, tends to heighten the group's longing for the therapist. This, in turn, tends to activate the internalized conflict with the rival parent, the observers constituting a convenient peg on which to hang the phantasies associated with the role of the rival parent. Disappearance of the therapist is felt perhaps as a triumph for the observers. When all members of the group seem to share a common deprivation in relation to the therapist, it is difficult to use any member within the group as a successful rival.

The impact of the holiday breaks upon the group's feelings towards the therapist leads directly to an examination of the nature of feelings prevalent in the group that tend to elicit a reference to the screen. These feelings were of two kinds: (a) feelings of dependence, or of frustration of dependent longings, and (b) sexual feelings associated with oedipal phantasies and strong rivalries. The screen acts as a powerful stimulus when it becomes involved in phantasies about the therapist's relationship with the observers, who then assume significance as people having close links with the therapist and stealing his attention away from the group.

We can see from the data given that most of the direct initial references to the screen were made by individual members in an attempt to displace the uncomfortable rivalry experienced in the group itself onto the observers. But whether or not other members took up the screen as a group theme depended on the presence or absence of certain conditions, which are given below:

1. The group are concerned with their relationship to the therapist.
2. This concern is expressed directly in the here and now.
3. The quality of their relationship to the therapist is triangular, in the sense that their frustration with, or deprivation by, the therapist activates phantasies about rivals.
4. The group are passing through a common or shared experience of their relationship to the therapist, so that all of them are in the same position and find it difficult to use members within the group as rivals.

To illustrate from the data, Miss C's attempt to displace the rivalry onto the observers failed in References 6 and 11 because the group were preoccupied with their perception of her as an immediate rival within the group itself. A similar situation existed in Reference 10 when the group were engaged in discussing Mr T's angry feelings directly in relation to them and the therapist, and they could not go along with Mr T's attempt to displace his anger to people behind the screen. In References 2 and 5, the screen failed to become a group theme because the group were unable to face directly the guilt-laden sexual phantasies about the therapist. In contrast, Reference 3 depicted the group as completely absorbed in discussing their feelings about the observers, since the group were concerned about their relationship to the therapist in the here and now, and shared common feelings of inadequacy, making it difficult for them to find a rival within the group itself.

SUMMARY

The main points emerging from this exploratory study are:

1. A one-way screen does not appear to act as a constant source of distraction or inhibition for patients in a therapeutic group.

2. The feelings projected onto the observers are typically those related to phantasies about the role of rival figures.
3. The group's concern about the screen is expressed both in a manifest and a latent form.
4. The effect of the screen on each group member varies in intensity as well as in mode of response, and is related to his particular character structure or symptomatology.
5. Reaction to the screen is influenced by certain factors in the group situation, such as holiday breaks, the significance of which can be understood in terms of their impact on the group's feelings towards the therapist.
6. The initial reference to the screen is often made by an individual member in an attempt to displace an uncomfortable rivalry experienced in the group itself onto the observers, but whether the screen becomes a group theme is a function of the following situation: The group members are concerned with their relationship to the therapist in the here and now, and are sharing a common feeling of frustration or inadequacy, making it difficult for them to "seek" a rival within the group itself.

In short, the data from the study of one group suggest that a one-way screen acts as a projective stimulus, the significance of which is determined by both the intrapsychic and the interpersonal dynamics of the group situation.

11. BION'S GROUP DYNAMICS

PERSONAL RECOLLECTIONS

During 1940–1941, the darkest days of World War II for Britain and her allies, I was a psychiatrist in a hospital for the war neuroses. It was my good fortune to be working closely with W. R. D. Fairbairn (hitherto the only psychoanalyst practising in Scotland) during this period when the pressure of his creative ferment was coming to full fruition. Inspired by Melanie Klein's writings—his contact with her before the war had been limited because of his geographical isolation in Edinburgh and was now nil—and by the impact of several markedly schizoid patients, he was recasting psychoanalytic psychopathology. Instead of Freud's foundations on the vicissitudes of instincts, Fairbairn described the development of the personality from a state of infantile dependence to the mature dependence of the adult on the basis of the structuring of experience within personal, or object, relationships. To put it into the terms Bion was to use later, he had moved from Freud's vertex with its penumbra of nineteenth-century energy concepts in which the second law of thermodynamics was virtually the ultimate truth in nature, to one from which the person at the personal or psychological level could be viewed as an organism perpetually requiring, and seeking, personal relationships for his development and maintenance.

The war neuroses had been a valuable stimulus to Fairbairn in consolidating his views. By the end of 1941, the change in the war situation to one of lessened demand on the psychiatric hospitals along with an urgent effort to build up the armed forces led to my being asked to join an experimental unit in the army whose task was to evolve a model procedure for the selection of candidates to be trained as officers. Located in Edinburgh, there was a small staff of experienced army officers along with three psychiatrists to provide a professional psychological component. The three of us were analytically oriented and, since I had been a psychologist before training as a psychiatrist, I acted as the psychologist for the first few months until Eric Trist could join the unit. My two colleagues were Eric Wittkower, later Professor of Psychiatry in Montreal, and who had been working in Edinburgh, and Wilfred Bion, whom I had not met before.

From the start we all got along well personally and our shared orientation to the task made work very congenial. Since Eric Trist (1985) has described the contribution Bion made within these early months, I shall confine myself to a few personal impressions, some of which will inevitably overlap with his. Bion had the great advantage of an imposing military presence. He was a large man wearing the ribbons of his distinguished record as a soldier in World War I—the British Distinguished Service Order and the French Legion of Honour. Apart from this visible record which, in the senior member of the technical team, was of enormous value in facilitating our acceptance in face of the widespread suspicion and underlying anxiety with which psychiatrists were generally received, he quickly made an impression on everyone of "power" in the best sense. He was quietly spoken, unfailingly courteous and attentive to others, and always sensitive and thoughtful about their views. His remarks were usually brief and penetrating and he had the most delightful sense of humor expressed in dry pithy phrases along with occasional amusing personal anecdotes to make a point.

As Trist describes, there were at times tensions between the technical and the military sides in the early days when the latter, for instance, found it difficult to accept that an apparently competent man would be rated too low in the intelligence tests for the arm of his choice or when some psychiatric features were uncovered that cast doubts on the man's stability despite an apparently good impression. The shared work helped to lessen those difficulties within the unit group, though they would emerge when groups of senior officers came to see the new methods at work. At one such meeting a visitor questioned somewhat sarcastically our low estimate of the intelligence of a candidate who had been the successful trainer of some well-known racehorses. "How could we account for that discrepancy?" Bion replied with a twinkle in his eye that "perhaps the man thought like a horse!" Bion's strength, however, would appear when he felt a criticism had a malevolent tone. Challenged about a psychiatric opinion on a similar occasion, he replied with considerable acerbity that he did not propose to defend the professional status of himself or his colleagues, whereupon the retreat was both rapid and apologetic.

At that time, it was the common practice in applied psychology to think of a vocational selection task as requiring on the one hand a job analysis from which the qualities required could be identified and, on the other, the devising of tests to measure these traits or qualities. Such a view had little appeal to those of us who had come to understand personality functioning in a very different way. When Trist joined us he conceptualized the selection task as, first, describing the basic features of the candidate's personality with all its uniqueness and, second, matching this picture of the man with the demands of the army. An underlying philosophy of this kind had been there from the start and, indeed, had been one of the reasons for the psychodynamic psychiatrists being recruited. When I went with Hargreaves and Rodger,[1] to discuss with the Adjutant-General, Sir Ronald Adam, and the General Officer in Charge of the Army in Scotland, General Sir Andrew Thorne, I had been deeply impressed by the wisdom and acuteness of their minds. They were fully alive to the complexities of appraising people. Sir Ronald Adam said we must not be daunted by the complexity of the job; it was of the greatest importance and if we were not in time to win the war, the work might help to win the peace. General Thorne emphasized that no methods must go after stereotypes and so deprive the army of its eccentrics. It was clear to both of these top-ranking generals that a great range of personalities could not only make valuable officers but was necessary for creative developments within such a multifarious institution as the army.

Trist's conceptualization of the task highlighted the problem of how to get data on what was basic in the officer. The technical side could go some way towards this goal through their interviews and psychological tests; the military members had more difficulty in getting data on which to make an opinion. It was here that Bion's genius showed up. I knew well that Bion had been wrestling hard from the start with this problem. Although he was a very private person, as Trist says, he kept remarking on the need to judge the "quality of contact" the candidate had with others. With his reserved way of communicating his ideas, and the highly condensed, almost cryptic, way in which he spoke of them, it took me some time to get at what he was after. I had learned early on that his terse statements stemmed from a great deal of hard thinking. He wanted to get at a crucial quality which was as his later words put it, "a man's capacity for maintaining personal relationships in a situation of strain that tempted him to disregard the interests of his fellows for the sake of his own." There was no doubt that his experience as a combatant officer in World War I, under the greatest of stress at times, was now fusing with his psychotherapeutic understanding. The popular way of trying to get some evidence on this general question, what kind of man was the candidate, was to ask in interview what he would do in certain imaginary situations. Bion's solution was the Leaderless Group method. Before it acquired this name, he tried it out by asking small groups to have a discussion. At first he was alone with the group, then he invited us one at a time to join him as observers. I can recall vividly how stunned I was by the simplicity of the notion, and yet what a stroke of genius it was to create in this way a living manifest sample of personal relationships in a situation in which the conflict between self-interest and a concern for others was an active reality. This was the man in actual open relationships with others and not within the constriction of the formal interview or test situation. As Trist points out, it had the added merit of making a radical change in the mode of working for the whole team because everyone could now relate opinions from a basis of shared experience of the

[1]The former from the Tavistock staff, and now the major innovative mind in the War Office psychiatric group under Brigadier J. R. Rees, and Rodger, a socially oriented psychiatrist with whom I had worked in Glasgow and now the psychiatrist to the Army Command in Scotland.

candidate in spontaneous interaction. From the discussion group, the method was quickly used with other situations, especially with practical tasks out of doors as the kind of setting with which the military staff was most familiar.

When the unit moved to near London to facilitate the training of staff for the many new Boards being set up, Bion was naturally hoping he would have more opportunities for training and developing the work. The blow he received (see Trist 1985) when he saw how he was to be cramped by the administrative arrangements angered him intensely. He felt there was a "sell-out" of the real importance of the development of the work by a special staff group in its own experimental unit. The staff who had been involved were now to be more like "sales representatives" or Inspectors, visiting other Boards to help them to use the "right technique." This was intolerable to Bion, who had to have his own thinking rooted in constant interplay with practice.

It was very difficult to understand why it had all happened. There were, of course, all the factors of the kind Bion was alive to, the envy and fear of creative ideas, and so forth. At the same time one had to ask whether he had contributed to the situation? There was only one way in which he may have done so; namely, in his own uncompromising attitudes on issues of this kind and in a reluctance to expand on the implications of his ideas so that it was not easy for the administration to work out their implementation with him. This is a very difficult issue on which to pass judgment. If the "establishment" of an institution, the term he was to adopt later in relation to the acceptance of new ideas, is not ready for innovation, then it crushes the disturbing source in one way or another. Not infrequently one argument used is that the creative innovator cannot be trusted to be "practical" about the changes or to deal effectively with the people who would be affected.

Bion may have been labelled in this way before the Research and Training Unit left Edinburgh because there had been a growing strain between him and the President there. The latter had begun to complicate his own role by behaving increasingly like an "amateur psychiatrist"—the term used by the soldiers as a cautionary "what not to do" in their own role—for example, in wanting various "experiments" tried out to which Bion objected on the grounds that they were using technical staff time in unprofitable work. His rather self-contained attitude may also have made the central administration feel uncertain of how he would operate if given full scope. Rees and Hargreaves had had Bion as a colleague in the prewar Tavistock Clinic and may have thought from this experience he was not "extroverted" enough to win the support of the wide range of senior officers the occupant of the senior post in the new unit would have to meet. He was certainly totally uninterested in, if not actively hostile to, playing politics. Such doubts, however, were an inadequate justification for thinking that he might not have been a realistic manager of a project with which he was so identified, and particularly in view of his previous record as a combatant officer. Perhaps if his thinking about all those aspects of groups related to power and the resistance to innovation had been more advanced, some of the sabotage meted out to his creative and courageous endeavours might have been obviated.

For Bion, there was a limit to compromise if the new ideas were to be given an adequate opportunity, and his extraordinary sensitivity to the unconscious negative forces around him had convinced him that nothing would mitigate them enough short of debasing his work, whose urgent importance at this stage in the war he appreciated with deep passion. In other situations he would have been tolerant of such resistance as he met. I am reminded, for instance, of meeting him once in a corridor of the Tavistock Clinic after the war when various members of staff were "taking groups," ostensibly following his inspiration. We were outside the door of a room in which a great deal of laughter was to be heard from a therapeutic group. Sensing the superficial use of his work that could be made even by close colleagues, Bion remarked, "Now that's a 'good' group—not like mine!"

I had been close to Bion during the whole of 1942; then, for the next 3 years, my contacts with him were few. The loss of his first wife in 1944 after the birth of a daughter was a dreadful blow. One felt fate was now carrying on the cruel experiences he had had. When he got his work established after the war he acquired a small house in the country with a housekeeper to look after the child. Though not an ideal arrangement, it gave him some quietness to find himself again and soon his extraordinarily resilient creative urge could be seen.

My contact with him resumed with the end of the war when the Tavistock Group[2] began to plan its future. Bion's deep commitment to pursue his understanding of human behaviour began to surface through his mourning. He asked me to join Rickman and himself in a trial "study group" (as it would be described later) with a membership of ten drawn from senior management in industry and other organizations by A. K. Rice, who was then working for the Industrial Welfare Society. Here I experienced Bion in action with a group that had few inhibitions about expressing its feelings, mainly very sceptical, for many months. Rickman and I felt ourselves lagging behind Bion's comments, yet we could appreciate how much his thinking had been developing. In spite of the denial mechanisms in the group, the impact was profound; two members got duodenal ulcer symptoms before the group finished and three decided to have personal analysis subsequently!

These effects served to bring out the depths of Bion's sensitivity and the validity of his conception of the close relation between the physical and mental at the primitive levels prominent in the group. His role was a stressful one much of the time and Rickman and I were not sufficiently on his wavelength to take the pressure off. He referred frequently in the group to the striking splits and

[2]The term applied to those members of the prewar Tavistock Clinic Staff who had been most involved in the development of the psychiatric services in the army along with a few recruits to the group who had no previous connection with the Tavistock, mainly Trist, Bowlby, and myself.

denials in the perception of what was happening, splits that he was relating in his mind to the earliest levels of development. It was in this group I first heard him comment on the irrational attitude to time so typical of the basic assumptions. The keenness of his sensitivity was all the more remarkable for a man still coming to terms with the loss of his wife and the absence of a normal home background. Thus while he habitually kept his painful feelings to himself, I well recall a very poignant occasion at this period when he was visiting my home. He said quite spontaneously, "You think you are out of it; then there is a day when everything brings it all back and you relive it all again."

On leaving the army, Bion resumed his training as a psychoanalyst at the London Institute. He continued to work with groups in the Tavistock Clinic though he did not wish to continue as a staff member, especially as it was to become a unit within the National Health Service. He had every reason to be chary of bureaucratic control and he seemed to be eager to give priority to his psychoanalytic work, for he did not stay within the independent Tavistock Institute either. His personal circumstances fortunately took a very favourable turn soon after he completed his analytic training. In 1952 his marriage began a sustaining relationship that brought him deep happiness. Also, he acquired the support of a group of Kleinian colleagues who, if not all sharing his interest in groups, did respond with active cooperation in his working out of some of the primary developmental processes in the individual. His creativity was very much the product of his own struggles and a group of even the most desirable colleagues could impose a certain pressure upon him, especially when he sensed there was a wish to keep him as a leader with the obligations that entailed. At any rate, that was the gist of some of the very last remarks I had from him shortly before he left for California in 1968. It may have been one element, if only a minor one, in the many that led to his decision to leave England.

Before turning to his work on groups, I should like to comment on Bion's apparent departure from the group field. It has often been thought that he gave up his interest in groups for the study of the individual in the psychoanalytic situation. I do not believe there was any break for him. Many years later he talked about Freud's remark on the "caesura of birth"—that there is much more continuity in development than the impressive act of birth would have us believe. The change was essentially the next step he felt his work required.

Bion's Switch from the Group Back to the Individual

As with Freud, Bion's dedication was to the human condition, as can be seen from the extent to which he was steeped in history and philosophy. What he observed in the group and within the psychoanalytic situation constituted a binocular vision of the same phenomena. The basic assumptions in the group crystallized for him replicas of the emotions with which the infant related to the mother and, later, the family. He emphasized that, while they provided a convenient way of ordering some of the phenomena in the groups, they were the product of complex fusions of emotions and ideas. That they derived from the earliest levels of psychological development he inferred from the strength and the quality of the emotions, along with the fact that the psychic and somatic expressions were closely interlocked. There was also the striking avoidance of any learning that they induced when they were dominant. The group revealed these primitive developmental phenomena with great clarity. Indeed, Bion stated that he knew of no situation in which the hatred of learning was more striking than in the group when in the grip of these basic emotions. Nevertheless, for the elucidation of the factors from which the basic assumptions were created, it was for him the microscopic vision of the intrapsychic that would be most productive. Accordingly, it was eminently understandable for him to transfer his attention to where these early phases of development could best be studied, namely in the psychoanalytic pair. This change of focus certainly coincided with an increasing absorption in the earliest stages of psychological development because of his own analysis with Melanie Klein. When he came to review his group papers about 2 years after he had written them there was such a marked linking of his previous views with Klein's theories that it was sometimes thought her work had influenced him too much. This opinion has to be assessed against a background of several considerations.

In the first place, Bion's decision to have Melanie Klein as his analyst was based on a considerable knowledge of her work. She had made a revolutionary impact on the psychoanalytic scene in London before the war and his first analyst, John Rickman,[3] had had a period of analysis with her, although he never became a "Kleinian." Her writings on the child's inner world of phantastic *objects* (parents and parts of parents), both good and bad, its intense emotional idealizations as well as its ruthless destructiveness, and the psychotic or splitting mechanisms used from the start in coping with the associated anxieties and impulses, could certainly make a profound appeal to someone all too familiar with the human scene from his psychotherapeutic experience, his knowledge of history, an intense involvement as a combatant in the most destructive war man had ever known, and now confronted with group behaviour, whose severance from reality made it describable only in terms of psychotic disorder. The splitting processes she stressed as characteristic of the earliest relationships with the breast-mother, with their projections and introjections, certainly fitted the savagery of the human scene. She also illuminated the way in which primitive

[3]Rickman had a keen interest in field theoretical concepts in his understanding of the individual. He had been in a Quaker ambulance unit in Russia in the latter part of World War I, where, although a noncombatant, he had been on the point of being shot after the Revolution started. They were both large impressive men who shared many attitudes and views, although I doubt that he was a major creative influence on Bion's thought; he was more a kindred soul. He had a more maternal component in his personality than Bion, which often made me think of him as the father of all mother figures, and Bion as the mother of all father figures. He published many psychoanalytic papers and collaborated with Geoffrey Gorer, the well-known anthropologist, in writing a book *The Peoples of Great Russia*.

internalized objects were projected into parts of the body, which then became the source of tension and anxiety leading to hypochondria and psychosomatic disorder. In short, her experience of these early processes as revealed in the phantasy play and behavioural difficulties of very young children matched closely what Bion felt when in contact with the primitive processes in groups.

Alongside her penetration into the role of the instinctive drives in the development of the infant's object relations, Melanie Klein in her writings had described the effects of disturbed emotional development on the child's *epistemophilic instinct*, her term for the dynamic origins of intellectual growth in relation to reality. The earliest object relations greatly affected the child's capacity to use symbols and so were crucial in facilitating the child's general intellectual development, its whole ability to learn from an enriching experience with reality. To Bion, it was the activation of these earliest emotions in the group that blocked learning and development. Klein had made her advances through the analysis of the play of young children whose phantasy life was vividly open to the interested student, as well as being much less overlaid with the experience of many years of ever-widening involvement with reality. In her first formulations, chiefly concerned with the factors causing inhibitions in intellectual growth, she did not elucidate the processes in the normal acquisition of knowledge. In her use of the term *psychotic mechanisms*, however, she stressed a mode of relating to reality that was dominated by universal processes belonging to the inner world. While these are modified in the course of ordinary interaction with reality, they persist openly in the schizophrenic as the result of various mismatches between the strength of the instincts and the failure of appropriate responses to them by the mother and, later, the family. Moreover, this persistence of psychotic mechanisms was much more widespread than was realized. Indeed, they were for Klein the chief underlying factor in the neuroses and character disorders, although commonly missed in the analysis of these conditions because of the degree of covering-up to avoid the intense anxiety associated with them.

In short, Melanie Klein's theories had a high degree of validity and relevance for Bion apart from any undue influence she might have exerted through being his analyst. It is true that her own pioneering courage and single-mindedness, qualities that appealed to Bion, were reflected in her associates, in whom she fostered inevitably a proselytizing zeal. Those qualities are necessary if new ideas are to be spread and developed, though the obvious danger is that there may be too little scrutiny of them. Bion was much too powerful and independent a person and a thinker to take up ideas without a deep critical evaluation of their relevance in making order out of the confusing phenomena of the earliest levels of psychological development. His appraisal of her views was his own and based on his own data.

There is one aspect that is at least of historic interest. He told me on the last occasion I saw him, not long before he left England, that, during his analysis and subsequently, he had felt Klein to be out of sympathy with, if not actively hostile to, his work with groups. She thought he was being diverted from more important psychoanalytic work. He could scarcely have convinced her, of course, of its value as a field for the study of psychotic mechanisms, bearing in mind her complete lack of clinical involvement with group phenomena—and, indeed, her tendency to underplay the role of the social environment in her theorizing. At any rate, Bion was not deterred from writing his *Experiences in Groups*!

When Bion did turn to the early levels of development, he soon focused on those around learning from experience problems for which there was no adequate psychoanalytic theory. The hatred of learning when the basic assumptions were active had struck him as a major impediment to work activity in the group, and further progress with his group studies would be held up because of this lack.

The readiest means of studying the most primitive emotions was in those adults in whom they overwhelmed ordinary rational thought, namely, schizophrenics. Bion accordingly took into analysis a few patients whose degree of disturbance had led to them being certified as psychotic. As he said later, had he known more of what he was going to be in for he would probably have decided against this course. His own epistemophilic drive, along with his extraordinary capacity to retain a sharp and objective sensitivity to what these patients were experiencing, saw him through in face of all his lonely doubts.

BION'S FIRST STATEMENT

Bion's account of his experiences with groups falls into two parts. The first contains the description of his method of work, the phenomena he noted by its use, and his tentative theories evolved to understand these. While he regards his views as an extension of Freud's, his whole thinking has a quite distinctive character. Like Freud, he refers frequently to very different entities by the word *group*, for example, to organizations, or institutions such as the church and the army, and to such an ill-defined grouping as "the aristocracy." These social references introduce so many complex factors that they are best left aside from our immediate concern. The fundamental features of human relationships are embodied in all social groups so that there is no question of the relevance of his references. His theories, however, stem from his observations in his "laboratory," the small group, and it is against the background of this "pure culture" that we have to appraise them.

Taking the origin of the group as the carrying out of its purpose, we note that he refers to two groups, each with a different task as perceived by the members at the start. In one, composed of "nonpatients," the accepted aim was to study group behaviour. In the other, the members were patients seeking help from a medical clinic. The actual situation was that, after an interview, the psychiatrist explained to each patient thought suitable that an understanding of their conflicts in personal relationships could help in the amelioration of their symptoms, because these conflicts were known to be at the root of many of these difficulties. Such understanding was facilitated by meeting in a group in which relationships could be studied as they developed. (Most of the psychiatrists involved had worked with Bion in some of his groups. There is thus a rather tongue-in-the-cheek disingenuousness in some of his remarks about the staff's beliefs! His serious point, however, is that the latter were not always subjected to the questioning that he himself felt they should receive.) It is not always clear at the start which of these two groups he is describing, although their stated tasks are different. To Bion, the use of his approach, that is, one in which the sole activity of the leader or therapist is to make interpretations of the phenomena in the group as these developed, made any difference between the groups irrelevant. The different expectations of members in the opening phase, however, are reflected in the groups. In fact his main references are to the therapeutic groups in which a strictly group-centred stance is stressed.

We readily recognize that the development of his method was in itself a major achievement. With a remarkable courage from his convictions, he showed that a psychoanalytic approach permitted the exposure of unrecognized, irrational, and powerful relationships that were specific to the group situation. Bion was explicit on the highly subjective nature of his method, especially in its use of countertransference feelings and in the detection of projective identification processes wherein the therapist picks up the feelings of the members through what he senses they are projecting into him. As in psychoanalysis, the observer learns to attend to two levels of mental activity: the manifest conscious and the latent subconscious and unconscious. It is its subjectivity especially of this degree that arouses so much antipathy in those who consider that "scientific" research into human relationships can rest only on behavioural data, albeit the ephemeral impingement of many studies of this latter type is in notable contrast with that of Bion's findings. That he had described something that illuminated the depths of group phenomena was clear from the remarkably rapid and widespread interest in his observations. There was little doubt that his work had made a profound stir in the new field of "group dynamics." Nearly four decades later it continues to be as evocative as it was at the start—and a short scan of the history of theoretical views in psychology and the social sciences during the century readily shows that to be a quite unusual distinction.

To sustain the efforts of any group around its task requires in the first place a readiness to cooperate, which, for Bion, is a sophisticated product from years of experience and training. Next, the mental activity required to further the task must be of a particular kind, because judgments about the nature and origin of actual phenomena and actions designed to overcome difficulties presented by them have to be tested against constant interaction with reality. In short, as opposed to any magical solutions, it must involve rational thinking with consequent learning and development, that is, ego activity. It is this capacity to sustain task-focused activity that the unorganized group greatly alters through the persistent interference from competing mental activities associated, in Bion's view, with powerful emotional drives. These conflicting forces at first seemed to have little in common except to oppose the task by creating a group that would satisfy the emotional needs of members as these become prominent. This state of the group Bion termed *the group mentality*, and the way in which it might express itself, for example, to find another leader, he described as *the group culture*. These concepts, however, he soon found did not clarify sufficiently what his further experience perceived, namely, patterns of behaviour that gripped the group into a relatively specific group mentality in opposition to the work activity. Bion named these patterns *basic assumptions* (ba's), of which he identified ba D (dependence), ba F (fight/flight), and ba P (pairing). In the *dependent group*, the basic assumption is that one person is there to provide security by gratifying the group's longings through magic. After an initial period of relief, individuals tend to react against the assumption because of the infantile demandingness and greed it engenders. Nevertheless, when he confronted the group with the dependence assumption taking over, Bion noted that a hostile response to any intervention by him frequently revealed more than a resentment against his refusal to provide the magical pabulum. A longing for a more permanent and comprehensive support was to be seen in the raising of religious themes, with the group feeling that its "religion," in which the therapist is a phantasied deity, was being taken from it. *Fight and flight* appeared as reactions to what the group wanted to avoid, namely, the work activity that forced it to confront the need to develop by giving up primitive magical ideas. The ineffectiveness of these solutions led at times to a different activity, for which Bion postulated the assumption of *pairing*. Pairing occurred repeatedly in his groups in the form of two members, irrespective of sex, getting into a discussion. To his surprise, this was listened to attentively, with no sign of the impatience from members whose own problems usually pressed them to seek the centre of attention for themselves. There seemed to be a shared unconscious phantasy that sex was the aim, with reproduction as a means of meeting a powerful need to preserve the group as a group.

As mentioned, the group dominated by an assumption evolves an appropriate culture to express it, for example, the dependent group establishes a leader who is felt to be helpful in supplying what it wants. Moreover, the assumptions can be strong enough for members to be controlled by them to the extent of their thinking and behaviour becoming almost totally unrealistic in relation to the work task. The group is then for each member an undifferentiated whole into which he is pressed inexorably to conform and in which each has lost his independent individuality. The individual experiences this loss as disturbing, and so the group is in more or less constant change from the interaction of the basic assumptions, the group culture, and the individual struggling to hold on to his individuality.

Basic assumptions originate within the individual as powerful emotions associated with a specific cluster of ideas that compel the individual to behave accordingly and also to be attracted to those imbued with the same feeling with an immediacy that struck Bion as more analogous to tropisms than to purposive behaviour. These bonds Bion termed *valency* because of this chemicallike nature of the attraction.

As primal motivating forces, the basic assumptions supply a fundamental thrust to all activity, yet the drive towards interaction with the real environment remains the more powerful dynamic in the long run, for, without that adaptive urge, survival would not be possible. The difficulties of reality interactions, however, are great. The physical environment may present insoluble problems; but it is the social factors that become prominent in their effects on the capacities of the individual when work demands cooperation with all the give and take that entails. The frustrations in sustaining work activity are thus perpetually liable to induce the regressed behaviour of the assumptions. The more the individual becomes identified with a basic assumption, the more does he get a sense of security and vitality from his fusion with the group, along with the pull back to the shared illusory hopes of magical omnipotent achievement inherent in the phantasies of the assumption. From all these sources there is derived what Bion described as a hatred of learning, a profound resistance to staying in the struggle with the reality task until some action gives the experience of mastery of at least a part of it, that is, until development of new inner resources occurs.

The appeal of each assumption rests in the associated emotion, which gets a characteristic quality from the specific phantasies and ideas it involves. The assumptions do not conflict with each other. Instead, they change from one to another and conflict occurs only between them and the work group. When one ba is combined with work activity, however, the other ba's are suppressed. A further observation Bion made was the way in which the ba group could change to its "dual." Thus the dependent group under the frustrations of the leader's failure to gratify its longings could reverse roles so that the group treated the leader as the one in need of help. In this connection, he also noted the tendency of the dependent group when left to its own devices to choose as leader the most disturbed member, as if it could best depend on someone of its own kind, as dependent as itself—the familiar "genius," madman, or fanatic.

The interrelations of the ba's, plus the tenacity and exclusiveness with which the emotions and ideas are bound together in each ba, led Bion to what he felt was a theoretical impasse, which no available psychological explanation could illumine. He therefore postulated a metapsychological notion that transcends experience in the form of a protomental system in which the prototype of each ba exists "as a whole in which no part can be separated from the rest." The emotion in each individual that starts the ba progresses to the psychological manifestations that can be identified.

The physical and the mental are undifferentiated in the basic levels of this system, a feature that led to his suggestion that certain illnesses, those in which a substantial psychosomatic component has long been recognized, might well be diseases of certain conditions in groups. To test such ideas needed much larger populations than the small group could provide, but he hoped it might be done in order to establish the basic assumptions as clinical entities.

Bion's concluding observations become increasingly concerned with aspects of group dynamics in general, for example, the oscillations in attitudes to the leader as leader of the assumption group or of the work group, or splits in the group, according as members wished to cling to either of these groups. On the relationship of the individual to the group, he agrees with Freud that a group instinct is not primitive and that much of his groupishness originates in his upbringing within the family. Bion adds to these, however, from his observations, the view that, while the group adds nothing to the individual, certain aspects of individual psychology cannot be explained except by reference to the matrix of the group as the only situation that evokes them. The individual loses his distinctiveness when he is in a basic assumption group, that is, one in which his individuality is swamped by the valencies in these. Such a group has to change when it has to deal with realities, or perish.

Earlier I noted that most of Bion's references were to his therapeutic groups, and he states how he believes their aim is furthered. His first and most emphatic view is that any help the individual may get from the group situation towards understanding himself more fully rests on the extent to which he can recognize himself as one torn between the pull of the basic groups and his membership of the work group that represents his ego functioning. For this reason, any interventions from the therapist directed to the psychopathology of the individual must be avoided because they are destructive of the experience of the basic group. He concluded that, by adhering strictly to his standpoint, individuals do become less oppressed by basic group activity within themselves. In other words, what he asserts is that by showing the group the ways in which it avoids its task through regressing to dependency, fight/flight, or pairing, it can become more work oriented and so further the development by learning of all members.

Much of the subsequent criticism of Bion's approach as a psychotherapeutic method arises, I believe, from a failure to keep his aims clear and especially to avoid the confusion which the use of the word therapeutic, and especially psychotherapeutic, has engendered. To those seeking to use the group situation in a psychotherapeutic way, that is, to cope with the enormous diversity of neurotic behaviour and its unique configuration in every individual, then work has to be based on our understanding of psychopathology. The group processes must therefore be directly relatable to the latter. Bion's approach in fact originated in the problem of neurosis as a social one, that is, how does the large organization cope with the failures of its members to comply with its work task. The opening sentences in his book make plain that, for him, group therapy can mean the therapy of individuals in groups, in which case neurosis is the problem of the individual, but in the treatment of the group it has to be a problem of the group.

His conception of group therapy may then be put as follows. The individual contains within his innate endowment certain potential patterns, which are released in the unorganized group. This unorganized group is not a special kind of group identifiable by its external features, but a state of mind that can overtake any group. Once elicited, these patterns or basic assumptions bond the individuals together to give security by preserving the group as a unity and by seeking a course of action for it governed largely by magical phantasies. These patterns remove the individual's distinctiveness, that is, his overall modes of dealing with his purposes as fashioned by his learning from the experience of reality. Because these modes, his ego functioning in short, are always present in some measure, a conflict between his ego and absorption in any basic assumption behaviour is never absent. Such group-determined behaviour is a serious limitation to the individuals in any group when faced with an unfamiliar task, because they then tend to feel in an unorganized group state and find their capacity to tackle that realistically as a group to have become quite unreliable. (The commonest remarks after intensive exposure to the unorganized group situation at Group Relations Conferences run on the Tavistock model are those describing feelings of being "de-skilled.") To have developed a method whereby these group dynamics can be experienced in adequate depth, and to have shown some of the requirements in the leader for the application of this method, is an extremely valuable contribution to the whole study of group dynamics. His findings can assist those responsible for groups coping with tasks to note when their effectiveness is impaired by bad behaviour, and this kind of experience features prominently in many management training schemes.

It is a quite separate issue, however, to appraise the value of the principles underlying Bion's work in relation to the use of groups for analytical psychotherapy. The distinction between the study of group dynamics and group therapy has become a clear one in the courses developed by A. K. Rice and his associates, as was seen, for instance, in the staff attitude to any individual who got into serious personal difficulties during a conference. The staff naturally arranged to get the help needed, but it would not confuse its own role by attempting to provide psychiatric or psychotherapeutic help, especially when psychiatrists or psychoanalysts were members of the staff. The strict use of Bion's approach has never in fact been widely adopted by analytical psychotherapists, not even in the Tavistock Clinic. Many have, however, made more systematic use of the group situation in their interpretations than have most other therapists, in the sense of trying to base these strictly on the here-and-now dynamics in the group situation as a whole.

Although we can agree on a separation of these two tasks, we are left with many unsolved questions that affect our understanding of both. To state that the individual's groupishness is an inherent property in his makeup as a social animal has not really carried forward our understanding of its nature and origin. Are the phenomena of the basic assumptions as specific to the group situation as he asserts? There is no question that, when activated by them, individuals can show a remarkable capacity to abandon their distinctiveness. The group gives a prominence to these responses by intensifying them, yet they do not appear to be different from the primitive relationships that can be seen in individual treatment, especially in the light of our further knowledge of the earliest stages of the development of the person.

One feature of Bion's thought that is unrecognized by him, I believe, is his underlying adherence to concepts of energy as in the classical psychoanalytic theories of Freud. Thus basic assumptions originate as emotions, which are viewed as sources of energy, and Bion is then puzzled by the specific clusters of phantasies around them. Phantasies are of imagined relationships, and if we take emotions to be the effective colouring accompanying any relationship, then their specific quality is determined by the specifics of the relationships. The dependence and pairing assumptions are much more complex in this respect than the others. They can be readily seen as the prototypes of human relationships, for example, as infantile dependence in which the self and the object are not differentiated, becoming the more differentiated clinging or attachment to a differentiated object in ba pairing. Fight and flight are the basic responses of all animals to the situation that evokes pain or the threat of danger. Bion seems to sense the problem of the individual and the group as needing a good deal of further clarification, and the choice he made for his next step was to turn his microscope, to use his own metaphor, back to the earliest stages of individual development. This move leads to a major amplification in his understanding of the dynamics of all groups.

THE REVIEW OF THE FIRST STATEMENT

In his review of the dynamics of the group, Bion (1961) "hopes to show that in his contact with the complexities of life in a group the adult resorts, in what may be a massive regression, to mechanisms described by Melanie Klein as typical of the earliest phases of mental life." This task of establishing "contact with the emotional life of the group . . . would appear to be as formidable to the adult as the relationship with the breast appears to be to the infant, and the failure to meet the demands of this task is revealed in his regression" (pp. 141–142). Two main features of this regression are, first, a belief that the group exists as an entity that is endowed with characteristics by each individual. Distinct individuals become lost and the group is treated as if it were another person. Second is the change within the individual that accompanies his regressed perception of the group. For this change Bion quotes Freud's description of the loss of the individual's distinctiveness, with the addition that the individual's struggle to retain it varies with the state of the group. Organization helps to maintain work-group activity, and indeed that is its aim.

In the work group, individuals remain individuals and cooperate, whereas in the basic assumption group they are swept spontaneously by the valency of identification, the primitive gregarious quality in the personality, into the undifferentiated unity of the group in which inner realities overwhelm the relationship with the real task.

Although starting his review with the regression in groups as their most striking feature, he emphasizes again the fundamental dynamic of the work group, which also has its combination of emotions and ideas, especially the idea that development and the validity of learning by experience is the impetus in the individual to possess the autonomy of his own mental life. It is as if there was a recognition "of the painful and often fatal consequences of having to act without an adequate grasp of reality." Despite the dominant influence of the basic assumptions over it at times, work activity is what takes precedence eventually—as it must. Freud, following Le Bon, believed the intellectual ability of the group was reduced, but Bion disagrees. His experience is that, even when basic assumptions are active, the group shows high-level intellectual work in the assimilation of interpretations. Although this work goes on in a segregated part of the mind with little overt indication, its presence has to be assumed from the way in which interpretations, ostensibly ignored, are nevertheless worked upon between sessions with subsequent reports from individuals of how they had been thinking of them, though they meant nothing at the time they were made. It is only in activity of the work group that words are used normally, that is, with their symbolic significance. The basic assumption groups, by contrast, he thinks, use language as a mode of action and are thereby deprived of the flexibility of thought that development requires.

When he relooks at the basic assumptions, there is considerable amplification in what he now discerns as presenting them. This development is apparently related to his much greater familiarity with primitive mental processes and their detection by an increased responsiveness to projective identification as described by Melanie Klein. He believes this method, which requires a psychoanalytically trained observer, is the only one that can detect the important subjective processes. Conclusions based on its use have to be appraised by the effect of interventions and by the experience of many observers over time.

In the dependent group, he adds to the expectation of treatment from the therapist a much more primitive phantasy of being literally fed by him. At a less primitive level he again stresses the presence of a projected deity who is clung to with tenacious possessiveness. The sexual phantasies which characterized the pairing group, with the possible implication of reproduction as preserving the group, are now taken to be the result of a degree of rationalization. Nevertheless, oedipal sexual phantasies are present much of the time in all of the assumptions. They are not, however, of Freud's classical type, but of the much more primitive nature described by Klein. According to her, the phantasies of very young children show, as the self is emerging in relation to its objects, themes of the parents mutually incorporating parts of each other with the hungry sadistic urges that the child attributes to one or both figures by its identification with them.

The child can then experience a psychotic or disintegrative degree of anxiety from the fear of being the object of retaliatory attacks and so it splits off the part of its self involved in the relationship with an attempt, then, to get rid of it by projective identification. These primitive oedipal relationships according to Bion are distributed in various ways among (i) the individual; (ii) the group felt as one fragmented individual with (iii), a hidden figure, the leader, used here by detaching him from his role as leader of the work group. A further addition to the oedipal figures, one ignored in the classical formulation, is the sphinx—a role carried by the therapist and the work group. The curiosity of the individual about the group and the therapist evokes the dread associated with the infant's phantasied intrusions to get at and to devour what is inside the mother and what goes on in the phantasied primal scene.

The anxieties inherent in the primitive phantasies, sexual and other, are instinctively responded to by an attempt to find "allies," figures with whom the feeling of a close contact can bring reassurance. Bion accordingly suggests this need as a powerful stimulus to the creation of the pairing group. Another factor in its establishment and maintenance, also operative with no regard to the sex of the pair, is the feeling of hope, not a phantasy of a future event, but a "feeling of hope itself." This feeling he takes to be the opposite of all the strong negative feelings of hatred, destructiveness, and despair, and it is sustained by the idea of finding a saviour, a Messiah essentially, an idea that must never be realized.

The fight/flight groups are, as would be expected, much less associated with complex phantasied relationships, since they have the relatively simple aim of getting rid of the threat of danger when no other assumption or activity seems appropriate. On this group Bion makes, almost as an aside, what I find to be a remarkable statement: "The fight/flight group expresses a sense of incapacity for understanding *and the love without which understanding cannot exist*" (my italics). I do not think its full implications are taken up by Bion in regard to the emergence of any of the assumptions and to the role of the leader, topics to which I shall return.

Recognition of their more specific contents leads Bion to reconsider the status of his notions about the basic assumptions. There was no doubt they were helpful in ordering the chaotic manifestations in the group, but, in view of the primitive phantasies related to them, they now appeared as derivatives of these more fundamental processes. All the assumptions drive the group to find a leader, yet none of them is felt to establish a satisfactory state in the group. There is consequently perpetual instability with changes from one assumption to another with all those remaining opposed to learning and development. For all these manifestations, and for their very existence, Bion could find no explanation. The exposure of primitive phantasies and the anxieties they induce now made it clear that the basic assumptions were derivatives whose function is to defend the group against these anxieties becoming too intense. As defences, however, they are all inadequate because of their segregation from any reality testing. For Bion, the dynamics of the group could now be adequately experienced and understood, therefore, only by the working out of these primitive primal scene phantasies as the factors underlying the basic assumptions and their complex interrelationships.

With these developments in his thinking, Bion has moved back to the nature of the individual and his groupishness. The new views brought him again closer to psychoanalysis and it is perhaps significant that their original publication was in *The International Journal of Psycho-Analysis* and not *Human Relations* with its social science readership. They were, of course, sought out, but their crucial position as the culmination of his work on group dynamics did not become widely manifest until 10 years later, when they appeared in his book. The time lag did not affect those students of group dynamics in close contact with his thinking. It helped to perpetuate, I believe, the separation of psychoanalysis and group dynamics when both disciplines needed each other. The obstacles to a wider acceptance stemmed from more profound sources. At the time of their appearance, Kleinian views were resisted among psychoanalysts in general, especially in the United States, and this rejection was scarcely needed to reinforce amongst nonanalysts what they were eminently prone to do by their disturbing unconscious resonances.

Bion always kept Freud's views on groups in mind, and so he now looked at where he stood in relation to these. Leaving aside the references both made to complex social organizations such as the church and the army, he reasserts his agreement with Freud in rejecting the need to postulate a herd instinct. For him the individual is a group animal by nature, yet at war with the group and with those forces in him that determine his groupishness. The latter is in no way created by the group; it is merely activated and exposed by it. The impact of the group on the individual's distinctiveness springs from the state of mind in the group, that is, the degree to which its lack of organization and structure fails to keep work activity, a contact with reality, the dominant activity. In the organized group the bond between members is one of cooperation, whereas in an unorganized state the bonds become the valencies of the basic assumption states. Bion sees McDougall's criteria for the organized group as the conditions that suppress the basic assumption trends in the members by keeping them related to reality. Freud's statement that the individual's emotions are intensified in the group while his intellectual functioning is lowered is not acceptable to Bion. For him the apparent intensification is the effect of tension due to the suppression of the basic assumption emotions. Bion's comment, however, hardly applies to Freud, since he is referring mainly to mobs in which the primitive instincts are released from normal controls.

The bonding from valency is a more primitive process than that from libido, which Bion takes to operate only in the pairing group. Freud's view of the bond to the leader as almost entirely an introjection of him by the ego (Bion does not mention Freud's ego-ideal as a separate structure) is again only part of the relationship to a leader. For Bion, Freud does not recognize the much more potentially dangerous bonding that arises in the assumption groups. Here the individual does not introject a leader who carries power for him through his contact with external reality. The leader in the basic assumption exhibits features that appeal to the assumption state in the members, who therefore projectively identify with him. This leader is thus as much a part of the assumption state as the members and just as divorced from external reality, so that he leads as often to disaster as not. Freud's view of the leader as the ego-ideal led him to see panic in military groups as following the loss of the leader. Bion thinks this account is not right, for panic arises when the situation might as readily give rise to rage as fear. Intense fight/flight behaviour may resemble panic, but for Bion the group can well be still related to the leader on such occasions. Panic occurs when a situation arises completely outwith the purposes of the group and its associated organization.

Bion thus adds to Freud's views rather than refuting them. Freud saw in the group the kind of relationships present in the family when the individual has developed to the stage of the traditional Oedipus complex, that is, its emotional features were neurotic in character with the main sources of anxiety being the fears of loss of love or of being castrated. Bion saw them as deriving from much earlier phases in which the fears are of disintegration, that is, loss of the self or madness. His belief that the only feasible therapeutic help in the group lies in the individual experiencing its primitive emotions and attitudes to him is again maintained. Here we are into debatable issues which I shall return to when the aims of therapy can be considered.

Much as Bion has contributed, we are left with what seem to be the crucial questions about groups unanswered. What does the individual's groupishness rest on? We have Freud's libidinal bonds supplemented by valencies from primitive projective identifications with a great deal about "mechanisms," all manifested as the individual's distinctiveness is removed. This regressed state, moreover, can come and go with a high degree of lability. For Bion, this distinctiveness is placed in opposition to the groupishness conceived as the expression of emotions with which the individual has to be at war. Freud, on the other hand, sees the conflict as between the id and the culture of the individual's society internalized in his superego and ego-ideal. Adult or mature groupishness, if we might put it that way, rests for Bion on cooperation, the sophisticated product of years of training. That is to say, it is like an activity imposed on the freedom of the individual to be "doing his own thing" and accepted more or less reluctantly. How can such an achievement vanish within a few minutes in the unorganized situation of Bion's groups? Both Freud and Bion from their psychoanalytic studies have emphasized that individual and group psychology constitute the same field of study. If we accept that position we are a long way from understanding it. The intimate interrelatedness of the individual with his social field strongly suggests to us that we are dealing with the individual as a highly open system maintained in his organization by appropriate input from a social field itself structured to provide this input. The phenomena seem to require the organization concepts of open systems, which neither Freud nor Bion had.

Freud, however inadequate his theorising may have been, as it was constrained by the scientific climate of his day, is universally recognized as a brilliant observer. I propose therefore to look back to what he said to see what can be taken from his observations.

Having eliminated the need for any such notions as a social or herd instinct, Freud (1921) stated that a psychology of the group had to answer three questions:

1. What is a group?
2. How did it acquire the capacity for exercising such a decisive influence over the mental life of the individual?
3. What is the nature of the mental changes which it forces upon the individual?

The latter is the one that is best studied first, and it is the one with which observers of group phenomena such as Freud and Bion are most concerned. Freud's data were largely the writings of Le Bon, McDougall, and Trotter, which he related to his own knowledge and experience of social behaviour, especially from the phenomena of transference. Groups brought together for the specific task of direct psychoanalytic observation had not yet occurred.

The changes made by the group were described by Freud in two different ways. At first, apparently influenced by Le Bon's description of mobs, he sees individuals in the group released from the inhibitions of civilization, with the consequent emergence of the unbridled instincts. He recognizes, however, that the same conditions can activate intense effort and self-sacrifice for the group's ideals. In other words, the group can convert the individual into one identified with all its members in the regressed expression of the repressed, or with its opposite, the repressing structure of the superego, although the latter can scarcely be regarded as regressed, at least in the sense used about the id. These changes do not fit well into any notion of a social instinct, or behavioural system, activated or inhibited by a social stimulus. They represent more of an organizational change in the personality from the normal degree of integrated functioning to one in which intense emotions are prominent and shared by the group and in which identification is a dominant mode of relating.

On how the changes are made, Freud rejects the concept of suggestibility as tautological and brings forward his libido theory, libido being his hypothetical instinctive energy that impels people into all the relationships commonly described as love. In using this theory, Freud has moved away from loose aggregates or mobs to highly organized, lasting groups in which he points out that role of leader is paramount. Thus in the Christian church or in an army, each individual has a bond of love with the leader and consequently all have a bond of identification with each other, that of brothers within the leader's family.

The leader, moreover, may be replaced by an idea or an ideal. This move to the group with a leader alters the description of the changes forced upon the individual to the following: "the individual, outside the primitive group, possessed his own continuity, his self-consciousness, his traditions and customs, his own particular functions and position, and he kept apart from his rivals. Owing to his entry into an 'unorganized' group he had lost this distinctiveness for a time" (Freud 1921, p. 86). Freud uses these two examples to bring out differences in the relationship with the leader and the associated characteristic of the behaviour when the group disintegrates. In the military situation, the loss of the leader can release "a gigantic and senseless fear" progressing to a panic, a reaction that cannot be interpreted as always due to the increase in external danger. The religious group, with a corresponding loss or threat to the leader or his ideals, does not produce fear. Instead a ruthless hostility is mobilized to those not sharing the group's ideals.

While the role of the leader is undoubtedly central, the nature of the libidinal bonds between him and the group remained for Freud rather mysterious. He was struck by their close affinities to hypnosis as a libidinal bond without conscious sexual trends to the powerful father, yet he also recognized the paralysed feeling of helplessness in the hypnotic bond as closely resembling the submission of the child to its parent. And beyond that, the "extreme passion for authority in the group" seemed to bring in the archaic residues of the dreaded father in the primal horde. With the bond to the leader being of the same nature as that of an idealized object, Freud defines the primary group as one in which the leader is put by all in place of their ego-ideal. The leader thus embodies the group ideal and is inextricably mixed with the aims of the group, both as the one who defines the task and as the one who will lead the group towards its successful resolution. The psychological situation within each member of these groups, however, is different. The soldiers are dependent on the actual presence of the leader for the survival of the group. On his disappearance, each member becomes totally disorganized and disconnected from everyone; and though this state may be seen as the response of any individual to an inescapable external danger, Freud points out that it happens in this group only as a result of the loss of the bond with the leader. This bond consisted in the replacement of their ego-ideal by the leader and we cannot but conclude that the organization of what is bonded to the leader in this situation resembles that of the young child to its parents in the quality of the powerful dynamic nature of the dependence on omnipotent parents. Without their manifest presence when stress has reached a critical point, the disintegration feared by the child increases with the terror of isolation. The inner situation of the group members, in short, is here that of a structural replica of this dependence which is too immature for them to function autonomously once it is not maintained by the reinforcement of the real external support. The ego-ideal has thus an immature status as well as the ego.

The bonding in the religious group has a different content according to Freud. Here the members are not only related to the leader or the ideal through these replacing their ego-ideal, they are also identified with him. The personality organization that is here tied to the leader has a more developed character in that it has assimilated the ideals so that they have become a part of this organized self. Moreover, the presence of the ideal is felt to be a matter of life or death in that its preservation has to be fought for at all costs, whether by the group or by the individual alone. The individuals in these two groups, as well as having different bonds, are in different situations externally and internally. What we see in the soldiers is a response from a group in which their distinctive identity has already been systematically diminished so that in the situation Freud described there is a predisposed state of immature dependence. Functioning is conditional upon the support of a highly personalized relationship with the leader. The religious group is promised great rewards for a course of conduct prescribed by the ideals and so enhances the individual's distinctiveness, albeit in conditional ways. Freud does not elaborate on the implications of his observations, yet he has made fundamental comments on the integration of the individual and its maintenance. He has shown that the individual keeps his distinctiveness by having built into the structure of his personality an imago of his parents, that is, an internalized representation of his social relatedness. Moreover, this inner imago has an open interchangeable relationship with external figures or ideas. The groupishness of the individual is thus placed as a dynamic within him which has developed from an early phase of almost complete dependence to one less comprehensive. Though stressing the highly tentative and limited status of his study of groups, Freud has reached conclusions of great significance. He has made it clear that what happens in any group is a particular instance of the relationship between the individual's inner world and his social world. Thus he has answered his questions about the group by expanding an answer to the unstated question of what is an individual. He had to advance the theory of the ego and its relationships by showing that a subsystem within the ego, the ego-ideal, entered into relationships that differed in character from those of the ego. Moreover, the most striking feature from his conclusions is the open and rapid dynamic transactions that can occur in the group whereby the individual, sensing his own inability and that of the other members to act effectively, can promptly alter the boundary of his self to internalize the leader as a part of it and so to surrender his previous distinctiveness in favour of a less mature organization of his self. Viewed in terms of Freud's metapsychology, and the metascience available to him, with the dynamics of the person based upon the redistribution of psychic energies, the phenomena could not be adequately conceptualized. We are clearly confronted again with problems of the organization of the individual as a highly open system in an environment that reacts with him in a correspondingly open way. Individual and environment are structured by, and within, each other.

To account for the group phenomena, both Freud and Bion have gone back to the dynamic structuring of the individual. Both have left many questions unanswered. Freud pays little or no attention to the individual's relationship to the common purpose other than to bring in McDougall's requirements for the organized group as the way in which he best furthers his contribution. Bion sees the grip of the reality task for the work group, like Freud's soft voice of the intellect, not resting till it has gained a hearing. His basic assumptions take over from the effects of valency, likened to a tropism, yet establishing a group mentality which has a much more purposeful quality than would arise in any lemminglike way. Both, of course, had views of the individual conditioned by their times. Recent trends in psychoanalysis, while not providing an agreed account, do give a different perspective on the dynamics of the individual in his groups. Of crucial importance for our evaluation of Bion's views in regard to therapy is how the experience of the individual's groupishness relates to the psychotherapeutic task for which *the therapist has suggested his joining the group*. For this purpose, I give in the next section a very sketchy and brief outline of the nature of his groupishness and of how his psychopathology enters into the group situation.

RECENT TRENDS IN PSYCHOANALYTIC CONCEPTIONS OF THE INDIVIDUAL AND HIS SOCIAL RELATEDNESS

Clinical work and child-observation studies of the last few decades have shown that the personality acquires the capacity to make effective relations with others only when there has been early experience of being treated as a "person" by the mother, and the father later, with stimulating encouraging interactions conveyed with joy. The satisfaction of physical needs has to be supplemented by a social input that meets the need "to become a person." There appears to be from an early stage an overall gestalt that gives to the potential self a feeling of "things being right or not." Bodily sensations and the affects accompanying many specific behavioural systems all contribute to the affective tone in the self, yet a general malaise, even to the point of death, can follow from a failure in "being personalized" by appropriate mothering. Child studies show the dramatic results under certain conditions of deprivation, for example, when a consistent maternal relationship is absent (see Spitz 1965). Clinical findings from the more seriously distorted personalities emphasize lifelong feelings of never having been valued for themselves as with cold or indifferent mothers or, more frequently, with mothers experienced as imposing preconceptions that denied powerful urges to develop autonomously (see Lichtenstein 1977). The self-system is thus structured by the internalization of the relationship with mother and child, undifferentiated at the start then progressively separated throughout the long period of human dependence.

Early structuring of the personality is inevitably dominated by the physical closeness in which the mother's attitudes are communicated through innumerable signals in her whole handling of, and responses to, her child. The emotional experiences are gradually cohered by consistent reliable mothering into a "primary or central self." This integration is a labile process with threats to it producing at times intense anxiety and aggression. Negative feelings from the inevitable frustrations are separated from this primary self, but with ordinary care these divisions are diminished so that a sufficiently coherent, resilient self becomes the dominant mediator in relating to the environment. The primary self remains the visible self, the one adapted to the mother. Should the latter have failed to facilitate development sufficiently well, this primary self acquires distortions of its capacity to relate, and when negative experiences have been strong enough, substantial divisions within the structure of the self-system are formed. These subselves embody frustrated needs, especially for unmet recognition as a valued person, and the aggressive reactions to the frustrating mother linked with fears of her talion retaliation. The self-systems each retain a self pole and an object pole, with an imago of the kind of parent desired or feared and hated. The primary self relates to the outer world and so learns from its expanding experience. The subselves, while remaining highly dynamic as portions of the original self, have to find covert outlets—the processes described in the whole of psychopathology—because their aims have to be hidden from the feared parental attacks.

Defences or control measures are evolved by the central self in keeping with its reality pressures and incorporated into its patterning. When the urges cannot be managed in this way then they constitute a secret self in conflict with the central one. Stabilizing factors such as family and work, or selected social groups, all assist in their control though the precarious balance shows when the functioning of the central reality-related self is altered as by drugs or by changes in the social environment. The central self ordinarily copes with changes in sections of the latter but removal of security-pinnings from it rapidly leads to the emergence of subsystem dominance.

When the imagos constituting the object poles in the inner relationships are facilitative, then the impact of infantile sexuality is worked through without undue trouble. Marked divisions in the self make for serious difficulties because the new urges to closeness are dealt with in their terms, for example, hostile imagos evoke anxieties about rejection and retaliation and so lead to the fusion of aggression and sexuality in sadistic and perverse expression in which the object becomes in varying measure depersonalized.

The essential change in this way of conceiving the person is from one based on theories of psychic energies to one dealing with the organization of experience of relationships in an open system interacting with the social environment. Because of the incomplete differentiation of self and object, relations in the primary self are characterized by identifications and urges to have omnipotent magical control with regressive clinging to objects for security against the threat of "going to bits." With growing appreciation of reality and differentiation of self and others, the primary self is progressively superseded by a strengthened definition of the self through satisfactions from talents and skills. Attachments to others changes to relationships based on shared activities. Goals and purposes become organized, and values add to the integration of the self. The personality acquires its characteristic configuration, that is, its identity (see Erikson 1959), and in keeping with the uniquely evolved patterns from its specific experience, the individual requires constant affirmation from the social milieu. The constant need for this "psychosocial metabolism" in maintaining a normal degree of effective integrated functioning is readily exposed when sections of the environment are removed, quite apart from any interference with the biologically rooted sexual and procreational needs. Populations displaced from their usual cultural setting show widespread indications of disorganization as in the rise of illnesses of all kinds, not only psychiatric. Again, when individuals lose a feeling of personal significance in their work, similar stress manifestations occur (see Trist and Bamforth 1951). These deprivations disorganize the most developed adaptive functioning of the social self leading to the increased dominance of the primary self with its insecurities and more primitive compulsive relations. Such regressive disorganization is almost universal. With individuals whose subsystems are a constant threat, the loss of their usual sources of relative security confronts them with the extra dangers of their "secret" selves being exposed.

The origin and nature of the individual's groupishness is thus no problem. From the very start he cannot survive without his needs for social relatedness being met.

As happens so often, Freud makes a remarkable description of the individual in relation to the group. He notes McDougall's conditions for the organized group as (1) a continuity of existence; (2) the individual should know the nature, composition, functions, and capacities of the group; (3) the group should interact with other groups partly similar and partly different in many respects; (4) it should possess traditions, customs, and habits, and especially such as determine the relations amongst members; and (5) the group should have a definite structure, exposed in the specialization and differentiation of the functions of its constituents. As stated previously, Freud (1922) takes these as precisely the features that characterize the individual and which are removed by the unorganized group. In short, although he could not fit it into his theories, he apparently sensed that the group and the individual structure each other in the closest possible way.

There is no phase in the life-cycle in which man can live apart from his groups. Bion's statement that the individual is at war "with himself for being a group animal and with those aspects of his personality that constitute his 'groupishness' " therefore has to be examined.

GROUP DYNAMICS AND GROUP PSYCHOTHERAPY

Group Dynamics

From the view of the individual I have sketched, the important questions about groups are those devoted to the conditions that take away the factors in the social environment that ordinarily keep his self-system in its normal integration. Bion stated that the basic assumptions are states of mind the individuals in the group get into. He then described these states and what seemed to constitute them. What he uncovered was the emergence of the primary mechanisms of relatedness, those of the developing infant to the breast-mother, and it is the intense anxieties associated with these mechanisms that drive the group into the assumptions. The individual's state of mind in them, however, remains a more developed organization than would pertain exclusively to their earliest phase. In the latter, differentiation of external objects hardly exists, whereas in the assumptions there are intense needs to relate to a leader and to each other. The phase in development that appears to be activated here is that of separation-individuation (Mahler 1975). As described earlier, this phase extends over several years, and a range in the depth of regression is to be expected. The dominant characteristic of this early self is its primal "instinctive" type of relationship, the precursors of the maturer ones in which the external reality of others is appreciated. The more the developmental elaborations around the earliest structures are put out of action the more primitive the levels that are exposed. Ba dependence can be interpreted as the reemergence of this stage in which the need for closeness gives to identifications a considerable urgency and immediacy; and the phantasy clusters around them represent the ways in which this is evoked, for example, by being fed, or protected, or held in parental security. Fight/flight responses similarly show this level of identification to provide security. As Bion described, the urgency of the identifications can make the whole group an undifferentiated object within which the greatest security is to be found. Pairing is clearly a more developed state in which more precise definition of the self is sought in the relationship with one other. At the deepest levels it can activate the mother–child pair, in which case the attraction affirms the existence of the self. As he puts it, an ally against the dreads of isolation in face of mounting anxiety is then provided. The fact that the rest of the group preserves it by giving the pair their rapt attention suggests that for them it has become their security, either from the primitive relationship or by this combined with the parental sexual couple, by identifying with the pair.

Regression to these stages represents the removal of the influence of later structuring and an inability to recover it. The awareness of the group remains in its regressed form because the group is there and so restrains further disintegration which would be tantamount to psychotic states, an eventuality that the early structuring of the self also resists desperately. The problems of group dynamics thus become those of how the normal affirmations of the self-system are removed. The situations of groups in this respect are of almost infinite variety. Thus when Bion said that certain illnesses might originate as diseases of the group, he thought specific illnesses might prove to be linked to specific states of the group. So far this has not been established, though there is much evidence now to show that disruptions of some areas of their normal relatedness, as in groups displaced from their familiar environment, lead to increased illness of all kinds, physical and psychological. In view of this complexity of factors, it is best for present purposes to consider Bion's groups only. Here the most prominent stem from the task. Although there may have been some nominal description such as "to study group processes," none of the members has any clear notion of what that task involves. There is therefore immediately a considerable loss for the self of its ego anchorage in reality. Important also is the realization that the task, in whatever form it emerges, will involve members in some exposure of their private and even hidden self. This factor I believe to be important in the "group dynamics" group, although much more so in the therapeutic one. Since the origin of the secret self was its unacceptability, there is a great deal of anxious suspicion among members, alleviated only as each member demonstrates his participation in the task by the freedom with which he expresses some of his feelings about the situation. Likewise the intense curiosity about the leader derives from wondering how he is going to help them with the task at its reality level and from the fears of what he will "read into their minds" and how persecutory or rejecting he will then be.

What characterized Bion's method of work is his waiting for developments to occur spontaneously no matter what the pressures on him "to help." There is no doubt his stance exposed the regressed basic states with, at times, considerable intensity and persistence. For him it is imperative that members should experience the primitive nature and power of these states, and to have contact with these layers of his personality contributes a great self-integration in that the boundaries of his self understanding are thereby extended. By focusing exclusively on the group, however, it is only those features in the shared assumption states that are noted. Such recognition is essential, but to learn more about how they are brought into being is as important.

Freud had noted early in his experience how individuals will only with the greatest reluctance give up a source of gratification. The group's hatred of learning has this quality for Bion when he confronts them with clinging to assumption behaviour instead of learning to cope with reality. In emphasizing this reaction we have, however, to balance it with the impetus to develop, the impetus which in the work group Bion notes as eventually overcoming the irrational resistances to it. We may then ask if Bion fosters an exaggerated degree of basic assumption behaviour by not giving help sooner. This is a question not easily answered. I referred earlier to his almost incidental remark on love as a necessity for understanding, that is, in this context, some fostering assistance. Bion was an extremely caring person and so one is left wondering whether he was in part fascinated by the assumption behaviour to the neglect of this aspect of how much help from the leader the egos of the members required to be reasserted for the learning task.

The assumptions made about the leader's role is that the group will by itself progressively learn to tackle the reality of the task through the leader pointing out what it is doing. Since, however, much of the overt behavior is determined by the need to avoid unrecognized feelings, these must require more explicit interpretation than Bion gives. Interpretations would seem to need more of a *because clause* (Ezriel 1952)—an attempt to identify what it is that is feared. Without this help the work group cannot function effectively. A group met to study its dynamics is like any other task group, a sociotechnical system, and here, as elsewhere, the technical job has to come into the sphere of the ego's resources for mastering and using it. The specific complexity of this situation is that undoing the depersonalizing of the members because of their lost ego-involvement is itself the aim of the "technology." A degree of understanding does go on much of the time, but it has to be asked whether it is at optimal proportions; especially when once in the grip of the basic assumptions it is all the more difficult to get back to normal ego-functioning. It thus seems that, as in analytical psychotherapy, a simultaneous relationship with the members' egos and the regressed state has to be kept alive.

When Bion referred to the struggle of the individual against his groupishness, we can put this in another way. The groupishness he describes is clearly that of the regressed separation-individuation stage from which the individual has developed to inhabit his adult distinctive identity. This new development, however, has its own needs for group relatedness, namely, in groups in which his identity is affirmed and enriched by the extent of the ego's reality involvement in them.

The situation created in Bion's groups takes away the anchorage of the adult self-identity and it has to be asked then whether the groupishness that is resented is so because of this loss. The self-identity requires identification by others of its ordinary status plus the engagement with the task in a meaningful way. The organization of the group has to match the nature of the work, and if the latter presents a puzzle the group does not see how to cope with, then the leader has the task of both dealing with the tendency of the group members to regress as well as enabling them to see that their belief that they have no resources is not entirely founded in reality. The experience of the latter, that is, of regaining ego-function, brings back the work capacity.

Group Psychotherapy

As Bion mentions at the start of his book, this term is itself ambiguous as to whether it means therapy of the group conceived as an entity and so concerned with facilitating the group to overcome barriers from its internal conflicts to its effectiveness as a work group or whether its purpose is therapy of the individuals comprising it. In practice, the latter purpose would be more accurately described as analytical psychotherapy in groups.

When Bion says that his method of work cannot be called psychoanalysis, he means that the fundamental principles of psychoanalysis do not apply to it. There is here a source of widespread differences of view even amongst analysts. Both the classical and Kleinian analysts believe that a comprehensive exploration of unconscious processes is possible only in the traditional setting with the analyst preserving a somewhat distant stance in the interests of objectivity, maintaining a certain intensity in the conduct of the process, usually five times per week, and avoiding any other activity than the analytic one, for example, no reassurances of any kind nor advice and only offering understanding of the unconscious solely by interpretation. The value of this approach is not in question. What is, however, is the common assumption that other less intensive and rigorous approaches are relatively poor substitutes and, in short, "not analysis." Analytical psychotherapy on a less intensive pattern than the standard psychoanalytical one has in recent years altered this view considerably to the extent that it is widely practised by analysts themselves with the conviction that it can be of considerable help for the individual. Many unconscious factors in the personality can be exposed and their disturbing effects ameliorated in a range of patient-therapist settings. The critical factors are not so much the latter as the therapist's understanding of the unconscious and the extent to which he focuses on that.

The general aims of analytical psychotherapy are the same as those of psychoanalysis, namely, to bring into consciousness the unconscious relationships structured from early experience and then segregated within the self with varying degrees of emotional distancing from awareness because they are not permitted by the opposing parental imagos reinforced frequently by further rejection by the ego. The work of treatment is to bring out in the transference relationship with the therapist both the forbidden aims and the defences against them. Because these conflicts are structured into divisions within the self from very early phases, the personality as a whole is damaged by them. Their roots cannot be extirpated or exorcised. We do not talk of cure but of achieving degrees of freedom for the person by lessening their power in relation to the central self. All psychotherapy, therefore, from intensive analysis over years to much less intensive and shorter-term treatments is ameliorative to varying extents. There is at present no accepted means of appraising the functioning of a personality in a comprehensive objective way, such as would be comparable with the assessment of the physical state of the person that the doctor makes by his examination of the main bodily systems. Careful interviewing can give some assessment of change, but even here the particular bias in any judge of what is important in the person limits the status of the findings. The important point about these familiar comments is that beliefs about what is and is not adequate therapy have to be evaluated by broad considerations.

The psychotherapeutic factor in Bion's method—again to be recalled as directed towards group dynamics—can be considered if we take one of his examples, the events in a group occasioned by a woman talking about a fear of choking in restaurants or, on a recent occasion, of her embarrassment during a meal in the presence of an attractive woman (Bion 1961, p. 182). About half of the group responded by saying they did not feel like that, and the others were indifferent. Bion notes that in analysis such a statement would have evoked various possible interpretations, none of which he felt could be regarded as appropriate to the group. What he did point out to the members was that the woman's difficulty was also theirs, although in repudiating it they made themselves superior to her. Moreover, in doing so they made it difficult for any member to admit any problem because they would then be made to feel more inferior and worthless. From an analytic point of view he appreciates that the woman got no help and is left in discomfort because in fact group treatment is the wrong treatment. He then adds that her manner of speaking suggested that she felt there was a single object, the group, that had been split into pieces (the individual members) by her eating and that being the recipient of the members' projective identifications was her fault and so reinforced her guilt which, in turn, made it difficult for her to grasp how the actions of the others had affected her. For the other members, they have not only rid themselves of the woman's troubles as part of their own, but they have also got rid of any responsibility for her by splitting off their caring parts into the therapist. The result of this process is akin to a "loss of individual distinctiveness" through the basic assumption state of dependence. The group dynamics are clear; the psychotherapeutic effect is not only nil, it is negative.

The question then is why Bion could not have made an interpretation along the lines he indicated in this reflection about the situation, at least to the extent of conveying the woman's hunger (perhaps felt as greed), destructive to the group, with the latter attacking her, as they did to these feelings in themselves. Also, by treating each other's problems in this way they were perpetuating the feeling there was no help to be had from the group, only from the therapist. The precise interpretation is not so important as long as enough of the underlying dynamics of the total situation are articulated. By focusing exclusively on the group as a whole, certain awareness of group attitudes is made possible. Has that been as helpful as it might have been for the development of each individual? Kleinian analysts frequently use the term "the correct interpretation." It is doubtful if such an achievement is ever possible, especially in the group situation, so that a degree of metaphoric latitude helps to catch some of the wide range of processes going on in each individual. Psychotherapeutic change is a developmental process requiring considerable time, and Bion mentioned, as evidence of intellectual work going on in spite of its covert nature, the fact that patients came back to his comments in later sessions. In other words, reflection on what is happening in the group with delayed assimilation is a necessary part of the individual's "work" activity. The therapist's task, I believe, is to further this by giving each individual as much awareness of all sides of his responses in the group situation, including especially the apparent reasons for abandoning his "distinctiveness" when faced with his intolerance towards his own unconscious processes. In my own experience with groups over 30 years, I have never ceased to be impressed by the importance that members attach to their group meetings, even though only once per week. It is common after only a few months for them to remark that what goes on in the session plays a prominent part in how they feel for the rest of that week. By commenting along the lines I believe Bion could have done in the light of what he described, he would have avoided in some measure in at least some of the members the depressing feelings of the badness of the group as almost inevitable.

In regard to pairing, he again warns against concentrating on the possible unconscious contents of the pair interaction. Here too, however, it is not at all difficult to comment on the group's interest in this interaction and in what this interest might consist. I have heard reports frequently in groups that certain sessions with marked pairing on which interpretive comments were made, were recalled vividly for long periods as having been particularly helpful.

Bion likened the problem of the individual coming to terms with the emotional life of the group as closely akin to that of the infant in its first relationship, namely, with the breast-mother. In his later analytic work he spelled out the nature of the infant's task in overcoming frustration, that is, when instead of the expected breast there was a "no breast" situation. For this achievement he took the mother's role as a "container" to be crucial. This is perhaps an inadequate term for the active contribution of the mother in making her comforting and encouraging presence felt. It could readily be said that, for the group therapist, Bion advocates a role of considerable withholding.

The importance of Bion's strictures can be granted and that the essential aspect in all these issues is whether or not enough of the total dynamics in the group are being brought to notice when an individual is being referred to. Basic assumption behaviour occurs in groups, whether the task is explicitly therapy or not. But when the aim is therapy, the individuals need to understand much more of themselves than the tendency to regress to the primal self of their separation-individuation stage of development. I have stressed that the paramount consideration is much more our understanding than using an assumed correct technique. Understanding the unconscious is notoriously subject to individual bias. Increasingly over recent years my "bias" has been a much greater focus on the state of the self that underlies the particular expression of the unconscious motives. Thus, to revert to the example just quoted, one can ask whether Bion's reluctance to use the individual in the group situation is influenced by the Kleinian view of greed as stemming from a high degree of oral sadism. I want to emphasize at once that Melanie Klein is far from ignoring object relationships, yet she retained the view that aggressive phantasies were mainly the product of the death instinct. If one takes the view that the most profound aggression arises from the universally desperate struggle to maintain the self—a view that Freud took, as I mentioned earlier—then the greed of the patient might well be seen as a primitive expression of her attempt to get possession of the object she needs to maintain a security in her self. In this case the social relevance of her symptoms, and hence its importance for the group is different from that were her greed to be taken as a problem of excessive oral sadism.

The need to cope with anxieties over the self can be seen in another of the examples he quotes (Bion 1961, p. 144). The members discuss a suggestion to use their forenames—three are for it as a good idea that would make things more friendly. Of the other three, one doesn't want her name to be known because she dislikes it, another suggests pseudonyms, and the third keeps out of it. I do not want to make unjustified use of the example, especially as Bion mentions only certain aspects of the episode to make his point. What he takes up is the way the group seems to regard friendliness or pleasant emotions in the group as a means of cure, as a contribution to their work group. Perhaps more immediately relevant to the work group are the anxieties about whether or not the self of the three dissidents will be secure if it begins to be looked at by the others.

The disadvantages of groups as a therapeutic medium are well known. They do, however, have several advantages. The sharing of humiliations, shame, and guilt is a different experience for many when they receive sympathetic understanding from other members. Also, whereas the projective identification of self-objects from the segregated systems has to be done mainly one at a time with the therapeutic pair, the projection of several around members of the group is active much of the time and its recognition can be used by all.

The individual in psychotherapy has to learn about his split-off relationships, his wishes, from maternal love for the infantile self that felt deprived to the full repertoire of sadistic coercion to get power, gratification, or revenge, and all his anxieties and despair about these inner situations. This task can become a life-long one for every individual. Therapy, as in other learning, has to give enough capacity to carry on the work. Psychotherapy in groups has to make much more of a contribution to this capacity than can be done through confining attention solely to the group dynamics equated with the basic assumptions.

Bion, like so many creative thinkers, confined his study of the work of others to relatively few. Perhaps he felt, as Winnicott once said to me, "I did not pay close attention to Fairbairn as I was too absorbed in my own pregnancies at the time." I never heard Bion discuss Foulkes, and I do not think he knew much about his work because he had left groups by the time Foulkes was publishing his accounts of it. He was not given to disparaging the work of others if it differed from his own; for him, experience would eventually find its survival value. Foulkes was convinced the total group interactions had to be used in therapy, and I believe that Bion, had he done more group therapeutic work, would have accepted that position though he would have insisted on what might be loosely put as more rigour and more depth, more attention to the primitive relationships.

None of Bion's Tavistock colleagues engaged in group therapy, in contrast with those concerned with group dynamics, adhered to his view about the sole use of the latter in their work. Ezriel's formulation (1950) of using a common tension in the group once it could be identified as coming from the wish for a specific relationship with the therapist, and adding to its exposure by showing how each individual dealt with it, was considered to be more appropriate. Revisiting both led me to conclude that Ezriel's views could not account for the group dynamics in general, and I believe our understanding of the individual should be such as to account for both. It has seemed to me for some years that a theory of the organization of the self is the emerging task for psychoanalysis and so I used my own rather rough and ready gropings in this direction. Analytic group psychotherapy has usually been considered by its users as a valuable therapeutic medium in spite of the negative findings of Malan and his colleagues (Malan 1976). Perhaps we expose here the inadequacies in our concepts of the nature of psychotherapy as well as our means of assessing change. Because of my interest in the self as an independent variable in the therapeutic task, Gill and I (1970) carried out an exploratory trial using spontaneous sentences as an indication of conflicts within the self system (see Chapter 6). Significant changes in patients after 18 months of treatment were found, so Malan's criteria seem to have referred to different processes.

For me Bion has always been the *preux chevalier* making his doughty forays into the confused tangles of psychoanalytic thought and the complexities of human relationships. His power to look at phenomena with fresh challenges remains a permanent questioning legacy. I started out by referring to Fairbairn as one of the first analysts to seek a conceptual basis for psychoanalysis that freed it from the shackles of nineteenth-century science. Fairbairn and Bion met on several occasions in Edinburgh, though in the circumstances of war with little chance of much sharing of work. It was a strange chance for so much creativity in psychoanalysis to be germinating in that city, so remote from Vienna and London and, in spite of its brilliant intellectual traditions, with a climate of opinion at that time not a little hostile to the new understanding of man that was being furthered in psychoanalysis. It is perhaps even stranger that the contributions of each can be seen now as needing that of the other and each, with its tough theoretical work, drawing its inspiration from the intuitive genius of Melanie Klein.

12. TWO INDUSTRIAL PROJECTS*

There is a growing tendency for industry to look to social science for assistance in personnel and training problems. Indeed, it might be said that in Britain at least, industry more than any other community group is likely to be a consumer of social scientific advisory services in the next few years. This together with the production crisis in Britain, which requires the rapid development of new production methods, makes industry a field of crucial importance for the application of social science.

One of the difficulties of collaborating in the solution of industrial problems is that the problem for which help is sought is so frequently only a symptom, an outer manifestation, of more deeply rooted difficulties. Autocracy or paternalism, for example, produces adverse effects whose causes are seldom recognized, and as these effects become increasingly severe, leads to attempts to cope with the difficulties by improving physical conditions, welfare services, personnel selection, and so forth, while the central problems remain untouched. Working in industry, therefore, requires that the social scientist maintain a position in which he is free to assess the total situation in a factory before proceeding to introduce special techniques to solve this or that isolated problem. Just as when a patient comes to a doctor with a headache it is the doctor's responsibility to find out what is causing the headache before prescribing aspirin, it is equally the social scientist's responsibility to find out what are the causes of trouble in a factory before fulfilling a request, for example, to introduce time-and-motion studies to step up production. It may well be necessary, however, once having diagnosed the problem, to work step by step towards the solution, proceeding from more symptomatic to more radical forms of treatment.

The two projects that follow are described merely to illustrate some of these problems. The first, on dealing with a morale problem among young textile workers, is presented to indicate some of the difficulties involved in coming to grips with more basic problems when one is called in to deal with a symptom.

---

*This chapter was co-authored by Isabel Menzies Lyth.

The second deals with the manner in which success in handling one project may facilitate grappling with industrial morale problems at deeper levels.

MORALE PROBLEM IN YOUNG TEXTILE WORKERS

A wool mill situated in a village a few miles from a large town was faced with the serious problem of labour shortage. For the previous century it had been the chief source of livelihood in the village, but in recent years, because of the drift of population to the town, the supply of young workers had become inadequate. The possibility of moving large sections of production to more populated areas was considered but it was felt that less drastic steps might be taken by making work conditions more attractive. The firm had advertised widely in mining areas about 40–50 miles away and had been successful in attracting a number of young girls. A great deal of effort had been spent on making a hostel for these girls and in organising recreational activities for them. Despite these efforts the girls seemed to be unresponsive; their work performance was mediocre, there were frequent differences with the foremen, and the native population seemed to be rather hostile to them.

One of the directors, a student of industrial problems, persuaded the Board to call in an adviser. The adviser was received well and made good personal relationships with the top management. He spent two days talking to management at the different levels and to many of the workers. The general opinion of the lower levels of management appeared to be that the girls were all rather a poor type, the typical irresponsible pleasure-seeking youth of today. The top level management leaned more to the view that possibly the working conditions were not all they might be, and thought better welfare might improve their attitude. The adviser after assessing the local situation concluded that a sufficient labour supply would have to be recruited from outside. He also interpreted the drift to the town as possibly an end product of a century of dependence on the mill-owners who had inevitably occupied what was tantamount to a feudal role. It was well known in the village that several large fortunes had been made from the mill in the past, and the latent hostility among the villagers was revealed by an instance in which property presented by the mill-owners to the village as a gift was demolished by the village shortly afterwards for no really good reason. The adviser suggested that improvement in welfare would not be enough but that more radical steps should be taken to secure worker participation.

The effect of the interpretation, which was not inaccurate, was to produce a sharp negative attitude in the top management. It is of the first importance that a development of this kind in the situation should be as fully understood as possible. It is likely that the latent guilt in the owners who were still the top management was exacerbated by the implication that the workers were now able to realise their wish to become independent of the traditional "benefactors." More important perhaps was the fact that the suggestion for radical changes to secure workers' participation raised anxiety, because the owner-managers sensed the feeling that they had not only ceased to be "good" but further were incapable of so providing for their flock that the latter would willingly stay. Anxiety aroused in executives seems to be most frequently expressed as hostility, and the situation is closely analogous to the reaction of the patient under analysis who has been given an interpretation beyond what he is able to experience as immediately throwing insight on his problem.

The "patient"–adviser relationship might easily have ended at this point except for the fact that the director who had introduced the adviser appreciated what had happened, and as the result of his efforts the directors agreed to meet the adviser along with a second adviser to discuss the problem afresh. The second adviser having been acquainted fully with what had happened proceeded with extreme caution and made a point at this meeting of trying to undo the anxieties aroused previously. Attention was focused on the fact that there were strange girls coming into a close-knit system consisting of the villagers and the owner-managers and that it was probably in this area that the management could take a lead in getting the girls to feel part of the community. In this way a process of growth could be started that did not deviate too much from their traditional role although there was no doubt that once started developments would proceed beyond what was envisaged at this early stage. The managers, having now sensed a positive role, welcomed the suggestion that the second adviser should go to the mill and speak to the girls. The adviser would make it plain to the girls that he had been sent as an outsider on behalf of the management to find out what they felt about working in the mill. As an outsider it was likely that the girls would talk more freely and they could be consulted on what points they would like reported back.

The second adviser thus started with strong positive support from the management. This support was reinforced probably by the fact that any doubts they may have had about an outside investigator were canalised onto the first adviser. Indeed, this phenomenon of ambivalent attitudes expressed as doubt against one adviser and trust of a second has led us to the motion that it is probably useful to work in pairs. Whenever this has been done it has become clear that one person collects most of the negative attitudes, while the other becomes highly regarded, and can therefore proceed more effectively with the work.

On visiting the mill the second adviser got much the same impression as the first had gained about the total situation. There was benevolent paternalism at the top and hostility in the lower levels of management because of their complete lack of insight into the problems of their girls. The adviser was told that the best way of seeing the girls would be to go to their hostel, which he did. He was warned beforehand that it would probably be difficult to get the girls to speak or even to stay in the hostel as all they were interested in was going to the cinema. When he arrived at the hostel he met a few girls in the common room and explained to them that he had come as an outsider on behalf of the management to find out what they felt about working in the mill and what their ideas were about improving things. The girls called in the others and in a few minutes the room was packed with over thirty girls. Having explained again to all his status, the girls began a nonstop tirade of their grievances. It was abundantly clear that very high degrees of tension existed and that little or no opportunity had been available for the expression of the grievances. The adviser did not say a word while this process of catharsis was going on and his expectations were confirmed when the process of reaction set in. The expression of grievances had reached a fantastic point when, for example, the girls were suggesting that the Company should take them on charabanc drives two afternoons a week. From this point more responsible attitudes began to be asserted. There then followed a period, still of complaints, but complaints accompanied by suggestions as to how the conditions could be improved. A long list of useful contributions was noted. A second wave of massive hostility against the Company developed but much less intense than the first. When the girls were asked at this point why they stayed in the mill when they felt all these grievances a number of them replied that the mill would go bust if they left.

The suggestions made by the girls were divided into three groups dealing with:

a. Working conditions
b. Conditions in the hostel
c. Relations with the village

The girls were then asked which points they would like reported back. They unanimously asked for all to be reported with the addition that some suggestions should be printed in capitals.

It was painfully clear after this discussion, which proceeded at a high level of activity for over 2 hours, that the major source of tension was that the girls were mistrusted. They complained of being divided amongst the local workers, of having recreation organised for them, and of being ignored by the local community. The contrast between the attitudes to themselves and to local girls was a recurrent theme. They reported that the only representative of the community who had visited them in their hostel was a priest. They were indignant at the attitude of the villagers which indicated that they were all hooligans. They admitted freely that there had been one or two girls who had misbehaved themselves, but added that if they had had their way these girls would have been sacked on the spot instead of which their dismissal had lingered on for weeks. The recreation organised by the management was resented. They felt that if they had to play games with the foremen blowing the whistle, they might just as well be staying on at work. This attitude was particularly interesting as one of the chief complaints of the foremen had been that the girls were so irresponsible that although the foremen went to a great deal of trouble to organise recreation *for* them there was very little response. The girls made many suggestions as to how they would discipline themselves in the hostel, such as having older girls look after younger girls. Their appreciation of the firm's responsibility for them when living away from home was extremely good. It was interesting that when they were asked if they could manage their own hostel with a committee their first response was a negative one with the addition that they would fight too much amongst themselves. That is to say although they were clamouring for more acceptance, they were anxious lest they might be faced with too much responsibility.

A full written report of the discussion with the girls was given to the management. The effect of this report on the management was most satisfactory. The statement that the girls had a kind of instinctive loyalty to the firm was very reassuring to them and the wealth of their suggestions was a great surprise. The management were astonished at the capacity of the girls for making sensible suggestions and of taking responsibility to a degree hitherto quite unappreciated.

Six months later one of the directors reported that the girls had elected a committee in their hostel, which met regularly with a representative of the management, and that many of their suggestions had resulted in a great improvement in their morale. Indeed the situation amongst the incomers became such that the local girls put forward a petition that they should have chances of developing group activities of the same kind and that there should be joint activities for making suggestions regarding working conditions.

SELECTION OF MANAGEMENT TRAINEES[1]

The initial contact in this case was a personal one between the Medical Officer and the Personnel Officer of the firm. The latter had learned from the Medical Officer about the developments in the Army of selection procedures for Officers and had been eager to hear more about this, as he was faced with the task of selecting from a large number of applicants a small group of men suitable for training to fill, eventually, top management posts. After an informal discussion in which the selection problem was explored and ways had been suggested for the Personnel Officer to overcome some of his difficulties, the latter discussed the position with his seniors and obtained permission for the adviser to work with him in making a survey of the problem. As usual the question of cost was one of the difficulties. The industrial pattern demands a cost estimate in advance whereas the psychological adviser cannot easily meet this demand, for he does not know how much work is involved until he is in the problem. His position is analagous to that of the physician who cannot tell beforehand what the complications in the treatment of an illness may be. It was agreed, however, that the plan should be to make a survey, which could be costed in advance; then, if agreed, to make an experimental trial over a period of say 3 months, this also to

[1]H. Bridger collaborated on this project.

be costed in advance; and finally, according to the experience from the trial, to decide what continuing assistance was desirable. The selection problem presented many interesting factors. The main steps were to provide the Personnel Officer with a satisfactory method of screening a large number of applications so that he could send forward to the Selection Committee the best material and at the same time as much relevant information about the candidates as possible. The Personnel Officer had been carrying out this screening by careful interviews. Applicants were given appointments as soon as possible with the result that he was having to devote a great deal of time to interviewing and most of his days were being occupied by the arrival of applicants. As many applicants were not available for interview except within a narrow time limit, there was no alternative to this procedure. A scheme was worked out, therefore, whereby the applicants could be grouped as far as possible and psychological assistance was provided for the administration and interpretation of written tests. The Personnel Officer was given further diagnostic equipment in the form of experience in handling group discussions prior to his interview. The impressions from group discussion enabled him to gain a better "man-to-man" comparison and also, when linked with the results of the psychological tests, enabled him to economise on his interview time. For the Selection Committee stage a similar extension in diagnostic equipment was provided so that judges felt more satisfied with what they had learned about the candidates.

In this case selection was a big problem by itself, but inevitably its link with other personal problems emerged. Thus a recurrent dilemma at Selection Committees was what could be done with candidates about whom the Committee had learned a great deal although they were not finally chosen for the specific vacancies as management trainees. Interest in the total recording policy was heightened and suggestions developed as to how it could be improved. More important perhaps, the amount of diagnostic material collected led to a rising concern with the quality of training and how specific opportunities could be given to the candidates accepted to give them the best chance of development. Shortly after the selection procedure had started its trial run it was felt that some of the principles in the selection methods could be used in training and the adviser was asked to collaborate with the Personnel Officer in an experimental training period. This proved to be a great success and further problems in morale began to be put before the adviser, including consultation on an overall education policy for the company.

The importance of the collaboration in the selection procedure cannot be over-emphasised. The Personnel Officer in particular felt that each day he gained something from his contact with the adviser. He became increasingly understanding of the complexities in personnel problems and correspondingly creative in dealing with them. Moreover after an initial period in which his uncertainties about his capacity to handle situations were outlived, he felt secure in his relationship with the adviser. The joint discussions of problems had made it plain that the adviser was not a magician from without who "knew all the answers" but that sound answers could only be reached when the Personnel Officer's experience and knowledge were used.

After the trial run had been completed, the Personnel Officer and the directors from whom the Selection Committee was drawn were sufficiently satisfied to make an arrangement whereby any senior member of the staff of the firm could call in the adviser on any problem. As a result of this the Institute has been called in to help solve a morale problem in one of the allied companies. This project, now in the survey stage, is not sufficiently advanced to report. The progression, however, from acceptance of help in relatively straightforward selection problems, to request for assistance in coping with deeper and more complex problems of morale and human relations, is of interest. This point is mentioned to illustrate the fundamental importance of the social science technician getting his relations with the client's representative right. Traditionally the pattern has been all too common for the expert to be called in and then leave after submitting a written report. The building of a sound collaborative relationship on the initial problem led in this case to the revelation of many other problems and to the continuing of a joint effort in tackling them.

In both these cases the actual techniques used and changes implemented were extremely simple. However, the establishing of a sound working relationship was not so simple, and it is felt that any success in instituting even simple procedures revolved around the degree of success in allowing those concerned with the problem to develop new and more creative roles. This showed particularly clearly in the second case where contact was through the Personnel Officer. Although desiring assistance, he naturally felt threatened by the entry of outside social scientists into the field. When this problem was successfully worked through and he realised that it was our aim only to collaborate with him and strengthen his own hand, resistances disappeared, and he is now championing improvements in other parts of the company based on the utilization of social science techniques, and is himself engaged in breaking down resistances in his own colleagues to the use of these techniques.

III
COMMUNITY MENTAL HEALTH

13. TOWARD COMMUNITY MENTAL HEALTH

That "mental health" was emerging as a new goal comparable with some of the master-values that have inspired various eras in our history, was suggested by Dicks (1950) 40 years ago. Since then, the subject has become part of our scene with a proliferation of associations and programmes devoted to improving mental health and, above all, with television bringing home to the public the great range of the psychiatric disorders and of the endeavours to treat and prevent them. This greater familiarity, however, is far from the acceptance of mental health as a master-value. On the contrary, there is a persistent and widespread tendency to restrict its import to those matters traditionally the concern of psychiatrists and the caring professions. It is for this reason that many have wished for another term. Yet, in spite of innumerable attempts to find an alternative, *mental health* has remained, perhaps reflecting an unconscious appreciation that these are the right words in spite of the common narrowing of their meaning—that they do signify a master-value.

The aspirations within the larger concept are plain. Can man, with the knowledge he has gained of how he grows and is maintained as a person in his society, put this knowledge to use so that he may realize more of his potential? Early gains in the first decades of our century raised many false hopes—ludicrous oversimplifications, from the retrospective standpoint of today. Understanding has progressed steadily and perhaps our most valuable advances are in a greater realism about the complexity of man's personal nature. Our increased knowledge is also shedding light on some of the thorniest of the problems in this task, namely, the resistances to the acceptance of man's nature—what Bion (1962) has referred to so arrestingly and yet with such depressing accuracy as our "hatred" of learning about ourselves. In this conflict, we have seen, oddly enough, science and religion with all the institutionalization of their stereotypes, as Dicks puts it, united Canute-like against the tide of the facts. But the voice of reason eventually gets its hearing. One of our sharpest theologians, Dr. Ian Ramsey, the Bishop of Durham, in a lecture (1970) described critically the devastating contrast that he noted between an ineffective, harsh theology like a polished cistern that contains no living water, and the knowledge and skills of the Behavioural Sciences that seem to minister so obviously and creatively to the spirit of man. Almost at the same time, and from the key position in British psychiatry, Sir Denis Hill (1970) challenged psychiatrists and psychologists on their restrictive views of science and their exclusive concentration on mechanisms underlying behaviour while ignoring the whole phenomena of meaning and its manifestly central role in man's personal behaviour.

If the urgency of our need to know more of ourselves as persons has been denied by our individual and institutional resistances, the technological revolution going on apace is breaking through these barriers in disturbing ways. The current changes in our society are great enough to warrant the sociologists' description of them as a movement into a new "post-industrial society." In a penetrating analysis of its implications for the individual, Trist (1968) remarks that the steps we take with regard to the welfare and development of people during the next few decades will be critical. What is most characteristic of the society into which we are now moving is the entirely new degree of interdependence of individuals and organizations. This vastly increased interrelatedness is leading to situations that inevitably challenge existing beliefs and values within the core of the individual and in the institutions that shape him and are in turn shaped by him. For instance, organizational philosophies are shifting the emphasis from competitive relations and separate objectives to collaborative relations with linked objectives. Above all, this new interrelatedness leads to the perception of many social problems, such as poverty and crime, as major integrated problems requiring central planning rather than as an aggregate of separate elements to be tackled piecemeal. Central appraisals lead to "ecological strategies" in which, for instance, crises are anticipated rather than responded to; measures are comprehensive with participation and confrontation of conflicts instead of being specific, requiring consent and covering up conflict. These new features forced upon us by the technological revolution demand that the individual move from such values as independence, achievement, and self-control to those of interdependence, self-actualization, and self-expression; from being one who endures a good deal of personal restriction, tension, and stress because of internal and external barriers, to becoming one who has a fuller and freer capacity for enjoyment.

In such a social scene, the relatively static notions of welfare as keeping people up to the standards needed by the industrial economy have to be complemented by the ideal of making personal development as rich as possible. The emphasis on the *self* in these emergent values is noteworthy. The *self* is the term we use for that core of the personality that preserves continuity in change and its integrity is what makes change acceptable. If this integrity of the self is threatened, change is resisted—often violently, as befits the defence of our most precious possession.

Several years after Dicks's paper, Marie Jahoda (1958) clarified some of the basic aspects implied by the term *mental health*. She also brought out the different meanings it could have for different people and in different cultures. Nevertheless, we are on firmer ground than the considerations of cultural relativity might suggest. The new theoretical trends in psychoanalysis that had been initiated by Melanie Klein, and systematically developed by Fairbairn in his object-relations theory of the personality, were helping to bridge the conceptual gap between what went on in the inner world of the individual and in the culture in which he and his family were embedded. It was the great merit of this approach that it conceived the structuring and functioning of the personality in terms of personal relationship systems. As with so many shifts in theoretical standpoints in the history of science, the new views could be seen as one expression of a fresh zeitgeist. Other psychoanalysts, from their detailed studies of profound disturbances in the capacity for relationships, were independently reaching similar conclusions, for instance, Balint and Winnicott; and there was the exciting support this relationship-systems approach began to receive from the ethological theories of animal behaviour stimulated by the work of Lorenz. These concepts have been notably applied to the psychoanalytic theory of child development by Bowlby. On the sociological side, the internalization within the person of the relationships he experienced in the family became a feature of the thinking of cultural anthropologists. Cultural patterns were thus seen as interdependent with child rearing practices, and so cultural values and their influence on the adult could be appraised on a more dynamic basis.

In the work of Parsons, Shils, and their colleagues, the structuring of the personality by the interactions within the family represented a most striking synthesis of the knowledge provided by the psychoanalyst and that from the social scientist about the forces from the social milieu that impinge on the development of the person.

The way in which these independent lines of thought confirmed each other is remarkable, and gives a reassurance that appropriate theoretical frameworks can be evolved for ordering this most complex area of the individual as a person, with all that this means, in his society. The essence of all this work is the emergence of an adequate model of the development and functioning of the person and of how culture mirrors and is mirrored by the inner world of the individual.

The impetus towards synthesis, springing equally from those psychoanalysts alive to social factors and from those social scientists who accepted the full importance of psychodynamic factors in the individual, has become a creative force in the theory and practice of mental health programmes. Those who share in this trend seek active relationships with sections of the community in which they may occupy a role closely analogous to that of the analyst in his psychotherapeutic relationships. That is to say, the efficacy of the part they play in any change process arises from what they help to release, from the removal of inner blockages to growth, and not from what they impose on the thinking and actions of others. The criticism that such socially active psychiatrists and allied colleagues take on omnipotent powers is for the most part based on fantasies of the same kind that attribute almost unlimited powers of suggestion to the analyst in his psychotherapeutic work. (Most analysts have wished at times that they did have such powers to influence behaviour in the relief of suffering!) The fact is that change processes within community institutions and ways are apt to evoke the same kind of anxiety as arises in the individual who seeks to alter his established patterns of relating to himself and others.

The belief that the psychoanalyst and social scientist have an influential role in community mental health endeavours is not as yet widely shared amongst psychiatrists partly because few psychiatrists have the necessary training. For those who do, their contribution, though vital, is only one component in an "ecological strategy." The comprehensive nature of what must be tackled is well expressed by Trist (1968):

> . . . at the higher level of complexity which characterizes the transition to post-industrialism a higher quality is required in all primary social units. By primary social units is meant the set of concrete social resources which exist in the life-space of the individual, i.e. the people and institutions with which he directly interacts and to which he contributes his own resources: his family, his work-place, the school his children attend, the particular community in which he resides, the services and amenities actually available to him: in sum, all those entities which compose his primary social world. The quality of those resources, in his case, determines for the individual his "quality of life", on which his welfare and development alike depend. The objective of taking the active role is to bring into being ecological systems able to maintain primary social worlds of high quality throughout a society. How to do this has now become the over-riding question as we move towards post-industrialism. [pp. 17–18]

Because of the extraordinary pressures our psychiatrists are subjected to in providing services to relieve the more urgent suffering in our society, the image of psychiatry has become too much associated with the attempts to mitigate personal pain by drugs. Few psychiatrists are really satisfied with this role. Only when our society begins to grasp the real nature of its mental ill health, however, will there be the opportunity to make adequate endeavours towards richer and healthier personal development for all.

At the W.H.O. conference on community psychiatric services, Peebles, Scotland, 1970

14. PSYCHOANALYSIS IN THE POSTINDUSTRIAL SOCIETY

Our changing society has become a byword, and the nature of the changes are such that sociologists view these as representing the emergence of a new social order. Because the most influential changes stem from our new technological resources, and especially because the energies of most people will cease to be absorbed in the processes of production, the new social order has been termed "the post-industrial society" (see Bell 1982). This changed order is only in the process of birth; but there can be no one who has been unaffected by what is already taking place. Striking are the changes in the existential quality of life for the individual. The traditional frameworks of control are being replaced by an enhanced permissiveness, a trend that evokes a rather widespread uneasiness because it outruns at times the complementary demands for increased responsibility on the part of everyone. Perhaps more disturbing are the new responses amongst whole sections of society, especially of violent protest and of a marked sense of alienation. Gaps between various groups, especially when these relate to the perception of privileged opportunities, are now felt much more provocatively—largely because of the rapid and vivid means of communication that television provides.

PSYCHOANALYSIS AND THE DEMAND FOR PSYCHOTHERAPEUTIC SERVICES

Closer to ourselves as psychoanalysts are those changes for which we have been in large measure directly responsible. It has been said that the face of the world was changed when Freud published his first five case histories. Psychoanalytic knowledge has permeated almost every sphere in which man's development and functioning as a person is the major concern. As this knowledge increased, our understanding of the psychological disorders, their enormous incidence and range, has become more widely recognized. Moreover, the intimate relationship between culture and personality is reflected in new symptoms. Our art and literature, and with their impact greatly intensified by the mass media, have made commonplace the vagaries of sexuality and the unbridled destructiveness which can be let loose in man. Our patients accordingly come less troubled by conflicts over instinctual impulses than by the bewilderment of a divided self. They present the schizoid futility of people alienated from those committed and responsible relationships to others, to themselves, and to their achievements, that give zest to living, and satisfaction and happiness at each phase of the life cycle.

Parallel with the increased awareness of the psychological disorders has been a great rise in the demands for help from those under stress. In the last decade the surging movement to create widely available mental health services is indeed an arresting feature of the more advanced societies. The psychotropic drugs have enabled psychiatrists and doctors to make life more bearable for countless numbers—and to permit many who would formerly have been long-term inmates of our psychiatric hospitals to manage in the outside world. Nevertheless, the main endeavour in the mental health services has centred on the provision of more and more groups of professional and semiprofessional personnel, or less highly trained groups of counsellors, who have developed experience and skill for helping persons in need towards a greater understanding of themselves and thereby, hopefully, increasing their well-being and effectiveness in the pursuit of their goals.

In this wide range of activity, psychoanalytic knowledge has been assimilated, often only in a very broad and general way, by the helping professions, and their skills have evolved in keeping with the extent to which they have been able to use this knowledge. Many of their leaders through their own personal analysis have raised the skill levels within their professions, have set new levels of expertise for others to emulate. These groups thus give help of a much more adequate nature than was previously available, usually in terms of support, advice, or exhortation. Amongst the social work professions, the evolution of skills has been conspicuously influenced by a further contribution from psychoanalysts, namely their involvement as consultants, often over long periods, in regular case seminars. Psychoanalytic knowledge differs from most other branches of knowledge in that its assimilation and use normally require some personal adjustment in the users. The collaboration of the analyst has permitted a substantial degree of working through of those restrictive attitudes, anxieties, and defensive traits that operate against the emotional freedom in the person necessary to transmute knowledge into personal skills; and it is only with such improved skills that these allied colleagues can gain sufficient trust from their clients for the latter to communicate more of their conflicts.

The stimulus of psychoanalytic understanding has not been confined to the kind of work just described. It has had a very great effect on the social sciences leading to a vast array of research into social behaviour. Most relevant in our present considerations have been the advances in our knowledge of, and skills in handling, the dynamics of small groups and the interactional processes within the family—advances which have added whole new dimensions to our resources for alleviating the stunting or crippling effects of certain conflicts in personal development and functioning.

SOME DANGERS

While psychoanalytic knowledge forms the core of much of this work, and although many analysts have played an active part in its furtherance, various dangers have inevitably been perceived (see Wallerstein, 1968). We are now less troubled by the justifiable concern of analysts about the early overfacile transfer of their insights into "wild analysis"; yet it is useful to consider some of the present dangers as aspects of the community's responses which have to be faced.

The first concerns the nature of the help which can be given by others and in settings different from that in which the analyst works. It would be universally agreed that the kind of therapeutic work that a social caseworker or other professional helper can carry out appropriately does not attempt what the psychoanalyst does. This limitation need not be further considered because what is normally attempted by others has its own validity as well as being so often the only help available. It must, however, be admitted that the attitudes sometimes conveyed by psychoanalysts that this kind of work is a poor substitute for what more thoroughgoing analysis might achieve, is more a professional fantasy than an established fact. For many, psychological help, and particularly in crisis situations, is probably best given by the kind of relationship the good social or other professional worker can make—one in which the whole person with his own resources and those of his life space are kept firmly as the focus of concern. The main danger here is thus not in the nature of the new facilities provided by well-trained professional groups. It consists in their too rapid expansion in response to public demand—with a dilution of standards and attempts to assert that less help than is really needed constitutes adequate services.

A few other trends are also noteworthy. The question of responsibility, especially in relation to medical considerations, was a highly sensitive issue years ago when the developments described were starting. It has now receded as a major source of interprofessional contention, largely because settings have been created in which medical and nonmedical groups can work together with the interests of the individual safeguarded. I should like to return later, however, to this question because it may well arise again as the personal welfare services expand on the scale foreshadowed by the present signs.

Another concern may be seen to emerge, somewhat paradoxically, from the influence of psychodynamic thought on the social sciences. We might perhaps put it as follows, albeit with rather gross oversimplification. Because personality development and functioning are closely interrelated to such social factors as family and group membership, and the culture in which the person grows and is maintained, there has arisen a widespread reaction against the slow and painstaking process that characterizes the psychotherapeutic model as a means of assisting the individual. The biological roots and the structuring of the personality then seem to get discarded in favour of what societal processes can do. There is no question that his social milieu can disrupt the individual's effective functioning, whether it is active through pervasive features of the culture in which he lives, or whether the noxious factors are confined to sections of his social environment, for example, his work situation. All research work on group functioning has demonstrated the constant need of the individual to have what we might term an adequate *psychosocial metabolism*. We know, too, that without such constant maintenance from the social milieu, highly developed, creative effective persons can with surprising speed be degraded into almost unrecognisable, and even irreversible, remnants of what they were. The horrors of the concentration camps made this fact so painfully manifest that it is still difficult for us to assimilate.

The failure here is that of not separating two groups of conditions, namely, (*a*) developmental anomalies leading to maladaptive structuring of the personality; (*b*) deficiencies in the social environment causing functional disorder. These two are, of course, closely interrelated, for example, certain cultural patterns of child rearing may be more pathogenic than others; but it is necessary to separate them if remedial action is to be appropriate.

While this danger of assuming that social action by itself is sufficient to deal with psychological disorder may come mainly from the ameliorative concern of social planners and administrators, yet it also permeates the efforts of those in the helping professions. Thus in our mental hospitals, the valuable advances in creating a therapeutic community are often taken as sufficient in themselves to meet the need for psychotherapy. There is a fairly common assumption that getting patients into groups will of itself be adequately helpful to them. It does not apparently matter whether the professional leader has any psychodynamic training or not; all he has to do is to get people "communicating more freely"—one of the clichés of today, as fashionable as it is often devoid of articulate purpose. The support and reassurance, and often the changes in attitudes that patients can achieve from participating with others in a permissive setting, are manifestly of considerable benefit. But a psychotherapeutically trained observer of these situations cannot but be struck by the difficulties of patients which might be given more effective treatment if some of their less conscious origins could be exposed in a therapeutic way.

The psychoanalyst has clearly a fundamental contribution to make in the social movements today. He is already making a substantial one in many ways, particularly in the expansion of our welfare services. Indeed, that to be involved in this activity is "in the air" can be seen from the fact that close to 80 percent of the younger analysts in England have part-time posts in some kind of community mental health service—and this pattern is common in many countries.

In addition to participating in the development of community services, psychoanalysis has a long record of involvement with many areas affecting the development of the individual—above all, in child development. This whole theme is clearly much too large to receive other mention than to remind ourselves of its history and its present scale.

IMPLICATIONS OF PSYCHOANALYSIS

If we are to make our contribution more telling, I believe that we have to give much more thought to the whole theme of the relationship of psychoanalysis to society. We have, moreover, a moral obligation to do so. From the very beginning of its growth, psychoanalysis has never fostered a sect whose knowledge has been kept within its professional boundaries. We have constantly attempted to influence our society and some of the most profound changes in it can be laid at our door. It is with a view to improving our contribution that I am venturing some reflections on this dauntingly complex, yet urgently pressing theme. In doing so I propose to take three aspects: (1) the nature of the society into which we are moving and its implications for personal welfare services; (2) the contribution of the analyst to the personal welfare services; and (3) the contribution of the analyst to a central feature of this new society, namely, the concept of personal development with a capacity to meet change as distinct from what we have traditionally subsumed under the term, the welfare services.

THE NATURE OF THE POSTINDUSTRIAL SOCIETY

In turning to the nature of the society we are entering, I mentioned at the outset that the social transition upon us is of a nature that warrants the conception of these changes as moving towards a new order. These changes are familiar to all of us; but their familiarity does not remove the need for us to try to make more specific their nature and hence to take more appropriate actions to manage constructively their effects. Change almost always evokes anxiety and one of the greatest contributions of psychoanalysis was to create the first setting in which the individual could change himself systematically, that is, with the possibility of the change process being understood both by the analyst as the person managing it, and the analysand as the individual achieving it. The changes made by the psychoanalytic method, however, have traditionally been within a relatively stable social environment. It may be that for this reason analytically induced changes have sometimes been rather pejoratively referred to as helping the individual to adjust to his circumstances. The issue at stake today is what we have to offer, by contrast, to people experiencing movement and change as part of their milieu.

In making some observations about this task, I shall borrow extensively from the writings of two social scientists, Trist and Emery (Emery 1967; Emery and Trist 1965; Trist 1968). As these writers remark, although we are acquiring the knowledge with which the current social transition could be managed, the availability of such knowledge does not ensure its use. Clearly, however, the steps we take in regard to the welfare and development of people during the transition, that is, during the next few decades, will be critical.

The most noteworthy development in concepts about *personal welfare* lies in its being bracketed with programmes related to *personal development*. It is not merely that these are related because they are both desirable values; it is the nature of the current social changes that puts them together as a necessity for adaptation and survival. Briefly, it is a new degree of interdependence of organizations in society that creates these new features. Such problems as poverty, water supply, and sickness or social deviance are now perceived by a community or society not as deriving from aggregates of subelements that can be dealt with piecemeal, but as integrated major problems requiring central planning. In this increased interrelatedness, the autoregulative mechanisms that were held to be adequate in our traditional industrial society (laissez faire) are no longer effective. This change, according to Trist (1968), affects the requirements of welfare and development in a new way.

> a. *Welfare or well-being*, to continue to function well, refers to states of a system under conditions which maintain the steady state. . . . This set of terms, therefore, is concerned with the "statics" of adaptation—with stability (not to be confused with stagnation which is a state of ill-fare) and with the regulation and maintenance of stability.
>
> b. *Development*, or *progression*, to continue to advance, refers to processes by which a system reaches higher or steady states of a more adaptive nature. . . . This set of terms, therefore, is concerned with the "dynamics" of adaptation—with positive change leading to the establishment of widened and preferred orders. . . . Development involves discovery and innovation. It is concerned with the regulation of growth. [pp. 10–11]

Trist then describes how in preindustrial societies welfare was maintained by the autoregulative processes operating through the kinship system. When these failed, development processes involved the taking of an active role by coercive methods, for example, autocratic regimes with armies. *Development here was thus a function of welfare.*

With industrial societies, the more dynamic environment created by technological change involved *welfare becoming a function of development*. Development was autoregulative, operating through the market process; but the welfare of more and more people required active or planned intervention because it was no longer autoregulative, being dependent on overall, economic developments.

With the society into which we are moving *welfare and development became interdependent functions*. The best welfare secures development and, conversely, adaptation of a society now depends on the ecological regulation of the interdependencies of the innumerable social subsystems that characterize large societies undergoing rapid but uneven change. If subsystems do not develop, they fall into states of ill-fare. But because of the interdependence, ill-fare in a few subsystems can produce widespread disruption. Thus the values and behaviour of one section of young people can cause major damage to others. Autoregulative processes such as the remedial efforts of other local organizations can no longer cope adequately with welfare or development in these highly complex situations, and so an active role, that is, a centrally planned and integrative type of intervention, involving the society as a whole, becomes necessary as a rule. Two options are then possible according to Emery (1967). One, modelled on the physical sciences, moves towards an engineered society. The other, more related to the behavioural sciences, seeks a more organic society. It seeks a higher quality in *all* primary social units (as contrasted with this higher quality primarily in the control parts). To quote again from Trist:

> At the higher level of complexity which characterizes the transition to post-industrialism a higher quality is required in *all* primary social units. By primary social units is meant the set of concrete social resources which exist in the life-space of the individual, i.e. the people and institutions with which he directly interacts and to which he contributes his own resources: his family, his work-place, the school his children attend, the particular community in which he resides, the services and amenities actually available to him: in sum, all those entities which compose his *primary social world*. The quality of those resources, in his case, determines for the individual his "quality of life," on which his welfare and development alike depend. The objective of taking the active role is to bring into being ecological systems able to maintain primary social worlds of high quality throughout a society. How to do this has now become the over-riding question as we move towards post-industrialism (1968, pp. 17–18).

The concepts of welfare and development relate to social values and do not originate in science. They belong to what Trist groups as *ideo-existential phenomena*. These include (1) such entities as ideals, philosophies, beliefs and values, and so forth, as make up the forces shaping the way in which the world is construed; (2) the activators of behavior—goals, aspirations, emotions, and so forth; (3) social practices and processes and social perceptions.

These phenomena are interdependent and, most important for the management of change, are the gaps that develop from the slowness with which beliefs and values change compared with the emerging social realities. This characteristic lag on the *ideo* side makes for great difficulty in effecting changes in core values and in the basic shape of institutions for conscious and unconscious reasons. This lag also presents serious problems in regard to the achievement of the kinds of thinking required for the conceptions of welfare and development adaptive to the conditions of postindustrial society.

In the industrial phase of our development, the state took an increasing role in providing welfare services for the sick and the poor—though in connection with the latter there was a conflict between this aim and the Protestant ethic. Moreover, a variety of *preventive*, as distinct from remedial, measures had to be instituted to cope with infectious diseases. Other state measures included what can be termed *social defences*, for example, to control the dangers of lawlessness or drunkenness. *Social security* measures were begun. A third welfare concept also emerged from the necessities of the ongoing changes, and one which began to relate welfare and development as interdependent. This was the concept of *improvement*, for example, by public utilities in the physical environment and on the personal side by education, better conditions of work, and so on.

The predominant values, however, created conflicts around these issues, especially the cost of the welfare function of the State.

In our current scene, these conflicts in values evidently persist. Yet, as stressed earlier, what the social scientists are establishing is that personal *development* as well as welfare is an inherent requirement besides being a desirable value if the new society is to survive. Actually there is already in the more affluent countries an impressive array of improvement activity especially in the field of higher education. Within these countries welfare rights are starting to be perceived also as development rights. Emphasis is no longer so much on minimum standards as on the realization of potential, both for the sake of the individual and for society—though the conflicts carrying over through our traditional ideas and values make for crises through very uneven acceptances of change, and the means with which to achieve the new goals.

Trist sets out some of the inevitable *changes in emphasis of social patterns* as follows:

Thus, *Cultural or Ideo-existential Values are changing*

From	To
Achievement	Self-actualization
Self-control	Self-expression
Independence	Interdependence
Endurance of distress	Capacity for joy

Organisational Philosophies

From	To
Mechanistic forms	Organic forms
Competitive relations	Collaborative relations
Separate objectives	Linked objectives
Own resources absolutely their own	Own resources as belonging to society

Ecological Strategies

From	To
Responsive to crisis	Anticipative of crisis
Specific measures	Comprehensive measures
Requiring consent	Requiring participation
Short planning horizon	Long planning horizon
Damping conflict	Confronting conflict
Detailed central control	Generalized central control
Small local gov. units	Enlarged units
Standardized admin.	Innovative administration
Separate Services	Coordinated Services

Many of these considerations are not new. As I have said, however, a comprehensive grasp of all these changing features is necessary if the psychoanalytic contribution to their transition, a process now in being, is to be an effective one.

WHAT IS PSYCHOANALYSIS TO DO?

If we assume that the changes in our society have the characteristics outlined, then we can reflect upon their implications for psychoanalysis. (I use this term as a convenience to cover the total activities and influence of psychoanalysis, that is, through the effects of its knowledge upon our society, the use of the psychoanalytic method itself, and all the ways in which analysts might facilitate the application of psychoanalytic principles by all those making practical use of them.)

The concept of welfare and development as interdependent, while representing a new aspect at the social level, has, in relation to the individual, characterized psychoanalysis from the start. The whole process of psychoanalysis was conceived as releasing the individual from forces holding back his development and treatment was judged to be successful in proportion as it enabled the individual to achieve full use of his resources. The intensely individual nature of psychoanalytic treatment has, however, been a major factor against the development of ecological strategies which could widen the use of psychoanalytic principles in the welfare services. Any therapeutic endeavour that can be used only for a privileged few is liable, in our current society, to evoke resentful turbulence when its existence is widely known. I believe it is this reaction that underlies such views as were recently expressed in an article in *Time* (March, 1969), when psychoanalysis was described as on its "way out" while all kinds of other methods were being acclaimed as answers to meet the clamorous need for more mental health services. We would all agree that the classical psychoanalytic method has never been "in" as a practical procedure in community services. If psychoanalytic views about people, their development, conflicts, and functioning, have the validity we believe they have after these 90 years of constant and progressive work, in what sense can psychoanalysis be on the way out? We are, of course, accustomed to this kind of rejection of psychoanalysis. In the past we have relied on the autoregulative processes of a free market in the acceptance of ideas to deal with these "attacks." The social situation now presents another problem. Community mental health services are emerging as an ecological issue so that they will tend to be planned with a growing degree of integration and on a wide scale. It is in relation to this dynamic in the social field that psychoanalysis could be on the "way out."

We have to ask ourselves if we are really keeping psychoanalytic knowledge in step with the times. Our understanding of human behaviour can be formulated at different levels of abstraction—from the personal to the more impersonal forces we postulate in our metapsychology to explain some of the problems at the personal level. There is a great deal in common amongst the various psychodynamic schools of thought as long as we remain at the personal level. It is differences in metapsychological theories that lead to what the intelligent outsider can only see as "religious" wars. And in regard to our own metapsychology, we really have to examine the degree to which it may now be anachronistic. We must ask ourselves whether or not it is out of line with modern behavioural science—and keep in mind that not all our critics have only resistances as the determinants of their thought processes.

A lack of congruence with the current scientific world is fostered by the organizational forms of psychoanalysis. These consist almost entirely of training institutes, and even though several of these conduct research programmes, the latter are frequently confined to the data obtained within the psychoanalytic situation. (Notable exceptions are child development studies.) Here I wish to emphasize that the basic task for psychoanalysts is, and remains, the improvement of their theory and practice, and to train practitioners to the highest level possible. The application of psychoanalytic knowledge to community problems is an additional role. Nevertheless, in so far as analysis takes this as a vital task, I believe the gains to its own fundamental work will be large.

Trist's three areas of emphasis, the cultural or ideo-existential, the organizational, and the ecological, provide a good framework for looking at this task of bringing psychoanalysis into an effective relationship with the needs of the community.

PSYCHOANALYSIS AND CURRENT IDEO-EXISTENTIAL ISSUES

The extent to which psychoanalytic views are accepted by the innovating sections of the public as relevant to the current ideo-existential problems will determine the use of these views in general measures for improving personal development, and in creating welfare services.

Taking the changing emphases for the individual, we see him as moving from an independent, self-controlled, achieving person who has to endure a good deal of restriction—both from his outer and inner environments, with associated tensions and distress—to one who will be much more interdependent, more self-expressing and self-actualizing, and with much more freedom as a result to enjoy living. To me, the most noteworthy feature of Trist's aspects is the use of the word *self*.

It may be a reflection of the interrelatedness of what is going on in society that this is the area now recognized amongst psychoanalysts as the one in most need of study. The self is the term we use for that core of the personality that preserves continuity in change—its preservation is what makes change acceptable. If the integrity of the self is threatened, change is resisted—often violently, in keeping as it were, with the defence of our most precious possession. With so much change in the fabric of society, it seems highly likely that it is the threat to the self that is most closely related to the many manifestations of anxiety that we see around us.

The self as a central issue for psychoanalysis is familiar enough, but we need a great deal more specific knowledge of what creates a good core to the self and what are the social settings required to maintain it in such a way that the individual is constantly enriching it.

The formulation of a good account of the development and functioning of the self would be of major value in helping society to cope with some of its current ideo-existential problems. A whole area that is pressing for more clarification is the study of the dynamics of the ego-ideal. Our patients have perhaps led us, understandably enough, to be preoccupied with the ego, the superego, and the instincts. The ego-ideal is as it were at the interface between much of our self-feeling and the values in society which are congruent with it.

In the anxious striving for more understanding of man as a person, for knowledge of how his positive attitudes are fostered as well as of the conditions which release his unique potential for losing his person-directed conduct and replacing this with sadistic and destructive behaviour of a kind unknown in the animal world, the existentialist philosophers have offered an appealing approach. Although it is difficult to discern a conceptual framework in their writings that does justice to the dynamics of the biological processes underlying human behaviour, they have with their phenomenological descriptions reinforced the view that psychoanalysis does not have at present an adequate psychoanalytic theory of the self. Here, however, we expose a paradox in the current psychoanalytic scene. As Weisman (1965) has put it, existentialists are concerned with the "hiatus between the *formulations* of psychoanalytic theory and the *problems* with which individual men are involved" (p. 10). The value of existentialist thought is to stress those subjective features that relate "to a unique responsible person from the *inside* of his experience, and which defy conventional categories and descriptions" (p. 11).

That the nature of man as a person has become a focus of psychoanalytic interest in the last 20 years is reflected in the widespread reference in our literature to such terms as the ego, identity, and the self. It must surely be important for us to devote more of our attention to the response to these ideas in various sections of the community. Allied professional groups can use our writings directly, and it behooves us, for instance, to ponder on the very wide assimilation amongst these groups of Erikson's studies on the problems of identity, so much so that the phrase "identity crisis" has become as popular as the "oedipus complex" became a few decades ago.

Similarly, the object-relations theorists such as Fairbairn, Winnicott, and Guntrip have also made a very ready appeal to the mental health professions in Great Britain. Unlike those of the Culturalists, their views represent an evolution from classical psychoanalytic concepts. These writers retain the fundamental importance of the very early structuring of the personality in the mother–infant interaction, and hence the interest in their work cannot be said to be dominated by a rejection of the importance of infantile sexuality and aggression. Their appeal seems to lie in the more direct relationship to the problems of intrapersonal and interpersonal conflict than is apparent in much of our writing couched in traditional metapsychology.

The relevance of these theoretical developments to current ideo-existential concerns is intuitively grasped by our writers and dramatists—the main transmitters to society of any new insights. Writers do not propagate our conceptual views; but when deeply affected by the human problems they illumine, they create archetypal characters who embody the preoccupations of the age. The mass media, and above all television, have immensely expanded the scope and rapidity of their influence so that they stimulate a restless dynamic in the social field. Writers, too, can have a remarkable sensitivity in regard to appraising psychodynamic theory—they respond to what makes sense amongst the inarticulate gropings of most people.

Underlining these responses in various sections of the community emphasises the dynamic properties of the social field. It is when we ignore the fact that the social field is itself changed by psychoanalytic ideas that we get such absurdities as the extrapolations that are made in relation to psychotherapeutic needs in the community. Thus one still hears the following kind of statement. One analyst can treat say 10 patients: there are x thousands potential patients in the community and so we need $x/10$ analysts—a statement made even when the size of $x/10$ is ridiculous. Such extrapolations really assume a view of society as composed of separate self-determining individuals.

The social dynamic aroused can be illustrated by various actions within sections of the community to give help to many whose troubles are either not met by current resources or who are not adequately relieved by them. To many of those involved in community mental health services, the disturbing issue recurs of how the growth of expertise in a therapeutic method tends to be accompanied by an increasing narrowing of its range of applicability. Movements such as Alcoholics Anonymous, The Samaritans, and so forth, come into being not only to fill a gap but also because the "experts" say so many people are unsuitable for their "treatment." These movements then tend to be ignored by the more highly trained psychotherapists—but may it not be that there are important aspects in the therapeutic relationships that these movements foster? At any rate, they are worthy of the psychoanalyst's interest.

We do not have to be the reformers of society. Our psychoanalytic model for the management of change is a unique one in relation to the ideo-existential problems of the age—for in our own work, our patients take their own destiny into their hands when we can assist them to learn more of themselves. It is a model that can be adapted by society in its own ways.

We may have to contemplate being more involved in creating opportunities for sections of the public to learn more about psychoanalytic knowledge—and the mass media make quite new possibilities in this respect. It is particularly important that psychoanalytic thought should permeate to a far greater extent than at present our views on education. Instead of being pejoratively linked in the public mind with neurosis, is it not timely for its "image" to be more identified with personal growth and development, that is, with education. This whole question, however, is so large that I cannot do other here than to bring the essential aspect before us, namely, that the nature of our relatedness to the social scene of today has a new dynamic and one on which we must reflect very purposefully.

THE PROVISION OF PSYCHOTHERAPEUTIC SERVICES: ORGANIZATIONAL PHILOSOPHIES

In contrast with the as yet scarcely developed contribution that psychoanalysis might make to the ideo-existential problems, I believe that we are much clearer in regard to how we can assist with the expansion of facilities throughout the community for offering psychotherapeutic help (Sutherland 1964, 1968).

The situation in the field is one of widening awareness of the nature of psychological stress and one that is now prompting remedial action. We have also to keep in mind that increasing permissiveness will mean more need to seek professional guidance. Thus freer divorce measures will inevitably entail more responsible and constructive steps in relation to each partner in the marriage and to the welfare of children, that is, there will be a greater demand for good counselling services. Psychological disorders vary greatly in their severity and in the ways in which the underlying conflicts may be expressed. A large range of agencies can therefore be appropriate as the first ports of call for help, or the first place wherein an underlying psychological problem will be exposed, for example, the family doctor, social work agencies of all kinds, the courts, the clergy, and so on.

The uppermost need within these agencies is to increase understanding and skill. We have now had a good deal of experience in methods of doing this; Michael and Enid Balint, for instance, have written extensively on this subject (M. Balint 1957; Balint and Balint 1961). The essential step here is to have consultants meet in regular seminars with the various professional groups. Conducting these seminars is best done by consultants who combine psychotherapeutic expertise with experience of group work as the group reactions can often be used to give a direct experience of how emotional difficulties interfere with the tasks people have to do—in this case, learning.

Although different agencies may be created in the community, these cannot remain discrete. They inevitably have to become integrated parts of a *sociotherapeutic system*—along with the specialist psychotherapeutic and psychiatric centre. In each agency, staff are constantly testing the limits of their skills because it is in the nature of much psychological disorder that a presenting difficulty, once it is brought under scrutiny, reveals more complex issues. The staff of each agency has therefore to have free and welcomed access to the specialist centre when they need further help. Again, a proportion of people using one agency as their first source may have to be transferred to another for a variety of reasons, for example, the other may be more appropriate for special problems uncovered. Such interrelatedness can only become effective in practice when the various units share a common core of understanding about human problems in addition to any special function each unit may have. Furthermore, the community has also got to share increasingly in this common understanding if the helping services are to be perceived as concerned with the welfare and development of its members. I believe the essentials of this common framework can be formulated in the vocabulary of everyday speech—or at least with very few technical terms.

With this kind of interrelated mental health service becoming available, we can see the position of the psychoanalytic/psychiatric centre as a pivotal resource for the whole. The most disturbed individuals are its concern and the staff therefore acquires more comprehensive and deeper knowledge about psychological disorders. Inevitably the staff groups within the specialist centre are looked to for helpful support and for the opportunities to increase understanding and skill.

The boundaries to what agencies can do will be pressed outwards all the time. This is in the nature of the work and in the situation. The staffs in many of the field agencies, particularly the social work ones, will have to become increasingly responsible in the professional sense. They cannot develop unless they see themselves as creating independent professions fulfilling the criteria of being a professional body, that is, (1) building up their own body of knowledge with constant scientific scrutiny of their working principles; (2) formulating these principles for training; and (3) creating a code of professional behaviour. The social work groups lean very heavily upon psychoanalytic knowledge, but they have their own specific tasks. The psychoanalysts within centres, however, can be invaluable sources of support to them in their professional growth—and conversely, analysts, can learn much from their work.

When the specialist centres take on this supportive and educative role, appropriate activities on their part are required. Psychoanalytic work has to retain its status within them as its detailed study of personal growth and functioning is our basic laboratory. In contrast with private practice, however, the psychoanalysts in a community-related centre should try to make special studies of current social problems, for example, of drug addiction or some such problem prominent in their area. It is only in centres with a group of analysts that the optimal conditions for such studies are normally available, especially the opportunity to integrate the study of intrapsychic with social factors.

Additional to psychoanalytic work, the special centre has also to use therapeutic methods akin to those usable in the field agencies. Thus it should develop considerable expertise in group psychotherapeutic methods, in marital and family therapies. With its resources of highly trained staff, it has to be able to offer consultative help to the other agencies in which these methods will play a prominent role. Moreover, within the specialist centre, it is particularly useful when representatives of all the relevant professions are engaged in this work. Thus, it facilitates the growth of the social work professions when these groups can relate to a member of their own profession as well as say to the psychoanalyst in the specialist centre.

I remarked earlier that these developments may raise again questions of professional boundaries, and such issues as when is someone "ill" (see Szasz, 1961). In our field *illness* is a term that has originated more out of professional rather than scientific roots. It may well be that it is the meaning of "medical responsibility" that has to be reexamined. As I see it, what is specific to the doctor are those people in whom there is (*a*) a somatic manifestation that needs elucidation; (*b*) a degree of disturbance that can be made more manageable with the aid of psychotropic drugs; (*c*) a severity of disorder that needs special inpatient care. Naturally many people will present difficult decisions in regard to who is to take primary responsibility. Such decisions should become much easier to reach as the whole network of service agencies builds up active collaboration. Faced with the anxieties of changing professional roles, interprofessional tensions will be inevitable. It is salutary to keep firmly in mind that, if there is one field of work in which there will be no redundancy problems, it is ours—the field of mental health in which demands are going to grow all the more as services become available.

THE RELATIONSHIP OF THE MENTAL HEALTH SERVICES TO THE COMMUNITY: ECOLOGICAL STRATEGY

A widespread network of therapeutic services will clearly be of the utmost significance in the community's striving for constant betterment. The people seeking help represent those who for a great variety of reasons are unable to function as they would wish in their community. The data available in all the of the therapeutic agencies must therefore be fed back to those in all key positions concerned with the improvement of our society. To do so involves much further work, for example, to elucidate some of the general processes underlying the very complex array of specific manifestations of disorder. The knowledge gained in the therapeutic centre about the intrapsychic factors in "breakdowns" has to be subjected to the expertise that social scientists can bring so that the social forces affecting the community can be identified. This could be achieved by having the specialist therapeutic centre as one unit in a complex—a group of units whose overall mission could be described as the study of human relations. The resources of this larger complex would be such that studies could be made of an appropriately comprehensive kind. This complex would, in addition to maintaining active internal scientific exchange, seek relationships with the relevant sections of the community, especially with those concerned with the planning for the main services affecting the social and physical environments.

SUMMARY

I have tried to show what I perceive to be the forces coming into more prominence in our society, and which are impinging upon us with increasing urgency. Far from being on the way out, psychoanalytic knowledge could, and should, be more than ever on the way in. It is incumbent upon psychoanalysts, especially those in specialist centres, as many of us now are, to study the current scene as carefully as we can and to act constructively to the best of our ability. I believe that, if we do not innovate in regard to our own roles, our mental health centres will shrivel and hence the welfare and development movements will be impoverished.

15. COUNSELLING SERVICES

SOURCES OF THE COUNSELLING MOVEMENT

Like most social phenomena the sources of the counselling movement are many, and they are clearly interrelated. I believe the major initiating stimulus was the result of Freud's discoveries. Freud made sense of what in people was dark, mysterious, irrational and, above all, frightening. He showed how the psychological disorders in the person could be correlated with failures in his social development. In the light of his views, the traditional moralistic attitude towards much human behaviour, suffering, and weakness could not be maintained. Strange thoughts, feelings, and actions could be understood, and if these did not vanish after their nature and origins were elucidated, they could often be managed better. The process of help, moreover, was located firmly within the personal relationship between the helper and the person in need.

Although psychoanalysis is the most intensively developed way in which this process is carried out, it was very early recognised by social workers and others that they could make use of the new understanding in a way appropriate to their setting. It was a criticism of the adoption of psychoanalytic views by social workers that in these early endeavours they followed the model of the psychoanalyst much too closely—a situation that was also fostered by the psychoanalysts who offered them consultative help. The social workers, however, gradually emerged with more confidence in their own ways of working and, correspondingly, the analysts became clearer in regard to how they could offer "training." The great step forward for the social workers lay in their regained confidence in working with the family on the basis of this enlarged understanding; and this was their usual "therapeutic unit," if one might use this term, rather than the individual.

Freud's views also had a profound impact on the social sciences, which in time began to bring new knowledge of how social forces affect behaviour. The result has been that the study of psychological disorders now emphasises what is happening in the family, at work, and in other sections of the individual's social environment. We know that even the most healthy people need certain satisfactions from the transactions they have with others. If deprived of too many of these, they can, with surprising speed, begin to show various stress manifestations or even to deteriorate into almost unrecognisable shells of what they were.

In short, well-adapted healthy persons are the product of a successful development in the various stages of their growth and then of continuing their inner satisfactions through their experiences in a good social milieu. Just what satisfactions are needed change with the different phases of the life-cycle. What appears to be the fundamental aspect is that, given enough satisfaction, people have an ongoing sense of self as "somebody's somebody" and so of "being" somebody. It is when this self-feeling is threatened that stress is felt and when, often enough, help is needed.

In the past, it was one of the great functions of the churches to affirm the sense of self, especially at times of crisis—the recurrent crises of sickness and death, of birth and marriage. The changes in the social fabric with industrialisation and urbanisation greatly increased the stressful situations, and these new situations along with the development of scientific knowledge, especially in biology and the human sciences, led to a recession in the use of the churches.

The need to care, however, was in no way diminished, and the new understanding of people and of social forces gave a new appeal. As Professor Halmos (1966) shows, the fall in church attendance has been paralleled by a rise in the size of the caring professions. This development was not institutionalised except in so far as certain professional groups developed organisations to safeguard their work and to train new members. As he further points out, it was inevitable that the counselling ideology, the belief that people could use a caring relationship in which to explore the nature of their difficulties with a view to enriching their own resources for managing these, should lead to most of the existing helping professions acquiring more understanding and skill in human relationships.

Out of this early development came two new professions: the psychoanalyst and the psychiatric social worker. Both of these groups had major influences on other professions with whom their work brought them in contact, for example, psychiatrists, general practitioners and other doctors, social workers of all kinds, teachers, the clergy, and psychologists. When the new knowledge spread through the community, the scale of need and the range of psychological disorders were exposed as very large, and in thinking of counselling strategies, it is therefore basic to keep in mind this great and diverse incidence. Thus, all estimates show that anything from 15 percent to 30 percent—some people put it at 40 percent—of people have their functioning as good human beings seriously impaired by inner conflict. These figures bring home the tragic loss of human creativity and human resources going on in our society. There is not only the scale and range of severity of the effects of psychological stress, but the multiplicity of ways in which it can manifest direct psychological disorder, from inhibited withdrawing attitudes to the infinite variety of impulsive and conflicted behaviour.

One result of the growth of knowledge and the urge to meet the emerging demands was that the professional workers devised additional methods of increasing their contribution, for example, through group work. Group work, however, is not a kind of "poor man's psychoanalysis"; it has a validity and value of its own. But there are other consequences of the growth of the helping professions that have caused concern. As skills have developed, the professionals have become more "professional." Skills can become a way of helping some, but of not helping other people. If the person does not fit one's skill, one cannot do anything, or one does not want to do anything. Another effect is that as skills get more expert, the work of giving psychological help gets more technical; it seems even to get "technologised." As Professor Halmos points out, the professional begins to get absorbed in the technicalities of the work and can lose sight of the fact that the fundamental and basic factor in giving personal help is the concern of one human being for another. Related to the acquisition of more professionalism has been the understandable caution on the part of the groups with more developed skills towards the groups with less skill, and a good deal of intergroup rivalries appeared. I remember 25 years ago (that was the time, as many of you will recall, when you could find several different social workers or agencies all at work on one family) how difficult it was to get creative collaboration amongst the different groups. Such difficulties arise most readily when groups are uncertain of what they are doing. Anybody who is in the counselling field, from the Samaritans to the psychoanalysts, is uncertain or confused some of the time. For free collaboration, the limits of understanding and skills have to be readily acknowledged without any sense of failure. At times professional and other groups have behaved as though they were going to be put out of business when their limits were exposed. Fortunately, this insecurity is disappearing as the scale of needs is appreciated, and as the value of many sources and kinds of personal help is recognised.

Great developments were stimulated when the National Health Service came into being. Needs became more pressing and the psychoanalysts became concerned to share skills with others. More striking was the way in which various groups of nonprofessionals began to appear to fill the many gaps in the services, a response influenced by the knowledge about human problems that was being transmitted to the public by our writers, dramatists, and artists, and especially by the mass media. The Marriage Guidance Council had been established before the war, but it began to develop its services rapidly. Counsellors also appeared in the schools. A new force was the self-help groups, such as Alcoholics Anonymous.

SOME DANGERS

The recognition of the scale of needs for personal help and the swell of personal services to meet these have not been without their counterforces. Two of these,

I believe, have to be watched. On the medical side, the whole training of doctors is to define the problem, and the great advances in medical knowledge have enabled them to do this in much of their work. The nature of the illness is to be identified and the treatment then follows. This has led doctors to think of personal problems and needs in the same way. Along with the almost impossible task of giving people with problems sufficient time to talk about them, there is a resultant tendency to treat human problems as something best dealt with by a drug, a de-tenser of some sort. And, of course, there is a great pressure from the public for the doctor to take this stance because of the powerful wishes for magical solutions rather than facing the realities that underlie our psychological makeup. The forces in the situation that drive us towards expedient measures would be serious enough as obstacles to the doctor giving adequate personal help without a further, and perhaps more dangerous factor, namely, the adoption of what might be termed a pseudoscientific view about human nature. In this respect the doctors are not alone, for many psychologists and others also share this outlook. People who are involved in a caring relationship with others find it very difficult to adopt this sort of simplistic approach. When studying isolated bits of human behaviour, the value of a reductive approach is very appealing, but the plain fact is that people are *complex*, that being a person and operating as a person, functioning on a personal level, requires a conceptual framework that does justice to these immensely complex forces. As a nuclear scientist said to one of his psychological friends when he had been watching a child at play, “My work is child’s play compared with the study of child’s play.”

We have got to watch these kinds of dangers because they can be part of a value system about people, which it is asserted is a scientific approach and hence the only one likely to give us true knowledge. Knowledge of people at this unique personal level can and must be checked and tested but this is not to assume that the best ways of helping people should be those based on experimental methods. To be concerned about others, the essence of simple help, is not a scientific activity. It is a human relationship in which validated knowledge about people can be used.

I have recently become apprehensive about a danger of another kind of which signs are visible at times in the social work world, particularly with the statutory provision for expanding the social services. The problems of giving help, of being concerned about human beings, of having the complexities and especially the dependent needs of people put upon one, are so disturbing to some, and this inner threat is reinforced by the external task of providing help on an adequate scale, that they wish to get rid of this task to promote, instead, social change. The assumption then becomes that casework and counselling are not really necessary if we get social conditions improved. This is again, to my mind, a dangerous oversimplification because it begs the whole issue of what *is* a person and what *is* personal help. Clearly I cannot pretend to answer these highly complicated questions; but at least we can keep in mind the important factors we do know about persons. The value of the psychoanalysts’ contribution comes from the fact that here the "counsellors" have studied people in detail and in depth to find out something of what they are about. They have, moreover, maintained these relationships over long periods and through phases when negative feelings could all too easily have led to the helping effort being abandoned. Working theories are naturally governed by the mode and setting of the investigating tools and a danger for the psychoanalyst is that he may refer too many things to what is going on inside the individual and not enough to what is happening in his social environment. The important thing for our understanding of others is to keep in mind these two sets of variables. There are the inner factors, our biological endowment and the structuring of the personality on this basis and the experiences of the individual during his growth. The other set is the social forces impinging on the person from his direct, close relationships to the more intangible pressures of the culture in which he is embedded and its values. These two are constantly interacting and any thinking about the social environment that ignores the inner personal factors is just as unrealistic as the converse.

THE NATURE OF THE PERSON

No individual reaches adulthood with a personality that is a coherent, completely integrated system. We all are split into subsystems of which three are Freud's familiar ego, id, and superego. I believe it is more useful to think of these systems not in this rather impersonal "scientific" language but in more personal terms because they operate in us as subselves. Instead of the ego, we can envisage a central self, the self that relates to others, that enriches us by learning from experience. Correspondingly, the id can be regarded as the part of our personality containing the frustrated relationships of our past. This part drives us to realise those goals that have become inbuilt from early experience, to seek relationships in which the other is someone to be coerced into the roles we wish, to dominate or to be dominated, to depend on in infantile ways or to be mothered, and so on. The superego part contains a range of primitive control systems with inner figures threatening us in varying degrees of severity with retaliation if we try to enact the frustrated needs.

This tripartite structuring of the personality has long been regarded as a useful framework against which to understand the human being. (Spirit, mind, and body as the great spheres in man have much in common with the systems I have been suggesting.) If the central self is founded securely on the basis of the individual having been loved and wanted, he has a core of security and confidence that can meet the uncertainties of the external world. In such persons, the conflicting needs and controls do not dominate behaviour by maladaptive clinging to ways of relating evolved to meet past needs. The subselves here can be realised in large measure, either by fusion with the activities of the central self as in adopting a particular career or in leisure pursuits. When the subselves are too strong relative to the central self, then we have people who become driven from within along certain lines and against all logic, although they may, as is well recognised, try to provide rationalisations. Here, for example, we may get a strong desire to follow a career, or to step out of one, in order to make a protest against a dominating parent rather than for more realistic aims.

Because the central self is founded in relationships, the continuation of our sense of well-being rests on our continuing to be involved in significant relationships and activities. The right foundations in the core of the self enable the individual to keep a strong sense of continuity of self while at the same time changing constantly as the different phases of life enrich personal experience. Change and crisis become challenges rather than situations in which to feel threatened to the point of losing our identity, of going to bits. In meeting change, however, the adaptive growth of the individual is normally anchored to the self-affirmation provided by sharing.

WHEN THE SELF NEEDS HELP

Needs to share uncertainty and threat may very enormously in their scope and intensity. For our present purposes it is useful to separate two kinds of problem for which this need commonly arises. The first stems from the major change points in ordinary growth, phases in which there are new experiences to be assimilated and adapted to—for example, learning to walk, to go to school, the bodily changes at adolescence, career, marriage, becoming a parent, retirement. The self is a dynamic organising system whose core we can describe only from subjective experience. It is what we mean when we use the word "I," and we cannot reduce this basic aspect of every person. The self has a constant forward reference; there is always a sense in which people are oriented to the future. At points of major change, if people do not see where they are going to fit, then they need to test out this area of uncertainty by talking to someone who has been there, who knows what this new world is like, and from whose experience one can affirm or feel oneself ahead in time. This seems to be the essence of the kind of help a counsellor gives at these normal turning points. It has been characteristic of our society to deny or keep away from the emotional needs in people at these times within our formal institutions. Perhaps the economic uncertainties of the industrial revolution led us to become obsessed with work, with achievement, and with acquiring knowledge or skills of commercial value. Our youth, however, is rightly protesting against the denials of the power of feelings in human development; and our greater affluence with increasing time to contemplate our lives is also pressing us towards the fuller recognition of what is going on inside ourselves.

The second kind of problem involves more than the need to share the new tasks of the future, although this group of problems may emerge at the great phase changes in development. The difficulties here are seriously affected by failures in the earlier stages of development. The individual has not a secure or strong enough central self and, indeed, what security he has in this part of himself is diminished by a threatened rise in the relative strength of his subselves. Such imbalances are most commonly seen at adolescence, but they may be precipitated by many later changes. To go to the other end of the life cycle we are all familiar with the person who goes to pieces on retirement, or with the loss of a spouse or the loss of some especially valued possession. In the adolescent, it is the drive towards new relationships occasioned by the development of sexuality that evokes profound anxieties leading to massive withdrawals from others or to impulsive, ill-adapted attempts to cope with the new tensions. With our older examples, we see individuals who have managed to cope with rather immature dependent needs by the particular people or jobs they could use. When these props are removed, the central self becomes overwhelmed by loss and often it requires special and intensive measures to redress the inner situation.

Now the great difficulty for counsellors is that presenting problems are often a mixture of these rather broad kinds of psychological situations, and, worse, not easily distinguished in advance. When developmental failures have been serious, the manifestations of difficulty are frequently plain enough to identify the problem as one of psychopathology rather than development crisis. In these cases the individual can be appropriately referred for specialist psychological help. What is to be done when the nature of the problem cannot be identified in advance, when we cannot say the individual should go for help to counsellor A in one kind of service rather than to counsellor B in a different type of agency? To make matters more complex, it is not only the counsellor who does not know what a problem entails. The individual himself may be quite unaware of the forces in himself. Take, for example, the student who is finding in the early stages of his university career that he is becoming increasingly unable to study effectively. He may wonder if he has chosen the right subjects, or if he should be applying himself in some different way. As he talks about himself it may soon strike the counsellor that the lack of the student's success is rooted in intense conflicts with parents, conflicts whose intensity is quite unrecognised by the individual. Counselling may then have to move into more prolonged psychotherapy, that is, into a longer relationship in which the conflicts can be exposed by the adequate understanding and skill of the counsellor who will now be described as a psychotherapist. There is thus no sharp line dividing these two activities. Counselling and more specialised psychological help merge into one another and it is certainly not always possible to say in advance what a particular individual will need.

One of the most successful pieces of psychotherapeutic work I ever did was in fact one hour's counselling. This concerned a successful man, aged 51, who was facing a critical decision in his career and who was referred to me because in the past such situations had usually been followed by bouts of physical symptoms for which he had had a great range of medical treatments. He happened to be a fairly insightful man and we were able to bring out the recurrent pattern of his crises as related to a conflict between him and his parents. Beforehand, the history had led me to expect that I should be recommending him for probably fairly lengthy psychotherapy and instead he was able to make such good use of our talking together that he went ahead from one success to another. (These success stories, I need hardly remind you, are sadly infrequent!)

ORGANISING THE COUNSELLING SERVICES

How then in the light of these complexities and uncertainties can we proceed? We must start from the fact that since personal problems arise in such diverse ways we must have a large range of different kinds of counsellors. We need people in roles or agencies whose image will be readily and hopefully associated with certain kinds of problems, for example, the school counsellor, marriage guidance, the probation officer, a social worker, the family doctor, and so on. Once inside the door, the counsellor may then find a situation for which effective help needs more expertise and/or time than he can give. This uncertainty is bound to be there and any system we may devise to improve the effectiveness of our counselling provisions must start from this fact. It is also the case that by the time an individual has talked fairly extensively about his problems, he will have become attached to this counsellor and too abrupt a reference elsewhere may be felt as a rather damaging rejection.

These kinds of complication are in the very nature of counselling and they suggest that any organisational system of our counselling services will require quite special flexibilities. In the first place all those in counselling services must feel they are sharing in a coordinated endeavour. They need a sufficiently common frame of reference to permit appreciation of what each component is doing, a common understanding of the main determinants of the effective and satisfying functioning of people. For instance, can we have a counselling movement making the progress we want if specific parts confront the individual with incompatible views? If, for instance, one agency has been trying to get the student I mentioned earlier to understand his difficulties, is it good enough that he may be told by say a family doctor that he should not fill his head with "all that introspective stuff"? What he needs is to snap out of it and get on to the sports ground, or to take these tablets for a few weeks! Again, what are we to do if say the clergyman also adopts a similarly antipsychological standpoint, but instead of a medical treatment suggests a "moral welfare programme" of exhortation to support a repressive attack on the inner sources of the disturbance. Naturally, I have taken rather extreme instances to make the point. Nevertheless, although they represent attitudes that are disappearing they are still to be found. It must be a task for any group concerned to advance counselling services that they can assert with conviction the kind of framework we need to do justice to persons without reducing them to oversimplified mechanisms. In this endeavour, counsellors have to be prepared to confront critics who seek to "blind with science," with masses of figures and data—all of them often irrelevant to the job the counsellor has to do. Research in the human sciences, and especially in the area of personal conflict, is too often conducted by people who have never had to talk to a human being in distress as part of their professional training. Indeed, they have not infrequently been told to avoid such "unscientific" situations.

Within a system in which free communication can be encouraged between the different units, a second major requirement is the way in which learning can be built in as a permanent process. Counselling is a personal relationship in which counsellors use their own experience of themselves to help their clients to enlarge their understanding—and so to make better decisions. The process of counselling is an educational activity for both parties, and each encounter is unique. The training of counsellors is therefore designed to give them more understanding of themselves, an objective which relies on appropriate opportunities for them to share experiences. Intellectual knowledge of personality development does little by itself to equip counsellors. Such knowledge has to be assimilated with recognition of the relevant processes at work in them if it is to be of effective help in the counselling task. Learning is best facilitated when we are up against a difficulty, a blockage in our understanding of what a client is bringing. What is needed then is an opportunity for counsellors to describe their difficulty within a trusted group. They have got to feel free to expose their confusions and secure enough to accept the implications for their own personalities of the comments that others will make. This sharing of experience is best done in a group of colleagues with the assistance of a consultant, someone with more experience than the members of the group. It is essential that all counselling services should provide for this continual learning process by arranging for regular seminar-discussion meetings. How frequently these may be held will be governed by various circumstances, but the essential feature is that they are maintained regularly. There must be no question of them being regarded as a fringe benefit or luxury. If the helping of others is to be given the serious status it deserves, then the ongoing learning of all must be built into the whole endeavour as a first priority in planning our programme.

PEOPLE AND INSTITUTIONS

In considering our services for the welfare and development of the person we must parallel any effort to assist inner growth by one that examines what is happening to people within the institutions concerned with their development, particularly, our educational ones. The data to be obtained from the counselling services are unique. People do not reveal some of the most significant factors influencing their behaviour except in a situation that offers help. Questionnaires or questionings cannot go below the surface, for often the person does not appreciate what is there. The knowledge gathered by counsellors must be made available to those who are responsible for our institutions. In the society into which we are moving, now known to the sociologists as the postindustrial society, new values are replacing the old. A complusive drive towards individual achievement is becoming less acceptable to our youth who are much more attracted by the values of self-realisation. More leisure time and activities will make people more critical of existing institutions and the values that have inspired them. In this society, the result of the technological revolution, sociologists put the dilemma thus. In the greatly increased interdependence of all the sections of our environment, change has become much more unpredictable and planning has to play a far greater role than hitherto. For such an increasingly planned society we have two choices; an elite group planning for the large majority or, as the Western democracies have chosen, planning as a process in which everyone must participate at some level. It is our belief that we enrich people best when they share in their destiny, in what is being planned.

For the creation of such a society, with its need to have all individuals realise to the full their potential, there must be widely available counselling services for all stages of the life cycle and at the same time, a constant scrutiny of the fit between our institutions and the kind of person we want them to produce. Thus we have to ask, what kind of schools and further education establishments will equip people to make this new society, in which the price of permissiveness is inevitably greater responsibility and concern for each other? Are their structures appropriate for this task or are they functioning on the basis of outmoded values? Can an institution in which there is an inbuilt hierarchial order imposed from without, a structure that assumes that only when the chief executive in the institution is appointed by some external body can the community rest assured that the staff will be properly supervised and controlled, really practise in a genuine way the exercise of responsible participation amongst its staff? And, if not, can a staff under these conditions be expected to educate others towards the kind of mature and independent persons we want?

These are the kinds of questions we must ask and I believe that those with counselling experience have a unique role in helping to answer them, for it is in the counselling situation that we pick up the frustrations and stresses that people are experiencing. There is no opposition between counselling services and the management of institutions. These two activities are more than complementary; they are necessary to each other.

16. PSYCHOTHERAPY IN COMMUNITY MENTAL HEALTH

Although the term community psychiatry has proved difficult to define acceptably, the ideas behind it are now initiating active programs in almost every country. The basis of this movement is an increased understanding of the person, not as an isolated individual, but as a being whose functioning must be viewed against the networks of social interaction in which he grows and lives. This "third revolution in psychiatry" is a logical development from the second one that was introduced when Freud showed that the psychological disorders of the adult could be correlated with failures in his social development. These views had a profound impact on the social sciences, which in turn began to bring new knowledge of how social forces affect behaviour. The result has been that the study of the psychological disorders now stresses what is happening in the family, the work situation, and the community. Correspondingly, the task of creating adequate therapeutic and preventive measures in a community has to be conceived and planned comprehensively from a wide background of knowledge and with the expertise of many disciplines.

In this collaborative endeavour, the psychotherapeutic clinic must play a fundamental role and in what follows are some brief observations on this role based on experience at The Tavistock Clinic over 20 years.

PROVIDING PSYCHOTHERAPEUTIC FACILITIES FOR THE COMMUNITY

To appraise the task of providing adequate therapeutic facilities, we have to remind ourselves of some of the essential features of the psychological disorders.

a. By "disorder" is meant a condition in the individual in which his functioning is felt by him, or by others, to be impaired in a way that needs the help of a specially skilled person to remedy it. In any comprehensive psychiatric service, many different therapeutic methods will be valued. However much physical methods facilitate matters, the need for psychotherapeutic help remains in

As Medical Director, The Tavistock Clinic, London, 1947–1968

practically all cases. By this term, I refer to the personal relationship with a professional person in which those in distress can share and explore the nature of their conflicts and possibly change some of the determinants of these through experiencing unrecognized forces in themselves. Further, I shall use "psychotherapeutic clinic" not necessarily as a separate institution, but also as the psychotherapy component in a comprehensive psychiatric service.

b. The psychological disorders comprise a wide range of complexity and severity with regard to their underlying causes and treatment. Various levels of skill can therefore be appropriate. The highest level of skill is ordinarily available in the psychotherapeutic clinic where the specially trained psychotherapist is based. Less specialized psychological help is given in many other professional roles.
c. The incidence of psychological disorders is widespread and demands for help are likely to increase as awareness of their manifestations grows.
d. Breakdown is governed by an interplay of both individual and social factors, and it is therefore particularly liable to occur at "crises" or points of change in the "life space." Help must be available at these times because the opening up of inadequate defensive patterns can often permit new growth processes to take place, both in the individual and in the family.
e. The nature of much disorder manifests itself indirectly. Help is frequently sought on the wrong basis and the source of help may collude in the avoidance of the important issues.
f. Many pathogenic social situations are unrecognized or denied, for example, one member of the family in the disturbed role hides the trouble elsewhere.
g. Even when recognized, resistance to changing dysfunction, both in the individual and in social groups or organizations, is a specific problem requiring special procedures.

Such considerations, and they are by no means exhaustive, force us inescapably to certain conclusions about how the task must be tackled.

1. There must be a large number of readily available sources of help throughout the community. The specialist psychotherapeutic clinic is not and cannot be the only source of skilled help.
2. These sources must comprise a range of different settings and roles. Psychological disorder is commonly manifested in a specific section of the individual's life. Help is therefore sought by "knocking on one or more of many doors" according to the nature of the trouble, for example, the family doctor, the probation officer, or the Family Planning Clinic.

   Many different professions and agencies are already involved in helping individuals and families and their great advantage is that they are the most acceptable doors for those in trouble especially at times of crisis. The important issue here is, therefore, the extent to which these groups can increase their contribution in quality and quantity.

3. More skilled contribution from the various professional groups, and especially as their work concentrates on the family and its social setting, entails progressively more cooperation among them and between them and the specialist centers. One or more workers will often be involved at one time with one family. Initial therapeutic work may lead to more serious problems being uncovered with the need to get help from the specialist center. This help may take the form of consultation enabling the field workers to handle the problems themselves; or it may mean that the treatment is taken over by the center. In this latter case it is clearly important that the process through which people get help should be felt as preserving a continuity. The specialist center must not be perceived in the community as doing something quite different in character from other agencies.
4. Optimal collaboration and flexibility in the use of resources must be achieved and this can be done only by fulfilling certain conditions:
   a. All the professional sources of help must *share the framework* on which the work is based. All personnel, including the specialist center, have therefore to formulate and communicate their working hypotheses in terms of the data of human relationships. No single theoretical system needs to be adopted, but all must know the significant phenomena that have to be considered and what is involved in treating these.
   b. *Consultative relationships* between the specialist center and sections must be maintained. Psychotherapeutic relationships, at whatever level of skill, impose uncertainties and stresses on all professional personnel who get involved with the strong emotional pressures of others. Increasing their skills is a constant aim of all, but unlike the acquisition of instrumental skills, learning in this field, like the psychotherapeutic work itself, needs ongoing personal relationships of trust within a group of colleagues, and between them and the groups on whom they rely for consultation. *An active commitment* to a permanent system of collaborative endeavour must therefore come from the centers of highest skill.
5. The fact that the kind of help given by the various professional groups for the psychological disorders has the common factor of dealing with conflicts in human relationships, and that this work begins to be perceived as closely connected with what goes on in the specialist psychological clinics, is of vital importance in getting the community to be more accepting of the nature and scope of human conflicts—and of the resources that people have for doing

something constructive about them. All those in familiar, respected, and trusted roles must be involved in a manifestly joint endeavour with the treatment of psychological disorders. Otherwise those figures are colluding in, and are seen to be colluding in, the defenses by which our society splits off and denies the recognition of what is happening psychologically to its own members. Resistances to the explicit awareness of the psychological nature of so much ill health and stress are a notorious obstacle to the development of the very services the community needs. Campaigns to popularize mental health knowledge have had only limited success in attaining their objectives. The helping professions have a crucial role in overcoming these traditional attitudes by bringing their work into a much more obvious relationship with each other and with what the specialist psychotherapeutic services are about.

6. In short then, when those needing psychological help are seen as breakdown products from the complex of the interacting social systems of which they are part, the services for giving them help have to function as an organized system itself related in comprehensive ways with the community. This organization, while requiring on the one hand administrative linkages with the relevant institutions, must on the other hand embody the internal means of maximizing the overall output and level of its technical contribution. For this purpose a permanent system of multiple relationships must be developed for the sharing of knowledge and skill.

WHAT CAN BE DONE WITH THE ALLIED PROFESSIONAL GROUPS?

From what has been outlined, a key role of the specialist center is the training of allied professional personnel. Assisting these groups to increase their *knowledge* of mental ill-health has long been a widespread activity of psychiatrists, and one that is not productive, because resistances to awareness of the psychological nature of so much ill-health and stress are a notorious obstacle to the development of the very services the community needs. Campaigns to popularise mental health knowledge are apt to have only limited success in attaining their objectives as the Cummings (1957) have demonstrated. The helping professions have a crucial role in overcoming the attitudes by bringing their work into a more obvious relationship with each other and with what the specialist psychotherapeutic services are about. That means sharing skill as well as knowledge. To teach an appropriate psychotherapeutic *skill* has not been a major effort, partly because effective practicable methods have not been available and partly because such an expansion of skills has raised many issues of professional policy. In the early stages of psychoanalytic psychotherapy there was great reluctance on the part of its practitioners to have their knowledge applied in any "diluted" form—a concern that was justifiable as the traditional caution of a professional group.

The development of therapeutic or mental health teams inside the child guidance clinics has shown that psychotherapeutic skills can be shared when a setting is found in which the interests of all parties can be protected. There are, however, important differences when the latter are in independent roles in other settings, in particular, the critical issues of responsibility and the kind of skill to be taught. The specialist psychotherapist in the clinic is not in a position to know the ways in which psychotherapeutic skill can best be used in the settings of various professional groups. It is our view that responsibility for what the worker undertakes in his own professional capacity must rest with him, not only because it is impracticable for the psychiatrist to take it, but because the worker cannot acquire skill without assuming responsibility. To take the clinic model for psychotherapy, especially the orthodox analytic psychotherapeutic one, would be manifestly unsuitable. For instance, most of the relationships that the family doctor has would introduce the complications of close physical and social contacts with the patient and his family. Again, the family social worker has usually to deal with more than one member of the family, and has often to give practical help in a variety of ways.

We have found the training method developed and fully described by Balint (1957) to be an eminently practical one for allied professional groups and it has been used by us extensively for many years. He thought that what was needed was not theoretical knowledge, but personal skill, and its acquisition entails a limited, though considerable, change in the personality. In this method, the workers meet weekly in groups of ten to twelve over a period of about 2 years for discussions of their ongoing attempts to give help. The sessions are not allowed to become therapeutic meetings, but making the group aware at times of how it reacts in tackling a member's account forms an essential part of the procedure. Understanding of how conflicting needs are expressed in human relationships thus goes hand in hand with the personal experience of experimenting with the relationships the members make with their own clients. Discussion of situations in which they feel blocked brings for all members opportunities to scrutinize their own attitudes, and to modify these. To go back to further sessions with their clients, and to bring the consequences for subsequent discussion, maintains a dynamic learning process, which combines new insights and skills with what is appropriate to the setting in which these are used.

A 2 year period appears to be adequate for most members to work through the excitements of new powers, the "depression" of coming up against their limitations, and then to reach a stage at which they can feel at ease with themselves in the new problems they tackle. To have benefited repeatedly from the inevitable self-revelation that is entailed in seeking advice on the handling of cases creates both a readiness to continue using consultative help and a model for their own work.

Specialist psychotherapists in the clinic, who take on this kind of commitment to the professional groups in its area, must have expertise in a range of psychotherapeutic work with individuals and families and in group dynamics. Our experience has shown that considerable skill can be acquired by all professional groups in the mental health field when they are given the kind of training outlined, and are provided with a *setting* in which it can be practiced with free access to the staff of the specialist clinic whom they have come to trust. The boundaries that a professional worker will set with regard to the complexity of the problems he will treat will expand with experience. The availability of regular consultation services enables him to advance under conditions of safety for all parties.

We have also found that a common framework for understanding the psychological problems of individuals and families has been of great value in facilitating the sharing of cases and families and accepting the work of members of other groups. Rivalries and tensions between members of different professional groups tend to be magnified when the nature of the skills that each group practices is not known to the other, or is of such a personal and intuitive kind that members of one group cannot communicate either within their own groups or with colleagues in other groups.

Consulting services of this kind soon acquire a multiplier effect for senior caseworkers, both in the clinic and in other agencies, who with good experience and training can themselves act as group leaders for their less experienced colleagues. With groups for group leaders, the clinic staff can help in improving training skills as well as keeping in close touch with a widening range of basic skill training.

As a result of such steps, The Tavistock Clinic has had a training program in which about 500 professional personnel have been attending weekly meetings during each of the last few years. These groups have included family doctors, specialist doctors working in other services—for example, for children, or in Family Planning Clinics—health visitors, social and family caseworkers of all kinds. Other groups were drawn from the staffs of approved schools and correctional institutions, the clergy, and others.

For this whole endeavour, the staff time required has been the equivalent of about two full-time psychiatrists and three full-time senior caseworkers.

DEVELOPMENTS ASSOCIATED WITH INCREASING PSYCHOTHERAPEUTIC SKILLS IN THE ALLIED PROFESSIONS

Increase of more intensive psychological work by the professional workers in the community carries immediate implications for the conditions and administrative arrangements of the work. The size of caseloads has to be reduced, and arrangements for regular consultative sessions within their own groups and with specialists have to be built into the working conditions and not left as a spare time "luxury." More comprehensive casework also brings, as a rule, the need for flexibility in regard to the type of case accepted.

When professional agencies adopt training programs as described, the staff of the clinic may have to play a part in ensuring that the implications are fully examined by all those affected. New skills for the field workers often change the relationships between them and their seniors, and between all the professional staffs of an agency and its administrative authorities. As a rule it is essential for the clinic staff to participate actively in discussions of these matters with the senior administrators of the services.

Questions may arise whether or not the right professional roles are available. Thus, while the role of the family doctor has tended to get lost with the rapid development of medical technology, all experience confirms his uniquely important role because of his involvement with the family at times of most stress. It has been an impressive experience to my colleagues and myself to see how many of our family doctors want to acquire psychological understanding and skill in family problems. The acquisition of many powerful therapeutic measures for the common illnesses has fortunately appeared to increase rather than decrease this interest. With new skills for helping emotional troubles, the general practitioner role may recover some of its appeal, for these skills can bring deep satisfaction from his greater contribution as a family caretaker. And this acquisition allows him to communicate more effectively with other professional groups.

Caretaking functions through ongoing relationships with the family, independently of a particular member seeking help, have assumed much more importance today with the detachment of so many families from their usual connections. The clergy, for example, have special opportunities of this kind, for example, in times of grief and mourning, and at marriage. Their role, if they acquire the necessary training, enables them to offer guidance and help that otherwise might not be given.

Most important in this connection are those services that have prolonged contact with the individual such as education. The growth of counseling functions within the schools and universities creates the same needs for ongoing training and close collaboration with the clinic.

The spread of facilities within the community may also expose a need for new types of service either within existing agencies or by creating new units. The Family Discussion Bureau was developed as a new type of agency after a group of social workers asked our Clinic to train them to deal with the recurrent marital problems they encountered in an agency that offered an advice service to families. In the first stages the social workers had to work together with the psychiatrists to define some of the problems, to work out an adequate conceptual formulation of their nature, and then to develop methods of skill training, along with the kind of conditions required. After a few years there emerged a casework agency that embodied a workable pattern for a service for marital problems—an essential feature being regular weekly discussions with their psychiatrists or consulting psychotherapists.

This model attracted considerable attention and it soon had to devote a large share of its effort to training staffs in other social work agencies. It showed that trained social workers, by creating a group that provided its members with support in the inevitable stresses and strains imposed by intensive casework, could acquire a very useful level of skill in handling the quite complicated marital interactions that were often presented.

Administratively it may fit our arrangements at present to organise separately the mental health services within the fields of medicine, education, and social welfare. Functionally, they cannot remain apart, and in my view the necessary collaboration to meet technical needs must correspondingly be represented by appropriate organisation.

The furthering of developments in skills and knowledge will require the professional services in an area to be coordinated by some kind of local Mental Health Council. The psychotherapist should play a key role in such a body. In doing so he should demonstrate by his own mode of participation in the common endeavour how constructive solutions to problems may be reached. Sensitive recognition of the interpersonal and intergroup tensions that are inevitably exposed at times, and a genuine mutuality in pooling knowledge and skills, must be his regular contribution; his training in the psychotherapeutic process of working *with* people rather than doing things *to* them remains his model.

THERAPEUTIC WORK IN THE CLINIC

When the clinic becomes a focal point in the services to the community, its own therapeutic work has to develop to match the new situation. Demands for psychotherapy increase enormously as services are created outside, not only because of referrals but also from greater awareness that "something can be done" for much disorder. Analytical group therapy can become a major psychotherapeutic method with many assets other than its contribution to therapeutic resources. It serves as a training component in group dynamics—mentioned as necessary in conducting training groups. The experience it provides of neurotic interaction in relationships is also invaluable in handling similar behaviour in work with disturbed marriages and in the family.

The choice of the family as the focus of therapy with children and adolescents is now taken as the rule. In recent years this approach for patients who are being returned from the hospital to their families, even with the more serious schizophrenic illnesses, has been shown to be an important advance. We have found, too, that for a considerable proportion of adult psychoneurotic patients with common symptoms and character problems, apparently "individual" in nature, it is useful to examine the marital situation. With many patients the intolerable parts of themselves are collusively projected into the partner and are never brought into treatment. To deal with the contribution of both to what is happening can frequently end a source of resistance that makes work with the individual difficult and, at the same time, will mobilize the therapeutic resources of both.

This new emphasis on family interactions is in our view an important advance in psychotherapeutic work. It becomes essential when the psychotherapist is engaged in consultative services with groups whose main work is with families. Unless the clinic's staff is keeping ahead in work which is similar to that of the allied professional services, the clinic cannot provide the expertise that these groups need. As was mentioned earlier, the mental health team comprising different professional skills becomes of paramount importance, with the therapeutic skills of all members being maintained at a high level.

Work with families also highlights the need for the consultant psychotherapist to understand intergroup as well as intragroup dynamics. When he works with staffs of residential institutions, knowledge of intergroup dynamics is indispensable. The specialist psychotherapist in the community clinic has therefore to acquire a much broader experience than has been the common pattern in psychotherapy. It may be added that we have found this broader experience sharpens appraisal in doing focal therapy with individuals.

In this task of creating more psychotherapeutic facilities in the community, I therefore suggest that *the crucial matter is the creation of a "sociotherapeutic system" amongst the helping professions* in which the psychotherapeutic centre has to play a fundamental part. The present skills of the helping professions derive almost entirely from the psychodynamic understanding that followed Freud's work. The psychotherapist in the specialist centre must continue in a joint collaborative endeavour with these professions to keep the skills of all growing.

AETIOLOGICAL THINKING AND THE ROLE OF THE SPECIALIST PSYCHOTHERAPIST

To describe the role of the consultant psychotherapist in the mental health services, we must start from the situation in regard to psychotherapeutic needs in the community and the kinds of resources that can be mobilized to meet them. I should make it clear that when referring to consultant psychotherapists in the psychotherapeutic clinic I assume that optimally these specialists would be part of a comprehensive psychiatric service. For convenience I shall use the term *psychotherapeutic centre* to allow for the location of the psychotherapeutic services to vary according to circumstances in any one area. Also, although I shall speak often of the psychotherapist as though his was a rather separate contribution, I want to stress that this is partly a reflection of the present situation. Much of what I have to say about his role must become increasingly a part of the work of all psychiatrists.

Compared with his traditional role, the specialist psychotherapist in the community centre has, therefore, to acquire a much broader experience of different psychotherapeutic endeavours. He has also to learn much more of how the community is served by the centre functions. In understanding the individual, he must marry psychodynamic knowledge of the inner world with a sociological sensitivity to the outer.

Three main areas of thought are now affecting our concepts of the psychological development and well-being of the person. Although psychotherapeutic theory and practice is responding in part to these influences, they have to be made explicit because their associated fields of knowledge must become, particularly for the psychotherapist in a community service, part of his training.

1. The stimulus that psychoanalysis gave to the social sciences has led to an enormous amount of research into the social development of the child and to the ways in which adult behaviour is governed by social relationships. The findings have provided a greatly enriched background on which thinking about the growth and functioning of the personality has to be based.
2. Parallel with these developments is the profound movement in our culture through which the whole orientation of people to society is in a state of flux, with marked effects on the functioning of the family and the individual.
3. Thirdly are the new studies of animal behaviour focused on the relations of innate behaviour patterns with the maturational environment, and the applications of this work to man's social development and functioning.

It is not uncommon now amongst psychotherapists to view the splits in the person as more like a number of incompatible subselves rather than as divisions arising along the lines of the familiar ego, superego, and id. In this development, it is thought that the subselves can be more usefully described in terms of system theory, each system having its own type of personal relationships as its inbuilt goal.

Symptom pictures have begun to alter as our society has exchanged its traditional values and its social conditions. Thus the disorders broadly subsumed under the notion of oedipal conflicts are emerging as manifestations of earlier and pervasive pathology. Our art and literature and our mass media have made commonplace the vagaries of human sexuality and aggression, so that our patients come, now, not only troubled by repressed instinctual impulses, but presenting the bewilderment of a divided self and the schizoid futility of people alienated from those committed relationships to others, to themselves, and to their achievements that give excitement to living and satisfaction and happiness for each phase of the life cycle.

As treatment of the person as a whole has proceeded, analyses have become longer and longer, and the place of such long-term treatment may appear even more difficult to envisage in our mental health services. Nevertheless, I believe it to be essential that some intensive long-term analytic treatment should be carried out in our National Health Service units. While acknowledging our very great indebtedness to the brilliant intuitions of our gifted analysts, it is doubtful if the conditions of private practice, where analysis is virtually exclusively carried out, should continue to provide the only setting for many of the developments we need. The importance of the study of the self and its identity—its intimate relatedness to the social transactions which constellate it and maintain its boundaries—makes it increasingly likely that detailed psychoanalytic work on the intrapsychic properties of the individual will have to be matched with equally intensive work into those social transactions that are essential to being a person.

In this endeavour the psychotherapist has a unique contribution, and I think this can best be realized in the setting of clinic or hospital.

Interactional processes are the essence of analytical psychotherapy with individuals, yet I believe that the understanding of individual psychotherapy will be enriched when those who make it their primary task bring to it a wider experience with the therapy of families and groups such as the clinic can offer.

Again, the development of the psychiatric hospital as a therapeutic community should be an area in which the psychotherapist can contribute to the ideas of his psychiatric colleagues. Much of the splendid work here is felt by many psychiatrists and others to lack a depth component that might well enrich its contribution. When there is the opportunity to work together, practical methods for introducing interpretative methods can be evolved.

I have elaborated the task of "aetiological thinking" because of its fundamental role for all mental health endeavours. It will be greatly advanced, however, when the specialist psychotherapeutic contribution is integrated into the work and thought of all psychiatrists that must go on in every psychiatric centre. Only then, too, will the general body of psychiatric trainees get the opportunity they need for acquiring psychotherapeutic understanding.

THE TRAINING OF THE SPECIALIST PSYCHOTHERAPIST

Just as the roles of the consultant psychotherapist must match the needs of the community situation in regard to psychotherapy, so must training equip the consultant psychotherapist to fill these roles. I have suggested that inside the clinics and hospitals we must have an ongoing proportion of intensive psychotherapeutic work done with the highest level of skill we can get. Only then will understanding and practice develop as they should both inside and outside the clinic.

The first requirement of the psychotherapist is to have training in intensive psychotherapy to the best available levels. This entails the following:

1. A personal analysis over some years.
2. Treatment under supervision of at least two cases, one of which must be continued for 2 years. It is usual for this stage to be begun after 2 years of personal analysis.
3. Theoretical and practical seminars over 2 to 3 years.

It is common for young psychiatrists who wish to specialize in psychotherapy to contemplate undertaking this training after 2 to 3 years of general psychiatric training, by which time they have obtained certification in psychological medicine. Should they proceed to the more advanced psychiatric qualification requiring a longer period, it should still be possible for trainee psychotherapists to start their personal analysis at about the same stage in their careers.

When the trainee begins supervised cases, it becomes appropriate to concentrate on psychotherapeutic work of various kinds, for example the treatment, under supervision, of analytic groups, families, and marital interaction. Towards the end of this phase, there must be added experience in providing consultation services to a range of allied professional groups and to getting familiar with the handling of community problems.

This phasing of the different parts of training need not be regarded as in any way rigid. The main point is the total ground to be covered.

Theoretical courses for the sociological background to the psychotherapist's work are at present difficult to describe, as much work has yet to be done on evolving the best content for these courses. Particular emphasis needs to be given to the sociology and psychology of the family, to the dynamics of small and larger groups and organizations. In the future, much of this background in the social sciences may be incorporated partly in the undergraduate and partly in the postgraduate period of the training of all psychiatrists. One aspect of the training should be stressed, namely, that a considerable proportion of it should be common to the postgraduate qualifications for all of the mental health professions. Working with the other professions in therapeutic and consultative tasks will be a major part of the psychotherapist's future activities and bringing these various groups together for common parts of their theoretical training has great advantages for the fostering of future cooperation.

Within the psychiatric services, the consultant psychotherapist has thus a particularly important part to play in establishing a collaborative "sociotherapeutic system" whereby all the mental health services can be functionally related.

This expanded role needs training in psychotherapy to the level of the psychoanalyst and theoretical and practical training in the sociological aspects of community mental health with special reference to the dynamics of the family, of small and large groups, and of larger organizations and institutions. An adequate overall training and experience can be achieved in the usual 8-10 years of the preconsultant phase.

CREATING CONDITIONS FOR OPTIMAL DEVELOPMENT AND FUNCTIONING OF THE PERSONALITY: PREVENTION

Access to many powerful forces in the personality is only to be obtained when the person is in the security of a therapeutic relationship. Accordingly, the role of the psychotherapeutic clinic in providing a laboratory for the study of the development of the individual personality, and hence for knowledge on which primary measures could be based, is well recognized.

That a much wider relationship must be developed by the clinic to more general problems of prevention and the development of positive mental health measures becomes clearer the more social factors are studied in their effects on the functioning of the person.

To illustrate this theme I shall take some recent findings on work stress and work satisfaction. When they investigated the high incidence of stress manifestations in certain groups of miners, Trist and Bamforth (1951) showed that a new technology in the mines had broken up the traditional working groups. These were replaced by work roles and groups based primarily on the machines. After prolonged working through of the various implications of change, a new social organization was then designed, which retrieved the old self-regulating patterns for small work groups and which was at the same time appropriate for the demands of the machines. The result was a marked fall in sickness and absenteeism rates, a recovery of work satisfaction, and a rise in productivity. Further work has emphasized this need to view the work group as a *sociotechnical system*, to use Trist's term, that is, as a system in which the social and personal needs of the worker must be satisfied by a work setting that simultaneously meets the technological requirements. Responsible participation in social tasks appears to exert a major influence on the feelings of security and competence in the individual.

Again, the study of Menzies (1960), investigating the high wastage rate in training nurses, suggested that the pattern of the nurse's work that has developed in recent years represents a social system evolved to operate as a powerful defense against the emergence of what are treated as uncontrollable feelings. In this particular case the defense not only denied the feelings involved, the emotions inevitably associated with the "nursing relationship," but the system also deprived the nurse of the necessary reassurance that the task could give in response to these feelings. In other words, the system failed with the primary anxiety and created a secondary anxiety from frustration and the inhibition of creative development.

This kind of study, and an enormous mass of other findings, raises many aspects of the relation between psychotherapy and the social sciences.

Affinities between the clinic and the social sciences have become clearer as group methods have been used by the psychotherapists. It is not only small groups, however, that can be described as microsociological. Detailed psychotherapeutic work shows that the study of the person can also be categorized in this way, for his personality carries within it a series of dynamic object-relations structures mediating a range of social relationships with figures in his inner world, and the patterns of relationships with people in the outer world. These theories in turn have led to several creative lines of thought on the functioning of small groups both in regard to the deeper forces influencing relations between members, and between members and the leader. Leading sociologists, for example, Parsons and Bales (1955), have interestingly enough reached similar conclusions.

Personality theory must account for the range and quality of the needs for belonging in various groups, for achievement, and for defining and maintaining a satisfying identity and self-feeling in cooperative relations with others on significant activities. Clinical work suggests that the integrity values of the central self are achieved for most at the expense of splitting off parts of the personality that embody repressed relationship needs. In spite of the familiar defense mechanisms, many of these needs remain as unconscious compulsions to re-create relationships in which they can be satisfied. For these relationships, objects are often selected from the groups in which people live or work. Such relationships may possibly underlie the "social atom" that Moreno (1956) has found to characterize group relatedness. Again, the need to exert some mastery over these inner relationships may have a close relationship to the kind of satisfaction many people require in work, for example, the feeling of being a responsible member of a self-regulating group. As automation progresses, new means of satisfying social needs will have to be evolved. And to all these problems, the psychotherapeutic clinic has a unique contribution to make.

In our modern world change has to become a normal and positive experience. Administrators and social scientists on the whole have been much more able to diagnose what has to be changed than to manage a successful change process. If we remind ourselves that the characteristics of a social system have been evolved in substantial measure to deal with the threatening tensions within it, then we will be prepared for the consequences of trying to change it. All psychotherapists are familiar with the anxieties aroused within the individual when he begins to alter his defense systems. It is inevitable that such alterations within the defensive patterns of a social system will also release anxiety and a degree of acting out. Social systems can create special difficulties during the change process; but members can also give each other considerable positive support during change.

New satisfactions have to be experienced and accepted before the old ways can be given up, and during this process the role of a therapeutic person or group of persons has a close parallel with the role occupied by the therapist for the individual or the family. Our experience has therefore been that the social scientist who wishes to be involved in change processes has to acquire, in addition to knowledge, skill that maintains the professional relationship while these processes with their inevitable anxieties and acting-out are being initiated and worked through. Such skills naturally have to be evolved with special experience, but the psychotherapeutic relationship, especially in analytic group therapy, can provide a valuable basic model. Some social scientists may seek personal analysis as a foundation, but where this is not adopted, experience, even as observers of therapeutic groups over a long period, is extremely useful as a foundation for professional skills.

The whole conceptual basis for research and development into the tasks of improving the social environment has fundamental problems that are common to the psychotherapist and the social scientist, and close collaboration between them must be a part of the activities of the psychological clinic. The psychotherapeutic clinic has a unique role as a control mechanism picking up critical data on damage being done within the current social processes. Use cannot be made of this role, however, unless the clinic is integrated with a wider group of institutions in the community, and especially those which can value its findings and on this basis initiate changes. In other words, while a comprehensive mental health service may undo some of the rejection by society of its psychological disorders, there is a danger that such services may merely develop "within" the community instead of getting into the integrated relationship with key institutions that is required.

The location of the clinic within its social space therefore assumes a new importance. It would seem that it has to become one component in a constellation of units—an institute or school of human relations—which together share the task of advising on the means to a better society.

SUMMARY

Expanding community mental health services entails new roles for the psychotherapeutic clinic. Its staff have to initiate and maintain a large-scale training program whereby the psychotherapeutic skill of all the helping professions can be raised. The clinic has then to remain a focal point in maintaining an increasing level of competence throughout this system. Inside the clinic, psychotherapeutic practice, as well as preserving the traditional role of providing long-term individual treatment for some, must comprise work that closely parallels much of the work in the community. In particular, high expertise must be maintained in the treatment of the family and in group therapy and group dynamics. Lastly, because of the clinic's role in picking up the breakdowns from the current social processes, it occupies a unique position to act as a servomechanism that must be integrated with key institutions concerned with evolving comprehensive knowledge for the management and development of the community.

17. RESEARCH IN PSYCHODYNAMICS

THE PRESENT POSITION

The provision of treatment for the psychologically ill is a task for the National Health Service, and it is a responsibility of all psychiatrists concerned to examine something of the nature of this task and what can be done about it.

In regard to the psychoses, our society has now accepted the provision of at least "an asylum" for most of these patients; but for the psychoneuroses and the character disorders, the existing facilities over the country as a whole for other than palliative treatment are almost negligible in face of the size of the needs. Nevertheless, the psychological illnesses despite their historical separation, form a continuum both in their manifestations and in the problems they present for treatment and prevention, and I propose, therefore, to have in mind the whole range of psychological disorders in looking at our task.

A little reflexion on the scale and cost of psychological illness is salutary.

1. In England and Wales there are approximately 150,000 people in mental hospitals.
2. Fraser (1947) and his colleagues showed that approximately 10 percent of the industrial population had suffered from definite and disabling neurotic difficulties, and a further 20 percent from minor forms of neurosis, during the course of 6 months. . . . Neurotic illness caused between a quarter and a third of all absence from work due to illness; neurosis caused more absence than colds and influenza. Of the total available working days, 1 percent in the case of men and 2.4 percent in the case of women are lost annually from psychological illness.
3. Such estimates as exist would tend to show that about a third of most general practitioner's work is concerned with illness in which the psychological factor is prominent.

The human suffering that this represents gives ample reasons for serious efforts. But if, in addition, we reckon the cost of these disorders, both the direct cost of their treatment and the indirect cost of the loss in productivity, a conservative estimate of the national bill for psychological disorders must be £100m. per annum. It would therefore appear that the need to take effective therapeutic and preventive action is urgent.

WHAT ACTION IS TO BE TAKEN?

Naturally a great deal of therapeutic effort is being expended on the more serious illnesses, especially in the mental hospitals. Furthermore, in preparation for an expansion of therapeutic services for the psychoneuroses, the Ministry of Health sponsored Dr. C. P. Blacker's valuable survey on *Neurosis and the Mental Health Services* (1946) in order that a comprehensive description of the psychiatric out-patient facilities would be available as a first step towards improving these. The essential points in Dr. Blacker's recommendations were:

1. The creation of more psychiatrists who would have had training at Teaching Psychiatric Centres for out-patient work.
2. A great increase of therapeutic facilities (including beds) for the neuroses.

However, when we look at our existing therapeutic activities we become less enthusiastic about these recommendations. It is no exaggeration to say that almost all actions taken at present for the psychological disorders, whether therapeutic or preventive, are completely empirical and palliative. All kinds of treatments are practised and incompatible measures are proposed for their prevention. The psychoanalysts and allied groups are perhaps the only therapists who would claim that their treatment is radical or rational in its aim, but their contribution to therapy must remain small because of the small number of cases who can be treated by their methods.

Now, although it should be unnecessary, I believe that the limited status of empirical methods needs to be emphasized in psychiatry to-day, both in treatment and prevention. In treating any illness about which we know little, all kinds of theories may be acted upon, and any treatment that relieves suffering is justifiable when rational treatment is either unknown or unavailable. From a coordination of all the available knowledge and experience, however, there soon emerge some general conclusions that limit the likelihood of some views on the nature and the origin of the illness, while at the same time they give to other lines of work a greater probability of reward. Any approach to illness that does not take into account these general findings is what we normally mean by an empirical one, and because it denies or ignores some of these findings, we imply that it is most unlikely to lead to the kind of knowledge upon which sound treatment and preventive measures can be based. It is my view that much current psychiatric treatment is empirical in this sense, and certain questions must therefore be faced. For instance, it has to be asked whether or not a problem of the size of psychological illnesses to-day must go on being treated almost entirely on empirical lines and whether or not it is justifiable to swell the number of psychiatrists when all they can do is to continue to expand this empiricism. Surely, our first priority is an acceptable approach to aetiology; we need some scientifically established principles and knowledge on which effective therapeutic and preventive action can be based.

The inevitable answer to this suggestion will be that we cannot get a sound aetiological approach without more research. That is to say, it is asserted that in psychiatry we are still at that stage where no general conclusions about the phenomena of mental illness can be accepted as setting limits to the probability of certain broad hypotheses regarding aetiology. Two points, however, must be noted about this reply. In the first place, a large amount of research has already been carried out in psychiatry during the last 50 years, and secondly, if it is true that more research is needed, one cannot but wonder why there is relatively so little of it in face of the scale and cost of the psychological illnesses. It is inconceivable that any enterprise with an annual loss of at least £100m. from say some kind of "wear and tear" should spend as little on investigating the cause of this loss as is being spent at present in this country.

Clearly, then, it may repay us to examine these questions of why current psychiatric research is so inadequate in both quantity and effectiveness.

THE INADEQUACIES OF CURRENT PSYCHIATRIC RESEARCH BOTH IN ITS SCALE AND EFFECTIVENESS

The main reason to my mind for the unsatisfactory state of affairs in regard to the amount of psychiatric research being conducted at present, lies in the fact that as a group psychiatrists have not yet been able to abstract from the available findings of psychological illness commonly agreed broad aetiological principles that group the phenomena in patterns related to the underlying dynamic processes.

But if we cannot show such an integrated approach, how can we expect the nation to support research on an appropriate scale? Naturally we do not know all the answers, but is it surprising that we are failing to convince the intelligent laymen, in particular our administrators, that we really could make a workmanlike attempt at finding some of the answers?

It cannot be said that psychiatrists are indifferent to the situation I have described. Every few years some fresh empirical approach to treatment leads to fairly widespread hope that an important gain has been secured, and a crop of papers follows from a surge of enthusiastic workers in hospitals scattered throughout the country. Here, however, history almost always repeats itself; the chimerical nature of the widespread hopes slowly emerges and the chilling fog of our ignorance descends once more. In contrast with this picture, the radical approach of dynamic psychology certainly presents a body of knowledge that is steadily, though slowly, being consolidated. However, this knowledge, which has been mainly derived from the work of the psychoanalysts, has not been placed upon a sufficiently scientific basis for it to be widely accepted and used as a scientific contribution.

The main reason for the ineffectiveness of most of our research would appear to me to be the lack of methodological clarity in much of the research going on in our field, and the absence of a thoroughgoing logical analysis of what is being attempted. It may be that it is because we are so much under stress from therapeutic pressures that we are not thinking enough about these problems. It certainly seems that recent psychiatric research has not only failed to help us adequately, but also that the lack of logic makes it such that much of it cannot possibly lead to that knowledge which would help us *to take effective action* in our situation.

This is a grave charge; I believe it, nevertheless, to be true. Any individual worker has the right to research on any topic he chooses if he can find the time and money. The vital question, however, is what lines of research are most urgent *for the National Health Service* if it is to deal in a practical effective way with the psychological disorders? I believe that this question is a very serious one indeed for the whole future of psychiatry and psychology in Britain. This will be seen if we put it in another way, namely, what lines of research should we have in mind and, if possible, what proposals would be put forward to secure these research aims, to obtain the most rapid advance along the most effective lines in our understanding of the development of personality both in its normal and pathological features.

A CRITIQUE OF CURRENT PSYCHIATRIC RESEARCH

It will help us if we look critically at the research that is going on to-day in the light of available knowledge.

Two basic methodological criticisms can be made against most of this work.

(a) The most serious scientific shortcoming in current psychiatric research is the widespread tendency to state antecedent conditions in static or classificatory terms, that is, in terms referring to aspects of the individual that are not essential to the dynamic interaction of the individual and his environment. There is a conspicuous lack of appreciation of the fact that research designed to explain psychological illness has to formulate the possible causes of the problem, not merely as antecedent conditions to be correlated with a certain end-result, namely mental ill-health, but it has to demonstrate the dynamic interaction of the various antecedent conditions leading to this result.

If, for example, we take the fact that studies demonstrate that constitution and environment are factors that play a part in mental ill-health, then it is virtually of no use whatever to correlate constitution in static terms, for example, asthenic physique, with the end-result that is called schizoid personality or schizophrenia. A satisfactory theory must state the antecedent conditions in *dynamic* terms on the appropriate dynamic plane. Only then can we demonstrate the interaction between constitution and environment that leads to the result we want to explain, that is, mental ill-health.

Let us take the treatment of this problem in a popular psychiatric textbook. (Although I have borrowed my illustration from one textbook, in fact all current textbooks are similar in this respect and I have therefore not specified this particular one lest it should be taken that it was exceptional.) In the chapter on aetiology, there are listed three types of causal factor: (i) constitutional, (ii) physical, (iii) psychological.

We hear, for instance, that a man with a certain depressive constitution which can be inferred from the family history, who in addition has influenza and who is unemployed, falls ill with a depressive illness. On the other hand, while unemployed several years ago, but when the physical factor of influenza was absent, he did not fall ill.

Here there are three causal factors listed in static terms, but there is no statement of how a certain constitution plus certain psychological stresses plus a physical illness interact in order to produce this particular condition that, it is claimed, is their outcome.

The unsatisfactory nature of this approach becomes apparent when we ask whether it is really claimed that whenever a similar family history (the only criterion used for the assertion of a depressive constitution consists of the presence of certain features in the relatives), plus unemployment plus influenza occur together they will cause a depressive breakdown, that is, whether it is claimed that these are logically sufficient conditions to account for their supposed effect. It is only too easy to cloud this issue by stating these supposedly aetiological conditions in nondynamic terms.

The absence of any attempt to demonstrate the interaction between the antecedent factors leading to a certain condition puts psychiatric research in the state of *claiming to have "explained"* the aetiology of a condition by making statements which, if applied to the field of infectious diseases, would sound like this: "there is some external agent (not further defined) and some undefined state of the body of a particular individual which interact in some unknown way to produce, say, typhoid fever." Naturally it is not possible at present to formulate these factors in detail with regard to particular mental conditions the aetiology of which we want to explain, but we must not give the impression of having solved the aetiological problem. This will not be achieved unless our research is conceived in such ways as to allow the formulation of these factors in specific dynamic terms.

(b) My second methodological criticism is the following one: *Hypotheses are formed from isolated observations without a thorough appreciation of the characteristics of the whole field. For instance, many studies in the physical sphere seem completely to ignore the fact that at least in our everyday life we are not indifferent to psychological experiences as dynamic agents in our own behaviour.*

One result of these partial approaches is that there are impenetrable barriers between the rival schools, most of which perpetuate their own inadequacies. There are many reasons for this one-sided development. Foremost, I think, we must place the completely inadequate training of most workers in our field. On the one hand, most psychiatrists have had little or no opportunity to acquire adequate experience and understanding in the principles of what is surely their basic science, namely, the science of behaviour or dynamic psychology. (In their training and in the qualifications demanded for most psychiatric posts at present, the place of psychology is at best a very uncertain one.) On the other hand, the contributions of psychologists to the problems of personality and the behaviour disorders are too often "academic," that is, of marginal relevance in practice—an unavoidable outcome as long as psychologists are kept apart, or keep themselves apart, from some of the most significant data underlying human behaviour and which are only accessible within the therapeutic relationships in the clinic.

In such a situation, it does not matter how brilliantly each group of workers develops its own special skills and knowledge, for the lack in each group of an effective knowledge of those other factors relevant to the understanding of mental disorders remains as a major obstacle to successful dynamically orientated research. Inevitably the methods of any one group are expanded into ways of dealing with the total phenomena, and because they cannot give a dynamic account of the specific features of psychotic and neurotic behaviour, especially in its apparently irrational aspects, the need to give such an account is lost under a cover of static formulations that can never explain the essential happenings in mental illnesses, and can therefore never be of value either in therapy or prevention. Thus, though few psychiatrists would admit to ignoring psychological factors, nevertheless, a very substantial part of current research and treatment seems to be based largely on the theory that they are at bottom irrelevant and that the important factors are organic derangements of the central nervous system caused by some intoxication or by some constitutionally determined disturbance in metabolism or by physical agents introduced from outside. Again, the psychologist, from the restricted nature of his background, has perforce concentrated upon attempts to develop refined measurements and to make statistical analyses of variables that have little or no dynamic significance and that can only be used to classify patients.

Perhaps we might avoid these pitfalls, of working with static concepts or of building up aetiological hypotheses on isolated observations that are contradicted by others, if we survey briefly the relevant findings of the most important lines of research carried on at present and if we try to evaluate their observations. This survey will necessarily be brief and it makes no claims to be comprehensive. I have made it essentially as a demonstration of what must be done in a much more exhaustive manner by others.

ORGANIC THEORIES OF MENTAL DISORDER

Let us examine first research based on organic theories. The first important problem is whether it is possible to correlate specific physical agents with specific mental syndromes. A tremendous amount of energy has been devoted to attempts to describe specific syndromes, for example, as alcohol hallucinations, drug intoxication, the grandiose delusions of general paralysis of the insane (G.P.I.), to quote but a few. Further investigations, however, have established beyond doubt that it is impossible to correlate any specific psychosyndrome with any specific external physical agent. Bleuler (1951) has brought out this point particularly well.

Three other questions interest us here:

1. Are lesions in the brain necessarily accompanied by psychopathological symptoms?
2. Can specific psychopathological symptoms be correlated with brain lesions of specific localizations?
3. If so, is this possible for all symptoms or only for some?

G.P.I. is often quoted as a proof that psychopathic manifestations are the direct expression of lesions in the brain, and in this case we know the spirochaete as the external physical agent that causes the brain disease. Some psychiatrists even use this example to point out the futility of a search for a psychological aetiology of the psychotic reactions accompanying G.P.I. For instance, Curran & Guttman (1949) say "no plumbing of psychological depths can bring to daylight the (unconscious) invasion of the brain by spirochaetes."

In spite of the assertion that psychological factors play a part in the aetiology of mental disorder, the implication in this case is that the psychologist cannot explain the occurrence of the delusion that is taken to be a direct expression of the brain damage by the poisons of the spirochaetes. It seems to me, however, that the keeping up of the organic hypothesis is only possible inasmuch as organically minded psychiatrists think of G.P.I. as a disease entity in a psychological sense because we happen to know a specific external agent that causes the disease of the brain. If we study the psychopathological pictures in G.P.I., the syndromes show a variation through the whole gamut described in any mental disorder. The only constant psychopathological change is the deterioration of the patient's intelligence and cognitive functions, that is, the individual's psychological *adaptive equipment* that allows him to perceive and order his perceptions into meaningful relationships in space and time and to integrate them with past experiences and with his expectation of the future based on them. (I am distinguishing this equipment from the conative and affective aspects of the personality based on needs, and drives to satisfy them, and which make use of the cognitive equipment for this purpose.)

The fact that the only constant symptoms of G.P.I. are the deterioration in intelligence and cognition forces us to conclude that the only psychopathological features that could be considered as the direct expression of the lesion caused by the spirochaetes is the deterioration of the intellectual and cognitive equipment.

As far as the explanation of the *in*constant psychological symptoms goes, for instance, the psychotic pictures that may or may not accompany the deterioration of the cognitive functions, we have therefore to look for other aetiological factors. I should like to draw your attention to the study by Hollós & Ferenczi (1925) who tried to demonstrate that the psychotic pictures, when present, can be explained as the psychological reactions of correspondingly predisposed personalities to the perceptions of their waning intelligence and to the conscious and unconscious meaning of the venereal disease. We thus find the manic denial of his deficiency, or depressive self-accusations, and so on. It is therefore not merely the content of delusions and other psychotic symptoms for which we have to take recourse to psychological explanations. The very existence of the delusions cannot be explained by the brain disease as such but only by invoking psychological factors. It is in keeping with this fact that in the majority of G.P.I.'s, where the brain disease occurs in fairly well-balanced pre-G.P.I. personalities, no psychosis develops. There is merely the simple deterioration in intelligence, and the most common form of G.P.I. is, as would be expected, simple dementia.

These findings are fully confirmed by the study of chronic circumscribed lesions like brain tumours, the results of which are well summarized in Bleuler's paper. They are: localized lesions in the projection areas may lead to "isolated" psychopathological symptoms, namely, hallucinations, which, we may note again, belong to the cognitive sphere. It is essential, however, to realize that they need not lead to any involvement of the rest of the personality, that is, there need be no psychosis. Apart from such lesions localized in projection areas, circumscribed lesions in the brain in any locality need not produce any psychopathic symptoms; and if the latter do appear, they cannot be correlated with any specific localization of the lesion. It is therefore impossible to consider psychopathological symptoms as direct expressions of lesions in the brain and we have to look for other aetiological explanations.

Space does not allow a detailed discussion of confusional states in acute intoxications of the brain, but delusions and hallucinations, which can be observed in such states, can again be explained as secondary phenomena based on a primary disturbance of the individual's cognitive equipment, which cuts him off from the controlling interchange with external reality and allows him, as it were, to dream while he is awake. In keeping with the findings from other organic states mentioned before, we have again only to assume the disturbance of cognition as the only direct result of intoxications. In spite of this, the similarity between the pictures in acute toxic states and the not infrequent confusional states at the onset of schizophrenia or other psychoses is apparently the mainstay of the approach of many organically minded psychiatrists who put forward the hypothesis that all psychoses are expressions of intoxications, especially those caused by disturbances of metabolism. This seems a very uncritical generalization, which neglects the psychological differences between the acute confusional state and the gradually developing psychoses. In the confusional states of acute intoxications we always find disturbances of the total cognition; we never find clinically isolated psychological disturbances like delusions appearing as a direct result of intoxications or morphological lesions when the general cognition is otherwise undisturbed, for example, when orientation in space and time are retained. In addition, no one has been able to produce the clinically isolated delusion of a paranoiac with otherwise undisturbed cognitive powers through administration of chemical substances as one can produce acute confusional states through acute intoxication.

If we go further into psychological studies of these phenomena, we can see periods of the classical picture of depressive psychosis alternating with schizophrenic pictures, states of persecutory delusions alternating with states of idealization, and so on. And in the analysis of psychotic patients these changes can be shown in a particularly impressive way to be the reactions of the patient to various anxiety-laden situations in his private world. The most improbable and complicated assumptions would have to be made to explain such phenomena on an organic basis, yet such hypotheses continue to be advanced even though they are usually introduced by their author as "speculations," not intended to be tested, and in spite of the incontrovertible evidence that makes them so improbable.

A similar discussion can show that pathological impulses are just as difficult to explain on the basis of an organic theory alone; it is difficult to imagine, for example, a biological hormone that could account for the object that is of sexual interest to a shoe fetishist.

CONSTITUTION AS AN EXPLANATORY FACTOR

Let us turn to another set of observations that appear to be isolated from other data and then given an undue importance—the investigations into *constitution*.

Such investigations are carried out mainly as statistical investigations of twins and familial incidence with regard to mental ill-health. There are, however, a number of basic methodological criticisms.

a. The statistical units used are not defined. It seems strange to be presented with correlations based on a supposedly precise percentage of schizophrenia or manic-depressive illnesses when the same authors often start their reports by pointing out that it is hardly possible to draw hard and fast lines between the conditions under consideration. Every clinician knows that the "mixed" forms are more frequent than the so-called pure ones. In his recent paper Bleuler particularly emphasized this point.
b. This lack of examination of the psychopathological details of the syndrome, and of the exact definitions of the mental pictures being referred to, leads to similarly unjustified claims as in the supposedly full explanation of the psychoses that may occur in G.P.I. through the discovery of the spirochaetes that cause the

brain disease. The oft-quoted classical example of a fully constitutionally caused mental disease is *Huntington's chorea*. It is said that it is a mental disease and that it shows a 100 percent dominance in its inheritance. It is then assumed to be a complete proof for the view that some mental diseases are nothing but the expressions of physical changes in the brain, and that their causation is explained solely by hereditary factors. However, if we examine which features are constant and which are frequently absent, and further, what kind of mental disorders we find in these cases, we discover just as in G.P.I., that the only constant feature in Huntington's chorea, apart from the physical choreic symptoms, is the diminution of intelligence. The psychopathological symptoms may be completely absent, or they may vary through the whole range known in psychiatry. Again, as in G.P.I., we come to the conclusion that it is the diminution of intelligence that can be considered as the direct result of the damage to the brain while the physical explanations fail us in regard to the psychological symptoms that may or may not occur. And for their explanation, we are again thrown back on the premorbid personality and its reactions to the psychological meaning for the individual of his physical disease and of the diminution of his intelligence.

Three further methodological points may be referred to briefly:

c. Constitutionalists show a conspicuous lack of appreciation of psychological environmental factors. Especially in identical twins is it the case that environment can work both to create identical attitudes and extreme differences. Where the environment operates to create identical emotions, this would account for a lot of what is attributed to constitution.

It is a striking feature of many case records quoted in twin studies to find the whole environment up to the age of adolescence or early adulthood dismissed in a sentence or two. With virtually no appreciation of what constitutes the psychological environment for the young child there is naturally little or no awareness of the tremendous range of differentiation possible in the psychological environment of siblings and of twins.

The observations reported by Sandford (1952) and others on the dramatic repercussions of the mothers' conflicts in the behaviour of their infants and young children illustrate the kind of phenomena that seem to be entirely unknown, or at least unassimilated.

Furthermore, recent work on the effects of foetal stimulation on behavioural development, for example, that quoted by

Ashley Montagu in the *Symposium on the Healthy Personality* (see Senn, 1950) suggests that environmental factors influence much of what has been attributed to inheritance.

d. The claim that identical twins are always psychologically so similar is, as Hartman's study (1933, 1935) shows, not borne out on closer investigation.

e. Finally, it must be asked whether statements about constitution made in static terms have much value when our aims are concerned with *what factors make for change*. To state that somebody's neurosis has a 10 percent constitutional factor, or that he is leptosomatic or cerebrotonic, or has an inherited factor of neuroticism, does not enable us to take practical action other than to label patients. That there is a constitutional factor we know anyway; as diagnostic indicators a Rorschach test or a clinical interview give us far more relevant information about the forces at work. Can statistical methods, and especially factor analysis, yield us anything other than nondynamic correlations? Or put another way, will they ever reveal to us the *dynamic laws of interaction* we need to know? In order to be useful, research into constitution has to be designed in such a way as to give results in dynamic terms. If, for instance, some of the physical bases of our psychological constitution could be related to specific chemical substances whose effects on the nervous system could be ascertained, then action could be taken.

However, allowing for these methodological deficiencies, even the studies of the most ardent constitutionalists provide foolproof evidence against the assumption of the fully constitutional nature of the functional psychoses. The classical investigation of Rosanoff, Handy, Plesset, and Brush (1934) on identical twins, and the many subsequent studies of this nature, showed that only in about two-thirds of identical twins is there concordance with regard to schizophrenia. This is conclusive proof against a purely constitutional theory.

Our attempts at integrating the findings in organic brain lesions with the existing studies on constitution therefore leave us with incomplete hypotheses regarding the aetiology and pathogenesis of mental disorder. The organic theories seem to explain the deterioration of intellectual and cognitive processes as a direct expression of physical damage to the brain, but leave unexplained the emergence of varying psychopathological syndromes. The constitutional investigations make likely the existence of a constitutional factor and an environmental factor without either indicating the nature of the constitutional factor or whether the environment is a physical or a psychological one. If we assume that the environmental factor is physical, this would lead us back to an organic theory the inadequacy of which has been mentioned. We must therefore conclude that the environmental factor is psychological.

This is confirmed by statistical evidence. Kallmann and colleagues (1949) quotes that nonconsanguineous step-sibs of schizophrenics show 1.9 percent incidence of schizophrenia, that is, twice as much as in the general population. It can only be the psychological environment of these families that raises the incidence of schizophrenia to twice as much as that in the general population from which these foster children originate. The same is borne out by another of Kallmann's findings, namely, that separated identical twins showed only 77 percent concordance in development of schizophrenia, while nonseparated ones show 91 percent.

PSYCHODYNAMIC THEORIES

Turning now to psychodynamic theories, what do they contribute to the problem of aetiology? (I shall refer mainly to psychoanalysis because it is the best known example of this class.) The most important finding is that the infant in his attempts to satisfy his biological needs encounters frustrations to which he reacts with aggression and in turn anxiety. Whenever such anxiety becomes intolerable some of the associated feelings and strivings get split off from the main or central part of the growing personality. Later, this process is the one usually referred to as repression and its aim is to prevent the recurrence of painful emotions by means of "defence mechanisms," which form the basis of his personality traits. If these prove inadequate, then the repressed breaks through as symptoms.

Psychoanalysts have shown that environmental differences explain to a large extent the development of different personalities, both balanced and disturbed. In the final analysis, however, they meet facts that suggest that different individuals must have reacted with different intensity to dynamically similar situations in earliest infancy, that is, they have to assume constitutional differences.

From time to time these constitutional factors have been stated in psychodynamic terms such as various sets of instincts differing in intensity from one individual to another, or as the ego's ability to master anxiety, and so forth. The growing influence of field theory makes us think of other types of factor as the important innate differences, for example, thresholds for frustration tolerance that seem closely correlated (as observations of infants have shown), with the individual's innate excitability. A child with a high degree of excitability reacts with more anger and subsequent anxiety to frustration than a placid child.

A further difference could be introduced by differences in the rates of the maturation of various functions. Differences in intellectual and physical equipment lead to differences in ability to cope with situations. One child may therefore find a situation frustrating while another copes with it. It would thus appear that biochemical and physical research might be more fruitful if it picked up these suggestions from dynamic psychology and tried to discover the physical basis of psychological constitution, for example, of excitability. We shall expect to find quantitative differences between various individuals in the first instance, and in view of the fact that a kind environment may do a lot to offset a constitutional handicap, and vice versa, we should not be surprised sometimes to find a comparatively balanced person with high, and a schizophrenic with low, excitability. On theoretical grounds, research into such dynamic organic factors in our constitution appears promising, but most present attempts of organically minded psychiatrists to discover the supposed metabolic disturbances underlying schizophrenia appear doomed to failure because they seek to correlate a highly complicated end-product produced by a multiplicity of intervening factors with a physical factor that could make for all kinds of development. It is, therefore, not surprising when Dr. McCowan (1952), in his presidential address to the Royal Medico-Psychological Association last summer, had to state with openly expressed disappointment, that in spite of the painstaking work done by many workers, surprisingly little has come out of biochemical, biophysical, and endocrinological research in psychiatry.

It is obvious that the discovery of the biochemistry underlying excitability would open up fascinating possibilities of preventive action in infancy. However, even if we could affect this factor, is there any justification to believe that once an individual has developed his distorted personality, mere change of his physically determined psychological constitution will be able to cope with his personality disorder?

I wish to emphasize here what Allport (1949) calls the *functional autonomy* of the traits of the personality. There is good evidence to suggest that these traits and symptoms are defences against the emergence of unconsciously determined anxieties, parts of psychological systems that have arisen out of the individual's infantile experiences and that are laid down in his nervous system in the form of highly complex "gestalten" apparently involving all areas of the brain. Once this has taken place, mere change in metabolic, perhaps glandular, processes that underlie the psychological constitutional factors that enter into the formation of personality in infancy can no longer materially affect the adult personality whose physical basis lies essentially in the brain. It is true that chemical substances may not only affect internal glands, but also the brain directly. However, the findings from organic brain disease lead us to expect that only the cognitive equipment will be affected. Equally, it is impossible to imagine any longer that psychological processes such as ideas and beliefs, which are based on all the areas of the brain, can be affected selectively by physical means.

Both the findings of organic brain disease and of physical treatment confirm this view. Without going in detail into the evidence from physical treatment, we have only to remember that the basic personality traits reappear unchanged whenever we stop the administration of chemical substances. Stilboestrol, for instance, may stop the sexual urge of a fetishist during the period of administration but his perverted sex interests reappear as soon as we stop the drug.

The same holds for attempts to remove specific traits or symptoms by means of brain surgery. Klein's (1952) recent study of postleucotomies shows this very well. The psychological effects seemed to correlate with the degree of brain damage. As expected, delusions and other pathological thought processes remained after leucotomy; in other words, the functional autonomy of the personality was preserved. On the other hand, comparatively slight damage of brain substance expressed itself in the most subtle disturbances of cognition, that is, in the individual's inability to integrate the present with past experiences and future expectations. The patient was thus reduced in this respect to the mental level of a child who lives entirely in the present. More severe disturbances created stronger disturbances of cognition, that is, amnesias.

It is not surprising to hear that though symptoms persisted after leucotomy, the "successfully" treated patients felt less worried by them. An individual who loses the ability to worry about future *real* danger would also lose his fears of *imaginary* dangers.

So far I have only spoken about those psychological effects of physical treatments that I believe to be the *direct* expression of organic changes brought about by drugs or surgical lesions. However, we must not forget their psychological meaning to the patient. Although only scanty investigations are available there are enough observations to prove that a great deal of what is often considered as a direct effect of the drug or lesion are in fact psychological *reactions* to the meaning of treatment, like E.C.T. or leucotomy representing punishment, symbolical suicide, killing of internal objects, and so forth. In addition, very often a better psychological environment is created for these patients. Although we shall not get a fuller understanding of the psychological processes accompanying physical treatment until such patients are analysed during its administration, I have presented a hypothesis which is in keeping both with facts observed in these patients and with our knowledge of organic brain diseases. It therefore seems unjustifiable to me to put forward hypotheses that contradict these facts and that try to perpetuate an untenable belief that psychoses are the expression of metabolic disturbances.

I must repeat that I do not wish to give the impression that I am opposed to all physical treatments if no other is available; but I should like it to be appreciated that it would appear to be partly a disguised form of palliative and uncontrolled psychotherapy, and partly, especially in leucotomies, psychologically nonselective damage of the brain which, by reducing healthy aspects of the personality, may also reduce pathological features.

An evaluation of all the known facts thus shows that the only therapy of mental disorder that would appear likely, selectively and radically, to remove pathological aspects of personality without harming the rest is a psychodynamic psychotherapy, and it is noteworthy that recently psychoanalysis has successfully dealt with some psychoses.

FUTURE POLICY

The Need to Integrate Psychiatric Research on a Psychodynamic Basis

I have put forward some considerations that must govern how we deploy our resources in the task for psychological medicine in the National Health Service. I have shown the paramount importance of research into the psychodynamic causes of the psychological illnesses. However, I have also pointed out that medical psychologists must do more than claim a larger piece of the research cake than we have been getting. Especially in times of economic pressures, it is attitudes of this kind that make the cake disappear. Cutting research grants is a familiar response of governments in critical times. But to be fair to our administrators, I believe that they only do that in the sincere belief that the research that suffers is a luxury. Now it is my opinion that a large amount of current psychiatric and psychological research would fall rightly within this category, because it is completely nondynamic in character and therefore not likely to make any effective contribution to our task of treating and preventing psychological illness. On the other hand, it must be shown that the present situation is the very time to concentrate resources on likely lines of approach.

Many psychiatrists, especially those trained in psychotherapeutic work, may feel "in their bones" the truth of all that I have been saying about nondynamic theories; but what is vital for us to grasp is that that feeling, however widely held, has no dynamic effect in our situation as long as it merely lies there—ossified. We must, as doctors, present to ourselves and to those responsible for administration that *compelling logic* that comes from the careful analysis of our situation and which is the essential precursor of effective action. Certainly the inexorable logic of the present situation in psychological medicine cannot go on being avoided as is happening at present. For example, Bleuler's review contains a sharp challenge to the organic school; but it is disturbing to get the impression that its implications are, and will continue to be, ignored. Are there any signs that these views, which in varying degrees are not at all uncommon, are being modified in order to establish an integrated body of basic psychiatric principles? Or are we to go on as at present with each school creating bodies of mutually incompatible theories? In such a situation how can any administrative body be well advised?

There is only one reality and to do justice to it there can be only one psychological medicine. It is my contention that we have enough evidence already on which to found a single integrated science of human behaviour, the basic science for psychiatry. It is no longer inherent in the situation that completely incompatible schools should be perpetuated. Furthermore, progress towards an integrated approach to the problems of psychological illness could be achieved rapidly.

Reorientation of Effort

I have tried to establish as essential for our task the combination of psychodynamic research along with the correlated research into the organic basis of such dynamic constitutional factors as excitability, frustration tolerance, and so forth. To my mind psychiatry will flourish or wither according to whether or not it accepts this view. If this view cannot be controverted, there must be a reorientation of our efforts.

I want to stress that I am not advocating that organic research is of little value. On the contrary, but it is essential to integrate it with psychodynamic work. Equally, I feel that the static nature of much psychological research into personality must be replaced by research into dynamic variables. I do not wish to attempt any kind of programme of research priorities in psychodynamics. Others, including myself, have made statements of this kind already. I should like, however, to refer briefly to what I consider to be some of the important tasks.

a. There must be an effort by the psychoanalysts and allied schools to state their theories in more strictly scientific terms. It is a valid criticism that these theories have not been stated in terms that are widely communicable. Even our most interested and benevolent friends find difficulties that are not all due to resistances. More important perhaps, for the advancement of our understanding, our hypotheses are not stated in a form that can be tested in a scientifically valid way. I do not believe that the forces we deal with in our therapeutic tasks fall outside the province of the natural sciences, for example, as Walshe (1950) suggested. The forces in psychological illnesses are very much present in the therapeutic relationship and they have been greatly clarified by what has come to be known as the unconscious object-relations theory of the personality. By the development of here-and-now techniques, many of these forces can be stated in precise communicable terms. Moreover, I think there are already developments that point to ways of making our dynamic interaction with the patient the subject of a strictly experimental approach without in any way sacrificing our therapeutic aims (see Ezriel 1951; Fairbairn 1952).

   If work along these lines can be developed by a number of dynamic psychologists, then our progress should be rapid in the creation of an acceptable and widely usable theory of the personality, healthy and otherwise.

b. The psychoanalytic method is particularly suitable for the study of the way in which environmental factors, especially the earliest ones in the family, act in favourable and pathogenic ways because it allows insight into the interaction between the psychological constitution of the individual with his early environment.

Knowledge in this field is obviously vital to the development of preventive measures.

c. Most psychological tests of personality factors have not proved of great value to psychiatrists. With better dynamic formulations, the development of more useful tests would be made possible with a gain in our work because of their help in assessing personalities and changes in them more precisely.
d. The extension of the psychoanalytic method to groups, again with an emphasis on studies using an experimental approach, opens up possibilities of studying such environmental factors as are transmitted through the medium of the family from society, and of investigating the way in which the difficulties of an *already established* personality are increased and diminished in groups such as at school, work, and so on, and what steps can be taken to keep these difficulties minimal.

Implementation within a National Health Service

If these are our views, what actions are we to aim at?

a. To return to Blacker's suggestions, there would appear to be no useful purpose served by adding substantially to the ranks of psychiatric specialists unless we approve of the roles they are to fulfil—unless we can answer satisfactorily, psychiatrists for what?

   It would surely be a waste of money to add to our ranks large numbers of these specialists merely to provide treatments which, if we are to be honest, are so often of a purely palliative nature; and I include here much of the physical treatment of mental illnesses.

   The apparently bottomless pit of needs for treatment must be handled by making widespread use of all possible therapeutic agencies. The psychiatric clinic must nourish and equip parents, teachers, managers, social workers, doctors, the clergy, and so on with more effective knowledge. And the more we apply our existing knowledge of pathogenic factors, the more will the preventive aspects of these steps appear in the oncoming generations.
b. Instead, money should be invested on a large scale in research by the creation of groups of psychiatrists and allied workers who have adequate facilities. Again, however, we must ask, and answer satisfactorily, research for what? It must be along the psychodynamic lines suggested if the barriers that are keeping the

rival schools apart are to be overcome. Money invested in this way will reduce the Health Service costs in the future by the effects of making available sound preventive knowledge.

c. Concern may be felt at the suggestion that large sums of money should be spent annually on research. What is large in this connexion depends on one's point of view. I suggest as appropriate the modest sum of one-tenth of the £6m. spent on placebo drugs last year, or less than 1 percent of the annual cost of psychological illnesses.

d. To give any attempt at a blueprint for implementing this policy is too large a task for an individual. It is one for discussion by groups that would include all the relevant knowledge including those who have to administer the National Health Service.

e. Suffering is the only motive that renders people at least partly willing to permit the exploration of the intimate regions of the mind and to reveal what really matters in human behaviour and in human relations (see Jones 1940). It is no accident that dynamic psychology developed from clinical work and in my view psychodynamic research is only possible within the therapeutic relationship to which people come with their needs.

   But we must not allow all psychiatrists to be overwhelmed by the demands for treatment. We must have groups of psychiatrists at work on such therapeutic tasks as can be handled under conditions which permit scientific investigation of the problems presented. We need clinics that can also be laboratories.

f. Such truly *Clinical Psychological Laboratories* ought also to be rooted in their local communities to get access to the therapeutic problems set by the various groups of which the individual is a member—school, work, marital, family, and so on. And such clinical psychological laboratories will have to draw on the resources of all the relevant human sciences. I think there might well be such a clinic, probably best associated with the facilities of a University, in many hospital regions. Again, however, it must be stressed that the present pattern of staffing University departments in psychiatry with far too few senior staff will prove futile. The necessary knowledge and conditions for progress will be likely to occur only when such clinical psychological laboratories have a substantial group of whole-time senior workers.

Although I imply that dynamic psychological work will contribute fundamentally to many of the troubles in our midst, it is not at all necessary to fear that the psychiatrist or psychologist must become a kind of supertechnocrat. The model of his relationship with the community was shown in my experience in the War Office Selection Boards where the psychiatrist and psychologist were in a purely advisory role helping those officers whose job it was to take responsibility for such actions as they thought wise.

This relationship is in contrast to what would really be one of neurotic collusion were we to go on providing more and more therapy. In this latter situation we should be allowing our society to park out its problems on us without once making it face up to its own sickness. Every psychiatrist knows the future of such a relationship to be the demand for more and more treatment.

I have managed to get near the end of this long paper without referring to the latest arrival in our field—cybernetics. However, it comes to my mind here as perhaps enabling us to describe the proper role of the clinical psychological laboratory and its staff as an ideal *servomechanism*, which would constantly pick up a sufficient sample of the flaws in our current social process and which would then, if our work goes ahead, "feed-back" the data for remedial action to its social administrators.

Many psychiatrists may feel that I have focused attention on what is really a dead horse, but even a brief survey of the titles of British psychiatric papers will show the extent to which psychiatric research goes on being impeded by its methodological confusions. I have pointed out already that this paper was not intended to be a comprehensive survey. It grew from an attempt some of my colleagues and I made to clarify our views on certain prominent psychiatric issues. I shall feel it has amply fulfilled its aim if it stimulates many other psychiatrists and psychologists to make much fuller clarifications in the issues I have touched upon. I believe that a clear logical statement of our tasks in the light of available knowledge would be enormously productive. Let me conclude by quoting you a passage from Robert Lynd's *Knowledge for What?* (1940) (in the original this passage refers to social science but by substituting in one place "psychiatry" for "social science" the quotation loses none of its point):

> The controlling factor in any science is the way it views and states its problems. Once stated, a problem can yield no further insights than are allowed by the constricting frame of its original formulation; although, in a negative sense, the data discovered may serve to point to the inadequacy of the original frame of reference. The current emphasis in psychiatry [social science] upon techniques and precise empirical data is a healthy one; but, as already noted, skilful collection, organization, and manipulation of data are worth no more than the problem to the solution of which they are addressed. If the problem is wizened, the data are but footnotes to the insignificant. In a positive sense, such data may be vicious, in that their very perfection may mislead others into regarding as important the problem to which they relate; for in science, too, "Apparel oft proclaims the man." If science poses questions within an unreal and mistaken framework, data and rival schools of thought begin to pile up behind the two sides of these questions, and the questions assume unwarranted dignity and importance. [p. 202]

I do not think that my eyes are on the stars when I state that a rapid advance in the integration of psychological medicine is possible. If a group of experts comprising the main disciplines relevant to our task were to make a critical evaluative statement of our knowledge and our methodologies, it would make it very difficult for what Professor Broad (1937) has called "silly" theories about behaviour and its disorders to go on hampering our work. It would, instead, reorient the contributions of all psychiatric skills and special knowledge towards a common goal.

Training psychotherapists in the National Health Service with Paul O'Farrell and Jill Savege, 1971.

18. THE NEED FOR A NEW PARADIGM

Confronted with the task of reexamining some of the fundamental principles that inspire their work, institutions are possessed by a lengthy process of reflection, review, resistance, and change. In this chapter, I reflect upon my experience of such a process at the Menninger Foundation, which I had visited since 1964 as a consultant for periods of 3–4 weeks most years for a quarter of a century. The length of this relationship affords an unusual opportunity for study. Clearly there were strong bonds on both sides to have kept it, at least for myself, as fresh as when it started; and this vitality could only have had its source in shared ongoing development. There is, of course, a highly personal side in my becoming involved in many varied roles and so I felt I should give a brief account of the background from which I responded to the perpetual challenges.

My first knowledge of the Foundation came from meeting Dr. Will and Dr. Karl at the end of the last war. I was a member of a group that had been formed in the British Army to help with several of its psychological and social problems. Its original members had come from the Tavistock Clinic in London, whose medical director, Brigadier J. R. Rees, had been appointed chief psychiatrist to the British army, and all of them were eager to apply what they had learned about psychological stresses from their psychotherapeutic experience. As they became more involved with groups and organisations, they recruited several psychoanalysts, psychologists, and social scientists who were sympathetic with their point of view. (Because of its origins the group became known as "The Tavistock Group" although most of the later members, including myself, had not worked at the Tavistock Clinic.) The group functioned closely with senior army officers in devising some strikingly innovative measures, for example, for selecting trainee officers, for rehabilitating returned prisoners of war, and for the hospital treatment of some psychological disorders. Dr. Will, in his capacity as chief psychiatrist to the American army, was keenly interested in this work and he sponsored a visit to its centre by a panel of eminent American psychiatrists one of whom was Dr. Karl. From the great encouragement of these visitors, the Tavistock Group decided to stay together and accept an invitation to reshape the Tavistock Clinic as a unit within the impending National Health Service and to establish an associated independent body to be known as The

Tavistock Institute of Human Relations, which would continue the study of groups and organisations. The planning work continued to be done by the whole group and within a few years various practical contributions emerged along with the formulation of the theoretical principles on which these were based. I was elected by the group to be medical director of the Clinic in which role I was soon engaged in the rapid development of psychoanalytical group therapy along with participation in the organisation and planning of both Clinic and Institute.

My first visit to the Foundation in January 1964 was devoted almost entirely to teaching group psychotherapy. The Tavistock approach had been stimulated by new psychoanalytic concepts about the fundamental part played in the development of the personality by early relationships with mother and family. From these experiences the individual's inner world was formed with imagined figures and relationships amongst them, which had a great influence on the capacities for future social behaviour. These concepts, loosely referred to as the "British Object-Relations Theories," were not acceptable at that time to most of the American psychoanalytic "establishment" and so I presented their essential features in a paper to the Topeka Psychoanalytic Institute, which responded with open-minded interest. Their main impact was upon those doing group psychotherapy, and especially upon Dr. Otto Kernberg who made considerable use of them in his subsequent important contributions to psychoanalytic theory and practice.

On this visit I also met with a lively curiosity about the organisation and administration of the Tavistock Clinic, especially within a state service. When I returned 2 years later, group psychotherapy was again my focus. Interest in it had grown, but I was struck most forcibly by the changed atmosphere within the Foundation. Dr. Karl's retirement was imminent and Dr. Will had a fatal illness. There was a widespread gloomy preoccupation about these losses and the future of the Foundation. The remarkable abilities and energies of the two brothers had established a leadership in the professional field for the Foundation along with an administrative structure that largely freed the staff from what professional workers so often regard as chores that interfere with their work. From the fact that the postwar Tavistock had grown from a similar situation I was asked to talk with many informal groups about its history. Any information I gave could not, however, remove their anxious insecurities—intensified by the growing realisation that they had become dependent upon a leadership that was most unlikely to be repeated. And crucial decisions and changes would have to be made soon.

There was a gap of about 3 years before I was asked back by Dr. Roy, who was now president. That in itself was significant because it implied I would be engaged in wider concerns than the group psychotherapy teaching for which my previous invitations had come from the school side. I had by this time retired from the Tavistock Clinic and I believe this added to the readiness with which I identified with him and the staff in their tasks. Tensions that had been held down were now erupting around the themes of leadership, authority, and responsibility. Formal authority had been given to Dr. Roy by the trustees of the

Foundation. His responsibility was to earn personal authority and he had made it clear that, in keeping with the times and with what he felt about his own capacities together with the staff, he wished to achieve a leadership rooted in full participation with them. I felt that staff reactions were mixed. Some regarded the change as what they had hoped for. Others appeared to me to be somewhat intimidated by the realities. Genuine participation can only come from the "gut" adoption of sharing in the destiny of the organisation as a fully personal commitment. Senior staff would not be concerned merely in decisions on practical matters but would have to be responsible for creating the ferment of ideas on which the success of an organisation such as the Foundation, with its reputation for high quality services, research, and training, relied absolutely. This creativity would be the wellspring to inspire the total overall effort and it must draw as widely as possible from the personal resources of the whole staff. The full implications of effective participation were slow to be realised. Inevitable frustrations and disillusionments about their own capacities led in several to a resurgence of the underlying dependence that had struck me previously. I would repeatedly hear that "this place needs leadership." For many others it was a painful experience to realise that they had to wear the hair shirt of torturing struggles with the problems along with the vagaries of personal behaviours that are invariably exacerbated in groups that have not yet formulated and assimilated what their tasks demand. It was readily understandable to myself that the learning the president and the staff would have to experience together would have to be sustained over several years; but I was reassured by "having been here before."

Investment in the work of the units went on steadily enough. What made for considerable tensions at times was the all too human difficulty in accepting that each unit belonged to a larger whole of which all were vital parts. The status of the whole was what brought the support from outside individuals and bodies for the training and research that a leading centre must maintain; and this overall image of the Foundation was also what played the major part in the supply of patients.

Workable management structures were eventually achieved over the next few years after much sturm und drang, though it then had to be learned by all that such structuring has to be constantly adapted to changing situations. Planning as an ongoing process is the reality, and not *plans* treated as fixed guides for the future. Thus when the financial situation was becoming more difficult, the corresponding component in management was felt to be overweighted. That challenge, however, was more readily adapted to, I believe, than was the case with the threat of an infectious invasion into the clinical philosophy of the Foundation by external trends, above all by the spread in general psychiatry of the use of physical methods almost to the rejection of the psychodynamic, and hence humanistic, concern for the patient as a person. From its start, a principle inspiring the Foundation was the belief that patients were to be accepted and treated with the respect due to all human beings and, as far as possible, this would apply to severely disturbed individuals. A paramount place in the values of the Foundation was thus to give care with all its implications. Professional care has, of course, to merge this humanistic concern with the best understanding available; and the psychoanalytic approach adopted by Drs. Karl and Will was to them the one that provided the basis for facilitating a regrowth of the person. Such a therapy is inevitably slow and uncertain in its results. The word *treatment* had come to signify in medicine something the doctor could administer to the patient irrespective of what was involved. Here what was offered were personal relationships within which a redevelopment could take place—a vastly different matter. The staggering advances in medical technology were unfortunately reinforcing the ever-present wish for short treatments, especially those that avoided the fears of looking inside oneself. Combined with the immediate appeal of reduced costs, and hence the reluctance of the insurance companies to cover long-term psychotherapy, the situation was at times a serious threat.

A more disturbing aspect of this development, however, were the beliefs about human nature that the physical methods tended to bring in their train. There was no question of the benefits to the increased therapeutic resources these advances could provide. But there was equally no doubt that the gains were limited for they were essentially ways of reducing tensions and not of understanding the nature and origin of the psychological disorders. Such is the fear of coping with our inner worlds that at times the transient gains from these methods were used in medicine to support philosophies that dehumanised man to the status of a machine. The split in the intellectual and academic worlds between those who would find reassurance in such a belief and those who could accept all the complexities and apparently insoluble problems that characterise human nature with its autonomous creativity and freedom to choose deepened. The reductionist views of man's nature were also supported amongst substantial sections of the rapidly growing body of clinical psychologists in their advocacy of behavouristic methods.

The threat here was potentially a profound one for the Foundation whose philosophy had attracted and held staff for whom the humanistic view of man carried convictions that could not be abandoned. There was not, however, a widespread understanding amongst psychoanalysts of the theoretical issues here. It was sad, too, that the psychoanalytical movement as a whole had not given them much attention, especially when enough knowledge was available to deal with them. Hence, when I say that I felt the Foundation senior staff might have done more to assert its position against the rising flood of doubt, if not overt hostility, in the academic and professional worlds about their approach, I must emphasize that this lack was almost universal amongst psychodynamic groups. It stemmed in my view from a deeper malaise to which I shall return presently. The absence of an active counterstatement was most noticeable in the public relations staff who in their job of seeking support from the outside world were not being given the arguments that could convince the sceptic of the reasons why an institution like the Foundation must be supported especially in face of this rising tide of *scientism*.

Despite the pervasively unfavourable climate that built up in the '70s, the staff held fast to its beliefs and fortunately we are to-day seeing a gradual recession in the so-called scientific methods as the modern biological views on the nature of the living organism as a self-regulating open system become more established. And at the grass roots, discontent amongst patients with what to them was a too ready resort to these mechanistic or placebo treatments is now increasingly manifest.

Linked with the philosophical challenge, and the misleading simplifications about disorders of the personality, there was a concomitant pressure from the other mental health professions for greater autonomy in their work. The greater responsibility given to relatively junior medical staff was often resented by highly experienced members of the other professions. Here again I thought that more clarifications of these issues was needed especially in relation to the position of the Foundation as an institution for which certain responsibilities were mandatory because of its medical status. In fact the issues raised could only be coped with at the level of the national professional bodies; and a year or two later this process was going on.

The complex psychological forces influencing all groups became of great interest during the '60s and '70s. To assist the staff in appreciating their nature, the president arranged for many members to attend the Group Relations Conferences sponsored by the Tavistock Institute. This experiential learning facilitated the development of group methods within the hospital and other units working with outside organisations. From observation of group work in many psychiatric hospitals I had been struck by the failure to use it for illuminating unconscious forces, focusing instead on the superficial content of what was happening. There seemed often to be no attention paid to the etiology of the psychological disorders, with a manifest ignoring of the crucial processes so far as concerned the improved understanding of these by the patients. Often, indeed, one felt group consensus about behaviour was replacing more adequate diagnosis. In these hospitals I attributed this deficiency to the fact that the staff had little or no psychodynamic training. When the group work began in the Foundation the senior staff, most of whom had had psychoanalytic training, were clearly operating in a way to be expected from a well established psychoanalytic tradition. By the later '70s, however, the work had become distinctly changed to a more superficial level with most of the staff participating irrespective of the differences in their training. For groups whose task was discussion of day to day issues that was fine; but when the aim was to increase patients' understanding of forces not ordinarily recognized, it seemed to me there was little awareness of these powerful etiological factors; and again, consensus seemed to be the touchstone for judging progress. Of course these views were impressionistic, but checking informally with staff confirmed them. The origins of this change were soon obvious—there were fewer staff in the senior hospital positions who had been psychoanalytically trained. Indeed, by the end of the '70s there were very few senior analysts in the chief posts within the sections. When I had first visited in 1964, almost all these senior posts were filled by analysts, several of whom were at the same time training analysts within the Institute at the Foundation. Around this time I also felt a growing lack of the excitement that should ordinarily be found in some sections of a large hospital from the challenges of the therapeutic tasks.

What was happening, I asked myself, in this hospital that was hitherto a leading centre in its contributions to the theory and practice of psychoanalytically based therapy? Hospital patients had been the main stimulus for a lively atmosphere whereas it now seemed that they were no longer felt to be so. There were many external factors making for this situation, for example, the greater financial rewards in other places where private practice could be combined with the hospital work. There was also the great pressure in the Institute resources forcing more of the seniors to devote increasingly large parts of their time to training. I felt, nevertheless, these external sources were not adequate to account for a kind of pervasive intellectual staleness. People were working hard and senior analysts acted as consultants to hospital sections, yet there was a distinct atmosphere of the work having become routine as far as analytic thinking went. Again, I want to emphasize that these were impressions that could well be regarded as highly subjective; but, as before, talking informally to individuals and to small groups I had them confirmed. Thus some senior analysts would remark, "We are needing some leadership here." I must confess I felt at times impatient with what I thought was an avoidance of a rather awkward situation. I asked on one occasion whether or not I was being told that the staff was incapable of producing ideas of their own. There was no awareness of what might be amiss and I was baffled. About 5 years ago I had some experiences that disturbed me and it was from reflecting upon these that a new perspective formed in my mind about an unrecognized yet apparently powerful factor that had had a stultifying effect throughout the Foundation for the previous decade. What had vitalised the institution in its first decades was usually thought of as coming from the outstanding personalities of Dr. Karl and Dr. Will. There was little or no distinction made, however, within the term *leadership* between charismatic personal qualities and the ideas that had inspired them. I now became convinced that what was missing was the creative enthusiasm that comes when the challenges of the work are felt to be met by the ideas available. What had gone was the inspiring lead given by concepts that offered exciting illuminations of the clinical problems now encountered. The specific experiences that crystallised my conviction were what happened at a few case conferences in the adult hospital. A few successive patients were all described as "difficult," by which was meant that they were persistently destructive to the therapeutic work of the staff. Indeed, all of them had been previously discharged from a few hospitals because the staffs could not tolerate the intensely stressful relationship these patients seemed motivated to create. The negativity was all too manifest and all too intractable. To account for such conditions psychiatrists commonly invoke innate factors, in this case too much aggression, a tautology designed to remove the problem. The impotent exasperation these patients aroused in the staff was striking as also was the absence of any consideration of the serious deprivations these patients had suffered. Not that the parents abused them. The deprivations arose often from such events as separations because of illness or, perhaps more frequently, from parental attitudes that frustrated the normal assertiveness of the healthy child. The new way, in which the patients' behaviour could be understood as the expression of hate and resentment because of the chronic frustrations of their natural assertive behaviour, now vitalised the whole staff. To the child, parental preoccupations and withdrawal of interest at times created a chronic rage that had to be split off into a separate part of the personality because it was so highly incompatible with all the good experiences from these same figures. The need to protest about his deprivations had never been accepted and he was now venting this hate on all those in close contact with him as though they were evoking the original situation.

Put in this way, the episodes seem extremely banal as examples of what I felt was the source of a pervasively deadening impasse. When we realise, however, the general position of psychoanalysis at this time it could readily be seen as an indicator of the deeper strains there. These patients could only be understood in terms of a divided self that is, in splits of a holistic organisation that determined behaviour from the start at the personal level. Despite the advances in ego psychology, the basic assumptions for the explanation of personal behaviour, for motivation and conflicts within the person, rested on the modes of regulation of the discharge of biologically conceived instinctual energies or drives. What these patients exhibited was in essence a bitter entrenched resentment that they had never felt responded to from the start with the joyous acceptance of the activities of their autonomous selves. Instead they experienced a coercion into being someone different from what all their inner pressures asserted as "being themselves." The framework of drive theory was deeply ingrained in the whole psychoanalytical movement especially in the U.S.A. It had a powerful grip because it had given so much insight into the unconscious functioning of the personality; yet there was wide recognition that its metapsychological assumptions had been largely laid aside, especially as more analysts treated serious personality disorders. The classical view was that the bulk of those conditions was not suitable for psychoanalysis. Clinical advances, nevertheless, were steadily disproving this belief and new theoretical concepts, affecting both theory and practice, were emerging. Resistance to potentially radical challenges to any widely accepted paradigm is the rule, and wisely so, until new data can carry conviction. To my mind it was unusually strong in the U.S.A. because of the nature of the "psychoanalytical establishment." The climate of opinion in Britain was a much more open one so that new ideas had been discussed openly alongside the traditional ones. In short, the intellectual flatness in the Foundation was a general one throughout the psychoanalytically oriented hospitals and academic departments in America.

The cases referred to illustrated the critical issue. The disorders in so many hospital patients were producing a sense of inadequacy in the staff from the rigidity with which their theoretical tools constrained their creativity. I got the strong impression that with this frustrating, and in some measure depressing, situation not being recognized, there was a "silent" withdrawal of most of the experienced analysts from it. Here I must emphasize again that I did not believe this drift reflected any lack of talent. This staff group was in the grip of forces typical of any group that has lost its confidence in tackling its task. The classical psychoanalytic paradigm had been in existence for decades and its very successes were adding to the reluctance to reexamine it. The adoption of a new one was certain to be a slow process for it was comparable to what any work force experiences when its old tools are threatened with new ones, or individuals are subjected to major attacks on their ideologies.

Within the years following the case discussions mentioned there was an increased interest in the hospital in treating the hitherto daunting problems presented by the compulsive negativity in so many patients. Though not a dramatic change it was a profoundly significant one reinforced fortunately by a new director of the hospital who grasped the need for a change extremely well. The focus now was on the development of the self as the central agency embodying the capacity for good social relations and a satisfying investment of the creative resources of the person in the business of living. Apart from its appeal in regard to the therapeutic work, there was also a growing awareness that the importance attached to the internalisation into the inner world of the experiences in early relationships illuminated human nature in a new way. It facilitated communication between the specialist staff in the Foundation and other mental health workers and with the outside world. There was a salutary emphasis on the inherent relatedness of the individual to others at all stages of the life cycle. The personality develops well and maintains its selfhood or identity effectively only through its facilitating experiences with others, a very different position from such achievements resting on the satisfaction of instinctual energies—a philosophy that had certainly contributed to the "cult of narcissism" with its disturbing implications for both the person and his society.

I now felt that the wellspring of the Foundation's professional morale could begin to flow strongly again. No area of psychopathology could be of greater importance than the growth of the self. It was also one that would require for its development a great deal of team work. The old pattern was for the analytic treatment of patients to be conducted completely apart from the staff of the unit who cared for the patient in "the other 23 hours of the day." I have long believed that a primary factor sustaining those who have to be close to the stressful impact of powerful emotional conflict is the opportunity for constantly enriching themselves through a deepening understanding of those they are helping. Psychotherapeutic work with divided selves demands especially such an ongoing learning. The splitting of the self into good and bad—loving and hating—parts induces intolerable tensions if the staff do not have the opportunity to discuss the particular ways they are disturbingly cast at times in the role of "all good" or "all bad" figures with the intensity of infantile demandingness or destructiveness. The senior staff therefore have to keep the whole team learning of the full nature of the patients' conflicts. This, of course, does not break the confidentiality of an analytic relationship; what has to be shared by all is an understanding of the overt relationships the patient is making with the staff, consciously and unconsciously. Without this overall collaborative involvement in the therapy the patients can avoid getting an appreciation of what they do to others and to themselves because of the compulsions from their inner worlds and especially the insecurities that are concealed by their destructive attitudes. It is this understanding that has to characterise a psychoanalytically informed approach to the use of groups and the whole social milieu of the hospital. The necessary study of the origins of love and hate and violence is obviously an urgent concern for society as well as for the staff. The scale of the complexities in this task with the interdependence of biological, social, cultural, and personal factors is enormous. Nevertheless, a new paradigm for psychoanalytic theory in terms of relationships would seem to be one that will facilitate a new level of collaborative thinking amongst all the relative disciplines and between them and society. And the hospital is uniquely placed to inspire the work needed, especially research into the adequacy of our guiding concepts, for the selves of the patients are living witnesses to the nature and origin of what can go wrong at crucial stages of their formation.

I have given a highly selective and sketchy account of my experiences with the Foundation over many years. What then has my role really been? I can only describe it as being that of a caring colleague who from his knowledge and objective appraisals tries to clarify with the staff what is happening. Above all, he makes a commitment to stay with the "family" while it works through doubts and blocks about their goals and the progress towards them; and by so doing he imparts his conviction that they have all the resources to do this. Some of the brilliant colleagues whom I was so fortunate to have had at the Tavistock had a gift for the apt slogan. Two that have remained as perpetual texts for myself are, first, "there is nothing so practical as a good theory," and the other, "no research without therapy," by which we believed that no one should try to understand the inner conflicts of others without the latter being personally enriched by the relationship. There is also implied here that only within a therapeutic relationship can individuals describe the most significant features of their inner life. Hence therapeutic settings are uniquely important for understanding people. No other method can reach the most crucial forces in the person. I think that, while the Foundation may not have used these mottoes in their work, the extent to which I felt it shared all that I believed in about psychotherapeutic institutions was what maintained the enrichment that gave so much to me in our bond; and I could only feel that if I sensed that, my friends must also have shared in what I gained.

With Eric Trist and John Bowlby at Menninger Conference, "Challenge to Psychoanalysis," 1985

19. THE PSYCHODYNAMIC IMAGE OF MAN

To be invited to give this first Malcolm Millar lecture is a great honour that I deeply appreciate. The psychodynamic approach of Malcolm Millar (Crombie-Ross Professor of Mental Health, University of Aberdeen, 1949–1976) inspired a practice and teaching that made a notable contribution to British psychiatry at a time when that approach was virtually denied scientific respectability. It is also a great personal pleasure as he and I shared a period of work together during the last war so that I got to know well his concern with providing care. It seemed appropriate, therefore, to choose a theme related to this concern.

A PHILOSOPHY FOR THE CARING PROFESSIONS

"A Philosophy for the Caring Professions" is a large assignment so I shall select a few broad issues that I believe to be crucial for the future of our work. There is an infinite range of care-giving activities, most of which I shall take for granted. In the present context I want to focus on care devoted to the development and well-being of the person—to those factors that equip and maintain the individual in the business of living with a sense of wholeness and responsible autonomy; of feeling "somebody" and being "a somebody" to others; and of fulfilment in the use of his talents. I shall return to this question of what we mean by a person and also by caring for him at the personal level. At the risk of oversimplification, let me put it at this point that my interest is care related to what goes on at the centre of the person, where he is, or should be, in himself as a responsible free agent, rather than with what he might present at his boundaries.

A few remarks are also necessary on my use of the word *psychodynamic*. Most of the insights about the person that have proved useful to the caring professions have come from the psychoanalysts. This knowledge, however, has been expanded by many groups outwith the formal psychoanalytic organisations, so I have adopted the more general term to cover the broad approach based on an understanding of the person in psychological terms and which emphasises the role of unconscious motives. Psychodynamic views have been widely disseminated and indeed are now part of our culture. In this process they inevitably get attenuated and distorted so that their full significance, and the way in which they are being developed, tends to get ignored. I shall thus try to emphasise what I see as important current trends.

Providing help for personal problems are several professions along with a great variety of counselling services. There are doctors and nurses, social workers, the clergy, and in recent years an increasing number of psychologists. To complicate matters, there is also a range of *therapists* practising one or other of the many methods evolved to help with personal problems, that is, Gestalt therapy, transactional analysis, encounter groups. True, these methods are mostly used by the professions, but there has been a trend for people both within and outside the professions to take a "training" in the method and then to set up as practitioners without an adequate experience in dealing with psychological conflicts. I shall confine myself to the professions because I believe that they must constitute the vital core of our overall endeavour to provide articulated knowledge and responsible practice.

Professions imply a corpus of knowledge and skills shared by their members. When duly recognised, they give to society an assurance of competence and its responsible use; and they maintain a steady research and development endeavour to keep enlarging their competence. In providing help for personal stresses there are good reasons why professional resources should be supplemented by agencies in which the expertise is not as specialised. We could not possibly cope with the demands without them; and in respect of the quality of their work, the best of our voluntary services maintain close collaboration with relevant professional groups so that the interests of all parties are protected. There is also another reason why a large voluntary movement is desirable, namely, that society is thereby confronted with the scale of stress and so can initiate steps towards its alleviation. It is the professions, however, who have to take a lead in helping all the allied services to keep adding to their expertise.

When we survey all these activities, we cannot but be struck by their diversity in theory and practice. A rough continuum can be based on the degree to which the approach is manifestly personal in depth. At one end we can place the intensive analytical psychotherapies, the distinguishing feature of which is coping with unconscious motives. There would then be a range of methods involving personal interaction at a conscious level. The groups operating in this way are by far the largest as they include voluntary counselling services as well as the professions. Next might come the relatively recent behaviour therapies in which the focus is on overt behaviour rather than on the inner world of the person. Lastly would be the "physical methods," which attempt to alter the mental state by changing the underlying physiology as, for instance, by drugs or other methods.

The increased facilities for personal help reflect the great rise in demands for it. The origins of this situation are complex. Many believe that changes in society are precipitating the demands. On the other hand, the nature of psychological stresses is more widely known. It is, therefore, difficult to ascertain whether there is a real increase in the incidence of stress or whether requests for help are more readily made. One thing certain is that the presenting complaints have changed towards a great rise in feelings of general personal malaise, for example, feelings of "depression" or futility, of loss of purpose, of not feeling sure of who or what one really is.

These features emphasise the point that we cannot consider the person apart from the society in which he has grown and is now functioning. There is no doubt at all that within the last few decades there have been very great changes in our social patterns and values with the result that appraisal of personal stress has become more complex. The assumed primacy of social factors led many young social workers some years ago to express vociferously the view that provisions for personal problems were useless—if not a bourgeois attempt to keep people adapted to society. What was needed was social change. There is no question that sections of the social environment can be unduly stressful and therefore every effort should be made to improve these. Nevertheless, there is no society in which individuals do not have problems of a primary personal nature. Personal conflicts are a product of the interaction of the social and the personal and we have to separate as best we can the contributions of each for remedial action. Also, we all have to keep in mind that society is not an entity as an agent of action. Changes in it come from the individual and our efforts must be to foster the kind of growth that increases his creativity.

THE SOCIAL AND THE PERSONAL

This theme of the social and the personal is so crucial that I want to enlarge on it to get a proper appreciation of the role of the caring professions. I believe important changes are occurring in this role in parallel with what is happening in society. For this purpose I shall draw upon the writings of two of my former colleagues, the social scientists Emery and Trist (1973). They describe the extraordinary technological advances of recent decades as having produced a profound change in the fabric of the social environment, especially in the modern Western nations. From a loosely knit laissez faire regulation of local and relatively autonomous social service and production units, our postindustrial society has changed this pattern to one of a tightly interwoven texture. This new interrelatedness gives a highly turbulent or unpredictable quality, because technological change can produce extremely rapid and extensive effects in large sections of our production system. Larger groupings result both in these systems and in the social services to create the necessary resources. The environment thus becomes more and more man-made with major problems not involving man versus nature so much as man versus man.

The survival of any society can rest on the maintenance of a steady state through established institutions and customs. Modern societies, because of external impingements and internal forces, are such that, unless they become adaptive learning systems, they perish. They must constantly develop, that is, meet challenge with creative changes in their internal structures. Such changes, on account of the high degree of interdependence amongst the component systems, have to be made increasingly by centralised planning for the society as a whole—and here we come to the greatly divergent philosophies of the modern world. Two options are available. One is the engineered society, modelled on the physical science, in which planning is done by a special section or elite group. This is the choice of the totalitarian countries. The other, the apparent choice of the Western democracies, rests more on the life sciences. It seeks to develop all members of society by a higher quality in all the primary social units, that is, the individual, the family, the work place, schools, the community and the services and amenities it provides. Securing the highest quality of life has now become the overriding question as we move towards postindustrialism.

The trends in these directions are manifest in the changing concepts of welfare. In the industrial era the state had to take an increasing part in providing welfare services for the sick and in providing measures against disease in order to maintain the work force. Gradually a new concept of welfare can be identified, namely, that the best welfare is secured by personal development, for example, by improvement in the physical environment and in personal resources through education, better conditions of work, and so forth. Today in the more affluent countries, emphasis is no longer on minimum standards for health and growth but on the realization of potential, both for the individual and society.

These concepts of welfare and development do not, of course, belong to the world of science. They are values or choices by which we shape our aspirations and goals, our social perceptions and practices. Our adaptive strategy is now increasingly towards the adoption of values that promote the optimal realization of individual potential. What is happening is far from a homogenous change since many of our old values persist even though detrimental to the newer ones. How then do we identify the adaptive values? This can be done by appraising the spontaneously emerging responses to what is sensed as inimical to development. Within organisations we have noted more collaborative groupings—changes from separate objectives to linked ones. In personal values, there is a very mixed array. Thus, as a reaction against the dehumanising effects of common situations at work, there have been movements against some of the hallowed values of the Protestant ethic, for example, from achievement to self-actualisation; from undue independence to interdependence; and from "grin and bear it" to a focus on joy. Contrasting with these ideals are changes that seem to have been initiated by the insidiously dehumanising influences of technology. Toffler (1970), for example, has vividly portrayed in his book *Future Shock* how our attitudes to the expendability of consumer goods have spread to human relationships, a change that does not appear to be adaptive for personal growth and development.

Older men with their family responsibilities have naturally not been leaders in finding more self-expression. The counterculture impetus has come from young people with the consequent disadvantages of their inexperience. To want to "do one's own thing instead of someone else's" is eminently understandable, but it can be a disruptive social philosophy, especially when human nature is viewed in an alarmingly superficial way. Envy, hate, and destructiveness were what the establishment had, or did to you. The beautiful people would achieve love. But with no realistic commitment of one person to another, love soon became essentially pleasure-seeking. Gratification and kicks became the goals as this "new narcissism" flourished. Although the excesses within these movements have abated, we have been left with a residue of belittlement of the person in some of his aspects. Thus at times sex therapy seems to get more emphasis than the need to improve personal relations. It is little wonder that a counterreformation has appeared in attacks on this *Cult of Self Worship*, or *Psychology as Religion*, as Vitz (1977) entitles his book.

A seriously disturbing aspect of these trends was the backing taken from the writings of some of our prominent intellectuals such as Sartre, Marcuse, and Norman Brown. The philosophies propounded, especially by Marcuse and Brown, were based on what they claimed, not without some justification, to be the essence of Freud's image of man, that is, the fundamental role of pleasure seeking from the satisfaction of the sexual instincts.

THE ROLE OF CARE IN THE OPEN SOCIETY

Assuming that the development of each individual is our accepted social philosophy, the role of the caring services must then be directed to this end. At first sight this may not seem much of a change but I believe it is. The traditional position of the carers has been very much one of ameliorating the lot of those extruded from the system, either temporarily or permanently, by picking them up in a net of charitable and philanthropic agencies. Beyond attempts to alter grossly harmful features of the environment, their main function was to keep those needing care out of the way until, hopefully, some could be returned to useful roles. Deviant behaviour too difficult to manage was treated with more active defences, for example, it had to be isolated or literally walled off. Such policies helped to preserve the status quo of existing institutions and their values, but only for a time.

True, we have now advanced a long way from that situation in regard to state provisions. I do not think, however, we have sufficiently considered the changed role of the caring services.

An open social system whose primary task is to develop all its members has to adopt a quite opposite attitude to disorders or deviance. The existence of everyone in trouble, whether ill-health, psychological disorder, or in a maladaptive group such as the poor, or in crime, now raises the question, how has this happened? What is going wrong in the system? From being largely a charitable endeavour with little expertise and almost no learning function built into it, caring is now at the centre of the social system. It becomes a servo-mechanism whose feedback is critical in evaluating how much people are not in a state of developmental well-being. A caring system becomes an essential component in all the main institutions of our living and so a built-in requirement in all social planning. The fundamental concern with development also means that we cannot separate education from the caring system in our overall considerations. In the United States, the administrative triad of Health, Education, and Welfare is a political recognition that development is the best form of welfare.

THE NEED FOR A DEVELOPMENTAL VIEW OF THE PERSON

The next question that arises is: do we have a concept of development of the person that can help us to realise our general philosophy? Our aim is not tied to a utopia nor to any specific ideological programme. It is the essence of open system development that its ongoing spontaneous creativity will make for unpredictability—both in the individual and in society. We can thus aim only at making the adaptive capacities of both as effective as possible so that action can be planned in the light of maximum knowledge of what is happening in all sections of society and in the environment. And when growth and development are paramount values the future is always in mind. Gaining relevant knowledge does not guarantee that we shall use it, yet at least it can guide those who wish to promote optimal planning.

For a congruent educational and caring endeavour there must be a shared view of the nature of man as a constantly developing person. We must have a framework that relates what happens at each phase to the next, and for matching what happens in the different sectors of the life space of the person. We cannot expect to foster responsible adults for instance, if we treat people as such in one sector and at the same time deny responsible participation in another.

I believe a useful image of man's nature is now being formulated amongst analytical psychotherapists, and following Chein (1972), I have preferred the term *image* to the word *model* with its mechanistic connotations and because the term *image* resonates with the unique feature of persons, namely their creative imagination.

The spontaneous trends that were noted all highlighted the importance of self-feelings: self-actualisation, self-esteem, self-expression. It is striking that contemporaneously the self is also appearing as a focus of study in several sections of our professions. What we most need is an adequate conceptualisation of the self. We have several incompatible claims here, for example, the Christian, the Marxist, the Behaviourist, and the Psychodynamic, and clearly we must examine and appraise their implications.

THE PSYCHODYNAMIC IMAGE OF MAN

Taking the psychodynamic first, the image of man left by Freud was of a titanic struggle between the powerful instincts of life and death and the need to control them. Personal development was governed by the vicissitudes of the instinctual drives, especially the sexual instinct with its progression through the zonal stages. The core developmental achievement was the surmounting of the oedipal complex—the child's conflicts from his sexual fantasies about his parents. The personality was structured in terms of the instincts or the id, the ego or the system adapted to reality, and the superego or internal image of primitive parental figures controlling the id. The general theory of man was thus couched in such scientific abstractions as energies, mechanisms, and functions together with a quite different level of functioning, namely, an internalised version of a relationship with "parents." There has been in recent years a growing dissatisfaction with this formulation and there have appeared attempts to bring the person into focus, notably those of Erikson with his concepts of *self* and *identity*. The word *self* has become more frequent in the titles of books and articles in psychodynamic journals, and the views of a number of British analysts have become specifically concerned with this topic, for instance; Balint (1968), Winnicott (1971), Fairbairn (1954b), Guntrip (1969, 1978). What they established from their work with persons having serious difficulties in coping with life was that in the very early development of the infant a basic psychological structuring takes place that determines the whole of its future development. They postulate that there is a unitary system from birth that is the potential self and that this system is personified, so to speak, into an "I" by the experience of a good fit between the personal care and love of the mother and the infant's needs. Instinctual satisfaction of bodily needs reinforces the development of this self system but it is not the essential factor, which is the experience of being loved for itself. The self then acquires a feeling of being integrated with the outer world in a way that promotes positive interaction with it—an attitude of "belief in" that gives zest to living and to the rapidly developing exploratory interactions of learning about the world. Development takes place by differentiation of subsystems or subselves within the original unitary matrix. Painful emotions are unavoidable even in the best mother-infant relationships, and "good" and "bad"—or pleasant and unpleasant—experiences cohere into the first divisions within the self, namely, a "good" mother/world system and another "bad" one. Further development follows a double path. The good self occupies a central position that enables it to be enriched by all the learning experiences within the powerful impetus towards independence. Simultaneously, frustrations lead to the creation of an inner world in which the self relates to a range of figures representing aspects of the frustrating situations. Thus, some have a frightening persecuting quality while others are excitingly gratifying. These inner relationships are imaginative creations that are actively expressed in play and fantasy in childhood. When the foundation self is established with security and confidence, the inner world is progressively modified towards the real external one in the ongoing interactions of the ordinary good family in which father and other members play a more and more prominent part. In the early phases, intense love and hate, and magical omnipotence, characterise the inner relationships in keeping with the dominance of the intensity of the child's feelings. Infantile sexuality is assimilated into the self-systems with the establishment of a sexual identity—one which is finally consolidated after adolescence.

When relationships with parents continue to be unsatisfactory, then these relationships acquire distorted or compliant patterns—as if the manifest ones are maintained with an outer layer of the self while the inner relationships are intensified to provide satisfaction in fantasy, both loving and hating. And the most primitive violence belongs to this area of having to fight to maintain one's self in a state of adequate autonomy against what are felt to be the parents' intrusive attitudes and lack of trust in the spontaneous expressions of the emergent self. The inner relations then operate in a maladaptive way by unconsciously dominating the relations with people in the outside world. The latter are responded to, not as they really are but as they are perceived through the patterns of the inner figures. Thus imagos of a frustrating "bad" mother that are too powerful may turn the later adult male away from women, or in marriage lead to his wife gradually being treated as this hated mother, so that she can do no right. Or his wife may find herself being progressively cast in the role of a mother who has to minister to the needs of a little boy. If father is built up internally as a persecutor we may later get the man who is afraid of all authority or who compulsively fights it. The permutations of these inner relationships are endless but it is their dominance over ordinary realistic relationships that gives rise to the infinite range of irrational attitudes and conflicts.

With normal good experience, the inner relationships are merged into patterns for relating to others as they really are, for enjoying the "otherness" of others. Such a person is not tortured with doubts about living and he enjoys a spontaneous creativity in his everyday activities. No one is free from conflict arising from the inner cast of figures with whom he is identified but conflicts are ordinarily manageable. Normality means this capacity to give and take freely with others on a basis of realistic appraisals of oneself and others.

The self is thus seen as a dynamic matrix with a predominant central identity though liable in certain situations to change its centre point to one or other of its inner figures—states we reflect in such simple remarks as "I was not myself then," "I was beside myself with rage," or "I was out of my mind." The self is established in relationships and preserves itself only by an ongoing *psychosocial metabolism*, so to speak, from constant relatedness. With growth, the relationship figures of early times become transmitted into wider and much less personalised goals so that we can describe or define a mature person, as Chein (1972) puts it, as, "one who has a commitment to a developing and continuing set of unending, interacting, interdependent and mutually modifying enterprises" (p. 289)—the latter, of course, referring to personal relationships as well as activities of other kinds. Cut off this relatedness and the whole person, mind and body, begins to fragment or deteriorate. Extreme manifestations of this state were made visible to us all in the tragic manifestations of the concentration camps and have now been studied more experimentally with periods of isolation and environmental deprivation. Less dramatic, but no less striking, is the fact that when people lose their main source of relatedness or significance, as with displaced people, or as happened in periods of chronic and despondent unemployment, the incidence of every kind of illness rises (Wolff 1960). As the familiar words of Yeats put it:

> The falcon cannot hear the falconer:
> Things fall apart:
> The centre cannot hold:
> Mere anarchy is loosed upon the world.
> (W. B. Yeats "The Second Coming")

The failure to establish a primary self-system of relatedness gives rise to the most serious consequences ranging from withdrawal from the external world to a great variety of tenuous adaptedness on the basis of a veneer of compliance. People who experience the reemergence of these earliest states feel as if "the power is switched off; nothing has any meaning"; a pervasive apathy supervenes, which removes even instinctual excitement. These states understandably pose the most serious therapeutic problems.

But while we encounter such states as a rule in people whose self-system has been severely crippled, we have to keep in mind that all the later structures of any self that mediate a satisfying and fruitful life can be overwhelmed if the social milieu does not support the maintenance of the vital core.

The psychodynamic image of man is thus one of the progressive organisation of relatedness. The foundation layer of this system, the primal organiser that holds the developmental differentiation together, is established effectively only when the relatedness is of love and care and, without a later input of that kind in maturer patterns, it becomes difficult to maintain the system as a whole.

THE PSYCHODYNAMIC IMAGE AND CARE

In the light of this image of the person let me revert to the word *care*. *Care* is one of those primal words whose antithetical meanings aroused Freud's interest when he was struggling to understand the strange phenomena of dreams. It means both the burden that weighs on people and also relieving the person of this load. It also signifies the relationship that fosters growth and development. The caring relationship has thus a pattern of reparenting, which allows new growth. This suggestion as the prototype of care commonly arouses negative attitudes on the grounds that it implies infantilising people, making them dependent. Further thought, however, shows this to be a quite unfounded view since the aim of good parenting is the very opposite, that is, to secure independence. What the caring professions have to appraise is whether or not their actions are appropriate to a philosophy that does justice to man's full nature as a person. If such an approach is shared, then they are, whatever their particular activity, part of a coherent endeavour. It is also one that can provide vital data on what society might be doing that is inimical to optimal development.

In being part of such an overall endeavour the carers also deal in substantial measure with what gives them care in coping with distress. The word *support* is frequently used in this connection yet we do not get its essence spelled out. To my mind what supports the carer is not encouragement in the conventional sense. Instead, it is to be part of a learning system greater than himself. Anxiety from puzzlement, and often a degree of feeling overwhelmed by human problems, are best alleviated when we understand what is going on. Here, as elsewhere, "there is nothing so practical as a good theory," as Kurt Lewin remarked. The opportunity to learn from discussion with others who take learning seriously is itself an experience of caring and being cared for—as in all good education.

The psychodynamic image of man thus puts care for the person as essential for growth and our maintaining well-being. We are not dealing with a sentimental value. Care is a necessity in our philosophy and a necessity established on scientific evidence.

SOME CURRENT IMAGES IN RELATION TO OUR PHILOSOPHY

Our image may be only a sketch map at present but I believe it is even now good enough to keep us away from directions which can, at best, take us into a no-man's-land but which may lead us into areas in which man cannot survive as the free creative agent we value. Let me take a brief look at the different approaches to personal problems—an array that bewilders the outsider.

In practice, the various approaches seldom draw on a single philosophy. This makes difficult the task of disentangling what assumptions are being made, yet I think we can see the important issues clearly enough. With the great middle range of the rough continuum I suggested, that is, those therapies that use personal interaction in an empirical way and largely avoid deeper motivation, we have no great problem. They all have their contributions. Their serious drawback is that, without a conceptual framework about the full nature of the person, they can become "techniques" applied at times by professionals and others with little knowledge of what they are dealing with. They thus do relatively little or nothing to advance our basic knowledge, and the failure is reflected in the common fate of "techniques," that is, they gradually disappear because they are boring to both therapist and client.

At the other end of my continuum I placed the physical methods. Here again there is no question about these being useful when used with adequate discrimination. Although few would now advocate a position held by some extremists in the past, one still meets the assumption that these methods, by altering an abnormal functioning of the brain, are "scientific" in contrast with approaches that assume that what goes on in the mind is the important question in the vast majority of psychological disorders. It is from this view, whether held openly or covertly, that the recurrent fantasies arise of the drug that will really do the trick—the wonder breakthrough.

We are here involved in a basic issue about what is scientific knowledge in this whole field of phenomena at the personal level. The danger of this kind of belief is that instead of understanding and development, we can readily produce a massive societal addiction certainly comparable with all the dangers of alcohol. The Office of Health Economics (1972) published a short report on *Medicine and Society* produced by a team of social scientists. Having shown the staggering rise during the previous decade of the use of drugs for psychological symptoms, they noted that much medical care was now concerned with symptoms that appeared to be of social or psychological origin. In many cases there was no scientific evidence that the prognosis could be improved. Devoting increasing economic resources to the application of medical technology in such cases could actually diminish rather than improve well-being. They concluded that it was not yet possible to define specifically the role of the health services in handling these new (social and psychological) problems.

I must emphasise that I do not put the sole responsibility for this situation on to doctors. Large sections of the community expect a magical solution for their problems and if not given one would merely move to the doctor who would—or, worse perhaps—resort to available drugs such as alcohol. There is clearly a collusion going on which can only be altered by massive educational programmes. Medical technology is no solution to the need for a personal growth-promoting care. Caring is far too deeply ingrained a human trait for us to believe that carers holding such beliefs do not care. It seems to be more a situation of people, possibly under the great pressure of too many demands, getting caught up in an unwitting drift towards substituting technology for care. Such trends must be watched.

This question of what is scientific knowledge in this whole field of behaviour at the personal level is raised sharply by the behaviour therapists. It is their contention that the analytical psychotherapeutic approach, as well as being ineffective, is also unscientific because in practice it is so subjective as to be incapable of offering testable hypotheses. Instead of starting from the exploration of all that might underlie a behavioural symptom such as a phobia, the behaviourist focuses on the external manifestations which he then tries to modify by specifically designed procedures based on theories of behaviour patterns as learned. There is thus a theoretical underpinning for what is attempted.

Again there is no question that useful changes in overt behaviour can be achieved and, indeed, more effectively at times than with other methods. Experience has led many behaviour therapists to become very interested in the characteristics of the personal relationship that develops between the client and therapist and so some of the initial simplistic notions are being modified. The issue is not so much the changes that can occur, for there are few approaches that do not produce some change, as what the implications of the underlying philosophy are for the individual and society. Many critics have dealt with the behaviourist standpoint and suffice it for me to refer to Barrett (1979), one of America's most distinguished philosophers. He has recently responded to its major implication, namely, that we can develop through such an approach a technology of behaviour, as Skinner has described it, with which we can shape the future of man. The important belief here is that man would be much better developed, not through our ideal of the free and self-governing personality—for Skinner, that is a pernicious belief that has blocked progress—but through a really scientific programme for his advancement. Such a programme would, of course, be designed by the few who "know" what is best for the rest of us. Barrett remarked that when Dictatorship acquires this kind of science then the revolution according to Marx had become the society according to Pavlov.

The pluralism in approaches thus reflects a situation not so much of stimulating differences within a healthy enterprise as of one with serious and potentially dangerous contradictions. If the caring and educational endeavours are to take their proper place in a society whose primary value is the development of its people as creative responsible individuals, then we must resist philosophies founded on scientific reductionism, that is, on the belief that the complex processes at a higher level of the personal organisation can be explained by the properties of lower order activity, that the whole does not have properties that cannot be accounted for with knowledge of the parts. Such beliefs lead us towards an image of man as a machine or a puppet programmed and controlled by an elite group or constantly searching for the magical drug that will remove human conflict.

The basic question we have to pose is how do we conceive of the person at the personal level. The Cartesian legacy, which separated the mental from the physical, still persists with extraordinary tenacity. The conceptualisation of the person, or the self, is now thought by several philosophers to be their major task. If we regard the inner world as not belonging to the real world, that is, the world we can study objectively, then we inevitably adopt a reductionist position. We believe the real processes governing our lives even at the personal level to be those that are reducible to neurochemical processes, or as some concession to the reality of emergent phenomena to processes at the level of stimulus–response organisation. The self or the person does not then require to be taken seriously, that is, as mediating emergent phenomena inexplicable by lower levels of organisation.

In facing reductionist beliefs we must ask ourselves, "Is anything more real for us than our 'self' as a free agent?" Nevertheless it is extraordinary how this reality of the self is ignored or denied. I have to emphasise here that I am not asserting the correctness of any particular psychodynamic theories. It is the legitimacy and the necessity of its approach that have to be accepted. Guntrip (1978) has argued this whole issue with great clarity. He points out that even if we accept Popper's criterion of falsifiability as a requirement for scientific theories, Popper's belief that "because psychoanalytic theories are not falsifiable, they cannot be scientific" is simply not true. Freud discarded his theories at various times when the evidence no longer supported them and this process has gone on constantly. What has to be appreciated is that the falsifying data in regard to a psychodynamic theory may take several decades to accumulate.

Research into the realities of the self cannot be studied by the experimental method. Bronowski (1965) recognised these realities but concluded they could only be studied in literature. Such study, however, is not a firsthand one of the psychic self at work, the phenomenal reality on the top of the hierarchy of existence! The self can be studied directly in action only within a therapeutic relationship. This most fundamental knowledge for man is thus the unique privilege of the caring professions. To quote Weisman (1965), another analyst, "Psychoanalysis is not a delusion, practised by the fanatical and perpetrated upon the gullible; nor is it a mere recital of psychodynamic litanies. Its basic fact is the *encounter*, which . . . is an effort to meet the patient as a unique being, with respect to himself, his world, and other people. . . . *The encounter is the fact of being in analysis for the purpose of the analysis of being*" (p 105). Therapeutic relationships are not scientific procedures, whether in general medicine or in psychotherapy. The scientific component resides in the kind of knowledge we use. We have to formulate our understanding of what happens in these encounters in the best way we can to do justice to the phenomena and to be open to constant checking against fresh findings.

As with the drift in medicine from care to technology, there can be a drift into reductionist standpoints without a full recognition of what is taking place amongst those helping with personal problems. Professions such as social workers and the clergy are much less prone to reductionism because they cannot use the "scientific" methods associated with it. They can, however, as can psychotherapists, become dominated by "techniques" and so lose the openness that should constantly develop practice and theory.

It is in our academic centres for psychiatry and psychology that there is the greatest need to have these issues examined because they are the prestige influences for our whole caring endeavour. Although most centres would deny an overall reductionist position, certain trends are ominous enough to warrant scrutiny. Thus, most students attending psychology courses in our Universities are greatly disappointed by failure of these courses to give a framework for understanding the individual or the family at a personal level. And we have only to survey the research output of psychiatrists and psychologists to see that an incredibly small proportion of their effort goes to a study of the dynamic processes underlying human relationships—those processes that constitute the essence of the therapeutic encounter. It seems to matter little how much the data studied are "trivialised" so long as the methods of using them, usually statistical, are of the requisite sophistication. By "trivialisation" I mean either the isolation of limited, or almost subpersonal, sections of behaviour or else the choice of what one might term the superficial indices of the underlying dynamics. What can one really do in a therapeutic situation with measures of a hypothetical entity such as "aggression," or masculinity-femininity, or a list of the roles family members commonly take in the "good" family? Is there not a concealed assumption that we have got "scientific" "data" or "facts" that we can "administer" to the client like a medical treatment and which should then lead him to alter his behaviour?

The reductionism here is compounded by the transfer of the traditional medical model of doing something to the patient whereas with personal conflicts we can only provide a relationship that lets the individual recognize his own nature. When we deal with subsystems of the organism that can be isolated and defined, we naturally have much more control; and this model has given us marvellous therapeutic resources for many conditions. With problems at the personal level this cannot be done. To revert to our caring prototype, it is noteworthy that we do not hear much of techniques of parenting. When we do, it is usually from those whose experience of "parental technique" has created their situation as patients. What they almost invariably describe is the lack of being treated as a person. The pressure to do this so-called scientific research is arguably one of the greatest drawbacks at present to the development of the therapeutic understanding and skills that are so much needed. The commonly expressed claims in academic centres that we have got to be scientific are seldom accompanied by an appropriate consideration of the meaning of this word—and why the assumptions made in using it are either not exposed or are denied.

There is also the fact that therapy as a goal is not a part of science. It is an act of human concern. Its effectiveness, however, rests on the adequacy of our validated knowledge.

The practice of analytic psychotherapy, with the time it takes and the highly specialised training its adequate use requires, of course precludes it from being an available therapy. Its value is in the knowledge it gives, knowledge which is already being wisely used in a great range of more practicable ways. The concepts it has provided underlie much of such widely used approaches as group and family therapy, counselling, and the therapeutic community.

True, it may press people to face up to what are painful aspects of themselves, but it does so on the well-founded belief that when they do so they are thereby maturer and richer personalities. When used well, psychodynamic knowledge is assimilated into the personality of the carer who then *is* that knowledge in his relationships; it is not a technique like a piece of gimmickry stuck on to the surface of the person.

In what I have said about the psychodynamic image, you may be thinking I have left out one of the great areas of experience, namely, religion. Obviously, I cannot embark on that theme here. Let me say, however, that Freud's views on religion as they were described over 50 years ago in "The Future of an Illusion" cannot be taken as representative of psychodynamic thought today. Freud at that time was greatly impressed by the role of infantile dependence in the creation of a God based on a needed father—a view reinforced by the images and metaphors of institutionalised religion. In recent years there has been much more detailed study of the development of the internal representation of God and the relationships, both mature and immature, with that inner figure.

As his consciousness of his situation in the universe expands, modern man cannot readily accept the old modes of representation. Nevertheless, we retain our powerful need for non-visible but meaningful realities capable of containing our potential for imaginative expansion beyond the boundaries of the senses (Rizzuto 1979). In this sense, religion is no illusion. For many, the position of feeling the lack of appropriate expression fits with Einstein's view of himself as a deeply religious unbeliever (see Pruyser 1974). An adequate psychodynamic image can help to separate what are personal stresses that originate from conflicting processes of development from those that may arise in a mature self reflecting on his relationship with something beyond what science can deal with. That there is a need to get these personal stresses distinguished from religious questions is seen, I believe, in the confusion several young clergymen experience over whether they should become social workers rather than stay in the ministry.

The psychodynamic image is thus not an antireligious image of man, though it may support a search for expressions that are congruent with the rest of our consciousness in the modern world.

To summarise what I have said:

1. Our current social philosophy is that the best hope for mankind is to foster the optimal development of the individual. To further that aim we must have society functioning as an open adaptive learning system.
2. Such a system has to monitor constantly what is happening in its various sections and this is the vital function of our caring and educational endeavours.
3. To fulfil that function there must be a shared philosophy on the nature of man as a person.
4. I have suggested that the psychodynamic image of man is the best guide we have at present.
5. I have stressed that caring and educational procedures based on a reductionist view of man can foster dangerous dehumanising trends and must be combated.
6. In this overall task of developing our image of man we need the caring professions, education, the Church, and all the other creative thought we can muster to realise the importance of their role and to fulfil it responsibly and assertively.

Our concern today must be less with "The Future of an Illusion" and more with "The Illusion of a Future."

IV
THE SELF

20. THE SELF AND OBJECT RELATIONS*

The self constitutes such an overriding challenge to psychoanalysis that it must remain the ongoing central issue for the next phase in the development of the whole field. Clearly, when one raises such far-reaching questions as the concept of the self introduces, one can only—almost absurdly—oversimplify. However, I risk oversimplifying because the implications of the concept of the self are so important. For many years, the absence of the essential nature of the personal from Freud's metapsychology has imposed more and more strain on psychoanalysis, creating an increasing need for a psychological theory of the self. In my own experience, I (1980b) have been greatly influenced by my British colleagues, especially Balint (1968), Fairbairn (1954b), Guntrip (1969), and Winnicott (1971), all of whom have contributed to the understanding of the self by advancing the theory from where Freud left it. I have been impressed by how much their work now has in common with that of many American analysts, for example, Erikson (1959), Kernberg (1976), G. S. Klein (1976), Kohut (1971, 1977), Lichtenstein (1977), and Schafer (1968). The emergence of such agreement from independent sources is particularly important in psychoanalysis.

In this presentation, I shall first outline my work with a patient over several years to focus critical issues in a way that relates to your own clinical experience and so keep before us the data on which to frame the questions to be studied. Then I shall draw some general features of this patient's difficulties that seem to require a change in our theoretical standpoint. In a third section, I shall sketch how the self might be conceptualized in its development and maintenance. Lastly, I shall reflect on some implications these views of the self have for the future of psychoanalysis. Again, I wish to stress that I offer no tidy theory. I hope, however, that you will share my interest in working toward a better understanding of the person.

CASE EXAMPLE: LENA

The patient, a middle-aged widow whom I shall call Lena, had had a difficult relationship with her mother from birth because

*Discussants are Leonard Horwitz, M.D., and Ramon Ganzarain, M.D.

of allergies, feeding difficulties, and fits for which she was in and out of the hospital much of her first year. From the time Lena can remember, she has believed that her mother hated her; her father just withdrew. Throughout her childhood and adolescence, her life was one long battle with her mother, and she also became more and more combative with the world.

Lena was bright intellectually and qualified to become a social worker. Soon afterward, she married a rather psychopathic man, who was killed in an automobile accident about 2 years later. Before he died, the husband was overseas most of the time, and so the marriage was hardly a relationship at all. Yet, in spite of the poor relationship, her husband's death intensified Lena's feelings that she was no good and there was no point in living. These feelings led to an attempted suicide and several months in a hospital. Lena was labeled depressive, although at times she experienced disordered thoughts with hallucinations, which suggested that she might be schizophrenic. She recovered sufficiently to manage her work for many years and sought help when she felt some of her lethargic, apathetic symptoms returning. She also became increasingly dependent on tranquilizers and alcohol.

Lena appeared constantly on the defensive against almost all close relationships, which she warded off either by withdrawing abruptly from people or by behaving aggressively toward them. Consequently, she became increasingly isolated. For example, her relationships with colleagues, the only people with whom she had much contact, were characterized by alternately thinking they were "not so bad" to more frequently thinking they were about to invade her. She achieved closeness with few co-workers, although she did establish responsive empathic relationships with her clients.

Lena believed that she had missed something in her childhood. Thus, she longed to get and to give affection, but she dared not express any lest she be "exploited." Her turbulent relationship with me brought out her destructive attitudes, not only as a defense but as a revenge—a quite prominent theme. For several years, Lena's treatment involved a struggle against her extremely tenacious clinging to an outer aggressive self, not only to avoid relationships but to ward off a greatly dreaded loss of herself such as had occurred during her breakdown. Her mistrust of finding a better world was almost total. It took her years to believe that I was concerned about her and thought she had good qualities to offer others. Moreover, she slowly realized that, by frequently attacking me, she was trying to destroy her treatment. Her treatment was made even more difficult to cope with because of her splitting off into a secret inner world a hidden self, with its rich fantasy world and its invulnerability and omnipotence.

The primitive nature of Lena's lack of a cohesive self behind her negative identity was evident during periods of particular stress. At these times, she became so disorganized that she would forget the meanings of familiar words—a serious handicap to her spare-time activity of writing freelance articles for the press. Words became just "sounds." Because of this loss of meaning, reading was impossible. Lena also believed that the words could jump out of the page as if to attack her.

Lena said that her body felt detached and strange, with little or no integration of either physical sensations or mental processes. She had difficulty speaking about the sense of self-loss because she feared that I would reject her for this "craziness." However, when she realized that I was trying to understand her experiences as repetitions of past terrifying experiences of being totally out of touch with any trusted figure, she was able to describe these feelings in spite of the intense anxiety and humiliation they aroused. Although she felt at her worst in this total chaos, she believed that she could regain an integrated self if someone made her feel that *he* thought she could do so. At the same time, I sensed her confusion and understood that she was desperate to "explode" something out from inside herself, namely, the intensely hated persecutory world. Perhaps most striking was the way she created in the outer world a replica of her inner world, that is, a world full of hate. At best, she perceived the outer world as being unconcerned about her, leaving her omnipotent in her secret fortress and ensuring inner survival as a person with a self.

CENTRAL ISSUES IN THE FUNCTIONING OF THE PERSON

Although some of these problems are specific to this individual, I believe they represent the central issues for most, if not all, patients. The following prominent features can be noted, leaving aside any claims to comprehensiveness or their relative importance.

1. Such patients are greatly preoccupied with insecurity about how other people accept and value them. Their powerful need for a positive response from others, frequently manifested in exhibitionistic components, may be hidden under extensive negativistic denials such as Lena employed. Even she, however, constantly hoped that people would see behind her aggressive front

a self wanting to be valued. Psychoanalysts must identify the nature of how their patients want to be valued by others and how these needs arise. They certainly concern a "whole," "the self," which cannot be broken down into components without disappearing. The nature and origin of this whole simply have to be understood as a gestalt.

2. Whether or not the self is a coherent unity in its earliest stages, it soon acquires divisions, or subselves, that are kept apart in their functioning by the incompatibility in the relationships each part seeks with the other parts. The splits clearly originate in the environmental mismatches. Nevertheless, the initial unity remains active in the awareness that the subselves are parts of the one self. However, there is a perpetual strain because of these divisions and because of the fluctuating struggle to integrate the splits. This strain, of course, is a powerful motive for seeking psychotherapy.
3. The subselves contain needs that press to be accepted as vital parts of the self, and, as such, these needs cannot be rejected; they are derivatives of the innate givens of the organism. But some of these needs are unacceptable to an infant's parents and therefore lead to painful consequences if expressed. Thus, the child has to cope with them away from the parents, for example, by fantasy activity or, later, by secret expression.
4. The integrative pressure brings out a basic feature of the self-system, namely, its active, initiating role with the environment. The self-system constantly strives to interact and establish compatible and reciprocal relationships with its surroundings. Underlying Lena's negativistic exterior was her almost intolerably painful feeling that everything she had ever given was rejected, and so she seldom offered herself to others.
5. One part of the self becomes dominant in the development of a *visible self.* The subselves are kept apart from this dominant one with varying degrees of splitting and repression; yet in many activities they are merged with the dominant self to achieve some expression, albeit unconsciously.
6. The activity of subselves creates symptoms, which may be relatively localized, as in perversions, or more general in their effects, as in Lena's lethargy and fears of disintegration. They cannot, however, be explained solely in terms of repressed impulses. They represent the solutions an original unitary self finds to express at a personal level its unmet or actively rejected needs.
7. From an early age, the self can be seen as a complex system that has internalized the important figures of the external world,

divided according to their different aspects. The inherent social relatedness of the self as a whole is manifest from the start. The instincts do not have their own internal templates to fashion the actual patterns of behavior that will satisfy them. These patterns come from the adaptive action of the self in its relationships with the real figures at hand, along with its inner-world figures and relationships, which can be manipulated with imaginative play.

8. I cannot go into all the intricacies of the numerous possibilities this inner world provides, for instance, by establishing relationships with objects that are fantasied as objects or by identifications with the objects, some with considerable stability, others with much more lability. These developments have been described in detail by Melanie Klein (1932), Fairbairn (1954b), Winnicott (1971), Kohut (1971, 1977), and many others. A primary patterning of the self is established in the earliest relationships, in which the acceptance of the self as a person is intimately involved with bodily needs, and in which the self and its objects are still incompletely differentiated. This primal patterning of the ways the self behaves to gain security and acceptance remains a powerful determinant of future development, particularly in social relationships. In keeping with the incomplete self-object differentiation, relationships in these early stages have a strongly compulsive character.
9. The primary patterns of the dominant self are elaborated by inner maturation and by increased experience of the world. In particular, the sexual instincts are fitted into these primary self-patterns in the evolution of the sexual identity, as originally described by Fairbairn (1954b).
10. Once a dominant self is fashioned and implemented, it forms what can be described as the individual's identity, that is, the self he makes visible because of its reality involvement and because others "identify" him by it. Thus, it is relevant to recall that Erikson (1959) at first chose the term *ego-identity*, an apt choice because it suggests the close connection of the visible self with reality relatedness. The concept of the ego as an independent entity, especially in motivation, seems unnecessary (G. S. Klein 1976). All the autonomous functions Hartmann (1958) described are employed by the self in action. Action, however, is controlled by the self-system, which is most active in relation to the environment. Lena's case is a striking example of how the self, especially in regard to its positive acceptance, can dramatically alter the individual's whole capacity to think and to hold on to meanings, that is, the structured layers of past experience. Her anxieties frequently prevented reality thinking because she had

withdrawn from the real world. Confidence in the mother's love seems to provide the foundation for the capacity to keep experience—and hence thought and understanding—continuous.

11. When the dominant self is established as an identity, a person clings to that self with the utmost tenacity no matter how restricted or distorted it may be because the dominant self is not only the visible mode of relating, it is also the cover for the whole invisible self in its closed world of secret inner relationships. As the individual's mode of surviving, the dominant self exhibits a profoundly aggressive attitude toward any attempt to take it away, even when the wish to alter that self brings the individual to treatment.
12. The ferocity with which the identity is defended calls attention to a puzzling phenomenon, namely, how this very structuring can be removed by a field change as opposed to a direct personal challenge. For instance, Lena's intense hate was aroused when she felt that I was forcing a different identity on her; yet she could lose her dominant self or identity when the external world felt empty of any source of reassurance to the self.

SOME GENERAL COMMENTS ABOUT THE SELF AS AN OPEN SYSTEM

Since Freud sought to keep psychoanalytic theory on a firm biological base, a few observations from this standpoint are helpful regarding one's perspective on any concept of the self. Freud's biological speculations, insofar as they impinge on clinical understanding, concerned mainly the origin and nature of the drives. It was inevitable that he should have reductionist science deeply rooted in him. Even when he had to give up the "Project for a Scientific Psychology" (1950) because of problems in dealing with the psychological, he remained wedded to his energy notions and to the second law of thermodynamics, which was then virtually the ultimate reality. However, advances in biology, cybernetics, and theories of open systems (such as living organisms, that is, those in which the system interacts incessantly and adaptively with an environment that in turn may show similar adaptive responses) enable analysts to establish a more appropriate basis for their views of both the psychological and the social and how their mutual relationships create the individual.

Apart from all the gains in psychoanalytic understanding, these developments liberate the thinking that is needed from the constant attack that psychoanalysis is outside "natural science." Prigogine (1976) and others (see Jantsch 1980) have now worked out the principles and associated mathematics of such open systems, in which there is the *necessity* for constant interactional developments, with structural changes to embody the "learning" that has taken place. Thus, predictability has a limited role in regard to open systems because unpredictable creativity in relation to unpredictable environmental change is the characteristic feature of these systems. Living systems survive by being negentropic, that is, they live outside the entropic principle inherent in closed systems. Death is not a running down of the machine but a "planned" event required by evolution. Concepts such as the death instinct must be appraised against the view that reactive aggressive behavior is required for survival. Within the evolutionary process, there is the thrust toward more and more freedom from environmental constraints. Man is not the blind, passive victim of chance and necessity Monod (1971) describes, for, as Jantsch (1980) puts it, "We are not the helpless subjects of evolution—we *are* evolution" (p. 8).

The evolution of man has taken him to his present place through his unique mental capacities, and in this development his simultaneous social evolution has been a necessity. The development of the individual and his resources and adaptive capacities is clearly inseparable from the social milieu which evolved in parallel. It certainly sounds platitudinous to make that remark and yet, as we are all aware, until recently, psychoanalysis has not paid adequate attention to the dynamic way in which social and general environmental relationships are built into the person. These relationships structure his eventual personal properties to create a system that cannot survive without appropriate responses from the environment which, in turn, has to change with developments in people. Man's relatedness to his environment depends on his unique capacity to transcend it by making a reproduction of it inside his mind, where he then manipulates possibilities, from which stem his creative alterations of it. As a result of this evolutionary process, a remarkable freedom from the uncertainties of the physical environment has been achieved. It is generally agreed that corresponding adaptations in the social world have lagged far behind. One change that has emerged, however, is the entirely new importance attached to the self. The individual has acquired a new status in Western democratic social and political philosophies, one in which the full realization of his personal resources is a requirement (Emery and Trist 1973). On all fronts, then, the individual, his self, and his identity have become central concerns, and it is no accident that these concerns have developed in psychoanalysis. The self as the controller of perception and action has become the focal concept in relating the individual to his environment.

In studying development, it is useful to have in mind its outcome. How, then, do analysts view the optimal condition of the individual? I believe that the starting point must be his "intentionality," his purposes, that is, the long-term relationships he wishes to make with his environment. Chein (1972) gives a useful description of this aspect when he states, "The essential psychological human quality is, thus, one of commitment to a developing and continuing set of unending, interacting, interdependent, and mutually modifying long-range enterprises" (p. 289). Love and work are central for the survival of these enterprises, but man's expressive needs, especially art and religion, must also be considered. The dynamics of these needs do not stem from the instincts alone. With the capacity to transcend the environment, they seem to represent a need to give meaning and significance to life and to move toward what can only be described as "betterment"—perhaps an expression of the thrust of evolution in relation to environmental stresses. When such commitment is within a self whose main aims are adequately integrated with reality, there is the foundation for a creative, satisfying, and enjoyable mode of living.

How are the self, its development, and its functioning to be conceptualized? The patient I have sketched and others who are similar, as well as the writings of other researchers, suggest the following diagrammatic outline.

Just as anatomical growth with all its differentiation appears to be ordered by an organizing ground plan operating as an overall gestalt, so the development of the self must have a parallel gestalt integrating its interactions with reality. However coherent its unity may be at the start, the self-system rapidly acquires divisions or subselves resulting from the incompatible affects associated with experiences. Even with all the limitations of present knowledge, the self can at least be regarded as an overall system in which experiences are brought into cohesion. The gestalt appears to have a "desired" state of positively toned affect that accompanies the interactions between the organism and the environment, with each affect having its own specific quality according to the particular features of any relationship. Innate behavioral systems have their own affective expectancies so that when the infant "needs" something that matches the "shape" of this need, the appropriate object gives the self the feeling that things are "right." It is now known that these innate expectancies include, in addition to the bodily or appetitive ones, powerful independent needs to satisfy the impetus toward autonomous psychological development. Adult patients all too often express the feeling that "something is missing" in their self from very early times, when these needs were not met. In short, the inherent "form" or "shape" that the gestalt "needs" is to be a person. The crucial factor for an infant's optimal development is an input of enjoyment from the mother that reflects her love and care for the child as a spontaneously developing, autonomous person. This experience imparts to the embryonic self a feeling of being a secure and "right" part of a world which is represented by this welcome into it. The self-system needs to be "personalized" by being treated as an autonomous person by other persons. The child sees and feels who he is by what is put into him by the mother and then by the other family figures. This process is a much more active one on the adult's part than is indicated by terms like "mirroring" or being a "container." This process needs all the shared experiences from encouraging stimulation and play that occur in everyday "tender loving care." In this mutuality, the child plays a decidedly active and evocative role toward the mother's responses.

Thus, the self-gestalt has to be viewed as becoming a proactive system, structured by an internal replica of its specific relationships with the outer world.

The differentiation of the self and its objects in this inner world is a familiar process, and the inevitable incompatibilities between some of the infant's self-needs and the parents' responses to them create divisions within the self. As Lena's case illustrates, these divisions contain both the infant's unmet or rejected needs and parallel structures of the controlling, rejecting parents. These divisions remain permanently because they are parts of the whole, stemming from the innate makeup of the child. Within the overall system, these divisions establish a complex set of processes, such as providing fantasy objects with which fantasy relationships can be enacted as substitutes for reality failures. These divisions also provide a great range of different imagos with which the self may be identified to varying extents and with varying stability. Because they are unacceptable for open expression, these divisions remain undeveloped by experience with reality. They persistently seek relationships with the outer world because they need people, but because their aims have remained unadapted to the outer world, the latter has to be coerced to fit them. A dominant reality-related self, in keeping with the gestalt nature of the overall system of which it is a part, tries to manage the activity of these subselves by merging them with selected reality relationships—the process Waelder (1960) describes as the "multiple functions" of most behavior. Should there be a regression in the integration of the self—which can happen with various environmental stresses—then the primary qualities in these subself relationships (for example, the lability of self and object differentiation) show in compulsive relationships and in identifications with the different inner objects.

In the early stages of the developing configuration of the self, the autonomous striving toward greater independence from the first symbiotic phase is characterized by labile fluctuations. On the one hand, there are regressions to the omnipotent and compulsive relationships and identifications of the undifferentiated phase, and, on the other hand, there are more mature patterns in which sharing with independent others for mutual gain replaces taking or wanting things for oneself. What might be termed a *primal self* is patterned in the early transitional stages of object differentiation, when the child acquires a feeling of the "shape" of the self he is free to have. In these early stages, the failure of the mothering and family relationships can create major distortions, either from deprivation of basic self-needs or from the not uncommon imposition of a parent's self-pattern onto the child. Early parental failures from accidental disturbances can often be overcome, at least in part, but all too often relationship failures are reinforced because of limitations in the parental personalities.

Lichtenstein (1977) suggests that this first personalization has a fixity in its patterns comparable with the early ethological concept of "imprinting." This first personalization certainly is extraordinarily persistent in the way it creates a scaffolding for future developments. Lichtenstein contrasts the development of the self in man with the situation in animals. Self-development is necessary for man to relate to his environment, while in animals instinctual equipment gives an inner *Umwelt* with which they can readily adapt to the particular environment for which their equipment has been evolved. Man with his man-made environment has to have his world internalized in a more complex and adaptive way.

An organization liberated from the stabilities of the instinctual systems has to pay a price for this freedom by losing the guaranteed, if inflexible, stability that instinctual systems provide. In the face of perpetual change, a sense of continuity is required for adaptive capacities. Also, with a structuring developed to cope with and anticipate the future in its own society, the affective tone of the self-system—its self-esteem—has to be maintained by affirmation. Lichtenstein (1977) suggests that, because the integration of the self is so important, an important inherited reinforcer of the self may have evolved in the form of nonprocreative sexuality. Such a function could explain the prominence of autoerotic activity for those selves that do not establish free relationships with reality, that is, most patients.

Affirmation normally comes from a range of social interactions. When reality freedom has been severely inhibited, the individual creates an inner world in which he compensates for this lack by omnipotent control of fantasied relationships. This inner world can become a serious maladaptive factor in the eventual self, for such a world is a distorted one with which to mediate relationships with reality. These relationships, instead of being established and enjoyed freely, become a safeguard of this inner world, where the individual protects his real self in a kind of fortress. Lena put up a hostile front to keep all possible intruders away from her secret world, where she felt at times an almost frightening omnipotence. Pure fantasy activity is seldom sufficient, and so the inner world has to coerce the outer to fit its requirements—a rather incompatible basis for adaptive relationships. This development is also the source of some of the most difficult negative therapeutic reactionships. The analyst is perceived as a menacing intruder to be fought off at all costs, even though little or no satisfaction is gained from the restricted mode of living this situation permits.

Although he has not elaborated the point, Lichtenstein (1977) suggests that work seems to be a highly important area within the wide range of interactions that provide affirmation. The instinctive roots of work are manifold, for example, its relation to physical survival, to provision for the family, and to satisfactions that skills and achievements bring. Personal needs, however, are central. Thus, many studies of work (see Emery and Trist 1973) have shown that unless personal needs are satisfied, there is a disintegration of the self, which is manifested in poor performance, high absenteeism, and high sickness rates. Such manifestations are also characteristic of groups that have lost their social connectedness, for instance, displaced populations. When expressive or ideo-existential needs are not met, effects of such deprivation are seen in the loss of the self-system's effectiveness, as in widespread apathy or "depression" or in violence by protest groups that arises from the loss of a sense of significance or meaning to life. With much of this kind of stress, it is often not so much the absence of ideologies, religion, or values that deprives the self of a sense of meaning as it is the dissonance between the inner image of man that is thought right for particular groups and the one that is proclaimed with intrusive force. Ideo-existential needs carry a considerable loading from the segregated subselves, and deprivation in regard to these needs exerts a disintegrative effect, both by weakening the reinforcing affirmation the dominant self needs and by altering the status of the dominant self in managing the subselves.

When the self reaches adulthood, its relationships with the social environment have patterned its *identity*—the characteristic visible way in which the individual functions. When I suggested earlier that a primal self could be described that was fashioned in the phases of infantile dependence, I was distinguishing its form from that of its later *social identity*, in which various accretions have been assimilated; and because of its intimate links with social interaction, this later self in its social identity seems particularly dependent on a requisite social connectedness.

Thus, it is not difficult to recognize the fundamental role that the dynamics of perpetual relatedness with society play in maintaining the integrity of the self. This relationship of the individual to groups naturally attracted Freud's (1921) interest, and he advanced his theory of the ego by postulating the separate function of the ego-ideal in binding the individual to the leader. In characterizing the distinctive identity of the individual outside the primitive or unorganized group, Freud described him as possessing "his own continuity, his self-consciousness, his traditions and customs, his own particular functions and position, and . . . [as keeping] apart from his rivals" (p. 86). Moreover, Freud noted that an individual would seek to preserve this identity against any negative impingement, with even a readiness to express hatred and aggressiveness, to which he ascribed the elementary character that he found in the death instinct. Since he believed that this identity was preserved by narcissistic libido, it is remarkable that he described the individual's distinctive identity on the basis of McDougall's (1920) conditions for the *organized group*: (1) the group should have a continuity of existence; (2) individuals within the group should know the nature, composition, functions, and capacities of the group; (3) the group should interact with other groups partly similar and partly different in many respects; (4) the group should possess traditions, customs, and habits, especially those that determine the relationships among members; and (5) the group should have a definite structure, exposed in the specialization and differentiation of the functions of its constituents (see also Freud 1921).

Bion's (1961) studies with actual unorganized groups show that, faced with a reality task the members cannot grasp, and given no help with this task by the leader, such a group rapidly regresses into what he called the "basic assumptions" of the group. He accounted for these states in terms of Melanie Klein's (1932) primitive mechanisms, yet the individuals showed a cohesion in regressing to their basic assumptions. Such behavior can be viewed as stemming from the loss of social identity and the emergence of the individuals' primal selves (see Chapter 17).

IMPLICATIONS FOR THE FUTURE OF PSYCHOANALYSIS

These somewhat discursive comments are intended to emphasize that the self cannot be conceptualized except as an open system developing and maintaining its identity through the social relatedness essential to it from the start. It must be questioned whether or not the classical psychoanalytical theory of the person and his development and functioning does justice to this fact. Therapeutically, the analyst's task is to achieve greater integration in the self-system by reducing the separateness of the subselves. I have no doubt that what has been encountered as a negative or rather partial therapeutic reaction frequently derives from the way the individual divides part of his self into a subself to be kept in virtually a secret fortress, with the rest of his relationships distorted to preserve this situation. This inner state, however, is entirely a product of his relationships within the family, and, even when he seems most cut off, the essential factors are the failed relationships and the terror of disintegration that remains. I have avoided using the term *narcissistic* because it has been connected for so long with the biologically oriented view that states of failed capacity to relate have their origin in the development of the libido rather than primarily because of failures of the social environment.

The implications of a comprehensive theory of the self and its personal (object) relations are, of course, much wider than the therapeutic problems. Although, as Freud (1926) pointed out, it is not the business of psychoanalysis to provide a weltanschauung or ideology, it is the concern of psychoanalysis to offer understanding of how the individual relates to reality and to himself. The inexorable thrust of evolution keeps man constantly seeking to improve his situation in relation to his environment, and the image of man within a society has a profound influence on his behavior. The psychoanalytic image, I must stress, is not of where man should go. Rather, it is an image of the way his functioning as a creator of guiding images for himself is determined by the properties of his self and its perceptions of the world. The image of man in this sense will be used by social philosophers, and there is already evidence of what can happen when man is seen as being created by his drives and their satisfactions (Brown 1959; Marcuse 1955).

By trying to belong to the "natural" sciences as they have been conceived following Descartes, psychoanalysts have alienated themselves in large measure from the humanities, and at the same time they have made even less impression on the "hard science" philosophy underlying medicine today. I do not believe that psychoanalysts have the right friends for making an effective contribution to the present climate of opinion. With a due importance attached to the self and its inner world as the mediator of social behavior, the works of the great writers and artists as well as developments in the social sciences should surely figure much more in psychoanalytic thinking. The human sciences badly need the kind of understanding of human relationships that psychoanalysis can contribute. Only in that way will the prevalent gap between psychoanalysts and other scientists be bridged. I also believe that the newer notions about evolution may well make it possible for psychoanalysts to be less dismissive of man's religious quests. Again, it is not a matter of saying "what should be," but of illuminating the nature and function of the great human expressive needs. When religion is seen as being rooted in man's innate striving to understand himself in his environment, its origins cannot be reduced to infantile dependence. Nevertheless, the mode in which it is expressed may have to be freed from these early influences and matured to fit man's expanding knowledge and understanding.

In a time of such turbulence as the present, with endless superficial remedies and treatments for personal problems, the psychoanalyst's task must be to get an account of the person that does justice to his full nature. This turbulence (Emery and Trist 1973) has resulted from the remarkable growth of the physical sciences with their technological advances, a growth that has reinforced the wish for "scientific" cures. In the view of many people for a long time, psychoanalysis has not been considered a science because of the failure to recognize that persons are complex, open, developing systems. I believe that this position is about to change radically throughout the scientific field, and that psychoanalysts must respond by putting people with all the subjectivity governing their actions to the front. I find it encouraging that in a recent book on ethology, Robert Hinde (1982), one of the leading scientists in that field (and, incidentally, John Bowlby's guide in his ethological thinking), states that it would be wrong to pretend there is extensive common ground between ethology and psychiatry. For Hinde, the psychiatrist's proper concern is subjective experience. This view constrains what ethology can offer psychiatry, although its indirect contribution in conjunction with the other behavioral sciences is great. The self is surely the heart of the matter regarding the organization and functioning of subjective experience.

DISCUSSION

Leonard Horwitz, Ph.D.

Dr. Jock Sutherland has a unique and highly valuable dominant self. The first part of his presentation, a beautifully concise clinical description followed by a series of clear formulations about the use of a concept of self in understanding the patient's struggles to survive, could easily stand on its own as a clinical and theoretical presentation. But Dr. Sutherland is one of those rare clinicians who views the clinical enterprise as rooted in a social order, part of an open system which requires our informed input about the scientific and philosophical basis of our work. A major difficulty we clinicians encounter with society is that we are not always clear ourselves about our own identity, where we have been, where we are going, and what we stand for. Indeed, we are obliged to articulate our own image of man as a first step in being persuasive and convincing about the validity of our efforts. Insofar as we suffer from professional identity confusion, we are in danger of losing our own anchoring as well as the confidence of those who should support us.

Dr. Sutherland's value to the Menninger Foundation over the past two decades has been his ability to impart a clear vision of what he believes we stand for and what we should aspire to become. Like all outstanding leaders, he brings needed perspective to our work, provides clarity about our scientific and therapeutic mission, and inspires enthusiasm in the pursuit of our professional goals.

By this time, you may have gathered that I hold the man and his views in high esteem. Let me first underline my agreement with his major ideas.

First of all, despite the difficulty most writers on the self have in clearly defining this concept, I believe that psychoanalytic theory requires an overarching concept of self that accounts for man's proactive, integrating activities. It also embodies such basic universal needs as the wish to be valued, the desire to be affirmed as a significant person in the lives of others, and the need to be attached in varying degrees of closeness to others while also being capable of autonomous functioning according to one's own internal standards. I believe that the present concepts of ego and superego do not sufficiently embody these important functions. However important the structures of ego and superego are in embodying necessary mental functions, present structural theory needs updating to deal with the accumulating body of evidence on the centrality of earliest relationships and identifications. Intersystemic and intrasystemic conflicts within the mental apparatus are not sufficient to explain all deviations in development. The first months and years of life give rise to a greater or lesser degree of cohesiveness in the sense of self, that is, one's identity and human relatedness. The self is a basic building block for all other mental structures.

Second, a useful and necessary concept is the view that splits in the self comprise subselves that express hidden or forbidden wishes, which often must be kept invisible and protected. Much of the goal of therapy, as Dr. Sutherland reminds us, is to help the person integrate the visible, dominant self with the hidden and shameful subselves.

Third, the healthy cohesive self is first nurtured in its earliest phases within a symbiotic dual unity of mother and child in which gratification and love predominate over frustration and anger. These internalized good objects require some degree of reinforcement from the environment throughout one's life. And, in passing, I would call your attention to a small gem our speaker dropped regarding the self and the negative therapeutic reaction: the self-disordered person tries to safeguard his true self by keeping others away from his secret fantasy world. The analyst is felt as a menace and an "intruder to be fought off at all costs, even though little or no real satisfaction is gained from the restricted mode of living this situation permits." I am not certain that a formulation of this kind about an important clinical phenomenon could be made without a theory of self, particularly Winnicott's (1960a) concept of true and false self.

Object-relations theorists and self theorists all have to reckon in some way with the dual instinct theory. I subscribe to the view expressed by most of these writers that instincts and affects must be conceptualized within a framework of the self-object internalized relationship. More simply put, the search for objects or persons may well be a more basic motivating force than the gratification of drives. Thus, I wonder whether Dr. Sutherland is implying the same solution recommended by his mentor, Ronald Fairbairn (1944), who reduced the instincts to mere "instrumentalities." In my view, the roles of libido and aggression still need to be reckoned with as significant motives, however influenced they are by a matrix of internalized relationships and relationship needs. I am aware that I am touching on an exceedingly complicated question, which is far from satisfactorily resolved. The problem of integrating instinct theory and self theory represents one of the exciting challenges of the future for psychoanalysts.

A corollary to the above point is to describe art and religion as expressions of the creative self; they reflect the universal human need to affirm and validate a healthy sense of self. Once again, I would not wish to subscribe to a reductionist view that religion is nothing but the sublimation of drives. Winnicott (1953) may have been on the right track when he described religion, art, and other cultural products as transitional phenomena, which are characterized by a partial retreat to an earlier desired relationship in which the pressures of reality and the strains of separateness are temporarily set aside. I am not certain that these creative expressions of the self as viewed by Winnicott are relational in a noninstinctive sense. Religion links the individual to his primary objects, but sexual and aggressive drives are important components of one's relationship to a loving and punitive God.

I have been privileged over these two decades, through a close association with our speaker, to learn and assimilate the major views expressed in his paper. I agree with him that it is important to enrich our present theory with a superordinate concept of the self in order to appreciate better our patients' inner worlds and struggles with reality. Whatever solution eventually emerges concerning the issues raised here, the specific content of the evolving theory will be less important than the thrust of the thinking we have heard this morning. Dr. Sutherland has presented us with an image of man as an open system with a need to be valued and affirmed, ever striving to integrate disparate and contradictory parts of his self and challenged by the need to deal realistically with a changing environment. This view clearly makes the mission of the mental health field one of fostering the process of human growth and development through understanding difficulties in personal relatedness. If developmental arrests have occurred, we try to use our scientific knowledge and human empathy to encourage growth to resume. In the mental health field, where a broad spectrum of therapeutic approaches beckon at every turn— particularly the simplistic ones promising quick solutions to complex problems—it is easy to lose sight of how our knowledge about human growth can best help our patients get back on the developmental track. I am indebted to Dr. Sutherland for what he has taught us in the past and for his enlightening statement today of the essential nature of human functioning.

Ramon Ganzarain, M.D.

Dr. Sutherland questions "whether or not the classical psychoanalytical theory of the person and his development and functioning does justice to . . . [the] fact" that the self is conceptualized "as an open system *developing and maintaining its identity through* the social relatedness essential to it from the start" (italics mine).

He briefly describes a case with negative therapeutic reactions, which derive

> from the way the individual divides part of his self into a subself to be kept in virtually a secret fortress, with the rest of his relationships distorted to preserve this situation. This inner state, however, is entirely a product of his relationships within the family, and, even when he seems most cut off, the essential factors are the failed relationships and the terror of disintegration that remains.

I was reminded of similar features in the famous case treated by Kohut (1979), "Mr Z," and the vicissitudes of his two analyses. During the first one, his failed relationship with the sadistic, psychotic mother was kept entirely hidden in a secret fortress.

After Dr. Sutherland tells analysts that they "have alienated themselves in large measure from the humanities, and at the same time they have made even less impression on the 'hard science' philosophy underlying medicine today," he declares that "the human sciences badly need the kind of understanding of human relationships that psychoanalysis can contribute." He suggests that the mathematics of open systems requires

> constant interactional developments with structural changes to embody the "learning" that has taken place. Thus, predictability has a limited role in regard to open systems, because unpredictable creativity in relation to unpredictable environmental change is the characteristic feature of these systems. . . . Man is not the blind, passive victim of chance and necessity . . . for, as Jantsch (1980) puts it, "We are not the helpless subjects of evolution—we *are* evolution."

As an illustration of such unpredictable creativity, the dramatic story of the *Birdman of Alcatraz* [Gaddis 1955] came to my mind. How could a man rise from being sentenced to life in prison for several murders to become a world-famous ornithologist, beginning by caring for a wounded bird that had fallen onto his window ledge? This man's wish to help a little creature began a new trusting relationship with his jailer that gradually allowed the prisoner to develop into a full-fledged scientist.

Dr. Sutherland continues: "Man's relatedness to his environment depends on his unique capacity to transcend it by making a reproduction of it inside his mind, where he then manipulates possibilities, from which stem his creative alterations of it." Psychoanalysts seem to be reaching a psychology beyond determinism and developing concepts that may enable them to study mental phenomena beyond the unconscious repetition-compulsion phenomenon.

Dr. Sutherland calls psychoanalysts to arms, stating that we "must respond by putting people with all the subjectivity governing their actions to the front . . . [because] the psychiatrist's proper concern is subjective experience." He concludes: "The self is surely the heart of the matter regarding the organization and functioning of subjective experience."

Dr. Sutherland's remarks reminded me of Zilboorg's (1941) criticism of the attempt by Kraepelinian psychiatry to classify mental illness in the same way the botanist Linnaeus classified plants. In so doing, Kraepelin and his successors erroneously attempted to achieve an objective diagnosis of every mental patient. Psychiatrists have not proclaimed emphatically enough that psychiatry, and particularly psychoanalysis, deals with the subjectivity of people, not with objective diagnostic categories. In every patient, analysts may help the important subselves abandon their secret fortresses. Patients may overcome their schizoid fear of psychotic disintegration by establishing a reliable, personal relationship with the analyst; analysis thus becomes a parentinglike labor of love and not a mere technical endeavor of deciding which button to push—when.

The concept of the self as a complex open system gives psychoanalytic technique a relatively new perspective. The old image of the analyst as a blank screen is exchanged for the picture of the patient-analyst relationship as an interaction. The fact that the analyst reacts to his patient—without necessarily losing his neutrality—is acknowledged and studied; attempts are also made to use such responses.

Racker (1957) did a meaningful review of the classical concept of countertransference. He first described the *countertransference neurosis* as a natural development within the psychoanalytic setting and then described two main types of countertransferences, concordant and complementary, whose significance and understanding he systematized by studying patient–analyst interactions from the viewpoint of projections and introjections. Grinberg (1962) contributed to the subject with his concept of "protective counter-identification."

Physicists acknowledge that material, physical phenomena cannot remain unaltered when someone observes them and that causality relationships between subatomic phenomena cannot be established with certainty because particles of matter respond unpredictably when under observation (Heisenberg's [1930] "uncertainty principle"). Psychological subjective phenomena, such as affects, transference, and unconscious fantasies, obviously are even more difficult to observe "objectively." Predictability remains only a probability, never a certainty, both in physics and in psychology. Thus, unpredictable psychotherapeutic developments can sometimes occur.

Psychoanalysis consequently becomes a "growth" experience, with a "hatching" of still unformed subselves that have been hidden in secret fortresses or that are still in germinal states inside their shells. Thus, analysis is like a trip toward spiritual achievement, a road to completion and perfection with quasireligious undertones, in search of a better integration of the self, almost à la Carl Jung." The analyst, therefore, views his technique more as an "artistic" endeavor than as a "scientific" enterprise. It requires an intuitive, creative attitude to promote—without undue interference—the best possible growth of a given patient, who is a unique individual in his own right.

Dr. Sutherland states that these concepts of the self give the individual "a new status in Western democratic social and political philosophies, one in which the full realization of his personal resources is a requirement." I personally believe that such "full realization of his personal resources" ideally should be an individual's right, granted to him by mother, family, and society. It should be stressed, however, that such realization is also the individual's responsibility. Increased autonomy and freedom of choice entail heightened correlative answerability. Such responsibility is important specifically in psychoanalytic theory and practice because it acknowledges the person's own (relative) power to shape his destiny and to modify and influence his relationships with the persons around him. Mental patients have a tendency to forget their active participation in shaping their fate, "disclaiming" it (Schafer 1976), while blaming instead "not good enough mothering" or another "faulty" environmental element. There is a risk of oversimplifying and forgetting the essential, constant interactional quality of the self that deals with the environment. Some analytic schools of thought offer "deficit theories" of poor mothering to explain the psychopathology of the self, while other schools minimize the role of human environment in the infant's development. Both extreme conceptual positions forget the essential interactional quality of the self within its human environment. Both of these diametrically opposed theoretical postures inspire exaggerated analytic techniques that risk limiting therapeutic effectiveness.

21. THE AUTONOMOUS SELF

Sutherland believed that a distinct self is present from birth, and that an innate organizing principle guiding development of the self is present from the beginning. The conceptualization of the self as, at birth, a dynamic structure that plays a crucial role in development challenges the theoretical assumptions of classical psychoanalytic theory, particularly drive theory. Psychoanalysis lacks a theoretical account of the person as inseparably interwoven with the fabric of society. Clinical evidence from disorders in the self that develop in later life, as seen in seriously disturbed patients, strongly suggests that effective development of the self rests on a joyful, empathic responsiveness from the mother. The infant can readily tolerate various limited frustrations of particular behaviors if the overall feelings communicated by the mother, and later the father, come from their genuine unqualified joy in the baby as it is.

In the late 1980s, Dr. Sutherland shared this paper with a small group of analytical therapists. He had been encouraging us to write up the cases we were presenting to him, and to use them as clinical examples of the kinds of pathology of the self he was describing. In the British tradition, he wanted us to criticize and debate his ideas so that we might clarify our understanding. Although Dr. Sutherland's emphasis in this paper is on the self, he strongly believed in the dynamic unconscious and the important place of dreams in psychoanalysis. The task of fully integrating the many aspects of psychoanalytic theory—drive theory, ego psychology, object relations theory, and the psychology of the self—still lies before us.

—Introduction by Stuart C. Averill, M.D.

EARLY THEORIES OF THE SELF

Several trends have contributed to the recent emergence of the self as a central issue within psychoanalysis. Common to all these trends has been the growing awareness that the fundamental assumptions of psychoanalysis did not do justice to new clinical findings. In contrast with the classical theories—which based development on the instincts and their vicissitudes, and from these, the tripartite structuring of the mind—more recent theories have increasingly seen psychopathological manifestations as being involved with the person as a whole, that is, the self. This self developed those disorders when it lost a core integration that had hitherto been referred to by such phrases as "an intact ego," or as a strength derived from a sufficient degree of cohesion in managing the instincts. Instead, the individual presented conflicts within the self or "identity." Divisions within the self caused doubts "about who one was" and other disturbing existential phenomena. Psychoanalysts were thus confronted with serious questions that exposed the inadequacy of current theory, which was considered to depersonalize individuals and especially their motivation. This belief was confirmed by what was happening in society, as poets and writers all too frequently expressed.

In Freud's first theorizing, he took for granted the personal level of conflict in the repression of painful ideas and feelings because of their incompatibility with the values of the central self. The "I," as Freud termed it, was clearly the self in all its subjective richness of meaning. A progressive depersonalization of this "Ich" seemed to begin when the instincts and their biological energies were conceived of as playing the dominant role in the unconscious psyche. This trend persisted for the next half century and was reinforced, as Bettelheim (1982) was driven to stress a few years ago, by the translation of the German "Ich" into English as the neutral word "ego" (p. 80); but its perpetuation almost certainly drew on the pervasive and tenacious influence of scientific materialism. Freud's genius, however, could not be wholly constrained by this limitation. In spite of holding on to this philosophy as part of his thinking until his death, he introduced into the self the personalized structures of the ego-ideal and the superego from his study of group behavior and the psychoses, while in the ego there was personification by identifications. When the tripartite theory emerged, there was thus a scheme of development starting from the drives of the impersonal biological instincts and proceeding with the formation of a person through interaction with the social reality of the family. This atomistic buildup of parts, however, fails to do justice to the uniqueness of the self as a functioning whole, especially in light of the growing awareness of existential issues that emphasize its central role. Nevertheless, as Franz Alexander maintained when the tripartite theory was formulated, there was now "a psychology of the total person."

The new formulation proved to have enormous appeal as well as great heuristic value. A wider range of disorder was investigated in depth to an extent not thought possible, and Anna Freud and Wilhelm Reich advanced the understanding of ego and character formation. The most radical development came from the work of Melanie Klein, who pursued the implications of Freud's views on the importance of early development by boldly and rigorously applying the psychoanalytic method to young children. The consequence was the rather startling finding of the rich content of children's inner worlds, worlds populated by a range of figures in fantasied loving and hating relationships with each other and with the ego. Because of the extreme violence and sadistic destructiveness in some of these relationships, Klein postulated that they were direct reflections of the instincts, and especially the death instinct. The destructive impulses aroused intense anxieties, which Klein related to a dread of disintegration of the ego, or to a loss of the cohering function of the internalized good mother. To lessen these inner terrors, the ego split into parts so that the dangerous impulses could be separated from the good figures. Impressed with the salient power of the instincts, Klein did not pursue the theoretical implications of her findings about the structuring of the self as vividly personalized in the inner relationships, except to assume that the ego must be a unity from the start. Thus she did not examine how perception and action were influenced by simultaneous dynamic effect from more than one of the internal objects. (At that time, the ego and the self were interchangeable terms, and they remained so until Hartmann separated them as a theoretical necessity.)

In contrast with the Viennese analysts, who gave Klein's ideas a hostile reception, the British analysts were divided in their response. A substantial group believed that her data warranted careful appraisal and assimilation. From this group, some became enthusiastic followers while others were stimulated to create their own lines of thought. Among these, the best known were Balint, Fairbairn, and Winnicott. Each was a highly independent thinker, yet all shared the attribution of a fundamental role in shaping the personality to the actual earliest experiences of the infant in its personal interaction with the mother and the family. From this common emphasis, they became known as the object-relations theorists, and many analysts subsequently developed their views further. For our immediate purpose, the most significant feature of their initial work was that they arrived at the need to conceptualize the self. Only Winnicott took the step of adopting the term, although, like the others, he did not formulate a systematic conceptualization. Fairbairn acknowledged, in his later years, that although he would have preferred to use the term, he believed it was more appropriate to retain the common psychoanalytic vocabulary at the time of his writing.

Balint's virtual arrival at the concept of the self is evident in his description of patients who regressed during analysis to a state in which the interaction between them and the analyst was dominated by its preverbal quality. Verbal interpretations then had little effect; instead, the patients responded to the experience of being "recognized." By this statement, Balint clearly implied a reaction of the person as a whole, whose unique feelings were being empathically understood and accepted by another person. The holistic quality of such an experience cohered in a relationship between two selves. Winnicott concluded that many, if not all, patients to some degree had a split in the self and its sense of being that led to a separation of the "false" or compliant self from the "true" self. (This repressed or "hidden" self became a central focus for Winnicott's pupil, Masud Khan, in his later clinical studies.) This split arose from a mismatch between the infant's needs and the mother's perception and reception of these needs, either through the mother's failure to recognize their nature by faulty empathy, or by an intrusive response based on her own conception of what the infant's needs should be. Whatever its origins, this division bedeviled the whole development of the individual; and it was extremely resistant to change because it had evolved as a defense against the dread of loss of the self, that is, of madness. Winnicott's work eventually had a growing impact on analysts because of the new way in which it illuminated many psychopathological manifestations.

Despite the genius quality in his work, Winnicott did not propose a revised metapsychology. Instead, he believed that Freud's libido theory and his own concepts could coexist as parts of the psychoanalytic understanding of the person. Greenberg and Mitchell (1983) found Winnicott's attitude toward his own theoretical contributions so bizarre that they devoted about five pages to its elaboration. They clearly found it difficult to understand his almost obsequious claim to be merely expanding some of Freud's ideas, while in fact he was emphasizing the crucial role of the earliest mother–infant relationship in shaping the structure of the personality. In their view, Winnicott's need to avoid challenging Freud's assumptions led him to concoct a viewpoint that differed from Freud's, and then to accept the simultaneous operation of two incompatible explanatory schemes. The Greenberg-Mitchell account of this anomaly is of special interest because of Winnicott's irrational attack on Fairbairn's confrontation of this issue. Instead of recognizing that Fairbairn was in fact spelling out, with remarkable conviction, evidence for what they were both advocating, Winnicott reacted as though Fairbairn had personally attacked Freud.

Fairbairn differed from most psychoanalytic theorists in having had philosophical training before he studied medicine and psychoanalysis. From his early years, he had shown a strong interest in identifying the basic principles underlying processes and making his own appraisal of these principles when applied to his own clinical findings. This attitude was reinforced by his geographical isolation from the other British analysts, which freed him from the pressures within the analytic movement toward strict conformity with Freud's writings. His thinking was thus individualistic, yet suffused with a disciplined critical approach, which led him to prospectively reject the views of others until he matched them against his experience. For Fairbairn, reaching conclusions that differed from others might be the greatest respect he could pay them, because it was from their work that he started.

After close study of a group of patients with schizoid personalities, Fairbairn summed up their psychopathology as resulting from failure by the mother to convey a feeling that she loved and valued them as persons in their own right. Fairbairn assumed an innate need in the infant that had to be met by the mother's emotional attitude toward her child. This need was thus unusual, as he conceived it, for it was a purely psychological holistic one arising in the self. It was not an appetitive bodily need to be gratified with pleasure as tensions terminated, as were the instincts in Freud's scheme, but rather a need for an ongoing personal relationship. The infant clamored for joyful, stimulating interchanges, as in playful baby talk and games, quite independently of the care ordinarily given in response to physical needs. For Fairbairn, the infant was thus "personalized" by being spontaneously responded to as a person right from the start, first by the mother, and later by the father and other family members. It was this welcome into the world of social relations that laid the foundation of the security essential for the development of potential personal resources through the resultant readiness to establish these relationships.

Because future personality structure was so closely determined by the quality of these early experiences, Fairbairn asserted that psychoanalysis would advance only by changing its underlying assumptions. Specifically, the crucial role attributed to the vicissitudes of instinctual energies and their satisfaction must be replaced by a theory of how the personality was structured as the consequence of its experiences, especially in the earliest stages of development. Fairbairn called this view an *object-relations theory,* a term that has stuck even though he later believed it would have been more appropriate to call it a *personal-relations theory*. *Object,* however, was the usual word for the aims of the instincts when these were conceived of largely as needs for which body parts might be the object.

CONTINUING EVOLUTION OF THE SELF

Despite the increasing inadequacy of the tenets of scientific materialism to explain the phenomena of living organisms, and even though the theory of open systems was developed to account for their properties, the grip of materialism has continued to exercise its influence. We have only to note the great reluctance to move away from concepts of drives as though they are biological energies pumped into the psychic apparatus and hence essential for any explanation of motivation. In this perspective, the evolution of an ego is an organization of experience forced on the person to cope with the id and its perpetual pressure to action in the outer world. Moreover, because the instincts constitute the supply of energy, they drive the organism to homeostatic constancy and eventually to the state of maximum entropy (that is, death). Fairbairn, on the other hand, postulated a holistic ego right at the center, which was structured from experience. Such a notion was in no way a naive separation of mind from body, but it employed the current biological concepts of holistic organizing principles. It also emphasized that new levels of organization invariably produce new properties that cannot be predicted from knowledge of the parts. No amount of knowledge about the hydrogen and oxygen atoms would let us predict that combining them results in a colorless liquid—water.

Fairbairn's line of thought, although starting from the clinical data provided by his schizoid patients, was also influenced by his antipathy to the atomistic approach that materialism engendered and by contemporary theories of embryology. The dominant concept was of a ground plan within the organism that controlled the emergence of its differentiated structures and maintained their interdependence. There was little understanding of how such an influence could be mediated, but Fairbairn's notion of a latent holistic force was supported by the growth of Gestalt psychology. During this period, the question of a holistic force independent of the instinctual drives was gripping the attention of other psychoanalysts. Hartmann made the first prominent contribution to this development. (Fairbairn and Hartmann were actually evolving their theories at the same time, but the outbreak of World War II prevented any mutual influence.)

The problem that Hartmann considered to be unsolvable, in terms of instinctual forces driving the individual to seek the pleasure of discharge, was how such motives alone could lead to the essential property of the ego—namely, the capacity to delay action by anticipating greater gains through knowledge and planning. For Hartmann, this capacity required an autonomous ego whose development had to be seen as that of a variable, independent of the instincts, with its own innate endowments governing its maturation. It also had to be distinguished from the whole person, which Hartmann held to be the self (that is, what was cathected in narcissism). In commenting on Hartmann's theoretical formulations, Lichtenstein (1977) noted that Hartmann saw the need for a radical rethinking of psychoanalytic theory if that theory were to rightfully claim the title of an evolutionary approach to human mental development. Hartmann, however, did not get beyond the concepts associated with ego functions, partly because of his adherence to mechanistic principles. Nevertheless, Lichtenstein followed up some of their implications. Thus, by assuming that "the whole person" was cathected by libido in narcissism, we have to ask whether this organizing principle is distinct in origin and function from a structure synthesized from the other psychic structures. What we observe of the "whole person" are the bodily and psychological transformations during the life cycle. The invariant self as a whole is the constant thread that gives the feeling of being the same person. Yet it cannot be derived from the parts. Thus we are aware of unrealized potential, of complex relationships, as in amnesias when the self-perception is changed, or when it is maintained in an unstable state against a feeling of not being the "true self." Lichtenstein believed that Hartmann's "third force," or independent variable, within the psyche must be invoked. As Masud Khan (1964) observed, "the discussion of ego-pathology has extended to the larger issues of identity formation . . . and the establishment of self" (p. 273).

The theme of identity is associated with Erikson, who located the development of the ego within the social relatedness of the person. Throughout his thinking, he has always integrated the biological with the cultural, but his scheme, unlike the theory of libidinal development, covers the whole life cycle. The epigenetic phases he postulated in development, from infancy to old age, have now become a part of culture. What we must note is that an identity principle, a biological organizing principle, underlies these phases. Indeed,

Lichtenstein asserted the establishment and maintenance of identity as the principle that defines the concept of living and the survival of life. In animals, as in man, this principle commands absolute priority over any other need.

In the lower animals, identity is largely that of the genotype, which is fashioned to a high degree by the genic endowment within a predictable environment. High up on the evolutionary scale, the saurian's development takes place entirely under the impetus of the innate behavioral mechanisms. The human being, in marked contrast, has prolonged gestation followed by years of nurturance from adults, without which the infant cannot survive. Spitz showed that the infant dies if no one gives enough love and care to set up a self, or organizing principle, that wants to live. The evolutionary endowment in the infant and in the mother is thus of a completely different order from that of the lower animals, one presumably evolved to cope with human survival through membership in groups. Humans also pose the problem of the plasticity of the phenotype. The behavioral characteristics of the adult human being vary greatly from culture to culture, within the same culture, and, to some extent, within the single individual when required. Any organizational principle is therefore concerned with the emergence of identity from potential forms of characteristics that are shaped by the experience in upbringing.

What Erikson described as identity was the objectification of the self into a person with a sense of being a "somebody" aware of personal history and whose self had been organized into patterns laid down by peer social groups. The person recognized by others was the identity as objectified, while the inner sense of being this person reflected this identity, although the existential awareness was absolutely unique to the individual. This inner core, which was distinguished from the public identity, could be carried only by an ongoing structure that psychoanalysis had not specified, although, as Lichtenstein said, an adequate knowledge of who a person was could never be inferred from what the person was.

Lichtenstein, from his remarkably comprehensive and penetrating considerations of the problem of identity, was one of the first psychoanalysts to offer a metapsychology of the self. Starting by assuming the existence of an innate organizing principle, he did not agree that this principle can be derived from the other metapsychological constituents. Spitz assumed its independent status from the work of the embryologists. Spiegel, however, accepted it on the psychological basis of its being the self. It acts from the beginning as a frame of reference against which experiences are judged. Sandler, although postulating an organizing activity that appears very early, saw it as a reflection of the synthetic function of the ego. For Lichtenstein, however, this latter conceptualization is a rather advanced ego property that would operate only later.

THE SELF AS "ORGANIZING PRINCIPLE"

The confluence of pychoanalytic thought represented by these brief references reflects a rising dynamic toward the recognition of the self as an independent variable. Couched in the tentative expression of "organizing principle," this force nevertheless has the most fundamental role in the very survival of the person as the agent responsible for the integration of experience. The abstract term "principle" indicates that although it determines the development of the future person, the only formal characteristic that can be attributed to it is that of coordinating the experiences from the rapid developments in bodily resources, the maturation of the innate behavioral systems, and their interactions with the mother, the father, and the family. To give more form to this potential, Lichtenstein suggested that, at birth, the infant's experiences with the mother start a transformative structuring or patterning into what he called a primary identity. This conclusion is inevitable, and all clinical experience confirms it. For this reason, I believe we must regard this variable as the self.

The potentialities are clearly plastic in that they determine what might be analogous to the trunk of the tree from which all the future shape—with its infinite possibilities in regard to the branches, the foliage, and the flowering for procreation—will emerge from the specific features of the environment that nourished it. The process of becoming is that of development with all the unpredictable distortions that may be induced by an unpredictable environment—either in pathological structuring in place of the normal, or in reactive deformations in the whole, to make good the absence of what should have been an available environmental constituent.

In the formation of identity, Lichtenstein attributed much more innately structured action to the infant than is usual. This assumption receives support from the subsequent studies of infant development. (From his philosophical training, Lichtenstein suggested that the theoretical barriers to linking the inner subject with the outer world have been created by entrenched Cartesian dualism.) Thus, from von Eüxkull's concept of an innate scheme in the embryo of the more primitive animals (wherein their drives have their object imprinted sufficiently for their behaviour to be directed to it from the start), Lichtenstein suggested that the infant self innately expects to find the constellation of a mother responding to it, and it responds at once to the mother as the object that completes its inner tension. Correspondingly, the mother begins to personalize the infant. It is the particular model that comes from her own needs, conscious and unconscious, that gives identity to the child. This initial "shaping" of the self operates permanently as "an identity theme" that persists throughout life, although modified by subsequent experience into many "variations."

Lichtenstein concluded that identity evolves into the structure through which the individual will perceive and interact with the world, and thus become responsible for survival as a human being. He further stressed that the identity must be constantly maintained against any tendency to regress, a task normally effected by membership in various groups to which the individual belongs. The two basic features of the self are thus brought to the fore—namely, its autonomy and its concurrent membership in a community. As a self-organizing, dynamic open system, the self places paramount emphasis on its autonomy, which is synonymous with survival. Nevertheless, as Angyal noted in his conceptualization of the person in terms of systems theory, the self must retain an *autonomy within a homonymy of relatedness*. Threats to the self evoke the defensive ferocity of the animal faced with a lethal predator.

In this connection, Freud (1921) discussed the libidinal ties among members of the group, noting the spontaneous intolerance to strangers that has to be overcome:

> This self-love works for the preservation of the individual, and behaves as though the occurrence of any divergence from his own particular lines of development involved a criticism of them and a demand for their alteration. We do not know why such sensitiveness should have been directed to just these details of differentiation; but it is unmistakable that in this whole connection men give evidence of a readiness for hatred, an aggressiveness, the source of which is unknown, and to which one is tempted to ascribe an elementary character. [p. 102]

In a footnote to this passage, Freud referred to his recent linking of the polarity of love and hate with the opposition between the instincts of life and death.

Lichtenstein's contributions thus clarified the position that the self should occupy in the basic assumptions of psychoanalytic theory. Although representing a radical change in theoretical principles, Lichtenstein's synthesis is a model for establishing the evolutionary status of the self from many trends in clinical thinking within psychoanalysis during the decades prior to his book, *The Dilemma of Human Identity,* in 1977. The importance of these principles is perhaps best indicated by Lichtenstein's (1977) comment concerning Hartmann's recognition that the "pressures of needs and drives appear as manifestations of personal will" (p. 235). Lichtenstein further reinforced this perspective by noting Hartmann's (1958) prediction "that the psychology of will-processes is destined to play a role in the psychoanalytic psychology of the future" (pp. 74–75).

The contributions of Lichtenstein and Erikson, because of their focus on the development of the self into an "identity," tend to be considered in isolation from their fundamental postulates regarding the development of the self. Both of these writers describe how the adult self is shaped by its identifications and internalizations. Erikson assumed the existence of the self as the central structured potential from which the eventual identity of the adult emerges. Lichtenstein suggested that this self-structure is so constructed that it "expects" from birth to be treated like a person. As he made clear, conceptualizing the self to be at birth a dynamic structure that will play a crucial role in development challenges all the assumptions of classical theory. Erikson had considered that the libidinal phases, as Freud described them, developed alongside the epigenetic stages in the formation of identity. Such a view, however, cannot be sustained because the libidinal theory accounts for the development of object relations in terms of the phases of libidinal development.

RECENT THEORIES OF THE SELF

Within the past few decades, the self has become the explicit focus for several analysts whose writings have in turn made it an issue of widespread interest. Prominent contributions, much influenced by Hartmann, have come from Mahler and Jacobson, and from Otto Kernberg (originally influenced by Fairbairn), who also acknowledged a debt to these two writers. These three, although accepting the self as a structure separate from the id, ego, and superego, nevertheless have held that their findings—thought by some to require an autonomous self of independent origin—can be accounted for in terms of classical theory.

Mahler's studies of young children, both observational and clinical, are now an integral part of the development of psychoanalytic theory. In contrast to Hartmann, who had left the self as a rather ill-defined entity, Mahler introduced a concept of the self as the whole person, which emerged as a coherent identity as the result of development through phases of differentiation from a symbiotic matrix. The experiences of the infant with its mother during the earliest phases had a crucial effect on the future personality. However, as Greenberg and Mitchell remarked, Mahler struggled to retain the role of drive theory in the face of evidence from later research strongly suggesting that the infant possessed independent resources and separateness from birth. Mahler did this by denying that what she had described was a metapsychological theory; it was essentially only a descriptive phenomenological account. It was the organizing function of the ego, as specified by Hartmann, that created the self through its representations within the ego becoming cathected by libido. Nevertheless, Mahler had moved away from the oedipal relationships as the foundation for "a totality of tenderness, security, and pleasure that is experienced in a full relationship with another person" (Greenberg and Mitchell 1983, p. 303).

Jacobson's seminal writings have demonstrated that she clearly saw some of the limitations of the drive theory. Her intensive work with very disturbed patients forced her to recognize the need to include the consequences of early relationships in the formation of the self. In her first theorizing, she adopted Hartmann's position of regarding the ego as a system of functions and the self as existing within the ego through its representations. She nevertheless concluded that the self contributed an independent dynamic influence; for instance, she believed that the ego acquired a likeness to the love object only by introjecting aspects of it into the self. The desire to be like the object contributed to differentiation of the self. Jacobson's acceptance of the fundamental importance of relationships led her to broaden the classical concepts. Thus orality for her included what the mother is for the infant in all aspects, and it operates to organize the manifold experiences. Here, too, Jacobson viewed affects, not as deriving from discharges of tensions, but as including the quality of the experience (that is, the factor added to it by the specific relationship). Of course, this line of reasoning raises a key question about the drive theory—namely, how the energies of the drives can account for the great spectrum of experiences. Jacobson believed that this is possible along the lines she suggested.

This issue is unavoidable for any theoretical scheme, and we see it again in Kernberg. Prior to the impact of Mahler and Jacobson, he was greatly stimulated by Fairbairn, a debt he acknowledged after his views on borderline patients had become established. Although he explicitly adopted the stance of an object-relations theorist, he disowned Fairbairn's position insofar as the latter asserted it to be incompatible with drive theory. For Kernberg, it is from the drives that representations of the self and objects are developed into internalized relationships. Because of this aspect of Kernberg's theoretical work, Greenberg and Mitchell have classified him as belonging to the current trend of "theoretical accommodation" that attributes much of the structuring of the ego and the self to a social origin apart from the drives. They added, however, that those who have adopted these theories, yet who also hold to the drive theory as essential for a metapsychological component in any psychoanalytical theory, fail to realize that in doing so they have constructed a theory that is quite different from Freud's.

Kernberg has postulated the internalization of dynamic systems with a self-image linked to an object. The introjection of the object, however, is not entirely at the behest of oral impulses. At this early stage, self and object are poorly separated and affects can be intense, especially in violently negative feelings. With maturity, the relationships of similar affective tone build up into identifications and eventually form the ego identity. The drives thus play an initial part in providing the affects from which the subsequent organization of the person is built. The self remains essentially as a phenomenological term in the experience of relationships and their subsequent organization by the ego.

Kohut is by far the most prominent writer to advocate a radical view of the self as the active agent in the initiation and organization of behavior. He conceptualized the self at birth as largely a potential only—one that is required to merge with the mother to function in a progressively organized way and with a sense of constancy and spontaneity. The essential dynamic system is thus that of a self with a self-object, or undifferentiated mother, operating in the earliest stages as an ego. As separation proceeds with development, the self becomes more autonomous and effective; but a tie to others remains throughout life even when the self fully recognizes the separateness of others. The closeness of the self with the self-object is such that it is the subjectivity of this latter to which the self mainly responds. With ordinary good parenting, the self works through two critical phases for its effective development. First, the mother, as the main influence, has to respond empathically to the infant's presence and achievements. From this experience, the self gains a sense of omnipotence and grandiosity that, in due course, through interaction with others, is transformed into a reasonable sense of security, self-esteem, and achievement from abilities. As this earliest structuring of a grandiose self is taking place, a second structuring begins from the internalization of the admired parents as ideals. At first, the idealized parents exist as undifferentiated self-objects, and are then replaced by more separated ideal figures that function as the ego ideal and superego. The behavior characterized in terms of the libidinal phases does not originate from fixations at the libidinal stages, but from "oral, anal, or oedipal disorders" in the parents.

Kohut's theory replaces the drives with factors arising from the experience of relationships. The analytic process does not reside in the interpretation of drives and defenses, but in the intersubjective field constituted by the analysand and the analyst. In his first formulations, Kohut stressed that he was not replacing classical theory, but was instead advancing a view wherein the dynamic structuring of the self can be considered alongside the independent processes of the libidinal stages and the drive theory. In keeping with this position, he regarded disorders of the self as separate from the neuroses, which are derived from conflicts between the drives that develop later. Some years later, Kohut concluded that the concept of "drive" was quite unsatisfactory, but he then decided to avoid breaking with tradition to preserve the sense of continuity of our science. Such an attitude from one purporting to make advances in a scientific theory cannot but remind one of Galileo recanting from fear of the Inquisition! It is the more extraordinary in that Kohut asserted, like Fairbairn, that the sexual and aggressive impulses, so prominent as symptoms, derive from disorders in the self and not from independent energies.

If we leave aside these "accommodations" as dictated by political rather than scientific considerations, Kohut certainly placed the conceptualization of the self in the forefront of psychoanalytic debate. His voluminous writings contain many valuable clinical observations. Nevertheless, he seems to present an oversimplified view that distortions in the bipolar structuring of the self, around the early grandiose needs and the attachment to idealized objects, explain all the major pathological developments of the self. He also underestimated, in the opinion of many analysts sympathetic to the object-relational focus, the ever-present manifestations of aggression aroused when the needs of the self are frustrated. But the essential limitation in Kohut's conceptual scheme is the lack of a convincing metapsychology, one that links the psychological to the biological factors that must be present for the evolution of a structure of such comprehensive responsibility for behavior.

Summarizing the progressive intrusion of the self into psychoanalytic theory over the past few decades, we note its growing prominence for theory and practice. The influence of ego psychology, so powerful among American analysts, has led to unresolved differences. The importance of conceptualizing identity formation emphasized the central role of early relationships and of subsequent relationships in the maintenance of identity. Only Lichtenstein, however, of those closest to ego psychology, favored the postulation of the self as an independent variable from which the identity is fashioned out of its relationships. Yet he stopped short of a theory of the origin of the self, even though he saw that the innately structured potential self must be the start of a metapsychology of the self. It is this problem of conceptualizing an adequate metapsychology of the self with biological roots that seems to have deterred most of those theorists inspired by Hartmann from moving from their acceptance of the essential role of early relationships in fashioning the personality on to a developmental origin independent of the biological instincts and the drive theory. It is this problem to which we must turn our attention.

I wish first, however, to refer to considerations from outside the clinical situation, because we seem to have created a major barrier by confining ourselves to it. Historically, Freud maintained that psychoanalysts should look to literature to learn what writers have to say about the psychological puzzles confronting us. As observers of the individual within society, writers are inevitably faced with the impact of various movements—intellectual, scientific, artistic, and sociopolitical—on the culture that in turn affects the individual. They can thus identify the features that bestow persistent personal characteristics.

SOME EXTRAANALYTIC CONCEPTIONS OF THE SELF

Just as we can see Freud's discoveries about the unconscious as only one manifestation among many related turbulences in the cultural scene of the Western world a century ago, so with the recent interest in the conceptualization of the self. From this complexity, I believe that some aspects of the fields of literature, philosophy, the social sciences, and psychiatry have crucial significance for psychoanalysis because it has claimed, following Hartmann's work, to be the path to a general psychology of the person.

From the start of his psychoanalytic studies, Freud was greatly influenced by what the poets and writers said about the nature of human beings as an essential source of insight. Masud Khan, although regarded as Winnicott's principal disciple, has made particularly relevant contributions. His unusual combination of a literary cast of mind and psychoanalytic training have enabled him to offer acutely sensitive observations of the phenomena within the psychoanalytic encounter. His observations are also relatively free of the insidious theoretical prejudices that accompany the use of technical jargon. In the opening chapter of his book of essays entitled *Hidden Selves* (1983), he quoted a passage from Trilling's Freud Anniversary Lecture of 1955 that goes right to the heart of our concern (p. 11):

> The first thing that occurs to me to say about literature, as I consider it in the relation in which Freud stands to it, is that literature is dedicated to the conception of the self [Trilling 1955, p. 17]. . . . In almost every developed society, literature is able to conceive of the self, and the selfhood of others, far more intensely than the general culture ever can. [1955, p. 19]

And, we might add, more intensely than psychoanalysis does. Khan's initial theme in his essay is the emergence in European culture of modernism, a trend characterized by "man's decision to be his own sole witness and exclude God, more and more, from his private relation to himself and his personal relation with others" (p. 12). Put another way, modern individuals recognize a new degree of autonomy in their whole being.

Trilling (1955) saw Freud's mind to be different from the literary one in allowing intelligence to play a greater part. Freud was born when science and literature were perceived as cultural antagonists. He was, above all, a scientist and proud of it, yet he was one of the greatest humanistic minds. By drawing on both sides of himself, he made a creative leap that enabled him to suspend his disbelief in his patients' fantasies and so to study the unconscious areas of inner reality from which they originated. The understanding of motivation was thereafter permanently expanded. Trilling, however, indicated various features of the person that did not receive as much attention from psychoanalysts as from writers. Among the Romantic poets, for instance, Wordsworth extended the role of pleasure from almost exclusive links with instinctual gratification to a principle by which humanity feels, and lives, and moves, but also *knows*. When Keats said "beauty is truth," he was acknowledging this principle in the gaining of knowledge. Moreover, when he added "truth beauty," he affirmed the kind of pleasure the developed self derives from perceiving some of the painful facts within it. The ever-resounding echo of his aphorism throughout our literature for the past two centuries testifies to the profoundly aesthetic affirmation for the self from embracing the experiences of distress into its wholeness.

These deep integrative trends appear to stem from a creative dynamic more inherent in human nature than is conveyed by the somewhat tautological phrase, "the synthetic function of the ego." Trilling believed that writers conceive of love as a principle of order and even a civilizing power. Thus, when Blake called in a great voice for the armaments of libidinal desire, his purpose was to build Jerusalem in "England's green and pleasant land." There are here overtones of an outreaching impetus that may be more deeply rooted than the acquisition of the ego-ideal from the social environment—perhaps the open-endedness of humanity at the edge of evolution.

The Two Cultures

Freud was born when science and literature were becoming seen as two antagonistic cultures. A degree of conflict stayed with Freud, as he made plain in his uneasy ambivalence about the relationship between the individual and the culture. Today, when culture itself is as much the object of study as is the individual, there is a greater appreciation of the necessity for both to establish a mutually adaptive partnership.

The movement toward modernism shows various attempts to find substitutes for the relationship with an external destiny that the human self appeared to need if it was to retain its cohesion and keep alive a sense of well-being. The close interdependence of the personal self with the characteristics of its culture became increasingly manifest in literature throughout the century after Freud's birth. The separation from religious belief following the Enlightenment had been followed by the Romantic movement's attempt to substitute a reverence for nature, including as part of nature the development of the self from childhood experience: "The child is father of the man." What then ensued was a progressive inner directedness, as though to find there some solution—for example, love or art—to what Robert Langbaum (1977) saw as a preoccupying concern in modern literature, namely, "the mysteries of identity."

Writers were too aware of the centrality of the self and its complexities to follow the scientific philosophy of humanity conceived of as a machine. For Coleridge, the crucial factor in forming and maintaining the autonomy of the self is the imagination—the unique capacity of the mind. And these writers were reinforced by the surging impact of the philosophies expounded by the phenomenologists and then the existentialists. There could be no question of the fundamental role played by the sense of being, the awareness created from the concentration of all the organized commitments to the more or less coherent aims that constituted the business of living. These commitments embraced the urges of corporeality, the essential relatedness necessary to preserve with others, and the appraisals of the constraints and the opportunities in the external world, all of which seemed to express a constant intentionality with the judgments and decisions for action into the ever-present future.

Although the theory of evolution at first led to some lowering of humanity's self-image, there was no widespread acceptance of this image as being that of a machine. The image of the individual as a unique development in the evolutionary scale was firm enough to reject any philosophy that ignored specific features. What disturbed writers more, however, was the effects of the social changes brought about by rapid industrialization. Marx had confronted society with the alienating, dehumanizing results of uprooting masses of people from social environments in which they could feel a sense of selfhood from being embedded in extensive networks of significant relationships, and placing them instead where they not only lost this relatedness but also were stripped of the essential affirmation provided by meaningful work. When no means was found to replace the contribution of these nutriments, so vital for maintaining the well-being of the individual's identity (as Lichtenstein had postulated), the effects of society evoked strong reactions in our literature. Without the cultural environment that had evolved from the interaction of individuals and their social milieu, writers became concerned with a chilling trend to fragmentation of the individual. The brittle attachment to the illusory substitutes that emerged in the social "wasteland" now evoked, not the death of God, but a depressing concern lest the individual die because of the loss of identity and the consequent isolation, as in Samuel Beckett's *Waiting for Godot*. There was also a depressing impotence from the absence of effective remedial ideas. To evolve such measures has never been the function of our writers, nor should we expect it.

Again Trilling (1955) referred, even if not explicitly, to this situation—to a characteristic of the literary, in contrast to the scientific, mind. He perceived Freud as not really a literary mind because he always wrote about writers and poets as an external observer. The feeling of writers when they produced their work was something Freud never conveyed. Instead, Freud fused a partly literary mind with a scientific one, and it is the analytic objectivity of the latter that is required to work out the origins of phenomena as experienced by others. The infinitely complex interdependence of psychological, social, political, economic, and other factors could not be studied by the psychoanalysts. They might, however, have been more interested in the striking psychological phenomena that emerged, for these were clearly determined by a serious change in the psychic economy of the person. There were, for instance, the diminished commitments to essential relationships such as marriage and the family, and the substitution for these of sexual gratification separated from love in personal relationships—the "cult of narcissism" as it was styled—and a rising greedy demandingness from the welfare state.

Psychoanalysts were not indifferent to these developments. It seemed that the development of their work within the isolated privacy of the consulting room had reinforced an underlying lack in their theoretical account of the person as inseparably interwoven with the fabric of society. Their research could be restricted to people regarded as closed systems within the boundary of their skin. Put like that, such a view would be vehemently rejected, especially today when the focus of the analytic relationship is on what happens between the patient and the analyst. This change, in fact, underlies what is perhaps the missing component. For this change has now shifted the center of our concern from the way in which drives and their derivatives are defended against (that is, hidden from the self and others) to the nature of the self that has to contain these conflicts.

For Freud, a scientist in the tradition of the nineteenth century, the whole problem of the self was scarcely conceivable, although its reality could be recognized. Even today there is a powerful tendency among scientists to view the individual as a machine, or at best to recognize the unique properties of the mind and then consider its study as being outside the purview of science. The core problem is the age-long one of how an immaterial mind can be related to its material body. If we approach that problem head-on, we inevitably encounter insuperable blocks. What we can do, however—if we accept the central role of the self as the agent that embodies the organization of our experience and hence controls the effectiveness of our behavior—is to study its mode of developing and some of its functioning; and these we observe from within ourselves and through the inferences we make from observing others, including their accounts of their inner world.

Existentialism naturally highlighted the problem of the self in relation to changes in the culture, and its contribution greatly influenced literature. Its effect, however, seemed to be mainly to sharpen and emphasize the phenomenological descriptions. The impact on psychoanalysis was limited, perhaps because of the inadequate attention given to unconscious processes. Among psychodynamically oriented psychiatrists, especially in Europe, existentialism aroused a widespread interest in directing therapy to understanding the individual's existential conflicts. Laing combined his training in psychoanalysis with a profound and extensive knowledge of the phenomenologists and existentialists to brilliantly expose the deeper conflicts in the self. Nevertheless, although he was widely acclaimed by writers and psychiatrists, his impact on psychoanalysts has been limited. His original data came from the treatment of schizophrenic patients, and his etiological factors were held to be psychosocial forces within the family. Because of their entrenched views linking the deepest disturbances in the personality to the libido theory, the analysts may have felt uneasy with theories involving only the dynamics of psychosocial interaction, and thus separated from the powerful biological origins of the instincts. In other words, it seemed that the Cartesian tradition might still be holding sway. Perhaps it would be more accurate to suggest that even though the framework of classical metapsychology might need replacing, it nevertheless attempted to root the personal level in the biological in a way that had a deep appeal. Even though Laing pointed out the failure of psychotic patients to achieve an "embodied" self, there was no ready way by which the self could be given a specific biological foundation.

The Self within Society

When we put together these impressions from some extrapsychoanalytic sources, we are confronted with direct references in much of our literature to an autonomous self as a structured entity that exerts a central control over personal behavior. This self is fashioned from early experience into an identity—the unique grouping that each individual has of character, abilities, and social relationships into a cohesive organization that preserves a sense of continuity throughout the life cycle. This identity or self is a dynamic structure in constant interaction with the social environment and its culture. When the latter no longer provides the affirmations the self requires, then the self tends to disintegrate, with widespread disturbances in the sense of well-being and hence various pathological reactions.

An investigation by my former colleague, E. L. Trist, and his associates contributed to an understanding of the nature of this deterioration in the maintenance of the well-being of the self. The study was carried out in response to a request to examine what was happening to coal miners who had been organized into work groups in which all the men had very restricted work tasks designed from a "time and motion" study of the job. Each group would take over from another group operating in one of three shifts into which the 24-hour day was divided. Coming to the situation with a psychodynamic approach to the whole person, Trist and his co-workers found, in free exploratory discussions with the men, a universal feeling that the job gave rise to a great deal of irritation, boredom, and frustration. Sharing tasks created little cohesion in the work groups because supervision was focused on the contribution of each man and each group separately. No sense of responsibility or autonomy was fostered in the groups, so that friction was prevalent within and between groups, especially because no regard was paid to how a group could assist the next one when it left the coal face. By switching to an allocation of responsibility for each group, to an overall sharing of the task, and to an organization of work related to both the human needs and the technical constraints, there was a significant change in what can only be seen as responses of the men as whole people. Absenteeism and sick leave diminished significantly and production increased. In short, the workers as a whole functioned better when the quality of their self-feeling improved from a recognition of their autonomy.

Another study also suggests that an unstable environment has a negative effect on a person's overall organization. Wolff, a physician concerned with community health, studied the health records of a large sample of people who had been displaced from their home countries to another. He found that the incidence of almost every kind of illness—physical as well as psychiatric—was higher than normal in the period following the change.

Whether or not a specific biological foundation can be established for the self, these findings strongly support the conviction among the most discerning writers that when the self is not functioning well, whether because of pathological development or current environmental stress, then the consequences of what Balint termed "the basic fault" can be seen, probably over the whole psychobiological structure of the individual, involving both mind and body in varying degrees. How, then, is this structure, which is crucial to the person, to be conceived of if we are to do justice to its origin and nature? It is clearly an open system, that is, one whose organization is maintained only when its interactions with the environment are appropriate to the needs of the human being—physically, socially, and creatively. This is the question to which both clinical and other sources of evidence force our attention.

THE NATURE OF THE HUMAN ORGANISM IN THE LIGHT OF MODERN EVOLUTIONARY BIOLOGY

The basic assumptions of Freud's thinking were those of scientific materialism and its view of what is "real." It is from these that the "drives" are made essential to subsequent theoretical development. As Greenberg and Mitchell (1983) emphasized in their excellent account of the mainstream of theoretical thinking in psychoanalysis in the past few decades, there is a striking paradox in the fact that, increasingly, the theory is recognized as inadequate to account for the person in his or her most characteristic aspects—namely, the autonomy of the self. The self, as the central agent controlling personal behavior, develops from its experience in relationships and its indispensable role as a dynamic structure that constantly maintains a process of interaction from which transformations take place. Moreover, despite the perpetual changes resulting from experience, the continuity of the individual self is preserved. This concept requires a different scientific paradigm.

The science in which Freud was reared sought to reduce "the human world to the equilibrium perfection, structural unambiguity and permanence, hierarchical control, and predictability of machine-like structures" (Jantsch 1976, p. 2). Freud never exclusively adopted all these beliefs, yet much of their spirit pervaded his thinking. The current biological paradigms offer some different lines of thought, but there is an overall change to a *process-oriented* understanding instead of one employing rigid system components and structures composed of them. In adopting what I find the most appropriate paradigm to fit the problems presented by the self, I have borrowed much from the views of Waddington and Prigogine, which in turn have inspired Jantsch to pursue their implications for the human sciences. The new perspective is, above all, a direct result of assimilating the fundamental place of evolution in considering living organisms. All present forms of life have originated from earlier forms, and what we must account for are such characteristics as self-organization and self-regulation, with nonequilibrium and unpredictability of differentiation in the development of new structures from interaction with the environment. What is *real* in these continuous self-renewals and self-expressions are the self-bounding processes rather than the changing structures. Although evolution has led to many organic subsystems that maintain an equilibrium, this "homeostasis" does not obtain for the organism as a whole. There, equilibrium means death because it ends the never-ceasing processes of self-transformation and self-organization that constitute life. As said by Sir Julian Huxley, our perspective must be *sub specie evolutionis* rather than *sub specie aeternitatis*.

Although the bodily structures have not changed much in humans since they acquired their distinguishing features, there have been relatively enormous developments in the human nervous system. The most significant feature of this development is that the brain structure of the saurians, the earliest animals in the most relevant level of the evolutionary scale, has proceeded to the later ones by the addition of two organizing structures. Each of these has mediated what we might term quantum leaps into a quite different level of flexibility in behavior from that of the previous level. The changes, of course, although resulting in enormous differences, are the end product of very long-term evolutionary processes. The result is that human behavior in its eventual mature form is influenced by these underlying earlier modes of responding to the world.

Clearly, we can refer to this evolutionary process in only the sketchiest diagrammatic way. But because the human position in the evolutionary scale is crucial in understanding human nature, even such a limited reference must be in our thinking. The first consideration, however, must be to note the characteristics of the living creatures associated with the quantum leaps into quite different modes of behavior compared with the earlier phases. The most relevant evolutionary stages for present purposes are those of (1) the land-dwelling reptiles, (2) the lower mammals up to the higher apes, and (3) homo sapiens. The crucial feature is the development of the brain achieved at these three stages.

Behavioral Evolution of the Self

Before considering brain development, the nature and organization of the behavior of the animals in each of these stages must be noted, because the behavioral changes evolve in parallel with structural additions to the brain that mediate the new behaviors. We assume, of course, that evolution is the means through which a given species increases its capacity to exploit the environment more flexibly and more creatively, so that its constraints are progressively overcome until the point is reached, with humans, where they largely determine the environment.

Evolutionary theory has changed in recent years from crude Darwinism, with its survival of the fittest (a distortion of what Darwin suggested), to the need to consider the population or communities from which genetic variations are selected. We then have to appreciate how the behavior of the phenotypes, or existing forms of the adult animal, as a factor independent of the particular genic inheritance, can decisively affect the latter. This view, as developed originally by Waddington, has shown how behavioral characteristics developed in various ways by the animals can lead to changes in the transmitted genes and so bring experimental evidence to justify the widely held view that evolution could not rest on chance and necessity in the blind way it was once held to operate. According to this view also, the genic inheritance increasingly allows the environment to play a greater part as the evolutionary scale is ascended.

What we must keep in mind is that an unconscious primitive organization, or "self," appears to continue to exercise an influence on brain functioning and thus on our behavior when the later evolutionary modes are overwhelmed. As we move up the scale to humans, the enormous complexity of the brain is difficult to appreciate, yet we must do so if we are to comprehend the human self, the essential organizing principle, in an evolutionary perspective comprising the distinctly human acquisitions. Assuming that the brain has evolved to provide for their growth and development, we must list these acquisitions as accurately and as comprehensively as we can. The following six elements are a tentative attempt at such a list and are intended wholly as a basis toward elaborating an evolutionary perspective.

1. The unique property of the human mind is consciousness of "the self" and the capacity to transcend itself, to look at itself in its relationship with aspects of itself, with others, and with the physical environment.
2. The dimension of complexity refers to many different functions. Thus, compared with the nearest animals, the higher apes, the

cognitive capacities permit an infinitely greater storage of information. There is also the unique degree to which humans evolve an "inner space" in which to create representations of themselves interacting with other figures and with things in their world. Also, these creations can be close to reality in form or completely changed to fit fantasy wishes.

3. While the "I" in these imagined relationships can have a representation to express its feelings in any particular relationship, there is ordinarily a continuity of feeling that it is the individual's own self within the changed character.
4. The self, or "I," is the agent responsible for all its varied motivations. This is the sense of autonomy of the self that is a normal characteristic. Although not in awareness most of the time, its perpetual immanent presence is at once revealed when it is threatened or ignored.
5. The autonomous self is the direct successor of the organizing principle in the embryo. After birth, however, it seems to act as we might imagine the reptilian brain mediating a sense of unity, that is, with peremptory action at the behest of the innate behavioral systems, only one of which (for example, hunger, sex, or attack) can assume a dominant position at any one time.
6. Although a primitive form of organizing principle may operate at early evolutionary stages, this principle is restricted by those genes that have been active up to that period. They have initiated the development of the behavioral systems required for the adult animal, which can then survive in the environment for which they have evolved.

Social Evolution

When we reach humans, there is a *radically different situation*. Humans have evolved to become *social animals* who can survive only in small groups—at the Neanderthal stage, and thereafter only in communities that rely on a high degree of control of the environment virtually to the point of creating it. Paramount in this development are the means for keeping the community organized into a functional whole; for protecting it and its resources against attack, a danger coming almost exclusively from other communities; and for creativity in adding new ways—especially technological ways—of increasing resources and then of transmitting this acquired knowledge.

To fulfill these functions as well as others that arise with new situations, evolution has created *homo sapiens*, and for present purposes we can single out only some of the characteristics that would appear to be crucial in human development: (1) the essential nature that makes a *social* being and how it is developed and maintained; (2) how instrumental resources develop; and (3) how, with the capacity to see themselves as actors within the world, that is, to experience and reflect on the existential situation, humans cope with the new situation of pondering the "meaning" of all that they are now aware of.

Lower forms of life evolve highly elaborate and effectively organized communities on the basis of simple innate patterns, with individual members carrying out prescribed functions. The whole thrust of evolution, however, has been to foster the flexibility, resilience, and persistence of human groups by maximizing the potential resources within each individual rather than to confine communities to rigid hierarchical organizations.

By *social being*, we refer to the human consciousness of being a unique person aware of one's own identity and boundaries in relation to others. We have noted how gradually and reluctantly the concept of an autonomous holistic organization has been recognized as necessary to account for the experience and behavior of the person. We also must recognize that its structuring is an ongoing process. Our experiences are encoded, ordered, and used to build up and apply knowledge, a process that seems to be required in an active intentionality of the whole. The self is more than a computer, although many of the activities of the brain make great use of such processes. But the outer world is a vast array of possible data from which the mind of the person selects and organizes, and our clinical and observational studies all suggest that the basis for this creative selection resides at first in the powerful innate impetus to make "personal" relationships with the mother and then others. The experience with the ordinary good mother seems to be a basic requirement for the development of the active exploratory behavior that the infant is equipped to release. Above all, human relatedness rests on each person being governed by a self that can be created only by other selves.

This development has complex roots. The genic equipment prompts the groping, but the effective behavior then has to be learned. Therein lies one of the great breakthroughs in our understanding of the nature/nurture controversies that gave rise to deep, bitterly defended schisms in the scientific world until a few decades ago. In mammals, the fertilized egg is kept inside the female, to be followed after birth by the closeness from the adult to equip the child to fit in with the environment it will inhabit. Although humans lived in the ape-man stage as a social animal with resources for communication with others, the evolution of language made them capable of a very different interrelatedness. Language made selves known to other selves. Suckling the young also introduced a new factor into development, namely, the giving and receiving of tender loving care. Prior to this, attachments were made, but the complex feeling of "love" now appeared for the first time.

It may well be thought that I am recounting what is all too familiar. It is, and yet it seems so familiar, so much taken for granted, that its significance for the evolutionary perspective on the functions of the self is often overlooked. To account for the incredible resources that humans have acquired in controlling their environment, psychoanalysts have been satisfied with extraordinarily simple ideas, such as the ego developing to satisfy the instincts by an atomistic buildup from experiences. I believe all the evidence points to what appears to be a logical necessity—namely, a much more prepared foundation within human inherited endowment. We know that humans are now born, whatever their race or culture, with the vocalizations necessary for language, and that the particular language they learn will be that of their culture, transmitted by their caretakers and then their family and peers. The experience of nurturance "completes" the self by personalizing it. The self is then permanently related to others because others have been built into it, with the intense need for changing from infantile dependence to that dependence between autonomous adults. In this later feeling is the need to belong, to which is added the role of sexuality, which itself expands to the creation of the family.

In place of the hunter-gatherer life, the place of "work" is difficult to specify because of the change in its character and function, especially with constant technological advances. The significance that work once brought has been disturbingly exposed, as technology removes its deeply felt role. What seems to be present among the effects of unemployment is much more than the loss of wages. With no prospects of work, people feel lost in a personal way, and the rise in explosions of violence seems to express a degree of frustrated rage, as though an attack or insult was being perpetrated on adult selfhood. It is perhaps noteworthy, too, that not only is a positive need denied satisfaction, but the autonomy of the person is also undermined by enforced dependence on the community. As well as apparently satisfying a need to be involved as a contributor to the community, work gives a great deal of expression to instrumental talents and skills.

Although these points are in no way meant to be a systematically ordered listing, I believe they are sufficiently indicative of the functions that the individual self has to fulfill if humans are to survive. The functions conspicuously characteristic of humans depend heavily on language. Social animals lower in the evolutionary scale use various sounds and signs for communication in specific situations, as in warnings of danger, in mating calls, or in shared contacts of limited scope. Language, however, represents what has already been described as a quantum leap in the capacity to share. In the first place, it is not learned by an atomistic buildup from sensory elements. It is assimilated from the communication of the subjective state of the mother with that of the child. Stern quoted Vygotsky as maintaining that the essential problem of understanding language acquisition is how meanings enter the child's mind through the process of mutual negotiation. This achievement follows the capacity to have representations of things by imagining them and so to use them as symbols. Imaginative play with symbolic objects and with words when these become the symbols permits enormously increased development in knowledge of the world and in the communication of subjective states and intentions. All these make possible the degree of sharing between minds that the constant close relationships of living in communities entails. The continuity of self-feeling must be maintained if this experience is to be preserved with a cohesion of vastly enriched organization. Only a unity could act as the agent employing all this knowledge in planning action; and with its consciousness, this gestalt is the self.

Early Development of the Self

The first preoccupying activity of the self is learning how to relate effectively with the mother. Feeding, of course, is dominant but not exclusively so. Sucking is mediated by a mother who, with the infant, fits the joint behavior into a successful pattern. The infant must be innately equipped to incorporate from the breast and to take in from the world, with a hunger originating from both sources, needs that can be recognized and responded to by the mother. At first, the self does not need to be conscious of itself in the manner of the adult. In an environment that is actively anticipating and providing for the needs of the self, the organization of experience can proceed by a sentience that monitors and distinguishes what feels "right" or "good" from what does not meet the tensions of need and so is affectively frustrating—that is, "bad" or "wrong." The growth of self-awareness, however, must begin early to develop the capacity to be alert to the attitudes of others by recognizing their emotional states.

The clinical evidence from disorders in the self strongly suggests that effective development of the self rests on a joyful, empathic responsiveness from the mother. Various limited frustrations of particular behaviors can be readily tolerated if the overall feelings communicated by the mother, and later by the father, come from a genuine joy in the baby as it is. Such an attitude puts no pressure on the baby's spontaneous maturational achievements to match preconceived images the parents may be using as molds into which, often unconsciously, the baby is to be fitted.

Good-enough mothering gives the first "layering" in the structuring of the self as a person. At this stage (I do not think we can be too specific in terms of age), the main achievement is a self that can feel secure and ready to explore and incorporate the world as physical and psychological capacities and talents emerge. From the start, an immense amount of experience with the social and physical worlds is rapidly acquired. A "person" seems to be being established at first without much differentiation of gender, even though babies are responded to somewhat differently according to their sex. The next main structuring is for this person to become more specifically a male or female. It would seem from disorders of the self that the relationship with the father now becomes of critical importance. The growing assertiveness of the boy must be responded to as before by the mother's joyful acceptance, but the father's acceptance now needs to be available as well for both the girl and boy infant. I have also concluded that, for the eventual integration of the self, the relationship between the parents and their joint attitudes toward the child are almost as critically important as that of each parent separately.

In the earliest months—the traditional oral stage—there seems to be no question that orality represents a more general incorporative need for which the alimentary function is the prototype. The infant needs to incorporate the mother in a personal way, that is, as having the significance of a whole object and not one confined to the feeding activity. The affective qualities of the physical and psychological incorporations, however, seem closely linked at this initial phase, if we are to explain how greed for food or drink is so often substituted later for personal deprivation. In addiction there is, of course, as the physiological result of the intake, the ensuing feeling of relaxation, of general loss of tension from frustrated social needs, and eventually of being in a state of some euphoria.

The question of how much the infant self is differentiated from the mother has tended to be regarded as settled by the assumption that there is a phase of nondifferentiation. This belief has been related to the phenomena of merging and identification, and also to the amount of differentiation or perception of a separate figure that would be possible with what is known of neurophysical development. Stern (1985) strongly advocates a recognized differentiation of the infant's own boundaries as present from birth, based partly on the grounds that it is difficult to see how two separate psyches could be undifferentiated, but mainly based on the findings from the infant–mother studies. From what we have stressed about the operation of an innate organizing principle, it would entail from the start in any organism a powerful assertion and maintenance of autonomy and of the integrity of its wholeness.

It is not at all fanciful to imagine such a powerful autonomy being present, yet covered over by the closeness of the attachment of the infant to the mother. When a self is postulated as the realization, from experience in relating to the mother, of a potential in the form of an innate gestalt that has the "shape" or "feel" of a person built into it, and that is strongly motivated to encounter this shape in the outer world, then a phase of undifferentiation is neither necessary nor conceivable. Such a gestalt would be activated not by energies external to it, but by its own nature to seek completion from the appropriate sources in the environment. This assumption implies nothing different in principle from the other innate behavioral systems, for example, seeking the breast and "knowing" when it is found. There is no doubt that the ordinary mother (and, indeed, adults in general) is highly and innately motivated to respond to the infant from the earliest stages as having this "potential person" quality.

We know, too, that sucking from the breast is not the action of a passive infant being supplied with all it needs. The infant shows a pronounced dynamic of its own to regulate the feeding process to match its own feelings, to train its mother, so to speak, in what is a relationship of mutual satisfaction. When things do not go well, there is marked disturbance in the infant's whole state. It is also well recognized that although various physical factors may cause difficulties, problems also commonly arise when the mother's attitude differs from that of the ordinarily spontaneously responding mother. Serious frustrations are then felt with great intensity, as witnessed in the infant's increasingly desperate signals that things should be put right. The self-feeling in these circumstances is undoubtedly one of disturbed security, with inhibitions in the readiness to relate to the external world socially and in instrumental inhibitions of various kinds. We also need to note Spitz's (1965) finding that meeting the bodily needs for food does not necessarily keep the baby alive. There is a hunger for stimulating exchanges with the caretakers that must be satisfied to foster a vital dynamic to go on living.

We cannot deal with all the specific features of the rapidly changing situation of the infant with its mother. I simply wish to indicate that autonomous reactions—either positive, in which case the dynamic of the self is encouraged, or negative, when it meets with varying degrees of deprivation, from the less intense to violent expressions of aggressive behavior—all point to affective experience and responses that constitute an independently operating infant self. The infant's recognition of the boundaries of its own body at quite an early age also suggests that this differentiated self is present then (as in Stern's striking data on Siamese twins).

Intentionality

The existence of a subjective sense of the self and its conscious intentionality is strongly suggested by the observational data on infants approaching the end of their first year. The infant also "understands" the mother's subjective state about this time (for instance, see Stern on infant and mother "pointing," and the "visual cliff" data). By the end of the second year, the subjective sense of self, and of the self as agent in creating imagined relationships to gratify fantasied relationships, is clearly established. Stern's account of the emergence of the core self, the subjective self, of each of these with "the other," and finally the verbal self and the narrative self presents a convincing picture. What I believe to be one of its most fundamental implications is the role of holistic patterns from the start. Particularly important is the discovery of the innate organization of transmodal perceptions with integrated modes of response. We cannot conceive of such integrated holistic activity without assuming an integrated whole that mediates it. Although not so confidently established, it seems to me of great importance that Stern virtually accepts Trevarthan's belief in the existence of an innate capacity for the shared awareness of human subjectivity. Moreover, I find highly plausible Trevarthan's view that this developmental leap represents the differentiation of a coherent field of intentionality.

Intentionality has recently become very much a focus of philosophical concern. Its existence is much more difficult to conceive and to establish when we do not take into account the evolutionary development of the self; and, of course, for the physically minded theorists, it is thought to be a vitalistic notion. Thus, assuming the absolute necessity of the organism to maintain interchanges with the environment—an assumption so obvious when bodily processes are considered—a necessary condition for the survival of homo sapiens, the social animal par excellence, is the constant outreach to grapple with and overcome the limitations of the environment, both social and physical. The cognitive explorations required here would alone make for a perpetual intentionality, but the innate dynamic of the person at all stages, apart from the need to relate to others, has this need to keep realizing the self through the incessant urge to know more. That was what the Romantic poets sensed in their appraisal of the pleasure from knowledge and the deep identity of truth and beauty. What evolution has created so far is this innate organization that, out of its experiences, evolves the personalization of the organizing principle in a creative interplay between the child and its family, and subsequently between individuals and their culture. The subjectivity of the person is an incredibly sensitive monitor for regulating personal well-being, a sense of being, and with the further sensing that this feeling is only "right" or "complete" when it incorporates the innate need for "being" to be always "becoming." This truth is proverbial in almost all cultures, and I shall mention only this saying in the Gaelic culture of Celtic Scotland: "Joy of seeking, joy of never finding!"

It is from the interplay of the self with its culture that Erikson's epigenetic phases evolved. Characteristically, his phases are not tied to libidinal zones, but to changes in the quality of the dominant self-feeling in its relationships with its society. The patterns of relatedness thought to be derived from the libidinal zones are there. As Stern stressed, these patterns do not constitute a succession of stages, with each replacing the predecessor. What we now see to be covered by "orality" is the behavior determined by the intense incorporative needs to secure the appropriate intake from the environment, bodily and personally, for the developments urged by the genic inheritance. The resultant oral structuring is one that maintains a permanent process in the continuing of the self-process. Our clinical work demonstrates daily the labile balance of the appropriate give and take in social relations. With the good-enough mothering experience, this balance is maintained from everyday transactions. Where this experience has been lacking, we see greed and infantile dependence reemerging as the regression to more primitive modes of "taking in" to make good the deficiency. Early stages never disappear but remain as modes of relating that can be reactivated by various environmental factors.

Intersubjective sharing, as mentioned earlier, is the means through which individuals can relate with rapid appraisals of intentions and affects in others. This sharing develops from the simultaneous acquisition of self-awareness and the knowledge of the self-states of others. In short, the person is created from interchanges with other persons. Infant development research shows the progressive gains and their extraordinary rapidity from the latter part of the first year onward. The period of the most intense socialization has been described by Bowlby and his colleagues in terms of bonding and attachment theory. The attachment phenomena are very real, but I do not think these terms are adequate for the ongoing inner processes. The period of intense closeness that lays the foundation for attachment is used by Mahler as the one for the symbiotic relationship from which individuation evolves. For myself, I find it clinically much more useful to see the closeness as necessary behavior for the gestation of the self. Far from being undifferentiated, the self is being formed steadily, and any interference with this self-determined dynamic elicits intense aggression. Not unexpectedly, the embryoniclike state of the self needs the closest contact with the mother's "self" as well as her care.

The concept of an *innate dynamic gestalt* underlying the formation of the person resembles Lichtenstein's organizing principle, which constitutes the potential self that is then personalized by the earliest relationships with the mother. Moreover, this potential being personalized by this specific experience becomes the unique identity of the person. I have suggested that this potential be conceptualized as an inherited gestalt that seeks to become a person by finding the "expected" encounters. (Such a possibility is fairly readily conceivable today with the discovery of such holistic fields of force in the organism as are revealed in holograms.) The fitting of a particular gestalt with its environment is a process going on all the time. Postulating a central agent implies a view of development proceeding from this center by differentiation, with the creation of various subsystems.

22. FAIRBAIRN AND THE SELF

In their superb account of the central issue in the development of psychoanalytic thought during the last few decades, namely, the dialectic between the drive theory and object relations, Jay R. Greenberg and Stephen A. Mitchell (1983) describe Fairbairn's contributions as having "a lasting place and a seminal role in the history of psychoanalytic ideas" (p. 176). Probably only a small proportion of analysts could evaluate such a judgment, because this work has been largely ignored. Apart from Guntrip's (1961) enthusiastic advocacy, few careful appraisals have been made, the most notable exception being that of Greenberg and Mitchell. They give various reasons for this neglect amongst which is the fact that he never produced a coherent and comprehensive theory but left a series of papers he described as "the progressive development of a line of thought" (1952, p. x). It occurred to me that a useful way of paying tribute to his work would be to consider the position at which he had arrived and then to suggest one direction in which his line seemed to be heading. Obviously this is a speculative exercise on my part; nevertheless I believe that an assimilation of his work and his personality lead one to ponder where psychoanalytic theory might go in furthering its development.

Like many thinkers, Fairbairn often stressed the importance of factors in the personality that would influence the form of his creativity. In formulating an alternative to the metapsychology underlying Freud's structural theory, I wish to refute Winnicott and Kahn's (1953) suggestion that Fairbairn's motives were in any way "to knock Freud." Fairbairn's attitude to Freud was never other than reverential, but he made a clear distinction, which Winnicott blurs by referring to the person and not his theories. For a cultured scholar, to challenge seriously the views of another thinker is the highest tribute that can be paid to him. Moreover, Fairbairn, while he naturally wished his contribution to be recognized, was dedicated to the development of the psychoanalytic endeavour as a whole. He rejected at once any attempt to make a distinct school from his views. He regarded his own work as a part of the developing understanding that he believed to be an urgent need in the current theory.

The essential personality features that fired his thinking were, of course, the main motives, and especially the unconscious ones, that determined his perceptions within the analytic situation. The following brief notes on his personal development will provide data for an appraisal of some of these forces.

FAIRBAIRN'S PERSONAL DEVELOPMENT

Fairbairn was the only child of middle-aged parents in whom the formalities of conduct had all the prominence given to them in the later stages of Victorian Britain. His father was a valuer whose background was socially limited and with the harsh religious Calvinistic values that were upheld with the particular sternness prevalent in Scotland since the Reformation. Attendance at Church twice on Sundays was maintained rigorously.

His mother, a surprising choice of wife for a strong Calvinist, was English and an Anglican. She came from Yeomen stock who had farmed their land in Yorkshire since Norman times. Any freer attitudes from her religion were overshadowed by her controlling nature; she was, in fact, somewhat of a martinet. Both parents provided devoted care but in an atmosphere from which much of the joyful spontaneity of the ordinary family was missing. A nanny, however, gave their son some of the vital quality. On the positive side, they encouraged him in his intellectual development, allowed him to share in their social life, and his father took him to places of interest. An important experience was the frequent holiday visiting of relatives and friends where he mixed with cousins and other children. Several of these families had close links with Anglican clergymen who introduced him to a very different picture of life within the Church groups, one in which there was a good deal of lively spontaneity.

Behind the social exterior, however, there were disturbing and puzzling forces. His father could not urinate unless all the rest of the household were out of sight. This difficulty, however, was painfully confused for him by an incident in a train. The family was travelling to go on holiday in the north of Scotland. There were no toilets on the train and the father got into a great state from a compulsive need to urinate. This was done in the carriage with Ronald sitting opposite his father, holding up a newspaper as a screen from his mother and other ladies while his father urinated on the floor in obviously great distress. This incident left a profound mark on the boy then 8 years old. Also about this period was a traumatic experience with his mother. He had seen some blood-stained diapers in a pail and expressed his curiosity to his mother. She flew into a frenzy of rage, beat him, and locked him up for several hours. She became preoccupied in these early years with a need to stop him touching his penis, a proscription that was accompanied by threats of the awful things that could happen to men who did this or who went with bad women. She thus became an extremely frightening figure in regard to the assertion of his masculine sexuality, while his father remained a mystery in this respect.

As the only child in this setting it was inevitable that he should turn to his inner world with a great deal of fantasy life. Nevertheless, he was not a social isolate. At school he held his own with others, largely relying on his intellectual interests, but never liked school because of a feeling he did not possess their ability to assert themselves in games and in sexual exhibitionism in adolescence.

His inner imaginative life, however, was responded to, and that a positive self-feeling was being established was seen in the way he adapted to the constraints of his environment. Amongst his interests he began to respond to the Church attendance by appraising the sermons and assimilating the Christian gospel. His early adolescence was beset with torturing conflicts about the emergence of his sexual feelings and the now perpetually active internalised mother keeping him under observation. The denial of his physical masculinity had inevitably left residues of hate and resentment tied to his internalised parents, the savage mother who had attacked him and the father who had failed to establish himself as a strong loving figure supporting his natural development. This sense of deprivation and the aggression associated with it had earlier roots, however. He seemed not to have felt an overall loving encouragement from his mother's controlled attitudes and, though there is a very early memory of a helpful father, he became mainly a part of the parental couple who excluded him. A reference to an early bed wetting scene that Fairbairn made later appeared to be associated with attacks on this parental relationship.

By the time he was about to enter the University, he had evolved an internal change that in many ways was an ingenious constructive solution to all these conflicts. He decided to become a clergyman. This choice was acceptable to his parents and, at the same time, it permitted him to aspire to owning his masculine sexuality within the confines laid down by the Church and in his immediate life, to explore intellectually what had become a powerful urge, namely, to understand the phenomena of conscience, sin, and guilt, which seemed to him so bound up with sexuality. Through this ego-ideal he could release the pent up forces in his repressed masculine assertive self. Through a relationship with God as his loving and beloved son, he could abjure hate and make reparation to his parents through the strong altruistic drive to help others in their psychological stresses. The intense confusion induced in his boyhood by his mother's branding of his penis as a potential source of so much evil was now replaced, in consciousness at any rate, by its acceptance for procreation. The resolution of his oedipal situation was, nevertheless, a complicated one. He had chosen to take the degree in philosophy before he went on to theology in the hope that he would clarify the moral issues his sexual feelings had raised. Also, as it was in the philosophy department of the university that psychology was taught, he would learn about sexuality as an innate propensity in man in an academic way freed from the irrational views he had encountered at home. However, a conflict between his parents now arose over his going to the university. His mother, who had become progressively ambitious for him, socially and professionally, wished him to go to Oxford. For his father, this was not to be contemplated. For one thing, it would be expensive and, if he had to go to the University at all, there was a highly reputable one on the doorstep. Furthermore,

Oxford was overrun with so many Anglican clerics who were morally lax and part of an episcopacy. This negativity was greatly resented by Fairbairn, and it stirred deeper levels because it was felt to be part of a long-standing disposition to deny him opportunities. The result was that, while his father accepted Edinburgh University, Fairbairn now felt his mother to be his ally and his father the castrating parent in regard to the thrust of his life.

Intellectually he was in his element at the university and socially he took part in various student societies devoted to scholarly issues or to social causes. The inhibition of his sexuality, however, was to be seen in the absence of any emotional relationships with young women though he made the acquaintance of several. His practical Christianity, which was sincere and deeply rooted, found expression in his work with youth groups in deprived areas. Though essentially introverted he had many friendships, mainly with people who shared his interests, and several of these were maintained throughout his life. With those with whom he felt at ease, he could be lively and entertaining, although the outer layers of reserve and formality were there. His dominant interest, however, in human and social problems usually focused on the need to understand the essential principles underlying the presenting behaviour; and he was sharp in his critical appraisals of the assumption made. Appropriate conceptual rigour was an absolute requirement for him as a basis for action. It represented a demystification about what was being felt by people, in other words, an undoing of his early experience with his parents.

The university teaching was a great disappointment in one respect when he found almost as much evasion over the issues of conscience, guilt, sin, and sexuality as he had found at home. The intellectual discipline, however, was congenial with its strengthening of his self-confidence in the intellectual field. The avoidance of open discussion of the issues that were so important to him may well have urged him when he completed his philosophy degree to spend a year on Hellenic studies with visits to some of the European universities.

In the autumn of 1914 when he was 25, he began the theological training in Edinburgh University. The First World War had recently begun so that there was the question of joining the armed service. His mother tried to keep him at home but he settled the conflict by joining the Royal Artillery the following summer. It was not until 1917 that his unit went to Palestine where a few months later he took part in the triumphant entry into Jerusalem. While in the army he had become keenly interested in the "new psychology" developing from the writings of Freud and Jung, and within a few weeks of his discharge from the army at the end of 1918 he had begun to study medicine with the aim of becoming a psychoanalyst. The determinants of this change were many, including an aversion that had grown towards preaching and the positive motives of acquiring sound understanding of human conflict along with the means of offering practical help. In the middle of his medical training he began a personal analysis with E. H. Connell, an Australian business man who had moved to Edinburgh to become a medical psychotherapist. He had had analysis with

Ernest Jones so that his experience had been in the Freudian approach. After gaining his medical qualification in 1923, he did a short spell in general practice and then proceeded with training in general psychiatry. In 1924 his father died unexpectedly from septicaemia and Fairbairn seemed to be liberated by this event. He arranged expeditiously for his mother to be established in a new home, and he began his private psychoanalytic practice in 1926.

In the spring of that year he met a young lady, a medical student, with whom he rapidly formed a close relationship and they married in the autumn. She came from an old landed family and was used to a more social life than Ronald. He joined in this pattern for a period that ended with the birth of a daughter in 1927.

Despite the radical changes in his life situation his intense investment in his psychoanalytic work grew steadily. He was brought into contact with Jones and Glover and with the latter he became quite close friends though they could meet only occasionally. To them Fairbairn was clearly a good recruit to the movement with his manifest knowledge and dedication. He considered a move to London, but with no suitable post available, he remained in Edinburgh. Appointments to the departments of psychology and psychiatry were very helpful, for though financially they were of little value, they gave what to him was of great importance, namely, membership in the academic world. His broad education in the humanities, theology, and then the medical sciences had given a greater definition to his profound impetus to further his understanding of the person. Intellectually, he had become completely convinced that scientific materialism and atomistic approaches could not account for the unique qualities of the individual. The psychological field was, for him, the study of the human being at the personal level, a view that assumed the personality to act in a holistic manner.

Fairbairn's devotion to the understanding of human nature was thus closely similar to Freud's. Unlike Freud, he was also imbued from his own early unhappiness with the therapeutic aim of relieving the suffering caused by psychological distress. For him, however, this motive in no way detracted from his scientific concern. To study the person at the personal level with all his subjectivity had to be the essential focus. Concepts that reduced personal phenomena to impersonal processes were not acceptable to him, a philosophical stance which, from his student days, he retained uncompromisingly all his life. In his first clinical paper, written in 1927 though not published until 1952 when he included it in his book, interestingly enough is a study of some features in the religious phantasies of a woman patient. He relates the patient's sexual feelings and phantasies to the classical oedipal situation and the libido theory, but there is at the same time a recognition of these and her religious phantasies as attempts to meet the need for a missing personal relationship with her father.

In the next few years he made an intense study of Freud and Jung for his postgraduate thesis on a comparison of Freud's concept of oppression with Jones's views on dissociation. Although he strongly favours Freud's line of thought, he criticises some of his concepts, especially that of the id compared with those of the British psychologists and philosophers who regard the innate propensities as structured by experience. As he mentioned later, he felt that he had now mastered the principles upon which his work was being based.

A second clinical paper was written in 1931, again on a woman patient, but with a physical genital abnormality. He was now particularly impressed by the multiplicity of personification she showed, and he was again critical of Freud's tripartite theory as not doing justice to the complexities of the structuring within the personality. He recognizes functioning structural units corresponding with Freud's theory yet in each there were components from all three of Freud's schemes. Each of these units operated as a separate self even though they were largely unconscious. Furthermore, he found that the common patterns of the neuroses, for example, hysteria, obsessional neurosis, phobias, and paranoid features, all appeared in the same patient at different stages of the analysis. He therefore concluded that these conditions were not nosological entities each related to a particular fixation at a libidinal stage of development but were labile defences adopted to deal with the unresolved conflicts from the schizoid or depressive positions.

This paper was read by request to the British Psychoanalytical Society. It made a highly favourable impression with the result that he was elected to associate membership of the society so that he was now formally recognized and accepted as a qualified psychoanalyst. At this period he was also becoming greatly interested in Melanie Klein's views. She had come to stay in London a few years earlier so that her work had become well known to the London analysts. He was particularly stimulated by her picture of the inner world populated by a range of internalized figures fashioned by the child from the experiences with his parents.

The personal and professional situation in Edinburgh for the first few years of his psychoanalytic career had been very favourable for his productivity. He was happily married with a young family so that any deep anxieties about his masculine gender from his mother's early persecutions were not manifest. The fact that he had rather belittled his father as unsupportive was also prevented from arousing disturbing guilt by the approval of the university professors in psychiatry and psychology of his growing standing professionally.

Sadly, there began in 1932 some changes that caused him considerable stress. A new professor of psychiatry had arrived who was hostile to psychoanalysis. A somewhat autocratic person, he soon made it plain that Fairbairn was not welcomed as a colleague. Simultaneously, the professor of psychology, a person who was widely respected and with a kindly disposition that aroused a good deal of affection, began to be deeply disturbed by his closer contact with the psychoanalytic viewpoint that he was increasingly encountering as they worked together on the cases seen in their Child Guidance Clinic. He distanced himself professionally from Fairbairn who was eventually forced to resign from both of his university appointments. Although not showing much, Fairbairn was rather depressed by this loss of the support he had enjoyed; but a much more distressing situation was developing in his domestic situation. His wife was becoming increasingly hostile to his psychoanalytic work, which isolated him not only during the day but in many evenings when he would retire to his study to clarify his understanding of the clinical problems he was identifying. Despite the strain, he remained deeply attached to his wife and family and he did his best to maintain a manageable compromise. There was, however, no question of his withdrawing from his work. From the time he had formulated his life purpose, his dedication to it was the paramount cohesive force in his being. To have given it up would have been an emasculation of his self with, almost certainly, psychic death.

By 1935 there were recurrent outbursts of acute hostility from his wife and there was now manifest a symptom that had restrictive effect on his freedom to travel. He developed the urinary symptom that his father had had: difficulty urinating in the presence of others. None of his friends or colleagues knew of it until after his death. Fortunately, there was no inhibition of his intellectual work. In addition to the stresses mentioned there seems also to have been some unconscious disturbance as his work became more and more involved with the earliest stages in the development of the personality and with Melanie Klein's views that he was progressively assimilating. Her paper on the psychogenesis of manic-depressive states (Klein 1934) had made a great impact on him in the way she brought out the powerful dynamics of unconscious phantasies of relationships between various internalised figures and between them and the central self or ego. (The effect of this paper was a startling one in the way it split the British Psychoanalytic Society and, indeed, threatened the unity of the movement in Europe and, years later, internationally.) Her views had a profoundly stimulating effect on Fairbairn and almost certainly facilitated the crucial observations that he made during the next 5 years of a group of notably schizoid patients. This paper appears to have disturbed Fairbairn by stirring up phantasies of the destruction of the parental couple by urinary sadistic attacks. It did not, however, interfere with his clinical work and the creative thinking engendered subsequently.

For 5 years after Klein's seminal paper, Fairbairn seemed to be assimilating her theories against the background of his growing experience. He wrote a brief clinical paper in 1936 in which he described the reactions of some of his patients following the death of George V and which supported Klein's views of the nature and origin of some of the phantasies evoked by this event. Other papers in this period, though not using clinical data, did make extensive use of her ideas. It was not until a year after World War II broke out that he gave the first indication of a major creative thrust that had gained momentum, and produced a series of papers in the next 5 years embodying the essentials of the new theoretical position that he considered to be an essential change from the assumptions underlying the classical psychoanalytic etiological principles. It was unfortunate for the reception of his views that the restrictions imposed in the United Kingdom by the war prevented the publication of his first paper for it was here that he described the crucial clinical data on which he founded his radically new position. This paper eventually appeared in 1952 when he brought it together with other papers that had appeared in journals during the later years of the war.

The first paper was entitled "Schizoid Factors in the Personality," and though not generally appreciated at the time, it indicated his holistic approach to the understanding of the person. A notable exception to this lack of understanding was the response of Ernest Jones who notes in his Preface that, in contrast with Freud, Fairbairn starts from the centre of the personality, the ego, and from there considers the vicissitudes of its attempts to relate to the external figures essential for its survival. Freud's theories were largely founded on the vicissitudes of instinctual gratification driven by the search for the pleasure that ensued and so he had to construct the self from these instinctual activities. This foundation had given rise to his theory of narcissism in which the libido, or energy of the sexual instincts, was invested in the ego whence it was progressively moved to external objects. Schizoid personalities were assumed to have failed to progress to this externalisation and, instead, to have remained with most of their available libido narcissistically positioned in the ego. They were on this account unsuitable for analysis because of their virtual incapacity to make emotional relationships with others. Melanie Klein had shown that such personalities had a rich inner world of relationships that, however, were largely used to compensate for the absence of relationships with others, and that their failure to make such relationships was caused by the anxieties associated with them. Fairbairn, working on this basis, found that when the origins of these anxieties were analysed, these individuals showed their longing for good emotional relationships with others and their capacity to make these.

Adults with marked schizoid personalities have three prominent characteristics that may be so successfully concealed that they are only discernible as analysis proceeds. These are: (a) an attitude of omnipotence; (b) an attitude of isolation and detachment; and (c) a preoccupation with inner reality. Of these, it is plainly the last that is the basic feature with the others stemming from it. It is also clear that these are the attitudes of a whole person and, since they have roots in the earliest stages of development, they suggest that this whole is present from the start. Fairbairn terms this original unity the *ego* though it would have been more appropriate to have used the *self*. The function of this self is the adaptation of primal instinctual activity to outer, essentially social reality. Perceptions of reality have to be integrated and behaviour matched accordingly, and with his capacity to make imagined relations, these have to be distinguished from the outer world. Such integration of experience can only be effective through the agency of a system operating from the start as an organized whole.

Psychoanalysts have long related the development of the ego or self as the infant's relationships within the family and to link distortions in development to the oral stage. Fairbairn accepts that what happens in these first relationships plays a crucial part in shaping the future personality. In considering this question he makes a radical departure from the classical position.

FAIRBAIRN'S ACHIEVEMENT

When I ask myself what the significance is of Fairbairn's contribution to psychoanalysis, my answer will strike most analysts as making grandiose claims. I believe, nevertheless, it is entirely accurate to say that he was the first to propose in a systematic manner the Copernican change of founding the psychoanalytic theory of human personality on the experiences within social relationships instead of on the discharge of instinctual tensions originating solely within the individual. In short, he replaced the closed-system standpoint of nineteenth-century science with the open-system concepts that were evolved by the middle of the present century to account for the development of living organisms, in which the contribution of the environment has to be considered at all times.

His viewpoint is receiving increasingly sympathetic and careful appraisal. Here I wish to stress that his specific theories about the structuring of the personality will certainly be amended, but such advances will be made by the adoption of his basic assumptions.

In judging the importance of his work, it is appropriate to comment first on his challenge to the fundamental assumptions upon which Freud's classical theories were based and which he retained until his death. Having asserted the vicissitudes in the personal relationships between the infant, his mother, and his family, as the primary consideration for the development of the personality instead of the instincts, there was, of course, no question of the instinctive endowment being ignored. The issue was how the interaction of the innate factors and the environment was conceived. Fairbairn was highly critical of the way in which instinctive energies were reified, one could almost say deified, in early psychoanalytic theory. Guntrip, following on this lead, has been interpreted as dispensing with "the instincts," and at times he can give this impression. Like Fairbairn, however, he was in no way a naîve thinker. What they both felt strongly about, and it was this aspect of Fairbairn's writings that attracted Guntrip in the first instance, was that the concept of "drives," the motivating forces originating in the instincts, was being used to create a quite inadequate picture of human nature.

The danger they reacted to was the insidious dehumanization of man with no adequate account of his nature at the personal level. With Guntrip's background as a clergyman it was easy to "explain away" his arguments, though these were put forcefully. (It was not so widely known that Fairbairn had started out to become a clergyman and had retained an active membership of the Church, otherwise he, too, might have had an even less serious reception.)

The accepted theory of the instincts had, therefore, to be questioned as an appropriate foundation for the understanding of the conflicts underlying the presenting problems. Though that was naturally of the first importance, there were also dangers from its influence on social and cultural values. The pleasure accompanying the satisfactions of instinctive needs did not lose its importance; it was essential in selecting and maintaining relatedness. When pleasure seeking became the foremost motive, however, this was the result of a deterioration in the essential relationships, a failure in the attainment of the capacity for rich and mutual relations with others in which the individuality of the other provides a deeper satisfaction than the use of him or her to provide gratification. The unfortunate consequences of adopting Freud's instinct theory as making gratification the aim could be seen when the writings of social philosophers like Herbert Marcuse (1955) and Norman O. Brown (1959) were taken to justify sexual indulgence as something with little or no restraint—for "kicks," as the saying went. Fairbairn was not concerned with moral values here. The biological importance of his views stemmed from his conviction that the family is the crucial agency in the development of healthy, creative individuals. For it to fulfil this function, sexuality is an essential component in the maintenance of the optimal relationship between the parents and between them and their children.

Both Fairbairn and Guntrip were trained in philosophy. Other philosophers, Yankelovich and Barrett (1970), gave a highly pertinent critique of psychoanalytic theory. While neither was a practising analyst, both were well informed and deeply convinced of the importance of psychoanalysis for the human sciences in general. Their concern was to further its acceptance and development by getting its basic assumptions right, for in their view no science can progress unless this is done, and they thought those of psychoanalysis were wrong. Despite a great deal of discussion with a group of distinguished analysts in Boston in the USA, they make no reference to Fairbairn, presumably because his book was not made known to them. (Elizabeth Zetzel, a leading figure of the psychoanalytical establishment in the Boston area, may have contributed to this neglect. In her article "Recent British Approaches to Problems of Early Mental Development" (1955) she treated Fairbairn's views as an ingenious intellectual exercise, without seeing the fundamental challenge that his powerful clinical data had forced upon him.) I have always felt this was a great pity, because these thinkers reached conclusions closely similar to his and so might have added to the impact of all of them. They propose as a fundamentally required step the replacement of the *id* by one of *developmentals*. These are the dynamic structures that are formed when instinctive activity interacts with critical experience at specific stages in the life cycle. Their concepts derive from a wide consideration of human development, social, cultural, and biological, and their arguments add up to conclusions that cannot be ignored, the more so when placed alongside those reached by Fairbairn 25 years earlier. Nevertheless, their line of thought has had little effect upon psychoanalysis. The response to their book reassured me that the reluctant recognition of Fairbairn's views could not be justified by the commonly expressed superficial reasons.

The issue that they and the "object-relations" theorists had introduced has been a preoccupying one amongst analysts for the last 50 years. In an admirably critical and comprehensive account of its history, Greenberg and Mitchell (1983) have described this dialectic as showing the progressive encroachments of the object-relationships viewpoint into the drive theory. These challenges have been met by a succession of accommodations made by tenacious analytic thinkers, which bring out the increasing strain of defending an untenable position. In their constructive critique of the psychoanalytic view of human nature, Yankelovich and Barrett (1970) describe a similar process with which they draw a parallel in the development of astronomy, with the constant addition of epicycles to the traditional scheme of the solar system.

As an evaluation of Fairbairn's views, I believe that that of Greenberg and Mitchell (1983) is quite unusual in its scope and penetrative accuracy. They note that the abstractness of his language can mislead the reader into thinking that, in his stress on libido as object seeking rather than pleasure seeking, these are somewhat Talmudic and arcane distinctions. What Fairbairn is suggesting, according to them, is really a fundamentally different view of human motivation, meaning, and values. The orientation of the infant to others is there from the very beginning because the infant has adaptive genic roots for his biological survival. Moreover, this urge to seek and maintain interaction with others is characteristic of adults at all stages of life.

Development begins in the total dependence of the infant, at which stage a security is normally established that lays the foundation for the later transformations towards the normal personality. Fairbairn's views of the transitional stage between this infantile dependency and maturity are not spelled out, and this is a weak feature of his developmental theory, though this lack is easily remedied from the wealth of data on childhood and adolescence. He does stress, however, that the earliest structuring from the experience in relationships forms a basic pattern that shapes the future patterns of relationships.

Clearly Fairbairn has left much that needs to be expanded, and what he ended with points to tasks for a more complete theory of the self as fashioned from relationships. His primary text, so to speak, is that the individual from the very start has to be loved for himself by the unconditional loving care of (at first) the mother. This loving care has then to be continued by the father as well, and adapted within the family to the specific behavioural stages brought about by maturation and the cultural environment. In all development and in maturity, persons have to be in satisfying relationships for their own survival together with that of their groups.

Assumptions about the infant not having any ego or self at the start contributed to the long period in which the self was scarcely mentioned. Freud's "Ich" had the significance of the personal self until, as Bettelheim (1983) suggested, the absorption in instinct theory led to it being replaced by the impersonal "ego." When Hartmann (1958) found it necessary to postulate an autonomous ego, he described the self as the separate structure that was cathected in narcissism. He did not elaborate the concept of the self, however, because of his inability to free himself from the traditional drive energies, even though he realized these were making a theoretical impasse.

If we take Fairbairn's basic statement we have clearly got to conceptualize a potential structure, operating as a whole, that only becomes functional, in the effective way for which it is designed, through certain experience with the mother, the father, and the wider society. It "seeks" to become the organizing agent of a conscious "person" who remains aware of the continuity of his past with his present and of the future as immanent, and with a unique sense of himself as having an identity in relationship with other persons.

As mentioned earlier, Fairbairn accepted that *self* is a more appropriate term in most of his considerations, since it refers to the whole from which subselves are split off. The ego is useful for the central self, that is, the dominant part of the self that incorporates the main purposes and goals of the individual in his relationships with the outer world and with which consciousness is usually associated.

Along with his humanistic and philosophical background, the understanding of the personality for Fairbairn had to be firmly based upon its evolution, that is, its biological roots. A modern image of man must illumine his essential properties, and for this I find Chein's (1972) definition invaluable. I have already referred to this but it will bear repetition. "The essential psychological human quality is, thus, one of commitment to a developing and continuing set of unending, interacting, interdependent, and mutually modifying long-range enterprises" (p. 289). When we start with a modern biological outlook, we depart from Freud, for whom the science available allowed only the Newtonian base with its emphasis on the second law of thermodynamics. Chein concludes that man's motivation is a unique development. As a living organism, man is removed from the closed systems characterized by entropy, and this focus has to be replaced by a commitment to accomplish something—even if only the survival of his family in the environment.

As an open system, the living organism is *negentropic*, a feature maintained by its perpetual incorporation of energy. All organisms are created from other organisms. (For a modern perspective on evolution I am indebted to Jantsch [1980] and Waddington and Jantsch [1976].) They are wholes that cannot be made from the aggregation of parts. Their constant exchanges with the environment mean that constant transformations are proceeding, despite which they maintain their own characteristic form by a process of self-regulation. What is essential in these continuous self-renewals and self-expressions are the self-bounding processes rather than the changing structures. While evolution has led to many subsystems in the organism that maintain an equilibrium or steady state, this homoeostasis does not obtain for the organism as a whole. At this level, equilibrium means death, because of the ending of the never-ceasing interaction with the environment in which processes of self-transformation and self-maintenance constitute life. As Sir Julian Huxley said, our perspective for man must be *sub specie evolutionis* rather than *sub specie aeternitatis*.

In the lower levels of the evolutionary scale the form of the animal along with its behavioural repertoire is directly determined by the genic inheritance. Thus, given that the dinosaurs lay their eggs in places that provide the appropriate environment, and with some early protection against external dangers, the embryo can emerge and fend for itself. An organizing principle within the fertilized egg provides for successful maturation under these conditions. Life can be lived in an action mode with learning restricted to the limited skills required to feed, to fight, and to mate. Evolutionary development does not greatly require increased adaptive capacities as long as the environment provides what is needed. Their huge physical bulk could evolve along with a relatively small brain being adequate for perceptual-motor learning and the coordination of all the bodily parts by the organizing principle its nervous system carried. Clearly this organizing principle is of the greatest importance, since it embodies the management of the life process as a whole. In the lower animals we can conceive of it carrying out this function on the basis of an affective field that controls the fitting together of sentient experiences from bodily and environmental changes according as the overall state is within the range of what feels "right" or not "painful." Innate patterns for finding the objects required for survival can be transmitted by the genic inheritance, as they are in the human infant in "desiring" and seeking the breast. In an unchanging environment little need for complex information storage arises. Any threat to its autonomy is a threat to life and so is reacted to ferociously and the individual and the species-group survive.

When man is reached, an extremely complex behavioural equipment has been evolved. In brief, he has become a social person who survives not only by adaptation to, but largely by the creation of, his environment. Social animals survive by the evolution of innate mechanisms to keep them together, thereby gaining protection against predators and facilitating the rearing of the young. The common mode of achieving this grouping is by innate mechanisms creating attachment to dominant members. With the enormously increased psychological resources and creative capabilities required to cope with life in human communities, there has been an evolutionary development in which these are maximized by each individual acquiring a high level of autonomous creativity. The innate equipment for each has to provide for such development and the relatively huge cortex in man's brain emerges to meet it. As well as the behavioural systems providing for basic actions, there is now a great range of behavioural properties required for community living, especially for the amount of activity that has to be shared if optimal creativity is to be achieved. Relationships are mediated by holistic features in each human being, the essential character of which we describe as "becoming a person." The individual becomes aware of having a self and, moreover, a self which can transcend itself in order to observe and appraise its inner processes and its position in the world. When this subjectivity can be shared an enormous facilitation occurs for cooperative action in joint plans and purposes. Homo sapiens has emerged with all his unique characteristics. Added to the innate equipment that provides for the specific behaviour survival requires, there is now much behaviour that has innate components sufficiently influential to ensure its emergence, although not such as to restrict too narrowly the fit with the environment. The adaptive behaviour is then given a final pattern by training within the family and its society. Thus, what has been evolved in the genic inheritance is not the complete structural basis for the required behaviour, but a "potential" for it, as in the acquisition of language.

The notion of inherited potential was thought by many biologists until recent years to be a somewhat vitalistic notion. Critical evidence came from the Cambridge ethologist W. H. Thorpe in the 1950s when he and his colleagues showed that while the basic song units in chaffinches were inherited, the young birds could not perform the adult song unless they heard this from the adults. The possession of the song as shared by all members of the species is critical for survival. Learning from experience provided by the parents or adults had thus entered the process of evolution. With the mammals, prolonged parental care has become a necessity for dependent young. In man this care becomes loving care, and powerful love feelings have evolved as the great means of creating and maintaining the most vital human relationships, those in the family and in the group. (In connection with this outline see also Artiss 1985.)

Yankelovich and Barrett (1970) quote from Cantril's (1955) study of functional uniformities in widely different cultures, which suggest a list of innate potentials in the individual for behaviour at the human or personal level. The potential has to be realized within a specific culture, and in this way great variation exists in specific characteristics such as in languages. Language plays an essential part in many other acquisitions in which a rich range of communication amongst adults and between parents and children is required, while its symbolic function underpins creativity and the extremely flexible use in the development of tools and shared skills. Other innate potentials seem to be the attaining of food and shelter, getting security in a territorial and emotional sense, a need for ordering the data from environment, the need to seek new experiences, for procreation and safeguarding the future, the capacity to make choices, to experience a sense of the individual's own value to himself and others, and the need for a system of values and beliefs to which he can be committed and even sacrifice himself.

All these potentials, when realized, have to be fitted together and in an overall way that is managed by an autonomous self. As Angyal (1965) put it, it is paradoxical that this autonomy can only be attained within the heteronomy of being raised in, and belonging to, the community. In short, optimizing creativity in the individual can be achieved with a simultaneous bonding of the self to the group. This list is not quoted to be a comprehensive one of essential capacities, but to bring out how the highly complex task facing the individual in his development towards being a mature member of the community can be seen from an evolutionary standpoint. These attainments are all expressions of what we mean by becoming a person, that is, of having a mature self. Without these innate potentials and their development within the group to which persons will belong, or enough of them in sufficient measure, and without the integration or cohesive functioning that only a whole can offer, the individual cannot become a person.

Several specific capacities have been listed, but the critical feature has been left, namely, how the "person" is formed as an essential unity. To put these capacities together in various ways does not add up to being a person. Indeed, to learn to fulfil most of them, the individual has to be a person in the first instance, for it is the sense of autonomous agency that determines the learning. Moreover, much learning, for example language, needs a shared subjectivity between mother and child (see Stern 1985). An intensely dynamic potential power in the self is thus what motivates the sustained purposiveness of the individual to contribute to the well-being of himself and the group.

The answer to how the whole is formed can be given as the simple one that it is there from the start, a view adopted by Lichtenstein (1977). All organisms are wholes, and they create other wholes for survival. Fairbairn long felt critical of the atomism of so much analytic theorizing. He himself found no difficulty in assuming the existence of wholes. That the infant gives the strong impression of being a whole "person" from a very early stage is certainly vouchsafed by all parents and most infant–mother research workers. Kohut (1971) quotes the way adults react instinctively to babies as persons and treat them as such, usually with expressions to indicate their pleasure in responding to this quality, as strong evidence in favour of a whole self being actively present. It is not difficult to conceive of this potential being present in the innate endowment and giving rise to the "expectation" to be treated in this way; and this does not only occur at the infant stage. The person at all stages of the life cycle resents not meeting this response from others, with intensities of feeling covering the whole range of aggression.

To return to Fairbairn, it is very much this trend of thought that can be seen in his conception of a unified self that is an autonomous potential, at first, and which is then suffused with a sense of being a person in proportion as the mother's loving care is assimilated. It can also be inferred that frustrations that interfere with this autonomous development are reacted to as with the animal fighting for its life, for the self is the living centre of the individual.

Since being a person, that is, having a self that is autonomous yet preserving its autonomy or identity by means of its matrix of relationships, is the essential resource for effective enjoyable and satisfying living, the nature and development of the self is the paramount issue for general psychology as well as psychoanalysis. For the latter, the immediate concern is the role of the self in psychopathology. Fairbairn attributes all psychopathology to the splitting of the self in early experience, and Melanie Klein also adopted this position.

Winnicott's therapeutic studies, together with the observation of mothers and babies in his paediatric work, fully supported Fairbairn's assertion of the primacy of personal relationships for the development of the self. He spelled out the mother's empathic responsiveness as establishing a positive attitude to others and to the outer world. This attitude characterized the child's "true self" in contrast with the conforming self that emerged to maintain the relationship with mother on her terms if not allowed enough scope to express his own. Bowlby (1960, 1969, 1973) has amply confirmed by his careful research studies the psychological necessities in the mother–child relationship. His theory of attachment stresses, so far, the conditions for the essential development of the self rather than the nature of the processes of the latter. He fully recognizes the complex developments involved in that process, a research area now receiving the attention of psychoanalytically trained workers (see Stern 1985).

Clinical data suggest that, while the mother's initial influence establishes security or otherwise in the sense of being a person, the interaction with the father seems to be essential in the realization of the full autonomous potential. Winnicott (1971) referred to "male and female elements" needing to be combined, and Fairbairn mentioned the need for a father. It would thus seem that while Fairbairn came to view the Oedipus situation in its relationship with infantile sexuality as a social situation and not a fundamental one for development as Freud had portrayed, there is another dimension to the importance of the relationship with the father in the maturation of the self. Indeed, Fairbairn's symptom can be seen as an attempt to bring back to life the father he had destroyed in phantasy, a need greatly increased when the imago of the castrating mother was revived by his wife's negative attitude to his work.

While it was the formation of splits in the self that formed the start of Fairbairn's line of thought, the defensive reactions against this situation suggest that the original self has retained a holistic dynamic within which these incompatible demands are dealt with, either by repression or by finding some substitute mode of satisfying the need. The structuring of these internal relations is much more complex than is apparent at first sight. Some of the internal objects have a relatively separate structure which is recognized as such, for example Freud's superego. The variety of objects and their topology seems to be quite large. Thus, Fairbairn regards dreaming not as wish-fulfilment but as the spontaneous "imaginative" playing out of relations amongst them. The person, in short, emerges as a cast of characters, each related to a specific kind of object. These systems of self–object relationships have constant dynamic effects on each other and are also in perceptual contact with the other world, so that when it presents a situation that fits what an inner split self is seeking, then the latter can become activated to the point of taking overall control of the self. We see here the mode of action in compulsive relationships when the activation is intense.

These subsystems, like the self as a whole, do not require to borrow energy from separate "drives." They operate in the quite different way that systems under cybernetic control do. The strength of the drive exhibited is governed by what is switched on by inner releasing mechanisms. The power of the whole self to manage behaviour with optimal adaptiveness is thus the resultant of the integrity of the whole self against the pressure from subselves, and these two sets of forces vary according to the past history of the person and the nature of the external environment to which behaviour is being directed. The outer world is frequently the main releaser of action, but more important are the internal goals and imagos embodied within the self, again with varying "distances" from the central self. All of these carry a dynamic of internal origin into the world to mould it, even with considerable coercion, to attain its goals.

With a subself becoming dominant, it is difficult to specify where the "autonomy" of the self is then located. Even under strong compulsions, there is usually an awareness of the situation of being "possessed," as though the observing self remains intact though powerless to exert enough control over it.

The compelling power of subsystems is not confined to instinctive action from sexual or aggressive arousal. Though less dramatic, it seemed that Fairbairn's ideal self could separate itself from these pressures and retain its own motivation in the sustaining of his creative work. Freud met this problem when he discussed the ego ideal and when he put civilization into an adversarial relationship with the autonomy of the self. His position is a complex one. On the one hand, he felt the individual has to accept tiresome constraints, yet he observed that with the development of the ideals shared by the group, the individual acquires an identity for his self that he defends against any threat. Furthermore, he does this with a ferocity that has to be conceived as coming from an elemental force, one he linked with his postulation of the death instinct. In short, if we adopt a theory of aggression as a reaction to danger, then threats to the autonomy of the self readily suggest the origin of hate; and its relative permanence follows from structured internal threats.

A comprehensive theory of the self will have to fill in the areas that are largely left out of consideration by Fairbairn. The whole of Fairbairn's transitional phase can be seen as occupied with the final structuring of the self under the influence of the realization of the various potential aspects, such as those listed by Yankelovich and Barrett (1970). In this development, Erikson's (1959) contributions at once seem to fill in the gap, with the epigenetic phases presumably deriving from the maturation of developmental potentials in the experiences that each culture seeks to provide at the appropriate period. Fairbairn gave a theory of the basic structuring that arises from the experiences in the earliest stages of mismatch between the child's needs and the parental responses. The schizoid split has a far-reaching influence because of the early highly formative stage in which it operates. Subsequent stages, for example the phallic-masculine-gender complex, can be more restricted in the disturbance they engender when the schizoid position has been free of deprivation. This freedom from inner constraints is especially important when the investment of the self becomes so much focused in the deep satisfaction of using special talents, for example in the acquisition of knowledge and evolving specific goals for the self. The split-off internalized objects can have a great range in the degree to which they deform development, and here we note whole areas in which much more research is needed. When mention was made of Fairbairn's relationship with his father, it seemed as though his father, at least as a sexual figure, had remained very much separated within his self, though very much present despite his repression.

When we take an evolutionary perspective for the development of the self as a fundamental characteristic structure, then the understanding of the dynamic of the ego ideal becomes much more plausible than that offered by classical theory. Thus in his introduction to Chasseguet-Smirgel's study, *The Ego Ideal* (1985), Lasch adopts her account, with all the richness of her observations of its development. Her basic assumptions, however, are strikingly rooted in a closed-system perspective from which all the commitments of man are seen to stem from his fear of death and a longing to reestablish a sense of primal unity with the natural order of things. Evolution, in contrast, can be seen as providing man with powerful innate potentials enabling him to strive purposefully, and not as a passive victim of chance and necessity, to alter this natural order. The prospect of death, moreover, is surely altered when it is seen as a planned necessity for the "progress" of life that evolution appears to embody. The Socratic injunction to examine one's life can thus focus on what has been given to life by the individual.

Jantsch (1980), in his view of the role of evolution, brings in the relevance of myths in man's awareness of his condition. For him, the striving after the "steady state" of an imagined perfection is reflected in the myth of Sisyphus. The evolutionary perspective on the other hand sees him as Prometheus. From our consideration of the self the vultures would then perhaps represent the deep hate over the frustrations of his autonomy—or the death instinct for Melanie Klein. It seemed to me that Fairbairn was always far more profoundly motivated by the "developmentals" in Cantril's list than by a longing to return to the "perfection" of the intrauterine state. If evolution has a thrust in it "to evoke," it is not too fanciful to imagine that man, or a proportion of men, get something of it within their nature. Hitherto his religions may have been one of its main expressions. Now he has to find ways in which selves in their groups do not need to eat each other, as the lower forms of life did, for survival. The development in social animals of the submissive action when a fight for domination has ended exemplifies evolutionary possibilities.

Fairbairn's emphasis on relationships started in his suffering from bad ones. His potential for an ideal self seized on Christianity as a means of realizing it. He then discovered, as Freud did, that only more knowledge of the self would in the long run sustain him towards his goals.

In the formation of commitments, the internal object may occupy a very different position in that it may be suffused in its influence by an assimilation into the central ego. We get a strong impression that Freud was internalized in this way following upon the similar internalization of Christ. The situation is then extremely complex when what was the bad mother becomes the adopted model after a change in her attitude from castration to active encouragement of a masculine autonomy. I am reminded here of Freud when puzzled to account for an instinctual demand being "tamed" when brought into the ego. His solution was to seek help from the Witch Metapsychology and I wonder if it was his "bad mother" who unconsciously prompted this suggestion (Freud 1937, p. 225). Fairbairn recognized the therapeutic problem here because of the deeper hate being overlain by so much gratitude that was felt later for the support of the realization of his masculine ideals. When he referred at various points to the intense resistance aroused by the therapeutic process, this seems to centre on the fear for self-structures that have become so important. In these later internalizations, there is also the problem of the relation between the parents being internalized, as when he felt in later adolescence he was in a secret collusion with his mother against his father. This enactment of the interparental conflicts within the self, with parts identified with each parent, is extremely common, highly destructive, and highly resistant to exposure because of the threat to the integration of the self.

In this rather personal version of where I believe Fairbairn would have continued his journey, a particular area is outlined, because I believe that the whole tenor of his work was steadily moving to the conceptualizing of the self. It was, after all, where he started.

23. AN OBJECT RELATIONS VIEW OF THE GREAT MAN

Early psychoanalytical studies of creative men have been criticized as reductionist. That certain unconscious fantasies might have played a fundamental part in what was created, both in determining its nature and in providing the relentless drive of genius, was not denied. What was seldom traced were the links between fantasies that were not unique in their pattern to the great man and the specific process whereby he fashioned his innovative thought and action from these primal motives and his later perceptions of his own and others' needs.

With *Young Man Luther* Erik Erikson (1958) established a new kind of study of the great historical figure. In it he combined the insights of the psychoanalyst with an appraisal of relevant historical factors to illuminate how the mind of the great man made him capable of leading his contemporaries from a major impasse.

I will explore these links in my discussion of the development of the self as I reconstruct it from the life and work of two great men, Mahatma Gandhi and John Buchan.

GANDHI'S TRUTH

In *Gandhi's Truth: On the Origins of Militant Nonviolence*, Erikson (1969), shows how the great man early in life evolves a special mission, a direction that must lead to all or to nothing. Such a structuring within his personality remains, however, a "developmental probability" whose subsequent realization is conditioned by an enormous range of influences from the social environment during the successive phases of development. The questions to be considered, then, embrace at least the following. What gives the developmental probability of the great man its specific content? That is to say, we want to understand how the essentials of his mature mission were shaped from his experience within his early family and social milieu. Allied with this question is that of the source of the necessary drive if his mission is to be transmuted into major social action. A third question takes us into his later experience. How does he, on the basis of his compelling potential, fuse his inner needs into an instrument that provides for others a way they intuitively sense as realizing what they have been unable to articulate and activate?

To appraise the theories offered about the origins of Gandhi's achievement we have to look at its nature. Here we note that Erikson is not making a comprehensive study of Gandhi's political life but is concerned specifically with his *Truth,* that is, the political tool he developed—*satyagraha*, or militant nonviolence as it has become known. Erikson is fully aware of the varying evaluations of Gandhi's activities for India and of the blood bath that flowed from the hatred constantly simmering between the Hindus and the Muslims. It is poignantly ironical that the last serious eruption from this chronic source occurred in Ahmedabad itself, the town in which Gandhi finally tempered his political instrument. Such occurrences do not remove the value of Gandhi's Truth; they are among the issues that it was evolved to tackle. A comparison of Gandhi's instrument and Freud's method is one that Erikson makes, and we do not ignore Freud's achievement because of the limitations of the psychoanalytic method. *Satyagraha* as used by Gandhi on occasion clearly carried inconsistent restrictions stemming from conflicts in his personality, which he managed not by understanding but by severe moralistic prohibitions. We can assume, however, with Erikson (1969, p. 32), and with Romain Rolland, whom he quotes, the greatness of a method that "stirred three hundred million people to revolt" and that "introduced into human politics the strongest religious impetus of the last two hundred years" (Rolland, 1924 pp. 3-5).

Gandhi's Truth as a method of conflict resolution involved various steps, some of which, though now taken for granted, were revolutionary half a century ago—for example, obtaining the full study of the facts including those factors that influence public opinion and making a genuine attempt at arbitration with the clear announcement of actions to be taken. It is over the meaning of the Truth for the contenders that Gandhi's views have provided a disturbing challenge. For him the clash between the inevitable relativities of the truth as discerned by each party would only be overcome by a truth that transcended both. In reaching such a truth Gandhi's assumption was that no harm was to be done. Erikson suggests convincingly that in translating *ahimsa* we have to accept Gandhi's meaning as no violation to the essence of the other person. Without such a respect for the other's truth we merely get violence and counterviolence. In the situation for which arbitration produces no acceptable solution, the test of truth in the campaigners is the conviction that they will suffer for their goal to the point of death, while holding to the code of nonviolence. A *satyagraha* campaign therefore has to convince its participants of these requirements, and it was Gandhi's extraordinary charisma that he did this on such a scale. For him it was the leader's task to decide on the "true" course, and here we can, with Erikson, allow for the rather special historical condition that determined Gandhi's individual power in reaching such decisions and the cultural features that gave such significance to actions like fasting. As Erikson points out, if truth is actuality it has to be achieved in each situation by fresh action and never by a mere repetition of ritualized acts.

The aspect of Gandhi's method that has aroused the most doubt is his belief, at least for himself, that its critical use demanded the abandonment of sexuality. It is here that an irrational manifestation of personal conflicts has taken over. His whole attitude to sexuality from early manhood was one of compulsive moralism against its "badness." It was a drain on the sources of the powers that man needs if he is to reach more mature ways. Erikson indicates that while Gandhi's personal choice in this respect does no justice at all to the role of sexuality in loving relationships, he was pointing to our need to understand more of what primitive phallic sexuality contributes to man's propensity to violence. For Erikson, Gandhi intuitively grasped that in situations of serious conflict each party must extend the boundaries of his self-feeling to include that of the other's. This was the essence of his drive and of his success. His capacity to speak for others down to the pariahs of his culture must spring from the fact that so much of his thought and action drew upon the deep and universal affects of mankind. What his failures have brought home is not the presence of basic error but his (and still our) lack of knowledge by which he could obviate the most urgent problems posed for mankind. It is here that Gandhi's method needs what psychoanalysis might help to supply. Erikson has been one of the most notable psychoanalytic thinkers—at times almost getting himself regarded as deviationist—trying to isolate at least some of the questions we have to study in regard to human violence, if not providing the answers. He likens Gandhi's contribution, admittedly with acknowledgment of the speculative flight, to an attempt in man to evolve a method of ritualizing aggression comparable with the instinctive inhibitors in most species. He has made it very clear that we cannot talk of aggression in the hydraulic metaphors of the nineteenth century. Neither can we account for violence with the conventional notions of instinct. Erikson, more than any other psychoanalyst, has stressed the need to understand what we mean by such terms as "identity" and "the self," for it is in these areas that violence is released. (Arthur Koestler has stressed that for many centuries wars have been ideological, not basically economic.) For Erikson it is the emergence in man of what he calls a "pseudo-species" mentality that is the lethal product. The ethologists have shown us how intraspecies rituals have allowed species to survive their aggressive potential. The creation of human identity, a richly plastic potential for increasing adaptive powers, has been very largely "pseudo" in the sense that it neither embraces the species nor gives stability to any section of man. Its unstable integration needs others into whom are projected the inner forces that cannot be managed. In such a situation only destruction or subjugation of the threatening others is felt to be the safe solution. Gandhi's mission was to create a method by which such impasses might be overcome, by the anticipatory development of more inclusive identities (Erikson 1969).

Though Gandhi studied the New Testament, his Truth was always intended to keep political action and religion inseparable. What was felt to be right had to be so central to man's sense of his self that he would gladly die for it. For him as in Christianity martyrdom included concern for the aggressor, but it was not to be invoked until all conceivable attempts had been made to replace the situation wherein "they know not what they do" by one in which both sides might see more clearly all the actualities—political, economic, and personal. By the time he ends his book Erikson confirms more than he expected his original intuition that Gandhi's Truth had much in common with the thoughts of psychoanalysis. What emerges is that Gandhi's method cannot be expected to solve conflicts that are the end product of too long-established pseudoidentities in man. Gandhi himself was notoriously unable to practice his method within his own family and at times within his ashrams, even when allowance is made for the fact that he was in middle age before he fashioned it. The aim of his method and much of its means are a legacy we cannot afford to ignore. Modern dynamic psychology—itself developed from a method in which a nonviolent endeavor to understand the other replaced a moralistic assault—is perhaps not so much required in the situations for which Gandhi sought a creative solution as for preventing the growth to the position in human identity formation where anxiety and fear preclude the capacity to enlarge the self's boundaries to admit the validity of the other.

Whatever value is given to Gandhi's Truth today, we cannot but admire and wish to understand what made him a great man of his age. Two questions are posed on this issue: what were the origins of his particular mission, and what gave it its consuming energy? In answering the first the speculative possibilities are endless. Great men, however, seem to convey a sense of their destiny so that data about their early characteristics can be assembled. Oedipal conflicts, the favorite resort in the past, can readily be detected, but psychoanalysis itself is passing beyond the stage where these conflicts are regarded as fundamentals to one in which they are seen as outcomes of much that preceded them. Erikson recognizes these early influences but does not make use of the extent to which primary structuring of the person by internalized object relationships has been described by those stimulated in varying degrees by the work of Melanie Klein. Thus much of what dominated Gandhi's mission incorporates a strong drive to make reparation. A difficulty for the Western analyst in speculating about the fantasy systems that Gandhi developed undoubtedly arises from the special setting of the Indian child in the extended family, with its compressed world of parental relationships complicated by the wider network in which they exist, the many children in the immediate environment, and the constantly impinging intensity of so many relationships with all degrees of intimacy in the closely packed life space. Nevertheless, Gandhi's fantasies of being the powerful father along with his reparative devotion to his father are prominent. The oedipal fantasies of Western culture are not ordinarily confronted with a father thrusting sexuality upon the boy in early adolescence, and Gandhi resented his arranged marriage most of his subsequent life. The closeness of his parents and the fact that he enjoyed an intensely affectionate relationship with them, as they did with each other, appears to have produced in Gandhi a most pronounced identification with the united and idealized good parents. But their relationship was to be freed from what he must have fantasied as dangerous sexual relations. As

Erikson notes, no great man has so explicitly avowed his wish to be a good mother to others. Nor is this striking component of his personality associated with the giving up of his masculine self. In all the challenges he accepted he displayed all the courage and toughness of any male leader. A complex personality such as Gandhi's—and his inconsistencies in action, in his relationships, and in his moods were ever prominent—is obviously structured by a great range of fantasy systems. Erikson makes a good case, however, for giving a central role to this theme of keeping the harmony of the parental relationship in the evolution of Gandhi's personality, in its earliest phases and in later life when he arrived at his method in Ahmedabad.

Erikson recognizes that place he gives to what he calls *the Event* in Gandhi's life is likely to arouse skepticism. Gandhi's disavowal in his autobiography of its importance is rebutted readily enough, for every psychoanalyst is all too familiar with the defensive processes that can belittle critical events. What may be asked by the reader is whether the fascination exerted by the Sarabhai family on the author has influenced his judgment unduly. Gandhi was certainly arrested by the situation in which a brother and sister, devoted to each other, were the protagonists in the struggle. Equally, there is no doubt that Erikson's experience of being in the ambience of this family, now greatly extended, and of being able to talk to each of them in the place where the drama had occurred, might have stimulated his rich imagination to exaggerate the Ahmedabad happenings. (As one who has shared this experience in Ahmedabad, I have no hesitation in raising these possible effects!) Erikson's account to my mind survives this criticism. The Event was a deeply formative experience for Gandhi, and the evidence adduced in spite of all the difficulties carries conviction.

Our second question as to the source of the drive that was transmuted into social action is one that Erikson does not answer, and no one else could in the light of our present knowledge. Erikson's probings, however, are surely pointing the way to where the answers lie. For what he is bringing out is that certain early experiences can create fantasy relationship systems that give an intensity of feeling to the self and that establish a constant inner pressure to reproduce their patterns within a constantly adaptive actualization. Cybernetic models will no doubt fill out from the data of the neuropsychological substrates of affective experience as well as its psychology what we cannot do at present, that is, account for the compelling intensity of certain emotional systems when they are combined.

JOHN BUCHAN'S "SICK HEART"

That *Sick Heart River* was notably different from Buchan's other novels was manifest from the start. "So unlike him, so introspective," was his secretary's comment as she began to type it. *Memory Hold-the-Door*, however, was far from being an autobiography "though he might later try to weave his experiences into a personal religion and philosophy." The outcome was *Sick Heart River* finished shortly before his death.

Always resistant to the direct communication of his inner self, Buchan resorted again to his fictional characters as though unable to depart from his habitual medium of telling a tale. *Pride's Purge* was an earlier choice for a title and at once we ask, what had this so admirable man to purge? His life was such an ideal and full one with extraordinary talents realised in so many fields along with the great joy he had in his family life and in his innumerable friendships. Nevertheless, there was for several of his friends a puzzling uncertainty about who was the real Buchan. His son, William, in his sensitive memoir (1982), describes being baffled by his father who was a mysterious person behind all his openness, and Buchan had said of himself in *Memory Hold-the-Door* that as a writer he must inevitably keep the best of himself for his own secret creative world. This unpromising prospect in regard to more understanding of his personality is less bleak when we recall Trilling's (1972) study of *Sincerity and Authenticity* in which he quotes Wilde's dictum: "Man is least himself when he talks in his own person. Give him a mask and he will tell you the truth" (p. 119). Buchan created an unusually rich array of masks through which he projected different aspects of his self into the dramatis personae of his tales.

His story telling had long struck me, because of the energy that went into its regular output along with the sustained pace of the action in each tale, as coming from powerful unconscious urges. It also seemed that this stream of activity constituted a segregated part of his self that had its own life. Moreover, the stories felt much more rooted in vivid dreams with all the compulsive intensity of that deeper process rather than being the products of the more superficial meanderings of daydreams. Their prominent unconscious themes were not uncommon or bizarre, though their variety was carried by a separate character thereby defending both dreamer and reader from the disturbing tensions of all being contained within the one person although this fragmentation naturally made the characters lack the roundedness of whole persons. The oedipal triangle was to the fore in the early romances while the thrillers suggested more primitive levels at which the hero had to contend with the ruthless omnipotence of the villains driven by their wish to control the world. To resist them evoked violent sadistic retaliation against which the hero had to protect himself, and his wife and family at times, by a secret flight. The villains did not remain solely a repository of primal sadism; they came to possess many of Buchan's own attributes as in the cultured interests of the characters Lumley and Medina. Pointing, too, to earlier levels of unconscious structuring than those of the oedipal stage was the way in which Medina's omnipotent realisations were shared with his blind mother. Her massage to induce the hypnotic submission of Hannay was not felt entirely by him as a soft feminine touch. Behind the airy touch of her plump hands was "a hint of steel as if they could choke as well as caress" (1924, p. 80).

There seemed therefore to be a separate part of Buchan's self that surged with a strong emotional pressure. What was most striking was the way his conscious ego, though heavily committed in his busy life, could transmute these imperative unconscious themes so readily into exciting adventures told with his vivid relationship with the countryside as a constant background. Readers could identify at once with the characters and the resolution of the sharply etched dramatic conflicts. Little suffering here from paralysing inhibitions or tortured guilts. No question either of Buchan seeking the costly process of psychoanalysis to alleviate their intrusion into his competent working self. On the contrary, he made his potential neurosis, so to speak, reward him handsomely. The integration of his ego must have been extraordinarily toughly welded by ideals embodying in his inner world the legacy from highly supportive loving parents.

These speculations that his stories drained off disturbing conflicts would also account for his own attitude towards his writing. He enjoyed telling a tale without ambition to be regarded as a writer; and he steadfastly avoided being any part of the literary scene. To have written novels of significance he would have had to unite the gamut of the human passions and their conflicts within the single person. For him, it appeared that he had to separate and then externalise into his "puppets," as he termed them, what he could not accept as latent parts of himself. The bad figures had to be conquered by the good ones who could then return to their idealised pastoral lives. The therapeutic function of his writing for himself served, however, to discharge tensions rather than to resolve their origins. They inevitably had to go on being repeated and their deep appeal, beneath the entertainment, gained them a sustained popularity.

The unique character of *Sick Heart River* stems from a very different state of mind in the author. The purpose and the impact of the story are no longer felt as entertainment as in the past. We are deeply moved by this journey of Leithen, a scarcely disguised representation of Buchan's ambitious and reflective self, into his own interior, albeit via his relationship with the separate figure of Galliard set in their struggle with the rigours of the Arctic.

When I first read this story I was much preoccupied with the newer concepts entering psychoanalysis about the self and its development. It seemed to me that a conception was cohering from these contributions, which resonated with Buchan's story. On rereading it, *Sick Heart River* was like a translation of this new line of thought into the medium of the novel. Writers have long familiarised us with divisions in the self. Explorations of the nature and origins of the phenomena, however, are absent as a rule as though close contact with them becomes too frightening to one's own integration. At any rate, the analytic pioneers who had gained access into these earliest experiences, at first only in very ill patients, had to work through considerable reactions in themselves, often over several years before they could understand some of the basic processes. It was thus of unusual interest to me to find Buchan's intuitive insights not only depicting the deep origins of the divisions in the self but also the terror of madness that a confrontation with them evoked. Furthermore, the essence of the therapeutic help necessary for achieving the integration that early experience had fragmented was there in the completion of his story. Instead of a final tragedy or an unreal ending there was a simple account of the power of unconditional care inspired by the understanding acceptance of the full intensity of madness threatening the self when its autonomy has given way to a total infantile dependence.

I propose now to outline the story and then to suggest from Buchan's history some powerful unconscious themes that gave it its form. Since these will inevitably strike some as the far-fetched fantasies of psychoanalysis I next quote from the story various features which to me confirm them. And in a final brief section I describe in bare outline a psychoanalytic theory of some aspects of personal development for which the story gives support.

The Story

Leithen, having been told he has not long to live, accepts a request to find Galliard, a brilliant New York financier who suddenly disappeared leaving only a note to his wife saying he is very sick in mind and will come back when cured. On learning that he belonged to an old French Canadian family, from which he had become disconnected, Leithen concludes that Galliard has gone back to his roots and with a guide, Johnny, he tracks him to the far Northwest. Galliard started out with Johnny's brother, Lew, as his guide. Johnny explains to Leithen that Lew must have become possessed by one of his mad streaks to find the valley of Sick Heart River, which, in Indian mythology, cures the ills of the soul. He has pressed on at a pace that has left Galliard behind and the abandoned man crawls into their camp injured and crazy, a state familiar to Johnny in those impelled by fantasies about the North. His obsession with Lew convinces Leithen that he will only recover mentally in a reunion with Lew. Leithen therefore goes off with an Indian porter only to find the valley to be almost inaccessible because of its mountainous sides. Descending a steep cleft they slip and career to the foot. Leithen is knocked unconscious and recovers to find the Indian trying to bring him round.

That night Leithen faces his religion and the feeling that all his achievements are pasteboard. Next day he goes alone to meet Lew and faints from exhaustion in front of him. On regaining consciousness he finds Lew has put him to bed and is tending him like a mother. He tells Lew that Galliard is very sick and in need of him. Lew is desperate to get away because he has found the valley to be a place of death. On the return journey, Lew's devoted care changes Leithen's stoical sense of duty over the undertaking to a warm personal concern for Galliard along with a deep experience of God's mercy in the world. He sees Galliard, tortured by guilt and remorse for what he has done to his family and driven to atone, the more so as he had been involved in the industrial development that had destroyed its heritage. Leithen tells him of his brave wife awaiting his return yet he realises that Galliard must get on terms with the North before he can leave it and get well. When news is brought that the local Indian tribe is succumbing to a suicidal apathy, Leithen finds inspiration for its rehabilitation through the care he received from Lew and Johnny, care that he feels to be an expression of beauty and tenderness concealed by the iron front of nature in the North. Sure that Galliard can find salvation from this reparation, Leithen evokes a new hope in him by getting him to participate in it. Leithen dies in serenity as the Indians recover. Galliard rejoins his wife to find again his great joy with her and to express his feeling that his life cannot be long enough to make up for all the suffering he has caused her.

Buchan's Early Development from a Psychoanalytic Perspective

While symbolic significance at many levels can be readily attributed to the story, its moving impact suggests that it resonates with universal emotional struggles in the evolution of the self towards a mature integration. To identify some of these conflicts in Buchan's psychological development, the inner depths he drew upon, we have to examine his history, especially the uniquely formative experiences in his infancy and childhood. Janet Adam Smith's excellent biography provides a number of clues which, along with the descriptions of the family life in his sister Anna's (O. Douglas) books, permit us to make reasonable inferences. I believe these carry a convincing picture of inner factors that shaped the future man and his writing.

Buchan was a fragile-looking infant who in his own words was "a miserable headachy little boy" (1940, p. 81) until he was about 5 years old. Since his subsequent achievements, physical and mental, suggest no major flaws in his constitutional endowments, this early condition points strongly to a seriously disturbed relationship with his mother. Barely 18 when he was born, and admittedly a very inexperienced mother, she also had a managing, controlling personality. Thus she would not have found it easy to provide the relaxed trusting attitude that allows a baby to make a spontaneous contribution to the patterns of its maternal relationships and so lay a foundation of security for independence with confidence in its autonomy. Any lack in his mother's personality must have been compounded during these first 5 years with the constant preoccupations to which several external events subjected her. She had been precipitated as this very young woman into the role of a minister's wife with her pregnancy following almost simultaneously. Then a few months after Buchan's birth, her husband changed his church so that she had to organise a move of their home to another part of the country and within the next year she became pregnant again. Furthermore, she had to cope with all those demands plus a husband who, though devoted to her, was a rather unpractical man in everyday domestic affairs.

It is hard to imagine any infant or child in this situation not being affected by gaps in the reliable availability of his mother with a joyful responsiveness most of the time to the assertion of his needs, bodily and psychological. We should also anticipate from psychoanalytic experience, that her possessiveness and the ambitions she had for her children, along with her puritanical upbringing, would inhibit the normal expressions of childhood masculine assertiveness and sexual curiosity, especially in a highly gifted boy. Some confirmation for this view is had in the fact that of her four children who survived to 30, Buchan was the only one to marry; and sexuality is scarcely in evidence in the idealised women of his novels. A considerable aggressive resentment against this intrusive controlling mother was highly likely to have been a main factor in his condition.

These psychoanalytic forebodings would be apparently made fanciful because of the way in which this miserable self was transformed into a zestful boy with boundless energies and enthusiasms. However, this striking change does not confirm the common belief that it was simply a case of "growing out of it." It was occasioned by a quite unusual and unexpected experience. Towards the end of his fifth year he sustained a fractured skull through a fall from a carriage. Instead of being separated from his mother by hospitalisation, as would have happened today, he was at once immersed in intensive care at home with his mother, aided by a friend, doing the entire nursing while he recovered during the next year. When we recall all the tasks she had to perform with her exacting standards, we cannot but be impressed by her as a powerhouse, an indefatigable manager, yet amply endowed with maternal devotion. From this surfeit of loving care the little boy emerged with a new self. Inner images of his early frustrating "bad" mother were no longer dominant with their depressing effects. They had apparently vanished into his unconscious and kept there by the almost saintly figure of a mother who had miraculously given him an exciting new sense of being. There was no question, however, of their early relationship structured over the five most formative years in the development of his personality having dissolved away. All psychoanalytic experience would be against that. It would stay although its effects would be covered over according to the amount of good experiences, especially immediately afterwards, and the effectiveness of the compensatory structuring from these. Fortunately, there was now in addition to what he got from his mother the rich relationship with his father, loved and admired for enchanting his children with endless stories and his love of the old Scottish minstrelsy. The joy in imaginative play from his fascination with these tales during his long illness and later must have been a creative experience of rare quality—one, incidentally, shared by the two other great Scottish story-tellers, Scott and Stevenson.

After his recovery, his enormously enriched and consolidated new self maintained a lively investment in his intellectual abilities both at home and at school. By adolescence the exciting world he had learned about, one he now loved intensely, was making the home environment too restrictive for his sophisticated ideals and aspirations. Little or no overt parental opposition was expressed, yet to pursue them must have entailed a sense of guilty betrayal, if not of rebellion, against what his beloved parents stood for. His longing for a more gracious and inspiring world was crystallised by the impact of Gilbert Murray, then a professor at Glasgow, and his fascinating aristocratic wife. Further encouragement from Murray saw him to Oxford. There his close friendships with a group of brilliant young aristocrats, of the mind as well as society, reinforced his goals for the future; and his literary talents allowed him financially to join their world. Yet he kept up active relationships with his family and his old friends of all kinds throughout his life. Buchan's attachment to this world was no snobbery. For him it was the appropriate environment for the realisation of his Greek ideal of the philosopher gentleman if not king. This was the road he had to follow. It was also the one that took him far from any threats of the return of a painful early past.

His gifts for outstanding intellectual competence and the ability to produce quickly with it, in literary and political reviews, and in legal and administrative matters, soon led to offers of important work. He never gave the impression of being rushed and he pursued his love of the country along with a lively social life. His genetic endowment was obviously superior, but the use he made of it conveys a sense of deep identification with his "second" mother whose highly organised energetic output was unceasing. His father, an intensely dedicated and evangelical preacher, was also perpetually driving himself in the service of others. Indeed his otherworldliness led to an ineffectiveness in everyday affairs such that his wife and family, in their great affection, assumed the role of watchfully looking after him. As Buchan's early model for manhood, his father's scholarship, his love of the old ballads, and his dedication to the welfare of others had a great influence. Later, his father's parochial outlook in intellectual issues generally led Buchan to have some patronising feelings to him, but with no diminution of his affection.

Overt attitudes to sexuality in the manse were, as would be expected, both Victorian and Puritan so that interest in the opposite sex and adolescent love affairs were strikingly missing in all the children. The family, of course, could hardly avoid the subject with their constant closeness to farm life and the familiar earthiness of the love life of Burns plus the perpetual biblical references. Furthermore, Buchan had the uncommon experience through being the first child of a very young mother of having the last two of her five succeeding children arrive when he was in his fourteenth and nineteenth years. Even here this last birth evoked considerable surprise in him when it happened. Romantic love thus inspired his first novels written while he was a student and they have all the stamp of the adolescent still constrained by the oedipal triangle and the almost excessively strong ties within the family group.

He was 30 when he first fell in love. Susan Grosvenor was closely related to a wide range of the upper strata of the London aristocracy and unusual in that her family had a large circle of friends within the literary and artistic worlds. Their relationship thus brought to Buchan a great deal of what he admired and aspired to. After about 18 months he was offered a directorship in Nelson's the publishers and with this economic security he was able to propose marriage.

There was no doubt that, however much his ambitions might be regarded as primarily for worldly success, they also included an ideal love relationship and this he realised. He was deeply devoted to her, his only love, and one which never faltered.

The successes of his later self, rooted in the miraculous therapeutic relationship with his mother, are remarkable when the serious insecurities of his first years are pondered. That pressures from the now hidden self had not been obliterated can be inferred from various aspects of his life, above all as the wellspring of the fictional side of his writing. Although he did not adopt his mother's ambitions for him to enter the ministry, he incorporated into his ideal self a strong intention to be involved in social affairs and to serve society from levels which he could exercise significant power; and he remained a staunch and devoted member of the Church of Scotland. Politics appealed and when he entered this field he impressed several of the political leaders sufficiently for him to be thought of as a future Prime Minister. Several of his friends eventually saw, however, that he was too "nice" a person to achieve the highest positions there. He himself felt that he was best placed as a number two in the leadership of public affairs. Here there was a characteristic noted by his friends, namely, that he could not readily "tick off people." That his deep ambitions, perhaps not fully conscious, to assume power at the top were curbed from within can hardly be better seen than in his becoming the monarch's deputy, with all the ritualised respect and acclamation accorded to the king. He was appointed for 2 successive years as the Lord High Commissioner in Scotland and then as His Excellency, the Governor General of Canada, a position for which he had to be elevated to the peerage. We may wonder to what extent omnipotent grandiose fantasies from early phases were competing with more realistic ambition for which his friends felt he never used fully his talents; or whether an unconscious guilt kept him from triumphing over his father.

Writing became an essential activity for him from boyhood. Creative urges were fuelled from the ambitions and ideals within his central self and from the ceaseless activity of his unconscious inner world. As described already, his great investment in the human scene and its history could pave the way for an entry into the influential commentators on current issues. From the split off self came a second group—the themes of his fiction. That this had potential dangers from its primitive destructive impulses and grandiose omnipotent aims was plain in the fantasies that surged up like dreams. Yet his central self, so firmly modelled from his parents, could always emerge as the dominant force. His leisure activities were also a great strength in the defence against the disturbing aspects of his secret self. His love of nature was of passionate intensity. In his descriptions of explorations into the countryside even in boyhood, there is a feeling of the child being close to his beloved mother, perhaps in the way he had missed in his beginnings. The quality of this feeling matured into his attachment to nature, which stayed firmly as an integral part of his self. This feeling also included his home and garden, his family and the servants, giving a depth of caring concern that obviously played a large part in his great gift for making and keeping his innumerable friends.

A third main grouping in his writings is his biographies. Perceptive and respected for their scholarly quality they include studies of men who challenged existing injustices yet who had tended to be negatively judged by history. His sympathy with their cause and his emphasis on its validity seems to draw upon his own struggle and to say something in defence of his hidden self and perhaps to achieve some integration of it with his centre.

Control over the constantly threatening tensions from the unconscious memory of his "bad" mother was reinforced by two other processes. He held on to the "good" mother who had saved him with a compulsive attachment, a familiar sequel to early insecurity in these relationships. There were ample grounds for feeling a great love and gratitude towards her, but a sense of compelling need to keep her presence perpetually there strikes us from the way he kept her in his mind. He wondered always what she would think before he made decisions. From adolescence they seemed to know each other's mind without anything said. No matter what pressures were on him he kept her regularly informed of his activities; and it may be more than coincidence that one of the worst spells of his recurrent gastric trouble occurred in the months after her death at the end of 1937. There was a contributing factor too in the close way his mother was involved with him.

The reference to his gastric illnesses introduces what was perhaps the most threatening and painful manifestation of the tensions from his hidden self. Becoming intrusive about the time when the relationship with his future wife began, spells of severe gastric pain drove him periodically to retire to bed for nursing care with the common régime which converts adult diet into what is much more like food for the baby. Recurrent attacks persecuted him for the rest of his life, defying all medical treatment including an operation for duodenal ulcer in 1917. This common trouble in men who live under too much stress is usually attributed to overwork and there was no doubt Buchan had periods when he was grossly overworked by ordinary standards. Nevertheless, he was a person who greatly enjoyed work for which he had an enormous capacity and competence. Often the source of such stress is to be found in the unmanageable interpersonal tensions at work rather than in the work itself. Here again, Buchan was seldom in that position with others.

That deeper psychological factors must have been involved was eventually decided by his medical advisers who in 1921 arranged for him to enter the clinic of a psychiatrist in Germany. After a few weeks of the usual remedial régime, inspired by physiological rather than psychological assumptions, Buchan was declared by him to be "free from frustrations, or crippling inhibitions and neuroses." His son William describes having long been unimpressed by this opinion. Apart from the disbelief it conveyed, the expansive tone of the doctor's pronouncement led him to conclude that his father had completely outwitted any attempt to get below the surface of his self. In fairness to the doctor, I do not think there would have been much of a battle of wits. He had no understanding of unconscious factors and even endless questions would only produce information from which little or no emotional insight could be developed by either doctor or patient. This lost opportunity to have helped Buchan was regrettable especially since he was sympathetic with the psychoanalytic approach to the mind. For someone of his sophistication, the doctor would have had to convey an understanding of what was beneath the surface of Buchan's personality before the patient could feel an evocative trust. The sick heart hidden within the tortured body had to be taken in hand.

Psychosomatic conditions have long been shown by psychoanalysts to have a meaning for the individual, that is, to express a hidden conflict within some infantile relationships. Avoiding guesswork about specific factors, we can say that certain stresses in his outer world could awaken in Buchan at a deeper level a feeling that his "good" mother was becoming lost to him. His illnesses then became miniature repetitions of the treatment that had worked so miraculously in the past, namely, the intensive care of devoted nursing when in the state of the dependent child. He felt better after these spells in bed but always this reassuring effect wore off.

In short, then, we can note ample cause for the creation of serious splits in Buchan's self and evidence of their persistence. As he faced the decline in his vitality he was drawn to a profound introspective look at himself in which some synthesis had taken place in those last years of his life. From this inner change, I believe he intuitively sensed some of the origins of the lifelong conflict in his self. This unconscious conflict was transformed by his rich imagination into Leithen's pursuit of Galliard, a man driven into his remote past, and then to effect a reparation by both for the destruction in their inner worlds of beloved parental figures. The question now concerns the evidence of this repressed conflict in the story.

Patterns of Early Experience in the Story

Leithen has been widely taken to be a central aspect of Buchan himself, and particularly so in this novel. He is, however, only one mask, namely, for his central reflective self, or ego, that has carried out his professional and intellectual achievements and which is now engaged on the most difficult of all appraisals, his total self, at a point in life where inner self-defensiveness is scrutinised. To the psychoanalyst, Galliard is just as much Buchan as Leithen, though embodying an alienated part, the secret self fashioned from the frustrated miseries of the little boy. Though described as extremely delicate by his mother, the boy would be all too capable of a violently protesting urge to get rid of the "bad" mother and have her replaced; for lack of manifest responsiveness in times of need can only be felt by a child as hostility. The wonderful transformation from finding a new mother behind what had been to him an ungiving front had produced an identification with her endlessly driving energy. To preserve this new relationship both internally and externally he maintained a compliance with her, which now made the achievements Leithen was referring to meretricious. Buchan, with unconscious wisdom, sets his story with Leithen in poor health to start the journey into his own interior, a regression to his own early condition. The setting drew on the great impression the Canadian north had made upon him. There was the beauty of the landscape and for him the idea of great riches under the surface. In the early years after he found his new self it was his exciting relationship with the environment, especially the hills and the woods, that he wrote about in *Memory Hold-the-Door* as his earliest memories.

I deferred speculation about the origins of Buchan's ulcer trouble, which can now be made. It is not too fanciful to suggest that in his poor state, colicky abdominal pains were a not infrequent experience. Whether or not, it is surely not "by chance" that Leithen's quest is instigated by Blenkiron, the American in *Greenmantle* with the bad duodenal ulcer. It was he who took part in the struggle against the dangerous fantasies of Hilda von Einem to scheme for omnipotent control of her world and to possess the freedom-loving Sandy Arbuthnot in whom Buchan seemed to have put his youthful longing to be a scholar-gipsy. And Galliard is married to Blenkiron's niece. Galliard's career has a close fit with Buchan's. He had broken away from the constraints of his family though only after a violent quarrel with his father who died not long after. His relatively late marriage is also a devoted one though the impression is given that for one part of himself it was the peak of his aspirations because of the glittering world his wife inhabits. She is described by others as possessive and ambitious for him and so we feel that her love could threaten him. The life longed for in his youth, with freedom from the family's impoverished situation, was now after its realisation not only felt as a hollow one, but one that in his inner world had become a cancer eating into his soul. The past was reliving itself in one part of him so that to continue to submit to it would be to go to pieces under the pressure of the frustrated rage of the gifted child's desperate struggle for his autonomy. Unconsciously, the inevitable violent infantile sadistic fantasies against frustrating parents become intolerably frightening with the anxiety and intense guilt from what one part of the self wants to do to all that in the central self is so precious. To lose his mother and his father spells terrifying isolation to the child. In Buchan, to attack his mother would have destroyed what she had put together and sustained for him, a feeling giving rise to unbearable anxiety and guilt. Though there is no open recognition of this destructive rage in Galliard yet we know that sadistic fantasies had been in Buchan's mind in the past. About the time his gastric troubles were becoming troublesome he wrote the short story *The Grove of Ashtaroth*. The central figure, a bachelor, creates a home of idealised perfection in a beautiful situation in South Africa. It has a grove in which there is an ancient phalliclike tower. He is eventually driven periodically to go in the middle of the night, naked and bearing a large knife, to the tower round which he performs a ritual dance. He returns covered with blood from self-inflicted lacerations like the devotees come to worship the goddess Astarte who demanded of them self-castration as they worked up to a frenzied orgy. In his first thriller, *The Power House*, Leithen had also to find a man who has left his wife without leaving any trace of his whereabouts lest she come to harm from the malevolent group pursuing him. *The 39 Steps*, which was written soon afterwards, opens with the dread of a man who has penetrated some of the secrets of a mysterious group plotting to take omnipotent powers and who are now trying to kill him. In spite of Hannay's efforts to help him, he is found on the floor stabbed through the heart. This fantasy gives some idea of the terror induced in the primitive infantile levels of the mind by the inevitable violent retaliation in kind from the hated figures.

From the unconscious dread of his destructive urges, there was only one choice in Buchan's mind, namely, to banish them into a segregated self where they could be hidden. It is a similar situation that has apparently built up with growing tension in Galliard until he has to take panic flight. This will protect his wife, and he will end the torture from an unconscious hate of her, perhaps evoked by a sense of her controlling ambitions for him, by a journey of atonement and reparation. Simultaneously he will assert his masculine independence in penetrating that forbidding land that his ancestors had possessed and find thereby the magic of a mother's acceptance of his manly self. This inner need, persisting so insistently, has made all his achievements a disillusionment and to be despised. When the feelings from this level return with self and mother merged together at times, and then in an unstable separation, Galliard gets the terror of being engulfed by a retaliatory mother. There is only one choice. He must flee and with little thought for his wife left in ignorance of his emotional state and where he is, and having to cope with her fears for him along with the pain of wondering where she failed him. This solution, though intended in one part of his self to protect her, inflicts very great pain. In a deep sense it is tantamount to murdering her. The violence here can be inferred from the intensity of Galliard's later guilt over his flight when he feels the rest of his life will be spent in atonement. Leithen regrets the absence in himself of simple earthy masculinity, such as Buchan felt to be the core of the Border shepherds he almost idolised, the men who had peopled his mother's world. For Galliard it was the courage and freedom of the men in his family who explored the North that he envied. For Buchan, there had been no instillation of this zestful self in his beginnings. Galliard had had a much more dramatic deprivation for we are told, in an almost casual passing reference, that his mother had died at his birth—perhaps a vivid expression of what Buchan's early misery felt like at times.

Before Leithen can get to the core of his inner situation he has to surmount some of its frightening nature. Galliard has been abandoned and cannot survive in this cold world in which he is a helpless babe. When he reaches Leithen's camp he is totally exhausted, injured and with his mind in a disintegrated madness. The guide Johnny takes his condition with a calm recognition of what it is about. Galliard is one of those travellers who go to the North with a fantasy of it being "a pretty lady" and then finding "it can be a cruel bloody-minded old bitch" (p. 95). These are strong words for Buchan which must have echoed his early misery and hate. Johnny says Galliard "wants nursin' and quiet, and a sort of feel that he's safe, and for that you need four walls" (p. 99). Leithen cannot understand how Galliard, after the way Lew treated him, is still obsessed with getting back to Lew, "like a child crying for his nurse" (p. 100). Johnny explains that "That's the way it works" (p. 100). Galliard does not know his troubles are "all Lew's doin" (p. 100). The terrifying loneliness has made him claw on to anything human, but if that were all, Leithen or Johnny might have taken Lew's place. Lew, however, has possessed Galliard's mind with "his Sick Heart daftness" (p. 100), the place where Lew and he will be put right; only the finding by Galliard of Lew in his right mind will change Galliard's mental state. In short, it is not "any" nurse who will do; it must be the one who induced this madness of his abandoned feelings—the one who is now merged in his deeper feelings with his mother.

Leithen now becomes possessed by this mission to find Lew and get him back whatever his state of mind. Johnny is greatly moved by his courage.

Buchan refound his good mother after he was precipitated unconsciously into her intensive care by a fall from a carriage in which he was being taken with her to a picnic. Leithen's journey with one of the Indians, agonising for him in his weak state, takes him eventually to the edge of the steep mountainous sides of the Sick Heart valley. Getting down looks impossible until he finds a cleft which they descend despite the risk. The Indian slips and both are plunged to the foot of the icy slope. Leithen, rendered unconscious, recovers to find the Indian massaging him. That night his mind is turned inwards. His achievements he had always known were pasteboard and he was now alone with God. Next day when he confronts Lew he falls unconscious from utter exhaustion. On coming to, he sees that he has been carried into a shelter in which Lew cares for him with great maternal tenderness. A remarkable detail is given at this point. Leithen is startled by Lew's hair, "as flaxen as a girl's" (p. 117), and by his piercing brilliant blue eyes—for both of which features Buchan's young mother had been well known and which would be deeply significant to the baby. Leithen gets from Lew the loving care and tenderness that had got lost behind Buchan's mother's preoccupied and frustrating front. He becomes a changed man, elated by a sense of God's mercy hidden beneath the iron front of nature. Having assimilated it in the upper levels of his self, he is then able to feel more strongly the necessity for Galliard to repeat the same experience in depth with Lew, the one who in his driven obsession became identified with the mother who had abandoned him. No reproaches are uttered to Lew for what he did to Galliard nor to Galliard for what he did to his wife. Instead there is an understanding acceptance of what has driven them. Galliard, like Leithen, appreciates the care, but for him it re-creates only his bodily strength. Leithen sees he must also create in Galliard's sick mind the only thing that will cure him, namely, a core self which has carried out an act of great reparation for what his destructive self has done. This act will give him the experience of restoring in his inner world the destroyed mother to her good state. Leithen takes him through this task by inspiring his participation in the rehabilitation of the Indians. And, though of a different tribe, the mother of Lew and Johnny was an Indian; she, too, had died at Johnny's birth. Leithen dies on the completion of their task in peace and serenity under the devoted care of the Oblate Father who served the little chapel for the Indians. Galliard is reunited with his wife. He feels that Leithen will live on inside him and the rest of his life will be needed for making reparation to the wife he cruelly abandoned.

Before leaving these observations on the repetition of his childhood experiences a brief mention should be made of the two guides. Apart from the more dramatic role played by Lew who has many aspects of Buchan's mother, Johnny, the younger brother, is an appreciative representation of the devoted care from his father as well. Aspects of each parent are mixed in the two men with the dominance of his mother reflected in Lew yet without effacing Johnny, the father who depended so much on his partner; Buchan had parts of both parents in his personality in much the way that the relationships amongst Leithen, Galliard, and the two guides have been depicted. Galliard and Lew link the deep threatened self with his mother while Leithen and Johnny bring together the solid virtues of his father. The unconscious family situation also seems to determine the close relationship between the guides as brothers whose father came from Border shepherd stock, the epitome of what Buchan greatly admired. The simplicity of the guides' attachment to their country of origin, their unhappiness when they left it and their need to return to what they fitted into so well, are contrasted by Leithen with people like Galliard and himself, whose abilities and ambitions for a spacious life beyond that of their parents, drove them inexorably to achievement in the wider world, success which he now questioned.

Buchan, through Leithen, seemed to have attained a profound resolution of inner conflict. He had started *Memory Hold-the-Door* about a year after his mother's death. He had now finished the personal autobiography and within a few months he died in his sixty-fifth year the same age as his father.

The Writer and the Psychoanalyst

My main purpose in presenting these reflections on John Buchan's last book is to share some suggestions about the unconscious themes that I felt illuminated the close connections between the novel and his own early history. It seemed to me that it was this wellspring that gave the novel its unique character amongst his writings. As a result of the particular impact it had on myself I was prompted to offer some brief thoughts on the relationship between the writer and the psychoanalyst. Poets and writers are our main source of knowledge of the deeper forces in the inner worlds of man; and for certain of these urges, for example, his responses to the changing image of himself in his world, they still have a unique role. They seldom, however, get to the origins of what they confront us with, as if that becomes too difficult, perhaps too frightening, for the single mind. This understanding has become more and more urgently required as man has expanded his awareness of himself and his responsibility *to be evolution* rather than the hapless victim of chance and necessity. If he is to manage more of his destiny effectively, he must have validated knowledge, especially this critically important knowledge of how he can direct the development of his personality—the instrument with which he appraises all. Here we have moved, as Braque put it, from the function of the artist to disturb us to that of the scientist who can reassure. For this task, he must articulate and validate knowledge of ourselves and so make it usable in our power to manage ourselves.

Freud's theories, evolved to their familiar form 60 years ago, made an epochal change in man's image of himself. It is still all too common to equate psychoanalysis today with these classical views. His lasting legacy, as he himself so often stressed, was not his theories—as in any scientific endeavour these must be constantly changing—but a method for exploring the unconscious processes in our inner worlds. It has in fact been one of my main aims to show how it is the recent changes in the perspectives of psychoanalysis that make *Sick Heart River* such a fascinating work. The rejection of psychoanalysis as unscientific, especially from the professional and academic worlds, is for the most part a demonstration of a widespread defensive ignorance and fear of psychoanalysis. The psychoanalyst in his practice is not primarily a scientist who can reduce and subject his data to the experimental constraints of the laboratory. He undertakes a commitment to develop with another human being a unique relationship in which to relieve as best he can the sufferings of his partner in a mutual endeavour. He cannot progress without making theories to organise and communicate what he finds; but some of the validation of these general hypotheses he seeks must come from the work and methods of others if they are to belong to science, that is, to tested knowledge. Writers in their descriptions of man's inner conflicts with himself and his society are in an obviously complementary role. They, too, use their insights, coming often in the intuitions from dreams and fantasies, and especially into man in his holistic aspects. Also, their commitment to their work must have a lot in common with that of the analyst as the relationships with his analysands develop.

As I said earlier, it was an impressive experience to me to find Buchan reproducing the essentials of the therapeutic task in the serious disorders of the self. His account of Galliard's psychotic distress and his rehabilitation after finding the concerned care in people behind their apparently unempathic surfaces was a striking confirmation of analytic work. Buchan's good fortune was to have had an extraordinarily intense compensatory relationship with his mother after what must have felt like one with a "cruel old bitch." The security with which he had established his second self was a buttress for the full realisation of his latent talents. The satisfaction from all his fulfilments was manifest though it never lessened the dynamic pressure of the early miserable one. It seemed as he faced death, his fear of the destructive aspects of his early self were now less of a threat and so he could let the unconscious levels come forward to be transmuted in a creative synthesis by his brilliant talents. The unique acts of creation in the production of the writer's work and its communicative power have essential elements beyond the psychoanalyst's resources. The existential position of man in his constant latent evolutionary thrust may well always be in this "beyond." That is where the artists' preoccupations are; yet their contribution will always need to be nourished by the advancing knowledge carefully established from the work of the analyst. Their unique contribution, especially with the newer views of the analysts, can serve to facilitate this mutual enrichment.

To make clearer the change in psychoanalytic theory from its assumptions of instinctual energies as the biological foundation for human development to a paradigm based on modern biological views of open systems, that is, living organisms and the transformation in their central organisation through interactions with the environment, I add a sketchy outline of the recent trends in self-psychology. I hope this may take those interested into the study of such writings as those of Bowlby (the most thoroughgoing and comprehensive), or Kohut, the American analyst, or of Ronald Fairbairn, the Edinburgh analyst who formulated about 50 years ago the first systematic attempt to move into modern science in contrast with Freud's adhesion to nineteenth-century assumptions about the nature of reality.

Psychoanalytic Notes on the Development of the Self

The adult self can be regarded as a system that has organised its progressive experience with the environment in such a way that the person manages the business of living with competence and a satisfying significance. Clinical experience and systematic studies of infant–mother development have now established beyond doubt that this successful development has to be founded upon appropriate experience from birth. The unit of study in this field is clearly that of the infant within the ordinary expectable family environment. The word "expectable" is crucial, for the infant has a surprisingly rich repertoire of activities which have an inbuilt goal that is at once felt as right when it is encountered. These inbuilt needs are not only around the bodily processes. There are just as urgent ones from the expanding psychological equipments to be met with the emotional equivalent of the "good feed." When a good measure of satisfactions is experienced and the mother communicates her joy in sharing the infant's achievements, it seems that a quality is established within the self as a whole of having a faith and trust in others, and consequently in himself. As wider relationships follow with father and other family members the secure self can cope with the instinctual forces of sexuality and aggressive assertiveness as these become more prominent.

When the environment fails the infant emotionally the potentials for all kinds and degrees of distorted development are laid down mainly in the form of excessive divisions within the self. A central self has to preserve a relationship with the mother for survival almost irrespective of the degree of any deprivation. When the latter is severe then the person has little or no security in his relations with others, though this inadequacy may be covered over by the acquisition of a compliant behaviour with no real conviction that this is what should be happening. There is little or no sense of the essential autonomy in doing "one's own thing" because it is essentially someone else's thing that has been forced upon the self. The experiences of frustration, however, do not disappear nor even wither. Instead they group to form the core of subselves whose aims have some of the dynamic urges of the primal self. Because they arise in opposition to the environment they must on no account be revealed. To do so would incur what is felt as the frightening hostility of parents or of their withdrawal of love. There is then a turning into an inner world in which the growing imaginative powers can fashion figures that will provide exciting substitute satisfactions. There are also, however, parallel figures which are hated for their frustration and dreaded because in the omnipotent magical modes of early mental processes there will be terrifying retaliation from them. Though these inner figures are created to be the objects of the repressed aims they are also in the mind and so are identified with. Thus, one part of the self comes to hate some of its repressed needs as a means of avoiding the dangers of their expression. The person becomes a cast of inner characters whose interactions are the source of our dream life, and of the main conflicts in relationships.

What has proved most striking about this inner world of the self is the intensity of the hatred with which the self responds to the parental figures who failed it. Also, the tenacity with which these inner relationships are clung to despite their maladaptive nature reflects a desperate need for the self to be attached to parental figures, no matter how bad they may be, to maintain any cohesion. When these attachments are threatened as in traumatic external happenings or in analytic work with their origins, then the anxiety aroused can be indescribable because isolation is felt as the dread madness or loss of the self. It is the difficulty in reaching these levels of development within the analytic relationship, and then usually only with seriously disturbed personalities, that made for the long delay in exploring these regions. What has emerged is that when the analyst has enough understanding to accept the intensely destructive hatred towards him when he is felt by the patient to be like the depriving mother, then working through the terrors of this relationship leads to the analyst being felt as reliable and concerned. An inner security is then established with a capacity to love in contrast with the permanent distortions of relationships that early deprivations leave especially when parent–child relationships remain bad.

While there seems to be a general pattern of the kind outlined, there is an infinite range of compensatory developments from better experience at later stages according as the talents of each child find a supportive expression from the parents and the family. In Buchan's development, the serious early deprivation was covered over by the extraordinary combination of the subsequent intense devotion of his parents, his unique talents fully encouraged, and energetically pursued, and a highly supportive family group. Nevertheless, his primal self remained unconsciously seeking the integration every child must achieve if its autonomous strivings, through their acceptance with parental joyous responsiveness, are to become transformed into good relations with others.

24. ON BECOMING AND BEING A PERSON

In recent years, I have got rather obsessed with the problem of the self because of what I feel to be the clamorous need for a new paradigm in psychoanalytic theory. One of the unfortunate features of psychoanalysis is the awful subservience to the tablets the master brought down from the mountain. Nobody dares say anything that would criticize Freud—he was regarded as the last word. I think it's terribly unfortunate that there isn't more openness.

I've chosen as the title for my theme: On Becoming and Being a Person. The agency of human motivation and conduct is the self, and we've got to understand more and more about its nature, its origin, and its functioning.

It has been remarked frequently that classical metapsychology has failed to do justice to the essential personal quality of the individual in its account of human nature. Moreover, I believe that it is the failure to give an acceptable theoretical basis for the personal level of behavior that has created the most prominent feature of the current psychotherapeutic scene; namely, a pluralism in theory and practice, with consequent confusion and uncertainty in those trying to appraise its various claims. Now, this development has been of concern to analysts in recent years. They've become concerned lest their work and its importance for society becomes discredited.

Three years ago the president of the International Psychoanalytic Association, Dr. Robert Wallerstein, entitled his presidential address "One Psychoanalysis or Many?"—a paper (1988) in which he provided a masterly survey of this aspect of the current scene. There, Wallerstein considers the anomaly of very different theoretical ideas being associated with comparable practice by analysts remaining within one professional body, the International Association. So they must feel that there is something common that keeps them and holds them together, and that can be recognized and evaluated.

The anomaly of this situation, with different theoretical ideas associated with comparable practice, led him to put forward some ideas based on thoughts from Joseph and Ann-Marie Sandler. In the early history of analysis, challenges to his theoretical principles led Freud to exclude the prominent dissidents from the psychoanalytic movement, because their views were associated with clinical work that abandoned what he deemed to be the essential core of psychoanalysis.

Yet, in Freud's view, any line of investigation that recognized the two facts of transference and resistance, and took them as the starting point of its work, even though it arrived at results other than his own, had a right to call itself psychoanalysis.

That was fair enough. Proceeding from his own metapsychological principles, Freud formulated his structural theory of the personality, which brought a period of outstandingly productive cohesion. As in all scientific work, developments inevitably exposed theoretical limitations, and in psychoanalysis these were plainly in the understanding of the ego. Anna Freud, followed by Hoffman and his colleagues, in a surge of fresh thinking, filled out a conspicuous gap in the structural theory with her creation of the psychology of the ego and so, in some measure, introducing a more holistic view of the person. Preserving much of Freud's metapsychology nevertheless, this line of thought was widely adopted as part of what has become known, certainly in the United States, as the mainstream development of Freud's work.

A different fate befell the work of Melaine Klein, despite her repeated emphasis that it, too, was evolved directly from Freud's theory of the instincts, especially his later concept of the death instinct. Her findings proved so disturbing that there were early reactions to them as not falling within the scope of psychoanalysis. Thus, the suspicion arose that inclusion within the analytic field was to be determined by theoretical conformity to Freud, rather than by the careful appraisal of new data, even though these were gleaned by the psychoanalytic method.

Now, the impact of Fairbairn's papers, published during and immediately after the War, was minimal, and this disregard has continued increasingly in the United Kingdom, though progressively less so in the United States. It's particularly striking that it was Fairbairn who introduced the term *object-relations theory* to describe views that challenged Freud's theory of the instincts radically. Many factors contributed to the neglect of his contribution, despite the fact that he was a devoted and highly sophisticated adherent to psychoanalysis as Freud had wished it to be. Indeed, it was soon after his first paper appeared that the term he introduced for his views—namely, an object-relations theory—was being used widely, for example, to cover the work of Balint and Winnicott as well. The views of Klein, who in her earlier writing stressed the importance of the influence of relationship, were also regarded as coming within the object-relations theory category. For myself, I believe the neglect of Fairbairn has been a serious loss in the development of psychoanalysis because of the closer links his views made with the person, links that he felt strongly were required.

Let me return to Wallerstein's address. He suggested that the anomaly of these different views being associated with acceptable practice could be resolved in large measure by the adoption of the Sandlers' suggestion that we distinguish a present unconscious from a past unconscious (J. Sandler and A-M. Sandler 1984). The present unconscious includes the derivatives of the past unconscious that are closer to experience, for example, the mechanism of defense. We deal with the past unconscious when we deal with the infant that is hidden by the infantile amnesia within the person. The nature of the past unconscious is inferred from its perpetual intrusion in fantasy and transference in the analytic situation.

The Sandlers point out that the understanding we gain about this part of the personality rests on creative acts of reconstruction. They make the further suggestion that in fashioning a general theory of infantile development, the different accounts are couched in metaphors, rather than in the real realities. When a metaphor captures enough real realities, then dynamically similar factors can follow from very different metaphors.

Wallerstein is somewhat pessimistic about achieving a widely acceptable general theory of development because the true factors lie too far beyond the realm of empirical study and scientific progress. He grants that this position will change, but he is not optimistic about achievement in the near future. The use of metaphors, Wallerstein reminds us, is common in all scientific endeavor at certain stages, when they are virtually indispensable, but the great danger they introduce, especially in the human sciences, is that the metaphorical factors all too readily become regarded as realities. When they're felt to fit aptly and closely with the phenomenon, they gain a powerful grip, both from their heuristic value and from unconscious sources.

Now, when confronted with the growing mass of new clinical data, along with the fact that modern evolutionary biology has advanced understanding to a point where the Newtonian principles of the science of Freud's day can no longer be regarded as a tenable foundation for comprehending the phenomena of living organisms, then Freud's metaphoric base for the understanding of human nature and motivation must be reappraised, despite the extraordinary tenacity with which the id metaphor has persisted. In his last contribution, "An Outline of Psychoanalysis," Freud (1937) opens his chapter on the instincts with the statement that the power of the id expresses the true purpose of the individual organism's life, namely, to satisfy its innate needs arising from the force of the instincts.

The International Congress in 1987 started from Freud's paper, "Analysis Terminable and Interminable" (1937). Exemplifying the tenacity of the id metaphor André Green, the French analyst, in his paper at this conference, expresses the view that it is Freud's concept of the instinctual nature of the unconscious that has given rise to significant reservations, both in regard to the specific instincts postulated and their mode of functioning. Yet there is a great reluctance to face up to this issue. When he lists some of the alternatives proposed, he selects, first, those who radically reject the concept of instinct in favor of the theory based on object relations. He then names primarily Fairbairn and Guntrip.

It seems to me that Green's way of putting things is totally misleading. Fairbairn regards instinctive endowment in man as an obvious necessity in accounting for development. What Fairbairn rejects is Freud's concept of *the instincts as somatic energies* that, in his phrase, give the ego a kick in the pants to get on with some activity, as a means of arousing action to discharge tension, rather than as an innate potential motivating an organism to seek relationships. The subsequent proactive transactions between organism and environment—that is, between the infant and mother primarily—give rise to the dynamic structures required for the organization of experience. They, thus, constitute the embryonic ego; for no learning can take place without such structures being involved from the very start.

The arguments of nature versus nurture, of instinct theory versus object relations, to me are thus largely irrelevant, as is also the adversarial relationship between society and the individual stressed by Freud. Instinctive endowment only becomes identifiable through its realization in the object relations it meets and seeks.

The viewpoint of modern evolutionary biology is radically different from the science available to Freud. In his day, the organism was described from a paradigm taken from mechanistic engineering in which the preservation of the structure is of foremost concern. The primary concern is how it maintains its equilibrium as a basic condition for achieving this, and the answer is found in homeostasis as the cybernetic mechanism.

Now, in the theory of open systems that constitute every living organism, the dynamic phenomenon of development and maintenance of life are conceived as permanent processes in which *positive feedback* is characteristic—not negative feedback, but positive feedback—that is, not coming back to the previous equilibrium, but breaking out of the boundaries of that to evolve new structures.

Now, from the original state of wholeness and order within the innate components that initiate the appropriate transactions with the environment, self-adaptation in a self-organizing whole preserves its identity, despite constant transformations. Such living systems cannot be built up from the aggregation of parts, but start from their living progenitors. Each organism contains an organizing principle that determines the potential shape of the adult organism.

I found myself many years ago using the idea that the organism's innate potential has some shape and characteristic activity. Activity, which is the constant motivation of the organism, ensures that it reaches outward until it meets in the environment something that fits the shape.

In her book on autistic children, Frances Tustin (1972) describes the dreadful, tragic situation of children who have failed to make a relationship with their mother or caring figures, and so fail to develop a self. But it's very striking that these autistic children have an intense interest in shapes, and circles appeal to them greatly, perhaps because a circle signifies a mother figure. My old idea of the potential having shape is not such a fanciful notion after all.

Holograms within the central nervous system demonstrate that shapes of the holistic form of the organ and of the structure can be contained in a potential form that permeates the whole structure. So the whole mind/body problem has changed radically since the days when Freud tied his theory to the prevailing science of chemistry and physiology.

I want to stress that living organisms cannot be built up from the aggregation of parts. They have to start from their living progenitors. Each organism contains an organizing principle that determines the potential shape of the adult organism. Development within an organism, which is an open system necessarily, demands an autonomous urge to maintain this wholeness of the shape; otherwise, the organism dies. A threat to the autonomy of the organism is tantamount to a threat from a lethal predator. To survive it has to assert itself autonomously at all times with varying degrees of force, up to the point of maximum ferocity. Paradoxically, its resources for doing so, however, have to be developed—and to an increasing extent as we ascend the evolutionary scale—from its relatedness with the adults. The organism's life becomes the dynamic process of preserving its autonomy within the heteronomy of relatedness with its social group and the physical environment.

In summary, the first principle to start with and grasp firmly is that the living organism has this inherent shape and that it is an open system. That is, it grows with organizing principles forming its interactions with the environment and transforming these into the shapes needed so that the adult form of the organism is reached.

The lower down the evolutionary scale we go, the more the behavioral patterns that mediate survival are ready-made. The tadpole can get off, swim away, and feed itself, and so on. It doesn't need a great deal of support from the adults. Dinosaurs are said to have done something similar, and recent evidence rather suggests that adult dinosaurs did do more than just protect the young. They could communicate to the young how to anticipate dangerous situations of a nonmanifest kind.

Resources for achieving this potential have to be developed. It's characteristic that, as we go up the evolutionary scale, the innate potential has more and more plasticity, more of a potential, rather than an inherited specific pattern. And the potential to reach adult development has to be realized within the framework of relationships with adults.

Based on the findings of human evolution, I conclude that the innate potential has to be highly complex and plastic because the human organism has become a social animal and its survival takes place only within social groups. In the lower levels of the evolutionary scale, the cohesion in the group is fairly largely concerned with protection, and so the group is tied together by attachment to the dominant male. In the human group things are very different. It seems here that to provide for the plasticity required to exploit the environment—and, indeed, as evolution has gone on, the capacity for man to *make* his environment—then we need very different resources.

Freud's method of reaching his views about the instincts was to make inferences from the neuroses of individuals; and, hence, sex and aggression were taken to be the dominant drives in man. But human nature was thus conceived as derived from forces internal to the organism, rather than through creative structuring from the interaction of a plastic potential with the environment.

The evolutionary value of a social approach to human development is evident; for a human group, a social group that got established in a certain environment, naturally needs its young to grow up with knowledge of and familiarity with the features of that environment. There is an immense need for communication, and so capacities for thought developed, with the associated requirement for language. The relatedness of the individual is increasing in depth, as well as extent, all the time.

From experience of encounters with the environment, the ego was created on the surface of the id, as Freud originally put it, although he later saw that id and ego could not be differentiated in the earliest stages of development. With greater importance attached to the role of the environment and to the importance of aggression, investigators find that the instincts appear to be much more complex and holistic—not so much a matter of ethologically proscribed behavior, but striving towards and reaching an end state—rather than following specific behaviors.

All embryologists, when starting their work, prepare themselves with a thorough knowledge of the adult or the mature organism to which development is headed. So if, rather than looking at individuals, we take the view of ethologists looking at what happens in species, then we ask what are the behavioral characteristics that large groups of animals have in common. If these can be shown to be relatively free from environmental influence, then they are not the products of training, and presumably we are dealing with innate potentials that underwrite those broad clustered features of behavior.

I doubt whether any valid generalizations about instincts can be made from clinical data, simply because the history of the environmental influence upon individuals is completely unknown. It's only when you've got a population to study that you can eliminate the specific features of individual experience.

Yankelovitch and Barrett (1970), in their book *Ego and Instinct*, have a remarkable critique of the basic principles of psychoanalysis. Two philosophers, one a social scientist as well, took such social studies as were available—namely, those of Cantril (1955), the social psychologist—of more than a dozen utterly different cultures, and they asked what were the common features of people in the groups? Rather than seeing individuals whose motivation is founded on instinctive forces of a totally impersonal kind driving the organism to seek pleasure, they found from the study of the social group quite a different collection of patterns that lead to a different theory of human motivation.

What they found in all thirteen cultures were characteristically human features that go beyond individual requirements, as follows: the quest for satisfying the needs for food, shelter, territorial security and for an individual security, and the procreation security for the future; a need for order, certainty and form to give assurance that experience could be repeated; a need beyond adaptation to the environment by a search for new experiences and a hunger for knowledge; the capacity to make choices, the freedom to do so, and the responsibility for acting upon the decision made.

(Most philosophers agree that freedom of will, the capacity to make a freely determined decision, is a characteristic feature of human beings preferable to their being compelled by instinctive patterns all the time.)

They go on to enumerate other characteristic features: a need to feel his own security and identity, and to have it maintained within his culture—that is, to be valued by others; the hope that the future of his society will fulfil his aspirations; to have a system of values and beliefs to which he can commit himself and even sacrifice himself. And then to facilitate all of these, he has the need for language. The characteristic that is new in the evolutionary scale is sharing, and individuals cannot share unless they can communicate what they are feeling and thinking. Language becomes a requisite for development of that kind (Yankelovich and Barrett 1970, p. 400).

From this list we can also infer the need to conceive a central organizing system of self, which not only mediates its internal organization, but which can communicate its thoughts and other mental activity freely, so that sharing with others can be carried out. The self is also facilitated in its functioning by the unique property in the animal world of being able to transcend itself to appraise its function. It can look at itself. When motives are conflicting, the self considers the conflict.

Now, the conception of a human nature that seeks to meet these needs is a very different one from the manifestation of instincts in the traditional form. As Isadore Chein (1972), that distinguished philosophical psychologist, puts it, the essential psychological human quality is one of commitment to a developing and continuing set of unending, interacting, interdependent, and mutually modified long-range purposes. The development of such commitment starts from the innate potential in the infant in constant transactions with the carers, chiefly the mother and family, transactions that are determined in the earliest phases by the innate factors in the organism, and also by the parallel evolutionary development in the mother, which equips the mother to take the right moves toward the needs of the infant at the right time.

So we can equate the human person with having a self. The development starts from an innate potential that finds its shape within constant transactions determined in the earliest phases by the innate factors in mother and child, and later with the carers in the family and in that particular culture, all of which, therefore, play an increasing part in the evolution of man.

The full development of this commitment to human group goals or end-states is what characterizes a mature person. Failure to achieve such development means that the person is not fully realized, though the potentiality to become so may well be there. But this realization needs an appropriately responsive environment from society to give the growing organism the care and concern that it needs for its evolution.

The function of the self, or the person, is to integrate a developing series of differentiated substructures within what has been an integrated whole to cope with various specific needs, but a structure that retains its holistic quality. I postulate an autonomous self.

You might object and ask how I can talk about a self before experience starts? Well, you get into a rather vicious circle about the cart and horse there. It doesn't seem to me that it's a problem nowadays, because if we conceive of the organizing principle, not as a content of behavior, but an affective tone that informs the organism that this is right or not, then we can see a monitoring system for development. If the infant is getting the right input of food, fine. If it isn't, it protests. It uses various specific methods for protests. But the same is true in regard to its psychological needs: if it's not being treated as a self, the infant protests. And that, indeed, may be the strongest argument for the existence of some innate holistic structure.

The developmental psychological work in recent years confirms this view that the infant behaves as a whole, and behaves as a person, and adults respond to the infant as a whole person. The infant has the inherent quality that it is going to become an adult human being, and that quality is responded to and fostered by the community. This ability to transcend itself, to look at itself and appraise its existential situation, is unique to humans in the animal world.

Our development is dependent on a certain affective tone: a sense that we're doing all right, that our self feels all right, that we don't feel deprived, and we don't feel we're doing the wrong thing. That affective tone is a plastic monitor for a wide range of different activities. The baby is given the innate impulse to grope for the breast. The baby doesn't know what it's going to find. All it has is this innate groping activity. When the mother puts the breast in front of the baby's mouth, the baby's feeling right away is, "This is what I've been looking for all my life, and here it is." So then you get experience beginning to be structured; but you can't learn without some previous structuring of the search, the groping, and the experience.

Freud himself and Melanie Klein introduce the ego and the self, but mostly ego, because "self" was regarded as a kind of nonword in scientific discussion, it was so subjective. But it's rather striking how both of them say "the ego does this" or "the self does that." In other words, the self's value as the agent of behavior is assumed, referred to, but never studied as such. It never becomes separated as a concept in the earlier stages of development.

In contrast, it was on the central place of the self that Fairbairn's work started; and this, I sometimes think, is not referred to enough. You cannot have an object-relations theory without a self. It's only a self that relates to other selves. As one of the philosophical biologists has said, it takes a gestalt to relate to a gestalt. An aggregate cannot produce this holistic quality of responding to what is essentially the quality of the whole in the organism, so that you have to have these holistic gestalts—that is, the self—developing in this way.

Now we know, of course, that from the structural potential the self grows rapidly, and we have a fair idea of what takes place there nowadays. When we see the work of the child development researchers like Daniel Stern linking up with the clinical studies of the analyst then we see a bipolar situation. The infant developers are starting from day one, working forward. The analyst starts from the adult end, working backwards. It's going to be like the Channel tunnel—hopefully, the two ends will meet. The two areas of study are absolutely complementary, and we need both. The infant developmentalists cannot, without knowing the features of the adult self, appreciate what is going on completely. Whereas, if we study only the adult self, we're apt to make theories about fantasy possibilities or to deny possibilities that are there.

There is no question, when you review classical analytic theory and psychological theory, that the whole potential of the infant is grossly underrated. The capacity of infants to smile knowingly, to recognize a human face, and to play is quite amazing. When you see videotapes of the early development of infants just a matter of a week or two old, it's astounding to see just how personalized they are.

Fairbairn started from the particular group of patients he was concerned with, schizoid individuals whose difficulties were that they couldn't make relationships. His conclusion about the common factor was that these people had never had their self developed because they were never loved for their own sake. Now to understand him when he states that the infant has a unique self that grows only when it is loved for its own sake, we've got to have some idea of what is the innate self and what we mean by love. And besides, it's only in man, you could say, that the particular quality and duration of nurturance establishes what we call love and care. We don't get socially related comprehensive love until we reach man. There is something like love in animals' protection of their young, but it does not extend to their injured. I suppose it was too dangerous to stay back with a sick one, because of the risk of predators. Only man deals with the injured of the species. Only man has care and concern for the survival of the person, the self.

This conception of human nature, then, is very different from the classical one. The defining characteristic of the human being is now seen as the capacity for commitment to a developing series of unending, interacting, interdependent, and mutually modifying long-range purposes. In other words, instinctual satisfaction, the quick-fix, is not adequate as the sole feature of motivation. Motivation has to keep the animal directed toward concern for the total community, for its survival, for the building up of experience and knowledge, and for its transmission. These are all part of the instinctive potential.

This was known quite early on. Malinowski (1927, 1929), the anthropologist, pointed out that the Western idea of primitive sexuality amongst savages was completely misleading. Sexuality was part of a highly social, organized behavioral complex to ensure the preservation of the group. The more we seek to exploit the environment, to control the environment, and to be self-actualized, the more we need learning, organization, and experience.

The more you think of the self, the more you realize that object-relations theory has acquired a misnomer that has given it a misleading status. It's really a theory of the self. The self makes the relationships, and the self is made by the relationships; the two interact, and the self is the agent of action. Now we all know clinically that neurosis is constructed by the person. It doesn't just happen. Symptoms don't just happen. They are created by the person as a whole.

If we study projection tests like the Rorschach, we can see that it is a total self that governs the perception because, while the self organizes a holistic precept, at the same time the substructures perceive details and interpret them in some other way. But the important point I think is that the total self is always in action. What we call the ego, I'm suggesting, is that bit of the self that is most developed around experience with the real world.

Although Wallerstein has difficulty with metaphors in analytic theory, I don't think we have that difficulty when we deal with the self. Is there anything more real than saying "I feel this" or "I think that"? In other words, what the self does is synchronous with reality in human contact.

Freud's concept of id postulates that while we appear to be one way in reality, really we are a mass of all these powerful instincts below the surface. There's increasing feeling, certainly amongst philosophers, that we're kidding ourselves here. This so-called real reality is a fantasy construct, simply because we have believed sufficiently in the fact that the higher levels of organization always produce a new repertoire of power in action, a new set of properties, which do not belong to any lower level and which are unpredictable. It doesn't matter how much we know about hydrogen and oxygen: no one can predict that the resultant product is the best additive to Scotch! These qualities are unique and emergent. The same thing is going on in the organism: properties are emergent all the time.

A common difficulty has been the theory that the infant at the start can't possibly have a separate self. It must be merged with the mother's as a kind of extension of the mother's self. Now, that is not what behavioral observation suggests. Watching the nursing couple, we note that, right from the start, a baby is a highly determined little creature that knows what it wants and gets it, and makes the mother adapt. So we've got to postulate this highly autonomous urge.

In his self-object theory, Kohut describes the need for a close, mirroring figure to maintain the sense of self. Without that, there's a nonfunctioning structure in the infant. But, to me, the self is not a passive extension to the mother's self. There's an autonomous, competent self there in the infant. The frustration of this highly autonomous quality sets the ground for most psychopathology.

Perhaps the autonomy of the self has been obscured because of the physical dependency of the infant and its need for closeness to the mother much of the time. Bowlby's work on attachment has given a widespread idea that attachment is the thing. I cannot see that attachment is anything other than a precondition for the development of the self. It's the first step. The baby has to become attached to the mother, to cling to, to hold onto the mother, and to find security there; and it's out of all the constant experience of being in attachment that the infant builds the self. Bowlby himself speaks of the self being evolved from the attachment situation by increasing modeling.

You can see that we are dealing, certainly, with a highly dynamic whole self with a powerful sense of autonomy. Certainly it needs to be developed by the input of loving models; but it also has its own capacity for fantasy, for play by which it can try out modes of behavior and build up possible self attitudes.

Psychoanalytic experience certainly suggests—and behavioral researchers would agree—that the inner security to do this, to set up an active, exploratory attitude to the world at large, comes from the experience of being loved. The plain fact seems to be that the infant has a powerful urge to get to the right experience, provided it's made reasonably available. So by denying the ordinary caring attention, we create intense situations of frustration that lead to splitting of the object and the self.

All I want to stress is that we've simply got to take as the basic feature in metapsychology the autonomous struggle of the self. Rather than the vicissitudes of instinct, let's think of the vicissitudes of the self in the relationships it finds.

Now I'll quickly give you two cases, the first from a British Independent point of view and the second from the Kleinian perspective, both of which bring out the kind of problems that have haunted us. I've also used these cases and two other cases of Fairbairn and Betty Joseph to elaborate upon my argument (Sutherland 1989) but here I'll confine myself to two cases by Patrick Casement (1990) and Terrtu Eskelinen de Folch (1988). First, I'll quote a case from Patrick Casement's book *On Learning from the Patient* (1990). It's always a good thing to quote from somebody else, because then I can't be accused of quoting evidence I've created.

> A young woman, Miss K, was referred for help with compulsive eating of several years' duration. She described her mother as manipulative and intrusive, preventing her from having any real independence. The mother had a flamboyant enjoyment of breast feeding, which could well have fostered an oral fixation. When 2 years old, a sister was born, and her mother withdrew to the pleasures of the nursing relationship, leaving the patient for several weeks with a nanny. Miss K then developed a highly seductive relationship with her father, which ended with his death when she was 17. Feeling bereft and empty, she dealt with her grief and depression by overeating. The intensity of her attachment to her father led her to feel that her sexuality was bad. Young men said she was devouring. Her mother's sexual orientation and her unusually seductive behavior with both her and Miss K's sister confused Miss K.
>
> Miss K's overeating also derived from her mother's ambition

With daughter Anne, first grandchild Phoebe, and Molly, 1973

Being a grandfather, 1979

to make her slim and beautiful, which was so possessive and overpowering that Miss K ceased to feel herself to be a separate person. Eating asserted an independence from the mother's control, yet she clung to her mother, despite the feeling that the mother was like a permanent cancer inside herself. The guilt she felt about her sexual contacts with men also added to her eating, which she thought would chase the men away.

Miss K had had a previous therapist before she had come from abroad to England, and he had fostered her dependence on him by offering extra sessions and physical comfort. Casement's attentions in the form of interpretations were taken by her as an attempt to control her. It became clear that her experience had led her to feel that all relationships were manipulative. When Casement resisted her demands for more and more of this and that, she reacted aggressively by having other treatments, outside of analysis, especially with her brother-in-law, who was a family doctor. These posed a serious problem at times. For instance, she got antidepressants secretly, and later had her jaws wired, despite which contraption she managed to feed herself with triumph. These measures intensified the hatred of her mother, which emerged as biting sarcasm to those who angered her. A behavioral therapist then repeated the physical acting out she had with her first therapist, until her sexual excitement frightened her away from him.

Casement interpreted these other treatments as enactments of the relationships she wished to make with him, but had to keep apart from him to maintain him in the image of the nonintrusive mother and the nonsexual father. Intense ambivalence evoked Miss K's wish to protect her mother against her murderous feelings. That, of course, is the primary reaction to frustration of the self: intense rage with murderous ferocity.

Some confrontations with the mother about her attitudes on a visit that the mother made to England improved the relationship. After a year in analysis, she began to free herself from her mother, but remained overweight, lest her mother and her brother-in-law could think they had been responsible for her progress. In her last session before leaving London, after about 18 months, Casement was impressed by her statement, "I am becoming my own version of myself."

Casement describes being made often to feel helpless and destroyed. He believed it to be essential that he had let Miss K come to her own realization of her unconscious need to experience the freedom to be destructive with no intrusion from him. The essential dynamics of the treatment, therefore, he took to be the opportunity to survive her intensely destructive efforts to wreck it and him. As

> Winnicott put it, when the assertive strivings of the baby are repeated in analysis, the critical thing is that the analyst should accept all these and survive, because that's what the ordinary mother does, thereby, of course, giving the deep physical instinctive proof that mother can take it. The very substantial change in becoming her own person was seen a few years later when Miss K wrote, telling him of how she had discovered her creative abilities with a newfound confidence.
>
> Using a classical formulation, her behavior would have been reduced to an oral fixation under the influence of oedipal guilt, while the Kleinian perspective might be that she had regressed due to preoedipal factors such as intense oral sadism from the death instinct. Casement, however, adopts another way of looking at Miss K's conflicts. We cannot but agree with him that Miss K's symptoms are pressing because of other, more complex purposes of the self than drive satisfaction.

The value of that case for my purpose is that it has all the drive manifestations from which Freud made his classical theories—oral, anal, and the next thing. But what seems to be the best explanation, the most plausible one, the one that is the best fit for the total situation, is simply that her mother had deprived her of a feeling that she was doing her own thing in her own way.

The other case that I would like to quote from was described by a Kleinian analyst, Eskelinen de Folch (1991). She notes—and, I thought, very sharply—that if the unresolved clinical problems prompting Freud to write "Analysis, Terminable and Interminable" are still with us, then our present-day explanatory capacity is not sufficient to resolve them. She then focuses on the analyzability of certain concealed nuclei of the personality that appear to be remote from the analytical relationship. Such patients, even after long analysis, have great difficulty acknowledging destructive impulses, such as hatred and envy, as belonging to them. They are terrified of disintegration, a dread that Klein described as aroused by primitive terrifying objects that are deeply repressed. Eskelinen de Folch believes that it is not necessary for these patients to be in a crisis for these primitive objects to appear, as she illustrates from a clinical case.

> The patient, a brilliant academic man held in very high regard, had come seeking treatment because he felt something lacking in his relationship with his wife and in life generally. He was burdened with a sense of impending disaster. In analysis, he began to have dreams of terrorists who set fire to book shops: sometimes he is the terrorist, yet he maintains he has nothing to do with it. Early in analysis, he dreamed of a small boy in danger of falling from a balcony. He then saw himself in a diver's suit, taking a shower and becoming excited. In the third part of the dream, he was carrying his own dead body to the little boy's mother, asking her for a death

> certificate, the cause of death being something like "death by annihilation."
>
> He kept impersonalizing his relationship with the analyst, which made her think that his terrifying object had come actively into their relationship and had to be defended against. In a subsequent session, he was intensely anxious, and said, quite unusually for him, that he felt some intense rage against her when he realized they might speak of important things. On the way to the session, he had seen one door of the lift labeled "exit," while the other opened into the void; and this idea related to his silences after moments of some true contact. He was horrified that the image of himself as warm and understanding, the goody-goody, was not at all accurate. He then had a silent period, after which he was surprised by how indifferent he felt. Just as the session was about to end, he revealed he had forgotten to tell the analyst that he and his wife had decided to have a child.

In discussing such material, Kleinians see the dangers of hate, but they account for that, as Freud did, by postulating an instinct of destruction within the organism, whereas people interested in relationships, like Fairbairn, see the hate and the aggressive phenomena as a violent reaction for the survival of the autonomy of the self. In Winnicottian terms, I might say that the patient had become an academic through a false self forced upon him by mother. In his dreams of the arsonists who came in and set fire to book shops, I might see a tremendous resentment that began to come out about his mother not allowing him a spontaneous self.

In response to that dream and the theme of death by annihilation, Eskelinen de Folch applies Kleinian ideas. With regard to instincts, ego structure, and object relations, she notes that:

a. highly destructive defence mechanisms are fuelled by the death instinct;
b. impulses to split are related to objects internal and external and to the analyst in the analysis. The patient may acknowledge these impulses after prolonged analytic work as his own but
c. he may then find himself caught in a painful repetitive experience from which he may derive a sadomasochistic satisfaction that seems to have a life of its own and which he strongly resists giving up.

Eskelinen de Folch then brings in some of Bion's ideas about a particular form of repetition compulsion, namely the fragmentation of objects that lead to intense persecutory anxiety by the objects into which they have been projected. The person makes a pact with these objects, which, while lessening the persecution, leads to compulsive acting out. The objects terrify the person while another part of the personality establishes other normal relations. Eskelinen de Folch thinks that this part of the personality that is struggling with psychotic anxiety is shaped not by love but by the strength of the death instinct. The possibility of changing these object relations is limited by the violence of the splitting process and by the amount of satisfaction derived from the situation.

Quoting work on this type of problem by Betty Joseph and Elizabeth Spillius, Eskelinen de Folch refers to serious countertransference problems. Through the exploration of countertransference, the underlying internal object relationships can be recovered. Eskelinen de Folch concludes that the concepts of the death instinct and the repetition compulsion can help us build our theory. The death instinct implements the splits while the integrative character of the life instinct acts as a counterpoint. The concealed nuclei of the personality appear as a sinister result of the action of the death drive. According to Eskelinen de Folch the repetition compulsion, however, may represent attempts to deal with the primary trauma in a less catastrophic way. This primary trauma arose because the death instinct was not mitigated by an appropriate external object—the good breast or the good mother.

I am impressed by Eskelinen de Folch's penetration into the primitive self levels, based on a highly developed sensitivity to the expression of early relationships in the transference created by a correspondingly sensitive use of the countertransference. It seems to me that this is where the advances made by Klein and her students lie.

Wallerstein notes comparable work with the present unconscious among analysts of different persuasions, but I do not want to underestimate differences among the various schools of thought in psychoanalysis. The identification of what is going on in the present unconscious in Eskelinen de Folch's case is to me of a different order than occurs in non-Kleinian analyses. She attributes her work to recognition of the impersonal death instinct along with mechanisms operating at a personal level, mainly projective identification and envy.

For Eskelinen de Folch, the concealed nuclei of the personality are intensely repressed object relationships, as a non-Kleinian might think. But the Kleinian concept of internal object relationships is based in instinct theory.

Early in analysis, Eskelinen de Folch's patient dreamed of a little boy falling from a balcony, then being excited by the prospect of engaging in deep diving, and then demanding from his mother a certificate of the cause of his death by annihilation. From my own object-relations perspective, I would conclude that he felt that his mother had annihilated his self. His manifest self was one of great academic success and popularity, but with failure in his close relationships. This suggests to me that his success came from a self adopted under his mother's pressure, a *false* self in Winnicott's terms. This self is inevitably identified with the mother that he wishes to destroy because of what she has done to an essential part of his self, namely the part that could have permitted him to make close relations with others. From his dreams of terrorists who set fire to bookshops, I suspect a denied, enraged self that attacks what his mother has made him into. To admit this, he would have to overcome the terrifying anxiety of a vengeful destruction of his mother who has given him what he lives by. More important than any guilt over this action, however, is his fear of disintegration if he carried out this murderous attack—a fear of falling into space with nothing to support him. I suggest that this rage burst out against the analyst when he thought that she might expose his secret intentions and he was shaken to feel that this might now destroy her.

To account for this patient's personality and his difficulties, I need a structural theory founded on the self and its needs, a theory that recognizes that failure to meet these needs in the earliest stages of development evokes intense aggression from the very beginning.

A crucial feature of working with the self as the agent in its presenting difficulties, is that we deal very little in metaphors. The self's experience is an ultimate factor, the thing in itself, and not requiring hypothetical realities other than itself.

The immense contribution of the Kleinians has been that their understanding of early phenomena has given them a capacity to use these manifestations in the analytic situation, working with transference, countertransference, projection, and projective identification; and that's been an enormous gift for psychoanalysis. But I don't think the theory is a help here. I don't think we need Klein's death instinct. What we need is a protesting organism.

SUMMARY

The complex issue of the self is a widely ramifying theme. For me it's such a critically important one. I think that the future of psychoanalytic theory will certainly rest on getting the self properly conceptualized. What I've tried to do is to give an evolutionary biological background to where the self is needed in the evolutionary scheme, to share my ideas as to how it could have evolved in that way, and to describe some of its properties and its necessity for man as a social animal, especially an animal that is self-organizing and able not only to adapt to, but to make its own environment. These, I think, are possible only through the development of this highly integrative structure, which can permit us to internalize the world, play with it inside, and make innovating possibilities: the autonomous self.

DISCUSSION

Male Questioner: In your extensive lecture, you talk about self that transcends itself. In other words, the self becomes critical of itself and objectifies itself. Will you discuss a little more what factors help the self to objectify itself?

Dr. Sutherland: The most obvious way to check up any subjective excess is to share it with others. They can then cut it down to size and so on. Individualism has tended to dominate in our culture, "keeping yourself to yourself." But the group could be very helpful, not attacking, and not belittling to the self. We've got to learn more and more, and use more and more, the phenomena of group relatedness in shared activity and study how to foster maximum freedom within that situation. That's how to address the problem of objectivity of the self.

Male Questioner: Dr. Sutherland, I wonder if you would agree or disagree that a future direction for psychoanalytic object-relations theory, in keeping with what your closing remark was, might be in the development of a dialogue with moral philosophy?

Dr. Sutherland: Paramount in groups, of course, is an active concern for others and respect for the individuality of others, so that certainly there's a high overlap with the moral philosophers. Charles Taylor, the professor at Oxford, has written a stunning book on the resources of the self. But some of the philosophers are ignorant of psychoanalytic developments. We can't expect *them* to know more—*we're* fumbling for our own knowledge. But if we can get our views of the self clarified, sharpened up, and presented in the literature so that philosophers could really absorb it more readily, then I think the dialogue will increase in its value greatly. But I would certainly say that it's an area where a coming together would be most helpful.

Male Questioner: I would say that the self is really a fiction, although a useful one, and that self is always in the context of relatedness, or in an open system. And if that's true, the self isn't at all divorceable from the ongoing relatedness. You can't convey the open-ended nature of what's needed and then talk as if the self is something that knows exactly what it needs once and for all, as in your example of the infant getting the breast, because that's already abstracting the self from the context of a workable relationship with the mother or the mothering one.

While I'm in line with what you're saying, I propose that to speak of an autonomous self, or a simple sense of self, without a lot of ongoing dialogue and reflection about what's happening with it and what the qualities of experience are, is reifying the concept of the autonomous self.

Dr. Sutherland: Well, I must say quickly that I don't accept that position because what is inherited in the potential is an affect, not a content. There's nothing specific psychologically in regard to the knowledge of the environment. What is inherited is a feeling tonicity, and if things are not right, then protest and reaction take place.

Now, the great philosophical argument at present, as I understand it, is this: is there anything corresponding to a self that's inherent in the organism, or is it all created by social relatedness? I don't think you can get social relatedness without this core, which is the monitoring, discriminating agent for what feels good or bad, or right or wrong, or painful or pleasant. So I think there is a core of a very plastic nature that is largely a kind of innate affective tone.

Dr. David Scharff: It seems to me that Fairbairn wrote about the object world with the assumption that it was the self reaching out to it; but he didn't talk much about the self that he assumed. And what you're talking about is that which remains undescribed and undefined. It seems to me that a balance will be found when we are able to talk about both poles of self and object and the way in which they are absolutely inextricable. Obviously, the self is not a fiction. It is the thing that keeps on going, keeps on being, has to be, has to do, and yet that cannot be without the object world.

Within its scientific and environmental background, you really bring to life in all its elegance the thing that keeps us going, including our practice of the science or art of psychoanalysis: the autonomous self.

25. REMINISCENCES*

Dr. David Scharff: We want to plumb the depth and breadth of Dr. Sutherland's experiences with object-relations theory, its founder Ronald Fairbairn, and its major theorists—Harry Guntrip, Michael Balint, Donald Winnicott, and the Kleinians Wifred Bion and Melanie Klein—whose contributions we value and about whom we're so curious. So I hope this will be an evenhanded balance between high-minded theory and low-minded gossip.

Dr. Sutherland: There's nothing so interesting as gossip. I never undervalue gossip. The trouble with gossip is it so often becomes malicious, but it's not necessary to behave that way with gossip. You could enjoy it as fun.

Dr. Gordon: In your book, you ask what took Fairbairn into psychoanalysis as a career and what sustained it in him. What I would like to do is turn the tables and ask you those questions of yourself.

Dr. Sutherland: Well, I can never remember at all being consciously ambitious to make a certain goal, and yet I must have been driven by something, because I subjected myself to terrible privations. I went through the medical course while I was teaching in the psychology department, because you couldn't become a psychotherapist then unless you were medical, you see. Fairbairn told me that. So I took 6 years to do that course because I had to keep my full-time job. I had no money then. As a result, I think I finished up the worst qualified doctor in Britain, but I was in on the right racket as far as I was concerned.

When the war started, I was asked to go to the hospital for war neurosis. They expected psychiatric casualties on a fair scale, and they took over this vacant building that had been used as a hospital for what were then called criminal lunatics. They didn't mince words in those days. It was out in the country in a kind of mordant place.

---

*A collage by Jill Savege Scharff from tapes of informal teaching interviews with Drs. Edward Corrigan and Pearl Ellen Gordon at the Insitute for Contemporary Psychoanalysis and Drs. David E. Scharff and Jill Savege Scharff at the Washington School of Psychiatry.

Then Fairbairn was asked to come as a part-time consultant. Fairbairn did a lot of his thinking there about the return of the bad object. These war veterans had a terrible, traumatic experience, where their outer world really fitted their worst inner fantasies. Fairbairn was struck by that and also by the quality of infantile dependence that he found. These men couldn't face being away from home. Fairbairn concluded that infantile dependency was often associated with the development of war neurosis.

Well, I had only been there about 2 years when I was asked, "Why don't you come into the Officers Selection unit?" Maybe they thought that I had the potential to rise to the top, but my army career was quite different. I started at the top and worked down. Before I had a uniform on, I spent 2 days with these two top-ranking generals in the British army, discussing the set-up of this unit. This is where I was absolutely stunned, because these men had vision and intelligence: they were so unlike the Punch cartoons of the regular army officers.

Well, then, after the war, a group of us planned to restart the Tavistock Clinic—a group of very powerful people. I'm not being funny here. I think this is realistic. I could never understand why they asked me to be chairman of the group. Then it dawned on me that I was the only non–prima donna. The others were all prima donnas with dedicated interests, and so they were a bit frightened of each other in some ways. But they had worked together during the war, and they could stand each other's faces.

Remarkably few people ever have the chance of going into an institution where the total staff in charge is self-selected. It was an extraordinarily creative group. We knew we would have to divide into a clinic and a group to study organizations. From early on I was the chairman of both efforts. By the end of the war, we had been visited by all sorts of people, including a team of American psychiatrists, who had heard about us through Will Menninger who was head of psychiatry in the United States army. The thing about our Tavistock group was that, having come from psychotherapy, we were interested in the social relatedness of psychiatry and institutions. Our staff was very good at grasping the principle that the most creative thing to do for people is to give them the chance to grow. The staff had outgrown the bureaucratic, authoritarian solutions that were characteristic of the army and had learned that there's nothing that crushes individuality and talent more, as Russia has found out at long last. Eventually it came time to form two divisions: the Tavistock Clinic and the Tavistock Institute of Human Relations. I chose to become chairman of the clinic. I think I was a bit frightened of the industrial and organizational side. So I was chairman of the clinic and my title was Medical Director. That's a funny story, the title of that role. My accurate title should have been "Medical Directed" because I did what the group decided. If I differed from the group, then I had to argue inside, till we had consensus. But the Health Service insisted, "No, no, we don't want this Bolshevik nonsense. We want to pin the responsibility on somebody. Your title will be Medical Director, and you're responsible to us." I said, "Well, that's all very well, but then it's up to me to bring the staff opinions fused together."

As an institution, I must say, compared with other places, it was a remarkably successful, democratic unit. The clinic decisions were made by the staff together with the unusual help from colleagues in the Institution of Human Relations who were studying organizations, their structure, and modes of functioning, and their ideas rubbed off on us. When I was chairman of the clinic John Bowlby was the deputy in the children's department. He's very different from me. He's an upper-class Englishman. I'm very attached to John. The work he does is terrific, and he's very dedicated to his own research. At the same time, he contributed enormously to the Tavistock Institute of Human Relations and to the British Psychoanalytic Institute. I have tremendous admiration for John and his capacity because, beside him, I felt a blundering idiot. He was so efficient.

There was a magic, serendipitous influence over me all the time, I felt, because things kept on coming, opportunities to do this and that, and meet people like Karl and Will Menninger and their team, which came to visit us at the end of the war when we were still in the Army. They had a very highly powered team, six international stars, and they were all very impressed with the creative institutions that they visited, places like units for the interned prisoners of war coming back to civil life. Returning prisoners of war got special units set up where they lived within their own boundaries under self-government. Then they made relationships with local industry. The men were allowed to go out and look at the different places to see what it felt like to get back to work before having to support themselves, because they had a big adjustment problem to overcome. As you know, when they came back from the war, they had enormous fantasies built up of getting back to life; and then it was very different when reality came along. So they needed therapy groups and these civil resettlement units.

These were great learning opportunities for working with social problems. The common pattern for industrial consultants—I think in many places it still is—is that they come in and go around the business, and then prepare a very elaborate, detailed plan, and then you're just left with it. But the Tavistock rejected that from the start and said, "No. We don't know that you even know your own problems." We got them to look at the real problems and then worked through to the solution with them. Sophisticated, professional consultants operating as facilitators.

That became known as the Tavistock approach to organizational work and it influenced a tremendous amount of organizational thinking the world over. My colleague Eric Trist eventually became chairman of the Wharton Business School. A number of the senior people left. The economic rewards were pretty thin, you see. We were fairly dedicated. We didn't starve ourselves, but we didn't take huge salaries or anything like that. That's fine when you're young. When you get nearer the fifties and you're looking out for the future, then people like A. K. Rice were enticed out into jobs.

Eliot Jaques was the first person to leave the Institute. That caused a bit of conflict because he had been working with this firm as their task worker, and I think people initially felt he was bought, and we felt that he was a traitor. He deserted the company. Now, looking back, of course, we don't see that at all. We're much more tolerant. If you feel there's an opportunity coming, you're in a very difficult choice. O.K., you've just got to do what you feel is right for yourself.

The group hung together pretty well for about 10 years, but there was a growing separation as it got bigger and more involved in various projects, so that it lost that very nice early feel, which I look back on with pleasure—and what a tremendous help it was to me in all sorts of ways. Still, it was all in the context of the National Health Service. When I first went to Menninger, they were talking about their administration and asked about ours. I said, "Well, you don't want to know what we do in our 'communist' health service, do you?" Then it came out, of course, that their problems were almost identical to ours but their controls were insurance companies. Ours were just set limitations laid down by the region, but we had, in fact, a very high degree of freedom.

The regional administrators got the feeling that we were serious about our job, because we thought about clinical policy. The policy of most hospitals is you take whom you get and you have as many beds as you can pay for and get them filled up. In other words, you don't see yourself as having to look to the outer world. But studies were just being made on the incidence of neurosis, and it was quite clear from the studies that something like 40 percent of the people who consulted their family doctor were really needing psychological help. Well, when you looked at the scale of the problem, you realized that the last thing that's of any help is to think of producing a large number of therapists.

I always remember the one analyst who hadn't a clue. I, myself, learned to think socially about the issues, really to see the social dimensions in a realistic way. He just sat down and he worked out that by the year 2050, we needed about 500,000 analysts. He had worked it all out! I thought, "This man needs to see a psychiatrist." It was totally out of touch with reality.

So we had this very interesting notion, which was to set up a thing called a psychiatric clinic where psychotherapy was going to be free. What do you do? We didn't quite envisage a queue stretching down toward Buckingham Palace. We saw ourselves out on the street grabbing people to keep up the patient load, saying, "What you really need is. . . ."

As it turned out, we did have more people than we could cope with, but we had to evolve a policy. Now there are two things you can do there. You can narrow the number of people you treat or you can expand your therapeutic methods. That was where Bion's group work came in. Of course, the group work was an enormous success, and I'm still very sad that analytic group therapy has not maintained a wider grip and been regarded with the seriousness it deserves because to me it's a very powerful therapeutic weapon. One difficulty is you've got to stay together, but the real trouble with group therapy—well, the same thing goes on in psychotherapy, doesn't it? You get too many ill qualified people coming in. In British psychiatry, of course, they're not taught any psychoanalysis at all, nothing really. The primary value system is the brain. In Britain, as one of my colleagues at times has said, "The mind is a kind of dirty spell around good clean neurons."

So you have to contend with a tremendous cultural opposition there. But in these early days, I think there was great enthusiasm for group work. At that time, of course, we had Bion and Ezriel. We all did one or two groups. By the end of the '50s, we were running fifty therapy groups, which was a quite considerable help in justifying ourselves as a service institution.

There were two or three other out-patient clinics in our regional group and that posed problems because we were compared with them, you see. We were regarded as rather a Rolls Royce place. In one of these other clinics, there was an odd man, a bit of a rogue, who prided himself on seeing about 600 patients a week with about one and a half psychiatrists. I worked out that he was really spending between five and ten minutes on each person, so I just said to our management committee, "If that's the help the patients are getting, then why pay an expensive psychiatrist because he can't possibly give any more help than a much cheaper level of employment would do?" At our clinic, we treated lots of people in groups, and the other thing we did was to see a few patients in as much detail as we wanted. That was our laboratory. We would do that as our research effort, but I don't regard that as a contribution to the community problem. The contribution to the community problem is the knowledge we get from that with which we can think of other methods. The group thing was one. Well, this is my spiel on the business of psychoanalysis.

Psychoanalysis had assumed that its business was the training of psychoanalysts. By the time the '50s came, that was all that psychoanalysts thought they were about, and that got more and more restrictive, because, not only did you have to conform with the theory, but you weren't a psychoanalyst and you couldn't help anybody if you hadn't gone to the Institute for so many years and if you weren't signed, sealed, and delivered. That might be alright in the Viennese society or the British society of 1900, when society consisted of individuals. But the social fabric is much more interlocked nowadays, and people can't survive in that isolated way. Now, Freud had the idea then, quite understandably at that time, that what he was learning was important for society. So he wrote books about his knowledge, and they sold as well, because he was such a good writer. He thought he was helping society.

It was only many years later that we realized that you can't expect that to be all that helpful, because psychodynamic knowledge is not like any other knowledge. You can talk about computers, you can talk about motor cars, you can send out a book of words, and, by and large, people can learn. You cannot do that with psychodynamic knowledge because it upsets the reader. The instrument that receives the knowledge is disturbed by the receipt of the knowledge. When you learn about psychodynamics, it's as if you were a kind of instrument that itself had to be treated. You have to have a personal experience that enables you to use psychodynamic knowledge. It's taken a long time for this to get across.

But the situation that intensive psychotherapy had set up was a very tantalizing one, because the practitioners became more and more insistent on their intensively trained settings and membership groups and rather contemptuous of others. A year ago I was talking to counselors who told me that analysts were saying, "Well, counsellors, of course, they're awful. They make such a botch of it." And I thought, "That's terrible, not to recognize their worth." So they make a botch, but is a botch always harmful? John Bowlby used to say he was a firm believer that a little knowledge is not always dangerous. It's better than no knowledge.

We could see ways of setting up systems or helping clinics to set up systems, but if we think our business is purely to train people like ourselves inside these walls and if we don't take the use of our knowledge seriously, then we'll be redundant. This is why the psychoanalytic business is almost going out of business—because it sets such rigid conditions, such rigid methodology, with the attitude that nothing else is any good.

Well, it's more and more difficult to get people willing to do the training and certainly more and more difficult to get people who can afford to pay for the treatment. Although they are publicly patronizing to anything that isn't the real thing, privately analysts are practicing psychotherapy like the very devil. The bulk of their patients are being seen twice or three times a week. Very few of them have got a practice based on five times a week. So there's a lot of hypocrisy going on here.

Well, what is the solution? To me, the real business we're in is not creating practitioners. That's a fundamental component of the business, like creating certain machines. Our real business is the export of knowledge. If we want society to look at itself more constructively and develop mental health objectives, then we are the most powerful source of knowledge for the variables that are important. Of that there's no doubt. It's only when people seek help that they reveal what is wrong. You can give people questionnaires ad nauseam, and you finish up with meaningless answers and a behavioral approach to them.

The danger a few years ago was the world according to Marx. Now the danger these people are presenting us with is the world according to Pavlov. And that is really dangerous, because the philosophy underlying behavioralism is a controlling one, treating people like machines. Now, who is going to decide what kind of machine they should be? The Western social trend toward maximizing the resources of the individual creates the strongest prospect for adequate creativity.

I remember a book that came out a few years ago, "The Rise and Fall of the Great Powers" by Paul Kennedy (1987). The striking theme to me there was that in the Middle Ages, the Ottoman Empire and the Chinese were infinitely more wealthy, had more educated people and resources and so on, than the West where there wasn't an emperor or some tyrant who said, "Stop that research." So Western societies got ahead with gun powder and technological weapons, which just destroyed the others in no time. So creativity and fostering the resources within the group is what gives the real power for survival.

People have got to be free from internal blockages in the development of their resources. That's a political problem. The problem for us to be concerned with is: What promotes maximum freedom of the use of resources? Now, that's the kind of knowledge that we've got to provide in an established way. We've got to validate our knowledge as best we can, and then let the community use it.

Now, the community will find ways of using it, I have no doubt about that. They'll find all sorts of ways. Some of them will be a bit California, but that will change as soon as they discover that primal screams and encounter groups have a fairly limited success when you're up against the intractable resistance of the unconscious. They don't take the time to know what people are about. That was the trouble with the hippie movement. The great love-in had no realization whatsoever how much hate existed in people and how you've got to treat it, not run away from it, pretend it's not there, or dismiss it. How do you think we might help people to cope with this? Not get rid of it. How will we manage it?

Increasingly, I think the proper setting of a clinic like this is to be a component within the wider issue of human relations. That's what we did in Scotland when I went back there from Tavistock. I was greeted by a number of senior psychiatrists, clergy, teachers, and social workers of all kinds, everybody on whose door somebody with a personal problem might knock for help.

What a lot of these people don't realize is that, when you take on personal problems, the stress can be very damaging. So, medicine became more captured by technology and a mechanistic view. You didn't need to get mixed up in that mind stuff, you see, because you've got the wonder drugs. This is still around. We won't say that that's a bad thing. Anything that removes suffering has got to be taken seriously, and medication can be a perfectly useful contribution. The trouble is that when people find something that relieves tension, they then draw the inference that you don't need to bother finding out any more about it; you just kill it. That's what happens. Medication becomes an explanatory philosophy quite soon, and not just a mode of helping.

So who is it helping? Bion had this cryptic way of talking, in nuggets you see. He had a discussion with me about all this drug business, and he just chipped in with his remark, "Well, the doctors need the drugs if they're going to get sleep at this point." That's the point. Who is the medicine for? The patient or the doctor?

It's a good idea to reach beyond medical people to senior social workers and educators. Helping them was one of the big things in our platform at the Scottish Institute of Human Relations in the '70s. We had three activities: we did clinical work; we did research and training; and we helped the allied professional and volunteer groups to increase resources in the community. We spent roughly a third of our time on each. It didn't mean that everybody shared everything, but the total personnel resources roughly added up to that division of labor.

Well, there's no doubt in my mind that the crossfertilization of the work, of us being involved with people in the outer world and social work organizations is quite a good thing. We need to be in touch with the poet's voice and the artist's vision. We meet with them and we listen. It's just being able to hear that matters.

I'll interrupt this with a little vignette I can't resist telling you. One of the young presidents of a big superhospital was stuck with a difficult suicidal patient. He was a man who had come to specialize a bit in what they call difficult patients. These would be patients who had been kicked out of about four or five other hospitals who couldn't cope with them because they were so destructive on the treatment. This young woman, who was about 28, had been a persistent suicidal since she was 16. She had undergone 14 attempts, which made me wonder if she really meant business. Anyway, they had a job because she had to be watched night and day, and she was very negative and very difficult. She was the bad object. Her doctor asked me, "Would you see her with me?" That's a tricky situation because, if you say something, the patient might use you to put down the staff there. Of if you say nothing, then you look a fool. Everyone wonders, "Why did you bring that man in?"

Well, this girl, she started talking to me and she said, "This place is a zoo. The patients are all animals and the shrinks are worse. Why can't I commit suicide if I want to? I want to do it. It's my life. It's terrible. Nobody's worth looking at, talking to, or anything." Just a stream of invective that went on for about half an hour. So she went on, and I just nodded my head at all this abuse, but I was included in it too. "You're another of them. I can see." Well, I suddenly stopped her. I was getting tired, and I said, "I'm told you write poetry." Well, she looked around and said, "Um," but then turned away. I said, "Well, that's interesting to me. When Freud started this kind of work, he was always interested in what the poets and writers said because it's poets who have told us most about human misery and the depths of the inner life of people. I wonder if your poems, you see, are not something you're trying to say to us."

She seemed so totally devoted to destruction and self-destruction, but this bit of her that wrote poetry was somehow calling out for a response. Well, we had to finish off, and I met the doctor the next day, and he said, "Oh, that woman. She thought you were God!" I said jokingly, "Oh, well, I know that. Tell me something new." He told me that she had made what I thought was a lovely remark. I had been sitting like this and she was there, and after I left, she had said to the doctor, "Does God wear a hearing aid?" I think that's the poetical remark of all time. I thought, by golly, that girl's not so hopeless as she makes herself out to be.

Going back to the Scottish Institute, we had our members who were qualified mental health professionals and then we made up an associate membership of people who were not qualified to do the specialist jobs that were being done, but were interested. So we got a link with the field, the relevant field. Then we said, "We will rely on you to bring in things that are coming up in the field, and then we'll just talk together about what can be done for it." So we made a social connectedness with a large group. When you work together, the others may feel a degree of envy—life is not a bed of roses—but at least they see that the specialist psychotherapy role is one that is helpful and might be one worth training for themselves.

The thing of value is to have an endless activity out into the community. So we have our therapy groups and application groups for the learned professions, social workers, teachers, lawyers, family doctors, poets, anybody who could want the group.

Of course, it was in this field that I think that Michael Balint made one of the most powerful contributions to the use of psychodynamic knowledge, when he took on the family doctors. He was a very able fellow, Michael Balint, a very trying chap at times. He was the one who said to me, "Well, don't worry. If you've got a Hungarian as a friend, you don't need an enemy." That was true enough. But he really was, he was a remarkable, creative man. He and Enid were quite a great pair together. I was very fond of him. I was very sorry when he died. He was a good fellow.

Coming from Middle Europe, of course, where they were used to old-boy networks and secret things, they didn't really grasp the democratic process. In the British health service, if you're going to ask for anything, you think of the number of committees you've got to go through, preparing your case, and this sort of thing. He thought you just rang somebody up, and it could be arranged. He was demanding more staff from me, and he said, "Ring them up, ring them up." I said, "I can't do that. It doesn't work that way." "Ah, you're no use at all," he complained. So I said, "Michael, you've convinced me I'm an administrative genius. I tolerate bastards like you." He jumped up and immediately took me around the neck. "Now we can be good friends," he said. Balint said that what the family doctors or social workers are trying to learn is a skill of how to work with personal problems and that learning that skill requires at least a minimal personal change in your own attitudes, because you've got to give up wanting to give advice. You've got to learn to listen—and he was very good with it.

I was talking about responding to demands from the field. There's another side to that. In turn, the professionals have got to be initiating toward the field. Well, Balint thought doctors might be ready, so he just put an advertisement in the local medical journal, saying that we were starting a pilot group for 10 weeks to explore the possibility of helping with the psychological problems of general practice. He said to the doctors right away, "Look, I don't do your job. I don't know how we can help, but the one thing I'm not going to do is give you lectures on psychopathology. I'm going to ask you to bring up a problem—anyone in the group—bring a problem that's bothering you, something you've got stuck with, and we'll talk about it together." Of course, the groups were a big success, because the members all began to look at themselves to see how their attitudes were conditioned or fixed. It was a very powerful method, but it's kind of faded out of the British scene. There is always a regressive tendency against growth. People don't always want to keep up because it's easier for the doctor to give them the drug sometimes. It's all very well criticizing general practitioners handing out tranquilizers, but the patients demand them. It's not just the doctor who wants to give them. The patients are as resistent to looking at the inner aspects of a personal problem as any health professional would be because, when you get into the inner world, you enter into a complex relationship with your helper.

The Scottish Institute has grown, and I'm very pleased. The teachers have their problems and that sort of thing, but they're working away. They've been given a sense of developing their own skills and resources, and they're going at it. There is a demand on their services. They don't make a lot of money, but there are enough people from the professions or industry who can afford private fees to offset that. They don't advertise the low-cost clinic. It's the staff that's the low cost, but they get enough now to keep the overheads going.

Dr. Gordon: I'm turning to another aspect of your career. During the time you were editor of the British Journal of Medical Psychology and, later, of the International Journal of Psychoanalysis, journals that published some of the most important papers in the history of psychoanalysis, what were your experiences of reading these papers and which ones in particular stand out as you think back?

Dr. Sutherland: Well, you'll be amused, if not horrified, at my first confession. It involves John Rickman, who, incidentally, was Bion's analyst originally. Rickman and Bion were huge men, both of them. I used to say, "Look at that pair. Now who's the mother of all father figures? Who's the father of all mother figures?" Between them, they contained all the figures that ever lived. They were huge. They were about 6 feet tall and about this wide. Rickman was a Quaker with a very good sense of fun. He had been in Russia at the time of the revolution, and was about to be shot at one point, being a Quaker there. He was interested in the British Journal of Medical Psychology, and I got to know him well. He came to me one day, and he said, "Look, will you take over the *British Journal of Medical Psychology*?" I said, "Any but the *Journal*, John. I don't even read the damn thing." Then he shook me; he said, "What better way of reading it?" So I started it. That's my first confession.

When I think of what goes on at the Menninger Bulletin, it seems to me that they have a staff of a hundred doing their editing. But we did it on a twentieth of my time, if that. I used to take the papers home. I was a great one for reading out of doors in the sun, if there was any, and so I used to say that the number of papers was directly correlated with the number of sun-hours a day!

The *British Journal of Medical Psychology* had room for various points of view, but most of the papers that came in were psychoanalytic and they did not have to conform to a certain point of view. The *International Journal of Psycho-Analysis*—just one of many now—used to be one of *the* places to publish, even for people in the United States. We didn't have to tout for papers; there wasn't a terrific number of outlets anyway. It always seemed to me that good papers were never much of a problem. You recognize fairly readily a thoughtful writer who has some objectivity. But when it comes to fringe papers, if one of them has come from Timbuctoo, rather than New York, we'd take it, because one function of a journal is to stimulate effort in the professional groups. I really see a journal as having a broader function than broadcasting ideas. Let's face it, what percentage of the papers really are new ideas? At the same time, they're valuable because often they make the way for new ideas coming.

Dr. Gordon: I'd like to turn now to Fairbairn who was your analyst in the 1930s for, I gather, about 5 years. I wonder if you can bring us into his consulting room, and tell us what Fairbairn was like. He's known to us as a theoretician. What was he like as an analyst?

Dr. Sutherland: Well, he was in his whole personality slightly formal, with an aristocratic type of bearing. He wasn't without a sense of fun naturally along the way, but there was a certain formality about him anyway. I would think if he lived today, he would find it not very easy to be anywhere without a tie. I could put it that way. Not that he looked stiff or starchy, no, but there were certain standards. "This is what the gentleman does," and he did it.

The way he talked about people was what attracted me in the first instance to him. He never proselytized. What converted me to his point of view was the way he talked about people. He was obviously concerned about their suffering. He remained very bothered about the recession of the therapeutic emphasis in psychotherapy. It was almost as if Freud said that the success of the treatment didn't matter, as long as the analysis worked. Fairbairn took the other view. His concern was, "If I'm not getting these people a bit better or into a state of less suffering or torment, then is what I'm doing wrong?" That was of foremost interest to him, and to me.

In his analytic approach, he didn't say much. He didn't work in anything like the way a lot of analysts would do who were influenced by the Kleinians. Nowadays, if I have a patient who is silent or tense, I speak up to take a hold of this person. I grab and I hook him. You remember that girl in the Institute, who wrote poetry—I thought, this girl has gotten to be taken hold of in some way, and I took up her poetry to try to get her to talk, to reach the split somewhere in her self. But none of the old analysts operated that way. They left everything to the patient. That was standard.

When I went to London, to Tavistock, I joined the British Society. I had to have another analysis. I said, "Look, I want somebody like Fairbairn." They said, "That's no good. You've got to go to a *real* analyst." I went to Sylvia Payne. Unlike many Kleinians, she didn't have that view. She seemed to me very similar to Fairbairn. She was quiet, waited, not asking, but just commenting what she thought. It was all very subdued. Things happened, but I don't think as much happened as might have happened.

One was always aware that Fairbairn was a concerned human being. When I look back on what I got out of analysis with him and with Sylvia Payne, I would have to say that my analysis really began when I began to think of my self. My analysis started about 10 to 15 years ago. That's when I really got the notion of looking at the inner self.

One of the things I noticed about my self was that I had permanent trouble with intellectual work. I could always sense the quality of papers, which were good or not, but I couldn't articulate why. I suddenly realized that I had been avoiding work for years by distracting myself all the time, and I realized that this should have been up for analysis. I mean that was the kind of analysis that people didn't seemed to do.

One of the nicest things about the National Health Service was you could take on an impossible patient if you wanted to. There was no question about the fee. If you thought there was something interesting, you could do that. I had a few fairly difficult characters for a very long time, so I was able to start looking at the development of their selves over time, and the development of my own self over the same time period. I could always see the splits in them, but I didn't think of my self in those terms.

Once I started to look at my self, I saw the split self there, too. I never realized that I suffered from this sort of thing. I had always been interested in gardening. But not when I was a boy. My father was a keen gardener and, of course, if you sensed you were being coerced into gardening, it's not a popular pastime with boys, so I wanted nothing to do with it.

But as I got older, I found that I was very interested in gardening. Early on, I just liked it. I didn't become a great authority, but I liked our garden. Sitting in the sunshine, this was good. I was allying myself with my father. My mother was the ambitious figure in my life, and all this academic stuff I was doing was really under her pressure. What my father did was rather enjoy himself. There was that tension between them. They weren't abusive, they didn't batter each other or anything like that at all, but I could sense a tension, and I could see that whenever I was confronted with serious intellectual work, I was tempted and inevitably seduced into doing some distracting thing, like thinking, "I've got the garden, I'll do some gardening." I found I was really wanting to say, "To hell with what you want me to do, Mother. I'm going to enjoy myself with Father." I became clued in to this, and the insight changed me considerably.

So, whereas in the past, I would go to Eric Trist and say, "Eric, I know what we should do. I know this is right, but you've got to tell me why. Why am I right?", now I began to get these things together, think them through for myself, and this had to do with the work I did on myself.

I mention that to say that there's hope for all. Even if you start at 70, there's hope for all.

I do think the formulation of self-knowledge is much more usable on one's self than trying to struggle with impulses, which is what Fairbairn said all along.

As an adolescent schoolboy with his father

He said, "What can you do with impulses?" But you can do something with yourself, your agent, choosing your activities.

Well, I realized, of course, that I had never had any ambition. Now where did that come from? I was obviously being driven by something. The role of images in childhood is very powerful. You know, a little boy wants to become a train driver or something. It's as if the in-and-out person who is there is seeking a guiding image. Kohut mentions this quite a bit. You are striving toward that image, and the person-you-might-be is not articulated, but it's there. Images are very powerful in that way, and I can think of various examples. There was one image—I can remember as a boy a figure who made a great impression on me was David Livingstone, the missionary/explorer. You probably don't know him, but, of course, he was very much respected in Africa. He was the first white man among so many tribes and they took to him. He made real contact with them. He didn't go in selling the gospel, and telling them what to do, or saying they were sinners. He just went in and taught them, helped them to fight their political battles, and saw to their needs. So he was enormously respected, as well as having this missionary zeal.

And talking to Roy Menninger one day, I said, "Good God, Roy, that's what it is—I've become a medical missionary!" In a sense, I had. Why had I gone through this medical course? I'm sure that the guiding image of that was a kind of ideal self that had been way down. That sort of thing never came out in 10

In his beloved garden, 1980

years of analysis. Why? It must have been a secret of mine. As Fairbairn says, the relationship between the internal objects is kept secret in case these interfering parents take it away from you. So there's my second confession.

The more we learn to work on self images, the more people could go on in life with relatively little help from therapy.

Dr. Corrigan: In your book *Fairbairn's Journey into the Interior* (1989a) you give a compelling picture of the interaction between Fairbairn's inner and outer worlds. You remark that Fairbairn often commented on the intimate interplay of theoretical preference and personality features. This question picks right up on what you've just been saying. How do you reconcile the intransigence of Fairbairn's neurotic symptoms with the continuous flow of his creative activity?

Dr. Sutherland: I'm very glad that came up. We have got into the way of thinking of the internal objects as rather crisply separated figures there, and that isn't really what happens, because they pervade the central self. Fairbairn's mother had been helpful with his career. His father questioned whether he should go to the university, or start doing something real and be earning money. But his mother was much more ambitious for him. So he developed negatively toward his father and, positively, ganged up with his mother. Well, I think that the problem there is that the central self has become so pervaded by the controlling mother, who is no longer felt as that bad. You come to accept that you are that person now. You can identify with that very much. So to start working on that is to threaten serious disintegration. You're confronted with Winnicott's false self. When you've got to give that up, there's a deep threat because you are existing on that. That's what's holding you together. There's a serious threat, and it takes the reassurance of trust in the therapist before you can begin to break that open.

Now, there was nobody Fairbairn could go to. So, I think, he just wrote all these notes to himself. It was a terrible problem for me. I thought, "Dare I use these notes? Have I betrayed him?" These were private, self-analytic notes. But they were so enlightening. Also, there was the other fact: he had written them and he had kept them 25 years. They were preserved. If he had been bothered about them—his last year or two, he was getting pretty old, he knew he was winding up—he could have destroyed those things easily or told his wife to destroy them, but they had been kept. So I have a feeling that perhaps he did think they might be used to understand things.

I think he tried to work it out himself, but I don't think he could get at enough of the destructive force toward the mother, the controlling mother. You see, Klein's depressive position is something that we need to do a lot more work on because she is talking about the mother becoming a whole person. Now, what she doesn't point out is that the mother cannot become a whole person unless the self is becoming a whole self in a different way, because it takes a gestalt to talk to a gestalt and understand it. So there's an inherent self-development toward wholeness going on with differentiation of the self and self-consciousness of the self as a self. These are the things that the infant developers have discovered. These changes take place especially dramatically in the second year. There's an awareness of the feelings of the other.

Now, there must then be a phase of awareness of self struggling free from mother. Now, if that's been a loaded struggle, it has a highly aggressive, destructive component. If when the child is in a raging tantrum, the mother does not say, "There, there, it will be O.K. Don't worry," but is very tense or alarmed about it, then it is felt to be very bad.

Fairbairn's mother was experienced as a martinet, and people who knew her said she was. She was a very formal person: tuxedos for dinner and that sort of atmosphere. I would think there was great anxiety. Dedication to his work, his hold on his work, was what kept Fairbairn's self together. No matter how chaotic his external life might be, the immense dedication with which he pursues the work to completion is a sign of a man's creativeness, the wholeness that's needed. I don't think we understand a half, a fraction, of what all these things are about, but we're beginning to see what the important issues are.

I would say Fairbairn's first wife was a very dependent woman. She had been brought up in a family of the country gentry and her only brother was a regular army officer. She had lived in that world where men provided the social life. When she found she was married to somebody who was absorbed with work, I think she was lost. She couldn't make a life for herself, and that's the tragic thing. Imagine—she had what nowadays would be a homemaker's dream: she had a nanny to look after the kids; she had two maids to do the domestic work; she had nothing to do but go ahead, and she could have pursued her own interests several hours each day. But she didn't do anything like that. She really wanted to be in on Fairbairn's mission, not wife to somebody who engaged in this horrid profession, closeted up with these bad creatures, his patients. It's often been said that had Ronald Fairbairn been Princess Di's gynecologist, Mrs. Fairbairn would have been in her element. She could have parties all around. All that was denied. All she knew was people moaning and groaning, awful people, patients around. He was the sort of man to whom marriage is a sacrament, and he wouldn't have thought of divorce or leaving the family, so he stayed. He did the best he could, you see, to make life possible, but she took to drink, and that was that.

Fairbairn had put his father into the role of bad object, and now without the support of his wife, his mother's support really, I think he was searching for something that was missing. And, he refound the bad object. Of course, when he brought back father as an important internal object he brought him back with his symptom. Fairbairn identified with his refound paternal internal object, and inevitably with the symptom. That's my speculation.

There was nobody that he felt he could have gone to. I can think of one therapist that he might have gone to. He might have gone to Melanie. Who knows? But obviously he didn't want to get into darkest Melanesia. Needed safer territory for decent Victorian behavior!

Dr. Gordon: Clearly, Fairbairn saw himself as taking Kleinian theories to their logical conclusions; but Melanie, on the other hand, seemed to feel he was going to absurd extremes. Phyllis Grosskurth comments that Klein was undoubtedly resentful that Fairbairn was developing concepts on his own and wasn't beholden to her. She even states that Klein may have felt competitive with

Fairbairn and was spurred on to get her ideas out before he did. How do you view her difficulties with Fairbairn?

Dr. Sutherland: Fairbairn was always very courteous. I often wonder if maybe he didn't exaggerate it, but he was a gentleman in every sense. He was very considerate and thoughtful about people, and very appreciative, and he had a great admiration for Melanie's contribution. He never had anything but a reverential attitude to Freud, but to him the best way of paying tribute to Freud was to look at what he was saying, examine it, probe it, and develop it. Classical Freudian instinct theory suggested that the evil inside one's self was something that we were afflicted with, not something for which we were responsible. He didn't see himself in opposition to Freud, but he thought that his theory would have to change. But Melanie wasn't like that. Melanie wasn't a scholar. She was intellectually untrained. By temperament, I think she was more of a flamboyant, exuberant girl in the European-Hungarian style. A very beautiful woman when she was young, very beautiful, a real sex kitten. Not like Anna Freud, who never seemed to get out of these hopsack skirts. Melanie stayed true to Freud's instinct theory, especially elaborating the death instinct. Fairbairn was a great admirer of Melanie and what she had done to understand the infant's object relations, even though her theory had an instinctual basis. But when Fairbairn rejected the death instinct and her notion of the instincts, he tampered with her safety measure.

Freud had stirred up the hostility of the world by bringing the unconscious in and confronting sexuality. Then this woman Klein came along saying we were all murderers, we were full of violence and destruction. I think it was too much for the analysts to take. In the modern world, it's taken the media working hard, night and day, to confront us with violence so that we have to see that it is all around. People have gotten a little more used to it, but at that time it was frightening I think in a personal way.

Guntrip said that there was a resistance in our culture and in analysis to the acceptance of the destructive part of ourselves, because it was uncomfortable. Our defense was to keep it as something impersonal with which we were afflicted. I have a feeling that Melanie was happier with something like that too. When Fairbairn was writing his papers, her glamorous daughter Melitta had really told Melanie to go to hell, told her she was a bitch. So Melanie was confronted: she had lost a son in a tragic accident but she also had this daughter who couldn't stand the sight of her, so she was in no mood to take responsibility that the parents might have something to do with it, as Fairbairn thought. That has been a constant criticism of her thinking, that she uses the words about the parents, but none of the music, I think, because of this powerful factor in her own life.

Dr. Corrigan: In your book, you're very respectful of Harry Guntrip as a friend and theoretician. Fairbairn accepted, later in his life, Guntrip's idea of a regressed ego. Greenberg and Mitchell, however, are quite strong in their feeling that Guntrip's emphasis on the regressed ego led to a distortion of Fairbairn's emphasis on object seeking.

Dr. Sutherland: I never understood that remark. What Guntrip says is that the object-seeking tendency, if you blank it out enough, retreats. That seems to me a perfectly ordinary phenomenon. If you don't mother it psychologically, it just shrinks. The self has no vitality going on, and you get death in a lot of cases. Well, that seems to me just a biological phenomenon, a fact. Guntrip has come in for a certain amount of the negative that people wanted to say about Fairbairn, but Fairbairn's writing was so timid they couldn't do it. Guntrip was looser, but Guntrip was no fool. He was a very sharp thinker, and that article he had which I published posthumously about science and psychoanalysis (1978) was very good. He had a very well trained, philosophical mind, Guntrip. He was a different man from Fairbairn altogether, of course. He was a rather intense chap, Guntrip was. He was always bustling—you felt he was driven all the time. Fairbairn never did have that attitude. Oh, he was active, but he had had some—not much, but just a whiff—of the enviable gentlemanly nonchalance that nothing is so important that you need to be bustling about it. Guntrip was much more driven and responsive and concerned and that sort of thing. A very active mind all the time. But inside he had a dead child part of himself. He wrote about seeing his younger brother dead on his mother's lap. I think he saw his own destroyed self, and there was a sense of saying to his mother in his theory: "that's what you did to me." So he wanted that destroyed self, or regressed ego, included in Fairbairn's theory. Guntrip's mother was really pretty awful. Even I got into trouble with her.

Although he didn't preach a word in the church for many years, Guntrip never gave up his ordination, and he was popular among the clergy. He took a very great interest in the clergy learning about psychotherapy in the cure of souls, and his writing appeals because he doesn't polarize religion against psychiatry. He doesn't do that, unlike Freud. Freud, by talking about the future of the religion, left us bothered by the religion of the future. It was really terrible. Guntrip and Fairbairn didn't polarize religion and psychoanalysis, but they both dismissed the concept of human motivation as originating in the bunkers of energy that come out of the soul.

Dr. Corrigan: Your theory of the self, to me, has a Winnicottian flair.

Dr. Sutherland: Winnicott carries the notion of the bad object into the central self by the creation of a false self. Fairbairn wasn't enthused about the false self, because he thought that it wasn't a good enough way of expressing the theoretical position. But he admired Winnicott's clinical work.

Winnicott was a maverick chap always. I did some supervision with him, and he was very informal. The first time I went, he walks into the room with his razor, shaving himself. That was the first thing. Then there was a plant on the window sill. He said, "Oh, somebody's just given me a plant. Bring me the pot.

Now we'll see who lives longer—your patient or the plant." He had a buoyant, boyish sense of fun. He was a tremendously intuitive person really. Again, he wasn't such a disciplined thinker as Fairbairn. Fairbairn's thinking was almost excessively disciplined. That's why people found his writing style so condensed, because it seemed to be a philosophical treatise for the scholar, not for the humble therapist.

Dr. Corrigan: What did Fairbairn make of Winnicott's ideas on integration and primary creativity?

Dr. Sutherland: Oh, I don't think Fairbairn got on to that. He got to this stage of writing about the endopsychic situation and the central self. I have a feeling that he kind of died then. Of course, that was the time when his wife was at her worst, and she died of alcoholism in 1952. Although he had to put up with this for some time, he was still very attached to her, so that he was depressed for a long time after her death. The domestic upheaval stopped the thrust of his thinking. I think that he would welcome a lot of what Winnicott and Guntrip have done.

Dr. David Scharff: Can you say some more about the relationship between Fairbairn as a man, his intellectual development from boyhood and his interest in theoretical elaboration?

Dr. Sutherland: Well, I think Fairbairn was an ordinary child, a thoughtful, intellectual boy with these somewhat overintrusive parents controlling his behavior. Very strong Victorian pressure to be good and proper. It was very important in those days, particularly in Edinburgh society. The class consciousness was almost unbelievable, and you had to conform.

Now, it always seemed to me that Fairbairn showed his independence in his attitude to the regular churchgoing that was imposed upon him. Each Sunday he had to go twice with his parents. Now, for a young child a Calvinistic sermon about an hour long is hardly an entertainment. Fairbairn made it into something he found of interest. He would go and copy down the sermon from a quite early age. He would pick out the flaws in the arguments. The one way he could be himself, assert himself, was through his intellectual activity. Of course, that was all right, because his parents would accept that, you see. That was quite nice behavior.

Well, at the same time, as he has said, he was perturbed about the issues of conscience, guilt, and sexuality that were mounting up toward adolescence. Of course, they were terribly forbidden activities in that household. I get the impression that the repressive attitude between the parents would be pretty heavy. I'm sure nothing like exciting sexual orgies were going on. I think that would be left to Fairbairn's fantasy. They were highly controlled people and preoccupied that this boy mustn't get onto the wrong track. He must be straight and well behaved.

So this forced the intellectual area on him. He got a lot of encouragement for that, because he went to this private school, and in these private schools there was a good deal of individual attention compared with the public school system. When he decided to go into the Church he found really rather a cunning solution to his situation, because he was going into a career where he could really look at sexuality and things of that kind under a very respectable cloak because, after all, it came up in the Bible quite a lot. So it gave him a way out. You get the impression of a boy rather left to himself, and his intellectual life was his field for asserting himself. That's what I felt.

Dr. David Scharff: You've been very interested in the relationship between his father's urinary phobia, Fairbairn's rather traumatic exposure to that symptom in the railway car when his father had to urinate in front of a number of women, and the onset of an almost identical symptom in Fairbairn . . .

Dr. Sutherland: Identical, yes.

Dr. David Scharff: . . . in his middle age.

Dr. Sutherland: Well, in many ways it brought out Winnicott's point about the male and female elements in the growth of the self. It seems to me increasingly that a prominent feature of the father's role is the symbolic value in asserting independence of mother. In the infant's world, father is independent. He goes out to work. He's not controlled, he's not subdued.

Now, Fairbairn's father, I don't think, could have been given much status by his mother, because she was the ambitious, socially climbing woman in some measure. The father had the typical, rather benign but somewhat controlling Scottish attitude, "What are these big ideas you're getting? You're good enough at the level you are, and you stay there. Going to Oxford and that sort of thing, what's all this nonsense? You don't even need to go to the university, and if you do need to go, Edinburgh is good enough." The mother was more expansive. Now, the mother, therefore, became a very important figure, because she really was encouraging the forward movement of his self into the academic world. She was his support figure against father.

Now, when Fairbairn's wife turned against him, he was, I think, rather in a quandary, because his internal objects vanished when his support figure vanished. Instead of a supportive mother figure, he found in her the repressed bad object, based on his experience of his father. As he wrote later, what were repressed were not impulses, but objects. He wrote in his diary that his father was a negative figure for him. I don't think there was much chatting with each other, not much in common. But, at the same time, I think the guilt came back tremendously about his father—had he destroyed his father? I think that his symptom was proof of the resuscitation of his reserved, stay-at-home, unambitious father and of the reparation to father internally, and bringing him back alive inside himself. He became like father in order to bring him back.

Well, then he continued with his work, because the surprising thing is it was around this point that his creativity was just growing, the tremendous creative urge was just beginning in those early thirties, and blossomed just at the end of the 30s. What it brought out for me was that the successful integration of the two parents in a constructive relationship in the self is an extremely important feature of development.

Dr. David Scharff: Did any of this insight about the self of Fairbairn reverberate with thoughts about your own self as you were writing his biography *Fairbairn's Journey into the Interior*?

Dr. Sutherland: There's a difference between Freud's self-analysis and analysis of the self. The self-analysis of the self has a totally different focus than what went on in the Fleiss correspondence, I'm sure. I was surprised by the number of people who have written to me to say that they found, by the time they had read the book, a considerable amount of analytical work had gone on in themselves about themselves. I certainly felt that in writing it.

I felt that Fairbairn had absolutely taken possession of me. I got worried about it. I felt I was living this man night and day. I really ought to have seen a good analyst about my writing before, because I've never written much. I don't like writing. I much prefer talking. I wrote the whole thing in 6 months, which was quite something; for I had passed my eighty-third birthday.

But I was aware of a profound process going on in myself, and I think that this is what it was about. It ran in parallel to Fairbairn's profound, essential struggle for the integration of the self; uniting the male and female elements that Winnicott later described. The female element is the establishment of the base from which you start as a person. The male element starts gender identity. You might say the first identity is being a person, a secure self; but the ultimate identity must be a secure gender self. I think Fairbairn never felt that he had a secure masculine self. He describes that. He felt different. He lacked the ordinary aggressive boyishness, and I think that's why, deep down, there was a deep resentment of his father for not asserting himself more in that area.

Self-analysis has acquired a new significance for me. I always said you can't do self-analysis because the perpetual problem is the countertransference! But I do think that people can do a lot of analysis of the self inside themselves, because once you've got the idea, you can look at it more, you can use art, you can use literature, you can use all these things far more readily, to look at the self. I think something of that kind was going on with Winnicott and Guntrip. They, of course, benefitted from Fairbairn's experience, and then they were able to do some self analysis that wasn't in the analytic culture, but they brought it into it.

Dr. David Scharff: So in writing this book and in thinking about it, you found an aspect of yourself that you had never found before, which really let you move on in a new way.

Looking at Sutherland's biography of Fairbairn with publisher Bob Young, outside Fairbairn's house in Edinburgh after the Fairbairn centenary, 1989

Dr. Sutherland: A very profound influence, because I was always hopeless at abstract thinking. I ran away from it, the way I kind of pushed my father aside. My mother was the dominant one, not outrageously so, but she was the ambitious one for her family. I was the sixth of eight children, that's why I can be bothered with all you lot, that's why I enjoy teaching, having been brought up to be surrounded permanently by people. That's when I really feel most at ease.

But I found, as I went on with this book, I suddenly began to be much more able to cope with abstract thinking. I had reinstituted my father and put that together with my ambitious mother. Had I done this, you see, years ago, I might have been able to write something. It was a terrible discovery late in life. Still, there it was. But I'm sure the valuable lesson I got out of it was bringing the parents together in that way. It really came up rather comically for me. I'll let you in on a dreadful secret.

My father was very Scottish. He loved the Highland traditions and the Highland regiments. He wasn't an Army man, but his ancestors had been in the Highlanders. He was very fond of the kilts of the Scottish regiments. Of course, when you were a boy in Scotland, you saw kilts all day long because the soldiers were always there, you see. As you know, of course, it's the only culture in which transvestism is a national pastime! I found myself, believe it or not, resuscitating the wearing of the kilt. I used to wear a kilt when I was a boy, but not as a man. Now I got one, and I realized that in my inner world I thought, "Now, this will please my father." It was a definite act to please him and to bring him back into my life. That really was quite an important self experience for me. It added to my whole feeling of freedom in the intellectual world. I felt much freer.

So I really began to believe in the self. I thought, "There's something in this." And I went on from there.

At the family country cottage, 1925, from left to right: Father, Martin, Jimmy, and Jock

Photo by Ann Applebaum-Slesinger

At Gifford, Scotland, 1990

Dr. David Scharff: Now, how do you think that had to do with the particular formulation of theory that Fairbairn arrived at?

Dr. Sutherland: Oh, I think that he had enough of the masculine from many support figures in childhood, especially around school. But I think that he was pressurized all the time from this bad, controlling mother. I think he was frightened internally, because when his own wife turned hostile to his analytic work, he walled off her objections. He had made enough contacts to reinforce his interest and he continued to work. His dedication to analysis was profound.

He had started as a theological student. He realized he couldn't be helpful to people in this way, but I have a very strong feeling that analysis was a kind of new gospel for him. People must get to know about this. It was a gospel that must be spread. It was real knowledge. It was the good knowledge. He was a very devoted analyst and he spent a lot of time talking to societies of all sorts. He had a very strong feeling for the social value of analysis. All these things went into making him the person he was.

Dr. David Scharff: Right, and a number of his papers actually were about the social application of the way of thinking.

Dr. Sutherland: Yes, that's right. Oh, yes, he would talk about communism and all these things, and relate them to analytic understanding. Analysts were incredibly naîve in their interpretation of complex social phenomena. Marx was left completely out, you see. But Fairbairn wasn't really foolish about that sort of thing, as some people said he was from reading his paper about communism. Guntrip, in fact, said he thought it was silly to reduce communism that way. Fairbairn felt a bit annoyed about the criticisms. He wasn't talking about political systems. He was talking about what might happen to the family in those cultures. That was what he was talking about, because he was concerned about the welfare of the family, very concerned.

Male Questioner: What would you write about now?

Dr. Sutherland: I want to write a chapter or a paper concerned with getting the self properly conceptualized. I want to think in terms of modern biology, with systems theory, because if you don't get that open systems type of thinking, it's very difficult to go forward and see how the different bits will build up and realize the necessity of conceiving of the self as a growing, dynamic process, needing to be constantly related.

I think a good concept of the self would unite the whole psychoanalytic movement, because that's what is lacking. The fights that go on are due to a lack of an acceptable central concept of personal development. If we get that, then I think we'll go a long way.

Dr. David Scharff: We may have been diverted from being aware of the self by the term *object-relations theory*. You've suggested renaming it *self and object-relations theory*.

Dr. Sutherland: Yes, I think object relations is in danger of becoming a misnomer and diverting people, because only a self makes object relations. I think we should bracket them together, the self and its object relations, a term that brings in the essential relatedness. They can't be considered apart.

Dr. David Scharff: The self psychology concept of the self that emphasizes only its use of objects and is shorn of the object's use of the person is an imbalance as well.

Dr. Sutherland: Well, I think it is, yes. I don't think they've got it right. I don't think there's enough biological foundation there. At least Freud tried to base psychoanalytic thinking in biology. But we've got to get the right biology.

When you go around psychiatric departments, especially academic psychiatric departments, you hear "Oh, no, we don't do this mind stuff. We do biological psychiatry." I say, "Do you mean to say—are you saying that the mind doesn't belong to biology? Where are you living?" For me, the mind is the end point, the absolute cutting edge of the evolutionary thrust in the biological sphere. Theirs seems to me the silliest statement. We've got to establish the right of the mind to be treated scientifically. We need to apply to the mind the new thinking by the systems theorists. They're very helpful about the self-organizing universe and the relatedness of systems and development. These are the models, rather than nineteenth-century science, that we need now.

Female Questioner: I just wonder whether you might comment on whether Piaget has something to give to the formulation of this biological theory of the developing self.

Dr. Sutherland: Oh, it's intensely relevant, but we've got to get it built in right, not just use it to underwrite cognitive therapy. We've got to get at the relationship between self development and cognitive development, because I think that only a holistic system like the self can organize knowledge. Difficulties in learning and using knowledge reflect splits in the self. The two kinds of IQ, the conformist and the open-ended one, are very much a product of the self. The self is the integrative body, the structure that integrates perception, thinking, feeling, and I think that cognition is centrally determined by that. So we've got to put what Piaget studied into the perspective of how learning is governed by the structural development going on.

Male Questioner: I think Bowlby has moved along the lines of the conception of self that you're talking about in terms of bringing in Piaget's sense that assimilation and accommodation are part of how we build internal working models. Although Bowlby certainly doesn't talk with the same kind of depth and poetry about the inner world, his concepts of internal working models certainly can accommodate the conceptions of Fairbairn and Guntrip. I think that Fairbairn's view of the internal world is one of several internal possibilities; and that we have to correlate these hypotheses with research coming from attachment theory, which throws light on how the self develops images of others.

Dr. Sutherland: I don't underestimate the work of John Bowlby, but I am nervous about attachment theory being used as if this is all that's needed. To me, what John Bowlby has done is to show that without attachment—that is, without the development of some inner structure attached to the mother—the self can't grow. The value of attachment is that it sets up the essential precondition for the further development of the self. Models of inner objects get built up inside us. I'm not sure that *models* is a good word, because we take bits and pieces from so many adults, and because it's really a fluid, dynamic process.

Attachment theory is a statement of the evidence for early structures in the organism, and these we are calling the self.

Dr. Jill Scharff: I would like to ask you about Fairbairn's idea that introjection was the first defense, and that the only motivation for introjection was bad experience, so that what is taken in is a bad object. Many people are puzzled by this emphasis on the bad. If so much is focused on the introjection of the bad, where, then, is the good? Is the unconscious entirely peopled with bad objects and, if so, is this not a very frightening prospect for the person?

Dr. Sutherland: There's no doubt he is confusing about this issue. But if you read him carefully, Fairbairn says that when he talks about internalizing the bad object, it's a deliberate act of incorporating a separate kind of person who has been frustrating. He's assuming that the original self structure has incorporated the good experience from mother, not by internalizing an image of the person, but just taking in all the things that have happened—the way he's been held and fed. All these qualities of goodness or nongoodness have come into the structure of the central ego there already. So he doesn't separate that as requiring the internalization of a separate object, although that develops later with the growth of perceptual capacity.

Better if he had made clearer that there is an identification with the mother, so there is an internalization. Mother's goodness has become dissolved inside, permeating the whole of the structure there with the qualities she has imbued. So that is there. If she has been good enough, it gives the self a feeling of great security that the outer world is a good place to relate to.

That's Winnicott's whole point: if you get that good feeling coming into you, then you're not afraid of the outer world. You enjoy exploring it. It's the necessary basis for all the exploratory activity that the child then needs, because you have no hostile or frightened feeling of the outer world. The good mother is built in.

Dr. Jill Scharff: So your point is that the good mother is taken in, but not as a defense. It's taken in as a healthy, normal mechanism.

Dr. Sutherland: Not as a defense. It's taken in and metabolized. Just as food becomes part of the body structure, the emotional experiences permeate the growing content of the structure we're calling the self, that becomes the ego.

When the frustration experiences render the child helpless because the child can't control the powerful adult you then get the frustrating outer adult being taken inside. As Winnicott would point out later, the capacity to play is what forms the foundation that will then need to manage the bad object. The infant can think, he can feel, he can invent ways of dealing with the bad object hopefully, you see. Internalization, as Fairbairn says, is to try to control the bad object, to manage it.

But you can see it's qualitatively a different kind of relationship and operation from the nondefensive internalisation of the good mother in the central self. In the case of the bad or frustrating object, the internalization is followed by splitting the bad object off from the good object and getting it away from the central self. Even the bad object is perhaps the wrong word because, as Fairbairn said, it is both good and bad at the same time. It has rejecting and exciting qualities, but it's always the frustrating object, the desired disaster, and it has to be kept in check.

Dr. Jill Scharff: Now, Fairbairn has been pretty clear on the need to split off an unacceptable part of experience and locate it deep in unconsciousness as a repressed object that either has rejecting or exciting aspects. Kernberg, in the United States, has pointed out how what's repressed is both the object, the part of the ego that is in relation to the object, and the affects that are involved in that cycle.

Dr. Sutherland: Yes, yes.

Dr. Jill Scharff: What is the place of affect in the central ego? Object-relations theory is quite clear about the affect that is unconscious. What do you think is the place of affect in the central ego?

Dr. Sutherland: Well, affect is an innate property of the organism, of the self. It's there from birth, and it's a sort of global quality carried by the structure. A living, feeling organism has this quality. If you think of it from the evolutionary point of view, it's a masterly creation. How can an organism deal with a multiplicity of experiences and stimuli coming in and how can it be prepared for what's painful and deal with each one? Give it a mechanism whereby anything that is disturbing the well-being is felt in the general headquarters as painful.

So affect has always struck me as an ingenious way of creating a monitoring system that could deal with all kinds of stimuli, and could set in motion internally a reactive mechanism—a cry of protest, a yell, a "go away"—specific responses triggered by this general message of unpleasant affect.

From early on I have not been convinced that repression is necessary for this. Splitting does seem to be an innate property of affect. If there's a painful sort of thing inside, the spontaneous tendency of such a system is to extrude the painful bit. So that gets split off. Naturally, what is split off is the bit of self that's feeling the affect and the relationship there. So the whole bit of the self system gets split off, not just the object.

Dr. Jill Scharff: I've always thought that affect at the conscious level had a lot to do with the infant's capacity to have an accepted object. In other words, a good baby can make its mother wonderful, whereas a baby with difficulties would experience the same mother as not such an acceptable object.

Dr. Sutherland: Well, the affect that comes into any experience is governed by the content of what's going on inside the organism and the nature of what's coming at it. So it's a combination.

You see, we've been so brought up with nineteenth-century science and Freud. The whole model for conceiving personality development was mechanical engineering. You're talking about solid structures all the time with cybernetic control of *negative* feedback. If anything gets out of place, you get it back to the same state that it was in. Whereas, we're dealing with open, growing, developing systems with *positive* feedback; that is, something is happening and you create a new bit so that there's expansion, growth and development, and permanent dynamics.

The whole model has changed completely. Equilibrium, solid structure, nineteenth-century stuff, that's only one area of science. It has no relevance in living organisms. The second law of thermodynamics has everything working toward a steady state. That's not the case in living organisms. Living organisms are negentropic: they are incorporating food stuff all the time to keep up their energy system. They're not dependent on something that was born in the system to start with. They're creating it all the time, so it's a permanent dynamic process.

We've got to think of the self and the personality as a constant, developing system, just exactly like the body, taking in all the time, keeping its structure going, adding new structures, and splitting off unwanted bits.

Dr. Jill Scharff: This idea of human personality and development as part of a cybernetic system, with other selves in a family group, in the peer group, in the society, in the species, seems to me much richer than the linear perspective of Freud, even when modified by a touch of Erikson. What I would like to ask you now is to comment on Fairbairn's view of the linear development of the oral, anal, phallic, and oedipal developmental stages, which he thought were driven not by the necessary unfolding of a set progression through the erogenous zones fueled with instincts, but rather by different techniques needed for dealing with objects.

Dr. Sutherland: Well, I don't think he discarded Freud's biological idea of libidinal development. There are two words I think could well be banished—narcissistic and libidinal—because we can now give them a more specific meaning. All we mean by narcissism is we've taken objects inside and we're living with them, rather than with outer people. And the libidinal drive is the interest toward the real world and the impulse to relate to it. The organism, as a potential person, has an insatiable appetite to encounter and incorporate other people to build up its own shape, and so the quality of the relationships encountered affects the final self. We're really in a state of scientific change, of moving from a linear concept of change to nonlinear concepts of growth and development.

I remember in an early day in the war, when we started those Officer Selection Boards, and the army officers were asking us, "We want you to be able to predict so and so." Bion, who had a great sense of fun, had the answer. An incredible character, he inspired the most terrific affection. He was a huge man, which was a great help in the army, of course. He had been in the Tank Corps in the First World War, and he almost looked like a tank. I felt a little shriveled wimp beside him, I can tell you. But I remember, he just looked at these senior officers, being himself with enough medals—he had the Legion of Honor with a Cross. He was recommended for the Victoria Cross, but he didn't get it. He led the first tank attack in the First World War. But people come in with all that colored brass on their chests, and make people like me feel about this size. But Bion, he could compete. Well he just looked and said, "Well, sir, if you will predict the environment, I'll have a chance of predicting how the individual will behave."

Dr. Jill Scharff: Well, I'm not going to attempt to predict how you're going to answer my next question.

Dr. Sutherland: You're wise not to do that.

Dr. Jill Scharff: Since you didn't specifically answer my question about the stages—oral, anal, and phallic—I'm guessing that maybe it doesn't mean as much to you as do other parts of Fairbairn's theory. I, myself, have never been as taken with, for instance, his view of the object being kept internally or being projected externally according to diagnostic type; and I would be interested to know if you have much interest in that or not.

Dr. Sutherland: Well, I think he never quarrelled with the libidinal stages, but they were just development phases. As Erikson put it, they form the pattern for the psychological disposing of experience, as it were. I cringe too when I hear people talking about anality or orality, as if they were special forms of electricity. What Fairbairn didn't like about the oral, anal, and phallic stages idea was that what were modes of dealing with the internal world were being given a reified status.

Now, the oral pattern, of course, there's no question about that. He talked about that, because the child's pattern for psychological taking in is the physical one. And there's no doubt that the foundation of self-security is physicalized, is very—I think of Ronnie Laing's word—corporeal. It's very much in the body, physical pleasures, getting the good. Mother's goodness comes in from the way she handles the baby.

Of course, the omnipotent or the potency feelings given by the father is a very direct experience, because the average father will pick up and lift a child in a different way from mother. The infant must feel a different quality of power. He's picked up and thrown about in a different way, than by mother, who would be more gentle in lifting and so on.

So one just has to imagine these different ways in which the physical experience could build up to patterns of relating. Fairbairn had no quarrel with that sort of thing at all. What he meant by anal behavior—and the Kleinians go partly toward this—is an advanced stage in which psychological reactions are symbolic. The feces and the excretory acts are taken symbolically.

Obviously, for him personally, early on there was conflict about urination and the parental couple: he was peeing on them. Well, we all know that that's a standard expression amongst kids of real contempt—"go and pee on them." So he was not treating excretion as the object as well, but as a mode, a symbolic mode of treatment of the object, a good way of getting rid of things.

Dr. Jill Scharff: A way of dealing with the object, not just a way of getting rid of instinctual tensions?

Dr. Sutherland: No, no. A way of dealing with the object all the time.

Dr. Jill Scharff: A way of relating.

Dr. Sutherland: Yes. Melanie was quite right, you see, when she spoke of infant terrors coming from projection. When things were extruded from the self, the child feels the edge of the cradle has become a terrifying object because of what got projected onto it.

Dr. Jill Scharff: Now you're mentioning Klein and projection. Fairbairn, of course, acknowledged that he was influenced by Klein. . . .

Dr. Sutherland: Oh, he was very much influenced . . .

Dr. Jill Scharff: But I haven't seen him use the term *projective identification*. Do you know anything about that?

Dr. Sutherland: She had only brought that term in *after* he had written his main papers.

Dr. Jill Scharff: In 1946, wasn't it, before his book came out?

Dr. Sutherland: Yes, but he had *written* his papers by '44 or '45. What's the third one called, where we get the internal structuring, the permanent structuring of the splits and so on? The endopsychic situation. She responded to him after that—and she didn't say much. Melanie simply said, "I disagree." Stop. No reasons. She didn't like what he was saying because he differed, and that wasn't done in darkest Melanesia. You didn't differ with the boss, you see. But

Fairbairn had that very good intellectual training. He didn't just differ, he argued systematically. Instinctive energies and the death instinct—these were nonconcepts to him. The death instinct is quite a useful metaphor for somebody who wants to murder; but, on the other hand, it is not so good when you take it on to a wider range of phenomena, like inner sadomasochistic relationships. Fairbairn had been trained as a philosopher, could think, could isolate principles, could make the challenge, and ask the vital question "Now, is that a valid concept?"

Here's my third confession: I have a feeling that I avoided the implications of what Fairbairn was thinking for most of my life. I didn't do a lot of thinking about his work, because I was caught up in Tavistock, which was so exciting for me, so different from anything that I had experienced in Scotland, so different from anything that he was living, too. He was also quite fascinated with my being in the Tavistock. He thought it was tremendous that he had a friend there. You get a certain kind of relationship with some people such that you always feel in touch with them, no matter if you are not seeing them every day. I had that kind of relationship with Fairbairn. He would tell me things about patients and send me his manuscripts. But I never really devoted myself to thinking about what he was saying. It was only when I started to do a self-analysis that I began to really think about his ideas on the self and its subselves. If I had the attitudes and feelings about thinking then that I have now, I would be much more informed.

All this is just to say, there's hope for us, hope for you all. Start at 70!

Epilogue

John Derg Sutherland C.B.E., F.R.C. Psych., F.R.C.P.E., Ph.D.
28 April 1905–14 June 1991
Psychoanalyst and psychotherapist, clinical psychologist and physician
Medical director, Tavistock Clinic, London, 1947–1968
Consultant psychotherapist, Royal Edinburgh Hospital, 1968–1974
Co-founder, Scottish Institute of Human Relations, 1970

Jock Sutherland's engaging personality, his respect for others, and his firm commitment to psychoanalysis and its application to psychotherapy had a profound impact on psychiatry in the United States. With characteristic humor and philosophical integrity, he persuaded American psychoanalysis to stretch its ego-psychology orientation to include the tenets of British object-relations theory. Beginning in the 1960s and continuing until 1990, he introduced the little known work of his mentor Ronald Fairbairn to American psychiatry, psychoanalysis, psychiatric social work, and nursing during his annual visits as a Visiting Sloan Professor to the Menninger Clinic, one of the most prominent American psychiatric training institutions. His classic (1963) paper, "Object-Relations Theory and the Conceptual Model of Psychoanalysis," given at the clinic and discussed there by Otto Kernberg, is one indicator of Dr. Sutherland's enormous influence on American psychiatry. Jock's teaching and consultation at the Menninger included organized formal consultation and participation on the editorial board of *The Bulletin of the Menninger Clinic* and, later, membership on the board of trustees.

> Jock's visits to the Menninger were anticipated by the staff in the same way children anticipate the annual arrival of St. Nick. The gifts he bore were inspiration, theoretical first aid, and a bottomless enthusiasm for the kind of work we had undertaken. Although the influence of Fairbairn and Winnicott was unmistakable, he often found the ideas of Melanie Klein useful. He would occasionally turn to a young psychiatrist with whom he was consulting and note with a twinkle in his eye, "To treat this patient you will need to enter darkest Melaniesia!"

Glen Gabbard
Director of the C. F. Menninger Memorial Hospital
Topeka, Kansas

In addition to his influence on psychiatry through his impact on psychiatric trainees who then settled throughout the United States, Jock Sutherland also made psychoanalysis relevant to the fields of education, counseling, and community development.

> Jock Sutherland's breadth of vision, keen open-mindedness, and inclusive spirit combined to render him a centrifugal force in the development and dissemination of British object-relations theory. He was committed to and deeply involved in making analytic understanding available to the broadest possible spectrum of the population, and instrumental in encouraging its disciplined appropriation and adaptation by human services professionals serving distressed people in settings well beyond the consulting room. Having organized his life work around the conviction that the fabric of the human psyche is woven from both deep interior and social experience, Dr. Sutherland recognized that he shared this conviction with the religious community of church, synagogue, and temple.
>
> Louis Reed
> Pastoral counselor,
> Jacksonville, Florida

In Britain some months after his death, many people gathered at a memorial service to celebrate Jock and let him go.

> We are not here simply to make a potpourri of good memories, to associate around the name of Sutherland. Jock would have disapproved of that. "What is the thesis from which you are operating?" he would have asked and reminded us, in his characteristic phrase, that there is nothing so practical as a good theory.
>
> The Right Reverend Michael Hare Duke
> Bishop of St. Andrews

Addresses and readings helped structure the recollections of the wide company while music made space for them in a context of Christian belief and tolerance of ambivalence.

> The service of thanksgiving for John Derg Sutherland (Jock) took place at St. Mary's Cathedral, Edinburgh, in the afternoon of Friday, October 4, 1991. It was arranged by the Bishop of St. Andrews, the Right Reverend Michael Hare Duke (with whom Jock had worked on several occasions at the Scottish Institute of Human Relations). It was a beautiful service, with various readings and addresses by people who had worked with Jock, and a cello solo, "The Swan" by Saint Saens, played by Jock's nephew, Dr. Robert Stobie. I had been asked to speak about Jock's contribution to psychoanalysis and the British Psycho-Analytical Society, which were in publications and training. Analyzed by Sylvia Payne, Jock qualified as a psychoanalyst in 1948, and became a member of the Society in 1952. In 1954 he was recognised as a training analyst and in 1956 he was elected to the training committee that reviewed the 1946 agreement with Anna Freud for parallel training courses A & B and introduced a common basic curriculum for all students. Editor of

the International Psychoanalytical Library since 1955 where he piloted 28 books to publication, Jock was also appointed as editor of the International Journal of Psycho-Analysis in 1960. This new office gave him a place on the council and the board of the society, and from that position he was able to have an important influence on the affairs of the society.

Pearl King (1992)
British Psychoanalytical Society

For him, the *purpose*, and the *means* to that end, were two distinct but essential components of every living system—and that unity entailed giving full consideration to both purpose and means in every aspect of life. This could be recognized in all his endeavours and relationships and that "double-task," as I like to refer to it, was basic in his concept of caring, psychoanalytic work, institution building, his group work, leadership roles, and to his marriage. What I might call his direct, concerned, but firm, insistence on that double-task of ensuring full attention to the unity of purpose and of the means of achieving it, encouraged others to search and explore rather than to occupy more resistant positions.

Harold Bridger (1992)
Organizational consultant

It was from Jock that I obtained that vision of a caring society as an infinitely preferable goal to a controlling, and at times a punitive, one. If Fairbairn initiated a Copernican revolution by rescuing the whole person from the clutches of a somewhat dehumanised psychoanalysis, it was Jock Sutherland who completed that revolution by focusing our attention not just on the whole person but on "the whole person in his or her whole environment"—his exploration of the inner world having led him back ineluctably to a study of what went on outside that inner world—of what went on in the larger society.

Drummond Hunter (1992)
Chairman, Scottish Institute of Human Relations

Jock was deeply concerned about the future of psychoanalysis, believing that it needed to broaden its theory to include more understanding of the development of the self. With Fairbairn, he saw the self as an open system that both moulds and is moulded by the caretakers. Every child, in this perspective, has a right to responsive, loving caretakers and, when these are absent or deficient, the child reacts with rage and seeks what it needs, albeit in distorted and seemingly pathological ways. He showed great concern for how damaged selves might be helped through human relatedness in hospital treatment and in psychotherapy. He believed that our patients are our greatest teachers. If we could understand fully what contributes to the etiology of their problems, we could make a major contribution to psychiatry and psychoanalysis. He would frequently remind us that it was our obligation to publish and let the world know about what we are doing and what we are learning.

Stuart Averill (1992)
Menninger Foundation

In addition to professional journals such as the *British Journal of Medical Psychology* (1992) 65:1–4, the *International Journal of Psycho-Analysis* (1992) 73:577–580, both of which he had formerly edited, and *Psychoanalytic Dialogues* (1992) 2(3):277, British daily newspapers such as *The Daily Telegraph* (6/24/91), *The Glasgow Herald* (6/20/91), *The Guardian* (6/21/91), *The Independent* (6/21/91) and *The Scotsman* (6/19/91 and 6/25/91) newspapers carried obituaries and appreciations:

> He was profoundly knowledgeable of the literature of psychoanalysis and its applications; firm in his view that good practice must be grounded in sufficient theory; and committed to promoting psychodynamic insights among the caring professions and into their work beyond the office and consulting room. He had striking success in this aim because of a warm-hearted, generous spirit; an irrepressible sense of humour; a continuing belief in the potential of others; and a constant willingness to share what he knew.
>
> Douglas Haldane, consultant psychiatrist, Scotland
> Eric Trist, formerly director of the Wharton Business School
> *British Journal of Medical Psychology* (1992) p. 1.

> Jock Sutherland was a man of prodigious energy, filled with interesting and challenging ideas and eager to communicate them. A natural teacher, modest to the point of self-effacement, he possessed the precious personal qualities of friendliness, toleration, and good humour. . . . He will be missed for his capacity for conceptualization and for his capacity to adapt his calm but amazing energies to working at the grass root level.
>
> Paul O'Farrell
> Consultant psychotherapist, Royal Edinburgh Hospital
> *International, Journal of Psycho-Analysis* (1992) p. 580.

> Jock, as he was affectionately known, was a psychoanalyst, an editor, a scholar, and an administrator of rare excellence. For his work as medical director of the Tavistock Clinic in London . . . he was awarded the Commander of the British Empire (C. B. E.), an honor given to only two other psychoanalysts, John Bowlby and Anna Freud. . . . In 1989, he published the first book on the life and work of Fairbairn—*Fairbairn's Journey into the Interior*. He was an elegant, humane man, infused with a great sense of humor, joyful, devilish, and peaceful at the same time.
>
> Edward G. Corrigan
> Director, the Institute of Contemporary Psychotherapy, New York
> *Psychoanalytic Dialogues* (1992) p. 277.

> I cannot really recall a time in my life when Jock Sutherland was not a part of it. I remember him as an analysand at my father's noble consulting rooms at 21 Grosvenor Crescent when I was 4 years old. . . . My father's philosophy of the workings of the human mind would never have received the acclaim that it now enjoys worldwide, but for the almost filial devotion of Jock Sutherland. . . . Jock was modest, almost to the point of self-effacement, but he was remarkably effective in achieving his objective of the

> compassionate cure of those who suffered from the deep well of mental anguish, and in promoting the explanation of their suffering.
>
> Sir Nicholas Fairbairn
> Lawyer, public servant, son of Ronald Fairbairn
> *The Scotsman* 6/25/91

> Jock was the youngest of an Edinburgh family of eight. A studious child, he first read chemistry and then psychology at Edinburgh University. There he came under the influence of Ronald Fairbairn. Determined to become a psychoanalyst, he took his medical degree at Edinburgh University. . . . With his wartime colleagues, among whom were Henry Dicks, John Bowlby, and Wilfred Bion, Sutherland led the [Tavistock] Clinic into its preeminent national and international position in psychoanalytically oriented psychotherapy and related health endeavours. . . . He devoted himself to furthering the development of the Scottish Institute [of Human Relations], using his great skills as an educator and facilitator, to make psychodynamic insights available to doctors, nurses, social workers, educationalists, voluntary workers, religious leaders, and others. "Working is fun," he used to say, and with such a dedicated man, it had to be that, and more than that.
>
> Anton Obholzer
> Medical Director, the Tavistock Clinic
> *The Independent* 6/21/91

It is for his personal facilitation that many of us will remember Jock. In his several visits to the Washington School of Psychiatry, a national postgraduate training institution for mental health professionals, he helped Margaret Rioch found the A. K. Rice Institute on the Tavistock model committed to the application of psychoanalysis to organizational and group relations; he led workshops on object-relations theory for faculty and students; and he was the distinguished Frieda Fromm Reichmann lecturer in 1979. His last and memorable visit to the Washington School occurred just a year before his death.

> During this trip he inspired students and faculty alike with his uncommon combination of common sense and profound knowledge. His message then, as it had been throughout his professional career, was one learned from his analyst and mentor, Fairbairn, refined in the cask of his own experience, and enacted in his work in what he called "the growth and development business." Jock taught us all: "What our patients want is only to love and to be loved for themselves."
>
> Jock loved his colleagues with the tough practicality of his tender knowledge of the human spirit. In Topeka, Kansas, Washington, D.C., and everywhere that he was known, Jock was unquestionably loved for himself.
>
> David E. Scharff
> Director, Washington School of Psychiatry, Washington, D.C.

The last word goes to Jock's wife of 51 years, Molly, who quotes E. M. Forster on Auden's death: "It is as though the temperature of felt life has dropped."

At home with Molly, Edinburgh, 1972

References

Allport, G. W. (1949). *Personality*. London: Constable and Co.

Angyal, A. (1965). *Neurosis and Treatment*. New York: Wiley.

Artiss, K. L. (1985). *Therapeutic Studies*. Rockville, MD: Psychiatric Books.

Balint, M., and Balint, E. (1961). *Psychotherapeutic Techniques in Medicine*. London: Tavistock.

Balint, M. (1952). *Primary Love and Psycho-Analytic Technique*. London: Hogarth.

——— (1957). *The Doctor, His Patient and the Illness*. London: Pitman. (2nd ed. 1964).

——— (1968). *The Basic Fault: Therapeutic Aspects of Regression*. London: Tavistock.

Barrett, W. (1979). *The Illusion of Technique*. London: William Kimber.

Bell, D. (1982). *Social Sciences Since the Second World War*. New Brunswick, NJ: Transaction Books.

Berne, E. (1963). *The Structure and Dynamics of Organizations and Groups*. Philadelphia: Lippincott.

Bertalanffy, L. von (1950a). An outline of general system theory. *British Journal for the Philosophy of Science* 1:134–165.

——— (1950b). The theory of open systems in physics and biology. *Science* 111:23–29.

Bettelheim, B. (1982). Reflections: Freud and the Soul. *The New Yorker* March 1st, pp. 59–93.

Bion, W. R. (1961). *Experiences in Groups*. London: Tavistock.

——— (1962). *Learning from Experience*. London: Heinemann.

Blacker, C. P. (1946). *Neurosis and the Mental Health Services*. London: Oxford University Press.

Bleuler, E. (1951). Psychiatry of cerebral diseases. *British Medical Journal* 2:1233–1238.

Bondurant, J. V., Fisher, M. W., and Sutherland, J. D. (1971). Gandhi: A psychoanalytic viewpoint. *The American Historical Review* 76:1104–1115.

Bowlby, J. (1960). Grief and mourning in infancy and early childhood. *Psychoanalytic Study of the Child* 15:9–52. New York: International Universities Press.

——— (1969). *Attachment and Loss*. New York: Basic Books.

——— (1973). *Separation: Anxiety and Anger*. New York: Basic Books.

Brierley, M. (1951). *Trends in Psychoanalysis*. London: Hogarth.

Broad, C. D. (1937). *The Mind and Its Place in Nature*. London: Routledge and Kegan Paul.

Bronowski, J. (1965). *The Identity of Man*. London: Pelican.

Brown, N. O. (1959). *Life Against Death: The Psychoanalytic Meaning of History*. Middleton, CT: Wesleyan University Press.

Buchan, J. (1924). *The Three Hostages*. London: Penguin Books, 1986.

_____ (1940). *Memory Hold-the-Door*. London: Hodder and Stoughton.
_____ (1981). *Sick Heart River*. London: Penguin, 1985.
Buchan, W. (1982). *John Buchan: A Memoir*. London: Buchan/Enright.
Buckley, W. (1967). *Sociology and Modern Systems Theory*. Englewood Cliffs, NJ: Prentice Hall.
Cantril, H. (1955). Toward a humanistic psychology. In *Etc.: A Review of General Semantics* 12(4):278–298.
Cartwright, D., and Zander, A., eds. (1953). *Group Dynamics: Research and Theory*. Evanston, IL: Row, Peterson & Co.
Casement, P. (1990). *On Learning From the Patient*. New York: Routledge.
Chein, I. (1972). *The Science of Behavior and the Image of Man*. New York: Basic Books.
Colby, K. M. (1955). *Energy and Structure in Psychoanalysis*. New York: Ronald.
Corrigan, E. G. (1992). J. D. Sutherland: In memoriam. *Psychoanalytic Dialogues* 2: 277.
Cumming, E., and Cumming, J. (1957). *Closed Ranks*. Cambridge, MA: Harvard University Press.
Curran, D., and Guttman, E. (1949). *Psychological Medicine—A Short Introduction to Psychiatry*. Edinburgh: Livingstone.
Deutsch, K. W. (1963). A simple cybernetic model. In *Readings on the Sociology of Small Groups*, ed. T. M. Mills and S. Rosenberg, pp. 56–74. Englewood Cliffs, NJ: Prentice Hall, 1970.
Dicks, H. V. (1950). In search of our proper ethic. *British Journal of Medical Psychology* 23:1–14.
Chasseguet-Smirgel, J. (1985). *The Ego Ideal*. London: Free Association Books.
Drever, J. (1917). *Instinct in Man*. London: Methuen.
Emery, F. E. (1967). The next thirty years: concepts, methods and anticipations. *Human Relations* 20:199–237.
Emery, F. E., and Trist, E. L. (1965). The causal texture of organizational environments. *Human Relations* 18:21–32.
_____ (1973). *Towards a Social Ecology: Contextual Appreciation of the Future in the Present*. New York: Plenum Press.
Erikson, E. H. (1950). *Childhood and Society*. New York: W. W. Norton.
_____ (1958). *Young Man Luther: A Study in Psychoanalysis and History*. New York: Norton.
_____ (1959). *Identity and the Life Cycle*. (Psychological Issues 1:1–171.) New York: International Universities Press.
_____ (1969). *Gandhi's Truth: On the Origins of Militant Nonviolence*. New York: W. W. Norton.
Eskelinen de Folch, T. (1988). Obstacles to analytic cure. In *On Freud's "Analysis Terminable and Interminable,"* ed. J. Sandler, pp. 93–105. New Haven: Yale University Press.
Ezriel, H. (1950). A psycho-analytic approach to group treatment. *British Journal of Medical Psychology* 23:59–74.
_____ (1951). The psycho-analytic session as an experimental situation. *British Journal of Medical Psychology*. 24:30–34.
_____ (1952). Notes on psychoanalytic group therapy II: Interpretation and research. *Psychiatry* 15:119–126.
_____ (1956–1957). Experimentation within the psychoanalytic session. *British Journal for the Philosophy of Science* 7:29–48; and, in continuation, reply to Mr. Spilsbury, *British Journal for the Philosophy of Science* 7:342–347.
Fairbairn N. (1992). Appreciation. *The Scotsman*, 25th June, 1991.

Fairbairn, W. R. D. (1944). Endopsychic structure considered in terms of object relationships. In *An Object Relations Theory of the Personality*, pp. 82–132. New York: Basic Books, 1954.

——— (1952a). *Psychoanalytic Studies of the Personality*. London: Tavistock.

——— (1952b). Theoretical and experimental aspects of psycho-analysis. *British Journal of Medical Psychology* 25:122–127.

——— (1954a). Observations on the nature of hysterical states. *British Journal of Medical Psychology* 27:105–125.

——— (1954b). *An Object Relations Theory of the Personality*. New York: Basic Books.

——— (1955). Observations in defence of the object relations theory of the personality. *British Journal of Medical Psychology* 28:144–156.

——— (1956a). A critical evaluation of certain psychoanalytical concepts. *British Journal for the Philosophy of Science* 7:49–60.

——— (1956b). Considerations arising out of the Schreber case. *British Journal of Medical Psychology* 29:113–127.

——— (1957a). Freud, the psycho-analytical method and mental health. *British Journal of Medical Psychology* 30:35–62.

——— (1957b). Reply to the comments of Balint, Foulkes and Sutherland. *British Journal for the Philosophy of Science* 7:333–338.

——— (1958). On the nature and aims of psychoanalytical treatment. *International Journal of Psycho-Analysis* 29:374–385.

——— (1963). Synopsis of an object-relations theory of the personality. *International Journal of Psycho-Analysis* 44:224–226.

Flugel, J. C. (1939). The examination as initiation rite and anxiety situation. *International Journal of Psycho-Analysis* 20:275–286.

Foulkes, S. H. and Anthony, E. J. (1957). *Group Psychotherapy*. London: Penguin.

Fraser, R. (1947). *The Incidence of Neurosis among Factory Workers*. London: H. M. Stationery Office.

Freud, A. (1946). *The Ego and the Mechanisms of Defence*. New York: International Universities Press.

Freud, S. (1914). On the history of the psychoanalytic movement. *Standard Edition* 14:1–66.

——— (1921). Group psychology and the analysis of the ego. *Standard Edition* 18:69–143.

——— (1923). The ego and the id. *Standard Edition* 19:12–66.

——— (1926). Inhibitions, symptoms and anxiety. *Standard Edition* 20:87–172.

——— (1937a). Analysis terminable and interminable. *Standard Edition* 23:216–253.

——— (1937b). An outline of psychoanalysis. *Standard Edition* 23:139–207.

——— (1950). Project for a scientific psychology. *Standard Edition* 1:295–343.

Gaddis, T. (1955). *Birdman of Alcatraz: The Story of Robert Stroud*. New York: Random House.

Ghent, E. (1992). Paradox and process. *Psychoanalytic Dialogues* 2:135–159.

Greenberg, J. R., and Mitchell, S. A. (1983). *Object Relations in Psychoanalytic Theory*. Cambridge, MA: Harvard University Press.

Grinberg, L. (1962). On a specific aspect of countertransference due to the patient's projective identification. *International Journal of Psycho-Analysis* 43:436–440.

Guntrip, H. S. (1961). *Personality Structure and Human Interaction*. New York: International Universities Press.

——— (1969). *Schizoid Phenomena, Object Relations and the Self*. New York: International Universities Press.

_____ (1975). My experience of analysis with Fairbairn and Winnicott. *International Review of Psycho-Analysis* 2:145–156.

_____ (1978). Psycho-analysis and some scientific and philosophical critics. *British Journal of Medical Psychology* 51:207–224.

Haldane, D., and Trist, E. (1992). Obituary Jock Sutherland. *British Journal of Medical Psychology* 65:1–4.

Halmos, P. (1966). *The Faith of the Counsellors*. London: Constable.

Hare, A. P., Borgatta, E. F., and Bales, R. F., eds. (1955). *Small Groups*. New York: Knopf.

Hartmann, H. (1933). Psychiatrische Zwillingsstudien. *Jahrbucher fur. Psychiatrie und Neurologie* 49:14–242.

_____ (1935). Zur Charakterologie erbgleicher Zwillinge. *Jahrbucher fur. Psychiatrie und Neurologie* 52:57–118.

_____ (1958). *Ego Psychology and the Problem of Adaptation*. (Original work published 1939). Trans. D. Rapaport. New York: International Universities Press.

_____ (1964). *Essays on Ego Psychology*. New York: International Universities Press.

Heisenberg, W. (1930). *Physical Principles of the Quantum Theory*, trans. C. Eckart and F. C. Hoyt. Chicago: University of Chicago Press.

Hill, D. (1970). On mechanism and meaning. The Ernest Jones Lecture, March.

Hinde, R. A. (1982). *Ethology: Its Nature and Relations with Other Sciences*. Oxford: Oxford University Press.

Hollós, S., and Ferenczi, S. (1925). *Psychoanalysis and the Psychic Disorder of General Paresis*, trans. G. M. Barnes and G. Keil. New York: Nervous and Mental Disease Publishing Company.

Jacobson, E. (1964). *The Self and the Object World*. New York: International Universities Press.

Jahoda, M. (1958). *Current Concepts of Positive Mental Health*. New York: Basic Books.

Jantsch, E. (1976). Introduction and summary. In *Evolution and Consciousness*, ed. C. H. Waddington and E. Jantsch. pp. 1–8. Reading, MA: Addison-Wesley.

_____ (1980). *The Self-organizing Universe: Scientific and Human Implications of the Emerging Paradigm of Evolution*. New York: Pergamon.

Jaques, E. (1955). Social systems as a defence against persecutory and depressive anxiety. In *New Directions in Psycho-Analysis*, ed. M. Klein, P. Heimann, and R. Money-Kyrle. London: Tavistock.

Jones, E. (1940). Sigmund Freud. *International Journal of Psycho-Analysis* 21:1–26.

Kallmann, F. J., Kluckhohn, C., and Murray, A. H. (1949). The genetic theory of schizophrenia. In *Personality in Nature, Society and Culture*, pp. 80–99. New York: Knopf. (Also London: Jonathan Cape, 1949.)

Kennedy, P. (1987). *The Rise and Fall of the Great Powers*. New York: Random House.

Kernberg, O. (1976). *Object Relations Theory and Clinical Psychoanalysis*. New York: Jason Aronson.

_____ (1980). *Internal World and External Reality*. New York: Jason Aronson.

Khan, M. M. R. (1964). Ego distortion, cumulative trauma, and the role of reconstruction in the analytic situation. *International Journal of Psycho-Analysis* 45:272–279.

_____ (1983). *Hidden Selves: Between Theory and Practice in Psychoanalysis*. New York: International Universities Press.

King, P. (1992). Note at memorial service. *British Psychoanalytic Institute Bulletin*, vol. 28 No. 1, January 1992.

Klein, G. S. (1976). *Psychoanalytic Theory: An Exploration of Essentials*. New York: International Universities Press.

Klein, M. (1932). *The Psycho-analysis of Children*, trans. A. Strachey. London: Hogarth.

_____ (1934). A contribution to the psychogenesis of manic-depressive states. In *Contributions to Psychoanalysis, 1921–1945*, pp. 282–310. London: Hogarth, 1948.

_____ (1955). *New Directions in Psycho-Analysis*. London: Tavistock.

Klein, R. (1952). Immediate effects of leucotomy on cerebral function and their significance: a preliminary report. *Journal of Mental Science* 98:60–65.

Kohut, H. (1971). *The Analysis of the Self: a Systematic Approach to the Psychoanalytic Treatment of Narcissistic Personality Disorder* (Psychoanalytic Study of the Child, Monogr. 4). New York: International Universities Press.

_____ (1977). *The Restoration of the Self*. New York: International Universities Press.

_____ (1979). The two analyses of Mr. Z. *International Journal of Psycho-Analysis* 60:3–27.

_____ (1984). *How Does Analysis Cure*? Chicago: University of Chicago Press.

Langbaum, R. W. (1977). *The Mysteries of Identity: a Theme in Modern Literature*. London: Oxford University Press.

Levine, R. A. (1966). Stand-patism versus change in psychiatric clinic practice. *American Journal of Psychiatry* 123:71–77.

Lichtenstein, H. (1977). *The Dilemma of Human Identity*. New York: Jason Aronson.

Lorenz, M., and Cobb, S. (1953). Language behaviour in psychoneurotic patients. *A.M.A. Archives of Neurology and Psychiatry* 69:684–694.

Lynd, R. S. (1939). *Knowledge for What? The Place of Social Science in American Culture*. Princeton, NJ: Princeton University Press.

MacMurray, J. (1957). *The Self as Agent*. London: Faber.

_____ (1961). *Persons in Relations*. London: Faber.

Mahler, M. S., Pine, F., and Bergman, A. (1975). *The Psychological Birth of the Human Infant*. New York: Basic Books.

Malan, D. (1976). Group psychotherapy: a long-term follow-up study. *Archives of General Psychiatry* 33:1303–1315.

Malinowski, B. (1927). *Sex and Repression in Savage Society*. London and New York: International Library of Psychology, Philosophy and Scientific Method.

_____ (1929). The Sexual Life of Savages in North-Western Melanesia. New York: Harcourt, Brace, and World.

Marcuse, H. (1955). *Eros and Civilization: a Philosophical Inquiry into Freud*. Boston: Beacon.

McCowan, P. K. (1952). Presidential address: "Whither Psychiatry?" *Journal of Mental Science* 98:1–11.

McDougall, W. (1920). *The Group Mind*. New York: Putnam.

Mead, G. H. (1952). *Mind Self and Society from the Standpoint of a Social Behaviorist,* intro. and ed. C. W. Morris. Chicago: University of Chicago Press.

Menninger, K. (1958). *Theory of Psycho-analytic Technique*. London: Imago.

Menzies, I. E. P. (1960). A case-study in the functioning of social systems as a defence against anxiety. *Human Relations* 13:95–122.

Miller, J. G. (1965a). Living systems: structure and process. *Behavioral Science* 10:337–379.

_____ (1965b). Living systems: cross-level hypotheses. *Behavioral Science* 10:380–411.

Mills, T. M., and Rosenberg, S., eds. (1970). *Readings on the Sociology of Small Groups*. Englewood Cliffs, NJ: Prentice Hall.

Mischel, T., ed. (1977). *The Self*. Oxford: Blackwell.

Mitchell, S. (1988). *Relational Concepts and Psychoanalysis. an Integration*. Cambridge, MA: Harvard University Press.

Modell, A. (1968). *Object Love and Reality*. New York: International Universities Press.

Monod, J. (1971). *Chance and Necessity: an Essay on the Natural Philosophy of Modern Biology*, trans. Austryn Wainhouse, New York: Alfred A. Knopf.

Moreno, J. L. (1956). *Sociometry and the Science of Man*. New York: Beacon House.

Morse, S. (1972). Structure and reconstruction. *International Journal of Psycho-Analysis* 53:487–500.

Obholzer, A. (1991). Appreciation. *The Independent* 26th June, 1991.

O'Farrell, P. (1992). Obituary John D. Sutherland. *International Journal of Psycho-Analysis* 73:577–580.

Office of Health Economics. (1972). *Medicine and Society*. Report No. 43. London.

Olmsted, M. S. (1955). *The Small Group*. New York: Random House.

Parsons, T., and Bales, F. (1955). *Family, Socialization and Interaction Process*. Glencoe, IL: Free Press.

Peterfreund, E. (1971). *Information, Systems and Psychoanalysis*. Psychological Issues, Monograph 25/26. New York: International Universities Press.

Pincus, L. ed. (1960). *Marriage: Studies in Emotional Conflict and Growth*. London: Methuen.

Prigogine, I. (1976). Order through fluctuation: Self- organization and social system. In *Evolution and Consciousness*: *Human Systems in Transition*, ed. C. H. Waddington and E. Jantsch, pp. 93–126. Reading, MA: Addison-Wesley.

Pruyser, P. W. (1974). *Between Belief and Unbelief*. New York: Harper & Row.

Racker, H. (1957). The meanings and uses of countertransference. *Psychoanalytic Quarterly* 26:303–357.

Ramsey, I. T. (1970). On not being judgmental. *Contact Journal of the Scottish Pastoral Association*, March.

Rapaport, D. (1951). The conceptual model of psychoanalysis. In *Psycho-analytic Psychiatry and Psychology*, pp. 221–247, ed. R. P. Knight and C. R. Friedman. New York: International Universities Press.

_____ (1960). The structure of psycho-analytical theory. *Psychological Issues*. pp. 7–158, vol 2. No. 2. Monograph 6. New York: International Universities Press.

Rice, A. K. (1963). *The Enterprise and Its Environment*. London: Tavistock.

Rickman, J. (1957). *Selected Contributions to Psycho-Analysis*. London: Hogarth.

Rizzuto, A. M. (1979). *The Birth of the Living God*. Chicago, IL: University of Chicago Press.

Rolland, R. (1924). Mahatma Gandhi. Trans. C. D. Groth. pp. 3–5. New York: The Century Co.

Rosanoff, A. J., Handy, L. M., Plesset, I. R., and Brush, S. (1934). The etiology of so-called schizophrenic psychoses, with special reference to their occurrence in twins. *American Journal of Psychiatry* 91: 247–286.

Rosenblatt, A. D., and Thickstun, J. T. (1977). *Modern Psychoanalytic Concepts in General Psychology*. Psychological Issues Monograph 42/43. New York: International Universities Press.

Sandford, B. (1952). Some psychotherapeutic work in maternity and child welfare clinics. *British Journal of Medical Psychology* 25:2–15.

Sandler, J., and Sandler, A-M. (1984). The past unconscious, the present unconscious, and interpretation of the transference. *Psychoanalytic Inquiry* 4:367–399.

Saperstein, J. L., and Gaines, J. (1973). Metapsychological considerations on the self. *International Journal of Psycho-Analysis* 54:415–424.

Schafer, R. (1968). *Aspects of Internalization*. New York: International Universities Press.

——— (1976). *A New Language for Psychoanalysis*. New Haven, CT: Yale University Press.

Scheidlinger, S. (1960). Group process in group psychotherapy. *American Journal of Psychotherapy* 14:104–120, 346–363.

Schmideberg, M. (1938). Intellectual inhibition and disturbances in eating. *International Journal of Psycho-Analysis* 19:17–22.

Senn, M. J. E., ed. (1950). *Symposium on the Healthy Personality*. New York: Josiah Macy Jr. Foundation.

Slavson, S. R. (1951). Current trends of group psychotherapy. *International Journal of Group Psychotherapy* 1:7–15.

——— (1962). A critique of the group therapy literature. *Acta Psychotherapeutica* 10:62–73.

Sofer, C. (1961). *The Organization from Within*. London: Tavistock.

Spitz, R. A. (1965). *The First Year of Life*. New York: International Universities Press.

Stengel, E. (1936). Prufungsangst and Prufungsneurose. *Zeitschrift fur Psychoanalytische Pädagogik* 10:300–320.

Stengel, E., Ezriel, H., and Farrell, B. A. (1951). The scientific testing of psychoanalytic findings and theory. *British Journal of Medical Psychology* 24:26–41.

Stern, D. N. (1985). *The Interpersonal World of the Infant*. New York: Basic Books.

Sullivan, H. S. (1953). *The Interpersonal Theory of Psychiatry*. New York: W. W. Norton.

Sutherland, J. D. (1941). Three cases of anxiety and failure in examinations. *British Journal of Medical Psychology* 19:73–81.

——— (1952). Psychological medicine and the National Health Service: the need for an integrated approach to research. *British Journal of Medical Psychology* 25:71–85.

——— (1957). Some comments on Dr. Fairbairn's paper. *British Journal for the Philosophy of Science* 7:329–337.

——— (1963). Object-relations theory and the conceptual model of psychoanalysis. *British Journal of Medical Psychology* 36:109–124.

——— (1965). Recent advances in the understanding of small groups, their disorders and treatment. *Psychotherapy and Psychosomatics* 13:110–125.

——— (1966). The psychotherapeutic clinic and community psychiatry. *Bulletin of the Menninger Clinic* 30:338–350.

——— (1967). The place of psychotherapy in community mental health. *Contact, Journal of the Scottish Pastoral Association*. January, pp. 2–18.

——— (1968a). The consultant psychotherapist in the National Health Service: His role and training. *British Journal of Psychiatry* 114:509–515.

——— (1968b). Unpublished paper. Training of psychiatrists for the psychotherapeutic needs of the community. July, Department of Psychiatry, Edinburgh University, pp. 1–8.

——— (1969). Psychoanalysis in the post-industrial society. *International Journal of Psycho-Analysis* 50:673–682.

——— (1971a). Introduction. *Towards Community Mental Health*, pp. vii–xii, ed. J. D. Sutherland. London: Tavistock.

——— (1971b). Reflections on the development of counselling services. *National Council of Social Services*, October. pp. 1–14.

——— (1979). The psychodynamic image of man: A philosophy for the caring professions. The Malcolm Millar Lecture of 1979, Aberdeen University. Also given as the Frieda Fromm-Reichmann Lecture, Washington School of Psychiatry, 1979.

_____ (1980a). Hate and the autonomy of the self. Unpublished paper. Published as The Autonomous Self. *Bulletin of the Menninger Clinic* 57:1–32, 1993.

_____ (1980b). The British object relations theorists: the contributions of Balint, Winnicott, Fairbairn, Guntrip. *Journal of the American Psychoanalytic Association* 28: 829–860.

_____ (1980c). The contributions of D. W. Winnicott. *Bulletin of the Association for Psychoanalytic Medicine* 20:18–25.

_____ (1983). The self and object relations: A challenge to psychoanalysis. *Bulletin of the Menninger Clinic* 47:525–541.

_____ (1985a). A start from the centre of the personality: The life and work of W. R. D. Fairbairn. Unpublished manuscript held at The Scottish Institute of Human Relations.

_____ (1985b). Bion revisited: group dynamics and group psychotherapy. In *Bion and Group Psychotherapy*, ed. M. Pines. pp. 47–86. London: Routledge & Kegan Paul.

_____ (1985c). The object relations approach. Unpublished paper presented at the Washington School of Psychiatry Sixth Annual Symposium of Psychoanalytic Family Therapy, Bethesda, MD, April 1985.

_____ (1987). The need for a new paradigm. Thoughts on my relationship with the Menninger Foundation, 1964–1987. Unpublished paper.

_____ (1988). John Buchan's "sick heart." Some psychodynamic reflections. *Edinburgh Review* 78–79: 83–101.

_____ (1989a). *Fairbairn's Journey into the Interior*. London: Free Association.

_____ (1989b). On becoming and being a person. Lecture given at the Washington School of Psychiatry, April 1989.

_____ (1989c). The significance of Fairbairn's contribution. Unpublished paper. Spoken at the Fairbairn Centenary conference, Scottish Institute of Human Relations.

Sutherland, J. D., and Gill, H. S. (1964). The significance of the one-way vision screen in analytic group psychotherapy. *British Journal of Medical Psychology* 37:185–202.

_____ (1970). *Language and Psychodynamic Appraisal*. London: Karnac Books.

_____ (1971). The object relations theory of personality. In *Language and Psychodynamic Appraisal*. London: Tavistock.

Sutherland, J. D., Gill, H. S., and Phillipson, H. (1967). Psychodiagnostic appraisal in the light of recent theoretical developments. *British Journal of Medical Psychology* 40: 299–315.

Sutherland, J. D., and Menzies, I. E. (1947). Two industrial projects. *Journal of Social Issues* 3: pp. 51–58.

Szasz, T. (1961). *The Myth of Mental Illness*. London: Secker & Warburg, 1962.

Toffler, A. (1970). *Future Shock*. New York: Random House.

Trevarthen, C. (1980). The foundations of inter-subjectivity. Development of interpersonal and co-operative understanding in infants. In *The Social Foundations of Language and Thought: Essays in Honor of J. S. Bruner*, ed. D. Olson. New York: W. W. Norton.

Trilling, L. (1955). *Freud and the Crisis of our Culture*. Boston: Beacon.

_____ (1971). *Sincerity and Authenticity*. Cambridge, MA: Harvard University Press.

Trist, E. L. (1963). *Organizational Choice*. London: Tavistock.

_____ (1968). The relation of welfare and development in the transition to post-industrialism. Los Angeles: Sociotechnical Systems Division, Western Management Science Institute, University of California.

_____ (1985). Working with Bion in the 1940s: the group decade. In *Bion and Group Psychotherapy*, ed. M. Pines, pp. 1-46. London: Routledge & Kegan Paul.

_____ (1991). Obituary. Personal letter to M. Leishman.

Trist, E. L., and Bamforth, K. W. (1951). Some social and psychological consequences of the longwall method of coal-getting. *Human Relations* 4:3-38.

Tustin, F. (1972). *Autism and Childhood Psychosis*. London: Hogarth.

Vitz, P. O. (1977). *Psychology as Religion: The Cult of Self Worship*. Grand Rapids, MI: Eerdmans.

Volkan, V. (1988). *The Need to Have Enemies and Allies*. New York: Jason Aronson.

Waddington, C. H., and Jantsch, E. eds. (1976). *Evolution and Consciousness: Human Systems in Transition*. Reading, MA: Addison-Wesley.

Waelder, R. (1960). *Basic Theory of Psychoanalysis*. New York: International Universities Press.

Wallerstein, R. S. (1968). The challenge of the community mental health movement to psychoanalysis. *American Journal of Psychiatry* 124:1049-1056.

_____ (1969). Psychoanalysis and psychotherapy. *International Journal of Psycho-Analysis* 50:117-126.

_____ (1975). *Psychotherapy and Psychoanalysis: Theory—Practice—Research*. New York: International Universities Press.

_____ (1988). One psychoanalysis or many? *International Journal of Psycho-Analysis* 69:5-21.

Walshe, F. M. R. (1950). Humanism, history and natural science in medicine. Linacre lecture. *British Medical Journal* 2:379-384.

Weisman, A. D. (1965). *The Existential Core of Psychoanalysis: Reality Sense and Responsibility*. Boston: Little, Brown.

Winnicott, D. W. (1953). Transitional objects and transitional phenomena: a study of the first not-me possession. *International Journal of Psycho-Analysis* 34:89-97.

_____ (1958a). The capacity to be alone. In *The Maturational Processes and the Facilitating Environment*, pp. 29-36. New York: International Universities Press.

_____ (1958b). *Collected Papers*. New York: Basic Books.

_____ (1960a). Ego distortion in terms of true and false self. In *The Maturational Processes and the Facilitating Environment: Studies in the Theory of Emotional Development*, pp. 140-152. New York: International Universities Press.

_____ (1960b). The theory of the parent-infant relationship. In *The Maturational Processes and the Facilitating Environment*, pp. 37-55. New York: International Universities Press, 1965.

_____ (1963). From dependence towards independence. In *The Maturational Processes and the Facilitating Environment*, pp. 83-92. New York: International Universities Press, 1965.

_____ (1965). *The Maturational Processes and the Facilitating Environment*. New York: International Universities Press.

Winnicott, D. W., and Khan, M. J. (1953). Book review of *Psychoanalytic Studies of the Personality* by W. R. D. Fairbairn. *International Journal of Psycho-Analysis* 34: 329-333.

Wolff, H. G. (1960). Stressors as a cause of disease in man. In *Stress and Psychiatric*

Disorder: the Proceedings of the Second Oxford Conference of the Mental Health Research Fund, pp. 17–33. ed. J. M. Tanner. Oxford: Blackwell, 1958.
Yankelovich, D. and Barrett, W. (1970). *Ego and Instinct*. New York: Random House.
Zetzel, E. (1955). Recent British approaches to problems of early development. *Journal of the American Psychoanalytic Association* 3:534–543.
Zilboorg, G. (1941). *A History of Medical Psychology*. New York: W. W. Norton.

Credits

Chapter 1 appeared as "Object-Relations Theory and the Conceptual Model of Psychoanalysis" (1963). *British Journal of Medical Psychology* 36:109–124, and is reprinted with permission.

Chapter 2 was published as "The British Object Relations Theorists: The Contributions of Balint, Winnicott, Fairbairn, Guntrip (1980). *Journal of the American Psychoanalytic Association* 28: 829–860, and is reprinted with permission.

Chapter 3 was a talk reported by M. Wasserman and published as "The Contributions of D. W. Winnicott" (1980). *Bulletin of the Association for Psychoanalytic Medicine* 20(1)(Nov.): 18–25, and is reprinted with permission.

Chapter 4 was extracted from an unpublished paper (1989) spoken at the Fairbairn Centenary Conference, Scottish Institute of Human Relations, Edinburgh, and is reprinted by permission of the Sutherland literary executor at the Scottish Institute.

Chapter 5 was previously published as a co-authored chapter with H. S. Gill. "The Object Relations Theory of Personality" (1971). In *Language and Psychodynamic Appraisal* ed. J. D. Sutherland and H. S. Gill. London: Tavistock Institute of Human Relations, and is reprinted with permission.

Chapter 6 was previously published as a co-authored paper with H. S. Gill & H. Phillipson. "Psychodiagnostic Appraisal in the Light of Recent Theoretical Developments" (1967). *British Journal of Medical Psychology* 40: 299–315, and is reprinted with permission.

Chapter 7 was previously published as "Three Cases of Anxiety and Failure in Examinations" (1941). *British Journal of Medical Psychology* 19(1): 73–81, and is reprinted with permission.

Chapter 8 was originally published as "Some Comments on Dr. Fairbairn's Paper" (1956). *British Journal for the Philosophy of Science* 7 (28) (Feb): 329–337, and is reprinted with permission.

Chapter 9 was published as "Recent Advances in the Understanding of Small Groups, Their Disorders and Treatment" (1965). *Psychotherapy and Psychosomatics* 13: 110–125, and is reprinted with permission.

Chapter 10 was published as a paper co-authored with H. S. Gill. "The Significance of the One-Way Vision Screen in Analytic Group Psychotherapy" (1964). *British Journal of Medical Psychology* 37:185–202, and is reprinted with permission.

Chapter 11 was published as the chapter "Bion Revisited: Group Dynamics and Group Psychotherapy" (1985) in *Bion and Group Psychotherapy*, ed. M. Pines. pp. 47–86. London: Routledge & Kegan Paul, and is reprinted with permission.

Chapter 12 was published as a paper co-authored with I. E. Menzies. "Two Industrial Projects" (1947). *Journal of Social Issues*, III (2) (Spring) pp. 51–58, and is reprinted with permission.

Chapter 13 was originally an introduction to the book *Towards Community Mental Health*, (1971) edited by J. D. Sutherland. London, Tavistock. pp. vii–xii, and is reprinted with permission.

Chapter 14 was originally published as "Psychoanalysis in the Post-industrial Society" (1969). *International Journal of Psycho-Analysis* 50 (4): 673–682, and is reprinted with permission.

Chapter 15 was previously published as "Reflections on the Development of Counselling Services" (1971). *National Council of Social Services*, October, pp. 1–14, and is reprinted with permission.

Chapter 16 was collated from "The Consultant Psychotherapist in the National Health Service: His Role and Training" (1968). *British Journal of Psychiatry* 114: 509–515, and is reprinted by permission of the Royal College of Psychiatrists; "The Place of Psychotherapy in Community Mental Health" (1967). *Contact*, published by the Scottish Pastoral Association, January pp. 2–18, and reprinted with permission; "The Psychotherapeutic Clinic and Community Psychiatry" (1966). *Bulletin of the Menninger Clinic* 30 (6) (Nov): 338–350, and reprinted with permission.

Chapter 17 was published as "Psychological Medicine and the National Health Service: The Need for an Integrated Approach to Research" (1952). *British Journal of Medical Psychology* 25 (2&3): 71–85, and is reprinted with permission.

Chapter 18 was an unpublished paper, "The Need for a New Paradigm: Thoughts on My Relationship with the Menninger Foundation, 1964–1987" (1987).

Chapter 19 was a paper, "The Psychodynamic Image of Man: A Philosophy for the Caring Professions" (1979). The Malcolm Millar Lecture of 1979, Aberdeen University. Also given as the Frieda Fromm-Reichmann Lecture, Washington School of Psychiatry, 1979, and is reprinted with permission of both institutions.

Chapter 20 was published as "The Self and Object Relations: A Challenge to Psychoanalysis" (1983). *Bulletin of the Menninger Clinic* 47(6): 525–541, and is reprinted with permission.

Chapter 21 will be published as "The Autonomous Self" (1980). *Bulletin of the Menninger Clinic* 57(1): 3–32, and is reprinted with permission.

Chapter 22 was created by combining an unpublished paper, "Fairbairn's Line of Thought" with part of the final chapter, "Fairbairn's Achievement" from *Fairbairn's Journey to the Interior*, reprinted with permission of Free Association Books.

Chapter 23 was created by combining two papers: Sutherland's part of a three-part paper co-authored with J. V. Bondurant and M. W. Fisher, "Gandhi: A Psychoanalytic Viewpoint" (1971). *The American Historical Review*. (October issue) 76(4): 1104–1115, and "John Buchan's Sick Heart (1988): Some psychoanalytic reflections." *Edinburgh Review* Vol. 78–79: 83–101, both reprinted with permission.

Chapter 24 was edited from transcriptions of published audiocassettes of an unpublished talk (1990), "On Becoming and Being a Person," presented at the Washington School of Psychiatry, April 1990, and is used with permission.

Chapter 25 was collated from transcriptions of audiocassettes made of informal teaching interviews with Edward Corrigan and Pearl Ellen Gordon at The Institute of Contemporary Psychotherapy in New York, 1990 (and may be published in the *Contemporary Psychotherapy Review*), and with David E. Scharff and Jill Savege

Scharff at the Washington School of Psychiatry 1990. Tapes used with permission from both institutions.

The epilogue is a collation of extracts from various obituaries in professional journals, newspaper appreciations, and tributes from the service of thanksgiving, all furnished by Molly Sutherland.

Index